AMERICAN FURNITURE IN THE METROPOLITAN MUSEUM OF ART

This publication is made possible by the
William Cullen Bryant Fellows
of the American Wing.

AMERICAN FURNITURE IN THE METROPOLITAN MUSEUM OF ART

I. Early Colonial Period
The Seventeenth-Century and William and Mary Styles

Frances Gruber Safford

Photographs by Gavin Ashworth

THE METROPOLITAN MUSEUM OF ART, NEW YORK
YALE UNIVERSITY PRESS, NEW HAVEN AND LONDON

Published by The Metropolitan Museum of Art, New York
John P. O'Neill, Publisher and Editor in Chief
Gwen Roginsky, General Manager of Publications
Margaret Rennolds Chace, Managing Editor
Ellyn Childs Allison, Senior Editor
Bruce Campbell, Designer
Paula Torres, Production Manager
Kathryn Ansite, Desktop Publishing Specialist
Jayne Kuchna, Bibliographic Editor

Copyright © 2007 by The Metropolitan Museum of Art, New York

All rights reserved. No part of this publication may be reproduced or transmitted in any form or by any means,
electronic or mechanical, including photocopying, recording, or any information storage and retrieval system,
without permission in writing from the publisher.

Separations by Professional Graphics, Inc., Rockford, Illinois
Printed by Brizzolis Arte en Gráficas, Madrid
Bound by Encuadernación Ramos, S. A., Madrid
Printing and binding coordinated by Ediciones El Viso, S. A., Madrid

Cataloging-in-Publication Data is available from the Library of Congress.

ISBN: 978-1-58839-233-6 (The Metropolitan Museum of Art)
ISBN: 978-0-300-11647-2 (Yale University Press)

Jacket illustration: Small cabinet, Salem, Massachusetts, dated 1679 (cat. no. 79)

Contents

Director's Foreword — vii

Preface *by Morrison H. Heckscher* — viii

Acknowledgments — ix

Notes on the Catalogue — xi

Introduction — 3

CATALOGUE

I. SEATING FURNITURE — 12

Turned Chairs with a Spindle Back — 13

Turned Chairs with a Slat Back — 34

Joined Seating with a Wooden Bottom — 51

Upholstered, Cane, and Related Rush-seated Chairs — 64

Miscellaneous Furniture for Sitting and Reclining — 104

II. TABLES — 120

Tables with a Stationary Top — 121

Tables with Hinged Leaves — 143

III. CASE FURNITURE — 168

Boxes and Other Small Case Pieces — 169

Chests and Chests with Drawers — 195

Chests-on-Frame — 253

Chests of Drawers — 263

Cupboards and Kasten — 279

High Chests of Drawers — 305

Dressing Tables — 331

Desks — 342

APPENDIX 1: ADDENDA — 353

APPENDIX 2: PHOTOGRAPHIC DETAILS — 372

APPENDIX 3: EXPLANATORY DRAWINGS — 404

Concordance — 417

Abbreviations — 419

Bibliography — 421

Index — 439

Photograph and Drawings Credits — 451

For Merritt

Director's Foreword

Among the urban art museums of America, The Metropolitan Museum of Art was the first to focus on the work of our nation's early furniture makers. This anomalous step taken by an institution originally devoted to the works of classical antiquity and Renaissance Europe must be credited to two museum men with a vision, Robert W. de Forest (secretary and, later, president of the board of trustees) and Henry Watson Kent (assistant secretary and, later, secretary). In 1909 they mounted a loan exhibition, principally of furniture, "to test out the question whether American domestic art was worthy of a place in an art museum." Late that year, buoyed by the enthusiastic public response, they began to acquire whole collections of American "antiques"—starting with some seven hundred pieces purchased from Boston lawyer H. Eugene Bolles. The intent, realized with the opening of the Metropolitan's American Wing in 1924, was to display the objects in context, in historic interiors or period rooms. Over the years—in good part through the gifts and bequests of such consummate connoisseurs as Natalie K. (Mrs. J. Insley) Blair—the collection of furniture from America's colonial and early national periods has grown in size and quality, until today it is unsurpassed.

The maturation of this great collection entails a responsibility to share knowledge about it with the Museum's various constituencies—the scholarly and collecting communities as well as the public at large. The foundation for such outreach is still the printed "collection catalogue," which assembles in one place the accumulated knowledge and judgments of generations of curators. The present volume, by Associate Curator Frances Gruber Safford, is a distinguished example of the genre. The distillation of a long and painstaking examination and scholarly assessment of the earliest American furniture in the Metropolitan's care, her catalogue now takes its place as the authorized record of this important collection.

American Furniture in The Metropolitan Museum of Art. I. Early Colonial Period: The Seventeenth-Century and William and Mary Styles is the initial volume in a chronologically ordered, three-part series on the Museum's American furniture that was first conceived back in the 1970s. The second volume, by Morrison H. Heckscher, Lawrence A. Fleischman Chairman of the American Wing, on the Queen Anne and Chippendale styles, appeared in 1985; the third, on the Federal or neoclassical styles, is currently being prepared by Peter M. Kenny, Ruth Bigelow Wriston Curator of American Decorative Arts. We are deeply indebted to the William Cullen Bryant Fellows of the American Wing for the funding that made possible both the writing and the publication of this catalogue.

Philippe de Montebello
Director
The Metropolitan Museum of Art

Preface

Catalogues of public collections form a critically important part of the bibliography of American furniture. They provide in-depth scholarly assessments of the finest and most familiar pieces, while also publicizing less well known institutional holdings. In recent years, upwards of a dozen stand-alone single-volume catalogues of such collections have appeared. But the vast scope of the grand old collections—at places like the Boston Museum of Fine Arts, the Yale University Art Gallery, and the Winterthur Museum—has meant that they required publication in multiple volumes with multiple authors over the course of many years. It is in that lavish and labor-intensive tradition that The Metropolitan Museum of Art is addressing the daunting task of publishing, in a manner befitting its importance, its superb collection of American furniture.

Such catalogues do not come about quickly. There is always the temptation to wait for one more acquisition to fill out the collection; research tends to be open-ended, reflecting the desire to examine every last related object; long-completed entries are rewritten to incorporate the latest published findings; and seldom is there an exhibition deadline or other terminal date to command closure.

So the appearance of this volume is indeed a landmark event. Its genesis, as part of a three-volume series devoted to the Metropolitan's colonial and Federal American furniture, dates back to 1972 and a tripartite series of small exhibitions on aspects of the collection, each accompanied by a modest printed pamphlet. One of these, on seventeenth-century joined case furniture, was the work of Frances Gruber Safford. In the years since that initial foray, in addition to many other departmental responsibilities, Mrs. Safford has mastered the field of seventeenth-century and William and Mary–style furniture.

To that fact the present volume is eloquent testimony. It is an unabashed collection catalogue, based on a deep and thorough examination of every object in the Museum's rich assemblage. It defines the collection, focusing upon those splendid pieces that deserve pride of place in a history of American furniture. It makes manifest the collection's geographic strengths (New England) and weaknesses (Pennsylvania and the South). It takes advantage of the wealth of pieces that retain their original painted surface decoration, presenting the results of scientific pigment analysis for the first time in toto. It groups, for comparison and study, large photographic details of other contemporary ornament, such as turnings, and drawings of molding profiles.

As a fellow author in this series, it gives me particular pleasure to honor a longtime colleague and friend for this extraordinary achievement, this labor of love. Among all the examples of the genre, Frances Gruber Safford's catalogue stands out for the precision and completeness of its observations, the elegance of its presentation, and the keen insight of its conclusions. If not the last word on the collection, it is as close to it as we are ever likely to get. Here is a shining exception to Henry Stevens's infamous rule, "If you are troubled with a pride of accuracy, and would have it completely taken out of you, print a catalogue."

Morrison H. Heckscher
Lawrence A. Fleischman Chairman of the American Wing

Acknowledgments

My first debt of gratitude is owed to Philippe de Montebello, Director of The Metropolitan Museum of Art, whose strong support of scholarly publications has made possible the undertaking of this collection catalogue.

Morrison H. Heckscher, Lawrence A. Fleischman Chairman of the American Wing and author of the second volume in the series to which this catalogue belongs, has given invaluable guidance and has been unstinting in his support and encouragement. He and Peter M. Kenny, Ruth Bigelow Wriston Curator of American Decorative Arts, have most generously shared their vast and discerning knowledge of furniture, and their great enthusiasm for American furniture has spurred me on. I gratefully acknowledge all my colleagues in the American Wing, who through the years have helped in many ways and provided moral support. They include curators Kevin J. Avery; Carrie Rebora Barratt; Alice Cooney Frelinghuysen, Anthony W. and Lulu C. Wang Curator of American Decorative Arts; Amelia Peck, Marica F. Vilcek Curator of American Decorative Arts; Thayer Tolles; Beth Carver Wees; and H. Barbara Weinberg, Alice Pratt Brown Curator of American Paintings and Sculpture. Elaine Bradson, the American Wing's associate for administration, has smoothed the way in day-to-day matters—as have administrative assistants Jeanne Ko, Catherine Scandalis, and Beth Wallace and their numerous predecessors, among whom Ellin Rosenzweig must be singled out for particular recognition. I am greatly indebted to Cynthia Van Allen Schaffner, my research assistant in the final stages of writing and during the completion of the book, who willingly and expertly dealt with tasks great and small and steadily cheered me on. Very special words of thanks go to Leslie P. Symington for her indefatigable and invaluable genealogical research. Over the years various volunteers gathered material for the object files and deserve mention: Gloria Abrams, Kay Freeman, Ruth Lederman, and Catherine Scheltema. Departmental technicians Don E. Templeton, Rob Davis, Sean Farrell, Dennis Kaiser, and the late Gary Burnett moved heavy oak furniture innumerable times for repeated examination, conservation, and photography, with professionalism and unfailing good grace.

In the Museum, archivists Jeanie M. James and Barbara W. File gave valuable and timely assistance. Many thanks are due to members of the Objects Conservation and Scientific Research departments for their skilled and sensitive treatment of the furniture in need of restoration and for the scientific examination of particular pieces: for upholstery,

Nancy C. Britton; for woodwork, Marijn Manuels, Rudolph W. Colban, and Mechthild Baumeister; and for pigment analysis, Mark T. Wypiski. Several conservators formerly at the Museum are owed a debt of thanks as well: John Canonico, Sherry Doyal, Mark Minor, Antoine M. Wilmering, and Keith Bakker, who as conservation intern examined painted surfaces.

For the wood analyses I am obligated to R. Bruce Hoadley. I appreciated having the opportunity to learn from him as we examined each object together.

Research for the catalogue depended upon the ready willingness over many years of numerous museums and individuals to make furniture available for study and to generously share information. I am indebted in particular to the following institutions, whose curatorial and other staff made possible lengthy, and in many cases repeated, examination of their collections and provided material from their files: Albany Institute of History and Art, Albany, New York; Art Institute of Chicago, Chicago, Illinois; Bayou Bend Collection and Gardens, Houston, Texas; Brooklyn Museum, Brooklyn, New York; Chipstone Foundation, Milwaukee, Wisconsin; Colonial Williamsburg, Williamsburg, Virginia; Connecticut Historical Society, Hartford, Connecticut; The Henry Ford, Dearborn, Michigan; Historic Deerfield, Deerfield, Massachusetts; Historic Hudson Valley, Tarrytown, New York; Historic New England, Boston; Milwaukee Art Museum, Milwaukee, Wisconsin; Museum of Art, Rhode Island School of Design, Providence, Rhode Island; Museum of Early Southern Decorative Arts, Winston-Salem, North Carolina; Museum of Fine Arts, Boston; Museum of the City of New York, New York City; New Haven Museum and Historical Society, New Haven, Connecticut; New-York Historical Society, New York City; Peabody Essex Museum, Salem, Massachusetts; Philadelphia Museum of Art, Philadelphia; Pilgrim Hall Museum, Plymouth, Massachusetts; Wadsworth Atheneum Museum of Art, Hartford, Connecticut; Winterthur Museum and Country Estate, Winterthur, Delaware; and Yale University Art Gallery, New Haven, Connecticut.

Many individuals—colleagues in other museums, scholars, collectors, woodworkers, and dealers—have given freely of their time and expertise, made furniture available, and helped in any number of key ways. I am especially grateful to: John D. Alexander Jr., David L. Barquist, Judith A. Barter, Luke Beckerdite, Karen Blanchfield, Leslie Greene Bowman, Michael K. Brown, Tara Gleason Chicirda, Wendy A. Cooper,

Abbott Lowell Cummings, Bert R. Denker, Anne M. Donaghy, Nancy Goyne Evans, Dean F. Failey, Jonathan L. Fairbanks, Jeannine Falino, Donald L. Fennimore, J. Michael Flanigan, Suzanne L. Flynt, Peter Fodera, Peter Follansbee, the late Benno M. Forman, Elizabeth Pratt Fox, Beatrice B. Garvan, Donna-Belle Garvin, Dudley J. and Constance Godfrey Jr., Lee Ellen Griffith, Tammis K. Groft, Erik K. Gronning, Barry R. Harwood, John Hays, Margaret K. Hofer, William N. Hosley Jr., Ronald L. Hurst, Brock Jobe, Kathleen Eagen Johnson, Phillip M. Johnston, Neil D. Kamil, Patricia E. Kane, Leigh Keno, Leslie Keno, Elizabeth P. Knowles, Thomas P. and Alice K. Kugelman, Joshua W. Lane, Bernard Levy, Frank Levy, S. Dean Levy, Jack L. Lindsey, Thomas S. Michie, Alan Miller, Christopher P. Monkhouse, Milo M. Naeve, Kenneth Needleman, Jane C. Nylander, Richard C. Nylander, Karin E. Peterson, Bradford L. Rauschenberg, Paula Richter, Cheryl Robertson, the late Rodris Roth, Albert Sack and his late brother Harold, Robert Blair St. George, John L. Scherer, Susan Prendergast Schoelwer, J. Peter Spang III, Kevin L. Stayton, Jayne E. Stokes, Robert Tarule, Robert F. Trent, Gilbert T. Vincent, Frederick and Anne H. Vogel III, Barbara McLean Ward, Gerald W. R. Ward, David B. Warren, Deborah Dependahl Waters, Martha H. Willoughby, Eric Martin and Ethel Wunsch, and Philip Zea.

Special thanks are due also to Catherine M. Ellard, Librarian, and the staff at the New York Genealogical and Biographical Society, New York City, and to the staffs of the libraries and registrar at the Winterthur Museum. Many others over the course of the last three decades shared their knowledge, answered inquiries, and gave access to their collections. It is not possible to thank them all individually, but their contributions are here very gratefully acknowledged.

This book would not have become a reality without the William Cullen Bryant Fellows of the American Wing, whose annual contributions support publications on American art at the Museum, and I am pleased to have the opportunity to extend to them my deep personal thanks.

Gavin Ashworth produced the excellent photographs for this volume. It was a pleasure to work with him as he strove to show each object in its best light. For the line drawings in this book I am obliged to Robert S. Burton.

For the production of this very handsome volume I am indebted to John P. O'Neill, Publisher and Editor in Chief, and his exceptionally skilled and experienced team. Particular thanks go to Bruce Campbell for the book's elegant design, which has benefited from his enthusiasm for American furniture, to Paula Torres for her commitment to the highest standards of production, and to Jayne Kuchna, who assiduously applied her superb editorial skills to the bibliography and notes. My most appreciative and heartfelt thanks go to my editor, Ellyn Childs Allison, who brought greater clarity and readability to the text and carefully guided the book through its various stages to completion. Her warmth and equanimity sustained me throughout.

The dedication of this book to my husband, Merritt, expresses in but a small measure my deep gratitude for his steadfast support of my endeavor and for his many sacrifices and stalwart forbearance throughout the duration of this project.

Notes on the Catalogue

The objects in the catalogue are organized into three main parts—seating furniture, tables, and case furniture—and then into chapters according to form. Each chapter begins with a brief introduction that touches on the history, the original function, and the extent of the representation in the Museum's collection of the form or forms included. Nomenclature in the early colonial period varied and is at times difficult to interpret, and it does not always allow for the distinctions we may wish to make today. The terms used in the catalogue for furniture forms are thus a combination of period and modern names, and they are discussed in the chapter introductions as well. The terms for furniture parts used in this book are given in the glossary drawings in Appendix 3.

Following the chapter introductions are entries on the objects that embody the form or forms under discussion. Each entry includes an overall photograph of the object (and occasionally two views). If detail photographs of the piece or drawings related to it are included in Appendices 2 and 3, respectively, the figure numbers of those illustrations appear under the main photograph in the entry. The designations "right" and "left" throughout the catalogue are those of the viewer when facing the object.

The section on *Construction* includes a description not only of the structure and particularities of workmanship of the piece but also of the profiles of its moldings. Line drawings in Appendix 3 illustrate the different types of joints referred to and the common molding profiles named, and serve as a glossary. Cross-reference is made to photographic details in Appendix 2 that show construction features of the individual object and to line drawings in Appendix 3 of particular moldings.

Under *Condition* are mentioned losses, additions, replacements, repairs, and other alterations that have occurred to the piece. When known or when it can be estimated, the date of restorations and repairs is indicated. Changes attributable to normal aging and usual wear and tear, including small shrinkage cracks and minor losses, are generally not noted.

The sections on *Painted decoration* and *Japanning*, when included, present the results of a project undertaken in collaboration with the Objects Conservation Department—mainly from late 1990 to early 1993—to investigate the technical aspects of the original ornamental painting on a group of fifteen early colonial pieces in the collection. The aim was to better determine the original appearance of each object and to begin to build a body of knowledge on the

methods and materials used for such painting in this period—an area then largely unexplored. Cross sections were taken and pigments were identified by energy-dispersive X-ray spectrometry. Binders were generally not identified.

Included under *Inscriptions* are transcriptions of original carved or painted initials and dates and of later inscriptions and labels (a slash indicates a line break). Joiner's, sawyer's, and restorer's markings, are transcribed or described. The presence of identification numbers added at other institutions and of illegible inscriptions and markings is noted. Not mentioned are loan and accession numbers or other notations added at the Museum.

Listed under *Woods* in the entries of the main catalogue are the woods of components that are (or could be) original. The woods of replaced or dubious parts, if identified, are mentioned under *Condition*. In the entries in Appendix 1, which includes objects with particular problems, all woods that have been identified are listed in the *Woods* section. For the identification of the woods, R. Bruce Hoadley, professor of wood science and technology, University of Massachusetts, Amherst, examined every object in the catalogue, together with the writer, over a period of several years, beginning in 1990. The determinations made by Hoadley were based on a combination of identification by eye and macro- and microanalysis, and took into consideration some earlier microanalyses performed at the United States Forest Products Laboratory, Madison, Wisconsin (detailed information on each object is in the departmental files). Woods are generally listed by their common names. It may be helpful to add that "yellow poplar" is used to designate *Liriodendron tulipifera* (also known as tulip poplar, tulipwood) and "poplar" a wood of the genus *Populus* (whose species—aspens, cottonwoods, poplars—cannot be separated with certainty). "Eastern white pine" refers to a species (*Pinus strobus*) within the white pine group. "Southern yellow pine" refers to an indeterminate species within that yellow pine group whose range extends north to southern Maine and whose species cannot be distinguished reliably.

Under *Dimensions,* measurements are given in inches to the nearest one-eighth of an inch, followed by centimeters in parentheses. The overall dimensions—overall height (OH.), overall width (OW.), overall depth (OD.)—are inclusive of all elements now present, even if replaced. On seating furniture, the seat height (SH.) is measured to the top edge of the front seat rail, the seat depth (SD.), given instead of overall depth, is measured from the front of the front seat rail to the back of the rear rail, and the seat width (sw.) is that of the frame as well; all easy-chair measurements are those of the frame. For tables, dimensions are given for the top and the frame. On case furniture, case dimensions—case width (cw.), case depth (cd.)—are exclusive of any applied elements, including moldings.

In *Exhibitions*, long-term loans to other museums and historic houses and loans to special exhibitions are listed together in chronological order. The respective exhibition catalogues are noted as such in *References*. Most citations in *References* and in the endnotes are in short-title form (with full information given in the Bibliography at the end of the book). Exceptions are advertisements and auction catalogues,

and also genealogical references pertaining to provenance. A list of the abbreviations used in the book for the names of institutions and collections immediately precedes the Bibliography

The *Provenance* gives the history of the object provided by the donor, vendor, former owners, or other sources. All vendors are mentioned, but dealers and those vendors whose identity is not known and who may be dealers are not included under *Ex coll.* (former owners). Neither are individuals named in the history of the object who acquired it by inheritance and are not known to be collectors.

At the end of each entry are the Museum's credit line and accession number.

AMERICAN FURNITURE IN THE METROPOLITAN MUSEUM OF ART

Introduction

A History of the Collection

Among the numerous collectors and benefactors whose discernment and generosity made possible the formation of the Metropolitan Museum's collection of American furniture, three were of critical importance to the holdings from the seventeenth and early eighteenth centuries. First in time came H. Eugene Bolles, of Boston, whose collection of American furniture was considered the finest of its kind, and Mrs. Russell Sage, who purchased it in 1909 and gave it to the Museum. That gift, which included representative pieces dating from the seventeenth century to about 1820, formed the nucleus of the Museum's American furniture collection. Bolles had a particular interest in furniture from the early colonial period, which is reflected in the fact that his collection is the source of half of the objects in this catalogue. Of paramount importance as well was Natalie K. (Mrs. J. Insley) Blair of New York City and Tuxedo Park, New York, who was collecting mainly in the 1920s, focusing on prime examples of the seventeenth and eighteenth centuries. Furniture from her collection, given to the Museum mostly in the 1940s and early 1950s, accounts for one-quarter of the entries. Of the remaining items in the catalogue a few also entered the collection as parts of larger donations—from the Sylmaris Collection, given by George Coe Graves in 1930, and from the large group of Pennsylvania pieces donated by Mrs. Robert W. de Forest in 1933—but they were assembled on the whole as single acquisitions through the years, as often by gift as by purchase.

H. Eugene Bolles (1853–1910), a Boston lawyer, began collecting in the 1880s, searching out antiques in eastern Massachusetts and also in Connecticut, buying usually from dealers and at auction but sometimes from individuals, including other collectors. By 1909 he had gathered hundreds of objects. Of the more than seven hundred items acquired by the Museum, about four hundred thirty were pieces of furniture—American, with perhaps as many as one-fifth English or European. The remainder of the collection consisted of numerous implements and utensils of metal or wood, miscellaneous items such as a tavern sign, as well as some textiles. In the parlor of Bolles's house, objects of various periods and types were crowded together, from early carved oak boxes and chests to a pair of Empire mirrors, and from a

veneered desk to fire buckets, a rolling pin, and an embroidered bodice. He was interested in it all—"that range of things from the simple and quaint to the really beautiful which are commonly called colonial" (at that time Federal-period objects were also called "colonial").[1] Bolles's main focus, however, was unquestionably furniture. He was collecting at a time when furniture was no longer just of antiquarian interest but was beginning to be classified. In 1891 Dr. Irving W. Lyon of Hartford, Connecticut, published *The Colonial Furniture of New England,* the first major scholarly study of American furniture and a work that has endured. And the idea that furniture should be collected to illustrate the various styles and forms that were made was starting to take hold.

In the introduction to his 1904 catalogue of the Charles Pendleton collection, Luke Vincent Lockwood, then the foremost scholar of American furniture, noted that there were three methods of collecting furniture: "The first is to collect specimens with respect to their dates, whereby upon completion the collection will contain examples of every style and date. The second method is to collect pieces solely because of some historic association, irrespective of date or style. The third method is to form a collection, having in view the furnishing of a house in the manner in which a person of taste and possibly of wealth could have done at the time the house or style was in fashion." The last referred to the Pendleton collection, bequeathed to the Rhode Island School of Design in that year. In describing the first, Lockwood probably had the Bolles collection in mind. He continued: "The first of these methods has many fascinations, requires a wide knowledge of the subject, and is the most generally instructive. When the collection is completed there is a museum. . . . Under the first, the collector seeks primarily for specimens not only of a pure, but of conglomerate and transition styles, as well as for the unusual and unique pieces, his question being: Does the specimen represent a style, or a stage in the development of a style?"[2]

By the beginning of the twentieth century there was also an increasing appreciation of the design and craftsmanship of colonial decorative arts and a realization that they had aesthetic value and deserved recognition as art and not just as representations of how earlier generations lived. There was also a growing feeling that Americans should be made aware of the artistic traditions of their own country. Although American paintings and sculpture began to be acquired by the Metropolitan Museum shortly after 1870, when it was founded—American artists were among the founders and first trustees—there was no interest then in the decorative arts of earlier periods. What few American decorative-art objects entered the collection before 1900 were principally examples of contemporary design from leading New York City firms—the aim being to encourage "the application of arts to manufacture and practical life," one of the Museum's purposes, as stated in its charter. Among those examples were objects shown at the 1876 Centennial Exposition in Philadelphia: the Tiffany & Company vase given by William Cullen Bryant in 1877, which had been commissioned by his friends in honor of his eightieth birthday and completed the previous year, and two upholstered chairs in the Henry II style made by Pottier and Stymus and donated in 1888.

That approach was to change after Henry W. Kent joined the staff of the Museum in 1905 as assistant to Robert W. de Forest, for many years a trustee and then newly elected secretary of the board (and in 1913 its president). Kent had acquired a passion for early American things while he was curator at the Slater Memorial Museum in Norwich, Connecticut (1888–1900). During those years he became acquainted and developed friendships with the major collectors of Americana at the time, in particular George S. Palmer of nearby New London, Bolles's cousin. In August 1907 Kent on his own asked Palmer in all confidence if Bolles might consider selling his collection, which Kent then knew only by its reputation for being, in Palmer's words, "far and away superior to any other collection of American Colonial furniture."[3] The answer was encouraging, and later that year Kent, without mentioning his real motive, went to see Bolles's house and collection for the first time.

Kent found his opportunity to further the cause of colonial decorative arts at the Metropolitan in the exhibition being planned by the Museum as part of the state- and citywide Hudson-Fulton Celebration commemorating both the discovery of the Hudson River by Henry Hudson in 1609 and Robert Fulton's first successful navigation of the river in a steamboat in 1807. Robert W. de Forest was the chairman of the celebration's committee on art exhibits, and Kent proposed to him that in addition to a showing of Dutch paintings from the time of Hudson there should be an exhibit of American objects to represent Fulton. Since the Museum owned virtually no decorative arts of the colonial or early Federal periods, the exhibit had to rely on loans, and the chief lender of furniture, particularly of the seventeenth century, was to be Bolles. When in March 1909 Kent learned that Bolles was about to lend part of his collection to the Museum of Fine Arts, Boston—just when Kent was planning to borrow furniture

for the exhibition—the time had come to push for the purchase of the collection.

Over the next several months Kent was able to convince de Forest of the desirability of acquiring the Bolles objects. Negotiations began in mid-September, immediately upon Bolles's return to Boston after three months in Europe. This was just before the opening of the Hudson-Fulton exhibition, on 20 September, and before its resounding success, which demonstrated that American decorative arts were worthy of a place in an art museum, was realized. In late September, de Forest asked Kent and Luke Vincent Lockwood to look over the collection and evaluate it, and to draw up lists.[4] Lockwood had assisted in planning the American portion of the Hudson-Fulton exhibition and in writing that part of the catalogue.[5] He had also advised the Museum in the 1908 purchase of a group of English Chippendale furniture, and in describing the acquisition in the *Bulletin* that June he had promoted the collecting of American furniture, pointing out that "the ideal collection . . . for the Museum, would be a combination of English and American pieces, the former to show the models from which the colonial workmen acquired their inspiration and the latter to show the independent development of the style far away from the influences of fashion."[6] Lockwood was a lawyer by profession, and he was charged with working out the details of the contract. For his part, de Forest persuaded Mrs. Russell Sage, the widow of a successful financier, to purchase the collection and give it to the Metropolitan Museum—all of which was accomplished before 30 November, when the Hudson-Fulton exhibition closed.

The Bolles collection provided both a broad range of representative objects of the colonial and early Federal periods and individual pieces of distinction. Among the highlights from that collection in this catalogue are a richly carved chest from Ipswich, Massachusetts (cat. no. 83), a remarkably well-preserved small cabinet with applied ornament from Salem, Massachusetts (cat. no. 79), a finely painted chest with drawer from the Connecticut shore (cat. no. 101), and a monumental Boston oval table of the type now called gateleg (cat. no. 59). The fact that eight other tables of this form in different sizes and with legs showing variations on the same turning pattern were also part of the collection illustrates how extensive it was. As the acquisition was described in December 1909, "It would be difficult to overestimate the value of this Collection to the Museum, not only because of the beauty and importance of many of the individual pieces, but because the Collection as a whole is a unit, the dominant idea being to portray the history of the development of form and ornament in furniture during a period of more than two centuries."[7]

As soon as the sale was certain, Kent and Lockwood, with de Forest's approval, set about devising a plan for the installation of the collection and in short order came up with a scheme comprising eight rooms. Their idea of showing the pieces "according to the German method, or 'room' arrangement,"[8] that is, in period-room settings, however, would have to wait until the building of an American wing—envisioned already in 1912 and opened in 1924. But within a few months a selection of objects was put on view in four galleries on the second floor of the new wing for Western decorative arts (now the Morgan Wing), which opened in early 1910.

The building of that wing had been prompted by the arrival at the Museum in 1907 of the Georges Hoentschel collection of French medieval and eighteenth-century decorative arts, which had been acquired by J. Pierpont Morgan and given in part the previous year. The Hoentschel collection also brought about the creation of the Department of Decorative Arts, with Wilhelm R. Valentiner its first curator in 1908. The installation of the decorative-arts wing was planned and executed by Valentiner and two associates, and they were responsible for the display of the American pieces, for Kent wrote to Bolles on 13 April 1910: "Your collection is temporarily arranged in four rooms of our new wing, much to my regret and under my protest. I had nothing whatever to do with the arrangement, nor, in fact, with the plan in any way. It was thought best, however, to put a portion of the collection in these rooms on the occasion of the opening of the wing which is supposed to contain our 'Western Art.' The selection was badly made, and the arrangement is worse, but I do not think any one except a hypercritical person like myself would find fault with it."[9]

American furniture and other decorative arts continued to be displayed in those galleries in various arrangements until the early 1920s. In addition, by 1916, there was in the basement of the Museum a large study room of American furniture where many of the remaining Bolles pieces could be seen—all tightly lined up.[10] With the opening of the American Wing in 1924, built with funds donated by Mr. and Mrs. Robert W. de Forest, there was available to the public a chronological display of interior architecture, furniture, other decorative arts, and paintings from the Museum's growing permanent collection complemented by some loans and dating from the seventeenth century to about 1820. On each of three floors was a central gallery surrounded by a series of period rooms; the early colonial objects were displayed on the third floor, the late colonial on the second, and the early Federal on the first.

Among those who availed themselves of the opportunity for study provided by the objects in the American Wing was Natalie K. (Mrs. J. Insley) Blair (1887–1951), who likely had previously visited the Western-arts wing and the American furniture study room. Married in 1912, Mrs. Blair and her husband first lived in New York City, and in 1914 they built a large neo-Jacobean mansion in Tuxedo Park, New York, which became their principal residence. At first Mrs. Blair collected English antiques, but by 1916 she turned her attention to American pieces. Between then and the 1930s, buying primarily from New York City dealers and one in New Jersey, she formed a superb collection of American colonial furniture. She took advantage of the increasing number of publications on and displays of Americana then becoming available in order to evaluate her prospective purchases. As she wrote in her unpublished memoir, she was "impressed with the wonderful collection Mr. Bolles formed and which is now in the Metropolitan Museum. . . . In my first years of serious collecting I used to compare each piece offered me with its counterpart in this collection."[11]

Although not as well known as other collectors of American decorative arts in her generation—Henry Francis du Pont, Francis P. Garvan, Ima Hogg, or Electra Havemeyer Webb—whose names are closely allied with individual museums, she played a principal role in shaping the Metropolitan's holdings of American furniture of the seventeenth and eighteenth centuries. She was exacting in her collecting, and many of her pieces in this catalogue stand out by virtue of their rarity, quality, and condition. Particularly noteworthy are a unique seventeenth-century folding table (cat. no. 58) and a grand spindle-back armchair with a wooden seat (cat. no. 2); two Turkey-work chairs (cat. nos. 23, 24) and a leather chair (cat. no. 27), all with their original upholstery; and several chests with painted decoration (cat. nos. 102, 104, 110, 112).

The American Wing inspired Mrs. Blair to create in the attic of her home in Tuxedo Park several "museum rooms," which housed most of her early material. The large room that contained the majority of the seventeenth-century objects had a beamed ceiling that recalled that of the Wing's Old Ship Meetinghouse gallery and a fireplace wall with sheathing based on that in the Hart Room (the Museum's room at that time was not yet the original but a reproduction).[12] In 1939, having in view the closing of the main house and its museum rooms and moving into smaller quarters on the Tuxedo Park property, she offered to lend furniture to the Museum. Joseph Downs, the curator of the American Wing, selected a group of about fifty pieces with an eye to prime objects that would enrich and upgrade the collection. Mrs. Blair began donating those pieces in 1943, and what remained on loan at her death in 1951 became a bequest. Additional furniture from her collection was subsequently given by her two daughters, Mrs. Screven Lorillard and Mrs. J. Woodhull Overton.

Mrs. Blair's decision in 1916 to begin buying American antiques was prompted by her realization that some of the English pieces she had acquired were of doubtful age. She later recounted: "At that time this faking in toto did not obtain in the American furniture—or rather not to any extent, except possibly in some of the elaborate mahogany pieces, for which people were beginning to give prices. The chief danger in those days was buying cripples—genuine enough pieces—with new legs—or feet—or drawers, or old tops and bases that did not belong together but fitted to match. There was still enough of the real to be found so that dealers often had it."[13] (Actually the reproduction and faking of early American furniture had been going on from about the 1840s, and from the 1870s into the early 1900s those activities responded to the particular interest in seventeenth-century pieces.)

While Mrs. Blair was carefully looking for objects in optimal condition, late-nineteenth-century collectors like Bolles were often willing to acquire furniture in disrepair—"in the rough," as they called it—as found by themselves or by dealers in old farmhouses, barns, or, as purportedly in the case of the cupboard cat. no. 141, even outdoors. Of the early colonial pieces in the Bolles collection that had seen hard usage and survived in poor condition, some had been restored before Bolles purchased them, some he had had repaired, and a good number still had to be "put in order" when acquired by the Museum.

Already in February 1910 Kent contacted Morris Schwartz, a restorer in Hartford, Connecticut, who did work for collectors in that area. Schwartz came to the Museum for a period of probably two or more months in the fall of 1912, Kent wanting him to put in condition the oak pieces in particular.[14] If and to what extent Schwartz provided his services over the next several years is not clear, but he was definitely involved with the Bolles collection prior to the opening of the American Wing in 1924, and he continued—at least in 1925—to work on those pieces not yet in condition to be exhibited. The notes on his collection that Bolles compiled for the Museum included in some cases information on the condition of an object and the repairs made, and in one rare instance, a cupboard, his verbal description was supplemented by photographs that show the piece before restoration (cat. no. 141, ills. 141a, 141b). But no record appears to have been made of which objects Schwartz restored or what was done by him or by any others who possibly worked on the furniture during the 1910s and 1920s.

The extent of the restoration that should be undertaken on a piece and especially how to deal with the surface were questions on which opinions varied considerably in the late nineteenth and early twentieth centuries and still differ today. On the one hand, Bolles in his notes on the collection and correspondence with Kent shows himself to be quite conservative, urging great caution, for example, in dealing with the japanned surface of a cabriole-leg high chest, stating he had "great fear of taking those steps which cannot be retraced." And in regard to a mahogany desk and bookcase he wrote: "To save the old color which was rich under the scale of dirt, I had the old finish rubbed down by hand nearly to the surface of the wood instead of having it scraped"—in opposition to others who did scrape and made the furniture look newer than new.[15] In dealing with some of the oak pieces, on the other hand, he was more aggressive and prone to stripping

and repainting, though he urged that careful notes be made of which molding or element had what color before any old finish was removed. The artist and collector Dwight Blaney recalled a visit to Bolles's home, where, he wrote, "I had a grand experience seeing his early American oak. I was horrified at his repainting his pieces in heavy oil paint, but of course did not criticize. He was so enthusiastic, it seemed unkind to destroy or interfere in his work."[16] One piece that Blaney surely saw was the cupboard mentioned above (cat. no. 141, ill. 141c), which stood in Bolles's parlor. The bright new paint on that cupboard did not meet with approval at the Museum either, for by 1916 the cupboard had been entirely stripped, as it stands today.

While the keeping of conservation records was slow in coming (brief notes on the furniture restoration began to be made in the 1930s and 1940s), Kent, a trained librarian, soon instituted a system of cataloguing and photographing all accessions, thereby making an important contribution to museum practice. Every Bolles object received a brief written description, which sometimes included the mention of paint, and its appearance at the time of acquisition was recorded in a photograph. The date of the photograph was inscribed in a ledger along with the negative number (and when the Bolles furniture was first photographed, the fact that a photograph had been taken and sometimes also the date might occasionally be noted in pencil or chalk in large characters on the piece itself, as a few remains of such inscriptions attest). Subsequent photographs, if such were taken, document any changes that had occurred in a piece after it was acquired (if discernible in a black-and-white picture) and make it possible to date those changes to a specific time period, as in the case of the cupboard.

On 27 December 1909, Bolles wrote somewhat apprehensively to Kent: "You speak of Mr. De Forest having under consideration the matter of restoring the pieces. I hope you will feel as I do, that a piece in its unrestored condition is much more interesting and attractive than after restoration, and that restoration should be limited to those pieces which physically require it for their preservation, or which have been so painted or otherwise dealt with that it is necessary to restore them to give an adequate idea of what they originally were. It is true that one can restore a piece at any time so there need be no hurry. He can never unrestore it, and an error in this direction is final." Two days later Kent wrote to reassure him: "I certainly should never think of really restoring a piece of furniture without consulting you. What I mean in the way of restoration is the putting in order where pieces are missing or where any part of the furniture is seriously damaged. So do not be afraid of me in this matter."[17]

The restorations on the Bolles collection that occurred, presumably in the 1910s or 1920s, sometimes went considerably beyond what one would today include in Kent's definition. If a component was damaged or had losses, it tended to be removed and replaced in its entirety, as happened in the case of the slats on the high chair cat. no. 11, which were missing their upper portion, or the base molding on the chest of drawers cat. no. 108, on which the remaining front molding was replaced along with the missing side moldings. The representation of the original design of the piece seems to have been of primary importance, not the preservation of all the old elements.

The alterations made to the upper front of that same chest of drawers (and since reversed) were on a different order, going beyond any evidence presented by the piece. The molding under the top, of a type characteristic of the Salem, Massachusetts, school of craftsmanship to which the chest is attributed, was removed and replaced with a molding similar to one on cupboard cat. no. 115 that featured serrations and is typical of case pieces in the main joinery tradition of Plymouth County, Massachusetts. (The three corbels just below that molding, then attached in an inverted position, were also removed and replaced with pairs of half columns.) One can only speculate on what happened. It may be that the type of molding on that chest of drawers was unfamiliar and therefore suspect, and thus it was replaced with one in a design that was known and associated with case furniture in the geometric applied-ornament style—in a presumably honest, but misguided, effort to better show what the piece originally was. Or possibly it was just thought that the Plymouth type of design was more desirable and would enhance the chest.

But the changes effected on cat. no. 51, a New York table with drawer—the addition of a front and rear stretcher (now removed) identical and parallel to the medial stretcher—can only be interpreted as a deliberate attempt to "improve" the piece: the photograph of the table as acquired does not show any evidence of a previous attachment to the legs at the location of those stretchers. For the stretchers to have been added, the table had to have been apart. It was then not uncommon to take joined furniture completely apart in order to make repairs or to tighten the mortise-and-tenon joints. Perhaps the reason for the table's disassembly was structural, and once it was apart, the opportunity for "improvement" was seized upon. When it comes to alterations and repairs on the Bolles furniture that were not noted by him and are not easily discernible in a Museum photograph, it is often difficult to say if they were made before or in the first two decades after the collection was acquired. The approach appears to have been similar, including probably the regrettable practice of staining or varnishing the interior surfaces of the furniture to hide replacements or just neaten the piece up.

How much oversight or freedom Morris Schwartz was given is not known nor is it clear who exactly was making decisions at what point on the American furniture collection during the 1910s and 1920s. In the early 1910s, basically only Henry W. Kent, who became secretary of the board of trustees when Robert de Forest was elected president in 1913, appears to have been involved. Wilhelm R. Valentiner, curator of the Department of Decorative Arts until 1915, did not have any expertise in American things and seems to have asked for assistance when it came to that part of the collection. In the spring of 1910 Lockwood was called in to help decide which of the Bolles pieces were duplicates and might be disposed of, and that appears to be the last time he advised the Museum. In 1912, after the restoration of the Bolles collection had apparently come under discussion, Valentiner indicated that he would be pleased if Kent, since his specialty was American furniture, would attend to the matter.[18]

R. T. H. Halsey, who had lent his silver and Duncan Phyfe furniture to the Hudson-Fulton exhibition, entered the picture in 1914, when he was elected trustee. Immediately appointed chairman of the committee on American decorative arts and later of the committee on the American Wing, he acted in fact as curator for many years. (Kent continued to play an important role, as did, in the realization of the American Wing, Robert W. de Forest.) From 1915 to 1917 Halsey was assisted in the planning of the American Wing and the quest for architectural elements and furnishings by Durr Friedley, the then-acting curator of the Department of Decorative Arts. In 1917 Joseph Breck became curator of that department, and the following year Charles O. Cornelius joined the staff to work with Halsey on the American Wing. After the Wing opened, to great acclaim, in 1924 and he received due recognition, Halsey, though he remained chairman of the American Wing committee, turned his attention to projects outside the Museum. Cornelius, who in 1922 had organized the exhibition "Furniture Masterpieces of Duncan Phyfe" and written an accompanying publication of the same title, was appointed associate curator in 1925.[19] He carried on as curator of the American Wing and its collections until his resignation in 1931, assisted since before 1929 by Ruth Ralston. With the death of Joseph Breck in 1933, the Department of Decorative Arts, which by then included only Western art, was divided into three new departments: Medieval Art, Renaissance and Modern Art, and the American Wing, as the Department of American Decorative Arts was then named.[20] Joseph Downs, who had joined the staff as associate curator in 1932, became in 1934 the first curator of the American Wing.

Downs began his tenure at the Museum (which lasted until 1951) by immediately organizing two exhibitions: "American Japanned Furniture" in 1933 and "New York State Furniture" with Ruth Ralston in 1934.[21] At the same time he focused his attention on the surface condition of the early furniture under his care. At this point the "restoration" that was undertaken was noted, but perhaps not in all instances, on the catalogue cards of the pieces involved in a standard statement: "Modern varnish removed and wood finished with linseed oil and turpentine." The date indicated is usually 1933–34, and in a few instances, later in the 1930s; who in the Museum was doing the stripping and rubbing in the oil was not noted. In some cases, where records indicate that a chair—for example, cat. no. 8 or no. 29—was painted black when received, it is not clear whether the paint had been previously removed and the chair varnished, or if the notation mentioned above was a general one that included the removal of paint (presumably all new). The almost total lack of color on the applied ornament on the facade of the chest with drawers cat. no. 92 or on the pillars of the cupboard cat. no. 113, for instance, dates very probably from the removal of "modern varnish" in the late 1930s. Whether or not oil was applied to stripped surfaces earlier at the Museum is not known, but in the 1930s it seems to have come into general use. Very likely, the practice of maintaining the furniture with a formula of linseed oil, beeswax, and turpentine was introduced at that time. It appears to have been continued well into the 1950s by some other museums and collectors as well. The present surface condition of a good number of the early colonial objects from the Bolles collection and of some of the subsequent acquisitions is the result of stripping and such oil or oil and wax finishing.

It was thanks in large part to Joseph Downs that so many superb pieces of furniture from Mrs. Blair came to enrich the Museum's holdings in the 1940s and early 1950s. Single acquisitions of great importance to the early colonial collection were also made during his tenure. Among the furniture, most notable are a Boston japanned high chest (cat. no. 125) and three rare New York pieces: a spindle-back armchair (cat. no. 1), a high chest of drawers with spiral legs (cat. no. 121), and a desk-on-frame (cat. no. 132). Downs also acquired architectural woodwork for the third floor of the American Wing, which houses the early colonial furniture—namely, in 1936, the seventeenth-century room from the Thomas Hart house in Ipswich, Massachusetts. The following year he saw to its installation and also to that of the room of about 1695–1700 from the John Wentworth house in Portsmouth, New Hampshire, which had been purchased in 1926. Both took the place of rooms with reproduction woodwork and are the Wing's earliest interiors. The representation of interior architecture on the third floor of the Wing remained basically the same from that time until the changes currently under way (which do not affect the two rooms just mentioned) and due to be completed in 2009.

After the early 1950s and under the curators who succeeded Downs—Vincent D. Andrus, James Biddle, and Berry B. Tracy, and now Morrison H. Heckscher—the seventeenth- and early-eighteenth-century collection has seen a slow but steady growth, with several objects acquired each decade. Noteworthy additions are a walnut Boston high chest said to

have belonged to Edward Holyoke (cat. no. 126) in 1975, a rare New York oak kast (cat. no. 118) in 1988, and a Massachusetts oak wainscot chair (cat. no. 18) in 1995. The recent acquisition of a New York Dutch vernacular room from the Albany area, which will be part of the reconfigured third floor of the American Wing, should also be mentioned.

Bolles himself realized that the Museum would not want to keep every item it had acquired from his collection, and the terms of Mrs. Russell Sage's gift allow for the sale of objects, with the proceeds to be used for the purchase of other examples of American decorative art. Thus already in 1910 a list of forty-seven "duplicates" was drawn up; six were sold almost immediately, others later, and some are still part of the Museum's holdings. Not just the building but also the refining of the American furniture collection have been ongoing processes since then.

The Catalogue

The furniture presented in this catalogue comes predominantly from New England, with fewer than a dozen examples each from New York and Pennsylvania, and none from the South. This reflects both the fact that considerably more furniture of the early colonial period, particularly of the seventeenth century, has survived from New England than from the other regions and the way in which the Museum's holdings of furniture from that period were formed. From the Bolles collection comes just one of the eleven New York objects and from that of Mrs. Blair three out of the same number of Pennsylvania pieces. The representation of early furniture from outside of New England has been built up slowly over the years with single acquisitions, and the strengthening and broadening of the geographic scope of the early colonial furniture remains an ongoing goal.

The design of early colonial furniture was influenced by two broad European stylistic movements, which were transferred to America primarily by way of England and to a lesser degree directly from the Continent, in accord with patterns of immigration. Of the objects in the catalogue nearly all have English antecedents, with just four pieces, all from New York, derived in toto from strictly Continental prototypes (cat. nos. 9, 118–20).

The first of the colonial styles, here called the seventeenth-century style, dominated American furniture making from 1620 to about 1690. Its manifestations were multifarious because of the diversity of regional and local craft practices transplanted by immigrant craftsmen, principally from all parts of England. The traditions they brought to the colonies during the early decades of settlement were indebted to influences that had reached England from the 1560s to the early 1600s, transmitted by Continental artisans and printed pattern books. The concepts they introduced were based on Renaissance classical design and reflected in particular the late northern European expressions of that movement that have been termed Mannerist.[22] Very generally speaking, those influences produced in England two different decorative trends. One, the earlier, was a carved style, which spread throughout England and became established in provincial areas, each region or locality developing distinct designs. The other, stylistically more advanced, featured applied ornament and gained favor by the early 1600s in urban centers—London and port towns on the English Channel, where European influence was the strongest.

Both ornamental styles, manifest mainly on case furniture, were transmitted to New England by the end of the 1630s, as immigrant artisans continued to use their particular idioms of design and construction where they settled. The urban style, which featured architectonic schemes that employed applied turnings and moldings in geometric patterns, was transferred by London woodworkers to Boston, where it took hold and then influenced surrounding areas, and also to New Haven, Connecticut. The greatest number of craftsmen came from provincial areas and worked in the carved styles familiar to them, which relied on a vocabulary of geometric shapes, including arches, and stylized plant forms. Furniture that combined carving and applied elements was also produced, either derived from an English school of joinery (cat. no. 79) or as the probable result of the interaction over time of two or more transplanted traditions (for example, cat. nos. 92, 93).

Underlying all the diversity were principles of construction and composition common to the seventeenth-century style. Whether it was a turned chair or a frame-and-panel chest, its design and structural system were based on a geometric arrangement of rectilinear verticals and horizontals. On furniture of frame-and-panel construction, which was characteristic of the period, the ornament, whatever its nature, was disposed in the same basic manner: as distinct units of design, each limited to an individual structural member; and in the applied-ornament style each member was itself often subdivided visually into smaller components. Out of such multiplicity and the play of shapes it created came the carefully crafted, at times highly complex, compositions typical of the seventeenth-century style.

Some towns or villages were founded by groups of settlers from the same region or locality, and the artisans among them could continue to ply their trade as they had learned it in relative isolation, at least for a time. In settlements with heterogeneous populations, there might be several diverse strains of craftsmanship present and coming into contact—as many as eight different shop traditions have been identified

in seventeenth-century Windsor, Connecticut.[23] Artisans also moved about, absorbing and disseminating divergent craft practices. American furniture in the seventeenth century presented a complex, evolving picture of local and sometimes multiple local styles. Urban artisans, responding to the needs of prosperous merchants with close transatlantic contacts, kept much more abreast of changing fashions abroad than did their rural counterparts.

By the 1690s the stylistic impulses that were setting the fashion in colonial urban centers were those of the early Baroque. In England the newer European design concepts, principally those of the court of Louis XIV, had begun to arrive with the restoration of the monarchy in 1660. A fresh wave of Continental influence came from Holland in 1689, when William of Orange and Mary Stuart ascended the English throne, and in America, the early Baroque movement now bears their name. The William and Mary style, which remained the ruling fashion in the colonies until about 1730, introduced a new feeling for form and its movement, which found expression in furniture that was no longer strictly rectilinear and was also lighter and more vertical in its design, and in turned elements that showed emphatic curves and sharply contrasting shapes. On case furniture, which was no longer of frame-and-panel construction but exhibited large, smooth surfaces, earlier modes of decoration were abandoned in favor of the patterning provided by natural wood grains, particularly of figured veneers. A different compositional aesthetic that valued unity and no longer multiplicity was also in evidence.

Fashionable furniture in all of the colonies emulated London or London-style design, but the American examples produced were by no means entirely uniform. The individual training of the craftsmen, the particular prototypes followed, local materials, and client preferences all differed to a greater or lesser degree and affected the objects made. In very broad terms, Boston, the largest colonial city until the mid-eighteenth century and a center of furniture making already in the late 1600s, was the only major urban center in this period that appears to have had a dominant style, with a large number of the craftsmen producing the same basic designs, not just for the local market but also for export. Boston furniture had widespread influence especially in New England, as illustrated, for example, by the fact that the turning pattern of opposed balusters that was employed on Boston William and Mary tables became the norm in nearly all of that region, whereas in the one exception (Rhode Island) and in the mid-Atlantic colonies and the South tables commonly exhibited various designs with a single baluster, which was the scheme preferred in England. In New York and Philadelphia, the two other major cities represented by objects in the catalogue, furniture production appears to have been not as unified as in Boston. Some distinctive London-style designs and specific shop traditions have been identified as particular to each of those two cities. In terms of case furniture, examples in the catalogue are a high chest with spiral legs (cat. no. 121), a type made in New York but not elsewhere in the colonies, and a dressing table with legs turned in an elegant pattern peculiar to a Philadelphia shop (cat. no. 131). A unifying, regional factor in Philadelphia furniture was the common use of solid walnut in its construction, no matter what the form or individual style.

Imported furniture, not just immigrant craftsmen, played an important role in introducing new ideas, particularly in seating. The design of William and Mary chairs was strongly influenced by English cane chairs, the production of which had by the late seventeenth century become a large industry centered in London. Cane chairs were exported in quantity to all of the American colonies as well as to Europe. From the 1680s, when they first appeared in colonial inventories, through the 1720s they were the major source of stylistic innovation in seating. Boston also had an export trade in furniture—chairs in particular—and its interpretations of English chair styles, which were shipped beyond New England to New York City, Philadelphia, and southern ports, exerted stylistic influence as well (and distinguishing Boston chairs from locally made copies can be difficult.)

Furniture in this period that was not emulating current English fashion exhibits some diverse, very distinctive designs that are clearly regional or local in character. Dutch-style cupboards made in New York and parts of New Jersey (cat. nos. 119, 120) are prime representatives of this category of furniture in the catalogue. Other examples are several New England chests with particular painted floral designs (cat. nos. 101, 103, 104, for instance) and a type of paneled chair peculiar to Pennsylvania that was seventeenth century in derivation but made at least to the mid-1700s (cat. no. 20).

The date ranges assigned to the seventeenth-century and William and Mary styles merely indicate when those movements were dominant. Certain types of furniture continued to be made at the middle or vernacular level long after they had been outmoded in fashionable circles; some William and Mary forms were particularly long-lived. Included in the catalogue are a considerable number of objects, mainly seating and tables, that have been given dates that extend beyond 1730 and in some cases are in the mid- or later eighteenth century. Styles not only overlapped but were also constantly evolving, as is clearly illustrated by the sequence of upholstered, cane, and related chairs in chapter four of the seating-furniture section of this book. Designs do not always fit neatly into the categories and style designations that have been formulated at a later time, and a few chairs that incorporate elements of both the William and Mary and the subsequent late Baroque or Queen Anne style have been included.

Not all of the early colonial furniture at present in the collection is being published in this catalogue. The preparation of the catalogue included the reevaluation of all objects of the period under question. In the process, a certain number were counted out for reasons of authenticity, condition, or quality of workmanship. Of those, some will probably not be kept permanently in the collection, while others will be retained for study and comparison purposes; examples of the latter are in Appendix 1. Admittedly there remain in the main body of the catalogue some objects, particularly from the seventeenth century, that show repairs and replacements of an extent that would, if the pieces were of a later period, exclude them from publication. Much less furniture was produced in the early colonial period than in later years when the population was considerably larger, and much of what has survived has seen years of hard usage, and a certain portion exists only because it was salvaged in disrepair.

The objects in the catalogue are not organized according to style but are grouped first into three broad sections according to the purpose they served: seating furniture, tables, and case furniture. Each of those categories is then divided into chapters that deal with particular types of pieces, such as boxes, chests, or cupboards. The arrangement within each chapter varies, depending on the particular individual objects it contains. In some cases a chronological-stylistic sequence is feasible. In others the order has been determined by the type of surface ornament or the form of the turned elements, for example, which may result in regional groupings. The aim has been to establish an order that is visually comprehensible.

This volume is intended to provide a careful and detailed record of the physical and design aspects of the individual pieces included and of their history and to serve as a work of reference. It makes available to the public for the first time in printed form the rich range of early colonial objects in one of the largest and finest collections of American furniture. It is hoped that the descriptions and commentaries and the photographic details will encourage readers to look more closely at the furniture of this period and gain a better understanding and appreciation of the craft practices and sense of design of its makers.

1. Letter of 29 October 1909 from Bolles to Henry W. Kent, Bolles correspondence, MMA Archives.
2. Lockwood 1904, pp. 1–2.
3. Letter of 9 August 1907 from Palmer to Kent, Bolles correspondence.
4. Letter of 16 September 1909 from Bolles to Kent, and letter of 28 September 1909 from Robert de Forest to Lockwood, Bolles correspondence.
5. See *Hudson-Fulton Celebration* 1909. The first volume of the catalogue, devoted to the Dutch paintings in the exhibition, was written by Wilhelm R. Valentiner. For views of the installation of the American section of the exhibition, see Safford 2000, figs. 2–4.
6. Lockwood 1908, pp. 111–12.
7. "Bolles Collection" 1909.
8. Letter of 29 October 1909 from Kent to Lockwood, Bolles correspondence.

9. Bolles correspondence.

10. For a view of the study room, see Safford 2000, fig. 5.

11. For more on Mrs. Blair and her collection, see Heckscher 2000; quotation on p. 184. Her memoir is in a private collection.

12. Mrs. Blair's "museum rooms" are illustrated in Heckscher 2000, pls. I–VI.

13. Quoted in ibid., p. 183.

14. Letters from Kent to Schwartz of 17 February 1910 and 14 May 1912 and memorandum of 30 October 1912 from Kent to de Forest, Bolles correspondence.

15. Letter of 11 February 1910 to Kent, Bolles correspondence (high chest); Bolles notes, MMA Archives (desk).

16. Letter [ca. January 1935] from Blaney to the Walpole Society, in *Meeting of the Walpole Society* 1935, p. 8; quoted in Stillinger 1980, p. 98.

17. Bolles correspondence.

18. Letter of 28 March 1910 from Valentiner to Lockwood and memorandum of 11 May 1912 from Valentiner to Kent, Bolles correspondence.

19. Charles O. Cornelius, *Furniture Masterpieces of Duncan Phyfe* (New York, 1922).

20. The 1924 American Wing building was intended for the display of decorative arts (with some paintings complementing the exhibits), and the building and the curatorial department were synonymous. In 1978, in anticipation of the opening in 1980 of the greatly enlarged American Wing building with galleries for American paintings and sculpture, the name of the department was changed to American Decorative Arts.

21. Downs 1933; Downs and Ralston 1934.

22. On Mannerism and American furniture, see Trent 1982a; Trent 1982b, pp. 501–4; Manca 2003; and Adamson 2005.

23. See Lane and White 2003.

I.

SEATING FURNITURE

Turned Chairs with a Spindle Back

Early colonial probate inventories indicate that chairs and other types of seating were more numerous than any other form of furniture and that households usually contained various kinds of seats. Seating furniture was made at different levels of production, which, especially in the seventeenth century, were basically differentiated by the craft skills and construction methods involved. The objects in the seating section of this catalogue are for the most part grouped along those lines. The most common and affordable chairs were those made by turners. Turned chairs were economical because their components could be quickly fashioned on a lathe and easily assembled by fitting round tenons into round drilled mortises (see fig. 163), and with rare exceptions they were equipped with an inexpensive woven seat of rush or other fiber. They were made of locally available woods, usually ash or maple.

Seventeenth-century turned chairs were made with a back that either was formed of vertical spindles set between rails—the type included in this chapter—or consisted of horizontal slats set between the stiles—the category contained in the one that follows. Both schemes were based on English and Continental antecedents, which had medieval origins. Seventeenth-century records do not differentiate between the two types, so the modern designation "spindle-back" must serve to distinguish the chairs in this chapter. By far the most common inventory listing is simply "chair" or "chairs." When qualifiers are added, they most frequently refer to the material of the seat, less often to the size, color, or type of construction. Chairs are occasionally described as "turned," but that they belong in that category is much more likely to be indicated by their being called "rush," "bass," "sedge," or "matted," for example. Chairs without arms were at that time simply called "chairs," and that practice is followed in the descriptive titles of the objects in this catalogue. Since they were not as big as armchairs, they were sometimes qualified as "little" or "small." Chairs with arms were described as "great" (meaning "large," a word that then also implied arms), "elbow," "armed," or occasionally "arm." Although one expression may have been more prevalent in one region or at one time than another, no one name was exclusive to any one area or period, and they were

often used interchangeably. Samuel Sewall of Boston, for example, employed all three terms in his diary, which covers the years 1674 to 1729.[1] The term still current today, "armchair," is the one used in this catalogue.

Spindle-back seating is represented in the Museum's collection mainly by armchairs. The rate of survival of this type has far exceeded that of the more common and more numerous small chairs without arms. They were sturdier and more valuable, and the fact that they were still regarded as symbols of authority, whether on an official level or within the individual household, no doubt also contributed to their preservation. The most elaborate of the armchairs, and the exception then and now, are those that are fitted with a wooden rather than a woven seat and that have spindles below the arms and/or the seat. Two noteworthy examples head this chapter. The first, which is distinguished by having a slanted back and rear posts in two sections instead of standard straight rear posts in one piece (cat. no. 1), is of a structural type of which only one other American representative is known. The chair comes from New York but its overall design, like that of almost all New England turned chairs, is derived from British antecedents. The second wooden-bottom armchair is from the Boston area (cat. no. 2). It represents a form that has long been associated with the earliest New England settlers because two well-known examples have traditional histories of having belonged to founders of Plymouth Colony, Massachusetts, namely, William Brewster and William Bradford. Its tall urn-and-flame finials and the squat vase turnings on its posts are characteristic of the seventeenth-century turned-chair style identified with the Boston area, whose influence is evident to a greater or lesser degree in five of the other chairs here included (cat. nos. 3–7).

Of the small chairs, one belongs to a turning tradition ascribed to coastal Connecticut (cat. no. 8). Another is in a distinctive design that originated in the Netherlands in the mid-seventeenth century. Made in New York City and environs where the Dutch settled, it reflects direct northern European influence (cat. no. 9). A New York spindle armchair in Appendix 1 (cat. no. 135) exhibits some traits attributable to direct Continental influence as well. The collection lacks any spindle-back chairs from farther south. Missing in particular is a distinct type with spindles set between sawn back rails that has French antecedents and is associated with areas of Huguenot settlement in the South.[2] Judging by the number of surviving examples, spindle-back chairs were the more prevalent type of turned chair in the colonies until the late 1600s. The form then became less favored, and it did not for the most part long outlive the seventeenth century.

1. Sewall 1973, vol. 1, p. 87, vol. 2, pp. 730, 963, 966.
2. See, for example, Rauschenberg and Bivins 2003, vol. 1, p. 17, fig. E1 (Bayou Bend Collection).

1.

Spindle-back armchair

New York City or vicinity, 1665–90

A complex structure is this chair's most distinguishing feature. Its unusual construction has antecedents in British three- and four-legged turned chairs that have a rectangular raked back emerging from a heavy lower back rail that overhangs the rear leg(s), such as the well-known President's Chair at Harvard University, Cambridge, Massachusetts. The use of a board seat, seat rails with intersecting tenons, and front-to-back rails below the arms seen on cat. no. 1 are part of that same chairmaking tradition. In other respects, this chair is quite different from the English or Welsh examples of this form, which typically display dense grids of elaborate allover late-medieval-style turnery and have an archaic look, whether made in the sixteenth century or as late as the early eighteenth century.[1] Here, the chair's members are widely spaced. The turnings reflect the Renaissance-inspired vocabulary of vase, ball, and ring shapes common to seventeenth-century American chairs with straight rear posts; and, as on those chairs, the ornament is applied selectively to create a subtle recall of forms. In addition, the thick lower back rail characteristic of British examples has been modified; the middle portion, where a large diameter offers no structural advantage, is thinner and more or less on the same plane as the spindles and upper rails. This not only lightens the design but also makes for more comfortable sitting.

Only one other American chair of this type is known, a similar example at the Connecticut Historical Society, Hartford. Its turnings are fewer and simpler in outline, but they are related in overall form and in a particular detail: on both chairs there is an analogous small thin disk below the flattened ball of the finials, which is recalled at the top of the stile balusters. On cat. no. 1 this disk occurs also at the bottom of the balusters on the front posts. The two chairs come out of the same school of chairmaking, but given the different quality of their turnings and their histories they were probably not made in the same shop or at the same time. The Connecticut Historical Society's chair was given in 1856 by the Rev. Dr. Thomas Robbins and may have come to him through ancestors in Wethersfield or Branford, Connecticut.[2]

The history of the MMA chair points to a probable first owner in Manhattan or in one of the early towns of Kings County (now Brooklyn), New York, whether it descended directly in the Strycker (Stryker, Striker) family or entered the family by marriage. The greater elaboration and sophistication of the turned forms on cat. no. 1 suggest that of the two chairs it is the one closer to the point of origin (in time

1

I

and place) of this school of turning in America and that this tradition was first established in the New York area and then diffused to the Connecticut shore, most plausibly by the movement of craftsmen.

A slat-back armchair with a wooden seat and straight rear posts at Historic Deerfield has deeply grooved balusters and compressed balls closely related to those on cat. no. 1.[3] Regrettably it has no history, but other chairs that provide parallels to the turnings on cat. no. 1 do have associations with the New York City area. The type of tall, grooved baluster featured on the arm supports of cat. no. 1 is found on all four posts of a spindle armchair at the Bowne House Historical Society, Flushing, New York, which has a local history, and on the arm supports of a chair that belongs to the same school of turning as cat. no. 9.[4] It may be reflected at some remove in the turnings of cat. no. 135 with a mid–Hudson River valley or perhaps Kings County provenance. A form of slat-back chair that is attributed to New York City or its vicinity also has rails below the arms, and those rails are ornamented with deeply grooved ovoid turnings analogous to those on cat. no. 1. Interestingly the under-arm rails of those slat-back chairs have loose rings—a type of virtuoso turning that is not otherwise known on American chairs but that is displayed on British chairs with the same type of construction as cat. no. 1 (and is found on northern European chairs as well). What relationship there may have been between the turner of this chair and the makers of the slat-back chairs it is difficult to say.[5] Given this chair's structure, he appears to have been trained in Britain; thus the chair most likely postdates 1664, when the English took over New Netherland, and it may not have been made as early as its archaic form might suggest.[6]

CONSTRUCTION

The chair is joined entirely with round tenons. The tenons, as was discovered when joints were disassembled to replace the seat, taper nearly ⅛ inch (about ⅞ in. to ¾ in.), as do the mortises, which appear to have been reamed. The joints of the top back rail, arms, and under-arm rails, and those of the stiles and rear legs to the lower back rail are pinned. Scribe lines mark the location of all the structural joints except those of the under-arm rails to the front posts. The scored lines on the rails of the back and on the front stretchers are irregularly spaced and do not mark the placement of the spindles. The front posts and rear legs taper slightly from top to bottom and the stiles from bottom to top; all measure close to 2¾ inches in diameter at their largest. The heaviness of the stock prevents the lower back rail from being weakened by the three mortises (for stile, rear leg, and under-arm-rail tenons) drilled in close proximity to one another at either end and allows the legs to safely accommodate the large size of the seat joints. The seat-rail tenons protrude and interlock: the thick (1⅛ in. diam.) tenons of the front and rear rails are intersected by the thinner (½ in. diam.) tenons of the side rails. The interlocking keeps the joints of the front and rear rails from pulling apart and assures that those rails will not rotate under the weight of the sitter and release the seat board, which is set into a groove on the inner surface of the four rails.

CONDITION

By the time the chair was acquired, the original board seat had been lost and the right seat rail replaced, and the seat was of rush. The present seat—of riven red oak like the original seat on the chair at the Connecticut Historical Society—was installed in 1999. The restoration included making a new replacement right seat rail and repairing the left seat rail and rotating it back to its original position (with the groove for the seat board on the inner side). The work entailed taking ten or so joints apart. Most of the chair's joints had already been apart and many repaired more than once: they had been reinforced with nails, many of which had subsequently been removed and the resulting holes patched; some tenons were broken and glued, and some were replaced; few if any of the joint pins were original. The 1999 restoration renewed the replaced tenons in both joints of the left seat rail and in the joint of the right arm to the front post and the right under-arm rail to the lower back rail, but it did not disturb the replaced tenons at the rear of the arms, which have been rotated somewhat. In addition, the spindles below the seat, which had been inverted, were reversed, and a replacement tenon on the left spindle was made new. The finials probably once terminated in small knobs, and the front posts are missing the handgrips. The top back rail may be an old replacement, for one would expect it to be more elaborately turned than the rail below it. The feet have been cut down. Many of the ring turnings have losses, and there are dents and surface cracks throughout as well as large splits with wood fill in the thicker portions of the lower back rail. The chair has been stripped and probably oiled and waxed; it retains residues of a dark coating and small traces of green over white paint, none of which is original.

WOOD

ASH. (According to R. Bruce Hoadley, microanalysis of the wood gave no indication that the ash might be European.)

DIMENSIONS

OH. 39⅜ (100); SH. 16 (40.6); OW. (lower back rail) 23¾ (60.3); SW. front 23 (58.4); SW. back 17 (43.2); SD. 16 (40.6).

REFERENCES

Hopper Striker Mott, "Jan and Jacobus Strijcker and Some of Their Descendants," *New York Genealogical and Biographical Record* 38 (January 1907), p. 9 (engraved illustration that shows the chair with a rush seat and the spindles below the seat oriented as they are at present); Downs 1944, p. 78 (this and all subsequent references show the chair with a rush seat and lower spindles inverted); "Additions to the American Wing" 1945; "Antiques in the American Wing" 1946, p. 247, no. 6; Schwartz 1958, pl. 1B; Comstock 1962, no. 19; M. B. Davidson 1967, no. 61; Bishop 1972, no. 15; Schwartz 1976, no. 1; Chinnery 1979, fig. 2:82; Kirk 1982, no. 698.

PROVENANCE

The chair was bought from Josephine Striker, New York City, with a history of having belonged to Jacobus Gerritsen Strijcker (ca. 1620–1687), who emigrated to New Amsterdam from the Netherlands in 1651, held public offices in that city, and eventually moved to Midwout (Flatbush) in Kings County (now Brooklyn), New York. The vendor was the second wife of Elsworth Striker (1858–1912), who had inherited from his uncle James Striker (1826–1900)—a lineal descendant of Jacobus—the family mansion in New York City and apparently its contents. An 1875 account of the house describes what may well be this piece, singling out from among the old chairs one that "is a veritable 'Mayflower,' and looks as if it might have come with the Pilgrims." The "old oak chair in the hall" mentioned as an early family memento in an 1883 article is also very likely this chair. (Both accounts refer to a portrait of Jacobus, presumably the painting sold to the MMA by the same vendor.) The house (at Fifty-second Street and the Hudson River) stood on land that came into the family through the 1780 marriage of James's grandfather James Striker (1755–1831) to Maria Hopper (1760–1786).

Given its style, the chair could have originally belonged to Jacobus Strijcker or to a member of the next generation. In direct line of descent to the above-mentioned Jameses are: Jacobus's son Gerrit Striker (b. Holland, d. 1694), who resided in Kings County and married in 1673 Wyntie Cornelise Boomgaert (d. 1700); his son Jacobus Striker (1682–1748), who married Martha Griggs of Gravesend and in 1722 moved from Gravesend, Kings County, to Oyster Bay, Long Island (Gravesend, chartered in 1645, was an English settlement); his son Gerrit Striker (1726–1775), who married Ann Alberston and lived in Kings County and then Oyster Bay until he acquired in 1764 a farm on Manhattan Island (at Ninety-sixth Street and the Hudson River).[7]

Rogers Fund, 1941 (41.111)

1. For British chairs of this type, see Ryder 1975; Chinnery 1979, pp. 93–97; and Trent 1990. See also Forman 1988, pp. 68–73. The Harvard chair is in Fairbanks and Trent 1982, no. 471. The writer is not aware of any Continental turned chairs with this type of rectangular raked-back construction. Depicted in northern European paintings and prints are three-legged chairs with board seats that have a straight rear post, to the top of which a crossrail is attached to serve as a backrest—a form of chair also made in Britain (Forman 1988, fig. 28).

2. The chair, shown in I. W. Lyon 1891, fig. 54, has been often illustrated. According to information compiled by Robert F. Trent and at the Connecticut Historical Society, it had been owned by the grandfather of the donor (1777–1856), Rev. Philemon Robbins of Branford (1709–1781) and may have come to him through his wife's Foote ancestors in Wethersfield or Branford. See also Forman 1988, pp. 71–72. This chair is close to cat. no. 1 in its dimensions, but the layout lines are not identical. It retains its original oak seat board but its two outer spindles are replaced, as is most likely its crest rail.

3. Fales 1976, no. 12.

4. Failey 1976, no. 17; Gronning 2001, figs. 6, 8.

5. For the slat-back chairs, see Dilliard 1963, no. 94; Randall 1965, no. 121; Bishop 1972, no. 33; Failey 1976, no. 18; Forman 1988, no. 17; Failey 1998, nos. 4A, 4B, 5A, 6A. Benno M. Forman considered this a Dutch chair type that may have been made also in England (Forman 1988, p. 110). While the New York chairs all have related turned rails under the arms, the differences they exhibit in other elements suggest that they were made in more than one shop and over time, with some examples dating probably as late as the early 1700s. This type of chair may have influenced the use of turned rails below the arms on eighteenth-century Connecticut chairs. For loose rings on British chairs, see Chinnery 1979, figs. 2:76–2:79.

6. There is always the possibility that an English turner was active in the area before that date. Chartered in 1645, Gravesend was an English settlement, unlike the other five towns established in Kings County under Dutch rule. In 1642, for example, an English carpenter, Thomas Chambers, contracted to build houses in New Netherland (I. N. P. Stokes 1915–28, vol. 4 [1922], pp. 95–96). However, a date of manufacture in the last third of the seventeenth century is much more likely.

7. The main sources of information are: William Norman Stryker, *The Stryker Family in America*, 3 vols. (Mount Vernon, Va., 1979–87), vol. 1 (1979), pp. 11, 16, 19, 36, 72, 243, 347, vol. 3 (1987), p. 838; I. N. P. Stokes 1915–28, vol. 2 (1916), p. 290, vol. 6 (1928), pp. 95, 141; William S. Strycker, comp., *Genealogical Record of the Strÿcker Family* (Camden, N.J., 1887), pp. 48–51 (on p. 51 is an excerpt from the 1883 article that mentions the chair). For the 1875 account, see Despard and Greatorex 1875, p. 119. For the portrait, see Gardner and Feld 1965, p. 281.

2.

Spindle-back armchair

Boston or Charlestown, Massachusetts, 1640–80

With tiers of spindles to the floor and a board seat, this type of chair was the ne plus ultra of seventeenth-century New England turned seating. The overall form (but not the turnings, which show Renaissance influence) is descended from the medieval secular and religious seats of authority that were enclosed below the seat and arms with grids of turnings.[1] Indeed cat. no. 2 has a commanding presence. While its boxlike design with ranks of repetitive spindles may appear simple at first glance, the chair is a carefully orchestrated composition with subtle variations in the arrangement of its horizontal and vertical members and of its turned motifs. The posts, tapered from top to bottom, have a slight outward slant so that the form widens toward the top making for a broader spread at arms and finials, which enhances the prominence of the sitter whom they enframe. In each two

tiers of spindles the upper is taller than the lower, though on the front and back the difference is small. The spindles enclose the form in a virtual screen—one that is vibrant not only because of variations in the execution of the design within the same row but also because of the greater or lesser attenuation of the vase and cone shapes according to the height of the tier. The turnings of the cross elements on the sides and back increase in elaboration from the bottom up. While the top back rail does not appear to be original, it is appropriate insofar as it is the most complex of the rails and as the pattern is organized around a central element.

The form of this chair's turnings, in particular the so-called urn-and-flame finials (fig. 1) and the grooved, compressed vase shapes on the posts, are key elements of a tradition of eastern Massachusetts chairmaking that originated in the shops of Boston and nearby Charlestown and was probably diffused through export and the movement of craftsmen.[2] Two features set cat. no. 2 apart from the majority of the chairs in this style of turning: ranks of spindles below the seat and a board seat that is let into a groove on the inner side of the rails, the joints of which interlock (see *Construction*).[3] Cat. no. 2 is one of three chairs in this category that have a history of ownership in the Boston area and are in all likelihood products of that dominant woodworking center, though probably not all the work of the same shop. One is an armchair said to have belonged to Rev. John Eliot of Roxbury, which has thick rings or flattened balls above the vase shapes on the posts and spindles; the other is a child's high chair with a history in the Mather family of Dorchester and then Boston, which has finials identical to those on cat. no. 2 and a similar seat-rail structure but a rush seat, not a wooden one.[4]

The best known of this type of chair are the two examples with histories of ownership in Plymouth, Massachusetts, by the Pilgrim Fathers William Brewster and Governor William Bradford, respectively. Both from the same shop, they do not appear to be by the same hand that produced cat. no. 2. Although they are similar to the present chair in many aspects, including the tapering of the posts, the turnings exhibit differences: the posts are ornamented not with squat vase shapes but with flat rings of the sort commonly found on crosspieces, and while the individual elements of the finials correspond quite closely to their counterparts on cat. no. 2, the design has only one disk between the ball and the flame. The pattern of the spindles is essentially identical to that seen here, but on the Brewster and Bradford chairs the vasiform turnings have a stronger ogee outline and are ornamented with a deep V-groove flanked by scored lines rather than with just a pair of lines. Listed in Bradford's probate inventory (d. 1657) along with other forms of seating are "2 great wooden chaires" (chairs with wooden seats)—evidence that he owned the type of chair that has been associated with him and that such chairs were being made at midcentury or earlier.[5] What has proved more difficult to establish is where the chairs of this form with Plymouth County histories were made; to date, no chairmaking shop in the Plymouth area that might have produced them has been documented. The eastern Massachusetts chairs with board seats show several different hands at work, but the vocabulary of the turned ornament is all interrelated. Whether this is because several immigrant craftsmen carried the same or similar schools of chairmaking to different Massachusetts towns or because one broad transplanted shop tradition was diffused from a single center is an intriguing question.[6]

CONSTRUCTION

The posts taper from 2½ inches in diameter at the top to 2 inches at the bottom. With the exception of the front and rear seat rails, the frame is joined with round tenons, which, as revealed by X-radiography, are slightly bulbous at the end. Those rails have ⅜-inch-wide rectangular tenons that go through the posts; they are intersected and locked in place by the round tenons of the side seat rails, which are secured with a pin. The rectangular mortises have rounded ends, indicating they were formed by first drilling a hole at either extremity. This is confirmed by the two ⅜-inch-wide holes that are bored from side to side on each front post (three of them through the post) and filled with wooden pegs; the holes are in line vertically and equidistant from a groove below the lower vase turning, and a short horizontal line is scribed at the top of the upper hole and the bottom of the lower hole. The lines are similar to those that mark the height of the front seat-rail mortises and are the same distance apart. Clearly the turner began making the seat-rail mortises at the wrong layout line and, unwilling to scrap the posts, simply plugged the holes. The inner side of the seat rails and of the four posts is grooved to receive the board seat. The round mortises for the seat rails, the arms, the lower of the two upper back rails, and the lower side stretchers are centered on a scribed line; those for the lower front and back stretcher are drilled tangential to a line. The location of the other crosspieces is not specifically marked. This suggests that the turner was working from basic layout lines that might be used for more than one design and that on this chair he positioned the lower back rail and upper stretchers to meet the needs of this particular scheme with multiple tiers of spindles. The rear rails are all the same length as the cross members of the sides, and the arms and adjacent rail of the back are in addition interchangeable in their turnings.

CONDITION

The top back rail is probably not original, and the handgrips (restored by Wallace Nutting), seat, and lower right stretcher are replacements. The present seat (red oak) dates from 1980, at which time the missing upper inner quadrant of the seat rails was restored and the grooves to hold the seat board thereby re-created. (The earlier replacement seat, on the chair when acquired by Nutting, was a thick pine board installed by removing the aforementioned segment of the rails so that the lower edge of the groove on the inner side of the rails formed a ledge to support the board.) While only the tenons of the side seat rails were probably pinned originally, all the structural joints except those of the top back rail now show what look like new wooden pins but are in some, and perhaps all, instances actually plugs hiding added nails. Small modern nails reinforce the joints of the top back rail, and the same type secures many of the spindles, all of which have small losses. The feet have been cut down an inch or more, and a large section has split off the right side of the right rear foot. The chair has been stripped and appears to have been oiled and waxed. It retains residues of black over red paint, which is not original.

WOOD

ASH.

DIMENSIONS

OH. 44½ (113); SH. 17¾ (45.1); SW. front 23¼ (59.1); SW. back 16¾ (42.5); SD. 16¼ (41.3).

EXHIBITIONS

"A Bicentennial Treasury: American Masterpieces from the Metropolitan," MMA, 29 January 1976–2 January 1977; "April Fool: Folk Art Fakes and Forgeries," Hirschl and Adler Folk, New York City, 1–30 April 1988.

2. See also fig. 1.

REFERENCES

Nutting 1921, pp. 182–83 (Tufts family history); Nutting 1924, no. 300 (owned by Mrs. J. Insley Blair); Nutting 1928–33, no. 1799 (this and the previous references show handgrips missing and the old replacement seat) and vol. 3, pp. 390–91 (story of purchase); Andrus 1951, p. 246; Andrus 1952, p. 167; Powel 1954, p. 201; Williams 1963, no. 4; Ripley 1964, fig. 4; M. B. Davidson 1967, no. 1; Margon 1971, p. 72; Bishop 1972, no. 10; *Bicentennial Treasury* 1976 (exh. cat.), p. 238; Chinnery 1979, fig. 2:90; Cooper 1980, fig. 140; Safford 1980, fig. 6; Fitzgerald 1982, fig. I-6; M. B. Davidson and Stillinger 1985, fig. 132; Pennington 1988 (exh. cat.), no. 39A; Greene 1996, p. 11; Manca 2003, fig. 7. For a reproduction of this chair offered for sale, see Nutting 1930 (1977 ed.), p. 80, no. 411.

PROVENANCE

Ex coll.: Wallace Nutting, Framingham, Massachusetts; Mrs. J. Insley Blair, Tuxedo Park, New York.

Nutting stated that he purchased the chair from John Tufts of Sherborn, Massachusetts, who told him that it had been in the family for eight generations. The progenitor of the Tufts family in America, Peter Tufts (d. 1700), was in Charlestown by 1638, and within a few decades the family became firmly established in Medford.[7] Mrs. Blair acquired the chair in 1921 from Collings and Collings, New York City dealers. It was on loan from her to the MMA from 1939 until it became a gift.

Gift of Mrs. J. Insley Blair, 1951 (51.12.2)

1. Ryder 1976; Eames 1977, pp. 192–95 and pls. 54, 55A, 55B.
2. This type of finial—Anglo-Dutch in derivation—has a form related to that found on turnings applied to Boston case furniture (compare G. W. R. Ward 1988, figs. 51B, 51C). For the Boston chairmaking industry, see Fairbanks and Trent 1982, no. 178; Forman 1988, pp. 75–78.
3. Wooden seats and interlocking seat rails are found on both English and northern European turned chairs, and they occur on a few chairs from colonies other than Massachusetts (cat. no. 1 and Hurst and Prown 1997, no. 3). Board seats were let into grooves in the rectangular seat rails of some joined chairs, mainly in Pennsylvania (*Philadelphia* 1976, no. 6; Forman 1988, nos. 48, 28, 30, 31; Hurst and Prown 1997, no. 1).
4. For the Eliot chair (location unknown), see Forman 1988, p. 77; for the Mather family high chair (American Antiquarian Society, Worcester, Massachusetts), see Fairbanks and Trent 1982, no. 183. A heavily restored chair, which lacks a history, at Historic New England (acc. no. 1971.67) has rings above the vases on the posts and spindles that are similar to those on the Eliot chair.
5. Both chairs are at the Pilgrim Hall Museum, Plymouth, Massachusetts (Pizer, Driver, and Earle 1985, pls. I, II). Portions of the Bradford inventory are quoted and interpreted in Fairbanks and Trent 1982, no. 504, and Forman 1988, p. 74.
6. Two other board-seated chairs have links to Plymouth County. One is a third example at the Pilgrim Hall Museum, with a traditional history of ownership by Myles Standish (Nutting 1921, p. 184; Pizer, Driver, and Earle 1985, fig. 4). Extensively restored, it retains spindles that match those on the Brewster and Bradford chairs but has straight-sided vase turnings on the posts much like those on the Historic New England chair (see n. 4 above). The other is a chair at the Museum of Fine Arts, Boston, with a history in the Keith family of Bridgewater, Massachusetts, that has spindles only in the back (one tier) and all seat rails round-tenoned. Its spindle turnings and rings on the posts are similar to those on the Bradford and Brewster chairs, but its one-disk finials differ in that the disk and flame are fused (Randall 1965, no. 119).
7. Thomas Bellows Wyman, *The Genealogies and Estates of Charlestown, Massachusetts, 1629–1818* (Boston, 1879; repr., Somersworth, N.H., 1982), pp. 957–63.

3.

Spindle-back armchair

Probably Boston or vicinity, 1650–80

Rush-seated chairs with two tiers of spindles in the back and spindles under the arms (and/or between the front stretchers), while not as rare as wooden-bottom examples (see cat. no. 2), are still not common. This is one of some eight such chairs known with turnings in the eastern Massachusetts style associated with the shops of Boston and Charlestown. On this chair the most conspicuous feature of that style—multitiered urn-and-flame finials—is missing; only the spherical turning at the base of the finials is original, and the upper elements are incongruous replacements.[1] Lost from the top of the front posts are the characteristic ball handgrips. The remaining turnings, however, place the chair squarely within that tradition: squat, grooved vase shapes on the posts, spindles consisting of a vasiform element between two cones, and stretchers with a scored ovoid turning at either end and a pair of incised lines flanking a single one in the middle. As on a number of other chairs in the same turning tradition, such as cat. no. 10, the posts are of poplar.[2] The turnings on the posts and spindles are

skillfully executed, with marked variations in the diameter of the elements and with a vital recall of form between the larger and smaller versions of the vase motif. On both, the shape is distinguished by a well-rounded base that narrows sharply to a short neck, which then flares out strongly to a thin disklike rim separated from the post or cone above by a deep cut.

This chair's design encompasses a series of equal horizontal spaces with the two tiers of spindles in the back, the spindles under the arms, and the void between the seat and the bottom back rail all virtually the same height. The gap above the seat is higher than usual, the result of having two equal tiers of spindles on the back between posts with the particular placement of vase turnings seen here, which limits the height of the upper spindles. It may be that this chair's stiles represent a shop pattern not intended specifically or solely for such a design but drawn up to accommodate more than one type of back; they could serve as well for a chair back with a single tier of spindles or three slats. While the top rail was virtually

3

always placed at a scribe line—as are the two uppermost rails here—the location of other crosspieces in a chair back was not necessarily fixed by a layout line. The turner apparently positioned the rails for the back he intended by measuring a set distance from an existing line. Grooves on seventeenth-century turned chairs formed part of the ornamental scheme, and the disposition of some, particularly on the stiles, appears to have been based on design rather than structural considerations.

A chair with closely related turnings is at the Museum of Fine Arts, Boston.[3] Its spindles are taller (the lower vase turning is lower on the stiles) and the back extends further down. With four spindles in each tier of the back and below the arms, it comes closer to achieving the substantial presence of wooden-bottom chairs like cat. no. 2 than does the present example. Although rush-seated chairs are bound to have a more open design because the spindles cannot go down to the seat rails, this chair with only three spindles in each row and a large void in the lower back (which would have been only partly filled by a seat cushion) has a quite airy aspect. Further examples of this type of seating within the Boston-Charlestown stylistic tradition include a group of three related chairs, on which the spindles under the arms are centered on those in the lower tier of the back and much shorter than the former. Several individual chairs, each the work of a different hand, represent yet other formats.[4] Rush-seated chairs that incorporate spindles below the arms and/or the seat were also produced by a distinct school of turning attributed to Plymouth County, Massachusetts (see the entry for cat. no. 12).

CONSTRUCTION
The chair's joints are all round-tenoned. The relationship of the mortises for the cross elements to the layout lines on the posts varies: some are tangential (two uppermost back rails and seat rails); some are centered (lower stretchers, upper front stretcher); others are a short distance from a line (upper arms, upper side stretchers); and the location of a few mortises was not marked by a work line (two lower back rails, lower arms). The posts do not have any consistent or appreciable taper. The cross members of the back and sides are the same length, and the rows of spindles are essentially all the same height. Many of the crosspieces were turned from stock that was too skimpy or not properly centered in the lathe, for there is a flat area on virtually all the arms and stretchers (turned to the under or inner side) and one visible across the front of the bottom back rail.

CONDITION
The upper half of the finials (above the ball) is new, as are all the spindles (ash) below the arms. The top inch of the front posts, which includes the uppermost part of the arm-joint mortises, is replaced. The seat rails appear to have been reworked or renewed, and the splint seat dates from the early 1900s; the original seat was no doubt rush. It may be that the flat area now on the front of the bottom back rail originally faced the rear and that the rail was flipped end to end at some point when the chair was apart for repairs (possible because the spindles are evenly spaced). The lower front stretcher has been rotated in its sockets. Heavy wear is evident at the front of the arms and on the posts, which show filled holes as well as gouges and losses. The chair has been mahoganized with stain and varnish or colored varnish, which has worn through in some areas and flaked off in others.

WOODS
Posts, POPLAR (*Populus* sp.); rails of back, seat rails, arms, stretchers, ASH; spindles of back, SOFT MAPLE.

DIMENSIONS
OH. 45 (114.3); SH. 15⅞ (40.3); SW. front 25 (63.5); SW. back 17¾ (45.1); SD. 15¾ (40).

EXHIBITION
"A Cubberd, Four Joyne Stools & Other Smalle Thinges: The Material Culture of Plymouth Colony, and Silver and Silversmiths of Plymouth, Cape Cod and Nantucket," Heritage Plantation of Sandwich (now Heritage Museum and Gardens), Sandwich, Massachusetts, 8 May–23 October 1994.

REFERENCES
Cullity 1994 (exh. cat.), no. 130; Trent and Goldstein 1998, fig. 10.

PROVENANCE
Ex coll.: Mrs. J. Insley Blair, Tuxedo Park, New York.
Mrs. Blair purchased the chair in 1918 from the New York City dealers Collings and Collings. The chair was on loan from Mrs. Blair to the MMA from 1939 to the time of the bequest.

Bequest of Mrs. J. Insley Blair, 1951 (52.77.47)

1. On the basis of the form of the replaced upper half of the finials, the chair has been mistakenly attributed to Plymouth County, Massachusetts (Cullity 1994, no. 130; Trent and Goldstein 1998, fig. 10).
2. See also Forman 1988, pp. 33, 90–92.
3. While the Museum of Fine Arts chair (Randall 1965, no. 117), which has also lost its upper finials and original handgrips, has very similar turnings, its posts are heavier, and the rear ones taper ¼ inch from top to bottom. From the seat down, the layout lines on the posts are close to those on cat. no. 3, but above the seat they do not correspond.
4. The group of three related chairs includes one in the Concord Museum, Concord, Massachusetts (Wood 1996, no. 21); one in the Detroit Institute of Arts, Detroit, Michigan (acc. no. 28.43); and one in the Winterthur Museum (Forman 1988, no. 1). Other chairs are in the Dietrich American Foundation (*Important American Furniture, Folk Art, Folk Paintings and Silver*, auction cat., Sotheby's, New York City, 24 October 1987, lot 533); Historic Deerfield (Fales 1976, no. 8); and the Wadsworth Atheneum (Nutting 1928–33, no. 1802). Also in the Winterthur Museum is a northeastern Massachusetts chair with turnings outside the Boston-Charlestown tradition (Forman 1988, no. 2).

4.
Spindle-back armchair
Northeastern Massachusetts, 1660–1700

In the use of urn-and-flame finials, ball handgrips, and vase turnings on the posts, this chair conforms to the Boston style enunciated, for example, by cat. no. 2, but differs in the details of its design, which suggests that it was not made in that urban center but elsewhere in eastern Massachusetts. Its turnings have some noteworthy particularities. The finial is distinctive in that it terminates in an ovoid that hardly narrows at the base and that the element below it is not a straight-sided disk, as on the typical Boston finial, but is a ring between fillets that is set above a well-defined reel (compare figs. 3, 1). A

peculiarity of the turnings on the crosspieces is a tripartite motif that consists of a flat ring flanked by half rings. It is found on the rails that support the spindles, on the arms, and on the stretchers. A larger version of this pattern occurs on the outer thirds of the top back rail; the middle third features opposed baluster forms that echo the three pairs of compressed vases on the bottom back rail and the vase shapes on the posts. The top back rail thus encapsulates the chair's major turned themes and brings unity to the design. The vasiform turnings on the stiles are considerably shorter than those on the legs

4. See also figs. 3, 122.

and arm supports, but even the shorter version is not as squat as the type characteristic of Boston work (compare cat. no. 2).

This armchair is one of a minority of seventeenth-century turned chairs with posts ornamented below the seat, and it represents a rare occurrence of turnings on both the rear legs and the front legs. Here, the particular placement of the vase motif on the leg has resulted in a totally atypical stretcher arrangement: in order to achieve a scheme in which the turning was more or less centered between the stretchers, the upper stretcher was positioned above and the lower stretcher below the respective side stretchers, contrary to standard practice, in which the front stretchers were both placed either above or below those on the sides.[1]

The type of spindle seen here, with a straight-sided urn form flanked by thin disks, occurs on several other eastern Massachusetts chairs, but those chairs do not relate closely to cat. no. 4 in any further details of their turnings.[2] No other chair from the same shop as the present example is known, and as is often the case, it is difficult to localize the piece. One can only speculate that it may have originated in Essex County since the turnings have a certain relationship—of generally similar aesthetics more than of specific patterns—with some of the applied ornament on case furniture that has been attributed to the Symonds shops of Salem and the northern Essex County shop tradition represented by cat. no. 58. That turned ornament exhibits a like taste for sequences of varied, rather densely stacked motifs with tight rhythms, as on this chair's back rails, and for multiple thin disks (see cat. no. 108), and it also includes rings and reels such as those that distinguish the finials (cat. no. 78).[3]

CONSTRUCTION

The posts do not have any consistent or appreciable taper, and they are meant to be vertical. The joints are round-tenoned, and the mortises in the posts are each drilled centered on an individual line that marks their location. The layout lines on the legs are for the usual two tiers of stretchers (with, in this case, the side stretchers on both levels positioned a short distance on the posts from the corresponding front and rear stretchers), but those work lines were reinterpreted to create an unusual stretcher arrangement. The horizontal elements of the back and of the sides are of equal length.

CONDITION

The vase turnings on the rear posts have a thicker rim than those on the front posts, but there is no indication that the posts do not

belong together. The right arm is replaced, and the left arm has been rotated in its joints to conceal wear. In the right rear and both front posts the mortises of the arm joints have broken through and the holes have been plugged. Holes dug out in the center top of the handgrips have been filled. The rear stretcher is a replacement, as is the lower front stretcher; the pins that were added to the joints of the previous lower front stretcher are no longer operative. The opening of the mortises for the upper front stretcher has been widened with cuts of a gouge and the end turnings of the stretcher slightly countersunk. It is not clear when that adjustment was made; it may have occurred initially, for X-radiographs show that the tenons fit snugly in the same manner as those of other original elements. Nails have been added to the joints of the rear and side stretchers and seat rails. The rush seat is modern; there is evidence that the seat was at one time upholstered. The rear feet have been cut down a good $\frac{1}{2}$ inch more than the front ones, causing the posts to lean backward. The chair has been covered in large part with brown paint applied over varnish.

WOODS
MAPLE; right front leg, bottom rail of back, SOFT MAPLE; seat rails, ASH.

DIMENSIONS
OH. 41⅝ (105.7); SH. 16⅝ (42.2); SW. front 23⅛ (58.7); SW. back 17¾ (45.1); SD. 16¼ (41.3).

PROVENANCE
Ex coll.: Mrs. J. Insley Blair, Tuxedo Park, New York.

Mrs. Blair purchased the chair from the dealers Collings and Collings in New York City in 1926. The chair was on loan to the MMA from Mrs. Blair from 1939 to the time of the bequest.

Bequest of Mrs. J. Insley Blair, 1951 (52.77.49)

1. With the exception of cat. no. 1, other known turned seventeenth-century chairs with ornament on the legs have a standard two-tier stretcher arrangement with a turning placed between the seat and the upper stretcher (see cat. no. 2), or between the two stretchers, or in both locations (see cat. no. 12). In most cases, turnings occur only on the front legs. One other Massachusetts-type chair with ornament on both rear and front legs is found in Forman 1988, no. 6. This feature is somewhat more frequently found on New York chairs (see cat. no. 1, cat. no. 9, and many related examples; and Forman 1988, no. 9).
2. Most closely related are the spindles on a chair at the Wadsworth Atheneum (Comstock 1962, no. 18) and one illustrated in "Made in New England" 1944, p. 26.
3. For example, a Salem cupboard at the Peabody Essex Museum (Trent 1989, no. 4), and from northern Essex County, a chest of drawers at the Winterthur Museum and a cupboard at the Museum of Fine Arts, Boston (Trent, Follansbee, and A. Miller 2001, figs. 1, 2, 91).

5. See also fig. 4.

5.
Spindle-back armchair

Eastern Massachusetts, 1650–1700

In overall format, type of finial, tapered posts, and spindles with conical ends, cat. no. 5 is indebted to the eastern Massachusetts style of chair developed in Boston and Charlestown, but in the details of the turnings it belongs to a distinct shop tradition. What sets the particular interpretation of the urn-and-flame finial design on this chair apart is the broad half-round groove, instead of a V-shaped line, that ornaments the midpoint of the ball turning and the fact that there is an incised line around the middle of all the elements above the ball, not just the ovoid knop at the top (compare figs. 4, 1). Such rounded grooves—in effect very short reels—are used throughout the upper part of the chair and give this piece a highly individual character. They occur singly on the lower stiles; on the upper stiles and the arm supports they flank flat-sided balls that take the place of the compressed vase forms typical of Boston-style chairs; smaller versions of the same reel-and-ball pattern are seen on the spindles; and reels, rather than the usual flat rings or grooves, punctuate the arms and the rails that support the spindles. Also to be noted are the extensive use of incised lines to demarcate and accent the turned motifs and the fact that the lines are most often paired or three together, and under the finials, even in a group of four. Lightly incised lines and grooves ornament the side and rear stretchers as well as the front ones, all of which have a greater than usual amount of decoration.

A chair advertised in *Antiques* in 1967 is the only other piece published that has like idiosyncratic turnings.[1] The patterns on the top back rail, other crosspieces, spindles, and posts are analogous to those on cat. no. 5, and as on the present example, the upper and lower tier of stretchers are uncommonly far apart. The ovoid top of the finials, however, is ornamented with the same narrow reel as the ball at the base, and the handgrips repeat the flat-sided outline and grooves of the arm-support turnings. Those handgrips are in keeping with the overall decorative scheme, in contrast to the replaced pommels on this chair, the smooth, rounded shape of which strikes a dissonant note.

There are no clear stylistic indicators as to where in eastern Massachusetts the shop that produced this particular design was located. A chair in the same general eastern Massachusetts style with a Scituate history has stile turnings related to those on cat. no. 5 in that a small reel occurs below the finials and above and below a ball motif; but that motif is not the same, for immediately flanking the ball shape is what appears to be a cavetto.[2] The type of rounded groove or short reel featured here, while not common on chairs, was in widespread use on turnings on case furniture; it is found on the pillars of cupboards made in the New Haven, Connecticut, area and in various parts of eastern Massachusetts, including Boston, Cambridge, Plymouth County, and particularly Essex County, where it appears as a repeat motif on applied turnings as well.[3]

CONSTRUCTION
The diameter of the posts tapers from about 2¼ inches at the top to about 2 inches at the bottom. They have a built-in backward slant (X-radiographs confirm that the mortises are drilled at an angle), and the taper gives them a slight lateral flare toward the top. The chair is joined with round tenons, which according to the X-radiographs have a slightly bulbous end. The mortises are each centered on an individual layout line. Two extra work lines were incised by error: one on the right rear post ½ inch above the groove for the bottom back rail and one on the right front post even with the lines on the rear posts for the rear stretcher. The horizontal elements of the back are equal in length to those of the sides.

CONDITION
The handgrips and lower side stretchers—missing when the chair was acquired—were replaced at some point before 1940, and the feet, which had been cut down and notched to receive rockers, pieced for about 2 inches. The manner in which the feet were ended causes the chair to tilt slightly to the left, and the rear stretcher slopes noticeably in that direction. The full height of the inner side of each finial is patched for a width of ¾ to 1 inch, to fill a notch cut in at one time, perhaps to insert a headrest or a slat from which to suspend a cushion. The chair was received with a splint seat, which has been replaced with rush. The surface has a shiny modern finish.

WOODS
MAPLE; left rear post, HARD MAPLE; seat rails, OAK.

DIMENSIONS
OH. 46 (116.8); SH. 17⅝ (44.8); SW. front 24 (61); SW. back 17⅛ (43.5); SD. 15⅛ (38.4).

EXHIBITIONS
"Seats of Fashion: Three Hundred Years of American Chair Design," High Museum of Art, Atlanta, Georgia, 11 September–18 November 1973; on loan to the Milwaukee Art Museum, Milwaukee, Wisconsin, from 1981 to 1988.

REFERENCES
Cornelius 1926, pl. II (as received); *Seats of Fashion* 1973 (exh. cat.), no. 1.

PROVENANCE
Ex coll.: H. Eugene Bolles, Boston.

Gift of Mrs. Russell Sage, 1909 (10.125.207)

1. Putnam House advertisement, *Antiques* 91 (January 1967), p. 20.
2. St. George 1979b, no. 32.
3. See Kane 1973a, no. XXIII (New Haven area); Arkell and Trent 1988, figs. 1, 9 (Boston); Wood 1996, no. 1 (Cambridge); cat. nos. 114, 115 (Plymouth County); and cat. no. 58 (Essex County). For applied turnings, see Fairbanks and Bates 1981, p. 14.

6.
Spindle-back chair

Probably Massachusetts, 1680–1720

Turned chairs without arms were more common in the seventeenth century than turned armchairs, but they have survived in far fewer numbers. Probably subjected to greater everyday use and not as strongly constructed as their armed counterparts, they were more susceptible to damage and, being less expensive, would then have been more readily discarded. Because it is a rare survival, this chair has a place in the collection despite the extent of its restorations. Not as broad, deep, or tall as contemporary turned armchairs, seats of this size were often described in probate inventories as "small" or "little," frequently as opposed to "great," as for example in the listing "3.great turned chaires and five small chaires" in the 1683 inventory of the parlor of Captain Daniel Fisher of Dedham, Massachusetts.[1]

The turnings on this example reflect the style promulgated by chairs made in Boston and Charlestown (see cat. nos. 2, 3), but at a remove. There is, on the one hand, an exaggeration of form, as in the overly large flame on the finials, and, on the other, a simplification and loss of vigor, all of which can be interpreted as signs of nonurban workmanship and also of turning produced toward the end of a tradition. The ball shapes on the stiles and front legs—those on the stiles perhaps alluding to a compressed vase form—are shallow in outline, and the rudimentary opposed urns in the spindles lack definition. That the top back rail is more elaborate than the lower rails and that its elements, which include a quasi-urn shape toward each end, are centered on a ring or ball are in keeping with turned-chair design of the period. Having a narrow square-edged ring abutting the tenon, however, is anomalous and raises the possibility that the top back rail is a reused turning that has been shortened.

6

CONSTRUCTION
The chair is joined entirely with round tenons. The mortises are each drilled centered on an individual layout line except for those of the joints of the bottom back rail and of the added rear stretcher, for which there are no scribe lines.

CONDITION
The legs are pieced at the bottom, starting from between 1 and 3 inches below the stretchers, and the turned front feet are conjectural. The present lower legs were installed at the MMA, probably before the 1930s, and replace earlier restorations that were on the chair when it was acquired (see References). Originally the legs were longer and there was doubtless a lower tier of four stretchers, but no upper rear stretcher; it has been added. The top back rail, one spindle, and the left stretcher are probably replaced. There are round patches on the legs

where the mortises for the left and rear stretchers appear to have broken through. The front and right stretchers have been rotated in their sockets. The tops of the front legs are marred by gouged holes and the left one also by a patch. Nails have been added to most of the seat-rail joints, and the rush seat has been renewed. At some point after the legs had been pieced, the chair was aggressively stripped; the surface appears to have been sanded and the posts scraped. Records indicate that in 1933–34 modern varnish then on the chair was removed and the wood finished with linseed oil and turpentine.

WOODS
Left rear post, SOFT MAPLE; remaining posts, spindles, MAPLE; rails of back, seat rails, stretchers, ASH.

DIMENSIONS
OH. 37½ (95.3); SH. 14½ (36.8); SW. front 19¾ (50.2); SW. back 15⅝ (39.7); SD. 14½ (36.8).

EXHIBITION
"Hudson-Fulton Exhibition," MMA, 20 September–30 November 1909.

REFERENCES
Hudson-Fulton Celebration 1909 (exh. cat.), no. 61; B. N. Osburn and B. B. Osburn 1926, p. 11 (this and the following references show the

chair as acquired; none of them includes a measured drawing); Hjorth 1946, p. 108; Margon 1971, p. 98; Shea 1975, p. 84.

PROVENANCE
Ex coll.: H. Eugene Bolles, Boston.

Gift of Mrs. Russell Sage, 1909 (10.125.694)

1. A. L. Cummings 1964, p. 46.

7.
Spindle-back armchair

Probably southeastern New England, 1660–1700

The finials on this chair fall within a broad category that features a prominent spherical form at the top (in this case, capped by a button) above one or two reels, a ring, or a ball, in many different configurations. Such finials are found on seventeenth-century-style turned chairs from southern New England—southeastern Massachusetts (see cat. no. 12), Rhode Island, and the Connecticut shore (see cat. no. 8)—to New York that appear to date toward the end of the 1600s, and in the eighteenth century they became ubiquitous.[1] In this particular interpretation, the ball at the base together with the reel and ring above it can be read as a vase with a narrow neck and a large flange, on which the sphere at the top is balanced (fig. 5). This version possibly reflects the influence of the urn-and-flame finials on Boston-style chairs, for the vase turnings on the posts have a form characteristic of such chairs. The additional decorative elements on the rear posts of cat. no. 7, however, are not typical of that tradition; they include flat rings (below the finials and arms) and a deep V-shaped groove (between the two upper rails). Also, all the posts are cut in at a sharp angle at the juncture with the top of the vase turnings.

Two chairs, one at the Connecticut Historical Society, Hartford, and the other in a private collection, have analogous flat rings and vase shapes on the posts and also spindles in a generally similar pattern of opposed balusters; the one at the Connecticut Historical Society also has a top back rail in a generically related design. In addition, both chairs, like this example, have posts with an intended backward slant and are entirely of ash. However, the finials on those two chairs differ markedly from those on cat. no. 7 in the elements below the prominent sphere at the top, and no deep V-grooves ornament the stiles. Thus this chair is not from the same shop, but the similarities suggest it is probably from the same region. The

Connecticut Historical Society chair is said to have been found in Fall River, Massachusetts, in the early twentieth century, and it and the related example have been attributed by Robert F. Trent to probably Rhode Island.[2] An origin in southeastern New England for this chair seems plausible; it allows for the type of finial used and for the influence of Boston turned-chair design.

CONSTRUCTION
The rear posts taper somewhat from the seat toward either extremity. Both front and rear posts have a built-in backward cant; the mortises for the side members are not drilled at a right angle to the posts. X-radiographs taken to confirm this revealed that the frame is joined with round tenons that have an unusual profile: toward the end the tenons are notched and beyond the notch the tenon tapers.[3] The mortises for the joints of the arms, seat rails, and stretchers are drilled tangential to a work line on the posts; those for the joints of the back rails are centered on a line. On the right rear post is a round hole where the maker mistakenly began to drill the mortise for the upper side stretcher below rather than above the layout line. The rear and side crosspieces are of the same length.

CONDITION
The legs are pieced from below the lower stretchers, where they were sawn off and notched in the center—presumably for the addition of rockers; the turned feet are conjectural. As restored, the front legs are shorter than the rear legs by about ½ inch, so that arms and seat slope toward the front. The narrow taper visible at the top of the spindles suggests that they are too short for the space between the rails and gives one pause, but they show a reasonable amount of wear. A thin slat has been nailed to the outer side of the seat rails, and the rush seat is modern. Significant losses occur at the back of the vase turning on the right stile and on the right handgrip; both handgrips have deep, gouged holes in the top. Records indicate that in 1933–34 modern varnish then on the chair was removed and the wood was finished with linseed oil and turpentine. The post turnings in particular show evidence of sanding and scraping.

7. See also fig. 5.

WOOD
ASH.

DIMENSIONS
OH. 46 1/4 (117.5); SH. 17 3/4 (45.1); SW. front 24 7/8 (63.2); SW. back 18 3/4 (47.6); SD. 17 5/8 (44.8).

EXHIBITION
"Hudson-Fulton Exhibition," MMA, 20 September–30 November 1909.

REFERENCES
Hudson-Fulton Celebration 1909 (exh. cat.), no. 59; B. N. Osburn and B. B. Osburn 1926, p. 11; Hjorth 1946, fig. 16; Williams 1963, no. 5; Margon 1971, p. 99; Shea 1975, p. 137 (includes measured drawings).

PROVENANCE
Ex coll.: H. Eugene Bolles, Boston.

Gift of Mrs. Russell Sage, 1909 (10.125.691)

1. See, for example, Forman 1988, no. 8 (Rhode Island); Failey 1998, no. 5A (New York).
2. Connecticut Historical Society 1958, pp. 64–65; Trent 1999, p. 217 and figs. 13, 14.
3. X-radiographs of the joints of the left rear post with the side stretchers and with the two upper rails of the back and of the left front post with the arm all show the same type of tenon. Since few X-radiographs of turned chairs have as yet been made, it is difficult to know how unusual this type of tenon is or if it indicates manufacture at any particular period. The X-radiographs, including one of the upper joints of the spindles, do not show any evidence of the use of modern tools.

8.

Spindle-back chair

Connecticut, Branford-Saybrook area, 1680–1710

A school of turning associated with the coastal Connecticut area between Branford and Saybrook produced this piece. Closely related are an armchair with a Guilford history (on loan to the Dorothy Whitfield Historic Society, Guilford), a small chair without arms said to have belonged to the Gardiner family of Saybrook (Yale University Art Gallery), and another lacking an early history (Mission House, Stockbridge, Massachusetts).[1] They have in common a back consisting of three spindles of an elongated ogee form flanked top and bottom by a ball, and stiles turned with tall grooved ogee balusters that have the particularity of being separated from the cylindrical post above by a deep V-shaped cut. Analogous grooved balusters are on the arm supports of the armchair. Like cat. no. 8, the two small chairs without arms are distinguished, in addition, by having a single upper rail in the back instead of the usual two. The three small chairs are similar enough to be from the same shop but not part of the same set. On the one hand, the layout lines scribed on the posts for the top back rail, seat rails, and stretchers are the same, as is the distinctive placement of the spindles in relation to the lines on the rails (see *Construction*). On the other hand, the chairs show some variations in elements that are not fixed by scribe lines, namely, the height of the spindles (since the location of the lower back rail is not marked), and the width and depth of the seat. Also, on cat. no. 8 the turnings at the top of the front posts and at the base of the finials have somewhat greater articulation (fig. 8) than on the other two chairs.

Two armchairs with histories in the area of East Haven and Branford have related but more complex turnings: opposed rather than single ogee forms on the stiles, a thin ring between the balls and the baluster on the spindles, and a finial with a large ovoid shape topped by a small ball above a ring, reel, and flattened ball. Patricia E. Kane has suggested that the simpler design of chairs like cat. no. 8 is probably later in date, perhaps the work of a craftsman apprenticed to the maker of the Branford chairs.[2] Indeed the back of this chair, with its attenuated spindles and single top rail, has the more vertical look adopted toward the end of the seventeenth century for joined upholstered chairs such as cat. no. 24. The double-reel-and-ball finials also point to a relatively late date of manufacture, since they are of a general form that enjoyed widespread popularity in the eighteenth century (see fig. 9).

While this chair's turnings can be attributed to a particular stretch of the Connecticut coast, they represent basic forms

8. See also fig. 8.

that had a wider regional currency; generically similar large ogee turnings on posts and elongated baluster-and-ball spindles are found on chairs with histories in towns that border the Long Island Sound from the New York City area to southern Rhode Island.[3]

CONSTRUCTION

The chair is assembled entirely with round tenons. The mortises in the posts are drilled tangential to a layout line with the exception of those for the lower back rail, the location of which is not scribed. On the back, the middle spindle is centered on a groove in the rails, as was common practice; but the mortises for the flanking spindles are bored with the inner side of the hole abutting a scribed line. On the right front leg, the lower line at the seat-rail joints is an error. The turnings on the top of the front legs consist of a broad button and an ovolo with a groove in the middle. A similar ovolo is at the base of the finials on the rear posts.

CONDITION

When the chair was acquired, the lower front stretcher was missing and 4 to 4½ inches of the posts were pieced at the bottom (see *References*). The stretcher was replaced and the posts newly restored with conjectural turnings at the bottom of the front legs. On the left finial, sections of the ring have been lost; on the right finial, the knob is worn off; and the turnings on the top of the front posts have lost definition. The rush seat is not original. Records indicate that black paint was on the chair when it was received and that in 1933–34 modern varnish then on the piece was removed and the wood finished with linseed oil and turpentine. The chair retains numerous residues of green paint (not original) and some traces of black over green paint.

WOOD

ASH.

DIMENSIONS

OH. 37⅛ (94.3); SH. 16 (40.6); SW. front 18⅞ (47.9); SW. back 14⅝ (37.1); SD. 14¼ (36.2).

REFERENCES

Lockwood 1913, fig. 412 (this and the following references show the chair as acquired); Cescinsky and Hunter 1929, p. 72; Kane 1973a, p. 77, fig. 10.

PROVENANCE

Ex coll.: H. Eugene Bolles, Boston.

Gift of Mrs. Russell Sage, 1909 (10.125.208)

1. In the order mentioned, they may be found in Kane 1973a, nos. XXXIII, XXXIV; and S. C. S. Edwards 1983, p. 589. Also related are armchairs in the Art Institute of Chicago, Chicago, Illinois (Naeve 1981, no. 1), Saint Louis Art Museum, Saint Louis, Missouri (Lockwood 1913, fig. 411), and Wadsworth Atheneum (Nutting 1928–33, no. 1820); and offered in *Important Americana: The Collection of the Late Dr. and Mrs. James W. Marvin*, auction cat., Sotheby Parke Bernet, New York City, 30 September–1 October 1978, lot 318. Bernard D. Cotton has noted similarities between these American small chairs and examples from the northwest of England and has suggested design transmission from that region to New England (Cotton 1990, p. 314, fig. NW7). His conjecture is based on English chairs he dates to the second half of the eighteenth century; no English chairs early enough to have served as prototypes for the American examples are known.
2. The Branford chairs are in Kane 1973a, nos. XXXI (New Haven Museum), XXXII (Bayou Bend Collection); see also no. XXXIII.
3. For example, Failey 1976, no. 17 (New York City area); Failey 1998, nos. 2A, 3A (eastern Long Island); Forman 1988, no. 15 (New London County, Connecticut); Monkhouse and Michie 1986, no. 83, and Forman 1988, no. 8 (Rhode Island).

9.

Spindle-back chair

New York City or vicinity, 1680–1710

This chair is a compelling display of the turners' art. Every member is decoratively turned, and the various rhythms set up by the repeated oval, ring, flattened ball, and short baluster forms create a vibrant counterpoint that gives the design an intensity of visual movement akin to that of contemporary twist ornament. The chair is of a distinctive type associated with areas of Dutch cultural influence in New York and northern New Jersey. Its overall design and turned motifs are based on a form of chair that originated in the Low Countries about the middle of the seventeenth century and that appears to be the turners' answer to the seventeenth-century uphol-stered joined chair with a low back (such as cat. no. 23), which it resembles in its general layout and proportions. It was an urban chair form that stood at a level above basic turned seating, as evidenced by Dutch examples at the Rijksmuseum in Amsterdam made of walnut or rosewood. This tradition of chairmaking was transferred to New York City and vicinity by craftsmen of Dutch or other northern European origin.[1] Elaborately and skillfully turned and made of cherry, cat. no. 9 also ranks above the everyday small turned chair of the period and has the attributes of an urban product.

About twenty small chairs of the overall format seen here are known, plus several related armchairs and child's chairs.[2] They all exhibit basically the same turned vocabulary as cat. no. 9, but the degree of variation in the details and disposition of the motifs suggests production in a number of shops and over a period of time. Characteristic of these chairs are finials with an urn-shaped turning at the base, from which rises an elongated reel that supports an ovoid knop (fig. 13). On the chairs on which the feet survive, the rear as well as the front ones are turned; and on the majority of examples the rear legs as well as the front ones are ornamented, as is the rear stretcher in addition to all the others. All those traits are associated with Continental chairmaking and not common on New England chairs.[3] This is one of four identical chairs (the others are one in the Bayou Bend Collection and a pair belonging to Historic Hudson Valley), all branded with the same initials of the first or an early owner "HH," conjoined (fig. 121). Such branding was a practice prevalent in the Hudson River valley during the eighteenth century, particularly in families of Dutch descent. A pair of chairs at the New Jersey State Museum, Trenton, branded "HG" are analogous to those four except that they do not have the small angular ring scored with a groove that is turned on the neck of the baluster at the top of the stiles and that distinguishes the HH chairs.[4] An identical ring is repeated at the top of the feet of the HH examples and is worked as an overhang—now largely lost—at the top of the front legs. They recall the similar, but larger, rings on the finials and lower arms of several slat-back armchairs attributed to New York City or the westernmost towns of Long Island.[5] Feet like those on the HH chairs in that they also have a narrow neck with a thin ring are found on several other chairs in this group. Related feet on a Pennsylvania table that shows Germanic influence (cat. no. 50) suggest that this was a generic northern European type.[6]

The vocabulary of ornament established by the school of turning that produced these chairs persisted in various manifestations throughout the eighteenth and into the nineteenth century on seating made in New York and northern New Jersey. Particularly long-lived was the urn-and-flame finial, which still appeared in essentially the same shape on slat-back chairs of Bergen County, New Jersey, dated to the 1850s. The motif of one or more flattened balls below a short ogee baluster occurs on the rear posts of William and Mary–style tall-back chairs with arched crests and straight, molded banisters, such as one in the Bergen County Historical Society, River Edge, New Jersey; on chairs with similar banisters and a crest rail in the shape of a shallow inverted arch, which, like the former, often have flattened balls on the front legs and sausage-shaped turnings on the stretchers; and finally on the stiles of "York" chairs with vase-shaped splats, a type that was developed by New York City turners about 1750 in response to the then prevailing Queen Anne style and that was produced into the early 1800s.[7]

CONSTRUCTION

The chair is joined with round tenons. The mortises in the stiles and rails of the back are centered on the layout lines that mark their location; those in the posts for the seat rails and stretchers are tangential to work lines. The two lines on the left stile at the joint of the top back rail indicate that an error was made in the scribing and then corrected. The turnings on the top of the front legs originally consisted of an overhanging grooved ring, two shallow convex moldings, and a central button.

CONDITION

The joints have been apart and glued. Filled holes in the legs at the joints of the side stretchers and lower front stretcher probably conceal nails added to reinforce those joints. The mortise in the top back rail for the spindle to the right of center was either drilled through or has broken through. There is a glued split in that spindle and in the left seat rail, and evidence exists to suggest that the seat was upholstered at one time. The present rush is a replacement. The feet have lost some height. Long usage has resulted in abrasions on the legs and the loss of most of the turnings on the top of the front legs. The finish is old but not original.

INSCRIPTION
The initials "HH," conjoined, of an unidentified owner, are branded on the back of the right rear leg below the upper turning (fig. 121).

WOODS
CHERRY; seat rails, ASH.

DIMENSIONS
OH. 35 5/8 (90.5); SH. 17 (43.2); SW. front 18 3/8 (46.7); SW. back 14 1/4 (36.2); SD. 13 3/4 (34.9).

REFERENCE
Important Americana from the Collection of Mr. and Mrs. James O. Keene, auction cat., Sotheby's, New York City, 16 January 1997, lot 33.

PROVENANCE
Ex coll.: Jess Pavey, a dealer in Birmingham, Michigan; Mr. and Mrs. James O. Keene, Birmingham, Michigan.

The chair was one of a pair purchased in January 1997 by the Museum of Fine Arts, Houston, at the sale of the Keene collection (see *Reference*) and subsequently sold to the MMA. The other chair became part of the Bayou Bend Collection.

Purchase, Gift of the Members of the Committee of the Bertha King Benkard Memorial Fund, and Bequest of Cecile L. Mayer, by exchange; and Fletcher Fund and Joseph Pulitzer Bequest, by exchange, 1997 (1997.68)

1. In its overall form and visual effect, this chair can be compared with two joined board-seated chairs with spiral ornament attributed to Philadelphia (*Philadelphia* 1976, no. 6; Forman 1988, no. 48), of a type that has English antecedents (Kirk 1982, no. 690) and also recalls low-back upholstered seating. For a comprehensive study of the chair form represented by cat. no. 9, including its European origin, the Rijksmuseum chairs, and immigrant craftsmen, see Gronning 2001. See also Kirk 1965, p. 798; and Forman 1988, pp. 114–19.
2. Almost all the chairs are illustrated in Gronning 2001.
3. Early southern turned chairs influenced by Continental traditions also exhibit turned ornament on all four feet and on all of the stretchers (Beckerdite 1997, p. 203; Hurst and Prown 1997, pp. 54, 64). Forman 1988, no. 15, is a rare New England chair with turned rear feet.
4. For the other HH chairs, see D. B. Warren et al. 1998, no. F7, and Gronning 2001, fig. 38; Butler 1983, no. 35, and Gronning 2001, fig. 39. For the HG chairs, see Lyle and Bloch 1972, no. 2, and Gronning 2001, figs. 41, 37 (detail of brand). See also Blackburn 1981.
5. Forman 1988, no. 17; Failey 1998, nos. 4A, 4B.
6. A broad northern European range is also suggested by feet of this general type on early French Canadian furniture (Palardy 1965, nos. 367, 370, 371).
7. For an 1850s chair with related finials, see Lynes 1934, fig. 22A. For the Bergen County Historical Society chair, see Gronning 2001, fig. 34. For chairs with an inverted-arch crest rail, see Scherer 1984, nos. 4, 126. For "York" chairs, see Heckscher 1985, no. 20. Tall banister-back chairs related to the Bergen County Historical Society example have been found in and attributed to Connecticut (Kirk 1967, no. 214; Kane 1976, no. 43). Whether they were exported from the New York City area or made in Connecticut in emulation of New York models (as were the later style "York" chairs) or by a craftsman who had migrated from New York or had similar training is uncertain, but their turnings from the lower stiles down, including the front feet, are indebted to the tradition represented by cat. no. 9. The use of sausage-shaped turnings, however, also had other sources, for they occur on the stretchers of eighteenth-century Massachusetts chairs as well (see cat. no. 15).

9. See also figs. 13, 121.

Turned Chairs with a Slat Back

The earliest type of turned slat-back chair that has survived from New England features three slats with incurved upper corners, flat arms, and Boston-style turnings similar to those on spindle-back chairs, and it is exemplified by the first chair in this chapter (cat. no. 10). A high chair in the collection—the one piece here included that is not an armchair—was designed with similarly shaped slats, but its finials cannot be linked to any particular known school of turning (cat. no. 11). Two of the armchairs, however, can be each attributed to a recognized local seventeenth-century New England turned-chair tradition, one identified with Plymouth County, Massachusetts (cat. no. 12), the other with New London County, Connecticut (cat. no 13). Both chairs appear to be late expressions of their respective shop traditions, made probably not before about 1700, for they show some evidence of the influence of William and Mary–style (early Baroque) seating. A New York chair dating from the same period has turned arms that extend over the front posts—a feature that reflects Continental rather than Anglo-American design (cat. no. 14). Not represented in the collection is a very distinctive form of slat-back chair with elaborately turned rails under its flat arms that is peculiar to New York City and vicinity and has Dutch and perhaps also English antecedents.[1]

Slat-back chairs appear to have increased in popularity toward the end of the seventeenth century. By the early 1700s they were being identified as such in colonial records, described by the number of cross members, which was a determining factor in a chair's value; namely, "two-slat" or "two-slatted," "three-slat" or "three-slatted," and on up to six. In New England, "two-back" or "two-backed," and so forth, was a common alternative locution. Unlike spindle-back chairs, which became obsolete in the early 1700s, slat-back chairs evolved in the early eighteenth century under the influence of the William and Mary style. A chair in the collection with a tall and narrow four-slatted back, ogee-baluster arm supports, and sausage-turned stretchers represents a widespread type that emulated the format of fashionable high-back William and Mary cane and leather chairs (cat. no. 15). The last two chairs in this chapter, characterized by five and six arched slats, respectively, illustrate a regional Delaware River valley type that became popular in that area toward the end of the early colonial period (cat. nos. 16, 17). The latter chair is in a design made only in Philadelphia and after the introduction, about 1730, of the succeeding Queen Anne (late Baroque) style; its turned slat-back frame has been updated with cabriole legs and represents a model that stood a level above the basic turned chair.

In the hierarchy of chairs, turned seating occupied the bottom tier, which was filled throughout the 1700s and beyond by slat-back chairs. While in the most modest homes turned chairs might be the only kind used, and in some rural areas the only sort available locally, they were found in the most affluent homes as well, where they provided practical everyday seating alongside more fashionable and costly forms. During the eighteenth century, turners produced in addition to slat-back chairs inexpensive versions of more stylish designs, adding banister-back chairs, which were a degree more fashionable than those with a slat back, to their repertoire toward the end of the early colonial period. The turning patterns introduced by joined high-style William and Mary chairs were copied on turned chairs and proved to be long-lived. They remained the basis of the turners' vocabulary well into the nineteenth century, for the designs of succeeding eighteenth-century styles relied on sawn and carved elements and thus did not provide any new turning patterns.

1. See, for example, Forman 1988, no. 17.

10.

Slat-back armchair

Probably Boston or vicinity, 1650–90

Characterized by a back that consists of three broad slats with a quadrant cut out at the upper corners and by flat arms similarly shaped on the outer edge, this piece exemplifies the earliest known type of turned slat-back chair made in New England. The slats are often graduated in height with the largest at the top. The turned posts feature the same motifs as spindle-back chairs in the style attributed to the Massachusetts Bay chair-making hub of Boston and Charlestown. This chair's posts, like those on cat. no. 2, for example, taper visibly from top to bottom and are ornamented with similar short vase turnings;

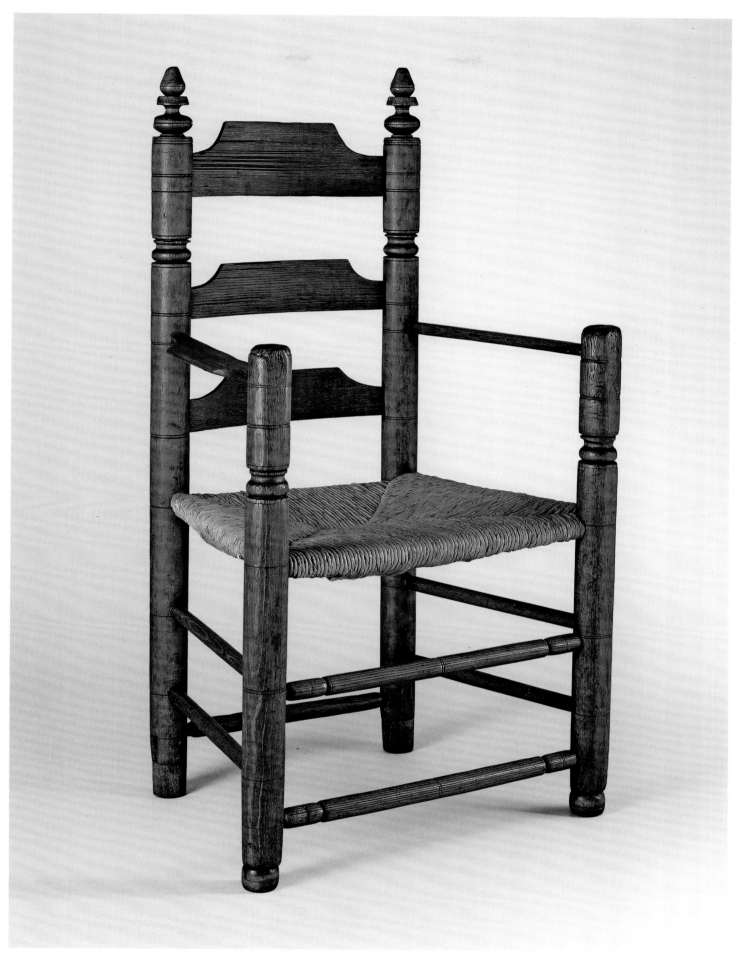

10. See also fig. 2.

the rear posts feature so-called urn-and-flame finials, and the front ones undoubtedly once terminated in ball handgrips. The posts, like those of some spindle-back chairs (see cat. no. 3), are made of poplar. Spindle- and slat-back chairs were most likely made in the same shops, and the latter, like the former, were probably exported and imitated in smaller centers.[1]

The urn-and-flame finials on this chair belong to a small minority in this general design on which the half ring that is usually turned just above the ball shape and below the angular disk has been omitted (compare figs. 2, 1). Here the ball turning at the base of the finial is quite flat, recalling the squat form of the vases on the posts, and its upper surface is adorned with several fillets; the disk has strongly angled sides, and the top knob is distinguished by its tapered shape. Pyramidal in form, the finials sit atop the posts like true pinnacles. Boldly turned, they are a summation of the synthesis of rounded and angular elements that underlies the chair's vital composition.

The use of an abbreviated urn-and-flame finial does not in itself help pinpoint the locality in which a chair originated; the shortened pattern does not appear to have been the province of a single shop or school of turning, for it occurs in several versions and on chairs that vary stylistically in other elements and have histories in different areas. The finials on a slat-back armchair at the Shelburne Museum, Shelburne, Vermont, are virtually identical to those on cat. no. 10 and are very probably the work of the same turner. Those on another related armchair (converted to a rocker) appear to have a similar profile and may have originated in the same shop. Regrettably none of the three has an early history.[2] A small spindle-back chair without arms at the Winterthur Museum that was probably made in northern Essex County, Massachusetts, or southern New Hampshire has finials close in outline to those seen here, but the tall baluster turnings on its posts bear no comparison. A slat-back armchair of the same type as cat. no. 10 at the Baltimore Museum of Art, Baltimore, Maryland, has a history of ownership in Exeter, New Hampshire, but the ball at the base of the finials is fuller and the knob differs in that it is bluntly rounded at the top. Yet another variant of the pattern is found on the two well-known board-seated spindle chairs that traditionally belonged, respectively, to William Brewster and William Bradford of Plymouth Colony (Pilgrim Hall Museum, Plymouth, Massachusetts). On those finials, the ball at the base is quite round, the top knob is ovoid, and the sides of the angular disk are nearly vertical, much like the corresponding elements on the full version of the urn-and-flame design on cat. no. 2, for example.[3]

CONSTRUCTION

The posts, 2 3/8 inches in diameter at the top, taper 1/4 inch to the bottom; the overall width of the chair narrows predictably toward the bottom at the front posts, but not at the rear posts, perhaps because of changes made when the frame was taken apart and then reassembled. The location of the rectangular mortises for the slats was probably just marked on the posts with short, light work lines that are no longer visible; only the lower edge of the bottom mortise corresponds to a groove in the post. The bottom and middle mortises are the same height. The joints of the top slat are pinned from the back. The arms have square tenons, which prevent them from rotating in their joints. They are shaped on the outer edge with a quarter-round cutout at each end and are flat on the upper surface but strongly beveled on the outer half of the underside. The base of the chair is joined with round tenons, with the mortises for the seat rails and upper stretchers drilled tangential to a layout line and those for the lower stretchers each centered on an individual line.

CONDITION

After the chair was acquired by the MMA, the missing upper right stretcher was replaced, the shortened posts were extended with the addition of 2 inches to the rear legs and conjectural turned feet to the front legs, and a splint seat was replaced with rush (see *References*). The pins in the joints of the top slat have been reset or replaced, and all the slat joints have been tightened with a wedge. The middle slat may not be original. The seat rails, the front one of which is strongly bowed inward, have probably been reworked or renewed. The front stretchers show too little wear to be original, and the rear and lower right stretchers have probably been rotated in their joints. The handgrips are missing, and deep holes have been dug into the top of the front posts, which are heavily abraded on the front surface. Records indicate that in 1933–34 modern varnish then on the chair was removed and the wood was finished with linseed oil and turpentine.

WOODS

Posts, POPLAR (*Populus* sp.); remaining components, ASH.

DIMENSIONS

OH. 43 1/8 (109.5); SH. 16 3/4 (42.5); SW. front 24 (61); SW. back 18 (45.7); SD. 15 1/2 (39.4).

REFERENCES

Lockwood 1913, fig. 419; Halsey and Cornelius 1924 (and 1925, 1926, 1928, 1932), fig. 8; Cornelius 1926, pl. II; Cescinsky and Hunter 1929, p. 72; Lynes 1933, fig. 2 (in this and the previous references the chair is shown as received); Halsey and Cornelius 1938 (and 1942), fig. 9; M. B. Davidson 1967, no. 7; Margon 1971, p. 149; Schwartz 1976, no. 2; Chinnery 1979, fig 2:101.

PROVENANCE

Ex coll.: H. Eugene Bolles, Boston.

Gift of Mrs. Russell Sage, 1909 (10.125.235)

1. For more on this type of slat-back chair, see Fairbanks and Trent 1982, no. 178; Forman 1988, pp. 80–84 and no. 14; Jobe et al. 1991, no. 1; Wood 1996, no. 22.
2. The finials on the Shelburne Museum chair (Bishop 1972, no. 32) differ from those on cat. no. 10 only very slightly in height and in having two rather than four fillets turned on the upper surface of the ball; the writer thanks Julie Eldridge Edwards for measurements and photographs of the finials. Lockwood 1913, fig. 422 (related armchair converted to a rocker).
3. Forman 1988, no. 3 (Winterthur Museum chair); Elder and J. E. Stokes 1987, no. 1 (armchair in the Baltimore Museum of Art); Pizer, Driver, and Earle 1985, pls. I, II (Pilgrim Hall Museum armchairs).

II.

Slat-back high chair

Probably southeastern New England, 1670–1710

The rarity of high chairs datable to the seventeenth century or even with seventeenth-century-style turnings warrants the publication of this example despite the regrettable loss of the presumed original, albeit reduced, slats that were on the chair when it was acquired (see *Condition*) and its other replaced or questionable elements.[1] The fate of those slats is a prime example of the unfortunate replacement in toto of damaged or partly missing elements that occurred at the MMA early in the twentieth century, also on other objects from the H. Eugene Bolles collection. The main bearers of the chair's stylistic message—the posts—have, however, survived in large part intact. The turnings are carefully executed, with the upper ball of the finials rising with assurance and some grace above the ring at midpoint (fig. 7). The vase forms on the stiles and arm supports have rims that jut out sharply and then are strongly cut in so that they resemble thin disks, which are recalled by the ringlike interstices between the deep grooves on the posts above and below the vases. Series of grooves also ornament the handgrips and finials.

Based on the design of the turnings, the high chair was most likely made in southeastern New England. Finials that end in a large ball that is set above two reels are found in various interpretations on turned chairs from southeastern Massachusetts on through coastal Rhode Island and Connecticut (see cat. nos. 12, 8) from toward the end of the 1600s, and they became widespread in the 1700s; however, no exact counterpart to the particular version of this generic pattern on cat. no. 11 is known to the writer. The vase turnings are straight-sided, rather than rounded as on Boston-style chairs, and they are set above a well-defined cavetto, which also occurs at the base of the finials and of the handgrips. A similar use of this profile is characteristic of the Plymouth County, Massachusetts, school of turning represented by cat. no. 12 and points to a possible origin for this chair in that general region.

A 1912 MMA photograph of the chair provides evidence that it once had slats of the same general outline as those seen here. The first set of arms was most likely turned, as indicated by the round mortises for those members. While the form of the original footrest is not known, there is precedent for a footrest being attached to the front of the posts with pegs into good-size round mortises.[2]

CONSTRUCTION

The frame is splayed on all four sides, with the posts deviating from the vertical the most across the front and the least across the back.

11. See also fig. 7.

Grooves on the stiles mark the top and bottom of the rectangular mortises for the slats; the upper mortises are scribed to be ¼ inch shorter than the lower. The joints of the upper slat are pinned from the back. The other crosspieces, except for the present footrest, are round-tenoned. The mortises for the arms and the seat rails are positioned each centered on a layout line, and those for the stretchers are tangential to a line. The footrest (replaced) is secured to the front of each leg with a headed wooden peg inserted into the ½-inch-wide hole drilled for the attachment of the original and positioned slightly above a layout line on the post.

CONDITION
The chair is shown in the 1912 photograph with two slats approximately the same height as their mortises but retaining evidence that they were once taller and had incurved upper corners. Those old, probably original, slats were replaced in their entirety (ash) at the MMA, as were the missing rush seat and upper front stretcher (oak), and the inner side of the upper left stretcher was pieced. Previous replacements include the arms (oak, shaved, not turned, the right one with a nail in each joint), the lower front and rear stretchers (oak, shaved), and the footrest (poplar [*Populus* sp.]). It is difficult to determine the age of the seat rails (the front one [maple] probably turned, the three others [ash], shaved) under the present tight rush, and the age of the side stretchers (ash, turned) is also uncertain. The two handgrips and the upper portion of the right arm support have significant losses. Records indicate that in 1933–34 modern varnish then on the chair was removed and the wood was finished with linseed oil and turpentine.

WOOD
Posts, MAPLE.

DIMENSIONS
OH. 40¾ (103.5); SH. 20¼ (51.4); OW. (front feet) 16¾ (42.5); SW. front 14½ (36.8); SW. back 12⅞ (32.7); SD. 12¼ (31.1).

EXHIBITION
"Hudson-Fulton Exhibition," MMA, 20 September–30 November 1909.

REFERENCE
Hudson-Fulton Celebration 1909 (exh. cat.), no. 63.

PROVENANCE
Ex coll.: H. Eugene Bolles, Boston.

Gift of Mrs. Russell Sage, 1909 (10.125.681)

1. Other known high chairs with seventeenth-century-style turnings have spindle backs. The prime example is one at the American Antiquarian Society, Worcester, Massachusetts, which has a Mather family history and was probably made in Boston or Charlestown (Fairbanks and Trent 1982, no. 183; Forman 1988, fig. 36). A similar chair is at the Art Institute of Chicago, Chicago, Illinois (Comstock 1962, no. 17). An unrelated example is at Colonial Williamsburg (Greenlaw 1974, no. 31). Two New York chairs—one at Historic Cherry Hill, once owned by Robert Sanders (Blackburn and Piwonka 1988, fig. 226; Gronning 2001, fig. 28), and a similar one at the Albany Institute that descended in the Ten Eyck family (Gronning 2001, fig. 29)—include seventeenth-century-style turnings but may date to the early decades of the 1700s.
2. The chairs at the American Antiquarian Society and the Art Institute of Chicago (see n. 1 above) both retain large broken-off pegs on the front of the front legs from the attachment of their now missing footrests.

12.

Slat-back armchair

Plymouth County, Massachusetts, 1695–1715

This is one of some eighteen stylistically related chairs, seven of which have histories in the Plymouth, Massachusetts, area. They represent a school of chairmaking that Robert Blair St. George ascribed in 1978 to the turner Ephraim Tinkham II (1649–1713), who in about 1694 moved from Plymouth to Middleborough, Massachusetts. The group consists primarily of spindle armchairs with either a single tier of turnings in the back or a double tier plus spindles under the arms and seat, and of armchairs with three slats in the back, one example of which has in addition spindles below the arms and seat. It also includes two other types of hybrid armchairs and two small chairs without arms. In a more recent study, Robert F. Trent and Karin J. Goldstein concluded that, given the variety of form and ornament this chairmaking tradition manifests, it represents the work not of an individual craftsman or shop but that of several shops which together were active for well over half a century.[1]

Cat. no. 12 differs from chairs in the dominant eastern Massachusetts style formulated in Boston in both its proportions and the profile of its turnings. Typically it is strongly trapezoidal in plan, and of the chairs in the group it presents one of the widest spans across the front. The finials, in the form of two spheres separated by an elongated reel indented at the midpoint (fig. 6), are in the more common of the two basic patterns associated with this so-called Tinkham school of turning. (In the other, a ball sits atop a double reel; there are also other variations.) It is noteworthy that on this chair the bottom of the reel does not terminate in just a fillet, but projects out to form a thin disk above the lower ball—a detail that is reminiscent of the flange above the ball on Boston-type finials (see fig. 1) and may reflect the influence of such urban chairs. Otherwise the turned vocabulary on this chair consists of one distinctive motif: a ball shape flanked by cavettos, a pattern that is one of the defining characteristics of this

12. See also fig. 6.

group of chairs.[2] In this instance, it occurs on the posts and the middle of the front stretchers and, in an abbreviated form, at the ends of the arms and stretchers. Here, as on many of the related chairs, the cavetto is broad and shallow, not only in conjunction with a ball but also when used at the base of the finials and of the arm supports. What distinguishes the front posts on this and virtually all the "Tinkham" armchairs is the fact that they are reduced in diameter above the seat. In most cases they also terminate in oversize, flattened ball handgrips, here nearly three and one-half inches in diameter. Generally the arm supports bear

little ornament; those on cat. no. 12 are among the more elaborate in that they are turned with a ball motif. They are distinguished also by another trait: while they are cylindrical at the base, above the ball motif they taper toward the top and then by way of a cavetto regain their former diameter.[3] A further characteristic of many of the "Tinkham" chairs is an uncommon stretcher arrangement: the rear and the lower front stretchers are not at the same level; rather, the bottom front stretcher is lower than the corresponding side stretchers but the rear stretcher is higher, though not often by as much as on this example.

The chair's high, relatively narrow back and the elongation of the reel on the finials, which convey a sense of verticality and upward movement typical of early Baroque chair design, indicate that it was probably not produced before the late 1690s or early 1700s. So does the rounded upper profile of the slats, a characteristic of eighteenth-century chairs. The character of the turnings on the posts is also consistent with a late date of manufacture; there is little variation in diameter within the ball shapes or the broad recesses that flank them, and the soft and shallow nature of those curves suggests a turning tradition that has lost its vigor.

CONSTRUCTION

The posts measure 2 inches in diameter; those in the rear taper from the seat up and those in the front are stepped in above the seat. The handgrips are one with the posts. The back narrows visibly in overall width toward the top owing to the taper of the stiles and the diminishing length of the crosspieces from the stretcher to the uppermost slat. Grooves on the posts mark the top and the bottom of the rectangular mortises for the slats, which have only a shallow bow; the scribing decreases the height of the mortises from the bottom up by increments of barely 1/8 inch. The joints of the top slat are pinned. The other crosspieces are joined with round tenons. The mortises for the seat rails and front and side stretchers are drilled tangential to a layout line; those for the arms and rear stretcher are centered on a line.

CONDITION

The bottom 1 3/4 inches of the legs are new—added at the MMA; the turned front feet are conjectural. The pins securing the top slat are original. All the slat joints and those of several other components have been tightened with wedges. The lower edge of the slats has suffered losses; wood weakened by worm damage appears to have been used. A 1/2-inch-wide channel of defective wood that runs from the seat down on the inner side of the left rear post has partly broken out. Deep holes have been dug out on the top of the handgrips, and the top of the arms is heavily worn. The rush seat is an old replacement. The chair retains traces of red paint (probably not original); records indicate that in 1933–34 modern varnish then on the chair was removed and the wood was finished with linseed oil and turpentine.

WOODS

Left front post, SOFT MAPLE; remaining posts, arms, MAPLE; slats, HICKORY; stretchers, ASH; seat rails, OAK.

DIMENSIONS

OH. 45 1/2 (115.6); SH. 16 3/4 (42.5); OW. (handgrips) 26 3/8 (67); SW. front 25 1/4 (64.1); SW. back 16 3/8 (41.6); SD. 16 (40.6).

EXHIBITIONS

On loan to the MacPheadris-Warner House (now Warner House), Portsmouth, New Hampshire, from 1946 to 1979; "Craftsmen and Community: The Seventeenth-Century Furniture of Southeastern New England," Brockton Art Center–Fuller Memorial (now Fuller Craft Museum), Brockton, Massachusetts, 15 September–30 November 1979 (not in St. George 1979b); on loan to the High Museum of Art, Atlanta, Georgia, from 1983 to 1984.

REFERENCES

Lockwood 1913, fig. 424 (right); Halsey and Tower 1925, fig. 33 (both references show the chair as received).

PROVENANCE

Ex coll.: H. Eugene Bolles, Boston.

Gift of Mrs. Russell Sage, 1909 (10.125.236)

1. St. George 1978 (St. George 1979b, pp. 26–27, 100, and nos. 46–49, presents some of the same material); Trent and Goldstein 1998. Chairs in this group not listed or illustrated in those publications are in *Sack Collection* 1981–92, vol. 7, p. 1766, and Cullity 1994, nos. 132, 135.
2. The Netherlands is probably the ultimate source of this pattern; similar turnings are on a Dutch chair (Trent and Goldstein 1998, pp. 217–18 and figs. 2, 5, 7).
3. Two other chairs have stepped-in arm supports decorated with one ball motif (ibid., figs. 18, 19). Two ball turnings occur on the arm supports of the two chairs in this tradition on which the front posts are not stepped in (ibid., figs. 1, 11). On several of the chairs with stepped-in arm supports that are ornamented with just a narrow concave or convex turning, the section of the post below that turning is somewhat tapered (*Sack Collection* 1981–92, vol. 7, p. 1766; Trent and Goldstein 1998, figs. 13, 16, 22, 23). This use of a taper appears to have come out of the same turning tradition as the distinctive ball-and-cavetto motif, for on the legs of the Dutch chair cited in n. 2 above such a ball is flanked by tapered columnar elements (Trent and Goldstein 1998, figs. 2, 5).

13. See also fig. 10.

13.

Slat-back armchair

New London County, Connecticut, 1695–1715

Several aspects of cat. no. 13 relate it to a group of chairs with a distinctive slat outline and form of turnings that have been attributed to the Norwich, Connecticut, area.[1] The design of the finial is similar, although on this chair the large ovoid shape that is set above two reels and is capped by a small reel and a knob (fig. 10) does not have the elongation characteristic of that element on the Norwich-school examples. Generically

similar patterns occur on two spindle-back armchairs from the New Haven, Connecticut, area and on two probably from New York, but this finial type is not known on Massachusetts chairs.[2] Also analogous are the large, flattened ball handgrips that overhang the posts, although not by as much as on the Norwich group (or on cat. no. 12). On both cat. no. 13 and the Norwich chairs, the front posts terminate below the handgrip with a ring and a reel, and the arms have a ring-reel sequence before they taper at either end. Other similarities are thick, sloping arms, which on this chair have a gentle rather than a steep pitch, and an intended backward rake of the posts. Notable on this chair is the difference between the two finials, which goes beyond the minor variations in turning normally seen in early colonial work, and points to a reasonably broad tolerance for inexactitude on the part of the craftsman and client in this period (see also cat. no. 33). Concomitantly, when a real mistake occurs, such as drilling at the wrong scribe line, the error may be simply patched, even if visible, as on the front posts of cat. no. 2.

Those features of cat. no. 13 that deviate from the Norwich formula are elements that can be associated with early-eighteenth- rather than seventeenth-century slat-back chair design: a high back with more than three slats; slats on which the upper contour is rounded; and the use of ball rather than vasiform turnings on the posts. The ball turnings in this instance are ornamented around the middle with a deep groove like the vase forms on Norwich-school chairs. The present back with its four slats not only is taller but also differs significantly in its organization from the well-ordered composition typical of the Norwich chairs, on which three equal slats, all with a flat upper edge that has an ogee profile at each end, are evenly spaced and alternate with identical vase forms on the posts. Here, while the turnings on the stiles and the spaces between the slats are obviously graduated, diminishing from the bottom up, no clear sequence is apparent in the three upper slats, which, at least in their present condition, vary only minimally in height. As a result the back is somewhat lacking in coherence. The tentative nature of that design suggests that the maker was working out an individual solution to the updating of an older model in response to the newer taste for chairs with tall backs. The less exaggerated size of the handgrips and finials and the gentler slope of the arms seem to indicate that he was working in an already weakened Norwich tradition.

CONSTRUCTION

The rear posts measure 2 inches in diameter and taper only slightly at the top. The front posts taper from 2¼ inches to 2 inches at the bottom and were turned from stock that retained a section of bark; the handgrips are integral to the posts. Both the front and rear posts have a built-in backward slant. Grooves on the stiles mark the top and bottom of the rectangular mortises for the slats; the mortises diminish in height from bottom, to lower middle, to top, to upper middle. None of the slat joints is pinned. The other crosspieces have round tenons with deep straight shoulders and flat sides. The mortises for the arm tenons are centered on a groove in the rear posts and drilled between two lines on the front posts. The seat rails and stretchers are positioned tangential to a layout line. The seat rails are turned; the side rails, accented with grooves, match the stretchers.

CONDITION

When it was acquired, the chair had shortened legs that had been notched at the bottom on the outer side—1½ inches on the back legs and 2¾ inches on the front ones—for the attachment of rockers (see *References*). (The lower side stretchers show nail holes from that attachment.) At the MMA, the legs were patched and extended with turned feet,[3] and the missing lower front stretcher was replaced, as was the broken rush seat. The upper middle slat may be an early replacement. A split in the right rear post, repaired with a nail, begins at the seat and ends in a loss on the front of the bottom stile turning and the cylindrical element above it. The outer side of that same post has been singed at seat level. The handgrips have significant losses. The right joint of the upper front stretcher has been reinforced with a nail. Records indicate that in 1933–34 modern varnish then on the chair was removed and the wood was finished with linseed oil and turpentine. Some areas of the surface appear to have been scraped.

WOODS

MAPLE; left rear post, bottom slat, SOFT MAPLE.

DIMENSIONS

OH. 48⅜ (122.9); SH. 16¾ (42.5); OW. (handgrips) 24¼ (61.5); SW. front 23¾ (60.3); SW. back 18⅛ (46); SD. 16½ (41.9).

EXHIBITION

"Hudson-Fulton Exhibition," MMA, 20 September–30 November 1909.

REFERENCES

Hudson-Fulton Celebration 1909 (exh. cat.), no. 107; Manca 2003, fig. 9 (both references show the chair as acquired).

PROVENANCE

Ex coll.: H. Eugene Bolles, Boston.

Gift of Mrs. Russell Sage, 1909 (10.125.676)

1. For the attribution of this group of chairs to the Norwich area and for existing examples, see Myers and Mayhew 1974, no. 3; Forman 1988, nos. 15, 16; and D. B. Warren et al. 1998, no. F2.
2. They are in Kane 1973a, nos. XXXI, XXXII; and Nutting 1928–33, no. 1804, and Forman 1988, no. 9.
3. The profile of the replacement feet is conjectural, but it is possible that the chair had turned feet at the back as well as the front, since that is the case on several Norwich-school slat-back chairs that retain portions of their original feet (Forman 1988, no. 15, for example).

14. See also fig. 11.

14.

Slat-back armchair

New York, 1690–1730

This chair is distinguished above all by having turned arms that extend over the front posts. In profile, they begin at the back with an ovoid defined by and accented with grooves, taper toward the middle, and then swell toward the front, where they terminate in a heavy barrel-like shape (now much worn) that is ornamented with two grooves at the joint with the arm support. They can be read as a turner's version of sawn and carved arms that bow down in the middle and end in a scroll handgrip. Turned arms that project over the front posts are known only on a few chairs from the mid-Atlantic region and are a characteristic of a larger number of southern chairs. The arms on a chair at the Albany Institute that belongs to the same New York school of turning as cat. no. 9 offer the closest parallel. They consist, like those seen here, primarily of a long plain turning that swells from the middle toward either end, and they terminate at the front with a barrel shape and at the back with a rounded form. The arms of a second armchair in that same chairmaking tradition, at the Morristown National Historical Park, Morristown, New Jersey, are also related in that they have a similar central section, but it is much shorter and there are a greater number of turnings at the front and back.[1] Other examples of turned arms that extend over the front posts have various different designs; they occur on a chair with arched slats and turnings typical of Delaware River valley seating and on southern spindle-back and slat-back chairs ranging in date from the late seventeenth century well into the nineteenth century.[2] Turned arms that pass over the front posts do not appear to be a part of the Anglo-American traditions of chairmaking. The occurrence of such arms in regions with significant numbers of artisans from northern Europe makes it likely that this craft practice was transferred directly from the Continent.[3]

The type of flattened ball motif used on the posts of this chair also link it to the New York turning tradition represented by cat. no. 9, and it is possible that the arm supports consisting of a vase topped by a rather straight-sided ring and then a rounded element are a distant echo of the design seen on the supports of the Morristown armchair. The strong ogee outlines of the vase shape on the present chair, however, relate much more closely to the early-Baroque-inspired turnings on New York tables, many of which feature two superimposed balusters (see cat. no. 65), a scheme that may also be reflected in these arm supports. The front stretchers, which are turned with ellipsoid and quasi-baluster forms, have much weaker cyma contours. The pattern seems to allude to the stretchers with opposed baluster turnings popular on Anglo-American William and Mary–style cane and leather chairs and possibly represents an updating of an older form under the influence of such models. The present stretchers have a certain affinity with those on a distinctive type of seventeenth-century-style slat-back chair attributed to the New York area. Those stretchers are likewise divided into five oblong segments (though in that case the center three are conservatively cylindrical) and terminate in the same type of long, rounded element with a taper at the end.[4] That the turner who made this chair was trained in a seventeenth-century tradition and was still working, at least partly, in that mind-set is evident in the extensive use of ornamental grooves—on the front stretchers, arm supports, arms, and finials. The finials (fig. 11) follow a generic design of a ball above one or two reels that was in use in some areas in the late 1600s and was widespread beginning in the early 1700s.[5]

CONSTRUCTION
The posts—a good 2 inches in diameter—angle out somewhat laterally toward the top. The stiles are grooved to mark the top and bottom of the rectangular mortises for the slats; the mortises are scribed to be equidistant one from another and to decrease in height from the top one, to the bottom one, to the middle two. However, since the mortises for the two middle slats extend beyond the upper layout lines, the actual decrease in height goes from the top mortise, to the middle two, to the bottom one. The slats themselves are all graduated starting with the largest at the top. A pin secures the joints of the top and lower middle slats. The chair's other joints are round-tenoned. The holes in the stiles for the arm tenons are drilled just above the bottom work line for the lower middle slat. A line scribed ½ inch below may have been intended for the arms; if it had been used, the arms would slant down toward the back. The arms are turned but have been flattened on the underside at the front for the joint (pinned) with the arm supports. The mortises for the seat rails and stretchers are drilled tangential to a layout line.

CONDITION
The rings on the finials are chipped on the front. The pin in the joint of the right arm to the front post is missing, as is a portion of two other pins. The top of the arms is not only worn but has probably also been shaved down. The front stretchers have been rotated in their joints to conceal wear. The feet have all lost a little height, and the rear feet (insect-damaged) have losses at the bottom. The rush seat is new. The black paint (not original) on the chair has worn off in some areas and is flaking.

WOODS
Posts, slats, SOFT MAPLE; arms, front and side seat rails, HICKORY; rear seat rail, stretchers, WHITE OAK.

DIMENSIONS
OH. 46¾ (118.7); SH. 15⅞ (40.3); OW. (arms) 25 (63.5); SW. front 24¼ (61.5); SW. back 17⅝ (44.8); SD. 15⅝ (39.7).

PROVENANCE
Ex coll.: Wunsch Americana Foundation, New York City.

The Foundation purchased the chair from dealer Jonathan Trace in Putnam Valley, New York, in 1993. The chair was on loan to the MMA from the Wunsch Americana Foundation from 1993 until the time it became a gift.

Gift of Wunsch Americana Foundation Inc., 1999 (1999.219.2)

1. Groft and Mackay 1998, no. 78A, and Gronning 2001, fig. 7 (Albany Institute armchair); Gronning 2001, figs. 6, 8 (Morristown National Historical Park armchair).
2. For the Delaware River valley chair, see Kane 1976, no. 18. For southern chairs, see Bivins 1988, figs. 5.4, 5.15, 5.16, 5.21; Beckerdite 1997, fig. 5 (now Bayou Bend Collection); Hurst and Prown 1997, no. 5; Leath 1997, fig. 16; and Gronning 2001, fig. 9.
3. Immigrant Huguenot artisans were probably largely instrumental in transmitting this practice to the South (Beckerdite 1997, pp. 203–4). Huguenot as well as Netherlandish craftsmen were active in New York.
4. For this group of slat-back chairs and stretcher type, see Forman 1988, no. 17, and Failey 1998, no. 4B.
5. Examples of New York chairs with a similar interpretation of this finial pattern are in V. I. Miller 1956, no. 8; Blackburn and Piwonka 1988, fig. 226; Failey 1998, no. 5A; Gronning 2001, fig. 27.

15.
Slat-back armchair

Probably eastern Massachusetts, 1720–50

Represented by cat. no. 15 is a popular form of slat-back chair that evolved at the beginning of the eighteenth century under the influence of William and Mary–style leather chairs and related banister-back chairs or imported slat-backs in the newer fashion. The back has been made tall and narrow and in armchairs incorporates four to six slats rather than the three characteristic of most seventeenth-century examples. The stock has become lighter; the posts have the standard one and three-quarters-inch thickness of posts on joined chairs of the period. The arms extend over the front posts instead of being set between the posts and are sawn. Of this chair's turned ornament, only that on the arm supports—a tall ogee baluster—bears a direct relationship to design elements introduced by William and Mary–style seating. The other motifs are indebted to the seventeenth-century-style vocabulary of turnings: ball shapes (here very flattened) on the posts, repeat rounded forms on the stretchers, and double-reel-and-ball finials such as those on cat. no. 8. However, the manner in which these elements are interpreted reveals a shift in aesthetic sensibility. The ball that tops the finials is not accented with one or more grooves but is entirely smooth (fig. 9). Similarly the work lines on the posts are no longer part of the decorative scheme but are scribed lightly so as not to be seen. The flattened balls flanked by broad hollows on the posts and the oval shapes on the front stretchers, particularly those at either end, have a softness of contour that is alien to the forms from which they are derived and that is associated with a turning tradition that has lost its vigor.

Chairs of this type with generally similar turnings were made from New England to New Jersey over a long period of time, and while they may exhibit certain individual characteristics, they have proved difficult to regionalize. The finials on this chair diverge from most examples in this pattern in that the ball is more elongated and seems never to have been topped by a button. The most distinctive feature of this chair is the outline of the slats; their upper edge is not arched, as was common in this period, but has the rare profile of two gentle ogee curves that come to a sharp peak at the center. Also, the overall scheme of the slats is not the usual one; the slats are not graduated with the largest at the top but are equal in size and evenly spaced, as designated by the work lines on the stiles for the placement of the mortises. Few chairs with such peaked slats are known, and all differ in details of the slats as well as in other respects. The slats on a chair at the Milwaukee Art Museum, Milwaukee, Wisconsin, are the closest in outline to

15. See also fig. 9.

those on cat. no. 15, but they have a double-curved bow not evident on the MMA chair. Because of the nature of those slats, the woods used, and other factors, that chair has been assigned by Robert F. Trent a probable New Jersey or Pennsylvania origin.[1] As far as cat. no. 15 is concerned, there is nothing in the character of its turnings or its woods (which are those typical of many eastern Massachusetts chairs) or in what is known of the H. Eugene Bolles collection, from which it came, to suggest that it was made elsewhere than in New England.[2]

With the undulating outline of the slats recalled in the curves of the finials, arm supports, and front stretchers, this chair has a certain refinement. One should bear in mind that the slat-back form per se was not always relegated to the role of a humble country chair. Slat-backs, certainly still during the first half of the eighteenth century, were popular in the city as well as in rural areas. In fact, there is evidence that in England and Europe in the late 1600s and early 1700s some types of slat-back chairs were to be found in quite grand settings.[3]

CONSTRUCTION

The posts are made from 1¾-inch stock, and the layout lines that circumscribe them are only lightly scored. The location of both the top and bottom of the rectangular mortises for the slats is marked; the mortises are all scribed for the same height (disallowing an erroneous line on the left stile that was corrected) and are evenly spaced apart. The slats are deeply bowed and are equal in size. A pin secures the joints of the top and the lower middle slats. The seat rails and stretchers are round-tenoned and placed tangential to a work line (but no lines are visible on the rear posts for the rear stretcher or the arms). The present arms are joined to the rear posts with a round tenon that projects from the inner half of the arm, and the shoulder on the outer half is shaped to conform to the curve of the stile.

CONDITION

When it was acquired, the chair had added rockers. At some point before 1924 they were taken off, the legs were pieced at the bottom for about 3 inches, and the right rear leg was also patched on the inner side from below the rear stretcher; holes from the attachment of the rockers remain. The arms are replacements. The arm supports lack the usual conical turning at the top and appear to have been shortened. To make up for that loss, the element on the arms that abuts

the supports is unusually high; its octagonal shape is anomalous. A nail has been driven from the top of the arms into the supports. The pin is missing from the left joint of the top slat, and a small area at the bottom of that slat has been singed. The lower middle slat has a long horizontal crack starting at the right end, and the pins in its joints may be later additions. The rush seat dates from before 1909 but is not original. Black paint on the chair when it was received was removed some time before 1933–34, when, according to records, modern varnish then on the chair was removed and the wood was finished with linseed oil and turpentine.

WOODS

Posts, POPLAR (*Populus* sp.); slats, stretchers, MAPLE; seat rails, undetermined.

DIMENSIONS

OH. 48⅜ (122.9); SH. 16¾ (42.5); OW. (arms) 25⅛ (63.8); SW. front 23⅝ (60); SW. back 16¾ (42.5); SD. 14⅛ (35.9).

REFERENCE

Dyer 1930b, p. 64 (with rockers).

PROVENANCE

Ex coll.: H. Eugene Bolles, Boston.

Gift of Mrs. Russell Sage, 1909 (10.125.241)

1. Jobe et al. 1991, no. 23. Other chairs with peaked slats are in Page 1969, no. 5; Fales 1972, no. 74; Kane 1976, no. 22; Monkhouse and Michie 1986, no. 88. See also cat. no. 14.
2. For chairs with similar turnings and eastern Massachusetts histories, see Jobe and Kaye 1984, no. 79.
3. For the ownership and production of slat-back chairs in Boston during this period, see I. W. Lyon 1891, p. 164; Jobe and Kaye 1984, no. 79. For English and Continental chairs, see Thornton 1997; and Thornton 1978, fig. 170.

16.

Slat-back armchair

Pennsylvania or New Jersey, 1750–1800

Slats that arch up gracefully on both the top and the bottom are the most eye-catching feature of a distinctive form of slat-back chair long identified with Philadelphia and the surrounding areas of Pennsylvania, New Jersey, and Delaware. The slats, which may number from three to six, are bowed to conform to the sitter's back and graduated with the largest at the top. As exemplified by cat. no. 16, other characteristics of this regional chair type are: plain rear posts that taper from the bottom up and have a peaked ball finial and a tapered foot; turned front posts that are smaller in diameter than the large ball feet with an inverted cone at the bottom; a

substantial front stretcher with ring-and-ball turnings; and sawn arms with an undercut that is straight at each end. In its turned elements and in the verticality of its tall narrow back with graduated slats that lead the eye upward, this type of chair is clearly expressive of the William and Mary style. The turnings on these so-called Delaware River valley chairs relate to those on couches from the same area (see cat. nos. 41, 42), particularly in the contours of the front feet and the pattern and large dimensions of the front stretcher. Both the couches and chairs are manifestations of the same broad school of turning that was based on forms introduced by the William and Mary style and that persisted regionally to the early 1800s and in some rural localities for yet another century.[1]

The general format represented by cat. no. 16 was probably established in Philadelphia and its environs by the 1720s. Such chairs continued to be made in basically the same overall form and proportions into the next century, with the passing of time reflected primarily in changes in the turnings, as on this example.[2] The character of its turnings suggests that it was made in the latter half of the eighteenth century and probably originated in a nonurban shop—one that was small, given the lack of examples with comparable elements. The front stretcher (three inches in diameter) is overblown and anomalous in having two rings at the center; it exhibits the type of exaggeration observed on some work done late in a tradition. The turnings on the front posts, with the exception of the feet, which have survived largely intact, lack clarity and represent a misreading or an idiosyncratic interpretation of standard forms. They are unusual in that the baluster at the top of the legs is inverted; so is the upper baluster on the arm supports, which may make reference to the more standard baluster-over-baluster pattern.

The full spectrum of Delaware River valley slat-back chairs includes more than three hundred examples, which, as determined by John M. Bacon in his thorough analysis of such chairs, fall into several groups, subgroups, and variants. One particular type, relatively small in number, has cabriole front legs and is exemplified by cat. no. 17. The present chair belongs to one of two major groups. It is defined by front posts with two or more turnings, a single front stretcher in a ring-and-ball pattern, and slats that are most often fully arched—the form commonly evoked by the term "Delaware valley chair." The other group, which is formally related to the first, has front posts with one or two turned elements, two plain, turned front stretchers, and slats that are most often arched on the upper edge and straight at the bottom.[3]

Benno M. Forman proposed a Germanic origin for the arched-slat form of chair (excepting the Anglo-American front stretcher). Chairs from the northwest of England, particularly Lancashire, have also been put forward as antecedents. Bacon concluded that the origin of the Delaware River valley slat-back is not to be found in any single prototype or in the tradition of any one country. The chairs appear to represent a fusion tradition that encompasses Germanic and Anglo elements, with different subgroups of chairs possibly reflecting different strains of influences, in accord with the heterogeneous character of the population of the region.[4]

CONSTRUCTION

The rear posts measure 1¾ inches at the bottom and taper a good ¼ inch to the top. Fine scored lines that circumscribe the posts mark the top and bottom of the rectangular mortises for the slats. Both mortises

16

and slats decrease in height from the top down, with the middle and lower middle elements equal in size. The joints of the uppermost slat are each secured with two pins. The frame's other components are all round-tenoned. The joints of the arms to the stiles and the front posts to the arms are pinned. The square ends of the arms are slightly let into the stiles. The edges of the cutout under the arms are chamfered. The front feet are one piece with the posts.

CONDITION

The top of the uppermost slat (that portion level with the finials) is replaced. The pins in all the arm joints are new, and the joints of the front seat rail have each been reinforced with a pin. There is evidence of insect infestation in the left front and rear legs and the lower left stretcher. The reason for the large hole that passes through the tapered portion of both front feet from side to side is unclear. The chair has a brown coating applied over red paint over bright green-blue paint, which is not original. There are numerous losses through one or more layers.

INSCRIPTION
The number 202 is inscribed in large black figures (modern) on the back of the left end of the uppermost slat.

WOODS
MAPLE; left rear post, SOFT MAPLE; side and rear seat rails, OAK.

DIMENSIONS
OH. 48¾ (123.8); SH. 16⅞ (42.9); OW. (arms) 24⅞ (63.2); SW. front 23⅞ (60.6); SW. back 18 (45.7); SD. 17⅝ (44.8).

REFERENCES
M. B. Davidson and Stillinger 1985, fig. 39; Bacon 1991, pp. 56, 200, and fig. 36.

PROVENANCE
Ex coll.: Robert R. Endicott, Washington Depot, Connecticut.
    The chair was on loan to the MMA from Endicott between 1959 and the time of its acquisition.

Purchase, Virginia H. Groomes Gift, in memory of her mother, Mary W. Groomes, 1975 (1975.310)

1. The most comprehensive study of this regional chair type is Bacon 1991. See also Powers 1926, Waters 1979, and Forman 1980.
2. For proportional systems and ratios, see Bacon 1991, pp. 66–81.
3. For a full typology, see ibid., pp. 36–42, 167–73.
4. Forman 1980; Forman 1983, pp. 103–6; Bacon 1991, pp. 82–90.

17.

Slat-back armchair

Philadelphia, 1735–50
Probably the shop of Solomon Fussell (active 1726–ca. 1750)

This armchair forms part of a distinct group of chairs within the broad Delaware River valley slat-back tradition (see the entry for cat. no. 16) that have cabriole front legs. This type of chair, made with and without arms, represents a rare instance in which an established chair form (in this case, in the William and Mary style) has been updated by having not the back—the more prominent portion—but the base modified to incorporate features of a newer style (here, the Queen Anne). In overall proportions and the design of the back, finials (fig. 12), arms, and stretchers, this chair follows the standard format of examples with turned front legs.[1] The back contains the maximum number of slats—six. Typically tall and narrow, it provides visual interest by playing the slats, which decrease in height from the top down, against the posts, which taper from the bottom up, and against the voids, which in the upper registers diminish in height toward the top. The arch of the slats is recalled in the curves of the cabriole legs and scalloped seat casings in a very pleasing integration of older and newer stylistic elements.

    The changes made to the traditional turned base are primarily visual, not structural. The base is joined entirely with round tenons, in the turners' fashion, with the seat casings merely boards nailed to the seat rails for show, providing the look but not the stability of a more fashionable and more expensive chair with joined scalloped seat rails. Boston joined chairs of about 1730 were the probable source for the square cabriole legs and shaped seat casings. It was Boston imports of a decade or so earlier that had most likely provided the model for the

ring-and-ball front stretcher, which appears to have been a feature of the arched-slat turned chair formula from the start. The Philadelphia version of that stretcher pattern differs from the Boston one primarily in that the conical ends have a concave outline and the ball shapes are incised with a pair of lines around the middle (which on cat. no. 17 are largely obscured by paint; fig. 31). Such grooves also ornament the balusters of the arm supports. They are a decorative device frequently found on William and Mary–style Pennsylvania turnings.

    The turnings on this chair are executed with flair and finesse, and the handgrips have a rare refinement: they are reduced in height and width in front of the arm support and end in a carved scroll. Similar handgrips are found on a nearly identical chair probably by the same maker. Eight additional related slat-back armchairs with cabriole legs have been published.[2] They exhibit some variations in the exact outlines of the slats, the shape of the seat casings, the taper or lack of it on the rear feet, and in one instance the pattern of the front stretcher. To what extent these differences indicate the existence of competing shops or are due to the subcontracting of parts, the turnover of journeymen, or the passage of time within the work of a single shop is unclear. Benno M. Forman has demonstrated that this type of chair was produced by Solomon Fussell, one of several Philadelphia craftsmen engaged in the rush-bottom chair business. Fussell's account books and ledgers for 1738–51 indicate that he was making slat-back chairs with cased seats and crooked feet ("foot" at that time referred to the

17. See also figs. 12, 31.

whole leg) and that maple examples were painted or stained—most often black or brown, rarely red or orange. Furthermore they reveal that a chair like cat. no. 17 was a middling product that ranked above two categories of cheaper slat-backs and below a considerably more expensive line of walnut or mahogany chairs, also available.[3]

CONSTRUCTION

The rear posts measure 1⅝ inches at the bottom and taper ¼ inch to the top. Lines scribed around the posts mark the location of the top of each rectangular mortise for the slats. The height of the mortises and slats decreases from the top down, but the distance between the mortises is the same throughout. The joints of the uppermost slat are pinned. The remaining structural elements are secured with round

tenons. The arm supports are separate from the legs; they are tenoned to the underside of the arms and to the top of the legs, and all joints are pinned. At the rear joint of the arms the tenon shoulders conform to the curve of the stiles. The scalloped skirts, or seat casings, are nailed to the outer edge of the front and side seat rails through the rush. They are shaped to extend partly over the upper edge of the seat rails and have a rounded profile at the top. A groove outlines the upper edges of the arms and handgrips and the top and sides of the step behind the scrolled ends. The lower edges of the arm within the cutout are chamfered.

CONDITION

The uppermost slat has a vertical break at the left end and an obvious loss along the bottom at the right. At the back of the right rear post a section that split out for about 5 inches from the top down and the adjoining mortise for the uppermost slat have been repaired with nails and fill. A nail reinforces the left joint of the uppermost slat, the right joint of the slat below, and the joint of the left arm to the stile. The seat casings have replaced and added nails. The casings on the sides have glued splits and are missing segments of the lower portion. There is a crack at the right end of the front stretcher. The outer corner of the left front foot has broken off. The rush seat is sagging and supported from below by modern webbing strips tacked to the underside of the seat rails. The chair has a coat of hastily applied orange paint over a red that does not appear to be original. The paint is crazed and shows many losses.

WOODS

MAPLE; left front leg, SOFT MAPLE.

DIMENSIONS

OH. 44 (111.8); SH. 16 3/8 (41.6); OW. (feet) 25 1/4 (64.1); SW. front 23 1/4 (59.1); SW. back 17 (43.2); SD. 16 (40.6).

REFERENCES

The Jacob Paxson Temple Collection of Early American Furniture and Objects of Art, auction cat., Anderson Galleries, New York City, 23–28 January 1922, lot 1494; MMA 1980, p. 57; M. B. Davidson and Stillinger 1985, fig. 37.

PROVENANCE

Ex coll.: Jacob Paxson Temple, Tanguy, Pennsylvania; Mrs. J. Insley Blair, Tuxedo Park, New York; her daughter Mrs. J. Woodhull Overton, Balmville, New York.

Mrs. Blair purchased the chair in 1925 from Mrs. George F. Baker. The chair was on loan from Mrs. Overton to the MMA from 1952 to 1979.

Anonymous Gift, in memory of Mrs. J. Insley Blair, 1979 (1979.305)

1. The proportional system of the chair's back posts corresponds to that found on the most common type of Delaware River valley chair: if the post below the finial is divided into eight equal segments, five are above the seat and three are below, and the arms are two units above the seat (Bacon 1991, p. 67 and fig. 50).
2. For the chair with identical arms, see *American Furniture and Decorative Arts: Part Two of the Collection of the Late Arthur J. Sussel, Philadelphia*, auction cat., Parke-Bernet Galleries, New York City, 22–24 January 1959, lot 693. Other chairs with six slats are in Nutting 1928–33, no. 1903, and Forman 1980, fig. 2 (Winterthur Museum); advertised by Joe Kindig Jr. in *Antiques* 53 (February 1948), inside front cover; and offered in *Important American Furniture, Silver, Folk Art and Decorative Arts*, auction cat., Christie's, New York City, 23 June 1993, lot 131. Five-slat chairs are in Lockwood 1926, fig. LXXVI; Hornor 1935, pl. 464; "Shop Talk" 1957, p. 30; and D. B. Warren et al. 1998, no. F53 (Bayou Bend Collection). An additional chair has joined seat rails and a rush slip seat (see Forman 1980, fig. 12).
3. Forman 1980, pp. 42–44.

Joined Seating with a Wooden Bottom

Seating made by joiners, who framed furniture with squared members and rectangular mortise-and-tenon joints (see fig. 161), represented a higher level of production than that made by turners. It was more expensive, since the fashioning of such joints was labor-intensive, and it was also sturdier. Grouped together in this chapter are various types of joined seating—stools, chairs with a paneled back, and a chair-table—that were fitted with a board seat, as opposed to chairs with joined frames that required for their completion the additional skills of a caner or upholsterer, the category presented in the following chapter. The forms of joined seating with a wooden bottom here included have English and European sixteenth-century antecedents. They were made in the colonies primarily in the seventeenth century, becoming obsolescent in the early eighteenth century.

For much of the seventeenth century, joint (joined) stools, made characteristically with legs splayed in two opposite directions, and "forms" (benches that were essentially elongated stools) provided ordinary seating in most households. They were usually listed in probate inventories in conjunction with a table and associated with dining. Although once common, joint stools are now few in number and only one "form" of the period is known.[1] Joint stools are represented in the collection by two prime examples from Massachusetts: one is of oak and has solid turnings in the seventeenth-century style (cat. no. 21); the other is of maple and has dynamic William and Mary–style turnings (cat. no. 22). The contrast between the turnings on those two stools vividly illustrates the change in aesthetics brought about by early Baroque design influences. The latter piece also provides evidence that while stools were becoming obsolete in the early 1700s, their production did not immediately cease.

Joined armchairs with a paneled back were much less common and considerably more expensive than stools, but they have had a relatively good survival rate. Now generally called wainscot chairs, they were most often identified in period documents by various designations that referred to their construction, such as a "joined," "joiner's," or "joinery" chair or one of "joined work." They were also sometimes described as "wooden" or "wooden-bottom," in reference to the material of their seat. The term "wainscot" is occasionally found. Since it was applied to chests, for example, as well as to chairs, the word appears to have been used in its early meaning of oak wood or paneling (made of oak) and not in the modern sense of a particular form of chair.

Colonial joined chairs with a paneled back fall into two broad categories, one stylistically earlier than the other. The first includes armchairs made of oak and usually embellished with carving, of which about two dozen examples have survived from New England, and of which one each is known from New York, New Jersey, and the South. Their basic format is derived from English chairs of the early 1600s. Representing this type in the collection is an Essex County, Massachusetts, chair that is one of several distinguished by having squared, rather than the usual turned, front legs and arm supports (cat. no. 18). One of the turning patterns often found on the front posts of wainscot chairs—a straight-sided baluster—is illustrated by the Museum's oak chair-table from Plymouth County, Massachusetts (cat. no. 19). Joined chair-tables are related in overall design and construction, from the arms down, to oak wainscot chairs, differing mainly in that the back is not paneled but made of boards and is hinged to fold down and rest on the arms. A paneled armchair that is made of walnut, lacks carving, and incorporates design elements introduced in the mid- and late seventeenth century illustrates the second type of wainscot chair (cat. no. 20). Such chairs are characteristic of Pennsylvania, where walnut was available locally, and they have survived in greater numbers than their oak counterparts. They were produced from the late 1600s to the mid-eighteenth century—an early form perpetuated for a conservative clientele. Large paneled armchairs were imposing and they conveyed status, particularly in the seventeenth century, but they already then had provincial connotations rather than a fashionable, urban aura.

Chairs of joined construction, whether fitted with a wooden seat or a cane or an upholstered one, were designed to provide more comfort than turned chairs in that their rear posts had stiles that canted backward so that the chair back was somewhat inclined. Whenever possible, the hard seats of wooden-bottom chairs and of joint stools were softened by plump, feather-filled cushions, as were rush and other woven seats, budget permitting.

1. Forman 1988, no. 40 (Winterthur Museum).

18.

Joined armchair

Essex County, Massachusetts, 1650–1700

This chair has an impressive monolithic quality, imparted primarily by its most distinctive feature—the massive square pillars on the front posts, which are quite different from the turned pillars normally found on joined paneled chairs, now commonly called wainscot chairs. As the lower pillars on cat. no. 18 are considerably taller than the upper ones, the posts firmly anchor the piece to the ground. Also conveying weightiness is the horizontal emphasis of the square back with its two equal-sized longitudinal panels and its low overhanging crest rail, which, instead of having brackets, is stepped in at the ends. Angular forms dominate the architectonic design and are offset by the interplay of circles and semicircles in the carving and by the shallow dip of the arms. In its proportions, cat. no. 18 relates not to the more typical New England wainscot chair with a tall imposing back, but rather to the squatter shape of low-backed seventeenth-century upholstered armchairs.[1] When the feet on the present chair were intact, the height of the back was the same as or slightly less than that of the seat. How consciously the maker emulated the proportions of the more fashionable upholstered seating it is difficult to say.

Five chairs related to cat. no. 18 are known. They have similar square pillars and tapered rear posts, a rear stretcher not in line with the others but positioned higher, and carved motifs in common. All have the same type of arcaded crest rail and S-scrolls with ligatures on the stiles and all but one, the pattern of intersecting lunettes filled with stylized foliage seen here on the upper back panel and rail. The scrolls are invariably carved within a rectangular reserve but the boundaries of the lunette design are defined largely by the outlines of the carving (fig. 54). A chair in the Bayou Bend Collection has the same combination of carved elements as the present example. The other chairs introduce four additional motifs: two (Winterthur Museum and Pilgrim Hall Museum, Plymouth, Massachusetts) feature an upper back panel with paired scrolls, and one (Museum of Fine Arts, Boston) has an upper panel with rosettes and lacks carving on the rail below. On another (Danvers Historical Society, Danvers, Massachusetts) the upper panel is carved with opposed lunettes and the rail below with strapwork, and the intersecting lunette pattern occurs on the front seat rail. The chairs vary also in their proportions—four have distinctly vertical backs—and in the height of the pillars in relation one to another and to the posts' blocks. The joinery, however, is consistent in its idiosyncratic pattern of two

different-sized joints, so that if this group of chairs was produced by more than one craftsman, it was probably a master and his apprentices. This shop tradition has been assigned to Essex County, Massachusetts; the known histories of three of the chairs associate them with that county, and this one descended in a family that settled just beyond its northern border.[2]

Square, tapering pillars are part of the Mannerist vocabulary presented in sixteenth- and seventeenth-century northern European printed furniture designs, such as those published by Jan Vredeman de Vries (1527–1604). Such pillars found their way into English provincial work, the most likely source of their use on this group of chairs and on the three other, disparate American, or possibly American, chairs with square pillars that are known.[3] A chairmaking tradition represented by several Massachusetts slat-back armchairs fashioned with heavy square posts may also have some bearing on the design of cat. no. 18; one such chair has rear posts that, like those on this and related pieces, taper on the front surface not only above but also below the seat.[4]

CONSTRUCTION

The rear posts are straight on the back surface, but on the front they taper in thickness from the seat, where they are 2½ inches deep, toward both the crest rail and the foot. The chair is framed with the front of the rear legs vertical. As a result, each entire rear post slants backward, and the incline imparted to the chair back by the tapering of the stiles is thereby increased. The rectangular mortise-and-tenon joints (all pinned) that secure the frame are of two different widths: about 5/16 inch and about ½ inch. The wider tenon was used at the top of the front and rear posts and on the side seat rails and side stretchers. On the two latter elements the tenons have just an outside shoulder. This simplified the joinery; it meant that just one tenon shoulder (rather than two, as on the joints of the arms to the stiles, which have a narrower tenon) had to be cut to accord with the oblique angle at which the rail or stretcher meets the post because of the chair's trapezoidal plan (see fig. 166b). The workmanship on these and nearly all other joints in the chair is not precise. The seat is formed of two boards joined with a half lap, and it is pinned to the top of the front and side rails; there is no rear seat rail. The outer side of the front and rear posts has been planed so as to be in line with the arms, side seat rails, and stretchers.

The carving on the upper panel and rail was laid out with a compass and it is centered, but the design on the stepped crest rail is not symmetrical and was executed entirely freehand. The ground of the arcades on the crest rail is crosshatched, but that of the other carving is worked haphazardly with a single punch. The upper front edge of the two back rails is beveled. On the arms, there is a groove along each side of the top, and the undercut has a cavetto at

18. See also fig. 54.

either end. The front of the seat is finished with an ovolo molding, the side edges, with rounded notches. A cyma reversa molding is worked at the bottom of the seat rails.

CONDITION

Two of the pins securing the seat are new, and the lower pins in the joints of the left seat rail are partly or entirely lost. Several loose joints have been tightened with small wedges. The top of the crest rail and of the well-worn arms is heavily nicked and gouged. Old nails and nail holes in the crest rail and arms suggest that at one point a cushion or other padding was attached. There is a shrinkage gap at the upper right of the lower panel and between the seat boards, and a split in the rear seat board. The feet have been cut down. The surface has been waxed and probably also oiled. It shows scattered specks of green paint (the analysis of one confirmed that the paint is modern), and there are large patches of green under the feet.

INSCRIPTIONS

A New Hampshire Historical Society loan number (see *Exhibitions*) is painted on the underside of the lower back rail (L1958.44.2). The remnant of a paper sticker under the seat inscribed in red ink reads: ". . . lder, C.E./ . . . mouth, N.H."

WOOD

OAK, probably WHITE OAK (not microanalyzed).

DIMENSIONS

OH. 36½ (92.7); SH. 17¾ (45.1); OW. (crest rail) 23⅛ (58.7); SW. front 23 (58.4); SW. back 19¼ (48.9); SD. 16½ (41.9).

EXHIBITIONS

On loan to the New Hampshire Historical Society, Concord, from 1958 to 1986; "The Decorative Arts of New Hampshire: A Sesquicentennial Exhibition," New Hampshire Historical Society, Concord, 28 June–29 September 1973.

REFERENCES

Keyes 1938, fig. 4; *Decorative Arts of New Hampshire* 1973 (exh. cat.), no. 18; *Important American Furniture, Folk Art, Folk Paintings, and Chinese Export Porcelain*, auction cat., Sotheby's, New York City, 24–25 October 1986, lot 279; Trent 1987b; *The Collection of Mr. and Mrs. Eddy Nicholson*, auction cat., Christie's, New York City, 27–28 January 1995, lot 1024; "Recent Acquisitions" 1995, p. 50.

PROVENANCE

Ex coll.: Charles H. Batchelder, Portsmouth, New Hampshire; Mr. and Mrs. Eddy Nicholson, Hampton, New Hampshire.

The chair came down in the family to Charles H. Batchelder, a direct descendant of Nathaniel Batchelder (or Bachiler, 1630–1710), who came from England to Hampton, New Hampshire, about 1645. It was presumably made for an early member of this family.[5] From 1958 until 1986 it was on loan to the New Hampshire Historical Society, from the Charles H. Batchelder collection (lent by Mrs. Charles E. Batchelder, Robert Batchelder, and Richard Batchelder). The chair was put up at auction by the family in 1986 (see *References*) and bought by Eddy Nicholson. It was purchased for the MMA at the sale of the Nicholson collection (see *References*).

Purchase, Friends of the American Wing and Sansbury-Mills Funds, Mr. and Mrs. Robert G. Goelet Gift, Mrs. Muriel Gluck Gift, in honor of Virginia and Leonard Marx, and The Max H. Gluck Foundation Inc., The Virginia and Leonard Marx Foundation, and Mr. and Mrs. Eric Martin Wunsch Gifts, 1995 (1995.98)

1. Only one American upholstered armchair of this form is known (Fairbanks and Trent 1982, no. 489). For English examples, see Chinnery 1979, figs. 2:132, 2:133, 2:155.
2. For the five chairs, in the order mentioned, see D. B. Warren et al. 1998, no. F1; Forman 1988, no. 18; Pizer, Driver, and Earle 1985, fig. 10; Randall 1965, no. 120; and Lockwood 1926, fig. LXXVII (Danvers Historical Society). An early discussion of this group is in Keyes 1938. For a compilation of the histories, see Forman 1988, p. 148.
3. Jervis 1974, nos. 146, 148. The square pillars in such designs, when they taper, narrow toward the bottom. On English provincial chairs they may taper down (Macquoid 1904–5, fig. 76) or up (Kirk 1982, no. 657). Other examples of square pillars are on a red oak chair-table base in the National Museum of American History (acc. no. 388039), a chair-table base in Failey 1976, no. 15, and a wainscot armchair in Nutting 1928–33, no. 1795.
4. Wood 1996, no. 23.
5. For the line of descent, see Frederick Clifton Pierce, *Batchelder, Batcheller Genealogy: Descendants of Rev. Stephen Bachiler, of England . . . Who Settled the Town of New Hampton, N.H., and Joseph, Henry, Joshua and John Batcheller of Essex Co., Massachusetts* (Chicago, 1898), pp. 76–77, 110, 115, 128, 135, 148–49, 183, 248, 249, and Batchelder correspondence at the New Hampshire Historical Society.

19.
Chair-table

Plymouth County, Massachusetts, probably Marshfield, 1650–1700

A convertible furniture form, the chair-table has a hinged top that can pivot up to become the back of a seat or down to serve as a table; often fitted with a drawer under the seat as here, it can also supply storage space. Well suited to limited living quarters, chair-tables are documented in New England from the 1630s on.[1] With its top (replaced) tilted up, this piece is an imposing chair; the expanse of the back provides an impressive backdrop for the sitter, and the base, on which virtually every element is ornamented, has a vigorous presence. This chair-table is a product of the stylistic tradition that dominated furniture making in the coastal towns of Plymouth Colony during the seventeenth century and of which two

cupboards in the MMA collection (cat. nos. 114, 115) are prime expressions.[2] Its history indicates that it was probably made in Marshfield. The chair-table base relates to the cupboards cited and similar pieces both in the degree of its elaboration and in particulars of structure and decoration, such as the use of white cedar in the drawer and of paired notches along the bottom of the seat rails and molding. The design of the scallops cut on the stretchers is a close match to that on the bottom rails of cat. no. 115 and the profile of the channel moldings, which consists of a flat band flanked by cavettos, is the same on both pieces. Three other chair-table bases in the same tradition of craftsmanship are known, but, given some differences in the construction and ornamentation of the drawers, they are probably not all from the same shop. They correspond to cat. no. 19 in the shape of the inverted baluster turnings, the contours of the arms and their embellishment with grooves, and the profiles of the moldings. The applied seat molding has an outline composed of a fillet, a horizontal ovolo, a large shallow vertical ovolo, and a fascia with paired notches. Moldings comparable in scale and overall concept but that incorporate a serrated band occur on related cupboards and chests. Two of the other three chair-tables have drawer fronts with incised carving rather than channel moldings; none other has scalloped stretchers.[3]

Not many seventeenth-century-style joined oak chair-tables have survived, and of the eight known to the writer, none is intact. (The fact that four of those eight are from the same area is probably just an accident of history.) This is the only example that has not lost its entire feet, and all but one have tops that are replaced or missing.[4] Cat. no. 19 was acquired with a modern rectangular top of anomalous proportions and manner of attachment (see *References*). The present replacement, of riven oak and installed in 2001, was made round—the most likely shape of the original.

CONSTRUCTION

The seat rails and stretchers are tenoned to the posts, which are a good 2¼ inches thick, and the posts, to the arms. The joints of the front seat rail are secured with one pin, and all others with two. The pins pass through the legs to a broad chamfer on the inner corner of the leg blocks; some of the pins that are at right angle to one another intersect. The seat—a single board—and the applied molding on the front and sides of the seat are attached with T-headed nails. The sides of the drawer are each secured to the rabbeted ends of the front with a single nail (T-headed), and the back is butted and fastened to each side with one nail (a rosehead, like all the remaining). The bottom—a wide front board and a narrow strip at the back—is nailed to a rabbet in the front and to the bottom of the other sides. The drawer is side-hung on runners that are let into the posts and nailed. Two pairs of parallel ornamental grooves run the length of the top of the arms and continue down the front of the handgrips, which are defined at the bottom on each side just beyond the posts with an incised inverted "V." The circular ends of the cutout under the arms were formed by drilling. The edges of the arms and the outer corners of the

19

posts are finished with a chamfer. The stretchers and some of the rails and posts are not fully squared on the inner side, and defective wood, which resulted in an irregularly shaped turning, was used for the left rear post. By mistake, the joiner initially made the mortise on the right side of the left front leg of a height to fit the tenon of a deep side or rear seat rail instead of the tenon of the shallow front rail above the drawer, and he then filled in the lower part of the mortise to correct the error.

CONDITION

The top (white oak) is new. There are losses at the bottom edge of the drawer front, at the left front corner of the seat molding, and at the bottom of one of the feet, all of which have been cut down. Nails have been added to the drawer and applied molding. The chair-table base has been stripped and appears to have been finished with oil and wax. Traces of green paint (not original) remain on the base.

INSCRIPTIONS

MMA Hudson-Fulton exhibition identification numbers (H. F. 40.31 [twice] and 498) are inscribed in chalk and orange crayon on the underside of the drawer.

WOODS

Posts, arms, rails, stretchers, drawer front and sides, drawer runners, applied molding, RED OAK; seat, SOUTHERN YELLOW PINE; drawer back and bottom, ATLANTIC WHITE CEDAR.

DIMENSIONS

OH. top up 58¾ (149.2), OH. top down 32 (81.3); top: DIAM. 43 (109.2); chair base: SH. 19¼ (48.9), OW. (seat molding) 23 (58.4), SW. 21¼ (54), OD. (arms) 20¾ (52.7), SD. 16⅝ (42.2).

EXHIBITION

"Hudson-Fulton Exhibition," MMA, 20 September–30 November 1909.

REFERENCES

Hudson-Fulton Celebration 1909 (exh. cat.), no. 58; Lockwood 1913, fig. 439; Halsey and Tower 1925, fig. 7; Cornelius 1926, pl. III; "Antiques in the American Wing" 1946, p. 247, no. 7; Williams 1963, no. 37; M. B. Davidson 1967, no. 42; Bishop 1972, no. 26; Schwartz 1976, no. 4; Fitzgerald 1982, fig. I-17; M. B. Davidson and Stillinger 1985, fig. 17. (All the references show the piece as acquired.)

PROVENANCE

Ex coll.: H. Eugene Bolles, Boston.

According to the MMA Hudson-Fulton exhibition catalogue of 1909 (see *References*), the chair-table was purchased by Bolles from a descendant of Peregrine White (1620–1704) of Marshfield, Massachusetts, with a history of having belonged to that noteworthy ancestor (the first English child born in New England). At the time of the exhibition Bolles considered the piece "the rarest and most distinguished American chair yet found" apart from the "sentimental value" it had because of its history. The vendor, as can be deduced from later correspondence between other family members and the MMA (ADA files), must have been Abigail Phillips (b. 1851), of Marshfield, the daughter of Nathaniel Phillips (1798–1884) and his second wife, Sarah L. Rogers (1811–1898). She was unmarried and had retained the old family homestead. The connection with the White family comes through her great-grandfather Nathaniel Phillips (1713–1795), of Marshfield, who in 1734 married Joanna White (1713–1798). This Nathaniel was the great-grandson of John (d. 1658), the first Phillips to settle in Marshfield. Joanna was a direct descendant of Peregrine through his son Daniel White (1649–1724) and Daniel's son Cornelius White (1682–1755), who was her father. The wives in both the White and Phillips families in this line of descent came from local, virtually all Marshfield, families—Bassett,

Hunt, Thomas, Randall, Rogers. Thus the chair-table originated in all likelihood in or near Marshfield, whether or not it belonged to Peregrine White. Such a piece cannot be identified in either his will or probate inventory.[5]

Gift of Mrs. Russell Sage, 1909 (10.125.697)

1. "A little chaire table, with a small carpet" is listed in a Plymouth Colony inventory from that decade (quoted in Bailey 1952, p. 237).
2. St. George 1979b, pp. 25–55.
3. The two with carving, one at the Henry Ford Museum (ibid., no. 5), the other in a private collection (ibid., no. 6), have the drawer front nailed to the sides through the front; they have later tops. The drawer of the third chair (*Property from the Collection of Peggy N. and Roger G. Gerry*, auction cat., Christie's, New York City, 7 October 2004, lot 1590), which is without a top, is partly rebuilt; the front has moldings similar to those on cat. no. 19.
4. Examples not related to cat. no. 19 are: two at the National Museum of American History, one of which (Kane 1973a, no. XXVIII) retains an old, probably original, top that provided the basis for the use of oak on the replacement on cat. no. 19, the other of which (acc. no. 388039) is lacking its top; one at the Old Saybrook Historical Society, Old Saybrook, Connecticut (Fairbanks and Trent 1982, no. 317); and a base (American or English) at the Smithtown Historical Society, Smithtown, New York (Failey 1976, no. 15).
5. Letter of 17 May 1909 from Bolles to Henry W. Kent (Hudson-Fulton exhibition correspondence, MMA Archives); Lysander Salmon Richards, *History of Marshfield* (Plymouth, Mass., 1901–5), vol. 1, pp. 13–14, vol. 2, pp. 12, 57–58; Robert M. Sherman and Ruth Wilder Sherman, comps., *Vital Records of Marshfield, Massachusetts, to the Year 1850* (n.p., 1970), pp. 32, 41, 57, 349, 406; *Plymouth County, Massachusetts, Probate Index, 1686–1881*, transcribed by Ralph W. Woods Jr. (Camden, Maine, 1988), unpaginated; Thomas White and Samuel White, *Ancestral Chronological Record of the William White Family, from 1607–8 to 1895* (n.p., 1895), p. 27. Peregrine White's will is published in Richards, *History of Marshfield*, vol. 1, pp. 37–38; his inventory in the *Mayflower Descendant* 3, no. 2 (April 1901), p. 119.

20.

Joined armchair

Southeastern Pennsylvania, 1690–1720

The use of walnut and the absence of carving characterize Pennsylvania chairs with paneled backs and board seats, of which many examples, made both with and without arms, survive. Cat. no. 20 represents the most common type, which was based on models from northwest England; the particular form of its sawn crest rail, which features partial crescents flanking a mushroom-shaped motif, has close parallels on chairs from Cheshire and southern Lancashire. The design is distinctive, the most striking of all the crest-rail patterns on Pennsylvania paneled chairs. Two joiners from Cheshire, who arrived in Philadelphia in 1683, the year after the founding of the city, may have been early bearers of this English provincial tradition of chairmaking. It probably first found expression in Philadelphia and then spread to surrounding areas, such as Chester County, where paneled seating was still being produced in the mid-eighteenth century.[1]

In its overall configuration—high canted back, heavy sloping arms, and turned front posts—cat. no. 20 is derived from the form of wainscot chair that was being made in England by the early seventeenth century, but it also includes later stylistic developments that are not found on New England wainscot chairs. Like virtually all Pennsylvania paneled chairs, it has not a low, but a high, front stretcher—a characteristic of English upholstered back stools beginning in the mid-seventeenth century (see the entry for cat. no. 23). Reflecting the influence of early Baroque design as promulgated by English cane chairs from the end of the century are the strong ogee form of the balusters on the arm supports and front stretcher (fig. 22) and the use of progressively less compressed bulbous shapes from the bottom of the front posts up (see cat. no. 27). Some if not all of these features were also part of the design vocabulary of emigrant joiners

20. See also fig. 22.

from northwest England, for they are found on the small oak chairs without arms that have wooden seats and backs and were popular in that region during the second half of the seventeenth and early eighteenth centuries and that emulated the design first of upholstered back stools and then of cane chairs.[2]

On Pennsylvania chairs, crest rails in the general design seen here are invariably flanked by round, sawn finials. The crest-rail pattern shows variations in the area between the crescents and the stiles. Three other chairs have not only the concave-convex outline found on this piece but also similar arms and turnings and a flat, rather than a fielded, panel (which on this example was in all probability originally edged with an applied molding, as it is on related pieces). Two show an alternate type of board seat found on Pennsylvania chairs—one in which the board is set into a groove on the inner side of the four seat rails. One of the latter chairs is not of walnut but of red oak and has a back panel surrounded on the front not by applied moldings but by a chamfer on the stiles and a molding run on the rails. Such a conservative treatment and the use of oak suggest that that chair was made early in Pennsylvania's history by an immigrant joiner recently arrived and still working entirely in the traditional manner in which he had been trained. Thus cat. no. 20 and the other closely related walnut chairs were probably produced in the first few decades after settlement rather than at a later date.[3]

CONSTRUCTION

The frame is joined with rectangular mortise-and-tenon joints; those of the stretchers and of the front posts to the arms are secured with one pin, the others, with two. The seat structure includes only front and side rails. The lower rail of the back is positioned so as to allow the seat board to extend below it, and the present board (a replacement) is pinned to the top of the seat rails and nailed to the bottom of the lower back rail. On the rear of the back, the edges of the two-board panel are beveled, and a broad chamfer finishes the lower edge of the crest rail and the upper edge of the lower rail. Two parallel grooves decorate the upper and front surfaces of the arms. The profile at either end of the cutout on the underside of the arms consists of a cavetto between fillets. The lower edge of the seat rails is finished with a fillet and a cavetto. No effort was made to remove the kerfs (from hand sawing) on the inner side of those rails.

CONDITION

The seat board, the front feet, and the bottom 1¾ inches of the rear legs are replaced. A molding that in all likelihood was originally applied around the edge of the front of the panel is missing. The convex segment at the upper right end of the crest rail has split off and been reattached with nails. The chair has been stripped and appears to have been oiled and waxed. Many of the small holes, nicks, and losses have been infilled with brown wax.

WOOD
BLACK WALNUT.

DIMENSIONS
OH. 45⅝ (115.9); SH. 17¼ (43.8); SW. 21⅞ (55.6); SD. 16¼ (41.3).

EXHIBITION
On loan to the William Penn Memorial Museum (now State Museum of Pennsylvania), Harrisburg, from 1968 to 1978.

REFERENCES
Early Pennsylvania and Other Colonial Furniture . . . from the Collection of the Late J. Stogdell Stokes, auction cat., Parke-Bernet Galleries, New York City, 20 March 1948, lot 120 (feet missing); Downs [November] 1948, p. 80; M. B. Davidson 1967, no. 487; Bishop 1972, no. 238; M. B. Davidson and Stillinger 1985, fig. 133.

PROVENANCE
Ex coll.: J. Stogdell Stokes, Philadelphia.

The chair was purchased by the MMA at the sale of the Stokes collection (see *References*).

Rogers Fund, 1948 (48.61)

1. The fullest discussion of Pennsylvania paneled chairs is in Forman 1988, pp. 138–43 and nos. 21–33. For related English crest designs, see Butt 1929, figs. 8, 12; and Forman 1988, figs. 68, 70, 78. The Cheshire joiners are mentioned in Forman 1988, pp. 140–41.
2. See Butt 1929; Forman 1988, figs. 68, 70, 78, 79, 86.
3. For the oak chair, see Forman 1988, p. 140 and fig. 69; for the walnut chairs, see Joe Kindig Jr. and Son advertisement in *Antiques* 60 (December 1951), inside front cover; and Kindig 1978, no. 4. A walnut chair with identical turnings but a slightly variant crest pattern and alternate type of seat is in Schiffer 1966, ill. no. 162. An oak chair (American?) similar to cat. no. 20 except for stylistically earlier front-leg turnings and four low, plain stretchers is in Keyes 1924, fig. 4a.

21.

Joint stool

Probably Braintree, Massachusetts, 1650–90
Probably the Savell shop tradition

With block-and-turned legs splayed in two opposite directions, rectangular stretchers, and a board top, cat. no. 21 illustrates the standard format of a joint (joined) stool. The most basic form of seventeenth-century seating, stools were subject to hard usage and thus, although they were common, relatively few have survived. This is one of only a small number known made of oak and having typically seventeenth-century-style turnings that are essentially columnar in nature, both in their solidity and in their close or distant derivation from the classical orders. Such turnings are of three general types, which have English antecedents. A strictly columnar design with a cylindrical tapering shaft is exemplified by two stools, one, at the Wadsworth Atheneum, that interprets the Roman Doric order, quite correctly, the other, at the Winterthur Museum, rather loosely. The overall sequence of elements on cat. no. 21 and two further stools at the Winterthur Museum reflects that same order, but, as seen here, the shaft has become a straight-sided vase and the astragal of the capital has been lowered and enlarged to a prominent ring. This latter formula but inverted (see cat. no. 47) occurs on a stool at the Scituate Historical Society, Scituate, Massachusetts, and two in private collections.[1]

The turnings on each of the known oak stools are individual interpretations and the work of a different maker. What most distinguishes the turning pattern on this stool is the short cylindrical element at the top of the leg, which is quite separate from the thick ring below it and is not an extension of an adjoining profile, as is the case at the bottom of the leg. The corners of the adjacent leg block were left quite angular so that there is a stark geometric juxtaposition of square and cylinder. As on some of the other stools, the uppermost motif on the leg is repeated at the top of the foot. No exact parallels to these turnings are known, and the piece has no early history; however, the stool's channel molding provides a link to a school of joinery with distinctive carving that has been attributed to Braintree, Massachusetts, and members of the Savell family (see cat. no. 71). The molding—a convex band flanked by fillets—is very close in overall dimension and profile to that found on several chests attributed to that school (see also cat. no. 45). A connection can also be made between the angularity of the leg blocks on the stool and the fact that the edges of the framing members surrounding the chests' panels were left straight and sharp rather than being finished with a molding or chamfer. The stool exhibits in addition the type of extremely careful joinery characteristic of that shop tradition.[2]

CONSTRUCTION
The frame is secured with mortise-and-tenon joints that were fashioned with great care: both the inner and outer tenon shoulders on the rails and stretchers fit tightly against the legs. The holes for corresponding pins at a right angle one to another were bored at about the same level, and the two pins come through the leg more or less together at a chamfer cut on the inner corner of the leg. The rake of the legs, about 7 degrees from the vertical and determined by the angle of the ends of the short rails, is such that the frame becomes square at the bottom of the stretchers. The one-board top was pinned to the legs; its edge has an ovolo profile. Evidence of riving remains on the inner side of two of the rails. The channel molding on the rails consists of a convex band flanked by fillets. It is worked the same distance up from the bottom of each rail, but because the short rails are somewhat deeper than the long ones, it does not line up all around.

CONDITION
The top is probably original. Heavily worn, warped, and split in two lengthwise, it has been pried loose from the pins that secured it to the legs and then reattached with two hidden dowels into each of the long rails and glued to the pins. Nearly all of the joint pins have been reset or are new. The wood of the legs has numerous small cracks. The feet have been cut down, and the deteriorated wood at the bottom has been consolidated; two are patched and two have modern gliders. The surface appears to have been oiled and waxed.

INSCRIPTIONS
Pencil reassembly marks (roman numerals and circles) match the legs with rails and stretchers and date from the time of modern repairs.

WOODS
WHITE OAK and RED OAK.

DIMENSIONS
OH. 20¾ (52.7); top: w. 17¾ (45.1), D. 10⅝ (27); frame: w. 14 (35.6), D. at top 9¼ (23.5), D. at feet 14⅜ (36.5).

REFERENCES
Halsey and Cornelius 1924 (and 1925, 1926), fig. 12 (1928, 1932, fig. 11; 1938, 1942, fig. 14); Halsey and Tower 1925, fig. 11; Cornelius 1926, pl. III; R. T. Evans 1928, p. 53; Cescinsky and Hunter 1929, p. 36; E. G. Miller 1937, no. 1694; Schwartz 1976, no. 19; Chinnery 1979, fig. 3:96; Follansbee and Alexander 1996, fig. 4.

PROVENANCE
Ex coll.: H. Eugene Bolles, Boston.

Gift of Mrs. Russell Sage, 1909 (10.125.330)

1. The stools, in the order mentioned, are in Kane 1973a, no. XXVI; Forman 1988, no. 37; Forman 1988, nos. 35, 36; St. George 1979b, nos. 28, 29, 40. Other oak stools are in Lockwood 1913, fig. 403; Fales 1976, no. 1; Failey 1998, no. 1A.
2. On both the stool and the case pieces, the fillet on one side is wider than on the other, but it is difficult to say if the moldings were all made by the same tool. For details of the moldings on case pieces, see Follansbee and Alexander 1996, figs. 5, 8, 14; for the framing around chest panels, figs. 1, 20–22; for the careful joinery, pp. 83–90.

22.

Joint stool

Probably Boston or vicinity, 1700–1725

The vitality of the turnings and the pleasing proportions of this piece (the seat and the top of the frame have a length-to-width ratio of three to two) make it an outstanding example of a stool in the early-Baroque-inspired William and Mary style. The turnings vividly demonstrate the dynamic quality achieved by this style through the use of emphatic curves and bold appositions of thick and thin and convex and concave. A comparison of the legs on this stool with those on cat. no. 21, an oak example, makes patently clear the entirely different spirit that infuses these early-eighteenth-century turnings from that which informed their seventeenth-century-style antecedents.

The turnings on this stool are finely executed, with the vase form well separated from the ring below it by a distinct cavetto, and the vase's bulbous base and thin neck recalled in the shape of the foot. The profile of the vasiform turnings relates directly to that on the front stretcher of contemporary Boston cane and leather chairs. The stretcher on cat. no. 27 (see fig. 24) provides a particularly close comparison, in that on both the stretcher and the stool's legs the ring at the end of the vase's neck adjoins the cylindrical element beyond it without an intermediary fillet. This affinity and the quality of the work suggest that the present stool probably originated in the Boston area. Two stools, one at the Yale University Art Gallery and the other formerly in the collection of Katharine Prentis Murphy, have turnings that are nearly identical to those seen here; they differ only in the profile of the disk that abuts the lower leg block and in that the neck of the vase form and consequently the entire leg turning are a good half inch shorter.[1] Stools are usually listed in probate inventories in multiples and often together with a table, such as, for example, the "Table & carpitt &. 8. joint Stooles" recorded in 1676 in the great parlor of Captain Hopestill Fostor of Dorchester, Massachusetts.[2] They were probably made in sets of six or twelve, but have virtually always survived singly. Whether or not any of them belonged to the same set, the survival of three stools that appear to have been made in the same shop is a rare occurrence.

CONSTRUCTION
The stool is framed in the standard manner, with the mortise-and-tenon joints of the rails secured with two pins and those of the stretchers with one. The angle of the legs (about 6 degrees from the vertical) is such that the frame became square at the bottom of the feet, when they were intact. The one-board top is now attached with a large wrought-iron nail into the top of each leg; its edge has an ovolo profile. A cyma reversa molding finishes the lower edge of the rails. The inner surfaces of all components have been planed.

CONDITION
The top, which is original, has two long shrinkage cracks running in from opposite ends and two screw holes on the underside of one long overhang, for which there is no apparent explanation; it is further marred by numerous scratches and dark stains. It was no doubt originally attached to the legs with wooden pins, which were replaced at one point with the current nails inserted into the existing holes. In 1979 the seat, which had come loose, was reset with the same nails into the same holes, which were partly filled with dowels. The feet have been cut down and have losses at the bottom. The stool, described when acquired as painted red, has been stripped; thin residues of red paint remain throughout and also some traces of green.

WOOD
SOFT MAPLE.

DIMENSIONS
OH. 21⅝ (54.9); top: W. 20⅜ (51.8), D. 13¾ (34.9); frame: W. 15¾ (40), D. at top 10¼ (26), D. at feet 15⅜ (39.1).

REFERENCES
Halsey and Cornelius 1924 (and 1925, 1926), fig. 12 (1928, 1932, fig. 11; 1938, 1942, fig. 14); Halsey and Tower 1925, fig. 11; Cornelius 1926, pl. VIII; R. T. Evans 1928, p. 53; E. G. Miller 1937, no. 1695; Hjorth 1946, figs. 11, 12 (measured drawing); M. B. Davidson and Stillinger 1985, fig. 135.

PROVENANCE
Ex coll.: H. Eugene Bolles, Boston.

Gift of Mrs. Russell Sage, 1909 (10.125.329)

1. Kane 1976, no. 199 (Yale University Art Gallery). The stool in Mrs. Murphy's collection is illustrated in a room view in "Living with Antiques" 1950, p. 436 (right); it was exhibited at the New-York Historical Society, New York City, from 1951 to 1981.
2. A. L. Cummings 1964, p. 16.

Upholstered, Cane, and Related Rush-seated Chairs

Joined upholstered chairs, which provided built-in comfort, represented the most advanced and the most fashionable form of seating in the seventeenth-century style. The earliest colonial type, popular in Europe and England since the beginning of the century, was essentially a square upholstered stool with a low rectangular back added on. Called a back stool in England, it was commonly identified in household inventories by its covering—leather, Turkey work, or serge (a wool fabric), for example. The first such chairs listed in New England inventories, in the mid-1640s, were most likely imported, but by the 1660s they were being made in Boston. This was the branch of chairmaking that was to remain at the forefront of evolving styles, continually responding to the latest trends coming out of London. Chairs were more affordable, wore out more quickly, and were thus replaced more frequently than case furniture, for instance. A new set of chairs in the parlor, where they were visible to visitors, was the perfect vehicle for remaining at the height of fashion. Chair design, at the higher end of the market represented by the objects in this chapter, was being constantly updated by means of small incremental changes. The one style that in period documents is regularly requested by clients and touted by makers and merchants is "newest fashion."

The various stages in the development of the joined upholstered chair from the 1660s to the 1730s are illustrated by the sequence of chairs in this chapter, four of which are notable for retaining their original Turkey-work or leather upholstery. The evolution is here documented by chairs made in Boston—which was the style and chairmaking center of New England—or, with one exception, in coastal northeastern Massachusetts or coastal New Hampshire. The two seventeenth-century Turkey-work back stools in the collection, the broad horizontal back of one extending up considerably further than the other, mark the initial step in the stylistic progression toward chairs with a higher back (cat. nos. 23, 24). Greater height was next achieved by having the back consist of a vertical panel set between turned stiles, as seen first on leather chairs with a plain crest rail—one in the collection that has stile turnings in the seventeenth-century ball pattern (cat. no. 25) and a pair with stile turnings in a complex scheme that reflects early Baroque influence (cat. no. 26). A yet greater elongation of the back characterizes the fully developed tall-back William and Mary–style chair, which features a carved crest rail and is represented by a prime Museum example with original Russia leather upholstery (cat. no. 27). The high back, turning patterns, and crest designs on such chairs were derived from English cane chairs, which set the style for seating in the colonies from the 1690s to the 1720s. The leather chairs were made to compete with the cane imports, and, in turn, chairs with banister backs and rush seats were devised as economical counterparts to tall-back leather chairs. Of the several banister-back chairs in this chapter, two have a carved crest rail in the standard Boston design (cat. nos. 28, 29) and a pair are distinguished by a crest rail carved in an exceptional pattern (cat. no. 30). Another pair of banister-back chairs—from Bermuda and outside the New England tradition—relate in their plain, sawn stiles and arched crest rail to the next phase of English cane chair design, which featured molded stiles and a crest that is a continuation of the stiles (cat. no. 31). A considerable number of cane chairs of this type, which have carved so-called Spanish front feet, were made in Boston. Regrettably the one example in the collection no longer has a cane seat (cat. no. 32). The last innovation within the William and Mary style is exemplified by a chair with molded stiles and original leather (cat. no. 33) and by a leather armchair similar in design (cat. no. 34). The back panel and the molded stiles on those chairs are not straight but have a novel shallow serpentine contour so as to conform to the sitter's back. The next step in the evolution of the chair back is a scheme characteristic of the succeeding late Baroque (Queen Anne) style introduced about 1730. The crest rail no longer rises but dips in the center, and in place of a vertical back panel there is a wooden vase-shaped upright, which then was called a banister—as were the narrower multiple uprights in a banister-back chair—and today is called a splat, which differentiates it from the latter. Chairs that combine such a back not with a cabriole-leg base in the new fashion but with an older-style William and Mary rush-seated base with Spanish front feet became a popular mid-level product made until at least the 1760s. Four chairs of this type (cat. nos. 35–38), including two from the Gaines shop in Portsmouth, New Hampshire, conclude this chapter.

The wood of choice for fashionable seating in the early colonial period, from the 1660s on, was walnut, but in New England, where it had to be imported from farther south, walnut was rarely used for chairs before the 1730s. The upholstered and cane chairs in this chapter are all made of maple or other local woods, which were usually stained walnut color. On banister-back chairs, which were not as stylish, the same woods were often painted.

During the seventeenth century, seating was constructed basically according to either the method of the joiner or that of the turner, but in chairs of the early eighteenth century the structural distinction became less clear. The joined frames of upholstered chairs, for instance, began to incorporate members with round tenons, following the lead of imported cane chairs; and some craftsmen who produced seating began to identify themselves by the more general name of chairmaker. Though the trades of joiner and turner were traditionally distinct, in actuality, especially in the absence of guilds in the colonies, the separation between the two crafts was often not maintained, and artisans, particularly in rural areas, practiced more than one trade. Only in large port towns were specialist turners and, more rarely, carvers, working in their own or the joiner's shop, readily available to execute the ornament on joined chairs.

23.

Turkey-work chair

Boston, 1660–90

The great rarity of this chair lies in its original Turkey-work covering and marsh-grass stuffing. Only three other examples of American seating with original Turkey work are known: cat. no. 24, a couch at the Peabody Essex Museum, and a chair with renewed upholstery foundation at the New York State Museum, Albany.[1] Chair frames of the same general type as cat. no. 23 have survived in far greater numbers than have their more perishable fabric or leather covers (estimates range from fifty or more frames in all to at least a hundred or so Boston examples).[2]

Cat. no. 23 represents the standard Boston version of a form of upholstered chair that was popular in northern Europe and England throughout the seventeenth century. It is characterized by a rectilinear frame that has a padded rectangular seat and back panel and a gap between the seat and the usually low backrest, which is capped by neither a crest nor finials. The stiles cant backward, and the legs are vertical. Such chairs correspond to the designation "back stool" in seventeenth-century English inventories;[3] they are commonly described in colonial records by the material of their covering. Typically, this example has a seat of greater height than the back and features ball turnings on the front stretcher and front legs; as is often but not always the case, there are also ball turnings on the stiles. Its legs are braced with a high front stretcher counterbalanced by a low rear stretcher, both of which are in line with side stretchers. The design is essentially an arrangement of rectangles formed by the seat, back panel, and the voids between the framing members. The base of this chair is regulated largely by symmetry: the blocks on each front leg are identical, as is the pair of turnings (evenly spaced above and below the front stretcher), and the seat rails and lower stretchers are equidistant from the upper stretchers. The ball turnings terminate in a fillet at the juncture with the block, and on the front stretcher they are characteristically centered on a ring flanked by a pair of spheres that are more elongated than the others. Variations on this chair's formula include a front stretcher with ball turnings of a uniform size, without or with a center ring (see cat. no. 25), one rather than two ball shapes on the legs and stiles, single side stretchers, and lower or higher seats and backs (see cat. no. 24).

Such back stools with ball turnings, based on English models of the second half of the seventeenth century, were produced in Boston from about 1660 on, both for the local market and for export.[4] Their simple turning pattern and straightforward structural system could be replicated readily by any number of craftsmen supplying frames to the city's upholsterers. The dimensions could be easily varied without changing the basic character of the form, and as far as Turkey-work chairs were concerned, it appears that the frames were adapted to the measurements of the coverings. On both this chair and cat. no. 24, the frame is dimensioned so that the border surrounding the floral pattern fits evenly down all the seat rails and along the bottom and sides of the back panel. Turkey work, a woven fabric with a knotted and cut wool pile, was produced in England by professional weavers in imitation of Turkish carpets and was exported to Europe and America.[5] The "2 turkie bottoms and backs for chayres" in the 1658 inventory of a Boston merchant, for example, document the practice in the American colonies of importing such covers to be put on locally made frames. They indicate that frames for such chairs were being made in Boston by that date. The "1 doz and 6 new backs & seats of Turkey work for Chairs" in the home of a Philadelphia merchant in 1685 and the "12 Rich new backes & seats of Turky work: for chear" included in the stock of a Charleston, South Carolina, merchant in 1686 imply that some upholstered chairs of this general type were also being produced in those localities, even though no surviving examples are known.[6] The Turkey work on this chair represents a pattern available in London in 1668, for the same stylized, rather geometric floral design appears on chairs with similar frames that were purchased there that year for Holyroodhouse in Edinburgh, Scotland.[7]

CONSTRUCTION

Frame: The chair is framed with rectangular mortise-and-tenon joints that are 3/8 inch wide. All joints except those of the stay rail and upper side stretchers are secured with a large square pin. The rear posts cant backward above the seat, and on the front surface they taper toward the top to the thickness of the crest rail, to which they are tenoned. The rear legs are vertical, and at the foot they are beveled on the front surface; exceptionally, they also angle back somewhat on the rear surface. Because the rear posts on cat. no. 23, as on all joined chairs, are not straight, the craftsman, in order to execute the turned ball ornament on the stiles, needed an extra device on the lathe that allowed him to do turning on more than one axis.[8] The top of the crest rail has a broad chamfer on the front and a narrower one at the back. The edges of the seat rails have been relieved with a fine chamfer.

As is often the case on chairs of this type, the seat rails and stretchers have for the most part not been completely squared or finished on hidden surfaces, with the result that there are variations in thickness between corresponding members and within an individual piece. In addition, there are differences due to the use of somewhat different-sized stock for specific parts. Thus, while the outer tenon shoulders of all of this chair's joints are of a uniform width, as was standard practice, the inner shoulders on the seat rails vary in width. Those on the lower stretchers vary as well, but they are minimal in size, since the stretchers are narrower than the seat rails. On the upper side stretchers, which are even thinner and also not as high as the lower ones, inner shoulders are entirely lacking. But on the front stretcher, which is of the same size stock as the legs, the inner tenon shoulder is much wider than the outer one (fig. 85).

Upholstery: The floral motifs of the Turkey-work covering are executed in lighter and darker blue, lighter and darker purple, red, green, browns, and white on a black ground. The pattern on the seat and back is the same, but the scheme on one is the reverse of the other (the cartoon was flipped from side to side). The design is framed by a border consisting, from inside out, of a band of white, one of light purple, one of red, and one of black. At the sides, the Turkey work is selvaged; beyond the borders that run perpendicular to the selvage, the fabric is also without knotted pile, and there it has been cut. On the seat, the fabric is turned under on the front and on the back edge and also where it is cut to go around the stiles. On the back panel, the covering wraps around the side of the stiles 1/2 inch or less and reaches two-thirds of the way down the rear of the crest rail. At the top and bottom of the back the edge was folded under.

The upholstery foundation consists, on the seat, of three webbing strips (two front-to-back and one side-to-side) followed by sackcloth and marsh-grass stuffing (see the entry for cat. no. 24) and, on the back panel, of a fine-weave linen support cloth tacked to the front of the frame and grass stuffing. The Turkey work is applied directly over the grass; it and the upholstery foundation are attached with wrought-iron tacks. A multicolor (red, blue, white) wool fringe

originally concealed the edges of the covering on all four sides of the seat and along the bottom of the back panel. Evidence also remains for fringe along the back of the crest rail and fringe or braid down the sides of the back panel. The fringe on the front and sides of the seat and the bottom of the back is affixed with dome-headed brass nails; the remaining trim is secured with wrought-iron tacks.

CONDITION

Frame: The joints of the front and rear stretchers have each been reinforced with a small wooden pin, those of the crest and stay rails each with a wedge at one end of the mortise, and the seat-rail joints at three of the posts with cut nails. Two large oval holes of uncertain origin are visible at the top of the crest rail where the upholstery is now missing. The frame has a modern finish; dark residues of an earlier coating render it uneven in color.

Upholstery: The Turkey work on the seat and back, the linen and grass stuffing of the back panel, and in all likelihood the grass in the seat are original; the webbing and sackcloth of the seat are replacements. Nearly all of the black ground of the Turkey work is now missing and there are losses to the flowers. Segments of the entire fabric have worn away along the top and at the upper corners of the back panel, where frayed edges have been secured with added nails, and along the front of the seat, where sizable areas have been repaired. Of the fringe around the seat and at the bottom of the back, only the heading remains. A section of trim has survived on the side of the left stile and fragments under tacks at the back of the crest rail. X-radiographs confirm that the entire upholstery of the back and the Turkey work of the seat have never been removed. It thus appears that the old seat foundation was taken out from below and that the losses in the Turkey work along the front of the seat (amounting, before they were repaired, to an opening three-quarters of the width of the seat) allowed for the installation of new webbing (at the same locations as the old), new sackcloth, and the old grass stuffing without disturbing any of the nails that attach the Turkey work and trim.

INSCRIPTIONS

Three words, as yet undeciphered, are written in ink upside down on the back of the stay rail. The two that are side by side are in an early hand and may represent a name. The third is partly covered by dark blotches.

WOODS

Posts, BEECH; left seat rail, front stretcher, HARD MAPLE; stay rail, remaining seat rails and stretchers, MAPLE; crest rail, WHITE OAK.

DIMENSIONS

OH. 37 1/8 (94.3); SH. 20 1/2 (52.1); SW. 19 5/8 (49.8); SD. 17 (43.2).

REFERENCES

I. W. Lyon 1891, pp. 151–52 and fig. 63; Iverson 1957, p. 22 and fig. 15 (drawing of the chair from a photograph provided by John H. Schmuck); Schwartz 1976, no. 5; M. B. Davidson 1980, pl. 17; Safford 1980, fig. 9; M. B. Davidson and Stillinger 1985, fig. 134; Swain 1987, fig. 36; Greene 1996, p. 11.

PROVENANCE

Ex coll.: Mrs. J. Insley Blair, Tuxedo Park, New York.

Mrs. Blair purchased the chair from the New York City dealer Charles Woolsey Lyon in 1926. His father, Dr. Irving W. Lyon, published the chair in 1891 (see *References*) as having a traditional

23. See also fig. 85.

history of ownership by Roger Williams (1603?–1683), founder of Providence, Rhode Island, and belonging to Henry M. Schmuck of West Springfield, Massachusetts, a Williams descendant. Henry Moore Schmuck was born in Hartford, Connecticut, in 1831. His father, Henry Schmuck (ca. 1801–1838), was recorded as "of Baltimore" when he married Sarah Moore (1801–1870) of Hartford in 1831. What connection there may be to the Williams family probably comes through Sarah Moore's forebears.[9] Regrettably the chair's inscriptions, which may hold clues to its history, remain illegible. The chair was on loan from Mrs. Blair to the MMA from 1939 until the time of the bequest.

Bequest of Mrs. J. Insley Blair, 1951 (52.77.51)

1. Swain 1987, fig. 35 (couch), fig. 38 (chair).
2. For the estimates, see Forman 1988, p. 216; Passeri and Trent 1986, p. 11C.
3. Thornton 1978, pp. 185–92.
4. Back stools with other styles of ornament were also made in America, but in far fewer numbers. Three have turnings of a type that has been attributed to Salem, Massachusetts (I. W. Lyon 1891, fig. 62; Fairbanks and Trent 1982, no. 285; Trent 1989, no. 7). Those with forms of decoration found on European prototypes include five Boston examples with twist ornament, which came into fashion in England about 1665–70 (Fairbanks and Trent 1982, no. 283), and four examples with vase-shaped turnings, one of which is a Boston example (Gonzales and Brown 1996, fig. 3) and three of which include an astragal on the neck of the vase and are thought possibly to have been made in New York (Hosley 1984, pl. IX; Trent 1987a, fig. 19; Yale University Art Gallery, acc. no. 1991.128.1). The type of chair base in fashion in Europe and England during the first half of the seventeenth century, which has columnar turnings and four plain stretchers around the bottom, is represented only by an upholstered stool without a back probably from the New Haven, Connecticut, area (Passeri and Trent 1986, fig. 5).
5. Swain 1987, pp. 54, 56–60.
6. Quoted in I. W. Lyon 1891, p. 150; Hornor 1935, p. 17; Beckerdite 1997, p. 208.
7. Swain 1987, p. 60 and fig. 30.
8. See Forman 1988, pp. 204–5.
9. *Vital Records of West Springfield, Massachusetts, to the Year 1850*, vol. 1 (Boston, 1944), p. 192; Barbour Collection of Town Vital Records to 1850, Connecticut State Library, Hartford, card catalogue, drawer 351; "Connecticut Headstone Inscriptions: Hartford Burials, Cemetery 3, Old North Cemetery," typescript, Charles R. Hale Collection, Connecticut State Library; 1850 United States Federal Census, Hartford, Connecticut (microfilm, roll M432-41, p. 334).

24.

Turkey-work chair

Boston, 1680–1700

The richness of texture and color that Turkey work imparted to an interior is evoked to a greater degree by this chair than by cat. no. 23, for the back retains remnants of what was once a thick pile, and the fresher colors on the reverse, now visible owing to the loss of the upholstery foundation, reveal something of the vividness, if not downright garishness, of the fabric when new. When the Turkey work was pristine and replete with a deep polychrome fringe that covered the seat and stay rails and extended down the blocks above the turnings, the frame on such a chair must have receded well into the background. The frame's secondary visual role and its small cost relative to that of the textiles may help to explain the extent to which defects in the wood and turnings and hastily dressed surfaces were tolerated on this and many other upholstered chairs of the period. One should also bear in mind that upholstery work during the seventeenth century made a good show of rich materials but did not achieve any refinement in technique.[1]

On this chair, the standard frame formula seen in cat. no. 23 has been modified by extending the stiles to allow for a higher back panel and by lowering the seat and eliminating the upper set of side stretchers. The taller back indicates that the present chair was made toward the end of the seventeenth century, when more elongated chair backs were becoming the fashion. The change reflects a stylistic progression documented in Britain by Turkey-work chairs acquired in London for Holyroodhouse in Edinburgh, Scotland. Chairs purchased in 1668 and similar to cat. no. 23 were described in a 1714 inventory as having low backs, whereas those bought in 1685, which, like this example, have higher backs, were called "newer fashioned."[2] While the wording of that inventory makes it clear that it is the back that is low, in colonial documents of the period the designations "high" or "low" are most often applied to chairs without further description, in which case these terms may equally well—indeed, much more likely—be referring to the height of the seat.

The pattern of the Turkey work on this and the 1685 London chairs is closely related and features tightly spaced flowers that are more realistically rendered than on cat. no. 23. The original Turkey work on two other Boston pieces with higher backs—a chair at the New York State Museum, Albany, and a couch at the Peabody Essex Museum—also has similar floral motifs,

24

though not entirely identical overall schemes. This suggests that the present type of design was the one in style in the late seventeenth century and that it was being formatted for taller backs. The couch frame, datable to the late 1690s, has a low seat with single ball turnings on the front legs and single side stretchers, like cat. no. 24. In a 1724 inventory the couch is listed as en suite with twelve Turkey-work chairs described as "large," which may have been similar in form to the present example.[3]

CONSTRUCTION

Frame: The chair is framed with rectangular mortise-and-tenon joints of standard 5/16-inch width; the joints of the seat rails and stretchers are secured with one pin. The crest rail has a broad chamfer on the upper front edge. A fine chamfer finishes that rail's upper rear edge and the edges of the seat rails and side and rear stretchers. The rear feet are beveled on the front surface and are characteristically vertical at the back.

The chair exhibits an inordinate number of examples of the less than perfect workmanship that may be encountered in such mass-produced frames. The mortises in the crest rail are too long by far for the posts' tenons. At the top of those posts hatchet marks remain visible where, on the back surface, the posts were quickly worked down to the thickness of the crest rail. Also on the rear posts, the ball turnings are flat at the back because the posts above the seat were not deep enough for a full spherical turning or the segment to be turned was not perfectly centered on the lathe. Knotty wood and torn grain mar not only some of the chair's interior surfaces but some of the exterior ones as well. On the side stretchers, which are not entirely flush with the outside of the posts, saw kerfs on the outer as well as the inner surfaces were only partially planed away. The inner sides of the seat rails were hastily dressed with a hatchet.

Upholstery: The range of colors of the Turkey work on this chair is similar to that on cat. no. 23, and the borders are identical. As on cat. no. 23, the pattern on the back is the same as that on the seat, but reversed. On the back, the pile runs from top to bottom, and on the seat, from back to front. The edges of the fabric are folded under, as on cat. no. 23. The upholstery foundation of the seat consists of four strips of webbing (two front-to-back and two side-to-side) and then sackcloth and marsh-grass stuffing. Through losses in the Turkey work and sackcloth one can see that a bundle of grass is laid parallel to and on top of the front and right seat rails. The bunch at the front goes across the top of the legs, as is evident also at the right front corner of the seat of cat. no. 23. In addition, a portion of the inner filling visible on the right reveals bunches of grass that appear to have been folded and the folded end placed against the bundle on the right rail.

CONDITION

Irving W. Lyon had the chair restored before publishing it in 1891. He had acquired it a year or two earlier in a dirty and "very rickety condition."[4] The chair appears to have basically not changed since the 1891 photograph.

Frame: Lyon had the chair taken apart; the joints have been glued and the pins replaced. On the right front leg, the right back corner of the block above the foot has split off and been glued. Two of the other legs show several splits, and there is a loss at the right end of the front stretcher. The finish is modern; the frame has been stripped and the turnings sanded.

Upholstery: The Turkey work on the back and seat and the upholstery foundation of the seat are original but were taken off for repair of the frame and reattached; the remaining brass nails look old, but most of the present tacks are modern. The black ground of the Turkey-work design is almost entirely lost, as are some parts of the flowers, but areas of the back panel retain a little pile. Portions of the cover fabric are missing on the front corners and edges of the seat and on the sides, upper corners, and upper rear edge of the back. Only fragments of fringe heading have survived, at the front of the seat and at the bottom of the back. The back now consists of just the Turkey-work fabric; the grass stuffing has been lost and also the support cloth, from the attachment of which tacks and tack holes remain. On the seat, most of the webbing strips have broken at the ends and the sackcloth has tears. A wooden frame holding a pierced Plexiglas panel, inserted under the seat and screwed to the inside of the rails, was installed at the MMA and now supports the sagging foundation.

INSCRIPTIONS

Scratched at center front on the front seat rail is a large X (probably old). Restorer's reassembly marks on the legs, seat rails, and stretchers (incised roman numerals and dots) date from the time of repairs.

WOODS

MAPLE; right seat rail, SOFT MAPLE; crest rail, RED OAK.

DIMENSIONS

OH. 40¾ (103.5); SH. 17 (43.2); SW. 19⅞ (50.5); SD. 16¾ (42.5).

EXHIBITION

"Hudson-Fulton Exhibition," MMA, 20 September–30 November 1909.

REFERENCES

I. W. Lyon 1891, p. 152 and fig. 64; *Hudson-Fulton Celebration* 1909 (exh. cat.), no. 66 (lent by Dr. Irving P. Lyon); Halsey and Cornelius 1924 (and 1925, 1926), fig. 11; Halsey and Tower 1925, fig. 15; F. Little 1931, fig. 24; M. B. Davidson 1967, no. 57; "Turquerie" 1968, no. 53; Chinnery 1979, fig. 2:138; Kirk 1982, no. 685; Swain 1987, fig. 37.

PROVENANCE

Ex coll.: Dr. Irving W. Lyon, Hartford, Connecticut; his son Dr. Irving P. Lyon, Buffalo, New York; Mrs. J. Insley Blair, Tuxedo Park, New York.

When I. W. Lyon published this piece in 1891 (see *References*), he noted that the chair, "belonging to the writer, was lately found . . . in an old house in the town of Harwinton, Conn. No history of it could be obtained."[5] Mrs. Blair purchased the chair from I. P. Lyon in 1923. He had lent the piece to the MMA Hudson-Fulton exhibition in 1909 and then placed it on loan at the Buffalo Historical Society from 1909 to 1923. Mrs. Blair lent the chair to the MMA in 1924–25 for the opening of the American Wing and again from 1939 until it became a bequest.

Bequest of Mrs. J. Insley Blair, 1951 (52.77.50)

1. Thornton 1978, p. 217.
2. Swain 1987, fig. 29 and p. 53. Similarly, Turkey-work chairs called "old fashioned" in a 1697 Boston inventory were later described as "small," and

those with a much higher valuation in the same inventory, which were presumably newer, were later described as "large" (Fairbanks and Trent 1982, no. 490).

3. Swain 1987, fig. 38 (chair) and fig. 35 (couch); see also Fairbanks and Trent 1982, no. 490 (couch and inventory).

4. I. W. Lyon 1891, p. 152; letter of 30 October 1909 from Dr. Irving P. Lyon to Henry W. Kent (Hudson-Fulton exhibition correspondence, MMA Archives).

5. The chair was discovered by I. P. Lyon, who purchased it from two old ladies for thirty cents (letter of 30 October 1909, see n. 4).

25.
Leather chair

Boston, 1690–1705

A high back with a vertical panel set between turned stiles was a dominant feature of early Baroque English cane chairs, from which American chairs in the William and Mary style were derived. In Boston, cane chair design began to exert its influence in the 1690s. On this chair, a back in such a format has been grafted on the frame of a standard seventeenth-century Boston back stool, the base of which has been modified to incorporate a seat that is no longer rectangular in plan but trapezoidal. Unaltered are the angle of the raked stiles, the distance between the seat rail and the back panel, the configuration of the stretchers, which are all essentially the same as on cat. no. 23, and the nature of the rear feet, which conform to those on cat. no. 24. Ball turnings now ornament also the upper stiles, which extend beyond the crest rail and terminate in spherical finials. The front stretcher, with its ball-shaped turnings all of the same size, exhibits a variant of the most common formula seen on cat. no. 23.

This is one of four chairs known to the writer that show a similar combination of older and newer stylistic elements, for which there is English precedent.[1] They exemplify the first of a series of incremental changes made to the traditional seventeenth-century upholstered chair frame by Boston joiners, as they, over several decades beginning in the late 1600s, repeatedly updated existing designs to reflect the fashion set by succeeding types of English chairs. Apparently made in relatively small numbers and for a short period of time, the form of chair seen here never developed into a standard model. This and the other three chairs—two in private collections and one at the Museum of Fine Arts, Boston—differ in many of their dimensions and particularly in the proportions of the back panel, and they also show variations in the manner in which the side members are joined to the posts in a base that is trapezoidal (using the two basic alternatives employed in seventeenth-century furniture; see fig. 166). One of the chairs has acorn rather than ball finials.[2] Each appears to be an individual working-out of an updated design with a

25

newer-style back and seat. The example at the Museum of Fine Arts is somewhat taller and narrower than cat. no. 25 and has nearly the same dimensions as the immediately following form of Boston upholstered chair represented by cat. no. 26. The two other chairs are shorter and slightly broader, and their more squat proportions recall those of the earliest types of English cane chair.[3]

CONSTRUCTION
The chair is framed with rectangular mortise-and-tenon joints that are 5/16 inch wide, with the exception of those of the crest rail and the uprights of the back panel, which measure just 1/4 inch. All joints except those of the uprights of the back panel and of the upper right stretcher to the rear post are secured with a pin. The base is trapezoidal in plan with the crosspieces of the back and sides equal in length. The tenons of the side rails and stretchers have virtually no inside shoulder but a large outside shoulder cut at an angle that takes into account the oblique angle at which those members meet the square posts (see fig. 166B). The outer side of both the rear and the front legs has been planed so that it carries on the line of the side rails and stretchers. The top of the crest rail has a broad chamfer on the front and a narrower one at the back. The finials have a single groove around the middle; the front feet had a double groove. The rear feet are beveled on the front face and vertical at the back. Less than careful workmanship resulted in ball turnings with flat areas on the stiles.

CONDITION
A 1912 MMA photograph shows the chair as received, with a broken splint seat and the frame of the back bare but retaining numerous nails from the original upholstery and a few fragments of leather under the nails (see *Reference*). At some point before 1939 the chair was upholstered in leather, after the seat had been reinforced with four screwed-on corner blocks. In 1988 those restorations were removed and the present nonintrusive upholstery was installed. The pattern of the nailing on the back follows clear evidence of the original treatment seen in the 1912 photograph and visible when the frame was stripped. Because the seat rails were rounded when the splint seat was put on and are damaged by tacking, little evidence remains of the nailing of the original trim strip around the seat. Splits, losses, and a small patch mar the left stile between seat and stay rail. The feet have lost more than 1 inch in height. The frame has been stripped and appears to have been oiled and waxed.

WOODS
Posts, front stretcher, MAPLE; remaining components, RED OAK.

DIMENSIONS
OH. 44 5/8 (113.3); SH. 18 1/4 (46.4); SW. front 18 1/2 (47); SW. back 15 1/4 (38.7); SD. 15 1/4 (38.7).

REFERENCE
Cescinsky and Hunter 1929, p. 74 (as received).

PROVENANCE
Ex coll.: H. Eugene Bolles, Boston.

Gift of Mrs. Russell Sage, 1909 (10.125.195)

1. Kirk 1982, no. 737.
2. The two chairs in private collections—one of which has acorn finials and an undercarriage similar to that of cat. no. 24—and the chair at the Museum of Fine Arts, Boston (acc. no. 1983.229) are all unpublished.
3. See Forman 1988, p. 239, table 3, and figs. 117, 125.

26.
Leather chairs (two)

Boston, northeastern Massachusetts, or possibly southern New Hampshire, 1695–1715

On this pair of chairs—only one of which is illustrated—the evolution of the standard seventeenth-century upholstered chair frame is carried a significant step further than on cat. no. 25; the turnings, and not just the shape of the back and seat (which have both become narrower), reflect designs associated with the early-Baroque-inspired William and Mary style. Most expressively Baroque in character are the complex stile turnings—a tight composite of ring, ball, vase, and short columnar forms. This sort of pattern is indebted to the elaborate stile turnings on a type of English rush cane chair that featured a back with carved rails and uprights and also provided prototypes for the other turnings seen here: vase shapes on the legs and above the seat and a stretcher with opposed balusters centered on a ball.[1]

In period parlance, this pair with flat crest rails falls within the broad designation of plain-top, as opposed to carved-top, leather chairs. Many of the surviving plain-top chairs have stile turnings on the general order of those exhibited here and, like the present examples, also other attributes (some held over from seventeenth-century back stools) that differentiate them from tall-back chairs such as cat. no. 27, which have long been recognized as Boston products. In his

26-1. See also figs. 14, 21.

study of chairs at the Winterthur Museum of the same overall type as those seen here, Benno M. Forman singled out many of those differences as being characteristics of leather chairs produced in New York and not Boston. The New York attribution of the majority of such chairs was subsequently challenged by Roger Gonzales and Daniel Putnam Brown Jr., who argued, much more convincingly, that those same features represent instead a phase of Boston chairmaking intermediary between that of back stools like cat. nos. 23 and 24 and the one exemplified by cat. no. 27, a high-back chair. Indeed if one applies Forman's criteria to the surviving plain-top chairs, the number attributable to New York far exceeds that attributable to Boston. This runs counter to what is known of chair production at that period. The thorny question of how to distinguish leather chairs that may have been produced in New York from the large output of the Boston chairmaking industry remains a challenging one.[2]

As far as this pair of chairs is concerned, there is nothing in their history of ownership in northern Essex County, Massachusetts, or in their construction to suggest they were made outside of New England. Existing records document a large export trade in chairs from Boston, including a delivery in 1696 of twelve leather chairs from a Boston upholsterer to a Newbury, Massachusetts, merchant, but they do not show any shipment of chairs from New York to Massachusetts.[3] Structurally, the present examples have close affinities with Boston chairs: seat dimensions and the manner of joining the side rails and stretchers to the legs that are the same as those on cat. no. 27; a stretcher configuration that duplicates the one on cat. no. 23; and the use of soft maple and red oak.

According to letters to two of his New York customers, Boston upholsterer Thomas Fitch had been selling both plain-top and carved-top leather chairs "for many year" by 1705.[4] Exactly how many years, what was the particular style of his chairs, and whether or not the two types were similar in design are all uncertain. The majority of surviving plain-top chairs are characterized, like cat. no. 26, by complex stile turnings and conservative double side stretchers, and no comparable frames with carved tops are known. Only stylistically later plain-top chairs—those, fewer in number, that have elongated columnar stile turnings and single side stretchers—can be matched with carved-top counterparts. Thus the form of chair represented here appears to have been in general production earlier than chairs with carved tops. It is difficult to say how much earlier, or if and for how long plain-top chairs with this style of frame were made alongside carved examples like cat. no. 27.[5]

Six other chairs are known with stiles in the particular pattern seen here, which is distinguished from the generically related design on other chairs of this type primarily by having a ball-and-ring motif at the bottom (below the superimposed vase turnings) rather than at the top (above

the column). They also have identical stretchers, which differ from those on the majority of flat-top chairs in that they show a ball flanked by reels, balusters, and thick rings (fig. 21), instead of double opposed balusters centered on a ring.[6] The finials on this group of chairs, which consist of an urn topped by a knob (fig. 14), are of a type that occurs also on some of the other plain-top chairs. The stile turnings on cat. no. 26 and related examples have vase forms with thick necks and rings that are rather fat. They are lacking somewhat in refinement in comparison with, for example, stiles in the same pattern but with greater modulation and precision of form on a chair at the Winterthur Museum that has the more common type of stretcher.[7] The present chairs were originally covered in Russia leather, the kind preferred during this period (see the entry for cat. no. 27), but the manner of their upholstery did not entirely conform to standard Boston practice, in that the trim strip around the seat was left loose at the bottom as if it were a textile fringe. This upholstery detail and the character of the turnings would seem to preclude that these chairs were made in a major Boston shop; they may have originated in a lesser Boston area workshop, or may possibly be copies of Boston chairs made in a smaller center in northeastern Massachusetts or southern New Hampshire.

CONSTRUCTION
On each chair: The frame is assembled with standard rectangular mortise-and-tenon joints, which, with the exception of those of the upper stretchers and of the uprights of the back panel, are secured with a pin. On the trapezoidal base, the back surface of the front leg blocks and the front surface of the rear legs have been planed so that the side seat rails and stretchers can join the legs at a right angle (see fig. 166A). The outer side of the front leg blocks (but not of the rear legs) has been planed to be in line with the side rails and stretchers. The crest rail has a broad chamfer on the upper front edge. There is little taper on the front or rear face of the stiles.

CONDITION
The chairs have a modern finish. Both have large splits in the stiles above the seat and have lost their feet almost entirely.

Chair 26-1 (acc. no. 29.133.2, illustrated): The left stile has been repaired at the baluster above the seat with a large wrought nail driven from the front and clinched in the back; the right stile has been similarly repaired with a nail at the top and bottom of the block at the stay rail. The left tenon of the front seat rail has been replaced. On the front stretcher, a section at the rear of each block has been reattached with glue, and there are fills in depressions at the back of the turnings. Some of the joint pins are new. As documented in a 1929 photograph (ADA files), the chair was acquired with original Russia leather on the back and, over the original leather of the seat, a second layer of padding and leather, which, according to the vendor, had been put on by his aunt. The present (1979) upholstery is the second on the back and the third on the seat installed at the MMA.

Chair 26-2 (acc. no. 29.133.1, not illustrated): The stiles have been repaired with large round-headed rivets that pass from the front through the baluster above the seat and the block at the stay rail; at the back, the rivets were hammered against diamond-shaped iron "washers." In addition, three wire nails have been driven into each block from the back. The chair, when acquired, had original Russia leather upholstery on the seat and back and a plain modern front stretcher (see *References*). That stretcher had been inserted by splitting out a portion of the block surrounding the mortise for the right tenon; the left front corner of that block is glued on, and a segment above the mortise is replaced. Records indicate that the present turned front stretcher was installed (presumably in the same way) at some point before 1946. In that year, the seat was first reupholstered and the front seat rail was given new tenons and all the seat joints new pins. In 1979 the deteriorated original leather of the back and the remaining fragments of its sackcloth backing and marsh-grass stuffing were removed to be retained as documents, and the 1946 seat upholstery was taken off. It was ascertained at that time that the only nail holes near the bottom of the seat rails were from the MMA upholstery. This confirmed what 1929 photographs indicate: the original trim strip around the seat was never nailed at the bottom. The present (1979) upholstery of both chairs conforms to that evidence and follows the original spacing of the brass nails on the seat and back seen in the photographs.

INSCRIPTION

A paper label (now lost) was glued to the reverse of the original leather on the back of chair 26-1. Its faded ink inscription was recorded in 1929 as: "This chair was once . . . / property of Rev. Caleb / Cushing first m . . . ter / of Salisbury Mass. in 1692 [*sic*]. / The Great Grandfather / of the late Caleb Cushing / (Mrs. A. W. [misread for M] Rubel)."

WOODS

Posts, front stretcher, one upright of back panel, SOFT MAPLE; crest rail, stay and seat rails, one upright of back panel, side and rear stretchers, RED OAK.

DIMENSIONS

OH. 46 (116.8); SH. 17½ (44.5); SW. front 17¾ (45.1); SW. back 14⅜ (36.5); SD. 14⅝ (37.1).

EXHIBITION

Chair 26-2: on loan to the Dey Mansion, Wayne, New Jersey, from 1946 until 1978.

REFERENCES

Halsey and Cornelius 1938 (and 1942), fig. 23 (chair 26-2 as acquired); Schwartz 1958, pl. 7B (chair 26-2 as acquired); Stillinger 1965, p. 194 (chair 26-2 at Dey Mansion).

PROVENANCE

The vendor, Walter H. Little (b. 1863), was a member of the eighth generation of the Little family of Newbury, Massachusetts. At the death of his mother, in 1929, he inherited one chair (26-2) and acquired another from a cousin, to which his aunt, Mrs. Andrew M. Rubel (née Jane Moody Little, b. 1835), had affixed a paper label associating it with the Cushing family (see *Inscription*). Walter Little provided a more complete history: "They came to my father, from his mother, who was a Moody; to her, from her step grand-mother who was a Cushing; to her from her grandfather the Rev. Caleb Cushing of Salisbury." According to this information the line of descent was as follows: Rev. Caleb Cushing (1673–1752), minister of Salisbury, Massachusetts, from 1696 to his death, who married

in 1698 Elizabeth Cotton (1663–1743), the widow of his predecessor, Rev. James Alling (1657–1696, m. 1688), the third minister of Salisbury (1682–1696); his son Caleb Cushing (1703–1797) of Salisbury, who married in 1730 Mary Newmarch of Kittery, Maine; his daughter Sarah Cushing (1738–1822), who in 1779 became the second wife of Col. Samuel Moody Jr. (1731–1790) of Newbury, whose first wife was Jane Dole (m. 1765) of Salisbury; her step-granddaughter Elizabeth Moody (b. 1799; daughter of Nathaniel Moody [1769–1815], m. 1794 Molly Moody [1774–1854]), who married in 1821 Joseph Little (b. 1799) of Newbury; their son Joseph Little (b. 1833), the father of the vendor.[8]

The chairs cannot be identified in extant probate papers of the above individuals. But while the original owner cannot be confirmed, there is no reason to doubt that the chairs descended in early families of northern Essex County.[9]

Rogers Fund, 1929 (29.133.1, .2)

1. These elements are all present, for example, on an English cane chair at the MMA (acc. no. 10.125.211), which has a traditional history of early ownership in Hartford, Connecticut (I. W. Lyon 1891, p. 155 and fig. 68).
2. Forman 1988, pp. 288–94, 320–26. Gonzales and Brown 1996 also advances the theory that New York and Boston chairs can be distinguished on the basis of specific techniques in the joinery of the base, a hypothesis that needs much further investigation. For New York chairs, see also Kamil 1995, which builds on Forman's attributions without questioning them.
3. Forman 1988, pp. 206, 284–85.
4. Ibid., p. 299.
5. In 1709, writing to Benjamin Faneuil in New York in regard to chairs he had shipped to Faneuil on consignment during the previous two years, which apparently had not sold, Fitch assured Faneuil that he made six plain chairs for every carved one and that the plain were not out of fashion in Boston (ibid., p. 321). It would certainly be enlightening to know what style of chair Fitch had sent and if plain chairs were really so very popular in Boston at the time or if Fitch was merely writing sales promotion.
6. The six are as follows: a chair belonging to the Chipstone Foundation (*American and European Furniture, Decorative Arts and Oriental Carpets,* auction cat., Northeast Auctions, Manchester, New Hampshire, 31 July 1988, lot 359); one at the Holy Trinity (Old Swedes) Church and Hendrickson House Museum, Wilmington, Delaware, which has stiles repaired with rivets in the same manner as chair 26-2 and is probably from the same set; one at the Los Angeles County Museum of Art, Los Angeles, California (acc. no. 53.19.2); a pair that was found in Maine (Gonzales and Brown 1996, fig. 31); and one of two chairs also said to have belonged to the presumed first owner of the present chairs, Rev. Caleb Cushing (*American Furniture and Decorative Arts,* auction cat., Skinner, Bolton, Massachusetts, 7 June 1998, lot 28).
7. Forman 1988, no. 71.
8. Letters dated 15 June, 27 June, and 11 July 1929 from Walter H. Little to Henry W. Kent (MMA Archives); George Thomas Little, *The Descendants of George Little, Who Came to Newbury, Massachusetts, in 1640* (Auburn, Maine, 1882), pp. 83–84, 386–87; James Stevenson Cushing, *The Genealogy of the Cushing Family: An Account of the Ancestors and Descendants of Matthew Cushing, Who Came to America in 1638* (Montreal, 1905; repr., 1979), pp. 32–33, 59–60; George P. Allen, comp., *A History and Genealogical Record of the Alling-Allens of New Haven, Conn., . . . from 1639 to the Present Time* (New Haven, Conn., 1899), pp. 18–19; *Vital Records of Salisbury, Massachusetts, to the End of the Year 1849* (Topsfield, Mass., 1915), pp. 65, 322, 422, 546; *Vital Records of Newbury, Massachusetts, to the End of the Year 1849* (Salem, Mass., 1911), vol. 1, pp. 328, 330, 332, vol. 2, pp. 292, 336–37, 663–64.
9. The 1752 probate inventory of Rev. Caleb Cushing groups all chairs together as "chairs" without number or further description. The 1696 inventory of Rev. James Alling lists leather chairs, but again without their numbers. A value per chair, had such been given, would perhaps indicate whether they were recently acquired and possibly in the newer style or older seventeenth-century back stools (Essex County Probate Records, microfilm, vol. 330, p. 382, and vol. 305, p. 163, Massachusetts Archives at Columbia Point, Boston). The extant probate records of later generations are also uninformative.

27.

Leather chair

Boston, 1700–1720

Tall and stately, and covered in its original Russia leather, this is a fine example of the fully developed William and Mary–style Boston high-back chair.[1] Its elongated back, typically crowned by a pierced and carved crest rail, has shed the last vestige of seventeenth-century-style upholstered chair backs, in that the panel is no longer padded but flat and thin like that of cane seating, which these chairs emulated. In the hierarchy of tall-back chairs, this one ranks a notch below the top model, which came with a stretcher carved in a design similar to that on the crest rail. Less expensive options were domestic leather, a plain top, and a banister back and rush seat in lieu of leather. Standard features of the high-back chair form, as exemplified by cat. no. 27, include rear posts that have urn-and-ball finials; a long columnar turning above a short baluster, reel, and ring at the height of the back panel; scored cylinders above the seat; and vertical legs that angle backward near the bottom to form raked feet that counter the cant of the long stiles. Characteristically the front legs are in a block-and-baluster pattern, and the side stretchers are plain and single and their top is in line with the bottom of the plain rear stretcher. Differences occur primarily in details of the turnings and of the carving.

The lower vasiform turnings on the front legs of these chairs are typically shorter than the upper—in contrast to the symmetrical formula usually seen on Boston-style leather chairs that are earlier and later in design (see cat. nos. 26, 33). On this and many other tall-back chairs, the lower vase shapes are strongly compressed and appear about to expand upward. A similar sense of Baroque energy is conveyed by the inflated bases of the balusters on the front stretcher. The front stretcher turnings have broken free of the convention that previously placed them between blocks and limited their diameter to the dimensions of those blocks, making possible the dramatic contrasts of thick and thin evident here. (And the attachment of the front stretcher with round tenons simplified the joinery.) The main motif on this stretcher—opposed balusters centered on a reel—is one of the two dominant stretcher patterns associated with William and Mary–style chairs. It is characteristically combined with terminal turnings that consist of a prominent sharp-edged ring—not set off by either a fillet or a groove—and a cylindrical end (fig. 24). As far as can be ascertained, reel-and-baluster stretchers occur on Boston chairs earlier than those with a ring-and-ball center motif, which do not appear to have been popular there before the

advent of chairs with molded stiles (see cat. nos. 32, 33). Reel-and-baluster is the design found on tall-back leather chairs with carved crest rails that have a turned rather than a carved front stretcher. Related stretchers with the same emphatic baluster profile are also on a small number of plain-top leather chairs and banister-backs, and, in combination with an additional terminal turning, on two uncommon forms of upholstered chair at the Winterthur Museum.[2] This baluster shape, with a full base that narrows gracefully to a long neck, is distinctive enough that it may represent the turning style of a particular shop tradition or a phase in the production of one or more such traditions. Boston chairs such as this one were the handiwork of several different craftsmen: the carving and the turning were done by specialists, who may have worked in their own shop or in that of the chairmaker, who in turn provided the completed frame to the upholsterer.

The chair's crest rail is in the characteristic Boston-school design of C-scrolls and foliage. On such crest rails the greatest variations occur in the carving of the pair of leaves below those forming the plume at the top. Here, a small lobe of each outward-spreading leaf reaches back in toward the center and is separated at its base from the stem of the uppermost foliage by a deep, gouged depression, which heightens the relief of the carving (fig. 15). This carefully executed passage and the degree of detailing on the leaves that rest on the top of the C-scrolls suggest that the crest was carved when this pattern was fairly new and had not yet been reduced to a more stylized treatment for production in quantity.[3] The fullness and vigor of the stretcher turnings also argue for a date of manufacture when early Baroque impulses were still fresh.

CONSTRUCTION

Frame: Rectangular mortise-and-tenon joints secure all parts of the frame, with the exception of the front stretcher, which is round-tenoned to the legs. The rectangular joints are 3/8 inch wide and single-pinned, except for those of the uprights of the back panel, which are narrower and not pinned. The front leg blocks have been planed on the back surface, as have the rear legs on the forward surface, so that the side rails and stretchers can meet the legs at a right angle (fig. 92, and see fig. 166A); the front leg blocks have also been planed on the outer side so as to be in line with the side elements. The crest rail is chamfered on the back along the top edge and around the piercings; the bottom of the crest rail is straight and has an arched recess on the front. The upper corners of the plain stretchers were finished with a fine chamfer.

27. See also figs. 15, 24, 92.

Upholstery: The back and seat are covered in Russia leather. On the back panel a linen liner was first secured to the front of the frame with iron tacks, and then the leather cover was affixed over the linen with brass nails. On the seat, the upholstery foundation consists of three strips of webbing (two front-to-back and one side-to-side) followed by sackcloth, marsh grass, and probably an upper layer of horsehair. The seat leather was tacked to the rails and its edge hidden by a trim strip that was attached in part with brass nails, in part with iron tacks. Originally there was stitching that formed a trapezoid in the center of the seat and passed through the under-upholstery and the leather to hold the stuffing in place.

CONDITION

Frame: A split at the right end of the crest rail has been secured from the back with two modern nails. Breaks in both stiles at the vasiform turning have been repaired with a 9-inch-long iron brace screwed to the back of each stile; in addition, a nail has been driven from the front into the vase turning on the left stile and the columnar section on the right stile. On the right front leg there are a split in the uppermost block, repaired breaks at the neck of both vase turnings, missing wood on the inner corner of the blocks, and glued sections on the foot. The legs and stretchers all show worm damage. The front feet, which most likely once consisted of a short vase form above a thick pad, have lost a little more height than the rear feet, so that the rake of the stiles is somewhat lessened. The frame has been painted brown.

Upholstery: The leather and under-upholstery are original. The leather of the back, seat, and trim strip is in brittle and fragile condition and shows losses, tears, and much surface flaking. A few brass nails are missing and some are replaced. Those at the top and bottom of the trim strip at the back of the chair, where it was standard practice to use just iron tacks (some of which remain in place), are surely added, and those at the bottom of the strip on the sides are probably also additions. In 1979 the leather on the back panel and its deteriorated cloth liner were taken off for treatment (not for the first time); they were both backed and reattached with the same nails. Modern webbing that had been tacked to the inside of the seat rails to support the sagging foundation was removed in 1994 to reveal that two of the original webbing strips had torn loose at one end and that the sackcloth had holes through which the grass stuffing protruded. The webbing strips are now secured to the sackcloth, and the under-upholstery is contained by a polyester scrim. Traces of the center stitching remain on the underside of the seat. There are numerous extraneous nail holes—through the leather and into the frame—around the edge of the back panel and similar holes on the outer side of the seat rails, which suggest that some sort of covering or padding was at one point tacked on over the leather.

WOODS

Posts, stretchers, SOFT MAPLE; stay and seat rails, uprights of back panel, RED OAK; crest rail, BEECH.

DIMENSIONS

OH. 48 (121.9); SH. 17¼ (43.8); SW. front 17⅞ (45.4); SW. back 14¼ (36.2); SD. 14⅝ (37.1).

REFERENCE

Schwartz 1976, no. 23.

PROVENANCE

Ex coll.: Mrs. J. Insley Blair, Tuxedo Park, New York.

Mrs. Blair purchased the chair in 1921 from Collings and Collings, dealers in New York, with a history of having been found in that city. The chair was on loan from Mrs. Blair to the MMA from 1939 until the time of the bequest.

Bequest of Mrs. J. Insley Blair, 1951 (52.77.58)

1. Russia leather, as it was called at the time, was the most desirable kind during this period and was exported to Boston via London. It underwent an elaborate tanning process, part of which gave the surface a characteristic pattern of scored cross-hatching. Imitations with a surface that resembled that of the genuine article were also made abroad and probably imported (Trent 1987a, pp. 46–47).

2. For related stretchers on carved-top chairs, see Gustafson 1977, p. 910; Forman 1988, no. 66; *Important Americana, Including Prints, Ceramics, Silver, Carpets, Folk Art and Furniture*, auction cat., Sotheby's, New York City, 16, 17, and 19 January 2003, lot 507; an armchair at the New Jersey Historical Society, Newark (acc. no. 1926.4) and one offered in *The Katharine Prentis Murphy Collection from the New Hampshire Historical Society*, auction cat., Skinner, Bolton, Massachusetts, 24 September 1983, lot 129. For such stretchers on plain-top chairs, see an armchair at Colonial Williamsburg (acc. no. 1976.431); Nutting 1928–33, no. 1963; and *The Collections of the Late Roger Bacon of Brentwood, New Hampshire*, auction cat., Skinner, Bolton, Massachusetts, 24–25 September 1982, lot 809. For banister-back chairs, see Kane 1976, no. 38, and S. C. S. Edwards 1983, pl. IX; for the two other chair forms, see Forman 1988, nos. 63, 85. Other interpretations of the reel-and-baluster design, usually found on chairs that are stylistically later than all of the above, have balusters that are more attenuated (see cat. no. 34), have a more spherical base (see cat. no. 40), or have different terminal turnings.

3. For crest rails with closely related middle leaves, see, for example, M. B. Davidson 1967, nos. 71, 71a; *Sack Collection* 1981–92, vol. 1, p. 161; Forman 1988, no. 65 (all chairs with carved front stretchers). On many, depressions at the center axis add varying degrees of depth to the carving, but the treatment of the adjoining pair of leaves is more stylized (Gonzales and Brown 1996, figs. 14, 15). The carving of foliage on the greatest number of surviving crests, particularly those on banister-back chairs, is very schematic (Jobe et al. 1991, p. 61 and no. 21).

28. See also fig. 18.

28.

Banister-back chair

Eastern Massachusetts, 1715–40

Banister-back chairs such as this example closely follow the format of tall-back leather chairs like cat. no. 27, for which they were economical substitutes. In the lightness and intricacy of their backs, however, in which both the banisters themselves and the voids between them create a highly patterned screen, they recall cane chairs, which set the style for leather chairs.

The silhouettes on the back of this chair are more animated than usual and stand out because the upper turnings of the stiles and banisters have a strong ogee shape rather than the more academic columnar form characteristic of Boston chairs. This individualistic interpretation of the generic Boston stile design (compare cat. no. 27) features unusually thick rings at the top and bottom and an urn profile below the uppermost ring, which repeats the urn form under the ball of the finial. The carving on the crest rail is distinguished by the fact that the veining in the foliage has a concave contour made with a small rounded gouge rather than the usual angular profile made with a V-shaped tool (fig. 18). A peculiarity of the stretchers is the bulbous shape of the turning at either end. The present chair numbers among those banister-back examples that have a traditional turned-chair type of seat with seat rails round-tenoned into front legs that rise slightly above the seat—the format initially used. Chairs with a stylistically more advanced form of rush seat—which imitates cane chair seat construction in that the front legs are round-tenoned into the front corner blocks of the seat rails, as on cat. nos. 31 and 32—represent a slightly later design. Boston-style banister-back chairs were first made in the same shops as tall-back leather chairs, which examples like cat. no. 28 emulate not only in the crest rail and general turning patterns but also in having rear posts that cant backward above the seat—a characteristic of joined chairs and of urban banister-back chair design. Banister-back chairs made in rural areas, where the form was produced until the end of the eighteenth century, typically have straight rear posts—standard in turners' work—and shaped but not carved crest rails.

Three chairs related to cat. no. 28 have been published: a chair without arms that is a close match (present location unknown) and two armchairs, one at the Hatheway House in Suffield, Connecticut, the other at the Philadelphia Museum of Art. All four chairs have similar stile, banister, and stretcher turnings and rear legs that end in feet that have only a hint of a backward rake. The armchairs both have arms in an unusual design: they incline from front to back and angle down noticeably a short distance before they join the stiles. The crest rails are all carved in the same manner, except for the anomalous, very likely replaced, crest on the Hatheway House example. That chair has a traditional history in Putnam, Connecticut. The armchair at the Philadelphia Museum of Art has a history of ownership by Anthony Morris II (1654–1721) of that city, in whose family it descended until it was bequeathed to that museum. Morris was a merchant who moved to Philadelphia from Boston about 1685, and the chair, a New England one, presumably entered the family through trade.[1] It was probably shipped from Boston and made there or in a nearby port town also involved in the export of chairs.

CONSTRUCTION

The rectangular tenons that join the crest and stay rails to the stiles are pinned; those of the banisters are not. The seat rails and stretchers are round-tenoned. On the lower front of the crest a scribed vertical layout line that marks the center and a horizontal one that marks the lower boundary of the carving remain partly visible. The bottom of the crest rail and the top of the stay rail are molded on the front with a bead. The upper back edge of the crest rail and the back edges of the piercings are chamfered. A small chamfer finishes the lower front edge of the stay rail, the outer front corner of the stiles, and both front corners of all four legs. On the right stile the cylindrical turning above the seat is scored around the middle with three lines. The front legs have a plain turned disk at the top.

CONDITION

The crest rail is warped and cups toward the back; it has suffered a horizontal break and loss at the left end below the lower volute of the scroll, and its bottom edge is gouged and dented. At the back of the crest rail, the mortise for one of the banisters has broken through. The rush seat is modern. The chair is partly covered with thin black paint, which is not old.

WOODS

Posts, crest rail, stay rail, banisters, MAPLE; right front post, SOFT MAPLE; seat rails, stretchers, ASH.

DIMENSIONS

OH. 46½ (118.1); SH. 16⅜ (41.6); SW. front 17⅞ (45.4); SW. back 14½ (36.8); SD. 12¾ (32.4).

REFERENCES

Halsey and Cornelius 1924 (and 1925, 1926), fig. 23 (1928, 1932, fig. 22); Dyer 1930a, p. 32.

PROVENANCE

Ex coll.: H. Eugene Bolles, Boston.

Gift of Mrs. Russell Sage, 1909 (10.125.218)

1. *Important Americana: The Collection of the Late Dr. and Mrs. James W. Marvin*, auction cat., Sotheby Parke Bernet, New York City, 30 September–1 October 1978, lot 321 (chair without arms); Kirk 1967, no. 218 (Hatheway House armchair). The Philadelphia Museum of Art armchair is in Nutting 1928–33, no. 1940, and Lindsey 1999, no. 136 and fig. 170; further information came from Jack Lindsey in conversation on 21 March 2000. The two armchairs differ in the turnings of the arm supports. Because the pattern of the turnings on the lower stiles and banisters replicates the one used on the chairs without arms and was not modified for the attachment of arms, the only blocks to which the arms could be joined are far down on the stiles. Hence their anomalous design.

29. See also fig. 16.

29.

Banister-back armchair

Northeastern coastal Massachusetts or Portsmouth, New Hampshire, or vicinity, 1720–40

The carved crest rails on tall-back chairs imparted an aura of importance to the sitter, whom they provided with a background of flourishes. This one is particularly effective in that regard because of its large scale and the verve of its carving. The stylized central leafage rises in expanding outward curving forms, the movement of which is reinforced by the assured lines of the veining. The whole composition is a vital play on C- and partial C-shapes, which are recalled in the small gouged crescents cut in the scrolls and at the tips of the uppermost outspreading leaves (fig. 16). A nearly identical crest rail (it has a little more detailing at the tips of the above-mentioned leaves) crowns a banister-back armchair of comparable proportions at the Winterthur Museum that relates to cat. no. 29 in other respects as well. While the finials are not the same, the columnar design of the stiles is similar and so are the somewhat unusual, vaguely vasiform turnings in the lower portion of the banisters (which on this chair are recalled in the shape of the rear stretcher).[1] A design challenge that faced turners of banister-back armchairs was what profile to give the lower banisters; because of the block for the arm joints, the base of the banisters could not simply replicate the lower stile turnings as they do on chairs without arms.

Both this and the Winterthur example have features that link them to splat-back chairs attributed to members of the Gaines family (see cat. nos. 36, 37). One of those chairs features a C-scroll at the center of the crest rail that is punctuated with pairs of gouged crescents very much like the scrolls on the crests of these banister-backs.[2] The same dynamic form of ram's-horn arm that distinguishes cat. no. 37 and related examples occurs on the Winterthur chair and may well have originally added gusto to this piece. Other similarities with cat. no. 37 include the pattern of the arm supports on the present chair and the shape of the side and rear stretchers on the one at Winterthur. Additionally, on both banister-backs, the front feet with a deep groove down the center ridge and the front stretcher with terminal turnings with a cavetto before the ring match the corresponding elements on cat. nos. 36 and 37 (see figs. 51, 30), but these forms had wider currency (see cat. no. 30). It is possible but far from certain that this chair was made by a member of the Gaines family. The account book of John Gaines II (1677–1748), of Ipswich, Massachusetts, records the sale of chairs described as banister-back (in entries dating from 1717 to 1741), crown-top or crown-back (1724–41), and carved-top or carved-back (1725–33)—all designations that could refer to the present example.[3] However, the considerable number of extant chair designs with "Gaines" attributes (see the entries for cat. nos. 36, 37) suggests that there may have been a broader group of craftsmen making similar local products.

CONSTRUCTION

The seat rails and stretchers are round-tenoned to the posts, and the front posts to the arms. The remaining components are secured with rectangular tenons; those of the crest and stay rails are pinned. The rear legs are vertical and do not end in raked feet. The front feet are carved from solid wood and are one with the legs. The upper back edge of the crest rail and the back edges of its piercings are broadly chamfered. A small chamfer finishes all the vertical edges of the four posts. The stay rail is molded with a cyma recta and a bead. Because the mortise for the stay rail in the left stile is further back than the one in the right stile, the rail is flush with the front of the stile on the right but not on the left; the shaving of the front of the left stile

at and below the rail appears to be an attempt to minimize that construction error. Many of the planed surfaces on the front posts show deeply torn grain.

CONDITION

The chair has been apart: the pins in the joints of the crest and stay rails are new (the latter pins are probably added) and the stretcher joints have been reset with wood shavings inserted to tighten the fit. The arms are replacements (probably fairly old), and their joints in the stiles are wedged; the stiles retain holes from the small pins that secured the original arms. There is a hole in the top of each arm where a nail driven down into the end of the arm support has been removed. The button on the right finial and a corner at the bottom of each front foot are missing. Small nail holes occur on the outer side of each stile down to the arm. The right stile and the stay rail, which has been bashed at the center of the lower edge, have splits. The rush seat is new. The chair appears to have been painted black when it was acquired. Records indicate that in 1933–34 modern varnish then on the chair was removed and the wood finished with linseed oil and turpentine. Some residues of black remain, particularly on the chair base, but the surface overall has a stripped look.

INSCRIPTIONS

At the Dey Mansion, Wayne, New Jersey (see *Exhibition*), an identification number was painted on the back of the crest rail and the inside of the right rear leg.

WOODS

Rear posts, banisters, POPLAR (*Populus* sp.); crest rail, HARD MAPLE; left front post, SOFT MAPLE; right front post, stay rail, front stretcher, MAPLE; side and rear stretchers, seat rails, ASH.

DIMENSIONS

OH. 44½ (113); SH. 16 (40.6); OW. (front feet) 26½ (67.3); SW. front 23¼ (59.1); SW. back 16⅞ (42.9); SD. 15⅜ (39.1).

EXHIBITION

On loan to the Dey Mansion, Wayne, New Jersey, from 1946 to 1999.

REFERENCES

Lockwood 1913, fig. 462; Halsey and Cornelius 1924 (and 1925, 1926), fig. 24 (1928, 1932, fig. 23; 1938, 1942, fig. 24); Cescinsky and Hunter 1929, p. 39; Salomonsky 1931, pl. 10 (includes measured drawings); Comstock 1954, p. 191; Kirk 1970, fig. 36; Margon 1971, p. 238.

PROVENANCE

Ex coll.: H. Eugene Bolles, Boston.

Gift of Mrs. Russell Sage, 1909 (10.125.219)

1. Richards and N. G. Evans 1997, p. 34, fig. 2. The finials on that chair consist of a reel and a ball (the same general type as on cat. no. 30) rather than an urn and a ball.
2. At the Winterthur Museum (Richards and N. G. Evans 1997, no. 18 [detail, fig. 1]). A similar crest rail on a chair at the Chipstone Foundation is replaced (Beckerdite and A. Miller 2002, p. 65 and figs. 23, 24).
3. Comstock 1954, p. 190; Hendrick 1964, appendices L, M, and N.

30.

Banister-back chairs (two)

Northeastern coastal Massachusetts or Portsmouth, New Hampshire, or vicinity, 1715–35

The unusual design of the crest rail on these two chairs—one of the most striking to be found on colonial seating in the William and Mary style—sets them apart (fig. 19). Reminiscent of engraved cartouches on contemporary silver, the pattern is clearly indebted to strapwork ornament. Two matching chairs, very likely from the same set, are in a private collection. A crest rail on an armchair that shows a similar use of strapwork and foliage but in a somewhat more complex configuration appears to belong to the same school of carving. It is executed with greater three-dimensionality than the more stylized design seen here, but the scrolls are notched in exactly the same manner. The armchair, which has urn-and-ball finials and also differs from the present chairs in details of other turnings and the shape of the stay rail, was probably made in another shop.[1] None of these chairs has an early history of ownership, but the sophistication of the crest design bespeaks production in an urban center.

This and the matching pair of chairs do not conform to the standard Boston tall-back model exemplified by cat. no. 27 in the style of the crest rail and in several other points: the form of the finials, details of post and stretcher turnings, and rear legs that are entirely vertical (they do not angle backward near the bottom to form raked feet). A more likely place of origin is a port town in northeastern Massachusetts or southern New Hampshire, for the MMA chairs and matching pair have some affinities with chairs from that region. The finials, which consist of a reel, ball, and knob, are similar to those on a banister-back armchair with a Boston-style crest rail at the Winterthur Museum, attributed to probably a member of the Gaines family, and they are also akin to those on a distinct group of banister-back chairs with crest rails sawn in a "fishtail" pattern that has been associated with the Portsmouth area.[2] Certain other features of the present chairs also have parallels in products ascribed to the Gaines school, but they may represent broader regional characteristics as well. These include prominent front feet that have a narrow groove down the center ridge and are carved from the solid wood of the leg, like those on cat. nos. 29, 36 (see fig. 51), and 37, and rear feet that lack a backward rake, as they do on cat. no. 29. In the turnings, there is a similar use of a cavetto at points of transition: for example, before the ring of the terminal turnings on the stretchers, as on cat. nos. 29, 36, and 37 (compare figs. 27, 30), and on the front legs between the base of the baluster and the small ring above the block, as on an armchair in a

private collection attributed to John Gaines III of Portsmouth, New Hampshire.[3] There are some very basic similarities between the crest rails on these chairs and the Gaines-type crest rails seen in cat. nos. 36 and 37; both designs are defined at each side by a scroll that flows down and outward and by a central element (curving up or down) that has an opening below it, out of which flows foliage (compare figs. 19, 20).[4] Whether there is any direct relationship between the two crest patterns or they are both just part of a broader design category that uses the same underlying concept as a starting point it is difficult to say. While firm evidence linking these chairs to Portsmouth is lacking, it is certainly possible they were made there. That town was a thriving port in the early eighteenth century, attracting not only native but also English craftsmen. The latter brought in fresh ideas, which could account for the novel crest design on chairs that are otherwise variants of a common model.[5]

CONSTRUCTION

On each chair: The back is joined with rectangular tenons, and the joints of the crest rail are pinned. The tenons on the crest rail are at the back edge of the board and have just a front shoulder, as was usual; but those on the stay rail are at the front edge of the board and have no shoulder at the back, having been formed by shaving down the back of the rail at each end. Because the mortises for both crosspieces were cut the same distance in from the front of the stiles, the stay rail is positioned nearly ½ inch further back than the crest rail. As a result, the banisters are more vertical in their orientation than the stiles. The seat rails and stretchers have round tenons that show flattened sides where joints have separated. The rear stretcher is shaved, not turned. Each front foot is carved from a solid block that is one piece with the leg. The top edge of the crest rail and the edges of the piercings have a broad chamfer at the back. The turnings that ornament the top of the front legs consist of a central button followed by a wide convex molding and then a narrower one. No two banisters within a chair or between the two chairs match exactly, suggesting that they came from a stockpile of banisters. Little effort was made to smooth not just the back of the crest and stay rails (a large sawyer's tally mark was left in evidence on the back of the crest of one chair; see *Inscription*) but also the front surfaces, and saw marks remain on two banisters.

CONDITION

On each chair: The frame is slightly racked and the back lists toward the left. There are some tack holes and small nail holes in the seat rails, and the rush is modern. The chairs have seen considerable usage.

Chair 30-1 (acc. no. 52.195.8): There is a loss at the bottom of the far left banister and at the back of the far right one. The left seat rail is replaced. The inner corner of the left front leg is split and repaired at seat level and the same corner of the two lower blocks shows losses—all probably owing to defective wood. The left stretcher has a split at the back. At the bottom of the right front foot small sections have broken off the center tip and the two outer corners. The black paint on the chair is not old; a few traces of an earlier light-colored coating remain.

Chair 30-2 (acc. no. 52.195.9): The joints of the crest rail have been reinforced from the outer side of each stile with a large screw (hidden by fill). Those of the rear seat rail and right stretcher to the right rear post have also been repaired, as has a break at the neck of the lower baluster of the right front leg. The front seat rail bows inward. Modern metal gliders have been added under all four feet. The black paint on this chair was applied over a coat of white paint with a brown glaze, which is visible on the inner sides of the posts just above the seat and covers an earlier layer of black.

INSCRIPTION
Scored on the back of the left side of the crest rail on chair 30-2 is a large sawyer's tally mark: || crossed by a diagonal line.

WOODS
Posts, probably banisters, POPLAR (*Populus* sp.); crest rail, front and side stretchers, SOFT MAPLE; stay rail, seat rails, probably rear stretcher, ASH.

DIMENSIONS
OH. 47½ (120.7); SH. 17⅝ (44.8); OW. (front feet) 21 (53.3); SW. front 18⅛ (46); SW. back 14¼ (36.2); SD. (30-1) 13 (33), (30-2) 12⅝ (32.1).

EXHIBITION
Chair 30-2: "Seats of Fashion: Three Hundred Years of American Chair Design," High Museum of Art, Atlanta, Georgia, 11 September–18 November 1973.

REFERENCES
Lockwood 1913, fig. 464 (chair 30-2; owned by Mr. G. W. Walker, of New York); Nutting 1921, p. 254 (chair 30-2; owned by Mr. B. A. Behrend); Nutting 1924, no. 473 (chair 30-2); Nutting 1928–33, no. 1923 (chair 30-2); "Recent Accessions" 1953, p. 263 (chair 30-1); Comstock 1957, p. 59 (chair 30-1); *Seats of Fashion* 1973 (exh. cat.), no. 2 (chair 30-1 illustrated; chair 30-2 in exhibition); Schwartz 1976, p. 23 (both chairs), no. 24 (chair 30-1); M. B. Davidson and Stillinger 1985, figs. 27, 28 (chair 30-2); MMA 2001, fig. 17 (chair 30-1).

PROVENANCE
Ex coll.: G. W. Walker, New York; B. A. Behrend, Brookline, Massachusetts; Mrs. J. Insley Blair, Tuxedo Park, New York; her daughter Mrs. Screven Lorillard, Far Hills, New Jersey.

Mrs. Blair purchased the chairs in 1922 from the dealers Collings and Collings, New York City. The chairs were on loan from Mrs. Blair to the MMA from 1939 to 1949.

Gift of Mrs. Screven Lorillard, 1952 (52.195.8, .9)

30-2

1. The matching side chairs were both formerly in the collection of Katharine Prentis Murphy ("Living with Antiques" 1950, p. 435), and one of them previously belonged to Louis Guerineau Myers (*The Rare and Extremely Choice Collection of Early American and English Furniture ... Formed by Mr. Louis Guerineau Myers,* auction cat., American Art Galleries, New York City, 24–26 February 1921, lot 514). A chair with a similar crest design but double-reel-and-ball finials is shown on the cover of *Antiques* 116 (December 1979). The armchair was advertised by Peter Eaton in *Antiques* 130 (October 1986), p. 714.
2. Richards and N. G. Evans 1997, p. 34, fig. 2 (Winterthur Museum armchair);

Jobe 1993, no. 75 (chair with a fishtail crest rail).
3. The cylindrical ends of the stretchers on Gaines-school chairs, however, taper much more strongly than on cat. no. 30. For the armchair, see Jobe 1993, no. 77.
4. The likeness is most evident on a Gaines-type chair at the Chipstone Foundation, on which the scrolls are more vertical than those on the standard Gaines crest rail and the carving is finer than normal (Rodriguez Roque 1984, no. 46).
5. Four English joiners arrived in Portsmouth between 1715 and 1720 (Jobe 1993, p. 41).

30-1. See also figs. 19, 27, 123.

31.

Banister-back chairs (two)

Bermuda, 1700–1740

Numerous chairs similar to this pair—only one of which is illustrated—have survived in Bermuda, where this general form was a regional type.[1] It represents a markedly different response to the styles set by English cane chairs from that seen in the North American colonies. A prime characteristic of these chairs (and most Bermuda furniture of the seventeenth and early eighteenth centuries) is that they are made of the native wood commonly called Bermuda cedar. The most distinguishing design feature is the back with its mushroomlike finials, three rectangular banisters, and a plain crest rail sawn to the shape of a central arch flanked by two serpentine curves, which is mirrored by the stay rail. The configuration of the stretchers seen here—an upper tier of four and a lower one of side stretchers connected by a medial brace—is common. Typically all the stretchers are turned but end in blocks with rectangular tenons that are secured with two pins, making for a solidly framed, labor-intensive undercarriage. The vocabulary of the turnings is all derived from English cane chairs, with the sequence of profiles on the stiles based on the same category of cane chair turnings that influenced the stile pattern on cat. no. 26, for example. The motif at the center of the front stretcher—opposed balusters separated by neither a ring nor a reel—is the most distinctive of the turning patterns and is characteristic of this type of chair.

Although seemingly simple, the back has a degree of stylishness. The crest and stay rails are gently bowed to conform to the back of the sitter.[2] The outline of the crest and stay rails relates to the shape of the back on English cane chairs of about 1700 that have molded stiles and a rounded crest rail mirrored by the stay rail. Here, as on many of those cane chairs, the curve of the crest's arch is greater than that of its inverted counterpart in the stay rail, so that the eye is drawn upward and the back achieves the vertical emphasis that is typical of early Baroque chairs. Backs with the same general crest- and stay-rail configuration also occur on other forms of English chairs—upholstered ones, fashionable banister-backs, and provincial paneled examples—so that it is difficult to say what was the actual source that inspired the Bermuda model.[3] The design represented by cat. no. 31 appears to be an updating of a stylistically earlier Bermuda chair form that also had three plain banisters, but sawn stiles, a crest rail shaped only along the top and a stay rail shaped just along the bottom, and plain stretchers.

The backs of this latter Bermuda chair type have a generic affinity with those of joined Pennsylvania chairs with sawn

31-1

stiles and plain banisters, permitting the speculation that similar traditions of British chairmaking were transmitted to Pennsylvania and to Bermuda.[4] Interestingly the same particular style of carved foot found on some London cane chairs—one in which there is a demarcation between the foot and the block above it on only the front and outer side—is reflected both in the present and other Bermuda examples and in several Philadelphia (but not Boston) chairs. The finials on this pair recall those found on a form of low joined English chair with a wooden seat, of which the only American examples are two made in Philadelphia, which have related finials.[5] This again suggests analogous English prototypes, but it also raises questions about the nature and extent of interaction in matters of furniture design that was fostered by trade between these two colonies in this period and of the possible movement of craftsmen. When in 1720 the Philadelphian Nathaniel Allen wrote to fellow Quaker William Tucker of Bermuda asking him "to send 3 red sedar chairs with white straw bottoms and of the newest fashion 16 inches high in the seate with Low Backs," as payment for a cask of flour, his description suggests that he was familiar with the type of chair he was ordering.[6] Because of their high seats and backs, the present chairs would not have fit the bill, but the above order indicates that they could have come to North America as new in the eighteenth century and not been collected at a later date.

CONSTRUCTION

On each chair: The backward cant of the stiles is moderate and that of the rear legs slight, and the rear feet have a strong rake. The frame is assembled with rectangular mortise-and-tenon joints with the exception of the front legs, which are round-tenoned to the blocks at the ends of the front seat rail (see fig. 165). The joints of the crest rail, stay rail, and stretchers to the posts are secured with two small pins, those of the seat rails to the rear posts with one. The base is trapezoidal, and the tenon shoulders of the side stretchers are cut to conform to the oblique angle at which they meet the square legs and those of the medial stretcher to the angle at which they join the side stretchers (see fig. 166B). The outer side of neither the front nor the rear legs is in line with the stretchers. The front feet are carved from the solid wood of the leg. All four vertical edges of the blocks on the stiles have a broad chamfer. A lamb's-tongue finishes the corners at the top of the rear legs and all corners of the stretcher and front leg blocks except the bottom of the block above the feet.

CONDITION

Both chairs have numerous cracks and have sustained minor losses, particularly at the bottom of the feet. Some of the many small knots in the wood are partially missing or have been replaced with wood plugs. The chairs have been scraped down, as is indicated by the flat lines running with the grain of the wood that are evident on the turnings. This aggressive treatment probably occurred when they were stripped of paint at some point before they entered the MMA collection; a few traces of green over a lighter color remain. The chairs, when received, had fabric-covered upholstered seats, which were subsequently twice re-covered in leather, but the seat construction calls for a bottom of rush or similar material.

Chair 31-1 (acc. no. 36.115.2, illustrated): In 1992 the modern upholstery was removed and a rush seat was installed. The front

corners of the seat frame, which had been shaved down, were built up again, and the joints of the front legs to the seat were reglued.

Chair 31-2 (acc. no. 36.115.3, not illustrated): There is a repaired break in the left stile at the top of the turning above the seat, in the right stile in the reel turning above the stay rail, and in the stay rail below the right banister. A pin has been added to the right joint of the stay rail. The wood of the left rear foot is worm-damaged and has been consolidated.

WOOD
BERMUDA CEDAR (*Juniperus bermudiana*).

DIMENSIONS
OH. 44½ (113); SH. 19 (48.3); SW. front 18⅛ (46); SW. back 14⅛ (35.9); SD. 14½ (36.8).

REFERENCE
Downs 1937b.

PROVENANCE
According to the donor, the chairs came from the Stamford, Connecticut, home of her grandfather Charles Hawley (1792–1866), who married in 1821 Mary Stiles Holly and was lieutenant governor of Connecticut from 1838 to 1842, and probably descended in the Hawley family.[7] Joseph Downs (see *Reference*) speculated that the chairs might have been owned originally by Samuel Hawley (ca. 1647–1734), of Stratford, Connecticut, from whom Charles Hawley was lineally descended, but no such chairs are included in his probate inventory.[8]

Gift of Miss Adelaide Milton de Groot in memory of the Hawley family, 1936 (36.115.2, .3)

1. For related chairs and for Bermuda furniture in general, see Hyde 1971; see also Tucker 1925 and C. Cooke and Shorto 1979.
2. This same feature occurs, for example, on a carved English leather chair (Gonzales and Brown 1996, figs. 8, 9).
3. For an example of this type of back on an English cane chair, see Kirk 1982, no. 728; on an upholstered chair, R. Edwards 1964, p. 131, fig. 58; on a banister-back chair, Kirk 1982, no. 743; on a paneled chair, Chinnery 1979, fig. 4:243. For related backs on cane chairs attributed to probably Philadelphia, see Forman 1988, no. 57 and fig. 148; for a Boston upholstered chair, see Forman 1988, no. 85.
4. For Bermuda chairs, see Hyde 1971, pp. 34–35. For Pennsylvania chairs, see Kindig 1978, no. 8, and Forman 1988, nos. 27, 28.
5. An English cane chair with a Pennsylvania history has this sort of foot (Mooney 1978, fig. 4). For Philadelphia examples, see Kindig 1978, no. 64, and Forman 1988, no. 57. For similar finials on English chairs, see Kirk 1982, nos. 690, 691; the related Philadelphia chairs are in *Philadelphia* 1976, no. 6, and Forman 1988, no. 48.
6. Quoted in Hyde 1971, pp. 19–20. For other early cedar furniture in Philadelphia, see Lindsey 1999, p. 116.
7. Letter of 9 August 1936 from Adelaide Milton de Groot to Joseph Downs (MMA Archives).
8. Samuel Orcutt, *A History of the Old Town of Stratford and the City of Bridgeport, Connecticut* ([New Haven, Conn.], 1886), vol. 2, pp. 1212, 1214, 1216; New-York Historical Society 1941, no. 330. The inventory of Samuel Hawley (d. 1734 and not 1737, as in Downs 1937b) lists only Turkey-work, leather, and five-back (slat-back) chairs (Fairfield County Probate, file no. 2785, Connecticut State Library, Hartford). The present writer is indebted to Richard C. Roberts, Head of the History and Genealogy Unit, Connecticut State Library, for a copy of the inventory.

32.

Cane chair

Boston, 1715–35

This is one of a group of more than thirty chairs of a similar type that form the largest coherent body of surviving early-eighteenth-century American cane chairs and represent the only significant response in kind to imported cane seating mounted by the Boston chairmaking industry.[1] Featuring a nearly vertical back, strongly raked rear legs, carved front feet, and a scalloped front skirt (missing on this example, on which the cane seat has been replaced with rush), these chairs cut a formal, elegant figure.[2] The design is derived from English models that are stylistically later than those reflected by tall-back chairs like cat. no. 27.[3] Innovations include stiles that are molded, not turned, and a crest that sits atop the stiles and carries on in carving their convex contour edged by a bead. The base, which follows the formula of English cane prototypes, represents a departure from that of the established upholstered chair tradition: the seat has its rails placed horizontally rather than vertically (see *Construction*); the rear legs are raked and ornamented with cylindrical turnings; and stretchers are configured differently. The stretchers are all turned. Those on the sides, which retain a block at the back and in the middle, where they are linked by an intermediary brace, are joined to the front legs with a rectangular tenon that issues not from a block but from a slightly tapered cylindrical turning (see fig. 89). The front stretcher with a central ring-and-ball motif (fig. 26) and the carved so-called Spanish feet seen here are typical of this Boston chair form.

At least nine different crest-rail designs, all of which incorporate foliate carving to a greater or a lesser degree, are found on this type of chair. The pattern on cat. no. 32 occurs on ten other chairs and has English antecedents. On this chair and four examples with related crest rails, the medial and rear stretchers are distinctive in that the characteristic swelled turning is not rounded at the center but comes to an apex and the conical turnings at either end are demarcated simply by a ridge rather than a ring.[4] As on the majority of molded-stile cane chairs, the side stretchers on this example have columnar turnings that are symmetrically arranged and a medial stretcher that is at the center and not toward the front of the chair; the former scheme appears to be an earlier formulation than the latter (compare cat. nos. 39, 40). The front feet on this chair are exceptionally high, but they are typical of Boston as far as the style of the carving is concerned: they have an outer concave groove that flares from top to bottom and is defined on both sides by a sharp ridge, and an adjacent inner hollow that adjoins

the rounded central ridge without a break (fig. 50). Finally, like many chairs of this general type, cat. no. 32 bears a punched "I" on the back, which is probably the mark of an unidentified caner (fig. 120).[5]

Documentary evidence as to when such cane chairs were first made in Boston is lacking. They have obvious similarities with molded-stile leather chairs like cat. no. 33, but if or by how much their production may have preceded the latter is unclear. The cane chairs do have certain features that are stylistically earlier: leaf carving in the crest; balusters of unequal height on the front legs, as on tall-back chairs with turned stiles; and a straight rather than a serpentine back. The straight back was probably preferred because it was easier to cane. Cane and leather chairs with molded stiles were doubtless made contemporaneously and most likely in the same shops. Elements of both carried over into the design of late Baroque (Queen Anne–style) Boston and New England cabriole-leg chairs: from leather chairs, the serpentine curvature of the back; from cane chairs, the shaped front skirt and the stretcher configuration and manner of attachment; and from both, the use of raked rear legs.[6]

CONSTRUCTION
The front, medial, and rear stretchers are joined with round tenons. All the joints of the back, including those of the stiles to the crest rail, and of the seat rails and side stretchers have rectangular tenons; those of the uprights of the back panel are thinner (¼ in.) than the others (a good 5/16 in.). The joints of the stay rail and side stretchers and those at the rear of the side seat rails are pinned. On the seat the rails are oriented horizontally; the tenons that join the rails to the rear posts are vertical, but those that join the side rails to the front rail are horizontal and are secured from below by a round tenon at the top of the front legs (see fig. 165). The tenon shoulders at the rear of the side stretchers have been cut to conform to the oblique angle at which they abut the square posts (see fig. 166B). The back surface of the front leg blocks has been planed so that the side stretchers, which terminate in a conical turning but have a rectangular tenon, can meet the legs at a right angle, and the outer side of those blocks has been planed to be in line with the seat (see fig. 166A). The inside corner of the uppermost front leg blocks has been cut away at the top to provide access to the seat rails for caning; the lower corners of those blocks were left square so that the front skirt that was originally set between them could be flush with the front and bottom of the blocks. The front feet are one with the legs (confirmed by X-radiography) except for the toes, which are carved from glued-on pieces. The molding on the stay rail and uprights of the back panel consists of a cyma reversa with a bead. A chamfer finishes the curved portions of the crest rail's back edge and the front edges of the rear feet.

32. See also figs. 26, 50, 120.

Condition

The caning on the back is modern, and on the seat it has been replaced by rush. The front skirt has been lost. The front and right seat rails are new; they were fashioned for a rush seat, and the two original rails have been rounded for rushing. At some point the chair was upholstered, as is evidenced by tack holes in the old rails and the numerous filled holes that mar the front and back surface of the frame of the back panel. The joints of the side stretchers and those at the rear of the side seat rails have replaced pins and added wedges. On the left rear leg there is a patch where the mortise for the side stretcher broke through, and a section of knotty wood near the rear stretcher has split off and been reattached with a nail. The upper baluster of the right front leg has a crack. The rear feet are chipped at the bottom, and the glued-on portions of the left front foot and a section on the outer side of the right front foot are replacements. The chair has a modern finish.

INSCRIPTION
On the back of the right stile just above the seat are punched dots forming an "I" with a center crossbar (fig. 120).

WOODS
MAPLE; left seat rail, SOFT MAPLE.

DIMENSIONS
OH. 46⅛ (117.2); SH. 19 (48.3); OW. (front feet) 18⅝ (47.3); SW. front 17½ (44.5); SW. back 13¼ (33.7); SD. 14½ (36.8).

PROVENANCE
Ex coll.: Mrs. Gordon Dexter, New York City.

Gift of Mrs. Gordon Dexter, 1948 (48.122)

1. This chair form is discussed in Forman 1988, pp. 258–67, and Adamson 2002. The earlier-style cane chairs attributed to Boston vary considerably in design and do not represent a recognizable local form. They have been identified as American rather than English on the basis of wood use. One chair has been catalogued as maple (Rodriguez Roque 1984, no. 71).

The attribution of others has been based on a distinction between American and European beech made by Gordon Saltar (former wood anatomist at the Winterthur Museum) in tests he devised but never published (Forman 1988, pp. 30, 37, n. 34). Chairs thus attributed are, for example, Baarsen et al. 1988, no. 114; and Forman 1988, nos. 52, 53 and fig. 126.

2. That a cane seat tended to have a short life expectancy and to be replaced by a more durable material is documented by a February 1718/19 Boston inventory reference to "3 cane back chairs with bass [bast fiber] bottoms" (quoted in Forman 1988, p. 266).

3. For example, Forman 1988, fig. 127.

4. For English precedents of this crest-rail design, see Mooney 1978, fig. 3, and Kirk 1982, no. 726. For chairs with similar crest rails and stretchers, see Lockwood 1913, fig. 482; Bernard and S. Dean Levy gallery catalogue, vol. 6 (New York, 1988), p. 9; Jobe et al. 1991, no. 20; and *The Collection of Noted Connecticut Antiquarians Priscilla S. and Howard K. Richmond,* auction cat., Northeast Auctions, Manchester, New Hampshire, 2 August 1997, lot 114. Other chairs with related crest rails are at Harvard College (see Forman 1988, p. 260, table 4); in Nutting 1928–33, nos. 2044, 2045 (pair), and Fales 1972, no. 73; and offered in *New Hampshire Weekend Americana Auction,* auction cat., Northeast Auctions, Manchester, New Hampshire, 6 August 2000, lot 848 (pair).

5. For the "I" mark, see Forman 1988, pp. 263–64; and Adamson 2002, pp. 188–89.

6. The stretchers that relate the most closely to those on Queen Anne chairs have the medial stretcher positioned toward the front (for example, Forman 1988, nos. 54, 56).

33.
Leather chair

Boston, 1723–45

Leather chairs of this type were being produced in Boston by early 1723, when the upholsterer Thomas Fitch described chairs he was selling as "crook'd back." In the following year he was promoting them as "newest fashion."[1] Truly new was the shallow serpentine curve—the "crook"—given to the stiles and back panel so that they would conform to the sitter's back—a significant advance in seating comfort. Derived from London cane chairs or English upholstered chairs in the cane-chair style, this form of leather chair has a number of features in common with Boston cane examples such as cat. no. 32. Foremost are the molded stiles, the general character of the crest rail, and the raked rear legs, which typically end in feet that have a yet stronger cant, as they do on cat. no. 32 and originally did on this chair. Also similar are the use of carved front feet and a front stretcher with ring-and-ball turnings. On both cat. no. 32 and cat. no. 33, the ends of the stretcher are turned in the same pattern, the one commonly found in conjunction with the ring-and-ball motif on Boston chairs; it consists of a fillet followed by a ring, one or two grooves, and a cylinder with usually only a slight taper (see fig. 26). On molded-stile leather and cane chairs, the upper blocks of the front legs (which house a round tenon) are shorter than the lower blocks (which house

a larger, rectangular tenon); but the upper and lower balusters on the leather chairs, contrary to those on virtually all cane examples (and earlier-style leather ones with carved crest rails), are typically of equal height. The latter trait may signal a waning of the early Baroque sensibility. It may have made for speedier (and thus more economical) production, which the elimination on the rear legs of the turnings found on cane chairs certainly did.

This form of comfortable, practical seating with pleasing outlines came in two basic models: the more prevalent featured a crest rail with a flat top and undulating shoulders and carved front feet, as illustrated by this example; the other had a low, rounded crest rail with round shoulders and often turned front feet.[2] A very popular product of the Boston chairmaking industry in the second quarter of the eighteenth century, such chairs were widely exported in coastal trade.[3] Evidence of the stockpiling of parts and hasty workmanship found in volume production is not uncommon. Cat. no. 33 was assembled with a left front leg that is noticeably thinner than the right one and that has not been planed on the outer side to be in line with the seat, and with uprights of the back panel that do not conform closely in their profile to the curvature of the stiles.

33

On the one hand, this chair has the distinction of retaining its original leather on the back and seat. The leather is no doubt of New England origin; it is not the more desirable imported Russia leather (see the entry for cat. no. 27), which by about 1725 was no longer readily available in Boston.[4] The frame, on the other hand, is compromised by feet that are replaced and inappropriate in design. The rear legs do not end with the typical backward-raked foot but continue at the same angle to the bottom. The front feet, with three narrow flutes on each side, are not carved in the characteristic Boston manner (compare fig. 50), and on the blocks above them the lower corners have not been shaped to match the upper ones. However, the chair's replacements and repairs are instructive as examples of fastidious late-nineteenth-century restoration work (see *Condition*), executed most likely by craftsman and collector Walter Hosmer, who worked in the Robbins Brothers cabinetmaking shop of Hartford, Connecticut.[5]

CONSTRUCTION

With the exception of the front stretcher, which has round tenons, the frame is joined with rectangular mortise-and-tenon joints; the joints of the front and side seat rails and of the side stretchers are secured with a pin. As is standard on this type of leather chair, none of the joints of the rear elements are pinned—the result of the continual trend in the Boston chair industry during the early eighteenth century to streamline production. On the trapezoidal base, the back surface of the front leg blocks has been planed so that the side seat rails and stretchers can join the legs at a right angle (see fig. 166A). At the back, the tenon shoulders of the side rails and stretchers have been cut to take into account the oblique angle at which they meet the rear legs on the horizontal plane (because the legs are square; see fig. 166B) and also on the vertical plane (because the legs cant backward). The outer side of the front leg blocks (but not of the rear legs) has been planed to be in line with the side rails and stretchers. The contour of the curves on the front of the uprights of the back panel matches that on the back of the stiles, and the profile on the back of the uprights is the same as that on the front of the stiles. This suggests that the uprights were made from wood left between cuttings of rear posts and that no effort was made to orient or shape them so that their curvature on the front would conform more closely to that of the stiles. The crest rail is chamfered on the back along the curved edges; it is straight at the bottom and recessed on the front for the attachment of the leather.

CONDITION

About this chair in his collection, H. Eugene Bolles wrote: "it was stated to me by Mr. Hosmer that the leather was taken off when the chair was restored and put back again" (Bolles notes, MMA Archives).

Frame: All the repairs made to the frame appear to date from that restoration. Face-grain plugs on the front and back of the left stile conceal the exact nature of the repair to a break about 5 inches above the stay rail, as does a thin facing (about 10 inches long) let into each side of that stile. On the front legs, the bottom blocks below the side stretchers and the feet are new; the join is concealed on the front and outer sides by a thin facing applied to the full height of the block. The rear legs are replaced from the bottom of the side stretcher down with a long splice extending 7 inches up the leg, and pins have been added to the joints of the rear stretcher. The other joint pins have been replaced. The tenon shoulders of the front stretcher appear to have been rounded. The frame has a modern finish.

Upholstery: The leather of the back and seat, but not of the trim strip, is original. That on the back panel has surface cracks and a tear; on the reverse, remnants of the cloth liner that was tacked to the front of the frame under the leather are visible around the edge. X-radiographs taken of the back panel show no extraneous tacks or nails or empty nail holes, so that the leather has probably never been off, or if it was removed, it was reattached with the same nails into the same holes. The seat leather, which has cracks, has clearly been taken off and reattached, as stated by Hosmer. The bottom of the seat now has tightly interwoven webbing not appropriate to the period. The sackcloth above it is old and possibly original, and the stuffing includes grass. The stitching in the center of the seat has been renewed. It goes through the original holes in the leather, which

typically form a trapezoidal outline and indicate a single stitch in the middle, and through the present webbing. The replaced trim strip has losses and is patched on two of the corners. It is double-nailed all around with older and newer brass nails. (The original strip would have been secured in part with just iron tacks.) Two screw holes on the underside of each side rail may be from a support attached at one point to hold up the under-upholstery.

INSCRIPTIONS

A portion of a printed paper label remains attached to the reverse of the leather of the back and reads: "Included in the collection [of Antique Furni-] / ture transferred to Mr. H. E. [Bolles, and Mr.] / Geo. S. Palmer. It is the or[iginal . . . illus-] / trated in 'Colon[ial F]urnitu[re of New England,'] / by Dr. Lyons." Restorer's reassembly marks (incised single and double notches) are at the joints of the right rear leg to the rear stretcher and rear seat rail. MMA Hudson-Fulton exhibition identification numbers (H. F. 40.32 and 488) are inscribed in orange crayon on the inside of the seat rails.

WOODS

SOFT MAPLE; stay rail, front seat rail, ASH.

DIMENSIONS

OH. 45⅝ (115.9); SH. 18½ (47); OW. (front feet) 19⅜ (49.2); SW. front 17¾ (45.1); SW. back 14¼ (36.2); SD. 14⅜ (36.5).

EXHIBITION

"Hudson-Fulton Exhibition," MMA, 20 September–30 November 1909.

REFERENCES

I. W. Lyon 1891, fig. 70; *Hudson-Fulton Celebration* 1909 (exh. cat.), no. 103, illus. opp. p. 52 (a photograph of a similar but different chair that did not enter the MMA collection was used by mistake for the illustration; the same wrong photograph was used to represent cat. no. 33 in the Lockwood 1913, Hughes 1962, and M. B. Davidson 1980 references below); Lockwood 1913, fig. 481; Cornelius 1926, pl. XVI; Cescinsky and Hunter 1929, p. 40; Hughes 1962, fig. 9; Randall 1963, fig. 3; M. B. Davidson 1967, no. 154; M. B. Davidson 1980, fig. 76; Fitzgerald 1982, fig. II-5; M. B. Davidson and Stillinger 1985, fig. 143.

PROVENANCE

Ex coll.: Walter Hosmer, Hartford, Connecticut; H. Eugene Bolles, Boston.

Bolles and his cousin George S. Palmer, of New London, Connecticut, purchased Hosmer's collection in 1894.

Gift of Mrs. Russell Sage, 1909 (10.125.698)

1. Quoted in Forman 1988, p. 335 (the date of the entry in Fitch's account book as cited in Forman is 27 February 1722/23—giving the year according to both the Old Style [Julian] calendar and the New Style [Gregorian] calendar, the one now in use).
2. For example, Forman 1988, no. 81.
3. See Randall 1963.
4. Jobe 1974, p. 39.
5. Stillinger 1980, p. 81.

34. See also fig. 25.

34.
Leather armchair

Boston or vicinity, 1725–45

Among the corroborating evidence of the extensive export of leather chairs from Boston during the second quarter of the eighteenth century are the oft-cited advertisements of Philadelphia upholsterer Plunket Fleeson. Clearly unhappy about the competition given by "Boston Chairs," he touted in 1742 "black and red leather Chairs, finished cheaper than any made here, or imported from Boston" and in 1744, "Maple

Chairs as cheap as from Boston."[1] Benno M. Forman sought to identify Philadelphia leather chairs made to compete with imports from New England and proposed as a candidate an armchair at the Winterthur Museum; he found that it differed from what he considered the typical Boston chair of this form in seven small details. Cat. no. 34 exhibits some of the same traits as the Winterthur chair, primarily the design of the arm supports and the unusual use of a ball rather than a baluster as the lower turning on the front legs, and he ascribed it to Philadelphia as well. The evidence presented by Forman, however, is not strong enough to attribute this chair to Philadelphia.

Forman conceded that six of his distinguishing details may just be differences of the type that occur between individual chairs and may not indicate regional preferences. (In fact, armchairs, produced in far fewer numbers than those without arms, which were often made in sets of six or twelve, tend on the whole to show greater variations.) On the one hand, he based the Philadelphia attribution chiefly upon the arm supports, relating the reel-and-baluster turnings seen here to similar forms on Philadelphia chairs, giving great weight to the fact that the balusters are ornamented with a pair of grooves—a feature that is characteristic of (but not entirely exclusive to) baluster turnings on Pennsylvania chairs and tables (see cat. no. 64). He seems to have disregarded the fact that on the typical Philadelphia arm support that he gave as an example, the uppermost turnings, which consist of a knop followed by a tapering form with concave sides, are not the same as on cat. no. 34 and the baluster has a more bulbous base.[2] On the other hand, close parallels to the entire sequence of profiles seen here, including the ring, groove, and cone turnings at the top, can be found on New England chairs of the period. Granted, the balusters generally lack grooves, as on the somewhat heavier version of this pattern on cat. no. 38, but grooves are present on the related arm supports of at least two splat-back chairs with the type of yoke crest that is characteristic of New England and seen on cat. no. 35. One of those chairs was meant to have an upholstered seat and has rectangular side and rear stretchers and, significantly, front legs that like those on cat. no. 34 substitute a ball for a short baluster—but in this case for the upper turning. The other chair has a loose rush seat, squared cabriole legs, and turned stretchers in a format typical of Boston.[3] The feet on the present chair, contrary to those on the Winterthur Museum example, conform to standard Boston practice in that they are carved with two broad channels on each side from a block with glued-on pieces. The front stretcher is a more attenuated version of the design on cat. no. 27, with the difference that the sharp-edged ring of the terminal turnings is here preceded by a fillet, as is sometimes the case in this pattern (compare figs. 25, 24).

While cat. no. 34 has front post turnings with a detail that is not common on Boston leather chairs, there is no compelling stylistic or structural reason to question that it was made in that city or its environs, where the production of such chairs was centered. Furthermore the chair's history of ownership in New York makes it unlikely that it originated in Philadelphia, which, unlike Boston, did not have an export trade in leather chairs. Nor has any evidence been found to date that this type of chair was being made in New York.

CONSTRUCTION

The chair is framed with rectangular tenons, with the exception of the joints of the front stretcher and of the front posts to the arms, which are round-tenoned. A pin secures the joints of the front and side seat rails, the side stretchers, and the right arm to the stile. The joinery of the side seat rails and side stretchers to the legs is similar to that on cat. no. 33, but here the execution is more precise; both the inside and outside tenon shoulders of those members fit snugly against the legs. The toes of the front feet are carved from glued-on wood. A broad chamfer finishes the back of the crest along the undulating edges and a narrow one the outer back edge of the rear posts and uprights, both front edges of the rear legs, the inner front edge of the front leg blocks, and the upper edges of the stretchers. On the rear surfaces of the chair, kerfs, hatchet marks, and torn grain remain visible, and the inner side of the seat rails was left irregular.

CONDITION

The rear joint of the left arm, which was never secured with a pin, has been repaired with a screw from the back (concealed by a wood plug) and a nail from the front. The top of that arm has a patch where it meets the stile and a round plug opposite the tenon of the arm support. An area under the right arm has been singed. Part of a ring turning on the right arm support is missing. The left joint of the stay rail has been wedged, and small nails have been added to both joints. The front seat rail is repaired at the joint with the left post, and modern corner blocks reinforce all the seat-rail joints. The toes of both front feet are replaced, and the left rear foot has losses at the bottom. Records indicate that in 1933–34 modern varnish then on the chair was removed and the wood finished with linseed oil and turpentine. The present leather show cover (cowhide) and upholstery foundation, installed in 2002, are nonintrusive. The removal of the previous MMA upholstery revealed that the tacking surfaces of the back and seat are riddled with holes and that the bottom ½ inch of the outer surface of the seat rails is pieced. Filled tack holes are visible on the rear of the back panel frame and on the four posts at seat level.

WOODS

MAPLE; rear seat rail, SOFT MAPLE; crest rail, BIRCH.

DIMENSIONS

OH. 48¾ (123.8); SH. 17⅛ (43.5); OW. (arms) 24⅞ (63.2); SW. front 23 (58.4); SW. back 17¾ (45.1); SD. 16⅞ (42.9).

EXHIBITION

On loan to the Columbia County Historical Society (for exhibition in the Luykas Van Alen House), Kinderhook, New York, from 1974 to 1979.

REFERENCE

Dyer 1930b, p. 63.

PROVENANCE

According to the donor, Emilie Vallete Clarkson (Mrs. William A. Moore, 1863–1946), the chair came down to her from Augustus Van Horne (1736–1796), who married in 1765 Anna Maria Van Cortlandt (b. 1736), the widow of Nathaniel Marston. The line of descent indicated is as follows: their daughter Ann Mary Van Horne (1778–1856), who married in 1797 Levinus Clarkson (1765–1845); their daughter Elizabeth Clarkson (1810–1883), who married in 1828 Thomas Streatfeild Clarkson (1799–1873); their daughter Ann Mary Clarkson

(1831–1895), the donor's mother, who married in 1852 Thomas Streatfeild Clarkson (1824–1902). The chair predates the marriage of Augustus Van Horne probably by a generation. It could have descended from his parents (Cornelius Van Horne m. 1735 Judith Jay), Anna Maria's parents (Frederick Van Cortlandt m. 1723/24 Frances Jay), from her first husband's family, or come into the donor's family by any number of other routes: included among the eighty-four family items given to the MMA by Mrs. Moore together with this chair are portraits, miniatures, and inscribed metalwork that can be identified with a wide range of original owners, all in related prominent old New York families.[4]

Gift of Mr. and Mrs. William A. Moore, 1923 (23.80.6)

1. For Boston's export trade in leather chairs in this period, see Randall 1963; the quotations are on pp. 12–13. It is generally assumed that Fleeson was referring to the type of chair represented by cat. nos. 33 and 34 and not to splat-back cabriole-leg chairs with leather seats (Forman 1988, p. 347).

2. Forman 1988, no. 80. The Philadelphia arm support he shows (fig. 183) is in the tradition of that on cat. no. 17 (see Forman 1980, fig. 15). Baluster arm supports that end in a ring and cone, as on cat. no. 34, are found on a few chairs of an unquestionably Pennsylvania type, but the supports usually differ in other respects: no reel below the baluster, which lacks grooves (Forman 1988, no. 28); more bulbous balusters (Lindsey 1999, nos. 148, 149); cone with concave sides (Lindsey 1999, no. 149).

3. *Sack Collection* 1981–92, vol. 3, p. 743 (chair with turned front legs); Gary C. Cole advertisement in *Antiques* 104 (September 1973), p. 375 (with cabriole legs). For leather chairs of the same type as cat. no. 34 with identical arm supports that lack grooves, see *Sack Collection* 1981–92, vol. 8, p. 2320, and *Important American Furniture, Silver, Folk Art and Decorative Arts,* auction cat., Christie's, New York City, 17 June 1997, lot 339.

4. Information from the donor in ADA files; [Matthew Clarkson], *The Clarksons of New York: A Sketch,* vol. 2 (New York, 1876), pp. 193–94 and charts opp. pp. 7, 118; J. Robert T. Craine, *The Ancestry and Posterity of Matthew Clarkson (1664–1702),* ed. Harry W. Hazard (n.p., 1971), pp. 37, 62–63; Laura J. Wells, *The Jay Family of La Rochelle and New York, Province and State: A Chronicle of Family Tradition* ([New York], 1938), pp. 45, 56.

35.
Splat-back chair

Boston, northeastern Massachusetts, or coastal New Hampshire, 1730–60

In the years just before and after 1730, when late Baroque influences were beginning to affect urban furniture design, Boston chairmakers devised a number of patterns that combined newer features of the Queen Anne style with elements of the then established molded-stile cane and leather chair forms (see cat. nos. 32, 33). Novel on this chair are a crest rail that dips at the center rather than rising to a crown, and a wooden splat with the outline of a vase in the place of a rectangular back panel. Carried over from leather chairs are the rear posts with molded serpentine stiles, the undercarriage, and the overall stance; from cane chairs, the molded stay rail and the seat construction (adapted for a rush seat, as on many banister-back chairs). The generic formula represented by this chair—an updated back with a yoke-shaped crest and vase splat on a William and Mary–style rush-seated base—proved to be an enduring one. Popular throughout New England and produced for many decades, it was the last major chair type to evolve out of the seventeenth-century upholstered-chair tradition.[1] This form of seating, commonly made of maple, was a mid-level product: it provided a degree of fashionability at a lesser price than walnut Queen Anne–style chairs with upholstered seats and cabriole legs.

Chairs with a back in the particular design seen here, which features a splat that flares at the top and a crest rail carved with a prominent ridge between the smooth saddle shape in the middle and the arched and molded shoulders, were the most common and have survived in large numbers.

While they can be separated into several groups according to certain details, assigning them convincingly to a particular region or locality has proved difficult; documentation is scarce, and given the Boston area's active export trade in chairs, a local history of ownership does not necessarily mean local manufacture.[2] This chair is part of a relatively small group that is distinguished by having sawn stretchers at the sides and usually also at the back. On these chairs the turning above the baluster at the top of the front legs is typically a sturdy cone. Also, the splat tends to be wider and the overall height of the chair less than on the much more numerous examples on which all the stretchers (usually double on the sides) are turned. The latter have a short bulbous turning or an abbreviated cone at the juncture of the legs to the seat. The profiles at the top of the legs (ultimately indebted to turnings on English cane chairs) parallel forms found at the top of Boston arm supports beginning with tall-back chairs.[3]

The base of cat. no. 35 closely resembles that of Boston molded-stile leather chairs in its plain stretchers joined with rectangular tenons and in the style of the carving on the feet. It probably originated in the Boston area or in a port town strongly influenced by that city's exports. In terms of labor and thus cost, it stands a notch above the many examples on which all the stretchers are turned. They represent a model—from the seat down identical to certain banister-back chairs—that was geared to faster, more economical production. Thus their undercarriage is entirely joined with round tenons; most

35

The outer side of the front leg and seat blocks has been planed to be in line with the side of the seat. The front feet are integral to the legs and carved from solid wood. The side edges of the splat cant in from front to back, and the stay rail is molded with a cyma reversa and a bead. The front corners of the rear feet are chamfered.

CONDITION

The lower left corner of the splat is replaced. A wooden plug on the back of the left post opposite the tenon of the side seat rail indicates a repair. The right seat rail has glued breaks. The upper surface of the rear third of the right front seat rail block is patched. On the front of both front seat rail blocks a hole left by a wooden pin that was at one time added to the leg joint has been filled. All the joint pins appear to have been renewed, and two small pins have been added to each joint of the right stretcher. The rush seat is modern. The chair has been stripped and the surface appears to have been oiled.

WOOD

SOFT MAPLE.

DIMENSIONS

OH. 39⅞ (101.3); SH. 18 (45.7); OW. (front feet) 20¼ (51.4); SW. front 19 (48.3); SW. back 13⅞ (35.2); SD. 14¼ (36.2).

EXHIBITIONS

"Hudson-Fulton Exhibition," MMA, 20 September–30 November 1909; on loan to the Dey Mansion, Wayne, New Jersey, from 1940 to 1978.

REFERENCE

Hudson-Fulton Celebration 1909 (exh. cat.), no. 129.

PROVENANCE

Ex coll.: H. Eugene Bolles, Boston.

Gift of Mrs. Russell Sage, 1909 (10.125.695)

often the joint of the splat to the stay rail has been simplified, in that the splat is thin and the entire bottom end is slotted into the rail, eliminating the need to cut a tenon; and the carving on the feet is more schematic than on the present example.[4]

CONSTRUCTION

On the rear posts, the cant of the stiles is such that the crest rail extends as far back as the feet, which have a stronger rake than the legs, which begin to angle back about 3 inches below the seat. The joints of the front stretcher, the front legs to the seat, and the seat rails to the rear posts are round-tenoned. The remaining joints have rectangular tenons; the tenons that join the side seat rails to the exposed ends of the front seat rail are oriented horizontally (see fig. 165). The joints of the stiles to the crest rail and of the side stretchers are pinned. The tenons at the top and bottom of the splat are at the back of the board and extend nearly its full width. On the stay rail and the rear and side stretchers, the tenons are set in a good ½ inch from the working surface so that they have in effect only a wide outside shoulder. The side stretchers join the front and rear legs at an oblique angle, and the tenon shoulders have been cut accordingly (see fig. 166B).

1. Other combinations of older and newer elements that were more short-lived or not as widespread in this period include chairs with a yoke crest rail and vase splat but a loose seat and scalloped front seat rail (Richards and N. G. Evans 1997, no. 2); examples with a high crest rail and a vase splat in the back and a base with a loose seat and turned front legs (Lockwood 1913, fig. 489) or square cabriole front legs (Richards and N. G. Evans 1997, no. 1); leather chairs (some of which have been attributed to Rhode Island) that have a yoke crest rail and a rectangular back panel and turned front legs (*Sack Collection* 1981–92, vol. 7, p. 1996; Rodriguez Roque 1984, no. 47) or cabriole front legs (Heckscher 1985, no. 1). See also cat. nos. 36–38.

2. For an early attempt to separate Connecticut chairs from Massachusetts chairs, see Keyes 1932. The distinctions, based on two dozen chairs that have local associations, suggested by Nancy Goyne Evans warrant further exploration (Richards and N. G. Evans 1997, no. 3).

3. Other chairs with a similar splat and crest rail and three sawn stretchers are in Fales 1976, nos. 55, 56, and Fitzgerald 1982, fig. III-4; and offered in *American Furniture and Decorative Arts,* auction cat., Skinner, Bolton, Massachusetts, 6 June 1999, lot 341. Armchairs include Greenlaw 1974, no. 43; Fales 1976, no. 50; Kane 1976, no. 77; *Sack Collection* 1981–92, vol. 4, p. 999, vol. 6, p. 1501; Venable 1989, no. 16. For arm supports, see Forman 1988, no. 64 and fig. 180.

4. These traits are found on six chairs, including one armchair, at the MMA (acc. nos. 10.125.248–.250, .262, .263 [M. B. Davidson and Stillinger 1985, fig. 41], .692 [armchair]). In other collections, see, for example, Monkhouse and Michie 1986, no. 95, and Richards and N. G. Evans 1997, nos. 3, 4.

36.
Splat-back chair

Portsmouth, New Hampshire, 1735–43
Attributed to the shop of John Gaines III (1704–1743)

A vivid composition in which the scrolls of the crest rail are recalled in the curves of the feet, and its inverted arch in the shape of the front seat rail, this chair is a skillful blending of older and newer style elements. Chairs in this striking design have long been attributed to John Gaines III, who in 1724 moved from Ipswich, Massachusetts, where he had been trained by his father, a turner and chairmaker, to Portsmouth, New Hampshire.[1] They are the most ambitious and individual representatives of the category of New England seating that is exemplified in its basic form by cat. no. 35. Nearly thirty chairs, including several armchairs (see cat. no. 37), are known with crest rails generically similar to this one.

The crest rail—inspired by Boston or English chairs—combines scrolls, piercings, and foliate carving, elements that were in fashion in the first quarter of the eighteenth century, with the hollow top and rounded shoulders that came into style about 1730.[2] The distinctive design of the crest is considered tantamount to a shop signature of John Gaines III or possibly the broader Gaines family. The crest rails show some variation in the width of the central hollow, in how far the scrolls extend toward the stiles, and in the details of the carving. On the whole, the carving is cursory, so that the considerably finer execution of the foliage in the variant interpretation of the pattern on one chair may represent the work of a specialist.[3] The formulation of the seat—a separate frame that sits inside rails that are joined to the posts and shaped along the bottom on the front and sides—follows that of contemporary Boston chairs, but not the profile of the front rail. The type of geometric rail seen here, with a half-round drop in the middle and a beaded edge, appears to be peculiar to the Gaines school of craftsmanship and is its most often used pattern. A less common outline features a center drop that has a straight bottom edge and sides cut to mirror the cavetto at either end of the rail.[4] Another characteristic of this and many of the Gaines chairs is the low placement of the stay rail, which probably reflects the fact that on Queen Anne–style cabriole-leg chairs the splat is connected to the seat rail. The front feet on Gaines chairs are typically carved with two wide flaring channels on each side in the Boston manner, but they have in addition a narrow groove down the center ridge, and they are carved from a solid block (fig. 51).

Except for the shape of the splat, cat. no. 36 is virtually identical in design to a set of four chairs that descended from John Gaines III in the Brewster family and form the basis for the attribution of his work.[5] In addition, it is numbered as part of a set in the same distinctive manner as those key chairs—with a large gouged roman numeral on the back of the front seat rail (fig. 119). The splat on the Brewster set is in the pattern that occurs most frequently on Gaines chairs and is seen on cat. no. 37. The pattern with fanciful prongs used on the present chair is less common. Splats cut from the same template occur on four other chairs, which match cat. no. 36 in all other aspects of the design as well and probably come from the same set of at least six. This chair, the only one from this set to retain its original loose seat frame, is numbered "VI"; two chairs at the Winterthur Museum are numbered "I" and "IIII," and two at the Henry Ford Museum, "II" and "V."[6] A splat with similar outlines but cut from a different pattern is on four chairs that have a cabriole-leg base, suggesting that cat. no. 36 may be among the later productions of the Gaines shop.[7]

CONSTRUCTION

The chair is joined with rectangular tenons, with the exception of the front and rear stretchers, which are round-tenoned. The joints of the stiles to the crest rail and of the stay rail, side and front seat rails, and side stretchers to the posts are secured with a pin. The tenon shoulders on the side seat rails and side stretchers are cut to conform to the oblique angle at which they abut the square legs, and the outer side of the front legs has been planed so as to be in line with the side rails and stretchers (see fig. 166B). On the loose seat frame, the rails are oriented horizontally, and the side rails are tenoned to the exposed blocks at the ends of the front and rear rails. The loose seat rests at the front on triangular ledges formed by cutting away the inner corner at the top of the legs and at the back on a slat nailed to the rear rail. Each front foot is carved from a 3-inch-square block that is integral to the leg. All the rear edges of the crest rail are chamfered. The sides of the splat cant in from front to back. The molding on the stay rail consists of a cyma recta and a bead. Heavily knotted wood was used for the left rear leg, and hand-tool marks were left very visible on the splat, which on the back surface shows, in addition, a large area of deeply torn grain.

CONDITION

A small section at the upper left corner of the splat is new, as is the segment of the left seat rail between the front leg and the cove of the cutout. The seat support nailed to the rear rail is a replacement, and adjacent small blocks nailed to the side rails are added. The loose seat frame is original, but the upper half of the left rear block is replaced, as is the rush. Small modern nails and numerous filled nail holes mar the seat rails and the adjoining portions of the legs and are evidence that the seat was at one time upholstered (happily without

36. See also figs. 51, 119.

impacting the loose seat frame). The upper front edge of the front seat rail has been roughly taken down. Initially there were probably thin strips nailed to the top of the seat rails to hold the loose seat in place. There are splits at many of the chair's joints. The front stretcher has been rotated in its sockets to conceal wear. A round hole (now with fill) at the back of the block that houses the right end of the front stretcher may stem from an original drilling error. The chair has been stripped but retains residues of a dark coating in all the recesses.

INSCRIPTIONS

A large roman numeral VI is incised on the back of the right end of the front seat rail (fig. 119) and under the right front corner of the loose seat. On the underside of the seat's right rear corner is a modern pencil inscription, "Snider."

WOODS

SOFT MAPLE; rear stretcher, front and rear rails of loose seat, ASH.

DIMENSIONS

OH. 41¼ (104.8); SH. 17¼ (43.8); OW. (front feet) 21 (53.3); SW. front 18½ (47); SW. back 14⅛ (35.9); SD. 14¼ (36.2).

REFERENCES

Downs 1944, p. 80; Comstock 1954, p. 191; Comstock 1957, p. 59; M. B. Davidson 1980, fig. 77; Jobe 1993, ill. no. 78C.

PROVENANCE

The chair was purchased from Israel Sack, a dealer in New York City. The information that the chair was found near Exeter [New Hampshire] published by Joseph Downs (see *References*) was probably transmitted to him orally; it does not appear in MMA records.

Rogers Fund, 1944 (44.29)

1. The literature on John Gaines III and his father, John Gaines II (1677–1748), and his brother Thomas (1712–1761), both working in Ipswich, includes Decatur 1938; Comstock 1954; Hendrick 1964; and Jobe 1993, pp. 43, 47–48, and nos. 77, 78.
2. For the type of Boston or English crest rail from which the Gaines design was at least in part derived, see Forman 1988, no. 63 and fig. 171. See also the entry for cat. no. 30.
3. Rodriguez Roque 1984, no. 46.
4. For example, Jobe 1993, ill. no. 77A.
5. The Brewster chairs are illustrated and discussed in all the references in n. 1 above. They remained in the Brewster family until 1998. One is now at the Strawbery Banke Museum, Portsmouth, New Hampshire, and another at the Winterthur Museum, and two are in private hands.
6. For the chairs at the Winterthur Museum, see Richards and N. G. Evans 1997, no. 17; for those at the Henry Ford Museum (acc. nos. 71.35.1, 2), see Bishop 1975, inside back cover. There were at one time three matching chairs at the Winterthur Museum (Downs 1952, no. 100); the present location of the third chair is not known.
7. See Jobe 1993, no. 78. The present writer is indebted to Jayne E. Stokes for a tracing of the splat on that chair.

37.

Splat-back armchair

Portsmouth, New Hampshire, 1735–43
Attributed to the shop of John Gaines III (1704–1743)

This chair's beautifully integrated design achieves a perfect equipoise between the greater than usual incline of the back and the relaxed slope of the arms, and the forward pull of the powerful ram's-horn handgrips, which are anchored by the vertical front posts. On the crest rail, the lower side leaves have a flowing outward motion that accords with the movement of the upper elements (fig. 20). This is one of at least six armchairs with design features that associate them with the Gaines shop tradition (see cat. no. 36). All six have similarly carved arms of impressive proportions, but in other respects no two chairs are quite alike. Two others have a crest rail in the characteristic Gaines pattern seen here. On three, the crest rail is also carved with William and Mary scroll and foliate motifs, but they are configured differently; they evoke the crest-rail profile of Queen Anne–style chairs with a carved shell in the center—a later stylistic development than that reflected in cat. no. 37.[1] In addition, the armchairs exhibit differences in details of the splat outline, in the turnings and

placement of the arm supports, in the shape of the front seat rails, and in particulars of the front stretcher. It is documented that John Gaines employed other craftsmen, but nonetheless the variety of the designs raises the question of whether these chairs were all made in the same shop.[2]

With a standard rush seat woven around rails that are round-tenoned to the posts, this is a more conservative and less expensive model than the other armchairs, which like cat. no. 36 and virtually all Gaines-type chairs have a loose seat.[3] On this and two further chairs, the arm supports are a continuation of the front legs in the traditional manner, but on the remaining three the arm supports are attached to the side seat rails behind the legs—a newer design concept introduced with the Queen Anne style. The arm-support turnings on this example match those on one of the chairs with supports set back from the front (and also those on cat. no. 29).[4] This pattern, with its reel-ring-reel sequence below the baluster and a reel above it, is more complex than the more widespread scheme of an elongated baluster above a reel found on the other chairs in this group. Below the seat, cat. no. 37 illustrates the standard Gaines formula: plain, sawn side stretchers; a turned rear stretcher with a swelled shape probably inspired by that on cane chairs (see cat. no. 32); and a front stretcher in the common Boston ring-and-ball pattern, with the difference that on this and numerous other chairs the end turnings have a cavetto rather than a fillet before the ring and a cone that has more of a taper (compare figs. 30, 26). The front stretcher on three of the armchairs is distinguished yet by another detail—a separate, extra ring toward each end similar to that on cat. no. 137.[5] The front feet are carved in the same manner as on cat. no. 36 (see fig. 51). The carved feet on Gaines chairs are notable for the length and breadth of their outward sweep, which on this chair has been somewhat diminished through wear and losses. The strong stance of the feet and the bold scale of the front stretcher counterbalance the chair's commanding arms.

CONSTRUCTION

The rear posts have serpentine stiles that have a strong backward cant with the result that the crest rail extends about 2 inches further back than the feet, which rake sharply at the base of legs that are only slightly angled. Round tenons secure the seat rails and front and rear stretchers to the posts and the arm supports to the arms; rectangular mortise-and-tenon joints secure the remaining components. All four joints of the arms and those of the stay rail and side stretchers are pinned. The tenon shoulders of the side stretchers are cut to conform to the oblique angle at which they join the square legs (see fig. 166B); the outer side of neither the front nor the rear legs is in line with the side stretchers. The feet are each carved from a solid block integral to the leg. The curved portions of the crest rail, its piercings, and the sides of the splat are broadly chamfered on the back edge. The stay rail is molded with a cyma recta and a bead.

CONDITION

Some of the joint pins have been reset or renewed. The arm joint in the right stile has been tightened with a wedge; the mortise of the arm joint in the left stile has broken through at the back. At the front, the top of the right arm is marred by a nail hole opposite the arm support, and the top of the left arm by a deep gash in front of the arm support. The rush seat is a replacement. Nail and tack holes in the seat rails and legs indicate that at some point another type of bottom was installed. The front feet are worn and chipped at the bottom and are missing the scrolls on the sides; the toes of the left foot are patched. A split on the inner corner of the lower left rear leg has been repaired with nails, and the right rear foot shows cracks and losses. The black paint on the chair—worn off in some areas and flaked in others—appears to be partly if not entirely modern.

WOODS

SOFT MAPLE; front posts, POPLAR (*Populus* sp.); side and rear seat rails, ASH.

DIMENSIONS

OH. 40½ (102.9); SH. 16¼ (41.3); OW. (arms) 27⅛ (68.9); SW. front 23⅝ (60); SW. back 16¾ (42.5); SD. 15½ (39.4).

37

REFERENCES

Nutting 1928–33, no. 2102; Bjerkoe 1957, pl. IX, no. 2; M. B. Davidson and Stillinger 1985, fig. 144.

PROVENANCE

Ex coll.: Wallace Nutting, Framingham, Massachusetts; H. Long, Boston; Mrs. J. Insley Blair, Tuxedo Park, New York.

Mrs. Blair purchased the chair from New York City dealers Collings and Collings in 1922. It was on loan to the MMA from Mrs. Blair from 1939 until the time of the bequest.

Bequest of Mrs. J. Insley Blair, 1951 (52.77.55)

1. An armchair with the same type of crest rail as cat. no. 37 is in a private collection (Jobe 1993, no. 77); another, formerly at the MMA, is now also privately owned (Comstock 1954, p. 191). Examples with alternate crests are at the Winterthur Museum (Richards and N. G. Evans 1997, no. 18) and the Chipstone Foundation (Beckerdite and A. Miller 2002, fig. 23); see also an I. M. Wiese advertisement in *Antiques* 120 (December 1981), p. 1464. There are three additional armchairs with a standard Gaines crest rail: one at the Winterthur Museum, described as "highly compromised" (Richards and N. G. Evans 1997, no. 217); and another shown in Barnes and Meals 1972, no. 4, which has had alterations; see also one with a broken crest rail advertised by the Candle Shop Antiques in *Antiques* 65 (June 1954), p. 455.

2. Other craftsmen are mentioned in Jobe 1993, pp. 296, 297, n. 9. Nancy Goyne

37. See also figs. 20, 30.

Evans has pointed out that channels of communication between John III and his father and brother in Ipswich, Massachusetts, very likely remained open, allowing for an exchange of design ideas (Richards and N. G. Evans 1997, pp. 31–32).

3. The front rail on three of the armchairs has the same design as that on cat. no. 36 (Comstock 1954, p. 191; Rodriguez Roque 1984, no. 75; Jobe 1993,

no. 77). That on two others is decorated in a scalloped pattern not seen elsewhere (Richards and N. G. Evans 1997, no. 18; and see also an I. M. Wiese advertisement in *Antiques* 120 [December 1981], p. 1464).

4. Comstock 1954, p. 191.

5. Rodriguez Roque 1984, no. 75; Jobe 1993, no. 77; and Richards and N. G. Evans 1997, no. 18.

38.
Splat-back armchair

Portsmouth, New Hampshire, or southern Maine, 1735–60

The back that has been grafted on this chair's William and Mary–style base is later in design than the type seen on cat. no. 35. It reflects Boston Queen Anne–style cabriole-leg chairs characterized by stiles that are not molded but flat on the front and by a yoke-shaped crest rail that is modulated but devoid of carved detail. On such chairs a portion of the rear legs—from a distance below the seat to the stretchers—is either rounded or has been given an octagonal shape by broad chamfers on the corners.[1] The latter treatment is recalled on the back legs of cat. no. 38: the rear corners are chamfered from top to bottom, but on the front the chamfers start about four inches below the seat, where the legs begin to cant backward, and the chamfer on the outer corner has a lamb's-tongue stop above the side stretcher. The serpentine outline of the stiles on this chair is somewhat shallow, and the splat has little curvature.

Several other chairs are known that share all of the above characteristics and also the following distinctive traits with cat. no. 38.[2] The most compelling feature is the front stretcher with its central ball flanked by large thin rings—a motif that on this chair is executed on a particularly bold scale. The pattern is uncommon in American furniture and finds its most dramatic expression on this group of chairs. Its source was no doubt English cane chairs, on which a ball flanked by rings occurs frequently in a more modest form at the center of medial and rear stretchers but exceptionally also in a larger interpretation on the front stretcher.[3] A peculiarity of the front-post turnings is that the element below each baluster does not have a rounded profile but consists of a cavetto above an ovolo. A further characteristic of this and related chairs is the use of an ogee molding on the upper edge of the side stretchers, which matches that on the lower edge of the stay rail.

Similarly molded stretchers, and feet that have the same strong outward sweep and sharp central ridge and are carved in the same schematic manner, are on an MMA table (cat. no. 55,

38

fig. 52), which is of a type attributed to the Portsmouth, New Hampshire, area. The chairs may have been made in the same shop.[4] They, like the table and also the Gaines chairs from the same region (cat. nos. 36, 37), represent a mid-level of production that provided furniture with a fashionable look but at a lesser price than contemporary high-style walnut pieces.

CONSTRUCTION

The joints of the seat rails and front and rear stretchers to the posts and of the arm supports to the arms have round tenons; rectangular tenons secure all other components. The joints of the arms, those of the stiles to the crest rail, and of the side seat rails and side stretchers to the posts are pinned. The side stretchers join the square rear legs at an oblique angle and meet the front legs, which have been planed on the back and outer surfaces, at a right angle; the tenon shoulders have been cut accordingly (see fig. 166). The front stretcher is made from 3-inch stock. The front feet are one piece with the legs, which have a section of bark running down the inside corner. A chamfer finishes the back edges of the crest rail (except for the central hollow) and of the rear posts and the front corners of the rear legs and feet. The side edges of the splat angle in toward the back.

CONDITION

The arms and the front and right seat rails are replacements, and the joint pins have been reset or renewed. There is a repair at the joint of the left stile to the crest rail, a fill on the outer side of the left stile where the stay-rail mortise broke through, and a round wooden plug on the outer side of the right front post where the front seat rail mortise broke through. Tack holes in the rear and left seat rails suggest the seat was at one time upholstered, and several nails and plugged holes on the front of the crest rail and top of the side stretchers indicate that fabric or padding may have extended beyond the seat. The front feet are chipped at the bottom. At some point the surface was not only stripped but also sanded, aggressively so in some areas. Records state that in 1933–34 modern varnish then on the chair was removed and the wood was finished with linseed oil and turpentine.

INSCRIPTION

At the Dey Mansion, Wayne, New Jersey (see *Exhibition*), an identification number was painted on the back of the crest rail.

WOODS

MAPLE; right front leg, SOFT MAPLE.

DIMENSIONS

OH. 41¾ (106); SH. 16½ (41.9); OW. (arms) 26¾ (67.9); SW. front 23¼ (59.1); SW. back 16⅞ (42.9); SD. 15⅝ (39.7).

EXHIBITION

On loan to the Dey Mansion, Wayne, New Jersey, from 1946 to 1999.

REFERENCES

Halsey and Cornelius 1932, fig. 26 (1938, 1942, fig. 30); Comstock 1942, fig. 1; Stillinger 1965, p. 192 (at Dey Mansion); Bishop 1972, no. 76.

PROVENANCE

Ex coll.: George Coe Graves, Osterville, Massachusetts.

The Sylmaris Collection, Gift of George Coe Graves, 1930 (30.120.72)

1. Richards and N. G. Evans 1997, nos. 7–10, for example. The shape of the splat, however, is the same as that on the type of chair represented by cat. no. 35.
2. Related are: a chair at the New-York Historical Society, New York City (acc. no. 1944.196), and one at the Rhode Island School of Design (Jobe 1993, ill. no. 46C [attributed to Portsmouth, New Hampshire, or southern Maine] and p. 219 ["a large group of related chairs"]); one advertised in *Antiques* 110 (December 1976), p. 1195, by M. Schorsch, one in *Maine Antique Digest*, August 1984, p. 25D, by Cobbs Antiques, one in *Antiques and the Arts Weekly* (Newtown, Connecticut), 6 August 1999, p. S43, by Hollis E. Brodrick, who knows of further chairs (telephone conversation with the writer, 14 April 2000), and one in *Catalogue of Antiques and Fine Art*, vol. 1, no. 6 (November–December 2000), p. 84, by Peter H. Eaton Antiques; and one offered in *Important Americana, Including Ceramics, Prints, Silver, Folk Art, Furniture and Carpets*, auction cat., Sotheby's, New York City, 15, 16, and 18 January 2004, lot 563. Dealer Teina Baumstone once had an armchair ("Shop Talk" 1957, p. 14).
3. American examples of ball-and-ring front stretchers, other than those on this group of chairs and the chair cited in n. 4 below, resemble in scale and overall design the medial stretchers on English cane chairs (Kirk 1967, nos. 215, 216; Lindsey 1999, no. 141; see also cat. no. 39). For this type of stretcher on English cane chairs with American histories, see I. W. Lyon 1891, fig. 68; Mooney 1978, fig. 3; Blackburn and Piwonka 1988, fig. 188.
4. A child's banister-back armchair with front stretchers related to the one on cat. no. 38 has a type of arm and finial associated with the Portsmouth region (Jobe and Kaye 1984, no. 88), confirming that this stretcher pattern was favored in that area.

Miscellaneous Furniture for Sitting and Reclining

The easy chair, fully upholstered except for the legs and stretchers, was introduced to the colonies in the early eighteenth century. Early examples—in the William and Mary style—are known only from Boston. The first fully developed type made there, which featured double-scroll arms, a high back with curved wings projecting from its sides, and a turned undercarriage, is illustrated by the chair that heads this chapter (cat. no. 39). The next stage in the stylistic development of the form, which is generally similar in design except for the short cabriole front legs that have taken the place of turned ones, is also represented in the collection (cat. no. 40). Easy chairs were expensive, for textiles were costly and the upholstering required considerable labor. They were found only in wealthy homes and were usually placed not in the parlor but in the best bedchamber, their fabric matching that of the bedhangings.

The form of seating that in well-furnished, affluent households complemented the chairs in the parlor or the best room—which customarily came in sets of six or twelve, sometimes augmented by an armchair—was a couch en suite with the chairs. The term "couch" referred in the early colonial period to either of two furniture forms. The kind of couch made to accompany seventeenth-century back stools was basically an extra-wide upholstered armchair with a hinged armrest at each end. It is a type rare then and now, of which only two colonial examples are known, neither in the Museum's collection.[1] According to Boston upholsterer Thomas Fitch, that form of couch was old hat by 1707—"as much out of wear as steeple crown'd hats."[2] In fashion was a type that resembled a chair with an elongated seat—now called a daybed—and that followed the style set by English cane examples. American couches made to compete with the cane imports had backs and turnings in the same designs as locally produced leather and banister-back chairs. Those that were joined had a canvas bottom to support a loose mattress or cushion, those of turned construction a rush bottom. The two couches included in this chapter are both turned and of a kind that is characteristic of Pennsylvania and notable for its robust turnings (cat. nos. 41, 42).

The settle, a bench with arms and a high back that extends down to the floor, was a much more ordinary piece, usually of board construction. It saw use in the kitchen or living hall and served to ward off drafts as well as for sitting or reclining. Settles, which had their origin in the Middle Ages, were present in colonial households from the earliest times, but none that can be securely dated to the 1600s has survived. A joined walnut and leather example in the collection, of a general type made in Pennsylvania during the first half of the eighteenth century, rises considerably above the merely utilitarian (cat. no. 43). The second settle here included (cat. no. 44), although it has a paneled back, illustrates in its overall design and construction the much more common board-sided pine settle, which was in widespread use into the nineteenth century.

Of the furniture designed specifically for sleeping, only one bedstead (turned) that stylistically dates distinctly within the early colonial period has so far been identified.[3] A bed's value lay in the textiles—hangings and bedding—that furnished it, which represented a major investment. The frames were generally of little value in comparison and appear to have been expendable. Joined oak cradles, preserved in part as family heirlooms, have had a better survival rate. The Museum's example, one of more than a dozen known, is among the less elaborate ones, but it is well proportioned and very carefully worked (cat. no. 45).

Cradles and chairs made of wicker—a distinct category of furniture—are both listed in seventeenth-century documents, but no example that is clearly American-made and from the early colonial period is known. Hardly any trace remains from that time of the lowest level of seating—plain utilitarian pieces of simple nailed board construction, such as settles, or stools and benches consisting of a plank or slab supported by stick legs.

---

1. Fairbanks and Trent 1982, no. 490 (Peabody Essex Museum); Forman 1988, no. 49 (Winterthur Museum).
2. Cited in Jobe and Kaye 1984, p. 317.
3. Fairbanks and Trent 1982, no. 297 (Museum of Fine Arts, Boston).

39.
Easy chair

Boston, 1715–30

The earliest known American easy chairs are in the William and Mary style and were made in Boston. This is one of a dozen examples that represent the first well-established Boston type: the proportions are tall, the undercarriage is turned, the wings have countercurves, and the arms are double-rolled with a horizontal outward roll on the armrest, a vertical one above the front leg, and a sloping curved connector between the two, all combining to form a large C-scroll. This fully developed easy-chair form with double-scroll arms was preceded by a stylistically earlier, short-lived model with arms that are squared in front and with a front stretcher, of which just two examples are known.[1] The type of chair illustrated by cat. no. 39 was probably first produced in the 1710s and is similar to Boston leather chairs with turned stiles in some design elements and to Boston cane and leather chairs with molded stiles in others. A few examples can be linked to Boston or its vicinity through traditional family histories.[2]

The bold outward movement of the prominent scroll arms that distinguish the standard William and Mary easy chair is countered on this example by the inward-curving sides of the crest rail. That rail with a high flat top that scrolls backward and the carved Spanish feet relate cat. no. 39 to cane and leather chairs with molded stiles (see cat. nos. 32, 33) and are its stylistically most advanced features. Two other easy chairs in this group have the same type of crest rail, and it may have been originally present and then lost on other examples. Spanish feet occur on all but four of the chairs (which have turned feet). Lacking on this piece but found on eight of the chairs under discussion is a scalloped front seat rail, a feature that relates specifically to contemporary cane chairs. All of the easy chairs use medial stretchers—an arrangement that is characteristic of cane chairs and found on a few Boston leather armchairs with a carved crest rail and turned stiles. Typically the side stretchers are turned in a symmetrical pattern (with either columnar or baluster shapes) so that the medial stretcher is positioned midway between the front and the back. With two exceptions, the medial and rear stretchers are baluster-turned in designs that are generically similar to those on the corresponding stretchers of the leather armchairs just mentioned and on the front stretchers of many leather chairs with turned stiles and plain tops (see cat. no. 26).[3] The most common scheme consists of a central ring flanked by short balusters, then half rings, long balusters, and half rings. On cat. no. 39 the formula is more abbreviated: a ball flanked by half rings centers elongated balusters (fig. 23).[4] Both of

these stretcher designs have their source in English carved tall-back cane chairs with turned stiles. On this and about half of the easy chairs in this group the joinery of the lower structure is conservative in that all of the stretchers terminate in blocks and rectangular tenons. An anomaly seen only on this example is the positioning of the rear stretcher level with the side stretchers rather than above them. In their profile, the rear posts of early easy chairs (including the type represented by cat. no. 40) correspond to those of leather chairs with turned stiles and carved crest rails such as cat. no. 27: the legs are vertical, and only the feet are raked to counterbalance the high, inclined back. The angle on this back is extreme and accentuated by the backward scrolling crest. The precarious balance of this tall back, offset somewhat by the unusually deep seat, makes a dramatic early Baroque statement.

Easy chairs were prestigious pieces, and this example with its high crest has an imposing presence. Featuring a padded back, wings, and arms, and a feather-filled seat cushion, the easy chair introduced a new level of seating comfort. Because of the cost of the textiles required for its upholstery, it was by far the most expensive form of chair available.[5]

CONSTRUCTION
The rear legs are vertical and the feet have a backward rake. The stiles are one with the legs and angle back at about 15 degrees from the vertical. The frame is secured almost entirely with rectangular mortise-and-tenon joints. The back of the front legs was planed so as to allow the side stretchers and side seat rails to join them at a right angle; at the back of the side stretchers and rails and on the medial stretcher the tenon shoulders were cut to accord with the oblique angle at which they meet the respective mortised members (see fig. 166). The crest rail is tenoned to the stiles; the wing rails to the stiles and wing uprights; and the wing uprights and rear scroll arm supports (which end in a roundel) to the seat rails. The joints of the medial stretcher are not pinned; those of the side and rear stretchers and rear scroll arm supports are single-pinned; and the others double-pinned. The armrests are nailed at the back to the wing uprights, and at the front they are nailed in place through the roundel of the rear scroll arm supports. The front scroll arm supports are formed by extensions of the front legs, which have been rounded on the inner side and have a vertical half-round section nailed to the outer face. The filler blocks between the arm supports are glued in place. The top of the crest rail is built out at the back with a half-round glued-on section. The corner brackets are separate from the seat rails. The feet were carved from glued-up stock.

CONDITION
On the visible frame, the feet have been shortened and the glued-on portions of the front feet have been lost. The finish is modern.

39

In 2000 the chair was stripped of all upholstery materials, and tacking rails that had been added at the bottom of the back and of each side when the upholstery foundation was renewed in 1968 were removed. Throughout the chair, most of the joint pins have been reset or replaced, and several are missing. The crest rail and the left rear scroll arm support have new tenons. The left half of the roundel of that arm support is replaced, and there are patches on the upper rear corners of the left wing rail, the outer surface of the left filler block, and the right front corner of the left front leg at the joint with the front seat rail. The corner brackets, with one possible exception, are replaced. Strips of glued-on fabric cover part of the wing-rail joints, and screws reinforce the joints of the armrests. The hidden frame has innumerable tack holes, many small losses, and some splits. The present upholstery, completed in 2005, is nonintrusive. The madder cover fabric is hand-woven wool (in a rep weave); the pattern of the trim, handwoven in matching wool and gold silk, is based on trim on a valance of about 1725 at the Peabody Essex Museum.[6]

WOODS
Front and rear posts, stretchers, rear seat rail, SOFT MAPLE; front and side seat rails, armrests, OAK; crest rail, left rear scroll arm support (and perhaps other elements of the hidden frame), BLACK TUPELO.

DIMENSIONS
OH. 48 7/8 (124.1); SH. 12 1/4 (31.1); OW. (arms) 32 1/8 (81.6); SW. front 27 1/2 (69.9); SW. back 23 5/8 (60); SD. 22 1/2 (57.2).

EXHIBITION
"In Quest of Comfort: The Easy Chair in America," MMA, 24 November 1971–30 January 1972.

REFERENCES
Andrus 1951, p. 247; Andrus 1952, p. 167; Schwartz 1958, pl. 5B; Comstock 1962, no. 43; Heckscher 1971a, fig. 1 (without upholstery); Heckscher 1971b (exh. cat.), no. 11; Butler 1973, p. 27; M. B. Davidson and Stillinger 1985, fig. 142.

PROVENANCE
Ex coll.: Mrs. J. Insley Blair, Tuxedo Park, New York.
   Mrs. Blair purchased the chair from Collings and Collings, the New York City dealers, in 1923. The chair was on loan from Mrs. Blair to the MMA from 1939 until it became a gift.

Gift of Mrs. J. Insley Blair, 1950 (50.228.1)

1. See Trent and Wood 2003, figs. 2, 3 (chair in a private collection; also in Forman 1988, fig. 186), and figs. 4–6 (chair at the Shelburne Museum, Shelburne, Vermont). A front stretcher occurs also on a chair with double-scroll arms (Lockwood 1913, fig. 507); since the chair is known only in a photograph, the age of the stretcher cannot be ascertained.
2. Chairs with histories are in the Bayou Bend Collection (D. B. Warren et al. 1998, no. F17), Museum of Fine Arts, Boston (Trent, Walker, and Passeri 1979; see also Fairbanks 1981, pl. VII), and Philadelphia Museum of Art (*Antiques* 120 [August 1981], p. 206 [John Walton advertisement]); and offered in *Important American Furniture, Folk Art and Decorative Arts,* auction cat., Christie's, New York City, 8 October 1998, lot 38. Others are in the Chipstone Foundation (*Important American Furniture, Folk Art and Decorative Arts,* auction cat., Christie's, New York City, 8 October 1998, lot 38, fig. 4), Colonial Williamsburg (Comstock 1963, p. 187), and the Winterthur Museum (Forman 1988, nos. 87, 88); shown in Lockwood 1913, fig. 507, and Forman 1988, no. 89 (formerly Winterthur Museum); and offered in *Fine Americana,* auction cat., Sotheby Parke Bernet, New York City, 27–29 April 1978, lot 920.
3. The exceptions (D. B. Warren et al. 1998, no. F17, and *Fine Americana,* lot 920; see n. 2 above) have the stylistically later type of stretcher arrangement and turnings seen on such chairs as cat. no. 40.
4. A similar central motif occurs on one of the chairs at the Winterthur Museum (Forman 1988, no. 88) and, with rings rather than half rings, on a chair similar to cat. no. 40 (*Sack Collection* 1981–92, vol. 1, p. 65).
5. For the origin of the form, upholstery, and usage of early easy chairs, see I. W. Lyon 1891, pp. 166–68; Trent, Walker, and Passeri 1979; Jobe and Kaye 1984, p. 366; Forman 1988, pp. 357–60; and Richards and N. G. Evans 1997, no. 78.
6. A. L. Cummings 1961, fig. 9.

39. See also fig. 23.

40.

Easy chair

Boston, 1730–40

This piece illustrates the second major stage in the evolution of the New England easy chair. The earlier scheme with double-scroll arms exemplified by cat. no. 39 has been updated in several ways, most tellingly with cabriole legs, a feature introduced in Boston about 1730 and characteristic of Queen Anne–style (late Baroque) design. The newer aesthetic with its predilection for flowing curves is reflected also in the lines of the crest rail. The undercarriage differs in that the medial stretcher is positioned toward the front and the joinery has been lightened: the front end of the side stretchers no longer terminates in a block, and the medial and rear stretchers are round-tenoned. Another structural difference as compared with cat. no. 39 is the addition of a tacking rail toward the bottom of the back.

Nearly a dozen easy chairs with double-scroll arms and related cabriole legs have survived. The legs are squared, and on many of them the edges are outlined with a groove. This type of cabriole leg is characteristic of chair designs devised when the Queen Anne style was just coming into fashion, as the retention of Spanish feet suggests. Similar legs occur on other forms of Boston chairs from this period.[1] The disposition of the stretchers and the manner of their joinery on this and almost all of the related easy chairs are the same as on some of the cane chairs of the general form represented by cat. no. 32 and are characteristic of Boston Queen Anne–style chairs, but not so the profiles of the medial and rear stretchers. These turnings nearly always correspond instead to those on the front stretcher of William and Mary–style chairs; they are either in the ring-and-ball pattern featured here on the medial stretcher or have a reel flanked by balusters (see cat. nos. 27, 34), a combination seen on the present rear stretcher in a somewhat modified version, in which the base of the vase form has been compressed to a near ball shape. The fact that both of these two basic William and Mary designs occur on the same chair (on this and several related examples) indicates that at least at this time in Boston the use of one or the other pattern was not shop-specific. The side stretchers are typically ornamented with balusters, with in some cases a ring and a reel at the back of the rear baluster, as on this example.

The combination of design elements on this chair and the variations among chairs in this group illuminate how stylistic changes in seating occurred through the accretion of small modifications to existing models. That a somewhat different mix of older and newer features is found in different chairs probably reflects the experimentation of several shops and

40

perhaps the passage of time. Three of these cabriole-leg chairs exhibit a high crest rail like that on cat. no. 39. Of those, one also has a scalloped skirt, common on easy chairs with turned front legs, and, in addition, variant stretcher profiles. On the one hand, another chair has a crest rail similar to that on this example but stretchers generally related to those on cat. no. 39. On the other hand, two easy chairs with turned front legs are fitted with the type of stretchers seen here. The present chair, which embodies all the stylistic elements common to most of the group, is one of only two distinguished by the use of walnut for the front legs and medial and side stretchers instead of the more common maple.[2]

CONSTRUCTION

The construction of this frame is similar to that of cat. no. 39 in many of its aspects, but there are also a number of differences. The rear and medial stretchers have round tenons (not pinned), and the rectangu-

40. See also fig. 89.

lar tenon (single-pinned) at the front of the side stretchers issues not from a block but from a tapered turning (fig. 89). The wing uprights are tenoned to the wing rails as well as to the seat rails (single-pinned). There is a rail joined to the stiles near the bottom of the back (not pinned). The armrests are rabbeted at the back to fit against the wing uprights. The filler blocks between the arm supports are nailed in place. The corner brackets on the front are integral to the seat rail. The front feet are each carved from a solid block and are of one piece with the leg. The right stretcher was made from an irregular billet that did not allow for fully squared-up blocks.

CONDITION

On the visible frame, a large portion of the right front foot has split off and been glued; both front feet are chipped at the bottom; and all four feet were at one time fitted with casters. The right stretcher has splits. The finish is modern. Throughout the chair, many of the joint pins have been reset or replaced. On the hidden frame, the tenon of the left rear scroll arm support, the outer two-thirds of the roundel on the corresponding right support, and the side and rear corner brackets are replaced (the last perhaps added), and the lower edge of the front seat rail has small patches. The inner edge of the top of the crest rail and of the front of the wings has been shaved. Later additions—tacking struts in front of the stiles, an extra rail at the bottom of the back, and inverted half cones nailed to the outer side of the front posts at the level of the seat rails—were removed in 1994 and have left their mark. In some of the heavily tacked areas the wood has been consolidated.

The modern green wool cover fabric, en suite with cushions and curtains of a period room in the MMA, is a tightly fitting slipcover over a nonintrusive foundation finished in muslin that was installed in 1995. The previous under-upholstery, removed because it did not have the proper contours, dated to about 1900. Evidence of the original, or an early, red wool fabric was found under old tacks.

WOODS
Front posts, side and medial stretchers, BLACK WALNUT; crest rail, lower back rail, probably left rear scroll arm support, BEECH; rear posts, front seat rail, SOFT MAPLE; remaining components, MAPLE.

DIMENSIONS
OH. 47½ (120.7); SH. 12¾ (32.4); OW. (arms) 32¾ (83.2); SW. front 28⅞ (73.3); SW. back 25¼ (64.1); SD. 20¾ (52.7).

EXHIBITION
"In Quest of Comfort: The Easy Chair in America," MMA, 24 November 1971–30 January 1972.

REFERENCES
Downs 1936; M. B. Davidson 1967, no. 94; Heckscher 1971a, fig. 2; Heckscher 1971b (exh. cat.), no. 12; Hornung 1972, no. 729.

PROVENANCE
The chair was purchased from Duval Dunn, Boston. The information published by Joseph Downs in 1936 (see *References*) that the chair had come from New Hampshire was probably received verbally; it does not appear in MMA records.

Harry Brisbane Dick Fund, 1935 (35.117)

1. For example, on cane chairs (Downs 1952, nos. 11, 12) and chairs with vase-shaped splats and upholstered seats (Richards and N. G. Evans 1997, nos. 1, 5).
2. Chairs with a high crest rail are in the Currier Museum of Art, Manchester, New Hampshire (Passeri and Trent 1987, figs. 6A–6E, with a scalloped front seat rail), Historic Deerfield (Fales 1976, no. 69), and the New Hampshire Historical Society, Concord (Bishop 1972, no. 38). Others are found in *Sack Collection* 1981–92, vol. 1, p. 65 (older-style stretchers), and Forman 1988, nos. 90–92 (Winterthur Museum; no. 92, walnut) and fig. 189; and advertised in *Antiques* 97 (March 1970), p. 305, by H and R Sandor, and in *Antiques* 130 (July 1986), p. 36, by Peter Eaton. For the two chairs with turned front legs and stretchers of the same type as cat. no. 40, see the entry for cat. no. 39, n. 3.

41.

Couch

Southeastern Pennsylvania, probably Philadelphia, 1710–40

The earliest style of Pennsylvania couch known is distinguished by a backrest with molded banisters and an arched and molded crest rail of the type seen here—a design that appears to have been peculiar to that region.[1] The backrest on such couches (as daybeds were called at that time) was hinged at the bottom so that its angle could be adjusted. Pennsylvania turned couches are remarkable for the vigor and heroic scale of their turned elements. The robust and shapely balusters, balls, rings, and reels on this example resonate with sonorous Baroque rhythms, and the solid cylindrical form of the legs recalls the substantial semicircle of the crest rail's arch. The profile of these legs—a cylinder with a vase form between the stretchers and the seat—is the most common one, as is the shape of the feet—a reel and a ball that tapers at the bottom (with the taper in this case almost entirely lost to wear). The turnings on these stretchers have one unusual detail: a ring between the ball and the end turnings (fig. 29). Also, while the cross stretcher at the head is most often plain like those between the middle legs, the one on this couch is ornamented.

The form of the finials was probably derived from the popular William and Mary–style urn-and-ball pattern and is found on several other couches of this type.[2]

Couches were often accompanied by a set of matching chairs, and their backs reflected current chair design. A back with a similar arched crest rail and molded banisters occurs on maple rush-bottomed chairs in the turned tradition and also on more expensive joined walnut examples with upholstered leather seats.[3] While the frames of couches such as this are entirely assembled with round tenons in the turners' manner, the head posts rake backward above the seat like those on joined chairs and the posts also show the influence of cane seating in that they have turned decoration below as well as above the seat. They were probably patterned on the head posts of imported English cane couches, which set the style and to which couches like cat. no. 41 were the local response. Most surviving examples are of maple and were designed to have a rush bottom, which was equipped with a squab covered in a fabric to suit the customer's taste and

41. See also fig. 29.

budget. More costly versions than the one seen here are also known: one of maple originally had an upholstered seat; one of walnut also has rectangular seat rails but was probably fitted with a canvas bottom to support a cushion.[4] The relationship with joined and cane seating suggests that the style of couch represented here had connotations of fashionability and was probably formulated in Philadelphia.

CONSTRUCTION

The couch's heavier elements are made from 2¾-inch stock. The frame is secured with round tenons; those that join the side seat rails and side stretchers to the head posts are pinned. The four middle legs are attached to the seat rails with through tenons. Those legs are each braced by two cross stretchers, the upper one just below the seat rails. The side seat rails are oblong in cross section; those at the head and foot are round like the middle transverse stretchers. The center side stretchers are placed higher than those toward the head and foot so that the mortises in the middle legs for the side and the lower cross stretchers can each be drilled at a different level and the strength of neither the legs nor any of the joints is compromised. The head posts cant backward above the seat. The backrest is assembled with

rectangular tenons; a pin secures those of the stiles and center banister. The backrest pivots on round tenons at the ends of the stay rail which are socketed in the head posts, and its incline can be adjusted by means of chains attached to the posts. The profile of the moldings on the backrest consists of a half-round flute flanked by half-round reeds. The top of the foot posts is finished with turned convex moldings and a button, as is the top of the finials.

CONDITION

The head and adjoining right side of the couch appear to have been damaged in an accident. The stay rail and the stiles of the backrest are replacements in walnut, and there are splits in the crest rail at the stile joints. The side stretcher connected to the right head post is new. A split in that post at seat level has been repaired with screws. The joints of the side seat rail and side stretcher in both head posts have been variously reinforced with new or added pins or a screw. The middle right leg toward the head is missing its tenon and is nailed and screwed to the seat rail. There are cracks and a replaced segment—all secured by nails—in the top 3 inches of the leg. The rush bottom is replaced, as are the chains for the backrest. A pair of small plugged holes on the back of each head post mark the location of staples that attached the original chains. On all but two of the feet the tapered turning at the bottom is completely worn off. The couch has been stripped, and traces of green paint remain on all but the replaced elements. The maple of the backrest has been finished to blend with the walnut replacements; the frame is generally lighter in color.

WOODS
SOFT MAPLE; seat rails, upper cross stretchers, RED OAK.

DIMENSIONS
OH. 37 3/8 (94.9); SH. (at foot) 16 5/8 (42.2); OW. (crest rail and foremost feet) 24 3/8 (61.9); SL. 67 3/4 (172.1).

PROVENANCE
Ex coll.: Harold M. and Cecile Lehman (later Cecile L. Mayer), Tarrytown, New York.

Bequest of Cecile L. Mayer, 1962 (62.171.23)

1. While this style of couch is usually not dated before the 1710s or 1720s, couches were in use before then; the form is first listed in Philadelphia probate records in 1693 (McElroy 1979, p. 65). The shop goods of joiner Edward Stanton, who died in 1689, included couch chains (McElroy 1979, p. 63). They may have been stocked for the repair of imported couches, but they also raise the tantalizing possibility that a type of couch earlier in design than cat. no. 41 was being made locally.

2. Similar finials are on a couch at the Philadelphia Museum of Art (*Philadelphia* 1976, no. 17) and one formerly in the Reifsnyder collection (*Sack Collection* 1981–92, vol. 7, p. 1696); and one included in *Hudson-Fulton Celebration* 1909, no. 64, and another in Hornor 1935, pl. 9. The first three have the same type of leg turnings as cat. no. 41 and also the middle side stretchers higher than the other stretchers. Other couches with arched crest rails are in Nutting 1928–33, no. 1618, Norman-Wilcox 1939, fig. 2B, and Blades 1987, no. 12; advertised by Willowdale Antiques in *Antiques* 108 (October 1975), p. 638, by Chalfant and Chalfant in *Maine Antique Digest*, December 1986, p. 44B, and by Indian Lane Farm in *Antiques and the Arts Weekly* (Newtown, Connecticut), 21 October 1988, p. 23; and offered in *Highly Important Americana from the Collection of Stanley Paul Sax*, auction cat., Sotheby's, New York City, 16–17 January 1998, lot 248.

3. For turners' chairs, see, for example, Nutting 1928–33, nos. 1953, 1954, and Lindsey 1999, nos. 148, 149. A joined walnut armchair with a leather seat is at Colonial Williamsburg (Kindig 1978, no. 11); a walnut armchair at the Winterthur Museum has a leather back and seat (Forman 1988, no. 82).

4. Lindsey 1999, no. 168 and fig. 179; the walnut example (Elder and J. E. Stokes 1987, no. 37) has leg turnings of a different character than those on other couches with the same type of back.

42.
Couch

Southeastern Pennsylvania, 1750–80

While settees had outmoded the couch form in fashionable parlors by the mid-eighteenth century, turned rush-bottom couches remained viable in Pennsylvania in less formal settings in both city and country for probably much of the remainder of the century—witness a reference to the production of "13 Rush bottom Chairs, & 1 Couch" in 1769.[1] The frames of couches basically did not evolve, remaining true to the general format established in the early 1700s (see cat. no. 41), but the design of the backrest was modified about the midcentury to reflect the yoke-shaped crest rails and vasiform splats of Queen Anne–style chairs (see cat. no. 35). As illustrated by this example, such crest rails typically took on generous proportions, in keeping with the substantial scale of the legs. The profile of the splats on this and several other couches is distinctive in that the shoulders of the vase are not rounded but angular. Splats of a similar outline occur on chairs that have been attributed to the Philadelphia shop of William Savery (1722–1787) and may have inspired the pattern seen here.[2] Although the turnings on this piece lack some of the assured vigor of the related forms on cat. no. 41, they are still entirely in the idiom of the William and Mary style and represent a long-lived tradition of turning that is manifest also in Delaware River valley slat-back chairs, in which it persisted at least through the end of the century (see cat. no. 16). The craftsman who produced this couch was working very much within the parameters of turned chairmaking: the head posts are straight members, and in order to have stiles that angle back, the entire posts were made to cant backward; they strive to emulate the joined-chair type of posts on cat. no. 41 also by having a block above and below the baluster on the stiles, but the blocks are finished in an idiosyncratic fashion—the vertical edges are chamfered on their full length rather than just on the corners as was standard practice—and below the seat the posts become turned chair legs.

CONSTRUCTION
The frame is assembled with round tenons. The joints of the side seat rails to the head and foot posts and of the side stretchers to the head posts are pinned. The four middle legs, which measure up to 3 inches in diameter, have tenons that pass through the seat rails and are pinned. At the head, the side seat rails extend about an inch further than the stretchers, causing the posts to angle backward. The backrest pivots on round tenons at the ends of the stay rail, which are socketed into the head posts. It is joined with rectangular tenons, and the joints of the two outer splats are pinned. A groove is worked a short distance in from the side and bottom front edges of the crest rail and of the upper front edge of the stay rail to create the effect of a bead molding. A broad chamfer finishes the back edges of the sides of the crest rail and splats and the vertical edges of the blocks on the head posts. The top of the foot posts and of the finials is finished with turned convex moldings and a button.

42

CONDITION

The two upper cross stretchers and the rush seat, all missing when the couch was acquired (see *References*), are new, and the splats, which were upside down and lacking joint pins, have been reversed and repinned. A large segment on the left side of the right splat is replaced. It may have been to facilitate that repair that a small section at the back of the right head post was cut out to expose the pintle on the stay rail and allow the backrest to be removed. The chains used to secure the backrest at the angle desired and the hooks in the posts are modern. The front of the ring on the baluster of the right head post is missing, and other turnings have lesser losses. Five of the feet retain stubs of a tapered turning at the bottom. The surface appears to have varnish over worn red paint.

INSCRIPTIONS

Inscribed in black crayon on the back of the lower block of the right head post are "16," within a circle, and "4 P" (both modern).

WOODS

SOFT MAPLE; seat rails, OAK.

DIMENSIONS

OH. 35⅞ (91.1); SH. (at foot) 14¼ (36.2); OW. (middle and foremost feet) 23¾ (60.3); SL. 67¾ (172.1).

EXHIBITIONS

On loan to the Art Institute of Chicago, Chicago, Illinois, from 1926 to 1933; "The Plenty of Pennsylvania," Museum of American Folk Art (now American Folk Art Museum), New York City, 9 December 1968–13 April 1969.

REFERENCES

Cescinsky and Hunter 1929, p. 74; Williams 1963, no. 20 (this and the previous reference show the couch as acquired).

PROVENANCE

The couch was purchased from N. D. Levin of Ye Old Curiosity Shop, Wilmington, Delaware. Its acquisition by the MMA was reported in the *Star* (Wilmington), for 23 July 1922 (MMA Archives). According to that newspaper account, the dealer had bought the couch from B. H. Davis of Milford, Delaware, in whose family the piece had been "for many years."

Rogers Fund, 1922 (22.126)

1. Quoted in Hornor 1935, p. 58.
2. Similar splats are on a couch at the New-York Historical Society, New York City (acc. no. 1944.201), and one at Wright's Ferry Mansion, Columbia, Pennsylvania (Bacon 1991, fig. 26); and on one advertised by Leon F. S. Stark in *Antiques* 91 (January 1967), p. 27. For chairs, see Forman 1980, figs. 15, 19, and *Sack Collection* 1981–92, vol. 2, p. 527.

43.

Leather settle

Southeastern Pennsylvania, 1710–40

Joined settles made of walnut and leather appear to have been produced only in Pennsylvania. While they varied considerably in some elements of their design, they were generally configured to shield the sitter from drafts; their high backs were either covered in leather or paneled, and protection below the seat was provided by extending the back down to the feet, as it is here, or by enclosing the front and sometimes also the sides, usually with paneling. The seat was normally of leather. How rare or common it was to have a seat with under-upholstery is uncertain. The original leather on a settle at the Winterthur Museum is a single large hide simply nailed to the frame of the back and seat, as was in all probability the case on this piece. On another example the original leather seat has foundation upholstery. The latter treatment may be the exception, since that piece, built with a space between the seat and the back and an open frame below the seat, is closer in form to a seventeenth-century couch than to a traditional settle.[1]

In its tall canted back and the overall design of its arms and turnings this settle relates to paneled chairs from southeastern Pennsylvania, such as cat. no. 20. In details of the turnings the piece exhibits several particularities: the baluster pattern on the arm supports consists of a clearly defined reel above and below a ball shape; there is a distinct reel on either side of the fat ring or very flattened ball on the legs and side stretchers; and the ovolos that adjoin the blocks are scored with a groove. The arm supports are not as heavy as usual because they end in a conical turning and not a block. The arms, with a deep bow in the middle, subtle tapering in thickness toward the handgrip, and molded detailing, are more refined than most. Identical arms occur on an idiosyncratic paneled chair that shares one other trait with cat. no. 43 not observed elsewhere—rear feet that curve in on the front surface.[2] What above all sets this settle apart is the use of a longitudinal brace between the side stretchers and the lack of a front stretcher—an arrangement not noted on any other settle and one not characteristic of Pennsylvania paneled chairs. Medial stretchers, generally used in conjunction with a front stretcher midway up the legs, are identified with more fashionable seating, such as cane chairs and related types of leather chairs. The configuration of the stretchers on this imposing piece and the design of the arms, arm supports, and rear feet all serve to lighten what is usually a massive furniture form and to give it a certain stylishness. The maker of cat. no. 43 appears to have been familiar with high-style seating, whether he worked in Philadelphia or in a nearby county.

CONSTRUCTION
The settle is made of heavy stock; the seat rails are nearly as thick as the 2¼-inch posts. With the exception of the front posts, which are joined to the arms with round tenons, the frame is secured with rectangular mortise-and-tenon joints, which are close to ½ inch wide and pinned. The back is framed with only a crest rail and a seat rail. The lower back is enclosed by a board that is attached to the rear of each leg with one long dovetail reinforced with T-headed nails; at the top, the board fits against a rabbet on the bottom of the seat rail, to which it is nailed. The dip in the arms is delimited at the back by a broad ovolo worked on the upper surface and at the front by a similar ovolo on the upper side and a narrow one on the underside. An ovolo finishes the bottom edge of the front and side seat rails. The front of the rear legs curves in at the bottom to form a foot. The leather is nailed to the frame without any under-upholstery.

CONDITION
The crest rail, rear seat rail, and medial stretcher are noticeably warped, and there are cracks throughout the frame. Large splits in the left front post and left handgrip have been repaired variously with screws (hidden by fill), nails, and wooden dowels. A good half of the right rear leg is pieced 8½ inches up from the bottom. A front-to-back center brace nailed to the underside of the seat rails is modern. Nail holes suggest there was a previous center brace, but there is no visible evidence that the seat originally had any braces. The frame has a modern finish.

The leather of the seat is replaced and does not entirely hide from view large nail holes near the upper edge of the side seat rails. The leather of the back, which has repairs to splits and losses on the left side, is original. At the top and sides it is fastened to the frame with wrought-iron nails; the narrow trim strip, which has breaks and losses and is attached with brass nails of various types, looks old. At the bottom of the back the leather has been cut down; it is nailed to the front of a slat that has been added above the seat rail, and that is screwed and nailed to the top of the rail through the seat leather; the trim strip and modern brass nails at the bottom of the back match those around the edge of the seat. Since the back was built without a lower rail, the back and seat were probably originally covered by a single hide that was simply nailed to the top of the rear seat rail to effect a change in plane, as is the case on the settle at the Winterthur Museum previously mentioned.

INSCRIPTION
A modern inscription in white chalk on the underside of the seat leather and front seat rail reads: "91" or "1b."

WOOD
BLACK WALNUT.

DIMENSIONS
OH. 45½ (115.6); SH. 16¾ (42.5); SW. 73½ (186.7); SD. 18 (45.7).

43

REFERENCES
"Early American Furniture" 1935; Downs 1945, p. 67; "Antiques in the American Wing" 1946, p. 249, no. 14; Downs 1946, fig. 3; Comstock 1962, no. 10; Bishop 1972, no. 56; Chinnery 1979, fig. 2:157.

PROVENANCE
Ex coll.: Mrs. J. Amory Haskell, Red Bank, New Jersey.

Gift of Mrs. Henry M. Post, Mrs. Lewis E. Waring, and Amory L. Haskell, in memory of their mother, Mrs. J. Amory Haskell, 1945 (45.46)

1. The Winterthur Museum settle has boards a short distance below the seat leather (Forman 1988, no. 43); there is no evidence of such boards on cat. no. 43. For the settle with under-upholstery, see Lindsey 1999, no. 109 and fig. 10. Other settles with leather backs include two belonging to the Chester County Historical Society, West Chester, Pennsylvania, one of which converts to a bed (Snow 1957, p. 64), and one at the York County Heritage Trust, Museum and Library, York, Pennsylvania (R. Davidson 1968, p. 54). Those with paneled backs include one at the Chester County Historical Society dated 1758 (Schiffer 1966, ill. no. 21) and one at the Winterthur Museum (Forman 1988, no. 42); one shown in Nutting 1928–33, no. 1634; and one advertised by Joe Kindig Jr. in *Antiques* 49 (March 1946), inside front cover. Examples of both types are in private collections.

2. Lindsey 1999, no. 144 and fig. 143.

44

44.

Settle

Mid-Atlantic region or New England, 1725–1850

With a high back that extends down to the floor and sides partly enclosed, settles were designed to ward off drafts and were generally placed by the hearth, where they also helped contain the fire's heat. The use of settles from the seventeenth century on is well documented, but none attributable to the 1600s have survived.[1] However, the underlying plan of pine settles made of nailed board construction remained the same throughout the two centuries and more when they were produced, so that the essential elements of this furniture form can be illustrated by this later example. The basic formula consists of having two high end boards serve as feet, provide arms, and support the seat and back. The outline of those end boards largely determines the design of such a piece. This settle is notable for the assured, well-balanced lines of those boards and hence of the overall form. On the front, the curve of the bracket for the top is echoed by the nearly circular handgrip and the arc of the arm by that of the cutout forming the feet. The top is angled, and at the rear of the settle the cant of the upper back is countered by a smart rake below the seat, which gives stability to the piece.

Cat. no. 44 belongs to a category of settles having a frame with fielded panels (rather than plain boards) that is attached to the back of the sides above the seat.[2] Some of them, like this one, also have a board across the top to create a hood. Settles with such backs, which relate to room paneling, were probably not produced before the second quarter of the eighteenth century, when fielded panels came into common use in interior woodwork, and they were made in both New England and the mid-Atlantic region. This example has several distinguishing features, but what significance they may have in terms of its date or place of origin is unclear. The profile of the molding on those edges of the stiles and rails that surround the panels is not the standard quarter-round usually found on eighteenth-century paneled woodwork (see cat. no. 82) but consists of a small ovolo followed by a fascia of the same width. The back is anomalous structurally in that its mortise-and-tenon joints are not pinned. Two further particularities of this piece are a seat board attached with tenons that pass through the side boards and a front seat rail with a half dovetail at each end. The last two traits can be observed also on a settle of the same type at the Winterthur Museum and one at the Museum of Fine Arts, Boston.[3] Benno M. Forman associated both of these features, and a third one present on those two settles—joints of the paneled back secured by two pins that are staggered rather than in line—with Germanic traditions of craftsmanship and hence probable manufacture in Pennsylvania. This piece lacks joint pins, and it should be noted that a front seat rail with half dovetails appears to have had wider currency, for it is found as well on a settle with a Connecticut history.[4] All in all, cat. no. 44 offers no stylistic or structural clues that in the present state of knowledge clearly point to an origin in a particular locality.

CONSTRUCTION

The settle is made of 1-inch-thick boards, except for the thinner top and panels. The hood board is nailed to the top of the back and sides. The framework enclosing the panels of the back has mitered mortise-and-tenon joints (see fig. 164), which are not pinned. It is attached to the back of each side with four screws and is nailed to the seat. The seat board has three tenons at each end, which pass through the sides, and it is nailed to the front seat rail. The ends of the front seat rail are cut to a half dovetail, which fits into a recess on the front edge of the sides and is nailed in place. The lower back, composed of a seat rail joined by tongue and groove to a board that extends to the floor, is nailed to the sides. Those nails throughout the settle that look original are sprigs. The lower front edge of both the front and the rear seat rails is finished with a bead.

CONDITION

There is a small patch at the back of the top board and a long one along the lower edge of the bottom back board. The bottom of both side boards is cracked and chipped, and a split near the front of the left board has been repaired with nails. Several of the structural nails

are added or replaced. Some of the screws attaching the upper back look old, others are modern; whether or not they are all replacing nails is not clear. The settle has been stripped but retains extensive residues of green paint, which does not appear to be original.

WOOD
EASTERN WHITE PINE.

DIMENSIONS
OH. 59 (149.9); SH. 17 (43.2); SW. 83½ (212.1); SD. 17¾ (45.1).

REFERENCES
Comstock 1962, no. 9; Williams 1963, no. 18; Bishop 1972, no. 55.

PROVENANCE
Ex coll.: Mrs. J. Insley Blair, Tuxedo Park, New York.

Gift of Mrs. J. Insley Blair, 1947 (47.103.13)

1. The basic function served by settles is reflected in a 1667 Boston inventory listing of "one pine settle to sett before the fyar" (quoted in Forman 1988, p. 192). The "bed settle" included in the 1659 probate inventory of Samuel Corwithy of Marblehead [?], Massachusetts, and the "old settle chest" recorded three years later in that of Thomas Antrum of Salem, Massachusetts, show that multipurpose settles in addition to those meant exclusively for seating were being made early on (George Francis Dow, ed., *The Probate Records of Essex County, Massachusetts,* vol. 1, *1635–1664* [Salem, Mass., 1916], pp. 276, 414).
2. Other examples are at Historic Deerfield (Fales 1976, no. 195), the Museum of Fine Arts, Boston (Randall 1965, no. 191), and the Winterthur Museum (Forman 1988, no. 44). They are shown in I. W. Lyon 1891, fig. 92, Nutting 1921, p. 309, Nutting 1928–33, no. 1625, Jeffcott 1944, fig. 12, and Kirk 1967, no. 260; and advertised inside the front cover of *Antiques* 48 (December 1945) by Joe Kindig Jr., in *Antiques* 111 (March 1977), p. 447, by Gary C. Cole, and in *Maine Antique Digest*, February 1995, p. 44D, by Samuel Herrup.
3. Forman 1988, no. 44; Randall 1965, no. 191.
4. Kirk 1967, no. 260.

45.
Cradle

Suffolk County, Massachusetts, 1640–90

Seventeenth-century cradles owe their survival at least in part to the fact that they were regarded by nineteenth-century antiquarians as symbols of our colonial heritage—relics treasured for their association with the Pilgrims and other early settlers. A cradle exhibited in the New England Kitchen at the Centennial Exposition in Philadelphia in 1876 received much attention because of a tradition (apocryphal) that it had rocked Peregrine White, the first child born of English parents in New England.[1] Of the dozen or so joined cradles from New England known, more than half have come down with histories in early families. The most elaborate

in design are five associated with Plymouth Colony, Massachusetts. They are all distinguished by a hood that incorporates spindles, and three of them have, in addition, a railing with spindles. One of the latter, which descended in the Thatcher family of Yarmouth, is a virtuoso piece of joinery composed of twenty-two panels and a multitude of turnings. A cradle that originally had a fully paneled hood with a top with sloped sides and that has been linked to the Pynchon family of Springfield, Massachusetts, represents a different joined type, two other examples of which have ties to Connecticut.[2]

This is one of several cradles with protective sides at the head but no actual hood. It was not made as a showpiece but was joined with care and finished in a very workmanlike fashion both inside and out. Its design is essentially a well-balanced arrangement of nine horizontal panels (in four sizes), their rectilinearity countered by the curves of the rockers and turned finials. The ornament is one that is basic to joined case furniture of the period: channel molding on the framing members and neat chamfering of the edges that surround the panels. A virtually identical cradle at the Old State House–the Bostonian Society, Boston, descended in the Minot family of Dorchester, Massachusetts. It matches cat. no. 45 closely in dimensions, joinery, profile of the turnings, and pattern of the channel molding; it differs only in that the edges around the panels are not chamfered on the interior of the piece. A cradle of similar overall form but with four new posts and other replacements and a history in Newbury, Massachusetts, has the same type of channel molding.[3] The molding on the present cradle and the Minot piece—a convex band flanked by fillets—is very close in contours and dimensions to that on a stool in the MMA collection (cat. no. 21) and, more importantly, to that on several case pieces that have been attributed to the Savell shop in Braintree, Massachusetts (see cat. no. 71). The writer has not observed that molding profile on any objects other than those mentioned just above, and it is possibly peculiar to that shop tradition.[4] On the basis of the Minot piece and its Dorchester history and the apparent links of that and this cradle to the Savell school of joinery, the cradle with a Newbury history notwithstanding, the present piece is here attributed to Suffolk County, Massachusetts, which in the seventeenth century was more extensive and encompassed Braintree.[5] It may be significant that the progenitors of the Minot and Savell families in Massachusetts probably emigrated from the same place in England.[6]

CONSTRUCTION

The cradle is framed with carefully worked mortise-and-tenon joints. The holes for the pins that secure the tenons at a right angle to one another are drilled at approximately the same height so that the pins more or less bisect; the pins come through at a broad chamfer on the inner corner of the posts. The posts, made from 2-inch stock, are notched at the bottom to straddle the rockers, which are held in place with wooden pins. The cradle bottom (now four transverse boards) rests on the inner upper surface of the $1\frac{1}{2}$-inch-thick bottom rails; the original bottom was not nailed in place. A channel molding is worked on all four upper rails of the body and on the muntin on each side. The framing members are chamfered along the edges that surround the panels on both the interior and exterior of the piece, and all surfaces except the inner side of the bottom rails (left with rough hatchet marks) are well finished.

CONDITION

The cradle bottom (white pine), the rockers (birch), and the stretcher (oak) between the rockers are all replacements. A section at the bottom of each head post is also replaced. Nearly all the joints have been apart and some of the pins are new. The foot panel and the two main panels of the right side have cracks and have buckled. There are losses on the knobs of the finials on both foot posts. The surface appears to have been oiled and waxed.

INSCRIPTIONS

Nearly all the framing members and panels are incised with reassembly marks (one to four small notches), which date from a time of repairs. More recent restorer's marks in pencil match up the bottom end rails, posts, and rockers. MMA Hudson-Fulton exhibition identification numbers (H. F. 40.6 and, in a circle, B/461) are inscribed in orange crayon on the underside of the bottom.

WOOD

WHITE OAK.

DIMENSIONS

OH. $28\frac{1}{2}$ (72.4); OW. (rockers) 24 (61); W. body 17 (43.2); L. $37\frac{1}{8}$ (94.3).

EXHIBITION

"Hudson-Fulton Exhibition," MMA, 20 September–30 November 1909.

REFERENCES

Hudson-Fulton Celebration 1909 (exh. cat.), no. 85; Nutting 1921, p. 316; Halsey and Cornelius 1924 (and 1925, 1926), fig. 18 (1928, 1932, fig. 17; 1938, 1942, fig. 8); Nutting 1924, no. 599 (called "perhaps English"); Davis 1925, p. 5; Halsey and Tower 1925, fig. 5; Cornelius 1926, pl. V; Nutting 1928–33, no. 1576B; Cescinsky and Hunter 1929, p. 44; Williams 1963, no. 23; Shea 1975, p. 102; Schwartz 1976, no. 20; M. B. Davidson 1980, fig. 73; M. B. Davidson and Stillinger 1985, fig. 15.

PROVENANCE

Ex coll.: H. Eugene Bolles, Boston.

Gift of Mrs. Russell Sage, 1909 (10.125.672)

1. Roth 1964, p. 60 and fig. 6. For the purported history of this cradle, now at the Wadsworth Atheneum (Hosley 1984, pl. XI), see Nutting 1921, p. 314.
2. The Plymouth Colony cradles have histories in the Thatcher (Jobe and Kaye 1984, no. 136), Cushman (Hosley 1984, pl. XI), Hinckley (Cullity 1994, no. 144), and Noyes (St. George 1979b, no. 39) families, and one (Monkhouse and Michie 1986, no. 159) was apparently found in Abington, Massachusetts. For the Pynchon cradle, see *Great River* 1985, no. 74; for the two similar to the Pynchon example, see Nutting 1928–33, nos. 1565, 1566.
3. The Bostonian Society cradle (acc. no. 1979.0006) has not been published. The writer thanks Robert Blair St. George for bringing it to her attention. It first came to the society in 1908 as a loan from a member of the Minot family, with a history of having been brought from Saffron Walden, Essex, England, by George Minot, one of the founders of Dorchester. The wood has been identified by microanalysis as red oak. The other cradle, with a history in the Plumer family (Benes 1986, no. 14), is in a private collection and has not been examined by the writer.
4. For the case pieces, see Follansbee and Alexander 1996, figs. 1, 2, 9, 21, 22. Because of wear on the moldings of the cradles it is difficult through normal measuring to determine how exactly they match the molding on the stool or on the case pieces.
5. It seems more likely that a cradle made in the Boston area or a joiner trained there would find the way to Newbury than vice versa. Another cradle with a Newbury history (Little family) is of a different design (Benes 1986, no. 15).
6. William Savell Sr. probably also came from Saffron Walden, Essex (Follansbee and Alexander 1996, p. 81).

45

II.

TABLES

Tables with a Stationary Top

The early colonial tables in the collection fall into two broad categories: those having a fixed top, included in this chapter, and those having a top with hinged leaves, grouped in the one that follows. The earliest form of American table with a stationary top to have survived from the seventeenth century has a massive joined frame with substantial turned legs braced by solid rectangular stretchers, a type that came into general use in England in the mid-1500s. Long joined tables of this kind, of which only a few American examples are known and none is in the collection, were the standard form of large table used for dining in the colonies for most of the 1600s. Traditionally accompanied by stools and "forms" (elongated stools), such tables, some of considerable length, were either freestanding or used along a wall with a fixed bench. The latter arrangement, common in the Middle Ages, is documented in an Ipswich, Massachusetts, contract of 1659 that specified the making of "a table and frame of 12 to 14 foot Long and a joyned forme of 4 foot Long and a binch Behind the table."[1] This general category of heavy joined table is represented in the collection by two examples from Massachusetts that are square in format and adorned with brackets and pendants under the rails—a type in favor in England in the first half of the seventeenth century (cat. nos. 46, 47). Ornamented all around, as were most square tables, and originally also embellished with graining, they were meant to have pride of place at the center of the room. The prime table at the start of the chapter is a stylistically late example of the type (cat. no. 46). Its maple legs have baluster turnings with an ogee outline—a profile introduced with early Baroque design in the late 1600s. The frame of the second square table, which is made of oak and with straight-sided balusters on the legs, is entirely within the seventeenth-century style, though not necessarily of earlier manufacture (cat. no. 47). The general design of turned legs joined by four rails and perimetric stretchers (commonly called box stretchers) served in the seventeenth century also for the frame of smaller tables—usually rectangular and sometimes with a drawer—and was a basic formula that continued in use in succeeding centuries.

A type of small rectangular table made only in the late seventeenth and early eighteenth centuries, of which three examples are here included, introduced a new scheme: the stretchers are turned and in a distinctive arrangement of a high front and rear stretcher combined with low side stretchers joined by a medial one. The turnings on the legs and stretchers of such tables correspond to those on contemporary joined chairs; they are either in a seventeenth-century-style repeat ball pattern or in a design that features William and Mary–style ogee balusters. A good number of these tables, most of them with ball turnings, like the two from Massachusetts in the Museum's collection (cat. nos. 48, 49), are ornamented with brackets in the manner of the square tables, and many, decorated all around, were also meant to be freestanding. A third example, from Pennsylvania (cat. no. 50), is the only early colonial table in the collection that incorporates a design element outside the Anglo-American tradition; its top is attached in a manner associated with Germanic craft practices. Its frame and that of one of the Massachusetts tables has been lightened by the elimination of the medial stretcher. Overall, however, it was the use of high longitudinal stretchers that was short-lived, for they made sitting at this kind of table impractical; it was the low "H" configuration that persisted throughout the eighteenth century and later as an alternative to the more conservative box stretchers. A New York table with drawer illustrates the latter arrangement (cat. no. 51). Larger in scale than the previous three tables and meant to stand against a wall, its legs exhibit urn-and-baluster turnings, a type of design favored in New York in the first half of the eighteenth century.

Large tables with stationary tops began to be outmoded for dining during the last third of the seventeenth century as the fashion of dining on oval tables with hinged leaves gained momentum. Consequently William and Mary–style tables with fixed tops are primarily small, many of them easily portable. A common type has a frame with splayed legs similar to that of joint stools, and the distinction between stool and table is not always clear (cat. nos. 52, 53). The tops on such frames were most frequently oval. Many oval tables of this kind were without pretension (cat. no. 54), but more elaborate versions of this form, which sport scalloped skirts and carved feet and of which a fine representative is in the collection (cat. no. 55), were made in Portsmouth, New Hampshire, and vicinity. Oval or round tops were the preferred shape on other types of frames as well (cat. nos. 56, 57).

Tables listed in early colonial household inventories, when they are qualified in any way, are most often described by their shape or size. The shape noted is that of the top: long, square (a term that was probably applied to any square-cornered form), round, or oval. "Little," "small," or "great" indicated the size. Occasionally tables were described as joined or framed, which were interchangeable expressions. In fact, all the objects in the table section and virtually all tables that have survived from this period—aside from William and Mary–style dressing tables of the type included in the case furniture section, which are a breed apart—are of joined construction, their rails and stretchers solidly secured to the legs with rectangular mortise-and-tenon joints.

1.   Quoted in Forman 1968, p. 27.

46.
Square joined table

Probably Boston or vicinity, 1680–1710

A rare surviving example of a distinctively seventeenth-century form of joined table, this piece has a massive square frame with four turned legs and rectangular perimetric stretchers and is ornamented with brackets and pendants. It is of a type that was being made in England by the early seventeenth century; a table generically similar in design at Chastleton House (Oxfordshire) is probably one of those listed in the "Great Parlor" and "great Chamber" of that house in an inventory of 1633.[1] In the colonies such tables, which were decorated on all four sides and thus designed to be freestanding, were doubtless also destined for the best room. That this one was meant to make a stylish statement is supported by its embellishment with graining that simulates an exotic wood and probably originally contrasted with pendants that were ebonized.

The most notable feature of this table is the graining, which is still largely intact on the upper frame (fig. 76). Painted with series of parallel wavy lines, it has the same general character as graining on case furniture from eastern Massachusetts dated to the late seventeenth or the early eighteenth century (see cat. nos. 110, 141), and it is one of several traits that indicate that cat. no. 46 is a late expression of this table form. Also pointing to a date of manufacture within this time period are the profile of the leg turnings and the use of maple and pine instead of oak in the frame. While the scheme of the turnings is generically the same common seventeenth-century one of an elementary vase form embellished with an astragal or ring seen on cat. no. 21, they reflect the influence that early Baroque design was beginning to exert in the late 1600s. The vase has been given a definite ogee shape, and it no longer extends upward to a cylinder flanked by rings but to a more modulated ring-reel-ring sequence. In fact, these turnings are not far removed from those on the legs of cat. no. 59, a Boston table with falling leaves. The distinct cavetto under the ring at the top of the ogee vase form, a fine point on the legs of this table, is an uncommon detail at this time. It is not present on a closely related table at the Milwaukee Art Museum, Milwaukee, Wisconsin, which never had graining or has lost it. The frames of these two tables are virtually identical not only in design but also in construction, down to the size and shape of the joint pins, and they were undoubtedly made in the same shop.

The Milwaukee table has a replaced top, and so it can shed no light on the possible authenticity of the two wide oak boards that now constitute the top of cat. no. 46 or on whether the original top was of oak or of another wood, given the maple and pine used for the frame. The two American square tables of this type that retain their original tops are totally within the seventeenth-century-style tradition, and they are made entirely of oak. Their tops consist of narrow, riven boards held by cleats on the cut ends, and they have a straight vertical edge, as do most tabletops of the early colonial period.[2] The broad ovolo molding on the long edge of the boards on this table is out of character, but it could have been added. The boards are not of riven but of tangent-sawn oak (see fig. 150). This does not, however, de facto preclude them from being original, for such wood does on occasion occur on New England furniture of the later seventeenth century.[3]

CONSTRUCTION

The frame, square in plan to within ¼ inch, is built of heavy stock, with the posts 3 inches and the rails up to 1½ inches thick. The

46. See also fig. 76.

mortise-and-tenon joints of the rails and stretchers are a good ½ inch wide and secured, respectively, with two and one large round pin. The brackets are separate and joined to the legs with tenons half that width, which engage narrow extensions of the rail mortises and are secured with one small square pin. A wrought nail fastens the bracket tip to the underside of the rail. The top, composed of two wide tangent-sawn boards 1 inch thick, is pinned to the legs. It is supported by a medial brace that has beveled ends that fit into a recess at the top of two opposite rails. The lower edge of the rails and both upper edges of the stretchers are finished with a cyma reversa molding. Areas of torn grain were left standing on the visible as well as the hidden surfaces of the stretchers.

The graining on the frame is executed in black on a brownish red ground that contains an iron oxide pigment. It is composed of series of four parallel squiggly lines, which are so consistently parallel that they must have been applied simultaneously with four brushes.

CONDITION

The boards of the top (red oak) are warped, heavily worn, and stained, and one has a full-length split. The cleats on the ends of the top boards are new; they were put on at some point between the time the table was first published in 1921 and when it was photographed in Mrs. J. Insley Blair's house in about 1935 (see *References*). During the same interval, probably when the cleats were added, the boards were removed from the frame, partly replaned on the underside to counteract warpage, and repinned to the legs turned 90 degrees from their previous orientation so that the grain now runs perpendicular to the medial brace. The boards show signs of age, but with the changes that have occurred, it would be difficult to prove that they are original. Two brackets have broken off and four others have splits or losses; one pendant is missing. The feet have lost some height.

The graining on the rails, brackets, and upper legs has in large part survived, and there are clear remains on one stretcher; on the rest of the frame it has been almost entirely effaced. In the early photographs mentioned above, much of the surface looks dark and the graining is barely discernible. Subsequently and before a 1950 MMA photograph, the surface appears to have been cleaned.

WOODS

One leg, SOFT MAPLE; remaining legs, pendants, MAPLE; rails, brackets, EASTERN WHITE PINE; stretchers, ASH; medial brace, RED OAK.

DIMENSIONS

OH. 29½ (74.9); top: W. 41⅜ (105.1), D. 39⅜ (100); frame: W. 33 (83.8), D. 32¾ (83.2).

REFERENCES

Nutting 1921, p. 407; Nutting 1924, no. 772; Nutting 1928–33, no. 877; Andrus 1951, p. 244 (this and the following three references show the table cleaned); Andrus 1952, p. 165; Schwartz 1976, no. 18; M. B. Davidson and Stillinger 1985, figs. 130 (detail of graining), 131; Heckscher 2000, pl. II (in Mrs. Blair's house about 1935).

PROVENANCE

Ex coll.: Ross H. Maynard; Mrs. J. Insley Blair, Tuxedo Park, New York.

Mrs. Blair purchased the table in 1921 from Collings and Collings, dealers in New York City. In letters written in 1933 she identified Maynard as a collector and in recent years a dealer, then living in Vermont but formerly of Boston (see also the entry for cat. no. 130).[4] The table was on loan to the MMA from Mrs. Blair from 1939 until it became a gift.

Gift of Mrs. J. Insley Blair, 1949 (49.155.1)

1. Marsden 2000, fig. 10 and pp. 31, 32, 38. See Chinnery 1979, pl. 7, for a grained square English table original to a library of about 1620. Other American tables include those at the East Hampton Historical Society, East Hampton, New York (exceptionally, with turned stretchers; Graybeal and Kenny 1987, pl. VI), Historical Society of Old Newbury (Fairbanks and Trent 1982, no. 177), Milwaukee Art Museum, Milwaukee, Wisconsin (Jobe et al. 1991, no. 7), and Wadsworth Atheneum (Nutting 1928–33, nos. 824, 825 [detail top]), and there are at least two in private hands. See also cat. no. 47.
2. See n. 1 above for the Milwaukee Art Museum table and for those with original tops at the Wadsworth Atheneum and Historical Society of Old Newbury.
3. See the entry for cat. no. 58.
4. Letters to Irving P. Lyon of 29 January and 6 February 1933 (Lyon Family Papers, box 7, Downs Manuscript Collection, Winterthur Museum).

47.
Square joined table
Southeastern Massachusetts, 1670–1700

The turnings on the legs of this square table follow a common seventeenth-century pattern that features a simplified vase, here quite straight-sided, that terminates at the neck with an astragal or a ring followed by a short columnar section; the vase form may be inverted, as in this case, or narrow toward the top as on cat. no. 21. The particular interpretation of this generic design seen here is distinctive because the columnar segment is not a cylinder but an extension of the vase's taper. The turnings relate closely to those on a group of chests-on-frame, represented in the collection by cat. no. 106, that have been attributed to southeastern Massachusetts—probably the Hingham-Scituate area—with the small difference that on this table's longer legs the midsection of the vase is ornamented with a shallow convex band flanked by thin grooves instead of with just one or more grooves. The fact that the channel molding on this piece, though slightly wider, is analogous in profile to that on cat. no. 106 strengthens the proposition that this table comes out of the same or a related shop tradition and probably also originated in the coastal area of Massachusetts south of Boston.

47

Although there is clear structural evidence that the table was meant to have decorative brackets—separate, as on cat. no. 46, and not integral to the rails as is sometimes the case—the present brackets raise questions in terms of their design, apart from considerations of physical signs of age or lack thereof. They are the only ones known on a square table of this type that are pierced. Solid and probably somewhat deeper brackets, which would give the table more mass and visually anchor it more solidly to the ground, would seem more in keeping with the character of the frame, which is otherwise entirely within the seventeenth-century design aesthetic. Graining, now almost entirely obliterated, once also enhanced this table. It is in a pattern not otherwise encountered by the writer. Instead of being applied in series of squiggly lines, as on cat. no. 46, for instance, or in swirls, as seen on some other late-seventeenth-century pieces, it is painted with parallel lines in a zigzag design, the continuous strokes often forming loops where they change direction.[1]

CONSTRUCTION

The rails are joined to the legs, which are a good 2¼ inches thick, with just ¼-inch-wide rectangular tenons. The ends of the brackets, which have been reduced to a ¼-inch thickness by beveling the back surface, engage extensions of the rail mortises and are single-pinned; the tips of the brackets are nailed to the underside of the rails. The joints of the stretchers are 7/16 inch wide; they are double-pinned like those of the rails. The holes for corresponding pins at a right angle to one another in a leg are drilled at approximately the same height, and some of the pins intersect. The channel molding on the rails is composed of a small cyma reversa at either side of a narrow recessed band. A shallow ovolo is worked along the bottom edge of the rails and on both upper edges of the stretchers. The inner side of the rails was roughly dressed with a hatchet and left unsmoothed; on the inner side of the stretchers, hatchet marks were planed but not entirely removed. The graining, executed in reddish brown paint, was applied directly to the wood; the paint has not been analyzed.

CONDITION

The top (pine) is a replacement and is loose. There are two sets of pins in the top of the legs and pin holes and broken pins in the top of two opposite rails. The frame has been apart and the joint pins reset or replaced. All four pendants are new, as are four of the brackets. The other four brackets are older. They appear to have been off and reattached—at any rate, the tips have been renailed—so that physical evidence that could help determine if they are original has been lost. The feet, except for the ring turning at the top of one, are MMA restorations. Records indicate that in 1937 modern varnish then on the table was removed and the wood was finished with linseed oil and turpentine. Traces of graining, varying in extent and degree of visibility, remain on the upper leg blocks, along the bottom of one rail, and on the inner side of the stretchers. The surface also retains scattered residues of red paint, which are sometimes partly under a dark coating.

WOOD
Frame, WHITE OAK.

DIMENSIONS
OH. 28½ (72.4); top: W. 41 (104.1), D. 38⅜ (97.5); frame: W. 30¾ (78.1), D. 30½ (77.5).

EXHIBITION
On loan to the Pierce-Hichborn House, Boston, from 1950 to 1981.

REFERENCES
Halsey and Cornelius 1924 (and 1925, 1926), fig. 16; Cornelius 1926, pl. III (this and the preceding reference show the table before MMA restoration); Halsey and Cornelius 1928 (and 1932), fig. 13 (1938, 1942, fig. 7).

PROVENANCE
Ex coll.: H. Eugene Bolles, Boston.

Gift of Mrs. Russell Sage, 1909 (10.125.105)

1. For an example of swirls, see *Sack Collection* 1981–92, vol. 6, pp. 26, 1592–93. In all three types of design, the graining was applied with several brushes at a time.

48.
Joined table with drawer

Probably Boston or vicinity, 1680–1710

Rectangular tables such as this, with a high stretcher at front and back and low side stretchers connected by a medial brace, represent a format that is peculiar to the late seventeenth and early eighteenth centuries and has English antecedents. The arrangement of the stretchers—an unusual one for a table— is identical to that on some English joined and cane chairs of about 1660–80, and one can speculate that it was simply transposed from one form to another—a reasonable supposition, since joined chairs and tables appear to have been made in the same shops.[1] This type of table was usually equipped with a drawer, and the top, contrary to the replacement with leaves on this example, was fixed and had a greater overhang on the ends than on the front and back. More often than not, the lower edge of the rails was shaped, generally to form brackets at the corners, as on the front and rear rails of this table, or had applied brackets (see cat. no. 49). When the rails were finished or ornamented on all four sides as they are here, the piece was designed to be freestanding. Such tables were made with turnings both in repeat ball patterns, in use since the middle of the seventeenth century, and in ogee baluster shapes, introduced at the end of the century and typical of the William and Mary style. While most examples have been attributed to New England, the form was not unknown in Pennsylvania (see cat. no. 50) and possibly the South.[2]

This table's turnings belong to the seventeenth-century design tradition, and so do its squarish proportions and deep rails incorporating brackets (see cat. no. 46), which give the piece a low-slung solidity characteristic of that style (compare with cat. nos. 49, 50). The ball turnings are not executed in the standard Boston manner exemplified by two MMA chairs, cat. nos. 23 and 24, for instance; they are not as spherical and are more closely stacked, and they bluntly abut the blocks with a full or truncated ball rather than being articulated at that juncture with a thin disk or partial ring. The table's leg and stretcher turnings do, however, have a close affinity to those on several chests-on-frame that are part of a group of such pieces distinguished by front panels that usually have canted upper corners and were decorated with a painted flowering tree or branch motif. Such chests-on-frame are thought probably to have been made in and around Boston, and so it is likely that this table originated in that area. The construction of its missing original drawer might have corroborated such an attribution.[3]

CONSTRUCTION
The table, its legs measuring 2⅛ inches and its rails a good 1 inch thick, is joined with 5/16-inch tenons. The joints of the side and rear rails are secured with two pins and the others, with the exception of those of the medial stretcher, which were left unpinned, with one. The present drawer supports are level with the top of the front rail, as were the original ones; there is no evidence that the table ever had a side-hung drawer. The outline of the lower edge of the back rail matches that of the front rail.

CONDITION
The top, drawer, and drawer runners (all pine) are replacements. The present top has a leaf at the front and the back hinged to a fixed

48

center board that is pinned to the legs. Support for the front leaf is provided by partly opening the drawer; the back leaf, when up, rests on a pivot support that was made by sawing out a rectangular section from the upper half of the rear rail and pintle-hinging it at top and bottom. The feet have been cut down and have some losses. There is a small split at center bottom of the front rail and what appear to be large insect boreholes at the bottom of the left rail. The runners and the inner side of the rails have been stained. Records indicate that in 1937 modern varnish then on the table was removed and the wood was finished with oil and waxed. There remain traces of red paint, sometimes under white, and many residues of black paint or a degraded finish.

INSCRIPTIONS
One large compass circle and two smaller partial circles are scribed on the outside of the back rail. A segment of the large one goes across the section of the rail that is now the pivot support.

WOODS
Right front leg, SOFT MAPLE; remaining legs, front, side, and medial stretchers, MAPLE; rails, RED OAK; rear stretcher, ASH.

DIMENSIONS
OH. 26½ (67.3); top: W. 36½ (92.7), D. open 36½ (92.7), D. closed 20⅛ (51.1); frame: W. 23¾ (60.3), D. 18¼ (46.4).

REFERENCES
Nutting 1921, p. 421; Halsey and Cornelius 1924 (and 1925, 1926), fig. 17 (1928, 1932, fig. 14; 1938, 1942, fig. 15); Nutting 1924, no. 766; Cornelius 1926, pl. XI; Cescinsky and Hunter 1929, p. 57; "Antiques in the American Wing" 1946, p. 247, no. 12; Fales 1972, no. 6; Hornung 1972, no. 860.

PROVENANCE
Ex coll.: H. Eugene Bolles, Boston.

Gift of Mrs. Russell Sage, 1909 (10.125.114)

1. For English tables of this type, see Chinnery 1979, figs. 3:175, 3:242, pl. 15; and Kirk 1982, nos. 1226, 1227. For the same stretcher scheme on chairs, see Symonds 1951, p. 8, no. II, p. 9, nos. III, IV; and Kirk 1982, nos. 688, 689, 693.
2. More than two dozen tables of this type have been noted by the writer. Examples in public institutions include those in the Bayou Bend Collection (D. B. Warren et al. 1998, no. F21), Brooklyn Museum, Brooklyn, New York (Stayton 1990, p. 47), Colonial Williamsburg (Fairbanks and Bates 1981, p. 63; attributed to possibly South Carolina), the Dallas Museum of Art, Dallas, Texas (Venable 1989, no. 2; attributed to the Delaware River valley, possibly Philadelphia), Henry Ford Museum (Lockwood 1926, fig. CXI), and Wadsworth Atheneum (Nutting 1928–33, no. 854).
3. For related turnings, see Lockwood 1913, fig. 236; *Sack Collection* 1981–92, vol. 6, p. 26; *Currier Gallery of Art* 1995, no. 33; D. B. Warren et al. 1998, no. F27. For the attribution of these chests to Boston, see Forman 1970, pp. 12, 14, 15; and Monkhouse and Michie 1986, nos. 21, 22.

49.

Joined table with drawer

Boston, 1690–1710

A very elegant example of its type (see cat. no. 48), this table is clearly a Boston product by virtue of its sophistication and the nature of its turnings. The ball turnings, which terminate in just a thin disk at the juncture with the blocks, are identical to those on Boston upholstered chairs such as cat. no. 23, and the same mind-set that elongated the spherical turnings at the center of the front stretcher on the chairs is evident in the slightly greater length accorded the central turned element of the front and back stretchers on the table. While repeat ball turnings are a standard seventeenth-century-style pattern dating back to the mid-1600s, this table, with its animated interplay of spheres and blocks, echoed in the circles and squares of the brackets, has a vitality that bespeaks early Baroque design. So does the relative lightness of the form, with its shallow drawer, pierced brackets, and lack of the lower medial stretcher that is usually found on this type of table.

The cast-brass hardware on the drawer, particularly the escutcheon with a cherub's head, adds a very stylish touch. The manner in which the escutcheon is attached, however, is not the most refined. It is secured with two small iron rosehead nails through voids in the casting (fig. 116) rather than with small brass nails—apparently not available to the maker—that would fit through the three holes provided. The escutcheon design is one found on late-seventeenth-century English marquetry pieces, and thus was clearly fashionable, but it is very seldom encountered on American furniture.[1] It is also noteworthy for the similarity that the cherub's head bears to cast heads on the handle terminals of contemporary colonial silver tankards. That English or Continental cast ornament for furniture probably provided the models for these tankard appliqués was put forward by Marshall B. Davidson in 1940, but examples of such imported cast decoration on American furniture are extremely rare.[2] The drawer front was, in addition, originally embellished with painted floral sprigs (see *Condition* and fig. 75). While decorative painting other than graining has survived on Massachusetts case furniture of this period, this is the only known table that offers evidence of such painting (for graining, see cat. nos. 46, 47).

A piece this elaborate would have been used in a parlor or perhaps in a dining room as a side table—in either case, very probably in the company of similarly turned upholstered chairs. With brackets and moldings on all four sides, it was designed to be freestanding, but what purpose it was intended to serve is uncertain. The height of the long stretchers precludes anyone's sitting at the front or back of the table; a sitter can only be accommodated at the ends, and wear on the side stretchers indicates such usage. The impractical stretcher arrangement, which limits the serviceability of this type of table, very likely was a factor in the short-lived popularity of the form.

CONSTRUCTION
The frame is joined with standard mortise-and-tenon joints. The legs and stretchers are made from 2-inch stock, and the riven, somewhat wedge-shaped, side and rear rails are nearly that wide at their thickest. The top is a single board that is pinned to the legs. It has a cleat attached to each end of the board with three T-headed nails, and the ends of the cleats fit against projecting corners of the board in a miter joint. All four sides of the top are finished with a shallow half-round molding worked on the perimeter of the upper surface and an adjoining one run on the vertical edge. A single such half-round is on the applied molding around the bottom of the rails. The eight brackets are nailed to the legs and rails. Each drawer side is joined to the front with one large dovetail; the back is butted to the sides and secured at each end with a single rosehead nail. The bottom, one longitudinal board, is beveled to fit into a groove in the front and is nailed to the sides and back. The drawer rides on its bottom and was never fitted with a lock. The runners are let slightly into the legs and nailed, and thin guides are nailed to the side rails.

CONDITION
The top and the drawer pulls and escutcheon are original, and so are probably the brackets, four of which have lost the bottom of the roundel. Nails have been added to two brackets, the applied molding, and the drawer runners. The drawer back has a gnawed top edge, and the drawer bottom a knothole. The left front foot and the front of most of the block above it are replaced, and the right rear foot has losses. All feet have been cut down and retain sockets from added casters. The table is covered with a dark coating composed of several layers of degraded varnish. It retains traces of red, black, white, and some green paint. Because the table was stripped, it has been difficult to determine from cross sections how many times it was painted or the distribution or layering of the colors. That the drawer front was originally decoratively painted was discovered by accident: X-radiographs taken to confirm that the hardware was original revealed the outlines of floral designs in a radiopaque pigment (probably lead white or red lead) still in the wood pores (fig. 75).

INSCRIPTIONS
The exterior of the left drawer side is scored with a vertical line and that of the right drawer side with a large X. On the underside of the drawer bottom are series of chalk numbers, perhaps accounts, partly effaced.

WOODS
Legs, stretchers, brackets, SOFT MAPLE; rails, drawer front and sides, drawer runners, RED OAK; top, drawer bottom and back, drawer guides, applied molding, EASTERN WHITE PINE.

49. See also figs. 75, 116.

DIMENSIONS
OH. 26¼ (66.7); top: w. 40¼ (102.2), D. 21¼ (54); frame: w. 32⅞ (83.5), D. 18½ (47).

REFERENCE
Williams 1963, no. 31.

PROVENANCE
Ex coll.: Mrs. J. Insley Blair, Tuxedo Park, New York.

According to Mrs. Blair's notes (ADA files), the table was bought in 1925 "from Mr. Louis Hurd, who found it in Connecticut."

It was on loan from Mrs. Blair to the MMA from 1939 to the time of the bequest.

Bequest of Mrs. J. Insley Blair, 1951 (52.77.53)

1. For English pieces, see Macquoid 1905, figs. 48, 52, 54, 120. According to Macquoid (1905, p. 60), escutcheons with a cherub's head were introduced in England about 1690. A walnut cabinet-on-frame at the Winterthur Museum is the only other American piece with such an escutcheon known to the present writer (Forman 1987, fig. 13).
2. M. B. Davidson 1940.

50.
Joined table

Southeastern Pennsylvania, 1690–1720

The manner in which the top is attached to the frame—by dovetailing cleats to the underside of the top and securing them to the end frame rails—is a northern European method of construction that is associated in American furniture primarily with craftsmen of Germanic background working in Pennsylvania.[1] Strengthening a Pennsylvania attribution for this table are the exclusive use of walnut and the similarities between the table's turnings and those on paneled chairs from southeastern Pennsylvania, such as cat. no. 20. The stretchers on these two pieces are related in their overall character and vocabulary of opposed ogee balusters, rings, and reels; moreover, the chair's front stretcher and the table's upper stretchers are virtually identical in length. Also, the same type of flattened ball set off by deep hollows found on the table legs occurs on the legs and at the end of the front stretcher of the chair. The table's turnings exhibit two distinctive features: a fillet between the block and the adjoining ovolo on the legs and stretchers and a foot with a narrow neck that terminates in a prominent thin ring just above a ball (or baluster). The general scheme of this foot, which is a cognate of that on cat. no. 9, seems to be northern European in origin, like the structure of the top.[2] The vigor of the turning on these feet suggests that the maker was working with a design that was still fresh in his mind at the time it was executed. In sum, the table appears to be the work of an immigrant German craftsman making an Anglo-American form (see the entry for cat. no. 48) that reflects both his background and the idiom of a transplanted English

regional chair tradition (see the entry for cat. no. 20). The end product is distinguished by the vitality of its composition and boldly turned forms.

CONSTRUCTION
The rails and stretchers are joined to the legs, which are made from 2¼-inch stock, with mortise-and-tenon joints that are nearly ½ inch wide. The joints of the rails have a haunched tenon and only an outside shoulder, and they are single-pinned like those of the stretchers. The top, composed of a wide and a narrow board, has a cleat toward each end attached to the underside with a sliding dovetail joint (see fig. 158) that stops short of the intended front edge of the top (at the back in the present photograph) so as not to be visible on that side. The cleats are secured to the outer side of the end rails each with two large rosehead nails. One of the rails has been lightly rabbeted to accommodate the cleat. The edge of the top is finished all around with a half-round molding and the bottom edge of all four rails with an ovolo; the outer edges of the cleats are broadly chamfered.

CONDITION
At some point in time, no doubt because the top boards had warped and become detached, modern screws and nails were added to secure the top boards to the legs and rails and the cleats to the boards. In 1979 the top was taken off for restoration by removing all nails and screws. The holes left in the top and cleats by the added screws and nails were plugged and the joints of the cleats to the top boards reinforced in a hidden manner. The only holes found in the top of the legs and rails were those from the added elements, confirming that the original method of attachment of the top to the frame was with two nails through each cleat into the respective rail. The top was reattached in this manner, using the three existing large old wrought

50

nails and one replacement. Both legs at one end of the table are racked, and all the feet have been cut down. The end stretchers are heavily worn. The top is scratched and stained. The frame is somewhat uneven in color with areas of lighter and darker finish, and there is black spatter on the rails and cleats.

WOOD
BLACK WALNUT.

DIMENSIONS
OH. 28½ (72.4); top: W. 31¾ (80.6), D. 19¼ (48.9); frame: W. 22⅝ (57.5), D. 14⅜ (36.5).

REFERENCES
Nutting 1921, p. 420; Nutting 1924, no. 775; Nutting 1928–33, no. 820.

PROVENANCE
Ex coll.: B. A. Behrend, Brookline, Massachusetts; Mrs. J. Insley Blair, Tuxedo Park, New York.

Mrs. Blair bought the table from the dealers Collings and Collings, New York City, in 1923. According to her notes (ADA files), it had been found in Pennsylvania. The table was on loan from Mrs. Blair to the MMA from 1939 until the time of the bequest.

Bequest of Mrs. J. Insley Blair, 1951 (52.77.52)

1. Forman 1983, pp. 110, 112, 115 and figs. 63–65.
2. For related feet on a northern German and a Dutch chair, albeit of a later date, see Schwarze 1979–81, vol. 2, fig. 15; and Deneke 1979, fig. 25. Similar feet are on a French Canadian chair (Palardy 1965, no. 273).

51.
Joined table with drawer

New York, 1700–1740

Urn-and-baluster turnings have long been associated with New York, for they are featured on the monumental, oft-illustrated table with hinged leaves at the Albany Institute, which was published as early as 1901. It and four other tables with such turnings can be linked to New York by their histories; all except one, which has a rectangular fixed top, are oval with hinged leaves.[1] Sources for the urn-and-baluster design are to be found in England—on table legs or on the stiles of some cane or banister-back chairs, where the pattern is part of a complex sequence of forms.[2] At least seven distinct interpretations of this basic scheme can be observed on New York tables. In three of them, differences are restricted to the shape of the baluster and of the urn and to whether there is just a reel below the baluster or, in addition, either a small ring or a flattened ball. Two versions in which there is a ring above the urn and one version with that added ring and a ball above the baluster are known.[3] The legs on this table present yet another variation. It is distinguished by the profiles just below the upper leg block. Instead of the turned element at the very top of the leg being a ring or an ovolo, as was common practice, there are, from the top down, a flat band or fascia, a cyma recta molding, and a fillet (fig. 37). A similar fascia is worked at either end of the center block of the medial stretcher and at the top of the feet. The motif of a double-ended baluster that occurs on the stretchers is also a recognizable New York form. On the medial stretcher it is compressed and used in conjunction with a long ogee baluster, as it is on cat. no. 65, an oval table with hinged leaves. A more expanded double-ended baluster ornaments the side stretchers and is recalled in the full shape of the feet. A particularity of all the legs and stretchers is that the corners of the blocks on those members were left nearly square.

With its carefully executed turnings and generous proportions, this is a substantial piece—an impression that could not but have been stronger when the table retained its original top and probably brass drop drawer pulls. It was designed to stand against a wall and may have served as a writing or dressing table. Fitted with low stretchers in an H-configuration, it can readily accommodate a sitter, unlike the stylistically somewhat earlier form of rectangular table with a drawer that has a high front and rear stretcher and is found primarily in New England (compare cat. no. 49). It is also deeper. The large majority of New York tables with early Baroque turnings belong to one of several types that are oval and have hinged leaves (and include some examples that, like

this piece, are made of cherry). Rectangular tables with a drawer from this period with turnings that are characteristic of New York are few.[4] Given the idiosyncrasies of cat. no. 51, its maker was probably working outside of the New York City area and may not have been producing tables on a regular basis. The large scale of the cyma reversa molding on the front and side rails is unusual, as is the fact that on the side rails it is an applied molding and not worked from the solid wood. Also anomalous is the single-pinning of the joints of the side and rear rails.

CONSTRUCTION
The stock of the frame is substantial, with the legs, stretchers, and left side rail $2\frac{1}{8}$ inches thick and the right rail nearly that size. The drawer front measures $1\frac{1}{4}$ inches thick. The tenons that join the frame are $\frac{7}{16}$ inch wide and are all single-pinned. The attachment of the original top was with a pin into each leg. The drawer, which rides on the bottom, has two dovetails at each corner; on the rear joints, the tails (the flaring tenons that resemble a dove's tail) are on the end of the drawer back rather than on the end of the side, as was generally the case. The bottom is secured to a rabbet in the front and sides and to the underside of the back. The top and sides of the front were made to angle in, and the upper edges of the sides were chamfered. There is a drawer guide on the inside of the right frame rail. The entire front of the rail under the drawer is a cyma reversa that was worked with two planes, one with a hollow and one with a round profile. A strip identical to that rail is secured with rosehead nails to the underside of each side rail.

CONDITION
The top, composed of five boards (sweet gum), is a replacement. It was once pinned to the frame and is now secured with angle irons. The frame has been apart, and many of the joint pins look replaced. At some point in time between 1912 and 1939, as indicated by MMA photographs taken in those years—most likely in the 1910s—the table was "improved" with the addition of a front and back stretcher identical and parallel to the medial one. (The 1912 photograph [see *References*] shows no evidence of mortises in the lower leg blocks at those locations.) The added stretchers were removed in 1980; the mortises were filled with cherry and the joint pins left in place. The rear two-thirds of the drawer sides have been pieced at the bottom, and the top of the front, sides, and back has been planed down. The original drawer bottom was nailed; the current one is attached with wooden pins and is formed of two newer narrow boards at the back and an old board at the front, which may be original but reset. The top of the front rail has been patched at each end. The drawer runners and the guide are replaced, as are the knobs, which do not match. The drawer was probably first fitted with drop pulls. The table has been stripped. Records indicate that in 1933–34 modern varnish then on the table was removed and the wood finished with linseed oil and turpentine.

51. See also fig. 37.

INSCRIPTIONS
Modern restorer's reassembly marks (Xs in pencil) are on the inside of the back rail and rear legs. A Dey Mansion identification number (see *Exhibition*) is written in ink on cloth tape under the right rail and twice directly on the drawer.

WOODS
Legs, stretchers, rails, applied moldings, drawer front, CHERRY; drawer sides and back, ASH; old board of drawer bottom, YELLOW POPLAR.

DIMENSIONS
OH. 27³⁄₈ (69.5); top: W. 42¹⁄₈ (107), D. 28 (71.1); frame: W. 34¾ (88.3), D. 23⁵⁄₈ (60).

EXHIBITION
On loan to the Dey Mansion, Wayne, New Jersey, from 1946 until 1978.

REFERENCES
Cescinsky and Hunter 1929, p. 63 (1912 photograph); Stillinger 1965, p. 191 (at the Dey Mansion; with added stretchers).

PROVENANCE
Ex coll.: H. Eugene Bolles, Boston.

Gift of Mrs. Russell Sage, 1909 (10.125.110)

1. The Albany Institute table is in Singleton 1900–1901, vol. 1, facing p. 260, and Kenny 1994, fig. 15 and pp. 126–27—two among many possible references. The other tables are in Kenny 1994, fig. 18 and pp. 127–28, fig. 20 (for history, see *Fine American Furniture, Silver, Folk Art and Decorative Arts,* auction cat., Christie's, New York City, 19 October 1985, lot 155), fig. 21; and Fairbanks and Bates 1981, p. 65.
2. See, for example, *Antiques* 120 (July 1981), p. 59 (Benjamin Ginsburg advertisement), and R. Edwards 1964, p. 124, fig. 34.
3. For the first three variants, see Kenny 1994, figs. 15, 20; Kenny 1994, figs. 18, 19; Kenny 1994, fig. 21, and Fairbanks and Bates 1981, p. 65. For other variants, see Greene 1996, p. 29 (ring above urn); Henry Ford Museum (acc. no. 30.834.3; ring above urn); and private collection (ball above baluster). While urn-and-baluster turnings are identified with New York, they are not entirely exclusive to that area (Jobe and Kaye 1984, no. 59).
4. For a full discussion of the oval tables with hinged leaves, see Kenny 1994. For rectangular tables with a drawer, see Fairbanks and Bates 1981, p. 65, and *Important Americana, Including Silver, Folk Art and Furniture,* auction cat., Sotheby's, New York City, 11 October 2001, lot 310 (both with perimetric stretchers); D. B. Warren et al. 1998, no. F22 (with H-stretchers). For a table with H-stretchers but no drawer, see Scherer 1984, no. 2.

52

52.
Small joined table

Rhode Island, 1720–50

Turnings of the type seen here—consisting of a baluster with a bulbous base and a long thin neck over a ball shape, the two separated by a ring or disk—are found on more than a dozen small tables with fixed tops and some fifteen oval tables with hinged leaves (see also cat. no. 63) and have been attributed to Rhode Island. This is one of several pieces with such turnings that are larger than a traditional joint stool but not any higher, or only slightly so, and were probably intended as low tables or stands rather than seats, though in practicality they could serve as both.[1] On the small tables as on those with hinged leaves, variations occur in the interpretation of the basic design, indicating the hand of more than one turner. The particular version of the pattern on this piece differs significantly from that on cat. no. 63, for example. Notably, the element between the baluster and the ball shape is a quite thick ring (which has lost some definition through wear) rather than the elegant, flat-bottomed disk seen on cat. no. 63 and several other tables or the thinner ring with a sharper profile otherwise characteristic. As executed here, the design

resembles the ring-and-ball front stretchers on contemporary Boston cane and leather chairs (see fig. 26)—but truncated and stood on end. The turnings on this and two other tables of similar form and scale lack the ring or astragal that normally enriches the baluster's long neck, but they conform to those on most other tables in the whole group in that they terminate at the blocks with a fillet rather than an ovolo.[2] Overall, the profiles on this piece lack the crispness and flair of those on cat. no. 63 and are somewhat pedestrian in comparison, but what the turnings may be wanting in finesse is partly offset by the smart rake of the legs.

CONSTRUCTION
The frame, secured with standard mortise-and-tenon joints, has legs that are strongly splayed in two opposite directions (about 9 degrees from the vertical). The outer corner of each leg block has been finished with a small chamfer. There are variations in thickness between and within the individual rails and stretchers. Evidence of mill sawing remains on the inner side of three of the rails.

CONDITION

H. Eugene Bolles had this table restored and the top "sawed through lengthwise to take out the warp" (Bolles notes, MMA Archives). The top, now in three glued sections and attached to the long rails, is narrower than when the object was published in 1891 (see *References*). It is probably a replacement. The upper surface shows patches of deteriorated wood, large fills, and plugged holes where it is now attached to the rails and was previously pinned to the legs. The frame has been apart and reassembled with new pins that caused splits and losses in the upper leg blocks. A split at the bottom of a long rail has been repaired with a modern nail. The feet have been cut down and are chipped at the bottom. The finish is modern.

INSCRIPTIONS

A printed paper label that came loose from the underside of the top (ADA files) reads: "Included in the collection of Antique Furni-/ture transferred to Mr. H. E. Bolles, and Mr. / Geo. S. Palmer." It is inscribed in ink (script) at the top "Spread Leg table." and signed in ink at the bottom "Walter Hosmer." A small paper sticker with the printed number 187 is on the underside of one corner of the top. Modern restorer's reassembly marks (roman numerals) are incised in some of the rails, stretchers, and legs.

WOOD

SOFT MAPLE.

DIMENSIONS

OH. 21½ (54.6); top: W. 26 (66), D. 14¾ (37.5); frame: W. 20 (50.8), D. at top 11¼ (28.6), D. at feet 18 (45.7).

REFERENCES

I. W. Lyon 1891, fig. 102; Hjorth 1946, fig. 11.

PROVENANCE

Ex coll.: Walter Hosmer, Hartford, Connecticut; H. Eugene Bolles, Boston.

Bolles and his cousin George S. Palmer, of New London, Connecticut, purchased Hosmer's collection in 1894.

Gift of Mrs. Russell Sage, 1909 (10.125.327)

1. Stool-like tables with the most closely related turnings are one at the Winterthur Museum (acc. no. 58.566) and one shown in *Antiques* 147 (April 1995), p. 498 (David A. Schorsch advertisement). Other tables are two at the Winterthur Museum (acc. no. 58.567 and one shown in Trent 1999, fig. 19); four published in Nutting 1928–33, nos. 1233, 1254, 1255, 2723; one shown in *Antiques* 101 (June 1972), p. 939 (Sotheby Parke Bernet advertisement); one offered in *The Contents of Thorntree, Mendham, New Jersey*, auction cat., Christie's, New York City, 11 June 1985, lot 95; and several unpublished examples. For the tables with hinged leaves, see the entry for cat. no. 63.

2. The two other tables are the first two listed in n. 1 above.

53.
Small joined table

New England, 1720–50

The pattern of the turnings and the tall, narrow proportions of cat. no. 53 suggest it was intended as a small table or stand rather than a stool, although the basic structural formula is the same. Legs with opposed baluster turnings are characteristic of New England tables of the first half of the eighteenth century and not typical of stools, and the relatively thin stock of the present legs corresponds to that of small tables of the period. Also, the splay of the legs is less than that usually found on stools, so that the piece has somewhat less stability, particularly given its height, which was a good twenty-four inches when its feet were intact. In actuality, cat. no. 53 no doubt served multiple purposes; given the evidence of wear on the stretchers, it probably saw usage as a seat for at least part of its life, but it is not clear under what circumstances. If it was used for sitting at a table, the table would have had to be quite high, as they generally were in the seventeenth century, when stools averaged about twenty-two inches in height and the sitter's feet were meant to rest on the table's stretchers, not the floor.[1] Eighteenth-century dining tables were lower and intended to be accompanied by chairs. Thus, this piece would not have done well as a stool pulled up to a contemporary table with related turnings, such as cat. no. 61, which originally was about twenty-eight inches high; the distance between the seat and the tabletop would not be adequate.

The turnings, with opposed balusters flanked by reels, are in a Boston-style pattern common to countless New England tables of the first half of the eighteenth century and are difficult to localize. The design as executed on this piece is distinguished by thin rings defined by fine fillets and particularly by the obvious division of the vase form into two segments of equal height and the abrupt change at midpoint from a convex to a concave outline. Whether this lack of modulation from one profile to another stemmed from a personal preference of the turner or reflects limited experience with flowing ogee contours is unclear.

CONSTRUCTION

The legs ($1^{5}/_{8}$ in. thick) are splayed in two opposite directions at about 5 degrees from the vertical. The frame is secured with mortise-and-tenon joints that have holes for corresponding pins at a right angle to one another in a leg drilled at approximately the same level so that the pins partially or entirely intersect. The loss of the inner segment of two of the pins reveals that the holes for the pins of the joints of the end rails and end stretchers were bored after the rectangular sides had been assembled. An ovolo is worked at the bottom of the rails and at the top of the stretchers. Mortise gauge lines are scribed the entire length of the underside of the rails and stretchers. There is evidence of mill sawing on the inner side of the rails.

CONDITION

The top, made of two boards which were perhaps originally one and later sawn apart to reduce warpage, is probably a replacement. It has been reworked, and the manner of its present attachment to the legs is hidden by large, square face-grain plugs. Some of the joint pins are replaced. The feet have been cut down. The piece has been stripped and has a modern finish.

WOOD
SOFT MAPLE.

DIMENSIONS
OH. $23^{1}/_{2}$ (59.7); top: W. 18 (45.7), D. $11^{1}/_{4}$ (28.6); frame: W. $11^{7}/_{8}$ (30.2), D. at top $8^{3}/_{4}$ (22.2), D. at feet $12^{1}/_{4}$ (31.1).

53

REFERENCE
Hjorth 1946, fig. 11.

PROVENANCE
Ex coll.: H. Eugene Bolles, Boston.

Gift of Mrs. Russell Sage, 1909 (10.125.182)

1.   Chinnery 1979, fig. 3:162; Forman 1988, p. 144.

54.
Oval table

New England, 1720–60

Small, easily portable tables came into common use in the early eighteenth century, and this piece exemplifies a type with a stationary top that enjoyed great popularity, for it has survived in large numbers. With plain rails and stretchers tenoned to turned legs that are splayed toward the front and back, it is essentially an enlarged stool equipped with an oval top—a then fashionable shape for tables. Characteristically there is nailed to the underside of the top a single cleat that runs perpendicular to the grain of the wood and fits into a notch at the center of the front and rear rails, and that invariably has failed to prevent warpage. This example, with the legs splayed in two opposite directions, represents the usual format. Occasionally

54

all four legs are vertical, and the more elegant versions have legs that are raked in all four directions and frame rails that are shaped on the lower edge (see cat. no. 55). Although named "tavern tables" by collectors early in the twentieth century, such tables surely saw mainly domestic use—as a serviceable piece in lesser rooms of affluent households and, the more elaborate ones in particular, probably as tea tables in the parlors of more modest homes.[1] The large majority were made in New England, virtually always of maple and with legs turned in a pattern of opposed balusters centered on a ring, like this one. Examples from other regions are rare.[2] The turnings on this piece, with a reel at either end, follow a standard Boston pattern that became widespread in New England. Here the execution is somewhat lacking in vigor and crispness: the cavettos that flank the central ring are quite vertical, allowing for little indentation at the base of the vase form, which has a somewhat shallow ogee outline, and the ring at the neck of the baluster is not sharply defined. The maker of this table seems to have been working at a little remove in time and/or place from the urban sources of this turning pattern.

CONSTRUCTION

The mortise-and-tenon joints of both the stretchers and the frame rails to the legs are secured with two pins. The legs are splayed in two opposite directions at about 6 degrees from the vertical. The holes for corresponding pins at a right angle to one another in a leg are drilled at approximately the same height so that the pins partially or entirely intersect. The loss of the inner segment of several pins confirms that the holes for the pins securing the joints of the end rails and end stretchers were bored after the rectangular sides had been assembled. The top is pinned to the legs; the seam of its two boards is not parallel to the frame. A center cleat with beveled ends is attached (was originally nailed) to the underside of the top and fits into a notch in the front and rear rails.

CONDITION

The top is warped and has splits, gouges, and stains. It is old and may be original. In 1976 it was found to have come loose from the frame and was reset using three extant pins and replacing the missing lower section of the fourth. Splits in the upper leg blocks were filled, and the top of two legs was built up to compensate for warpage of the boards. The nails attaching the cleat had pulled loose, and two modern screws were added. There is evidence of an earlier repair that at one time attached the top to the end rails with a pin on either side of the join of the two boards. The feet have lost some height. The age of the red brown color on the table is uncertain. It has been lost in some areas, and there are remains of subsequent finish.

WOOD
SOFT MAPLE.

DIMENSIONS
OH. 25½ (64.8); top: W. 31⅜ (79.7), D. 22⅛ (56.2); frame: W. 17¾ (45.1), D. at top 10¼ (26), D. at feet 16⅛ (41).

EXHIBITION
"The Bicentennial Barge," New York State Education Department, Division of Historical Services, 3 June–1 October 1976.

PROVENANCE
Ex coll.: H. Eugene Bolles, Boston.

Gift of Mrs. Russell Sage, 1909 (10.125.101)

1. The term "tavern table" does not appear in period documents (Jobe and Kaye 1984, p. 165).
2. A Pennsylvania table of this form is shown in Lindsey 1999, no. 91, and one from Virginia in Horton 1967, p. 76; the turnings on both feature a single baluster. Chinnery 1979, fig. 4:267, shows an English example.

55.
Oval table

Portsmouth, New Hampshire, or southern Maine, 1735–60

This arresting table, which features legs that are splayed in four directions, a scalloped skirt, and carved Spanish feet, is an elaboration on the basic form of oval table with fixed top that became popular in the early eighteenth century and is exemplified by cat. no. 54. Its dynamic composition sets the oval of the top against the rectangle formed by the stretchers and those horizontals against the smart rake of the legs, which is extended outward by the sweep of the feet and inward by the arches of the frame rails. This is probably the best preserved of a group of seven tables, to all appearances from the same shop, that have rails cut in an identical pattern of an arch with a flat top and sides that have a profile consisting of an ovolo, fillet, and cavetto; on three of the tables, that design occurs on the two ends as well as on the front and back. All seven are further distinguished by stretchers that are finished on the upper edge with a large cyma recta molding and by rails that are recessed and in line with the top of the stretcher molding. Four of the tables, including this one, have carved (instead of turned) feet, which are all worked in a similar stylized manner with a sharp central ridge and narrow flutes (fig. 52). The ring-and-baluster turned legs here have an elegant elongation. In all cases they are executed with a neat cavetto not only on either side of the ring between the balusters—a common formula—but also adjoining the ring at either end. Three tables in this group have histories linking them to the area of southern Maine in close proximity to Portsmouth, New Hampshire.[1] This general form of oval table—one with four raked legs, a shaped skirt, and Spanish feet—was first associated with that region through an example at the Old York Historical Society, York, Maine, that is the product of a shop tradition distinct from the one represented by cat. no. 55. Other tables of this type show further variations in design and have no local history.[2]

The particular shaping of the skirt on this and the related tables dates them to no earlier than the 1730s, for the arches on the rails do not resemble those on William and Mary–style case furniture but recall the flat-headed arches with ogee sides found on the skirts of some Boston and Boston-influenced Queen Anne–style high chests and dressing tables.[3] This table represents the same level of production as chairs with a traditional turned base that have been updated with a newer design element—in that case a vase-shaped splat (see cat. nos. 35–38).[4] In fact, cat. no. 38 is one of several such chairs that exhibit the same distinctive carved feet and molded stretchers as this table and may well have been made in the same shop. The table, like the chairs, provided a conservative fashionability. That it had some pretense to stylishness is borne out by a related example at the Wadsworth Atheneum that is made of walnut, the color of which the red brown that this table was originally stained was probably meant to emulate.

CONSTRUCTION
The legs are splayed on all four sides; they deviate from the vertical approximately twice as much (about 12 degrees) on the ends as on the front and back. The mortise-and-tenon joints of the frame are secured with small square pins—one in each stretcher joint and two in each rail joint, with the exception of one joint on a long rail, which is not pinned. The rails are recessed; they are flush with the outer face of the mortises (their tenons have only an inside shoulder), so that they are aligned with the upper edge of the cyma recta molding on the stretchers. The feet, including the toes, are one piece with the legs. The top is formed of two boards and secured to each leg with a large square pin. A center cleat with beveled ends is attached with rosehead nails to the underside of the top and fits into a notch in the front and back rails. The top is beveled on the underside around the edge. A small ovolo is worked on the lower outer edge of the end rails, a broad chamfer on the lower back edge of the scalloped rails, and a small chamfer on the inner and outer corners of the leg blocks.

CONDITION
The top is strongly warped. Extra nails and a modern screw have been driven through the cleat into the top in an attempt to offset the

55. See also fig. 52.

warpage; the tips of the cleat show losses caused by added nails no longer in place. Splits in the upper and lower blocks of one leg and at one end of a long rail and of two stretchers have been repaired with nails. Reddish brown stain, probably original, remains visible on under and inner surfaces. The black color now on the frame appears to be paint that has been varnished. The top, which is marked with numerous stains and scratches, has a clear finish.

INSCRIPTIONS
A large inverted V is inscribed in white chalk at the top of the inner side of one end rail. There are modern doodles in pencil under the overhang of the top.

WOODS
SOFT MAPLE; cleat, RED OAK.

DIMENSIONS
OH. 27 (68.6); top: w. 31¾ (80.6), D. 26¾ (67.9); frame: w. at top 16⅛ (41), w. at feet 23¼ (59.1), D. at top 8⅜ (21.3), D. at feet 21½ (54.6).

EXHIBITIONS
"A Bicentennial Treasury: American Masterpieces from the Metropolitan," MMA, 29 January 1976–2 January 1977; "Portsmouth Furniture: Masterworks from the New Hampshire Seacoast," Currier Gallery of Art, Manchester, New Hampshire, Wadsworth Atheneum, and Portland Museum of Art, Portland, Maine, 15 September 1992–11 July 1993; "American Furniture and the Art of Connoisseurship," MMA, 7 April–4 October 1998.

REFERENCES
M. B. Davidson 1967, no. 144; *Bicentennial Treasury* 1976 (exh. cat.), fig. 8; Schwartz 1976, no. 26; M. B. Davidson 1980, fig. 71; Kirk 1982,

fig. 391; M. B. Davidson and Stillinger 1985, fig. 141; Jobe 1993 (exh. cat.), no. 46; Heckscher 1998, pl. III.

PROVENANCE
Ex coll.: Mrs. J. Insley Blair, Tuxedo Park, New York; her daughter Mrs. Screven Lorillard, Far Hills, New Jersey.

Mrs. Blair purchased the table from Collings and Collings, the New York City dealers, in 1923. According to her notes (ADA files), it came with a history of having been "found north of Boston." The table was on loan to the MMA from Mrs. Blair from 1939 to 1951 and from Mrs. Lorillard from 1951 until it became a gift.

Gift of Mrs. Screven Lorillard, 1952 (52.195.4)

1. Five of the related tables are in public collections: the Bayou Bend Collection (D. B. Warren et al. 1998, no. F23), Historic Deerfield (Fales 1976, no. 295), Historic New England (Jobe 1993, ill. no. 46B), the New Hampshire Historical Society, Concord (Guyol 1958, fig. 7), and the Wadsworth Atheneum (Nutting 1928–33, no. 1225). One was advertised in *Antiques* 132 (September 1987), p. 483, by the Cobbs Antiques. For the histories, see Jobe 1993, p. 218.
2. The Old York Historical Society table (Fales 1972, no. 38) has a scalloped skirt with round-headed arches that is flush with the legs; the stretchers are plain, the leg turnings have a reel at either end, and the feet are carved in a different manner and are each surmounted by a turned ring. A table at the Winterthur Museum (Fairbanks and Bates 1981, p. 65) has feet and legs similar to those on the Old York example, but the rails are cut in a single broad, peaked arch. See also Comstock 1962, no. 133, for instance.
3. For example, a 1739 veneered high chest at the Museum of Fine Arts, Boston (Randall 1965, no. 54), and a 1747 japanned high chest and matching table at the MMA (Heckscher 1985, nos. 153, 154). See also the bracket feet on a Portsmouth 1735–55 bureau-table (Jobe 1993, no. 5).
4. A further adaptation of the oval splay-legged table form to the Queen Anne style involved the use of turned legs with pad feet and the elimination of stretchers (for example, Nutting 1928–33, no. 1240).

56.
Oval table

New England, 1720–60

Among the smallest and lightest of the easily portable tables that came into use in the early eighteenth century are those with a fixed top set on a base that, instead of having four legs, has a trestle support at each end consisting of an upright—a turned leg—joined to a shaped crosspiece at top and bottom, the lower one serving as a foot. The tops are usually oval and the legs virtually always turned in a pattern of opposed balusters. Variations within this form include framing the base with just a lower stretcher instead of the two used on this example or having a plain rectangular upper stretcher rather than one that is turned, as it is on this piece. Also, the legs sometimes incorporate a short block and a turned motif between the foot and the block (below the opposed balusters) to which the lower stretcher is joined.[1] The frame of this table is totally symmetrical, with the upper half mirroring the

lower half. A table in the Bayou Bend Collection shares the same design and construction features and has turnings with identical details. A peculiarity of these turnings is that they terminate at either end, not with the usual ring but with a ball that is grooved and has a tiny cavetto where it meets the baluster. The idiosyncrasy of these terminal elements and the soft, quite flat-sided shape of the vase forms suggest the two tables are the work of a rural turner. Neither has a history that goes back beyond the 1920s and might point to a particular place of origin.[2]

CONSTRUCTION
The frame is made of 1¾-inch stock. The tenons of both the legs and the stretchers are ¾ inch thick, centered on the width of the block, and single-pinned. The leg tenons go through the feet, and presumably

56

also the trestle heads. The top is one board, attached to each trestle head with two T-headed nails that pass through the head and are clinched on the underside.

CONDITION

The top is warped, well worn, and split at one end. The joints of the legs to the trestle heads have each been reinforced with a large nail toed in from below. The joints of the lower stretcher and those of the legs to the feet have been apart and their pins replaced; the tenons

that come through the feet were wedged at two different times. An inner corner of the lower block of one leg has split off and been secured with small wire nails. A section is missing on one side of a block of the upper stretcher. The table, except for the underside of the top, is covered with thick brown paint, which obscures the grooves on the turnings. There is evidence of green over red paint under the brown.

WOODS

SOFT MAPLE; top, EASTERN WHITE PINE.

DIMENSIONS

OH. 26 5/8 (67.6); top: W. 27 5/8 (70.2), D. 19 7/8 (50.5); frame: W. 16 1/8 (41), D. 15 (38.1).

EXHIBITION

"Early American Furniture and the Decorative Crafts," Park Square Building, Boston, 8–29 December 1925.

REFERENCE

Early American Furniture 1925 (exh. cat.), no. 189.

PROVENANCE

Ex coll.: Herbert Lawton, Boston; Mrs. J. Insley Blair, Tuxedo Park, New York.

Mrs. Blair purchased the table in January 1926 from Herbert Lawton, who had lent it the previous month to an exhibition at the Park Square Building in Boston (see *Reference*). The table was on loan to the MMA from Mrs. Blair from 1939 until the time of the bequest.

Bequest of Mrs. J. Insley Blair, 1951 (52.77.59)

1. The range is illustrated in Nutting 1928–33, nos. 1196, 1204, 1205, 1208, 1211. Of the fifteen such tables noted by the present writer, one has repeat ball turnings rather than opposed balusters (*Antiques* 119 [January 1981], p. 106 [Lillian Blankley Cogan advertisement], and also in *Antiques* 158 [October 2000], p. 440 [Anthony S. Werneke advertisement]).
2. The Bayou Bend Collection table (D. B. Warren 1975, no. 20) was first published in 1921 as belonging to Mrs. Anna H. Howard of Whitman, Massachusetts (Nutting 1921, p. 449); by 1924 it was owned by Dr. Mark Miner of Greenfield, Massachusetts (Nutting 1924, no. 791; Nutting 1928–33, no. 1204).

57.

Round table

Probably southeastern Pennsylvania, 1720–50

The scheme of the turnings and the use of walnut and yellow pine point to a probable Pennsylvania origin for this table. Turnings in a repeat pattern of a ring alternating with a rounded form appear to be more prevalent on Pennsylvania furniture than on that of other colonies. They occur on types of furniture considered exclusive to that region, such as paneled chairs of the sort represented by cat. no. 20 and pieces with inlay in a line-and-berry pattern, and on other objects that

have histories in the area.[1] This generic design has English antecedents and ultimately Continental sources. Interestingly such turnings can be observed on joined chairs from Lancashire and adjacent areas of northern England, including examples that have the same crest design as many paneled Pennsylvania chairs (see the entry for cat. no. 20).[2] Thus this type of turning was plausibly in the repertoire of the craftsmen from northern England who introduced to Pennsylvania the form of paneled chair characteristic of that colony. Most Pennsylvania (and English) examples of this turning scheme exhibit a bold rhythmic pattern that relies on strong contrasts between full ball shapes and thin rings, all separated from one another by deep hollows. On this table, the rounded elements are elongated, have a groove around the middle, and do not narrow sharply at the juncture with the rings, and those rings are rather thick and also grooved. These turnings have no known exact counterpart and probably represent a late interpretation of the general formula. A parallel to the profile of the feet, however, does exist on a walnut Pennsylvania stool that is in the collections of the Philadelphia Museum of Art and has legs in a baluster-over-ball design. On both pieces there is a similar sequence of a ring, followed by a broad reel defined by crisp fillets, and then a ball that tapers downward.[3] The X-shaped construction of this table base is an unusual one. One other such piece with legs that are vertical, like those on cat. no. 57 (but with an elongated baluster turning), has been published. It was advertised as "from Delaware," raising the possibility that this is a form to be identified with the Delaware River valley.[4]

CONSTRUCTION

The X-shaped frame consists of two rails and two stretchers that cross in the center with a halved joint and are tenoned to the legs. The legs and stretchers are made from 1¾-inch stock; the rails are half that thick. The joints in the legs (5/16 in. wide) are just about centered on the width of the leg blocks; they are single-pinned, as is the joint at the center of the stretchers. The top, formed of four boards, is pinned to the legs and to the rail that runs perpendicular to the width of the boards. Its edge is slightly rounded.

CONDITION

The top, discolored by numerous dark stains, is old and may be original. It has been off and reattached with added pins; the joints of the boards have been reglued, nailed at the rim, and reinforced with two transverse braces (chestnut) nailed to the underside. Notches were cut in the top of the rail that the braces cross. There is evidence of a previous brace across one joint. A section of one rail has been broken out by a pin, and one top board and the upper block of one leg have a split. A defect in the wood has caused another leg to rack at the bottom and the loss of a section of the block above the foot. The table has a modern finish; it has been stripped and the turnings sanded.

INSCRIPTIONS

Modern restorer's marks (Xs in pencil) are on the underside of the rails and top.

WOODS

BLACK WALNUT; rails, SOUTHERN YELLOW PINE.

DIMENSIONS

OH. 28¼ (71.8); top: W. 29½ (74.9), D. 28⅞ (73.3); frame: 17¾ (45.1) square.

57

REFERENCES

Nutting 1924, no. 770 (owned by Mr. L. G. Myers); Nutting 1928–33, no. 863 (owned by L. G. Myers, New York).

PROVENANCE

Ex coll.: Louis Guerineau Myers, New York City; Mrs. J. Insley Blair, Tuxedo Park, New York; her daughter Mrs. Screven Lorillard, Far Hills, New Jersey.

Mrs. Blair purchased the table in 1926 from Mr. F. Dunn, Boston. It was on loan from Mrs. Blair to the MMA from 1939 to 1949.

Gift of Mrs. Screven Lorillard, 1952 (52.195.6)

1. For example, paneled chairs (Keyes 1924, figs. 2c, 4a; Kindig 1978, no. 3; Forman 1988, nos. 22, 25; Lindsey 1999, no. 147), an inlaid table (Schiffer 1966, ill. no. 122), other tables ("Shop Talk" 1958, p. 32, and Lindsey 1999, no. 48), and a miniature high chest (Lindsey 1999, no. 41 and fig. 165).
2. Kirk 1982, figs. 319, 320. For such turnings on chairs from northern England, see Chinnery 1979, figs. 3:490, 4:139, 4:151; Kirk 1982, nos. 664, 667; Forman 1988, no. 34.
3. The stool (acc. no. 28-7-54) is part of a large gift from Lydia Thompson Morris.
4. *Antiques* 132 (July 1987), p. 206 (Chalfant and Chalfant advertisement). Three stands with this type of construction but splayed legs (and New England type of opposed baluster turnings) are also known (Nutting 1928–33, nos. 1215, 1243; Kirk 1967, no. 151).

Tables with Hinged Leaves

Tables equipped with leaves so that they could be made larger or smaller according to need came into general use during the sixteenth century. They provided a greater degree of flexibility and were far less cumbersome than trestle tables made to come apart that could be set up or removed as required (see cat. no. 138). One new form was the draw or drawing table, a joined rectangular table fitted with a leaf at either end that was housed under the main top and could be pulled or drawn out as an extension; lopers affixed to the underside of the leaves provided the necessary support. Such tables were more prestigious than long joined tables with stationary tops and in England were the most fashionable form for dining from the late 1500s to about 1660. In the colonies they were the exception, and only one American example of the period is known.[1]

The other means of varying the size of a table that came to the fore during the sixteenth century was the addition of one or two hinged leaves, the method employed on the tables in this chapter. The leaves were attached in either of two ways: hinged so as to fold over the stationary top (with leaf and top identical in shape) or so as to hang down from the sides of a fixed top. The table that heads this chapter illustrates the first manner of attachment; tables with such tops were often designated "folding" tables (cat. no. 58). With a half-round (when closed) top set on a polygonal base with turned pillars, it represents a form that was in fashion in England in the first half of the seventeenth century and of which just two other American examples are known. The three are the only early colonial tables with this type of top, which was derived from folding game boards and became commonplace on late colonial card tables. The leaf on the Museum's table, when in use, rests on an auxiliary swinging support now called a "gate," which consists of two uprights and two stretchers and pivots out from the frame when the top is open and fits against the back of the table when the top is closed (fig. 90).

Early colonial tables with hinged leaves that hang down from either side of a stationary top set on a rectangular frame generally employ the same type of leaf support and are now commonly called gateleg tables—a strictly modern term. In documents of the period such tables were most often just designated by the shape of the top when open—oval, which was the style. A much more descriptive appellation was "oval table with falling leaves." Other names that were applied to the leaves of such tables in England or the colonies were "sides" and "flaps," and they might be described as "folding" as well as "falling." A "folding" or "folded" table, however, could be either one with falling leaves or one on which a leaf rests on a similarly shaped top. Oval tables with hinged leaves

came into fashion in the colonies during the last third of the seventeenth century, and they had generally supplanted long joined dining tables by 1700. With the introduction of oval tables, dining in stylish circles became less formal. Guests were now seated in more intimate groups at several tables in the same room. Thus, in 1685 William Penn wrote from England to the steward of his manor in Pennsylvania instructing him to have made, among other furniture, "two or three Eating Tables to flap down—one less than another as for 12-8-5."[2] Somewhat less specifically, William Byrd I of Virginia ordered from London in 1690 "1 Small, 1 Middling & 1 large Ovall table."[3] The tables when not in use were placed with the leaves down along the wall, beside the chairs that accompanied them. Oval tables were to be sat at on chairs—no longer stools—and their turnings were similar to those on contemporary joined chairs. The stylistically earliest oval tables have repeat ball turnings, but virtually all American tables, and all those in the collection, feature ogee balusters and are in the William and Mary style.

The oval tables with falling leaves in this chapter represent a range of sizes and turning patterns. The first is an impressive Boston example, one of the largest American oval tables from this period and one of the few with two gates rather than one supporting each leaf (cat. no. 59). Made of fashionable walnut, its well-executed turnings are in a symmetrical design of opposed balusters centered on a ring, the scheme that was favored in Boston and became widespread in New England. The turnings on the three smaller tables that follow it in this catalogue (nos. 60–62), which like many made at this time in New England are of maple or some other local wood stained to resemble walnut, exhibit different versions of the same basic pattern. A table from Rhode Island (cat. no. 63) is one of a group from that area characterized by leg turnings in a distinctive asymmetrical pattern of a tall baluster over a spherical form. Asymmetrical patterns dominated by a single baluster are otherwise associated mainly with tables from the mid-Atlantic and southern colonies. The turnings on a hefty table from Pennsylvania (cat. no. 64) and a small example from New York (cat. no. 65) present different variations on this scheme. The New York table has a trestle base, as do the two New England tables that follow it here (cat. nos. 66, 67). This form of base, constructed somewhat differently in New York and New England, made for a very compact piece when the leaves are down.

The same type of base with splayed legs that was popular for small tables with a stationary top was also equipped with a top with hinged leaves, as exemplified by the last two objects in this chapter (cat. nos. 68, 69). The pivot supports for the leaves on such tables consist of shaped boards—the outline of which prompted the modern designation "butterfly table"—and were economical substitutes for the more labor-intensive and costlier joined gates. The latter of those two tables, made decades after early Baroque designs were out of favor in fashionable households, is here included to illustrate the longevity of certain William and Mary furniture forms and of that style's turning patterns. Since the furniture in the

eighteenth-century styles that ensued featured sawn and carved elements, there was no infusion of new designs to be used by makers of economical tables and chairs with turned legs, which continued to be in demand for everyday use.

1. Fairbanks and Trent 1982, no. 286 (Connecticut Historical Society, Hartford).
2. Quoted in McElroy 1979, p. 62.
3. Quoted in Alexander 1989, pp. 3–4.

58.
Folding table

Northern Essex County, Massachusetts, 1680–85

The table's history points to an origin in northern Essex County, Massachusetts. Its style and structure link it to a major unidentified shop that was active in that area principally during the 1680s and 1690s and is notable above all for the unusual variety and elaboration of the cupboards it produced.[1] Very generally, the boldness of design and a sense of movement uncommon in seventeenth-century forms that distinguish the complex compositions of that shop's cupboards are reflected in the table's vigorous interplay of angular and circular shapes. Much more specifically, the half columns that are applied to the stiles under the top and flank what was originally a center drawer are in the same pattern as those that flank the drawer under the middle shelf on two cupboards at the Winterthur Museum, dated 1680 and 1684, respectively, and on a cupboard in a private collection dated 1683.[2] The turned pillars on the table (fig. 46), ornamented with the broad concave bands flanked by fine grooves that are typical of this school of craftsmanship, relate the most closely to those on the same cupboards, but in this case there is no exact match. The baluster profile seen here—round shoulders, straight sides, and a taper toward the bottom with a shallow S-curve outline—is rendered with a stiffer, virtually straight taper at the base on the 1680 cupboard. The interpretation of this form on the 1684 cupboard, on the other hand, exhibits curves that are somewhat fuller than those on the present balusters and a neck that is narrower. The dated pieces in this shop's production show an evolution of the turning style toward more graceful forms, with the pillars on later cupboards having quite thin necks and emphatic curves.[3] In that stylistic development, this table's pillars stand between those on the 1680 and 1684 cupboards. The type of baluster shape used for the table's pillars occurs on the cupboards in this Essex County group specifically in the lower

case portion of the piece. In fact, the table's overall structure corresponds to that of the lower part of a cupboard with an open bottom shelf—a tier with drawer(s) supported at the front by pillars resting on a platform—except that it has the trapezoidal shape of a cupboard's upper storage unit.

Characteristic of this school of craftsmanship are the table's extensive use of layout marks and its very solid construction. The front and rear stiles are pentagonal so that the rails can all meet the stiles squarely at a right angle, as they do on the trapezoidal storage compartment on cupboards from this shop.[4] The table incorporates mill-sawn oak, which occurs also on at least two of the cupboards. The use of such oak is rare in seventeenth-century joined pieces but not exclusive to this Essex County group.[5] The later, painted surface, applied after the drawer under the top was lost, has altered the appearance of the table; originally the pillars, feet, pendants, and applied turnings were ebonized and may have been the only elements painted. The present decorative painting does not relate in style to that on any other known piece and is not the work of a trained painter or grainer. The more or less parallel black streaking over white on the top is presumably meant to be marbleizing. What, if anything, the black over red on the frame (including the pillars, feet, and applied turnings) was to represent, particularly the diaper pattern with large blotches in the interstices on the platform, is unclear. While the colors are those used in the eighteenth century to simulate tortoiseshell and in the nineteenth for rosewood graining, the painting bears no relationship to either.

This table, with its polygonal frame, two-part hinged circular top, pillar legs, and open shelf, is of a form that was being made in England by the early seventeenth century. The type is rare in American furniture; only this and two other

58. See also figs. 46, 87, 90, 91.

tables, one at the Chipstone Foundation and one in a private collection, are known.[6] The two others, attributed to Boston, closely recall English examples. On cat. no. 58 this table form is eloquently expressed in the particular idiom of the northern Essex County shop that made it. Such tables fell at the time into the general category of "folding" tables; their tops consist of two identical leaves, one fixed and the other hinged to fold over the first—a scheme that became standard on eighteenth-century card tables. The leaf, when open, rests on a framed pivot support (fig. 90) of the type that is now commonly called a gate and that became widespread on tables in the William and Mary style with two falling leaves (see cat. nos. 59–67). With the leaf closed, the table can stand against a wall. Often equipped with a drawer, as this example once was, or other storage compartment, and with a shelf, this form may have been intended as a side table associated with dining, as Victor Chinnery suggested was probably the case with English examples.[7] In practice this table was likely put to multiple uses.

CONSTRUCTION

The table is built of heavy stock: the stiles and pillars measure more than 3 inches across, and the rear rails are nearly 2 inches thick at the bottom edge. It is framed with mortise-and-tenon joints $7/16$ inch wide, secured with two pins, except for those of the shallow front rail, which are single-pinned. Two sizes of pins are used ($1/4$ in. and $3/8$ in.) in a somewhat haphazard way, with some joints having one pin of each size. The upper and lower stiles (or corner blocks) are pentagonal in section so that the rails (which are wedge-shaped and have the thicker part toward the bottom) can be all joined to the stiles at a right angle. The pillars and feet are each separate pieces with round tenons that engage holes drilled in the stiles. Below the shallow upper front rail there was originally a drawer that was side-hung on runners let into the front stiles and the back rail. The open shelf is fastened to the lower rails with T-headed nails; it consists of one tangent-sawn oak board, which retains evidence of mill sawing (fig. 91). Each section of the top is a thick (ca. 1 in.) single oak board that was cut along the radial plane. The lower, fixed leaf is pinned to the stiles and the back rail. The upper is attached to the lower with two hinges that have long narrow straps that are inset and were secured with nails. The folding leaf, when open, rests on a pivot support formed of two legs and two stretchers; the inner leg is round-tenoned to the upper and lower rear rails so that it can rotate; the outer leg has cutouts at the top and bottom that fit into corresponding recesses in the rails so that it can be in line with the back of the frame when the top is closed (fig. 90). Joiner's assembly marks on the gate (see *Inscriptions*) indicate that its mortise-and-tenon joints were worked so that, whether by intent or error, the baluster on the pivot leg faces in the opposite direction from that on the outer leg. A slat nailed to the outside of the upper back rail, and flush with its top edge, gives support to the inner edge of the open leaf; the ends and the lower edge of the slat are beveled. The upper edges of the gate's stretchers are finished with a chamfer.

CONDITION

The top is original but has been reset. The hinges appear to be old but may not be the first; the left one is secured with modern screws but was once nailed on; the nails in the right one do not look to be of the seventeenth century; at both locations there are traces of nails that do

not readily line up with perforations in the hinges. Two holes drilled in the back edge of the upper leaf are later additions, as are the protruding dowels on the lower leaf that fit into those holes when the top is open. The drawer and runners have been lost, and a board has been affixed under the top front rail in place of the drawer front. All five feet have been cut down and are fitted with metal sockets for casters. The front and right pendants are replacements, as are some of the bosses and probably the two applied columnar turnings in a variant pattern. The applied elements are all secured with small modern nails and covered with heavy paint.

The red paint patterned with black that covers the frame and the white with black streaking on the outer surfaces of the closed top are not original; they were applied after the false drawer front was installed. There is evidence of black under the present paint on the pillars, feet, and applied turnings, of an earlier red on other portions of the frame and under the marbleizing of the top, and of more than one coating on the top's solid red inner surfaces.

INSCRIPTIONS

Joiner's assembly marks are at the joints of the upper and lower side rails to the front and rear stiles and consist variously of single or double chisel strikes, either perpendicular to the side or diagonal, and of a diagonal scored line. Very short chisel strikes (single or double) are at two of the joints of the gate (fig. 87).

WOODS

Top, stiles, rails, shelf, slat on back rail, WHITE OAK; pillars, feet, gate, applied turnings, SOFT MAPLE.

DIMENSIONS

H. closed 28 (71.1), H. open 27 (68.6); top: w. $36 3/8$ (92.4), D. open $35 3/8$ (89.9), D. closed $17 5/8$ (44.8); frame: w. $27 5/8$ (70.2), D. 14 (35.6).

EXHIBITIONS

"A Bicentennial Treasury: American Masterpieces from the Metropolitan," MMA, 29 January 1976–2 January 1977; "Puritan Classicism: Seventeenth-Century Cupboards of Massachusetts," Milwaukee Art Museum, Milwaukee, Wisconsin, 4 May–2 September 2001.

REFERENCES

Keyes 1923, pp. 162–64; Lockwood 1926, fig. CVIII; Nutting 1928–33, no. 1011; I. P. Lyon 1938c, fig. 51; Downs 1940b, p. 21; Andrus 1951, p. 244; Andrus 1952, p. 164; Powel 1954, p. 200; Comstock 1962, no. 111; M. B. Davidson 1967, no. 46; Fales 1972, no. 11; Butler 1973, p. 17; *Bicentennial Treasury* 1976 (exh. cat.), fig. 3; Schwartz 1976, no. 17; Chinnery 1979, fig. 4:218; Fairbanks and Bates 1981, p. 25; Barquist 1992, fig. 47; Trent, Follansbee, and A. Miller 2001, fig. 22 (details, figs. 24–26).

PROVENANCE

Ex coll.: Mrs. J. Insley Blair, Tuxedo Park, New York.

Mrs. Blair's records (ADA files) note that she purchased the table in 1924 from Charles Woolsey Lyon, a New York City dealer, less than a year after it had been published in the October 1923 issue of *Antiques* (see *References*). At that time it belonged to George Choate Furness (1884–1944), son of James Choate Furness (1854–1925) and Lillie May Appleton (1858–1930). According to information Mrs. Blair received from Mrs. George Furness, the table was discovered in 1922 in the attic of her in-laws' house in Manchester, New Hampshire, and it was subsequently offered for sale through their Marshfield, Massachusetts, friend the dealer Edward Ford. The table had come to Lillie Appleton Furness from her parents, George Appleton (1825–1907) and Esther Knowlton Annable (1824–1894), and she remembered it as her mother's "parlor table" that always stood in the little best room of their farmhouse outside Haverhill, Massachusetts. If the table descended lineally in the Appleton family, its first owner would have been Samuel Appleton (1625–1696) of Ipswich, but its ownership cannot be established through extant probate papers. Samuel married first in 1651 Hannah Paine of Ipswich and second in 1656 Mary Oliver of Newbury; his son Oliver (1677–1760) married in 1701 Sarah Perkins of Topsfield. Marriages of succeeding Appletons in this line raise the possibility of the table's having been acquired collaterally through the Whipple, Patch, Lovering, Kinsman, and Annable families of northern Essex County.[8] The table was on loan to the MMA from Mrs. Blair from 1939 until it became a gift.

Gift of Mrs. J. Insley Blair, 1951 (51.12.1)

1. For this anonymous shop and a comprehensive in-depth study of its cupboards, see Trent, Follansbee, and A. Miller 2001.
2. Ibid., figs. 8, 40 (detail, fig. 45), 27; similar turnings are also on a chest of drawers dated 1678 (ibid., fig. 1).
3. Ibid., pp. 28, 40.
4. For a diagram of such framing, see ibid., fig. 14. In all other New England shop traditions known to the present writer, only the front stiles of such trapezoidal units are pentagonal; the back and the canted sides are framed with separate stiles and nailed together (see cat. nos. 113, 116, 141).

5. Trent, Follansbee, and A. Miller 2001, caption to fig. 27 and p. 62, n. 48. For the use of mill-sawn oak by other shops, see cat. nos. 87 and 110 and the entry for no. 116.
6. For English tables, see R. Edwards 1964, pp. 549–50, figs. 1–4; and Chinnery 1979, figs. 3:204–3:210. The Chipstone Foundation table is illustrated in Trent, Follansbee, and A. Miller 2001, fig. 23; the table in a private collection is unpublished.
7. Chinnery 1979, p. 305.
8. Letter from Betty Furness (daughter of George C. Furness) to researcher Leslie Symington, 11 August 1992 (also family data supplied by Betty Furness [ADA files]). Letter from Natalie K. (Mrs. J. Insley) Blair to Irving P. Lyon, 27 September 1936 (Lyon Family Papers, box 7, Downs Manuscript Collection, Winterthur Museum); the present writer thanks Robert F. Trent for bringing this letter to her attention. Obituary of George C. Furness, *New York Times*, 11 April 1944; William S. Appleton, *A Genealogy of the Appleton Family* (Boston, 1874), pp. 5–6, 8, 44; George Francis Dow, comp., *Vital Records of Topsfield, Massachusetts*, vol. 1 (Topsfield, Mass., 1903), p. 175. The Samuel Appleton probate papers contain only an inventory of his estate still in the possession of his widow (and executrix) at her death in 1698. It lists "three tables" in a group of items and a single table at half the value of a chest of drawers (Essex County Probate Records, docket 815, Massachusetts Archives at Columbia Point, Boston). Two of the tables in the inventory of Oliver Appleton are described as "oval"; from their context and valuations they are not out of fashion (Essex County Probate Records, microfilm, vol. 336, pp. 143–45, Massachusetts Archives at Columbia Point, Boston). There is no will or inventory for Esther K. Appleton (d. 1894; Essex County Probate Records, docket 75432, Essex County Probate Court, Salem, Massachusetts); the inventory of George Appleton (d. 1907; Essex County Probate Records, docket 100696, Essex County Probate Court, Salem, Massachusetts) is brief and uninformative.

59.
Oval table with falling leaves

Boston, 1690–1720

The skillfully turned balusters, rings, and reels on cat. no. 59 display the strong forms and rhythms that characterize early-Baroque-inspired turnings in similar patterns on other large walnut (and in two instances mahogany) oval tables with falling leaves that have been attributed to Boston by virtue of the quality of workmanship, the use of imported woods, and the history of two examples in prominent families in that city. Owned also by important families in the broader region, they represent the highest level of production of this form of table in New England.[1]

This impressive piece is exceptional on several counts. Built on a grand scale, it is among the largest American oval tables in the William and Mary style and one of a small number with two gates, as they are now commonly called, supporting each leaf.[2] Its twelve legs and numerous stretchers, executed with precision and vigor, present an imposing array of turnings that is masterful in its complex rhythms and recall of forms and incorporates a greater diversity of motifs than is

characteristic of such tables. On the four frame legs and the end stretchers, the central ring is separated from the vase forms not by the usual cavetto (seen on the legs of the gates, for instance) but by a broader concave profile tantamount to a reel (fig. 32). On the gate stretchers and matching segments of the side frame stretchers the opposed balusters are centered on a reel rather than a ring—a variation found on contemporary chairs (see cat. no. 27), but not known to the writer on any other New England table of this type. A very distinctive sequence of a ring, cavetto, and shallow ogee separated by fillets is found above the ball of the foot and on either side of the fat ring at each end of the side stretchers. An anomaly in New England turning, this sequence of forms is generically related to the profile on the feet and above the trumpet shape on the legs of some William and Mary–style Philadelphia high chests and dressing tables (see cat. no. 131). The similarity may indicate that certain turners in both cities were trained in the same or a related English tradition or reflect the migration of craftsmen from one city to the other.[3] Finally, the table exhibits exceptional attention to detail: a bead molding was run not only on the lower edge of the rails under the drawers but also on that of the side frame rails and on the two outer edges of the upper stretchers of the gates; in addition, on the outer legs of the gates, the outer top corners of the upper blocks were shaped to mirror the turned corners at the bottom of those blocks. The greater diversity of motifs and the very careful finishing on cat. no. 59 point to its being a custom piece, made before this form of oval table was produced in quantity and became more standardized.

This type of table, which corresponds to the period description of an "oval table with falling leaves," is based directly on a form that became fashionable in England after 1660 for dining. However, the turning pattern of symmetrically opposed balusters centered on a ring that is characteristic of Boston tables is much more the exception than the rule on English examples. The latter most often have leg turnings that feature a single baluster form, as is typical of American tables made from New York on south.[4] Both basic schemes have their source in classical antiquity and are shown used in balustrades in Renaissance architectural books.[5] Why the opposed baluster formula came to dominate the design of William and Mary–style tables in Boston (and as a result in most of New England) has not been addressed. Since turnings for tables and joined chairs were made by the same craftsmen, the existence in Boston before the end of the seventeenth century of a large, well-established chairmaking industry may have been a determining factor. One can speculate that whatever the actual source of the pattern in Boston may have been—immigrant craftsmen or turnings on imported chairs or tables—it took hold because it fit in with the ingrained working habits of turners who had been producing bilaterally symmetrical designs centered on a ring for the stretchers of seventeenth-century joined chairs (see cat. nos. 23, 24); and in an industry probably already organized in part at least on piecework, it answered the need for a stock pattern that could be easily replicated and proportioned and adapted to different lengths.

CONSTRUCTION

The turned members and the side frame rails are a good 2 1/8 inches thick. The mortise-and-tenon joints are carefully worked and nearly 1/2 inch wide; those of the side rails are secured with two pins, all others with one. The three sections of the top are each composed of two boards with a thickness of 1 inch. The center was attached with one wooden pin into each frame leg and two pins into each side rail, and the leaves abut it with tongue-and-groove joints. Originally each leaf was attached with one hinge at either end where there is a cutout in the top of the side rail. The leaves are each supported by two gates that swing out from either end of the frame and meet in the middle when closed. The pivot leg is round-tenoned to the frame rail and the stretcher, and the outer leg has cutouts at the top and bottom that fit into corresponding recesses in the rail and stretcher. The foot below

each pivot leg is attached to the stretcher with a rectangular tenon that is pinned. Scribing for the placement of the pivot legs remains visible on the underside of the frame rails: two parallel lines perpendicular to the rail to delimit the location and between them intersecting diagonal lines to mark the center for the drilling of the mortise. At each end of the frame there is a drawer with a rail both above and below it, and at the center of the frame, a cross brace with a through tenon that fits into a recess at the top of each side rail. The drawers are supported on narrow runners that are nailed to the side rails with sprigs.

CONDITION

The top is original, but it has been off, and the glue joints have probably been renewed. The center section is now attached from below with three screws that go through large holes drilled in the outer upper portion of each side rail and one screw up through each upper end rail. Six of the wooden pins of the first attachment—or at any rate their upper portion—remain intact in the top and they match the joint pins in the frame in size and character; round face-grain plugs mark the location of the other two pins, which went into one of the side rails. The top boards all show some warp and larger and smaller knots, and one leaf has a 2-inch-square surface patch. The present replacement hinges—two on each side at the cutouts in the rail and one in the middle—are let into the surface and screwed on. Evidence remains at the cutouts of the original larger hinges that were surface-mounted and attached with nails. The drawers (with a dovetail at each corner and a nailed bottom) are not original and the runners are probably replaced. The wood in parts of the base has cracks. On the feet all or most of the pad under the ball turning is missing. The table has a modern finish with residues of an earlier dark coating visible throughout the base. Dark brown stain remains on the frame rails.

WOODS

BLACK WALNUT; side rails, cross brace, WHITE PINE.

DIMENSIONS

OH. 29 3/4 (75.6); top: w. open 74 1/2 (189.2), w. closed 26 1/2 (67.3), D. 71 3/8 (181.3); frame: w. 23 1/2 (59.7), D. 55 1/4 (140.3).

REFERENCES

Lockwood 1913, fig. 680; Halsey and Tower 1925, fig. 14; Cescinsky and Hunter 1929, p. 58; Halsey and Cornelius 1938 (and 1942), fig. 21; "Antiques in the American Wing" 1946, p. 247, no. 11; Schwartz 1958, pl. 5C; Comstock 1962, no. 124.

PROVENANCE

Ex coll.: H. Eugene Bolles, Boston.

H. Eugene Bolles wrote at the time the MMA acquired it: "This table was bought by me 15 or 20 years ago at Leonard's auction rooms in Boston. It was said at the time to have come with other things from some storage warehouse in Boston" (Bolles notes, MMA Archives).

Gift of Mrs. Russell Sage, 1909 (10.125.129)

1. Large oval tables with histories are in Fales 1976, no. 237 (Bowdoin family, Boston); *Sack Collection* 1981–92, vol. 1, p. 190 (Franklin family, Boston; with Spanish feet); Baarsen et al. 1988, no. 101 (Isaac Winslow, Plymouth, Massachusetts, married in Boston, 1700); Jobe 1993, no. 53 (a mahogany table in the Wentworth family, Portsmouth, New Hampshire; another table in the Pepperrell family, Kittery, Maine, is mentioned therein); and a sixth

59. See also fig. 32.

example included in Bernard and S. Dean Levy gallery catalogue, vol. 6 (New York, 1988), p. 5 (from the Joseph Reynolds House, Bristol, Rhode Island). Of the other larger examples, those in public collections are Jobe and Kaye 1984, no. 58; Monkhouse and Michie 1986, no. 62; Venable 1989, no. 3 (mahogany); Barquist 1992, no. 40; D. B. Warren et al. 1998, no. F24 (with Spanish feet).

2. Other examples with two gates that also swing from either end are shown in Nutting 1928–33, nos. 935, 936, 960. The large New York table at the Albany Institute (Lockwood 1913, fig. 681) has two gates swinging out from the middle of each side. The biggest American oval table of this period

known, from Pennsylvania (Schiffer 1966, ill. no. 85), has each leaf supported by a single gate, as does that with a Winslow family history (see n. 1 above), which is also larger than cat. no. 59.

3. For a similar foot on an English case piece, see Bowett 2002, pl. 2:33. It may be relevant that upholsterer Edward Shippen and furniture- and chairmaker Thomas Stapleford moved from Boston to Philadelphia in the 1690s (Forman 1988, p. 295).

4. Chinnery 1979, pp. 190-b, 191-b.

5. For example, see Serlio 1537–47 (1611 ed.), bk. 4, chap. 8, fol. 52; Palladio 1570 (1738 ed.), bk. 2, pls. X, XII.

60. See also figs. 33, 124.

60.

Oval table with falling leaves

Probably Boston or vicinity, 1715–40

This piece exemplifies the standard turned vocabulary characteristic of William and Mary–style Boston and Boston-inspired tables of this form: opposed ogee balusters centered on a ring, a motif that on the table's longer components is usually augmented at either end by a reel, as on this piece, or by a ball (see cat. no. 62). While the same core pattern is repeated on all of the table's turned members, variety and visual interest are provided by its adaptation to the several lengths dictated by the structure and by the resulting differences in the curvature of the balusters. The longest version of the ring-and-baluster pattern on this and most tables with falling leaves occurs on the frame legs (fig. 33); in this case, it is repeated with increasingly shorter dimensions and thus more compressed balusters on the legs of the gates, the gate stretchers and matching center turnings of the side frame stretchers, and finally, with the center ring omitted, on the end stretchers. The turnings at either end of the side stretchers here feature a flattened ball; the usual alternative in that location is a single vase form, its base toward the center of the stretcher.

The feet, which have survived with little loss to height, echo the profile of the balusters, and their long necks give the table a nice visual lift.

The end rails are neatly finished with a bead, a feature associated with Boston tables. The turnings are elegant and precisely executed: the serpentine lines of the balusters are fluid, the corners of the blocks are turned far down, the cavettos that link the center ring to the balusters are well defined, and the terminal rings are separated from the blocks by a deep cut. The table has the traits of an urban piece and was probably produced in Boston or its immediate vicinity. Made of maple rather than the more expensive imported walnut, of a small to middling size, and originally without a drawer, it appears to represent a good-quality stock model of that furniture industry.

CONSTRUCTION

The turned members and side frame rails are only 1 5/8 inches thick. The mortise-and-tenon joints of the frame rails are secured with two pins, all others with one. The center top, composed of a single board, is pinned to the frame. The hinged leaves, each formed of two boards, abut the center with tongue-and-groove joints. The top of the side rails has a recess toward each end to accommodate the hinges. The pivot leg on the gates is round-tenoned to the frame rail and stretcher, and the foot below it is attached to the stretcher with a rectangular tenon that is pinned. A bead molding is worked on the bottom edge of the end rails. Evidence of mill sawing remains on the inner side of the frame rails and the underside of the leaves.

CONDITION
The center section of the top has large lengthwise splits down the middle. Its surface is marred by dark stains, possible scorching, scratches, and gouges, and so is to a lesser degree that of the leaves. The center section has been off and the underside probably replaned. It was reset with a pin into each leg supplemented by modern screws up through the inner side of the rails. It appears to be original, as are probably the leaves.[1] On the leaves, the joint of the two boards has been reglued and reinforced at the rim with pins or nails. The hinges are replacements, and on one side there was more than one previous set. One end rail is marked by a deep gouge. The other has been cut down to make room for an added drawer (pine, nailed) that runs on an added center support. The lower portion of the original rail now serves as the rail below the drawer, and the mortises in the legs were extended down a short distance to accommodate it; the mortises at drawer level and one of the upper pin holes remain empty. A large section of one foot has split off. Neither the dark mahogany-color finish on the base and underside of the leaves (thin or worn off in the more exposed areas) nor the red paint on the lighter color top (remaining mostly on the leaves) is old.

INSCRIPTIONS
A paper sticker with the printed number 190 is under the rail below the drawer. A piece of cloth tape inscribed with a William Trent House identification number (see *Exhibition*) is adhered under one end of the center top, on the outside of a side rail, and on the inside of the drawer bottom.

WOODS
SOFT MAPLE; side rails, PINE.

DIMENSIONS
OH. 26¾ (67.9); top: w. open 42⅞ (108.9), w. closed 14½ (36.8), D. 37½ (95.3); frame: w. 12 (30.5), D. 28¾ (73).

EXHIBITION
On loan to the William Trent House, Trenton, New Jersey, from 1945 to 1977.

REFERENCES
Nutting 1921, p. 367; Nutting 1924, no. 718; Nutting 1928–33, no. 957.

PROVENANCE
Ex coll.: H. Eugene Bolles, Boston.

Gift of Mrs. Russell Sage, 1909 (10.125.130)

1. In the microanalysis of wood samples from the center top and a frame leg, R. Bruce Hoadley noted that the rays in both samples were unusually narrow in width and cell count, suggesting that the wood might be from the same tree.

61.
Oval table with falling leaves
New England, 1720–50

The large number of surviving oval leaf tables with generically related turnings suggests that the Boston furniture-making industry was producing not only quantities of chairs but also many tables for both the home market and export. The exports disseminated Boston-style table forms and turnings and inspired locally made copies. Turnings with opposed balusters became widespread in New England, and this popular motif was produced in countless different versions that are difficult to localize and exhibit varying levels of skill.

The leg turnings on this table have the same sequence of motifs as those on cat. no. 60, but the manner in which the design was interpreted gives this piece a quite different character. Although the baluster turnings are just one-sixteenth inch thicker than on cat. no. 60, they look decidedly heavier. The vase forms are indeed stockier; on the frame legs they are shorter by nearly one-half inch because the turned segment of

the leg is not as high overall and the reels at either end are taller. Also the base of the vases—fuller and with a lower center of gravity—is weightier. In this interpretation, the bulbous base reads as a sphere distinct from the neck, which is only slightly concave. The turner was apparently not well versed in flowing, serpentine lines. While the turnings follow a standard Boston formula, the execution of the forms is lacking somewhat in élan and refinement. Made of maple, without a molding on the end rails, and without a foot under the pivot leg of the gates, the table is a model at the lower end of the market that probably originated in a smaller town.

CONSTRUCTION
The turned members and the side frame rails are all about 1¹¹⁄₁₆ inches thick. The mortise-and-tenon joints of the side rails, the deep end rail, and the upper stretchers of the gates are secured with two pins,

61

all others with one. Each of the three sections of the top is a single board. The center board is pinned to the frame legs, and the joint with the hinged leaves is a tongue and groove. The top of the side rails is ¼ inch lower than the top of the legs, which provides the clearance for the hinges. The pivot leg on the gates is round-tenoned to the rail and the stretcher. The drawer is supported by a center runner, on which one end is beveled on the underside to fit into a conforming recess in the rail below the drawer and the other end is nailed to the underside of the opposite rail.

CONDITION

The top—in particular, the center section, which is split at one end—is heavily stained, scratched, and gouged. The center board has been replaned on the underside and reattached to the frame with four nails in addition to the pin into each leg. It is old and possibly original; the leaves are probably not, since they are a little small for the frame. However, the leaves and the center have been together for some time: dovetail hinges have been added or reset on one side, and more than one change of hinges has occurred on the other. Both the drawer (pine, with two crude dovetails at each corner and a nailed bottom) and the runner have been replaced. On the end stretcher below the drawer, the left block has split and been repaired with nails, and there is an added pin in the right joint. At the back end of the left frame rail, pressure from joint pins has split off two large sections on the inner side. The feet have been cut down, and one has sustained large losses. The base is mostly covered by a brown coating, the leaves retain residues of red paint, and there is dark stain on the side rails and the underside of the leaves.

INSCRIPTION

Paper tape with an identification number applied at the Pennsylvania Farm Museum of Landis Valley (see *Exhibitions*) is inside the drawer.

WOODS

SOFT MAPLE; side rails, EASTERN WHITE PINE.

DIMENSIONS

OH. 26⅝ (67.6); top: w. open 43½ (110.5), w. closed 15⅜ (39.1), D. 42¼ (107.3); frame: w. 12½ (31.8), D. 31¾ (80.6).

EXHIBITIONS

On loan to the Baltimore Museum of Art, Baltimore, Maryland, from 1952 to 1965 and to the Pennsylvania Farm Museum of Landis Valley (now Landis Valley Museum), Lancaster, Pennsylvania, from 1968 to 1972; "The American Christmas," Museum of American Folk Art (now American Folk Art Museum), New York City, 27 November–31 December 1972; "The Bicentennial Barge," New York State Education Department, Division of Historical Services, 3 June–1 October 1976.

REFERENCES

Nutting 1921, p. 367; Nutting 1924, no. 719; Nutting 1928–33, no. 958; Shea 1975, p. 23.

PROVENANCE

Ex coll.: H. Eugene Bolles, Boston.

Gift of Mrs. Russell Sage, 1909 (10.125.131)

62

62.

Oval table with falling leaves

Eastern Massachusetts, 1720–50

The turnings on the frame legs of this piece represent a formula found on many of the large walnut tables attributed to Boston, but with a difference. On those examples, whether the ball on either side of the opposed balusters is rounder or flatter, it is separated from the rings that flank it by narrow hollows, making for a strong and compact juxtaposition of convex and concave shapes. The ball usually has enough fullness to stand out from the rings and to recall the bulbous base of the balusters, creating a design that is more complex and more clearly in the early Baroque idiom than the arrangement of the more repetitive forms on this table.[1] Here the ring-ball-ring sequence at either end of the legs is more drawn out, and the broad reel shapes that separate those elements provide a less dramatic contrast in diameter; the flattened ball (it is that rather than a ring since it is not defined by fillets) is the same size as the ring above and below it, and works in effect as a repeat motif with the rings. The table derives its particular animated effect from the pulsating rhythm of its many rings and reels, which catch the eye more than do the balusters,

which normally dominate the turnings on tables in this period. The balusters on the frame legs are in fact quite short (because of the height of the ring-ball-ring segments that flank them), and they are equal in size to the vase shapes on all the turned members except those on the end stretchers. Similar turnings are on a small walnut table formerly at the Wadsworth Atheneum.[2] The turnings on that and this piece include an uncommon detail that occurs on some of the tables attributed to Boston: the rings that adjoin the blocks were turned with a distinct fillet between the ring and the block.[3] It thus appears that the maker of cat. no. 62 was trained in or directly influenced by a school of turning that was active in the Boston area.

The use of beech for a table base is unusual, but the frame, which has admittedly seen some changes, gives no indication that it did not originate in the eighteenth century. What does ring a false note is the size of the replaced top; it is larger in its depth than across the open leaves, which are too narrow for the gates.

CONSTRUCTION

The turned members and the side frame rails are all about $1\frac{7}{8}$ inches thick. The mortise-and-tenon joints are double-pinned, except for those of the side stretchers and of the rail above and below the drawer, which are single-pinned. Each of the three sections of the top is a single board, and the joint between the center and the hinged leaves is a tongue and groove. The top of the side rails has a recess toward either end to accommodate the hinges. The pivot leg on the gates is round-tenoned to the rail and stretcher. The drawer runs on thin supports nailed to the side rails. The lower edge of the end rails is finished with an ovolo.

CONDITION

The top (maple) is a replacement, and both the center section and the leaves are too narrow for the frame. The center board has a split at one end and shows the top of a pin above each frame leg but is now primarily secured with large cut nails into each side rail. The drawer (maple and pine, with a dovetail at each corner and a nailed bottom) is not original. The drawer runners are questionable. So is the rail (pine) opposite the drawer, and perhaps also that above the drawer. There is no evidence on the end rails of the usual medial drawer runner. Some of the joints have been apart and the pins replaced. A large split down the upper block of the left rear leg has been repaired with modern screws. On the right gate the joint of the lower stretcher to the pivot leg has a new tenon. There are losses on the inner side of the end blocks of the left stretcher, on a turning on the left gate (defective wood), and at the bottom of two of the feet, all of which have been cut down. The top is stained and scratched under a clear finish; the base shows remains of red paint under one or more finish coatings and is uneven in color.

INSCRIPTION

An identification number painted on at the Dey Mansion (see *Exhibition*) is at the top of the left rear leg.

WOODS

Frame legs and stretchers, gates, rail above and below drawer, BEECH; side rails, EASTERN WHITE PINE.

DIMENSIONS

OH. $28\frac{1}{4}$ (71.8); top: w. open 41 (104.1), w. closed $15\frac{5}{8}$ (39.7), D. $42\frac{3}{4}$ (108.6); frame: w. $13\frac{3}{4}$ (34.9), D. $34\frac{3}{4}$ (88.3).

EXHIBITION

On loan to the Dey Mansion, Wayne, New Jersey, from 1938 to 1999.

PROVENANCE

Ex coll.: H. Eugene Bolles, Boston.

Gift of Mrs. Russell Sage, 1909 (10.125.673)

1. See, for example, Jobe and Kaye 1984, no. 58; Monkhouse and Michie 1986, no. 62; and Venable 1989, no. 3.
2. Nutting 1928–33, no. 949. The table was sold in 1991 (*Fine Americana, Including Furniture, Folk Art, and Folk Paintings,* auction cat., Sotheby's, New York City, 26 October 1991, lot 210).
3. On the Boston tables, see n. 1; others are in Wood 1996, no. 16, included in Bernard and S. Dean Levy gallery catalogue, vol. 5 (New York, 1986), p. 13 and advertised by Peter Eaton in *Antiques* 134 (September 1988), p. 350.

63.
Oval table with falling leaves

Rhode Island, 1715–40

This table is part of a group of about thirty tables of several types that have related turnings. They compose the largest coherent body of such objects from early-eighteenth-century New England that do not have legs turned in a pattern of symmetrically opposed balusters (see also cat. no. 52). Instead they feature a very individual interpretation of the generic design of a baluster above a spherical form—a formula that was much more common on tables made from New York on south (see cat. nos. 64, 65). The leg turnings on this group consist of a high baluster characterized by a globular base and a long, straight, tapering neck above a ball form that is set between taller or shorter segments that range in shape from cylindrical, as here, to clearly concave. The baluster and the ball are separated either by a ring or, more distinctively, by a disk with an ovolo upper profile and a flat bottom, as on this

piece. The finely executed, quite stylized version of this scheme on the present table is noteworthy for the sharp variations in the diameter of its elements: the neck of the baluster is particularly slender and the thin ring near the top projects out prominently and appears quasi-free-floating; and the full, round base of that vase form rests on a narrow point of the leg, where it is stepped in by means of two cavettos above the ovolo of the disk (fig. 34). The turned profile that adjoins the blocks is a thin, crisp disk. The terminal turnings on these tables typically have little height, whether they are straight-edged, as on this and some of the other examples, or have a rounded contour.

Some fourteen other oval tables with falling leaves and legs in a similar asymmetrical pattern are known, and they reflect in their turnings the work of more than one shop. Differences occur in the details of the individual turned elements, including,

63. See also figs. 34, 117.

on six of the tables, the addition of a shallow astragal midway up the neck of the baluster.[1] The tables also vary structurally, and some of them exhibit features that diverge from common construction practices of the period. On more than half of the examples the gates that support the leaves swing out from the same end of the frame as they do here, instead of from opposite ends. On this and at least two other tables, the top is pinned to the side rails rather than to the legs and the hinges are located outside the legs; and on this and at least one other table the pins go through to the bottom of the rails. A further characteristic of some examples is that the rail under the drawer extends down no further than the side frame rails, as is the case on this piece.

The school of turning represented by this table has long been ascribed to Rhode Island. The attribution is based at present on two tables with histories that link them to that area: one is said to have descended in the Easton family of Newport (present location unknown) and the other (private collection) in the Alden-Southworth-Cooke families of Little Compton and Newport.[2] Stair balusters in the Seventh Day Baptist Meeting House in Newport (1725–30) confirm that an asymmetrical turning pattern of a vase form over a ball shape was in use in Rhode Island at that time. The vase form is similar to that on this group of tables in having a globular base and long thin neck, but it is separated from the ball below by just a narrow fillet.[3] A stylistically earlier version of the general baluster-over-ball scheme was present in eastern Massachusetts by 1700, as is documented by stair balusters in the Isaac Winslow House in Marshfield, Massachusetts, and by those from a house formerly in nearby South Scituate, both of about 1695–1700.[4] Such a pattern is rare on New England furniture outside the group of tables under discussion (it may be that it was more widely used in interior woodwork). Interestingly one of the few other examples, a walnut stool attributed to Boston and at the Winterthur Museum, provides a precedent for the type of ovolo disk seen on cat. no. 63. Stylistically the turnings on the stool appear to date from very early in the 1700s, and the disk, likewise separating the baluster from the ball below, is not just flat on the underside but undercut.[5] The profile of the vase turnings on the Rhode Island tables bespeaks a somewhat later period and suggests the influence of Boston cane and leather chairs of the later 1710s to the 1730s (see cat. nos. 32, 33). The shape of the baluster bears a striking resemblance, particularly on this piece, to the contours on the ring-and-ball stretchers of such chairs. The similarity is especially clear on the table's stretchers.

CONSTRUCTION

The frame has broader than usual proportions, with the ends half the length of the sides. The turned members and the side frame rails are made from 2-inch stock. The mortise-and-tenon joints of the back and side frame rails are secured with two pins, all others with one. The center top consists of a single board and is affixed to each side rail with two long wooden pins that pass through the rail. The leaves, each formed of a wide inner board and a narrow one at the tip, abut the center with tongue-and-groove joints. They are attached with a surface-mounted iron butt hinge at each end installed outside the leg and secured with rosehead nails with leather washers (fig. 117). (There are no recesses in the top of the side rails to accommodate hinges on the inner side of the legs.) Both gates swing out from the same end of the frame—opposite the drawer. The pivot leg of the gate is round-tenoned to the rail and stretcher, and the foot below it is attached to the stretcher with a rectangular tenon that is pinned. There is a rail above as well as below the drawer, which rides on runners attached to the side rails with T-headed nails. Evidence of mill sawing remains on the underside of the top and the inside of the back rail.

CONDITION

The top, including the hinges, is original. It has been off, and the center section has been reattached with new pins. (X-radiographs confirm that no top was ever attached to the legs.) On the leaves, which are noticeably warped, the seams between the boards have been reglued and the joints reinforced at the rim with pins or nails. While a 1912 MMA photograph (see *References*) shows the tip of one leaf missing, records indicate it had merely come loose. On the left gate, the upper stretcher is split at the outer leg and repaired with modern

screws; a portion of the ovolo disk turning on that leg is missing; and the joint of the insect-damaged foot under the pivot leg has a new pin. The feet have all been cut down. The drawer (maple and pine, with a dovetail at each corner and a nailed bottom) and the drawer stops are replacements. The top, which has been stripped and refinished, has residues of red paint. The table base is still painted red (not original); there are losses to the paint and dark residues of a later coating. Parts of the understructure have been stained dark brown.

WOODS

SOFT MAPLE; side rails, drawer runners, EASTERN WHITE PINE.

DIMENSIONS

OH. 28 (71.1); top: w. open 57¾ (146.7), w. closed 20¾ (52.7), D. 48½ (123.2); frame: w. 17¾ (45.1), D. 35¾ (90.8).

REFERENCES

Schwartz 1976, no. 28 (1912 photograph); M. B. Davidson and Stillinger 1985, figs. 33, 34 (detail of stretcher); MMA 2001, fig. 18.

PROVENANCE

Ex coll.: H. Eugene Bolles, Boston.

Gift of Mrs. Russell Sage, 1909 (10.125.133)

1. The six with an extra astragal are illustrated in Gronning and Carr 2004. The others are in Rodriguez Roque 1984, no. 129 (Chipstone Foundation); advertised in *Antiques* 117 (February 1980), p. 298, by Nathan Liverant and Son; and offered in *Fine Americana*, auction cat., Skinner, Bolton, Massachusetts, 30 May 1986, lot 132, and *Annual Summer New Hampshire Auction*, auction cat., Northeast Auctions, Manchester, New Hampshire, 4 August 1996, lot 811. In addition, several have more recently come on the market and Erik K. Gronning has kindly brought them to the present writer's attention.

2. The first published attribution of such turnings to Rhode Island was probably in Sack 1950, p. 240; no basis for the attribution was given, but a small table with this type of turning had been published in 1928 as belonging to Henry A. Hoffman, Barrington, Rhode Island (Nutting 1928–33, no. 2723). Benno M. Forman recorded the Easton family history of the table in question (Gronning and Carr 2004, fig. 5), which was for a time on loan to the Redwood Library and Athenaeum in Newport (Rodriguez Roque 1984, p. 278; Trent 1999, p. 222, n. 14). The owners of the second table (Gronning and Carr 2004, fig. 3) kindly provided the present writer with its history (see also Gronning and Carr 2004, p. 125).

3. Beckerdite 2000, fig. 19.

4. St. George 1979b, no. 34; a table with similar turnings is shown in no. 33.

5. Forman 1988, no. 39. A similar disk, used in the same manner, is on a table at the Isaac Winslow House; the present writer is indebted to Beverly T. Thomas for a photograph of the table's turnings and the information that it is of maple. Ovolo disks or half rings, usually flat-bottomed, occur on English cane chairs and can be observed on the stiles and stretchers of some Boston plain-top leather chairs (Gonzales and Brown 1996, figs. 1, 6b, 6c) and the stretchers of Boston easy chairs such as cat. no. 39.

64. See also fig. 38.

64.
Oval table with falling leaves

Southeastern Pennsylvania, possibly Philadelphia, 1700–1730

Massive, and with vigorous turnings juxtaposed to heavy blocks and echoed in the shape of the skirts, this table is related to examples with histories in southeastern Pennsylvania in the substantial weight of the stock, the use of scalloped end rails, and the nature of the turnings.[1] While the basic formula of a baluster over a rounded form is not exclusive to any one region, it is much more common in the mid-Atlantic colonies and the South than in New England and it is characteristic of many oval tables with falling leaves that have been attributed to Pennsylvania, where the baluster is frequently ornamented with grooves, as it is here. What

distinguishes the turnings on the legs of this table is the particular shape and sequence of the elements below the baluster, which consist of a ring, short reel, very flattened ball, and an ovolo (fig. 38). A close parallel to those forms, below a somewhat taller baluster, can be found on a walnut table at the Germantown Historical Society that descended in the family of John Ashmead, one of the first English settlers of that locality (now part of Philadelphia).[2] The turnings on the stretchers of that piece are also related in that they consist of opposed balusters flanking a full ball, but the balusters are less compressed, because that table is larger, and the ball and balusters are separated by rings rather than concavities. On the Ashmead table, as on this one, the turnings on the legs of the frame and of the gates are identical and at the same level—a design feature that appears to be more prevalent on tables from Pennsylvania and the South than from New England. Consequently the lower blocks of the frame legs are of a greater than usual height, which is exceeded slightly on both tables by that of the upper blocks. The monolithic quality imparted by the size of those blocks is heightened on this piece by the sharp square corners that terminate them and reinforced on both tables by the heft of the upper gate stretchers, which have the same width as the legs and are molded on all four edges.

This table does not lack in sophistication, and the design elements it has in common with the Ashmead example suggest that it was produced in close proximity to Philadelphia if not in the city itself. Although of hard pine rather than the more prized walnut of which the majority of surviving Pennsylvania tables from this period are made, this piece cannot be discounted as a possible urban product because of the wood used. Ruth Matzkin in her study of the Philadelphia County inventories from the period 1682–1710 found that of the tables described by the wood of which they were made, slightly more than half as many were of pine as of walnut. A pine oval table with carpet listed in one inventory likely referred to one with falling leaves such as this one.[3]

CONSTRUCTION

The frame is made from stock close to 2¾ inches thick and joined with substantial tenons ¹¹/₁₆ inch thick. The tenons of the side rails are haunched and double-pinned. The other joints are single-pinned, except for those of the end rail above each drawer and of the cross brace under the top at the center of the frame, which lack pins. The brace doubles as a stop for the two drawers, which slide on a medial support that is let into a notch in the rails below the drawers. Each of the three sections of the top is composed of two boards. The center is pinned to the frame, and the leaves, each attached with three large flared hinges secured with screws and rivets, meet the center with plain butt joints. The leaves are each supported by a gate that pivots and fits against the frame in the standard manner. The gates were designed with an eye both to what is the outer side when the gate is closed and to the inner side, visible when the gate is open, rather than just to the outer side, as was almost always the case. For example, rather than being thinner than and flush with just the outer side of the legs, as was common practice, the upper gate stretchers, like the lower stretchers, are as thick as the legs and flush with them also on the inner side; and the joints of both stretchers are centered on the width of the legs, and not worked a set distance in from the outer face, as they are invariably on the fixed frame and as a general rule also on the gates. All four edges of the upper stretchers are molded with a small cyma reversa. The shaped end rails are lightened on the lower inner edge with a chamfer.

CONDITION

The top has undergone several changes and has some problematic aspects. It appears to be old and may or may not be original. At one time, perhaps to counter warpage, large nails driven through the center top into the side rails and legs were added. The nails have since been removed, leaving the surface marred by empty nail holes in addition to deep gouges and nicks, and the top has been reversed end to end and reset with a new pin into each leg and two additional pins into each end rail. The outer board on each leaf is a modern replacement, and the glued joint is reinforced on the underside with two dovetail keys and on one leaf also with two screwed-on metal straps. The joint between the two center boards has been altered, probably as a repair to a broken lap joint; each board now has a rabbet at the upper edge and the resulting recess is filled with a narrow strip of recent date. The plain butt joints between the center and the leaves are somewhat questionable and may represent another type of joint that has been taken down. The large hinges, which may be hiding evidence of earlier ones, are unusual, and the rivets with a broad, flat head that protrudes prominently on the upper surface have an Arts and Crafts look of the late 1800s and early 1900s. The drawers (Atlantic white cedar and probably yellow poplar, with two dovetails at each corner and a nailed bottom) and drawer runner are replacements. Nail holes remain where, at a point when the top was off, the drawer fronts were nailed in place through the upper and lower rails. The feet are new—from below the ovolo under the leg block—and were added by the donor, Mrs. Robert W. de Forest; in the 1929 Reifsnyder sale catalogue (see *References*) the table had only worn stumps for feet. She recorded in her notes on the piece (ADA files) that she had the table "slightly repaired" by Morris Schwartz (a Hartford, Connecticut, cabinetmaker and restorer). The table has been stripped but retains residues of modern red paint. The wood has raised grain and appears to have been oiled and waxed.

INSCRIPTIONS

A restorer's mark ("I") is incised on one lower end rail and the underside of the corresponding drawer. The right outer side of the same drawer is inscribed "#366R" in chalk.

WOOD

SOUTHERN YELLOW PINE.

DIMENSIONS

OH. 29¾ (75.6); top: W. open 57¾ (146.7), W. closed 19⅛ (48.6), D. 50⅜ (128); frame: W. 16⅞ (42.9), D. 40¾ (103.5).

REFERENCES

Storey 1926, p. 12; Holloway 1928, pl. 2B; *Colonial Furniture: The Superb Collection of the Late Howard Reifsnyder,* auction cat., American Art Association, New York City, 24–27 April 1929, lot 661 (this and the previous references show the table before the feet were restored).

PROVENANCE

Ex coll.: Howard Reifsnyder, Philadelphia; Mrs. Robert W. de Forest, New York City.

Mrs. de Forest acquired the table in 1929 at the sale of the Howard Reifsnyder collection (see *References*). According to a letter of 1 October 1934 from Thomas Curran, Philadelphia dealer and friend and aide of Reifsnyder's, to Joseph Downs (ADA files), the table had been purchased in Bristol, Pennsylvania, with no known history.

Gift of Mrs. Robert W. de Forest, 1933 (34.100.16)

1. Tables of this type with histories are in Schiffer 1966, ill. nos. 85, 120; Lindsey 1999, no. 77; Zimmerman 2004, pl. I; see also the table cited in n. 2 below.

2. Lloyd 1983, fig. 1. The present writer thanks Mary K. Dabney for providing the requested information on this table. The same sequence of turnings below a more elongated baluster is on a walnut table advertised by Thurston Nichols in *Antiques* 161 (January 2002), p. 50.

3. Matzkin 1959, pp. 29 (25 pine, 48 walnut), 106.

65.
Oval table with falling leaves

New York, 1690–1730

Although found in Rhode Island, this table, by virtue of its particular form, the woods used, and the nature of the turnings, was unquestionably made in New York. The type of trestle-base table with falling leaves popular in New York, which was based on English models, is characterized by a one- or two-board flat stretcher, plain flat gates, and at each end a turned leg of substantial proportions (compare cat. nos. 66, 67).[1] Structurally these tables are distinguished by having the top supported by a board that is parallel to the stretcher and to which the frame legs are joined, in some cases with a dovetail, as they are here, in others with a rectangular tenon. On the gates, made of boards less than an inch thick, the stretchers are characteristically joined to the uprights with through tenons.[2] Peculiar to a number of New York leaf tables of various types from this period is the manner in which the hinges on this example are attached (fig. 118)—with a rivet, the head of which is concealed by a face-grain plug, supplementing the nails.[3] The fact that this piece is made of sweet gum and yellow poplar provides another strong link to New York (see cat. nos. 121, 132).

The design of the turnings on this form of New York table varies. The most common one, used on approximately half of the some two dozen such tables known, consists of two superimposed ogee balusters, a pattern that is associated with New York and has been found also in South Carolina work. The basic scheme of the turnings on this table (fig. 35)—an ogee baluster above a more or less ball-shaped form—is a generic pattern that is more widespread and appears in many different interpretations from New England to the South.[4] The version seen here, in which the lower element is set between rings and reels and can be read as a double-ended baluster, appears to be peculiar to New York. The same sequence of turnings occurs on the legs of two other trestle-base tables and of two gateleg examples with rectangular frames and, minus the reels, on the stretchers of cat. no. 51.[5] The compressed double-ended form on this piece and the tight reels that flank it convey a sense of energy ready to be released. They exhibit the Baroque vigor that characterizes many New York turnings of the period and here stands in contrast to the rectilinearity of the remainder of the table base, on which a large ovolo toward the ends of the feet is the only decorative detail.

CONSTRUCTION

The turned legs—2½ inches thick—are each joined at the upper end with a dovetail to a board that lies flat under the top and serves as a rail and at the lower end with a rectangular through tenon (double-pinned) to the foot. The stretcher is joined to each foot with a broad tenon that is pinned on either side of the leg. Each of the three sections of the top is a single board. The center one is fastened to the flat rail with a wooden pin at the middle of each end and of each side. The leaves meet the center board with tongue-and-groove joints; they are each attached with two dovetail hinges secured from below with a nail at each corner and from above with a rivet in the center, the head of which is countersunk and hidden with a round face-grain plug (fig. 118). The upper surface of the rail has recesses to accommodate the hinges. The pivot leg on the gates is round-tenoned to the rail and to the stretcher, and the outer leg fits into a cutout in the rail and stretcher when the gate is closed. The stretchers of the gates are joined to the uprights with through tenons that are double-pinned.

CONDITION

The table has no replacements but numerous repairs. The top has suffered from the heavy warpage to which tangent-sawn sweet gum is prone. The center board has numerous splits, and its attachment to the rail has been reinforced from above at each end with three nails or screws (hidden by fill) and from below by two modern screws. The leaves are now in sections—one in two, the other in three—probably separated at splits. The adjoining edges have been planed and glued, and the outer edge of the leaf has been shaved where two segments no longer met flush. On the two-part leaf, the joint has been strengthened at the rim with screws or nails, and there was once a reinforcing strip nailed to the underside. The hinges are original, and some of the nails retain remnants of leather washers. Four of the plugs hiding the rivet heads are missing. There is heavy wear on the stretchers and the leaves from the movement of the gates, and the top of the outer leg of one gate has been patched. Nails have been added to the stretcher joints and secure splits in the stretcher and rail

65. See also figs. 35, 118.

near the holes that engage the gates' pintles. The feet are heavily worn; the wood is weak on account of insect damage and has been partly consolidated; gliders were added underneath. The table base is covered with brown paint (not original), which has been largely removed from the top. The underside of the top and rail has been stained brown.

WOODS
SWEET GUM; rail under top, YELLOW POPLAR.

DIMENSIONS
OH. 26¼ (66.7); top: W. open 35 (88.9), W. closed 11¼ (28.6), D. 30 (76.2); frame: W. at feet 11¼ (28.6), D. 23⅞ (60.6).

REFERENCES
Kettell 1929, pl. 89 and measured drawing, no. 31; MMA 1981, p. 57; Kenny 1994, fig. 22 and pp. 117, 122, 125.

PROVENANCE
Ex coll.: Earle W. Sargent, Greenville, North Carolina.

Sargent found the table in the cellar of an old house near Warren, Rhode Island, in the vicinity of his parents' home in Barrington, Rhode Island. The table was lent to the MMA by Sargent in 1925 and remained on loan until it became a gift from his widow.

Gift of Eleanor G. Sargent, 1980 (1980.499.1)

1. For English tables, see Chinnery 1979, figs. 3:215–3:224. For a comprehensive study of early Baroque New York tables with falling leaves of this and other types, see Kenny 1994.

2. Three trestle-base tables with flat board stretchers but turned gates are known to the writer. They differ structurally from the type represented by cat. no. 65 in that the frame legs are tenoned at the top to trestle heads that are connected by one or two flat rails, a method of construction also seen on English tables. On two, the leg turnings have the heft of those on New York tables (Winterthur Museum, acc. no. 64.1041; Lockwood 1913, fig. 689). The third, because of the scale and character of its opposed baluster turnings, may be a rare New England table with a board stretcher ("Shop Talk" 1960, p. 442, said to be from the Luke Vincent Lockwood collection).

3. For an illustration of such plugs, see Kenny 1994, fig. 33.

4. New England turnings in this general scheme (see cat. no. 63 and St. George 1979b, nos. 33, 34) are less common than those from Pennsylvania (see cat. no. 64) and the South (see Barquist 1992, no. 43, for example).

5. For the trestle-base tables, see *Maine Antique Digest,* August 1990, p. 33B (Fred J. Johnston advertisement); and *Fine American Furniture, Folk Art, Folk Paintings and Silver,* auction cat., Sotheby's, New York City, 26 June 1986, lot 112. The rectangular tables are one at the Van Cortlandt House Museum, Bronx, New York, and one in *The American Heritage Auction of Americana,* auction cat., Sotheby's, New York City, 27–30 January 1982, lot 783.

66.

Oval table with falling leaves

Probably eastern Massachusetts, 1690–1720

This table features finely articulated turnings that consist of a baluster over a reel, with the greatly attenuated vase form on the frame legs playing against a more typical William and Mary–style ogee shape on the legs of the gates. The overall scheme of the turnings has seventeenth-century-style antecedents (see cat. nos. 21, 46), and the very slight curvature given to the balusters on the frame legs recalls that tradition. More specifically, the marking of the fullest part of the baluster with a groove was a seventeenth-century practice. A convex band flanked by grooves virtually identical to that on this table occurs on the legs of cat. no. 47, for example.

Such single-baluster turnings are not common on New England tables of the William and Mary period, but the trestle-base form of this example is characteristic of that region (see also cat. no. 67), and the woods of which this piece is made are not inconsistent with an attribution to that area.[1] Maple and oak, used for the less visible parts of this table, were the principal woods employed in the Boston area for the joined frames of upholstered chairs—from seventeenth-century back stools to early-eighteenth-century tall-back chairs (see cat. nos. 24–27)—and would have been the stock-in-trade of an urban shop making tables alongside such chairs; the oak upper stretchers on the gates of this piece could easily be shortened chair stretchers or stay rails. The quality of the table's turnings and the fact that it is primarily of walnut, which had to be imported into New England, suggest that the piece originated in a larger port town and indicate that it aimed at fashionability, even though the maker chose to use a conservative, single-baluster design for the legs. Not many New England examples from the first half of the eighteenth century of legs turned in an elongated, slightly shaped baluster over a reel are known, and they occur usually on pieces of moderate or little pretension made of local woods. This form of turned leg seems to have moved into the realm of a

66

traditional pattern used on economical, serviceable furniture, and as such persisted into the nineteenth century.[2]

CONSTRUCTION

The turned members and the frame rail are 1½ inches thick. The rectangular tenons that join the frame legs to the feet are secured with two smaller pins (¼ in.), those that join the frame rail to the legs with two larger pins (5⁄16 in.), and all others with a single larger pin. The pivot legs of the gates are round-tenoned to the rail and to the stretcher. They are installed ½ inch apart, following the layout lines visible on the frame rail; and to assure clearance when the legs pivot, the corners of the blocks on the sides that face one another when the gates are closed have been lightly chamfered. On the replacement top the leaves are composed of a wide and a narrow board and meet the center section with tongue-and-groove joints.

CONDITION
The foot on one frame leg has a split near the top, and the weakened joint with the leg has been reinforced with a large dowel that goes up through the foot. The top (walnut) is not original. The center section is attached to the rail with two wooden pins capped with face-grain plugs, and it is supported underneath on each side by two long blocks nailed to the rail; an earlier top was attached to the legs (confirmed by X-radiography). The present top shows some signs of wear and has repairs at the joint of the two boards in each leaf and replaced hinges on one side. A thin slat has been nailed under each leaf at the point where it is supported by the outer leg of the gate. The foot on one of those legs has been cut down. The table has been refinished but retains dark residues from an earlier coating. The underside of the top and the blocks have been stained brown.

WOODS
Frame legs and feet, frame stretcher, legs and lower stretchers of gates, WALNUT; frame rail, SOFT MAPLE; upper stretchers of gates, OAK.

DIMENSIONS
OH. 25⅝ (65.1); top: w. open 27⅝ (70.2), w. closed 7 (17.8), D. 28½ (72.4); frame: w. at feet 9⅝ (24.4), D. 23¼ (59.1).

PROVENANCE
Ex coll.: Mrs. J. Insley Blair, Tuxedo Park, New York; her daughter Mrs. Screven Lorillard, Far Hills, New Jersey.

Mrs. Blair acquired the table from Henry V. Weil, a New York City dealer, in 1920.

Gift of Mrs. Screven Lorillard, 1952 (52.195.5)

1. Turnings of this type occur on Pennsylvania walnut tables of the mid-1700s (for one with legs that are similarly grooved, see Scott 1979, fig. 2). However, this trestle-base table form is not known to have been made there nor is the combination of woods used characteristic of furniture from that area.
2. Related turnings (grooved) are on a stool at the Museum of Fine Arts, Boston (Randall 1965, no. 115). Generally similar long balusters (without grooves) occur on a number of tables of the type represented by cat. nos. 68 and 69 (see, for example, Nutting 1928–33, no. 923; Kirk 1967, no. 146; Fales 1976, no. 242; and *Sack Collection* 1981–92, vol. 6, p. 1573), some of which date no earlier than the mid-1700s, and they are found on plain rectangular tables from the mid-1700s to well into the 1800s.

67.
Oval table with falling leaves
Eastern Massachusetts, 1715–40

In its overall design, this piece exemplifies the type of small oval or round table with a trestle base and falling leaves that is characteristic of New England. All the uprights and lower stretchers are turned, and the frame rail is oriented vertically, which makes for a very compact unit; such tables sometimes measure barely six inches across with the leaves down. (The center board of the replaced top of this example is unusually wide.) Tables of this form appear to have been made only in New England. They are smaller on the whole than their New York counterparts, the frame rails and stretchers of which are formed of boards oriented horizontally, making for an inherently more stable structure (see cat. no. 65). They are also generally lower, measuring in most cases between twenty-five and twenty-six inches high, about three inches less than was normal for a dining table. (Cat. no. 65 is among the lowest of the New York examples.) Easily portable and taking up little space when put away, such tables were probably put to multiple uses wherever needed in the home. That this furniture form had a place in well-appointed households is borne out by examples made of imported walnut rather than local New England woods.

This walnut table shows refinement in its nicely shaped high-arched feet and its well-executed ogee balusters, reminiscent of those on cat. no. 60. It differs from almost all other New England gateleg tables of any type in that the opposed baluster motif on the frame legs is exactly the same as that on the legs of the gates rather than being in a design that has greater height. Another particularity of this table is that the pivot legs of the two gates are positioned tightly together (see *Construction*). A related, somewhat smaller, walnut table at the Pilgrim Hall Museum, Plymouth, Massachusetts, with a history of ownership in the White and Warren families of Plymouth, exhibits these same two traits and has opposed ogee balusters virtually identical in profile to those on this piece (but the feet on the frame legs have different contours). It was possibly made in the same shop.[1]

CONSTRUCTION
The turned members and the frame rail are at most 1⁷⁄₁₆ inches thick. The rectangular tenons that join the frame legs to the feet and the frame rail to the legs are secured with two pins, all others with one. The pivot legs of the gates are round-tenoned to the rail and stretcher, but contrary to the norm, they are installed with no space between them, in accordance with the scribed layout lines visible on the rail. The legs are able to rotate the requisite 90 degrees because on the side

67

on which they abut when the gates are closed the corners of the blocks have been taken down and rounded. The upper edges of the plain stretchers on the gates are finished with a small chamfer. Some of the less visible surfaces of the base were left with torn grain, and wood with a disfiguring knot was used for the frame stretcher. The center section and the leaves of the replacement top are each a single board, and they come together with a rule joint.

CONDITION

The top (soft maple) is a replacement. It is pinned at each end to the frame leg and at the middle of each side to a large, added half-round block (soft maple) nailed to the frame rail. The center section may be a reused board. On the underside of one leaf are two thin nailed-on strips to hold the gate in place when open, and under each leaf is a wedge, attached by means of a nailed-on leather thong, to be inserted at the top of the outer leg of the gate. The top of those legs has been crudely chamfered on one edge. The foot on one of the frame legs is split at one end. The table base shows moderate but consistent wear. It has been stripped and has a modern finish; dark residues of an earlier coating remain. The top has graining in dark brown or black on red paint, which has partly worn off on one leaf. Red brown stain has been applied to the frame rail, blocks, and underside of the top.

INSCRIPTIONS

Inscribed in white chalk on the underside of one leaf are script initials that appear to read "JRT." Inscribed in ink on a piece of paper glued under the other leaf is: "PROPERTY OF / Ca . . . / W . . . / 1926."

WOODS

Frame legs and feet, frame stretcher, gates, BLACK WALNUT; frame rail, EASTERN WHITE PINE.

DIMENSIONS

OH. 25¼ (64.1); top: w. open 32½ (82.6), w. closed 9¼ (23.5), D. 32⅞ (83.5); frame: w. at feet 10 (25.4), D. 23⅞ (60.6).

REFERENCE

Schwartz 1976, no. 27.

PROVENANCE

Ex coll.: Mrs. J. Insley Blair, Tuxedo Park, New York.

Mrs. Blair purchased the table from Hyman Kaufman, a Boston dealer, in 1931. The table was on loan to the MMA from Mrs. Blair from 1939 until the time it became a bequest.

Bequest of Mrs. J. Insley Blair, 1951 (52.77.57)

1. Pizer, Driver, and Earle 1985, fig. 10. The frame of the Pilgrim Hall Museum table is only 18½ inches deep. The present writer is indebted to Karin J. Goldstein for detailed information on this piece.

68.

Oval table with falling leaves

Connecticut, 1740–60

This type of table with falling leaves, which appears to have been made only in New England, enlarges upon the form of oval table with a fixed top exemplified by cat. no. 54. Portable, but not as compact as small leaf tables on a trestle base (see cat. nos. 66, 67), such tables, with their wider frames and splayed legs, offer greater stability when the leaves are down and also a larger usable surface. The pivot supports for the leaves, sawn out from flat boards, are more easily produced than are turned and framed gates; they are not, however, as substantial and not practicable for large tables. Today, this form of table is commonly known as a butterfly table, in allusion to the shape of those supports.[1] The majority of these tables have plain rectangular stretchers like those on similar frames equipped with a stationary top. This is one of a good dozen examples that are distinguished by having turned stretchers.[2] The use of such stretchers, which represented an added cost, cannot be linked to any particular shop or locality; the variations in the turnings—which all feature opposed balusters, the pattern seen on most tables of this form—indicate they are the work of many different craftsmen, and the shape of the supports—based on ogee curves and compass arcs—also varies.

Most of the tables of this type that have histories, including four out of the five examples with turned stretchers, have associations with Connecticut.[3] That and the frequent use of cherry in that region in the mid-eighteenth century point to a Connecticut origin for cat. no. 68. The shape of the pivot supports on this table has a certain flair, but the turnings, with their rather flaccid vase forms and shallow reels, lack vigor. They appear to have been made by a rural turner at a time when early Baroque design impulses were no longer fresh. Indeed the use of rule joints in the top supports a date of manufacture not earlier than about 1740. This form of table with hinged leaves was an economical one, made of local woods and geared more toward practicality than pretension. As such, it seems to have found favor mainly outside major centers and it continued to be produced well past the period when opposed baluster turnings were fashionable in urban areas (see the entry for cat. no. 69).

CONSTRUCTION

The legs and stretchers are made from 1¾-inch stock. The legs are splayed (about 7 degrees from the vertical) in two opposite directions.

One of the mortise-and-tenon joints of the rails is secured with three rather than two pins; the joints of the stretchers are single-pinned. The holes for corresponding pins at a right angle to one another in a leg are drilled at approximately the same height so that the pins partially or entirely intersect. Each of the three sections of the top is a single board. The center board is pinned to the legs; the leaves abut it with rule joints and are attached outside the legs with butt hinges that are recessed and affixed with screws. The pivot supports for the leaves rotate on round tenons, one socketed into the underside of the center top, the other into the stretcher. The edge of the top and the vertical edges of the leaf supports are rounded. The bottom edge of the end rails is finished with an ovolo and a fillet. There remain visible on many of the blocks of the legs and stretchers the lines that were scribed perpendicular to the length of the blocks to indicate how far the corners of the blocks were to be turned.

CONDITION

The boards of the top are warped and marked by stains and scorching, and two have splits. The attachment of the center top has been reinforced with two pins into each side rail. On one side of the table, the side edge of the center board is pieced for about 5 inches at one end, and the inner edge of the leaf has a patch at the other end. On the other side, the edge of the leaf is heavily worn at both ends. The tenon at the bottom of one pivot support has been replaced with a dowel. The upper blocks of two legs have splits. The feet have lost most of their height. Notes by the donor, Mrs. J. Insley Blair (ADA files), describe the table as "Refinished"—its present condition—and state that it was "Bought in rough. Painted Red." The table retains traces of red paint and evidence of stripping and sanding.

INSCRIPTIONS

Joiner's assembly marks, consisting of one or two notches, match up the side rails with the legs—at both ends of one rail and one end of the other.

WOOD

CHERRY.

DIMENSIONS

OH. 25¾ (65.4); top: w. open 42⅜ (107.6), w. closed 14⅝ (37.1), D. 34¾ (88.3); frame: w. at top 10½ (26.7), w. at feet 16½ (41.9), D. 21⅛ (53.7).

REFERENCE

Schwartz 1976, no. 25.

PROVENANCE

Ex coll.: Mrs. J. Insley Blair, Tuxedo Park, New York.

Mrs. Blair purchased the table from Collings and Collings, New York City dealers, in 1916. Her notes also state: "Maurice Schwartz

68

knew of it and sold it to Collings, I think." (She is probably referring to Morris Schwartz, a cabinetmaker and restorer in Hartford, Connecticut.) The table was on loan from Mrs. Blair to the MMA from 1939 until the time of the bequest.

Bequest of Mrs. J. Insley Blair, 1951 (52.77.54)

1. The term appears to date from the last decades of the nineteenth century (Barquist 1992, p. 126).
2. Four of the tables with turned stretchers have histories in Connecticut: Keyes 1927 (Portland); Bissell 1956, pl. 10 and p. 37 (Norton family, Suffield); Connecticut Historical Society 1963, p. 28 (North family, Colebrook); Kirk 1967, no. 145 (Windsor area). One has a history in New Hampshire: Guyol 1958, fig. 2 (Dover). Others are in Lockwood 1913, figs. 693, 694, Nutting 1921, p. 394, Dyer 1931b, p. 44, and Comstock 1962, no. 118; are advertised by Benjamin Ginsburg in *Antiques* 111 (March 1977), p. 431; are included in

Bernard and S. Dean Levy gallery catalogue, vol. 6 (New York, 1988), p. 14; and are offered in *The Rare and Extremely Choice Collection of Early American and English Furniture . . . Formed by Louis Guerineau Myers,* auction cat., American Art Galleries, New York City, 24–26 February 1921, lot 524.

3. See n. 2 above. Other tables with histories are in Keyes 1935, fig. 5 (Wyckoff family, Windsor, Connecticut); Connecticut Historical Society 1958, pp. 124, 125 (two tables, Churchill family, Newington, Connecticut); Kirk 1967, no. 143 (found in Putnam, Connecticut), no. 146 (found in Higganum, Connecticut); and Monkhouse and Michie 1986, no. 59 (West Newbury, Massachusetts). One was advertised by Florene Maine in *Antiques* 80 (October 1961), p. 325 (Westbrook, Connecticut); and others were offered in *Colonial Furniture, Silver, and Decorations: The Collection of the Late Philip Flayderman,* auction cat., American Art Association, Anderson Galleries, New York City, 2–4 January 1930, lot 453 (Gould family, North Bridgton, Maine), and in *Americana,* auction cat., Skinner, Bolton, Massachusetts, 14 January 1989, lot 119 (North Branford, Connecticut).

69.
Oval table with falling leaves

New England, 1770–1800

While the general plan of this table and the basic scheme of its turnings represent designs identified with the William and Mary style, this piece was probably not made before the end of the eighteenth century. It is included in this catalogue as an example of the longevity enjoyed by some of the furniture forms and by the turning patterns characteristic of that style at a conservative level of production, particularly in nonurban areas. It also illustrates how later fashions influenced the interpretation of those forms. The maker of this table had in his vocabulary stylistic details associated with furniture of about 1740 to 1790. He used a rule joint (documented from about 1740 on) between the center top and the leaves rather than a tongue and groove, and he gave the outer edge of the top an ovolo profile instead of leaving it straight or making it rounded, as was customary in earlier periods.[1] In addition, the drawer front is not entirely flat and inset, but is finished with an ovolo around the perimeter and overlaps the frame. The early-eighteenth-century turning pattern of opposed balusters with reels on the legs has been simplified; there is a plain, thin disk between the balusters in place of the usual ring flanked by cavettos, and the rings at either end are not much more than ridges. The stylized treatment and attenuation of the forms suggest a date of manufacture late in the century, as does the small scale of the stock; they give the frame a dainty lightness reminiscent of neoclassical-style tables of the early Federal period. The table has the distinction of having the legs splayed in all four directions. This enables the slight frame to better counterbalance, both structurally and visually, the broad, flat expanses of the top and leaf supports.

CONSTRUCTION

The frame is made from 1¼-inch stock and is joined with tenons ¼ inch thick; those of the side and back rails are secured with two pins, the others with one. The legs are splayed at the same angle (4 to 5 degrees from the vertical) on all four sides. The three sections of the top are each a single board. The center board is pinned to the legs; the leaves abut it with rule joints and are attached well outside the legs with butt hinges that are recessed and screwed in place. The pivot supports for the leaves rotate on round tenons, one socketed into the underside of the center top, the other into the stretcher. The drawer, designed to conform to the trapezoidal shape of the opening, rides on the bottom of the sides on L-shaped runners nailed to the side rails. It is joined with two dovetails at each corner, and the bottom fits into a groove in the front and sides and is nailed to the back. The drawer front is molded around the perimeter with a small ovolo, and its ends are rabbeted so that it overlaps the frame at the sides for the width of the molding. The same molding finishes the lower outside edge of all four rails and the two upper edges of the stretchers. The edge

of the top has an ovolo contour, and the vertical edges of the leaf supports are rounded. The maple of the legs and stretchers shows a curly figure.

CONDITION

The top is stained and heavily scratched. The leaves have each lost a segment of the edge of the rule joint at the back, and the center section is split at the front and strongly warped. Because there is no rail above the drawer, the warping has drawn the front legs together at the top so that the drawer can no longer slide in all the way. On the drawer, a strip along one side of the bottom is replaced, the upper edge of the back is partly missing, and the joints have been reinforced with either a nail or a wooden pin. The runners are probably replacements. The upper outer third of the left leaf support has split off and been reattached. The right support is worn thin along part of the outer edge. The feet have been cut down. The table has a modern finish. It was at one point stained a deep mahogany color, which still covers a large part of the pivot supports and of the underside of the top and of which there are remains on the frame.

INSCRIPTIONS

A large X is scratched on the inner side of the right side rail (probably modern); a smaller one (in pencil) is inside the same rail, and another (scratched) is inside the drawer back.

WOODS

SOFT MAPLE; drawer back and bottom, PINE.

DIMENSIONS

OH. 24½ (62.2); top: w. open 33⅝ (85.4), w. closed 13⅛ (33.3), D. 34¼ (87); frame: w. at top 10¼ (26), w. at feet 13½ (34.3), D. at top 14¼ (36.2), D. at feet 17½ (44.5).

REFERENCES

Halsey and Cornelius 1924 (and 1925, 1926), fig. 14 (1928, 1932, fig. 15; 1938, 1942, fig. 20); Halsey and Tower 1925, fig. 29; B. N. and B. B. Osburn 1926, pp. 48 (measured drawings), 49; Cescinsky and Hunter 1929, p. 57; Salomonsky 1931, pl. 45 (includes measured drawings).

PROVENANCE

Ex coll.: H. Eugene Bolles, Boston.

Gift of Mrs. Russell Sage, 1909 (10.125.124)

1. An early reference to this type of joint occurs in the ledgers of joiner Joseph Brown Jr. of Newbury, Massachusetts, who in 1741 was paid three pounds for a "table rule joynted" (Mackiewicz 1981, p. 70). That tongue-and-groove joints were no longer fashionable on tables in the mid-eighteenth century, though they might still be used, is indicated by a 1757 list of prices for joiners' work in Providence, Rhode Island, which included both "Maple rule Joynt tables" and those with "old fashen Joynts," the latter costing less than the former (I. W. Lyon 1891, p. 265).

69

III.
CASE FURNITURE

Boxes and Other Small Case Pieces

The most common small storage unit in the seventeenth century was the rectangular box with a hinged lid. Boxes provided a place to keep belongings of many kinds, such as documents, writing implements, and books or jewelry, currency, and small items of apparel. The boxes in the Museum's collection were all made in New England, and as is the case in general, the large majority are carved. The carving, which utilizes a vocabulary of stylized plant forms and simple geometric shapes, displays a variety of designs and several different methods of execution.

The first two boxes in this chapter—one that was made in Connecticut (cat. no. 70) and one from Massachusetts (cat. no. 71)—are the most elaborately ornamented. They are carved not just on the front, as was common practice, but also on the sides. The main motifs, defined by deeply incised lines, include some three-dimensional modeling, which was the exception rather than the rule in colonial work at the time. The borders surrounding those motifs, however, were decorated by the simplest of means; the ornament was stamped with a punch or impressed with strikes of a gouge or chisel. Probably the most common type of carving was that executed on two planes—in which the design lies flat on the surface and the ground around it has been sunk. Such carving is represented by four of the boxes, three from Connecticut (cat. nos. 73–75), which have generally related designs but are each from a different shop, and one from Massachusetts (cat. no. 72). Gouge carving distinguishes the decoration on another box, the only one in this group not assigned to a particular shop tradition or locality (cat. no. 76). This type of carving was most often employed to form bands or borders; its use to create floral motifs, as on the sides of cat. no. 76, is exceptional. On the last carved box (cat. no. 77), which is attributed to New Hampshire, the main motifs have been basically just outlined with incised lines.

Boxes with applied ornament that consists of mitered moldings and half turnings were very much in the minority; only one, from Massachusetts, is in the collection (cat. no. 78). The rectangular box generally went out of fashion after 1700, but some eighteenth-century representatives of the form are known, such as the Museum's example with painted floral decoration from coastal Connecticut (cat. no. 80).

The boxes are typically of board construction, with the front and back nailed to the sides and the bottom nailed on from below. The lids are attached, as they are on chests, either with iron snipebill hinges or with cleat-pin hinges. (On the latter, a wooden pin protruding from the case engages the thick back end of the cleat under the lid.) Seventeenth-century boxes generally have the four sides made of riven oak; on a few examples, the lid and more rarely the bottom are of oak as well, but most often those elements are made of mill-sawn pine. The interior of some boxes is fitted at one or both ends with a small separate compartment, a till.

Other types of small case pieces made in the seventeenth century were considerably less common. They include the rectangular box with a drawer below and the dressing box, a miniature joined chest with several drawers underneath—both rare forms not represented in the collection. Another seventeenth-century form, the small cabinet of nearly square proportions that contains ten or so drawers of varying size behind a locked door, has survived in somewhat greater numbers. The Museum's example, from Massachusetts, is inscribed with the owners' initials and the date [16]79 (cat. no. 79). While it served a practical storage purpose, it was also a showpiece, for the applied elements adorning its joined door suggest an architectural facade. In New England, small cabinets did not remain in fashion beyond about 1700. Known from that region from the first half of the eighteenth century are small chests with a drawer or chests of drawers of dovetailed board construction, some of which, like that in the collection, are embellished with decorative painting (cat. no. 81). In Pennsylvania, square or rectangular small cabinets, made most often of walnut, were produced until past the mid-1700s. A particular type of cabinet favored only in that area set the unit enclosing the small drawers behind a door or doors on a stand, so that the whole resembled a miniature full-size case piece. The stand of the one in the collection (cat. no. 82) is a reduced version of the base of a William and Mary–style Philadelphia high chest.

70.

Box

Windsor or Killingworth, Connecticut, 1660–80
Attributed to the Buell shop tradition

The degree of elaboration exhibited by this box and by two related examples—one at the Oneida County Historical Society, Utica, New York, that descended in the Buell family and one at the Yale University Art Gallery—is not matched by any other American box of the seventeenth century.[1] The ornamentation on these pieces goes far beyond the carving of the sides as well as the front, which in itself is unusual. Not just the front corners but also those at the rear of the case are notched (with alternating concave and V-shaped cuts), as are the ends of the top, the front and rear edges of which are molded; the top has, in addition, a border near each end in a pattern formed by circular punches and arcs made with the strike of a gouge, and the same design adorns the projecting front and side edges of the bottom. The cleats underneath the ends of the top are notched at the back and have circular punched decoration on the underside. Finally, the back of the box is finished at each end with a vertical band of two parallel scored lines (fig. 53).

Joiner William Buell (or Buel, 1614–1681) is thought to have been the first owner of the Buell family box and its maker. He arrived in Windsor, Connecticut, in 1638. Rosettes within a guilloche dominate the carving in the joinery tradition that is represented by these boxes and was presumably endemic to County Huntingdon, England, where Buell was born.[2] The rosettes have a geometric quality—on the MMA box they are divided neatly into quarters—and are characterized by a foliate motif that consists of several leaves or petals defined by deep gouging, such as the four in the larger rosettes on the front of this piece. The carving on the Buell family box is the most complex; it has three distinct rosette designs within guilloches that completely fill the front and sides except for a plain margin all around. On the front are two rosettes divided by narrow grooves into eight segments, each with the typical foliate motif; they are separated and flanked by three rosettes that contain an outer band with eight of the same motifs and an inner circle with four single leaves similar to those seen here in the smaller rosettes. Three identical rosettes adorn each side of the Buell family box; they have a foliate motif in each quadrant of a cross that is formed by a small central cluster of petals and four elongated leaves. A simplified version of this cruciform pattern, in which the cross is formed by plain bands, appears in some of the rosettes on the Yale box; in the others, grooves take the place of bands, as on the present example.[3] The carving on the Buell family

box compared to that on the two other pieces suggests, by virtue of the greater diversity and complexity of the main motifs, that it is the earliest of the three and was produced by a first-generation joiner still closely adhering to patterns acquired during his training. The MMA box appears to represent somewhat of a diminution of the tradition. The rosettes, here in groups of three, not only have a simplified design but they also have been much reduced in size, cutting down on the amount of deeply gouged carving required. The portion of the space filled with shallower schematic foliage punctuated with a star punch has been increased, and easily executed borders that enlarge on the pattern used on the lid and on the projecting edges of the bottom have been added. William's eldest son, Samuel (1641–1720), who moved to Killingworth, Connecticut, in 1662, followed his father's trade, so there is the possibility that he made this box. Carved motifs related to those on these boxes occur on the panels of one published chest but are not otherwise known.[4]

CONSTRUCTION
The front and back are rabbeted to accept the sides; the front is secured with six nails at each joint, the back with five. The bottom is a single board nailed to the four sides that retains evidence of mill sawing. The one-board top, to the underside of which a transverse cleat is nailed at either end, rotates on pintle hinges. A pin-shaped projection at either end of a slat nailed to the back of the box engages each cleat and serves as a pintle (fig. 53). The molding worked on the front and back edges of the top consists of two ovolos separated by a small hollow; that on the edges of the bottom, of an ovolo. Both upper edges of all four sides and the two lower edges of the cleats are finished with a chamfer. The scribed lines and compass points from the laying out of the carving are clearly visible.

CONDITION
The right cleat is a replacement, and on the left cleat four of the six nails have been replaced with screws and one is missing. Most of the nails on the front (apparently all once T-headed, like those that secure the back) are now without heads; one or two may be replacements. At the left end of the slat attached to the back, one nail is missing its head and there is an empty hole—not made by a wrought nail but perhaps from an added screw. The lock in the front and the plate with a staple in the top have been lost. The box has been stripped and appears to have been oiled and waxed; it retains traces of red paint.

INSCRIPTIONS
Scratched on the top edge of each side is a V with the narrow end facing out (joiner's marks). Carved at center front of the box within

70. See also fig. 53.

the lower border is a barred "I" and at center front of the top is an S. Inscribed in pencil on the inside of the bottom are IP and other markings (all modern).

WOODS
Front, sides, back, cleats, slat, OAK, probably WHITE OAK (not micro-analyzed); top, bottom, SOUTHERN YELLOW PINE.

DIMENSIONS
OH. 9⅜ (23.8); OW. (top) 28¼ (71.8); CW. 24⅞ (63.2); OD. (top) 18½ (47); CD. 16⅜ (41.6).

EXHIBITIONS
"The Art of Joinery: Seventeenth-Century Case Furniture in the American Wing," MMA, 18 October 1972–18 March 1973; "Woodworkers of Windsor: A Connecticut Community of Craftsmen and Their World, 1635–1715," Flynt Center of Early New England Life, Historic Deerfield, and Windsor Historical Society, Windsor, Connecticut, 25 April 2003–15 April 2004.

REFERENCES
Lockwood 1913, fig. 227 (also shown in fig. 38); Margon 1954, no. 31; Margon 1965, p. 85; Safford 1972 (exh. cat.), no. 16; M. B. Davidson and Stillinger 1985, fig. 125 (the corresponding caption is wrongly numbered 126); Lane and White 2003 (exh. cat.), no. 20.

PROVENANCE
Ex coll.: H. Eugene Bolles, Boston.

Gift of Mrs. Russell Sage, 1909 (10.125.2)

1. The Buell family box is illustrated in Kane 1970, fig. 11, and Fairbanks and Trent 1982, no. 173; the Yale box, in G. W. R. Ward 1988, no. 3.
2. For William Buell and his sons, see Kane 1970, pp. 78–79; Fairbanks and Trent 1982, no. 173; and Lane and White 2003, pp. 49–51.
3. The Yale and MMA boxes also share the unusual manner in which the cleats are hinged (see *Construction*). The cleats of the Buell family box now rotate on iron pins, and the top has little or no overhang at the front. It seems unlikely that its cleats originally revolved on pins that were integral to a slat nailed to the back, for in that case the top would barely extend as far as the front of the box.
4. Lockwood 1913, fig. 11; the panel motifs are closest to those on the Yale box.

71

71.

Box

Braintree, Massachusetts, 1660–90
Attributed to the Savell shop tradition

This box is part of a group of ten chests and chests with drawers, two other boxes, and a fragment of a cupboard, all ornamented with similar carving. The particular tradition represented by these pieces—for some time associated with Connecticut—was attributed in a 1996 article by Peter Follansbee and John D. Alexander to Braintree, Massachusetts, and the Savell family of joiners.[1] The primary motifs that distinguish this school of carving are a lunette that encloses two buds (on the front of the boxes and the top front rail of the chests), a roundel with four such buds (on the drawer fronts), and a large palm leaf set within an arch (on the four front panels of the chests and the door of the cupboard). While the profile of the band that defines the arches is convex, that of the lunettes and roundels is concave and contrasts with the slightly rounded contours of the buds, as seen on this piece. Characteristically the main outlines of the designs on this box are formed by deep grooves made with a V-shaped gouge expertly handled: the concentric grooves of the arcs and those of the buds are here very precise and controlled, and the buds are defined by one more groove than was usual. The work is marked by exactness of execution rather than flair. A round gouge was used to add definition to

the buds and to render the schematic foliage that surrounds them, and also to provide decorative accents on plain surfaces. On all of the pieces the band that defines the lunettes, arches, and roundels bears a pattern of two adjoining arcs, impressed with strikes of a gouge, alternating with a small cross, applied with a punch. Peculiar to the three boxes is the border seen at the top and bottom of the front and sides of this example. Delimited by double lines, it contains pairs of straight diagonal lines, made with strikes of a chisel, which alternate with the stamped cross motif. The boxes in this shop tradition are carved on the sides as well as on the front: this and a smaller example at the Museum of Fine Arts, Boston, bear on each side a lunette enclosing a pair of ellipses with foliage that is delineated in the same manner as the fronds on the chest panels; the third box (private collection) has a slanted lid and higher sides that feature the roundel design and a short lateral frond. Structurally, the three boxes are distinguished by the fact that the front and back are attached to the sides with wooden pins rather than nails. The same method of construction is used on one of the chests and on the cupboard fragment: on those pieces a joined paneled front is secured to board sides with wooden pins.[2]

CONSTRUCTION

The front and back are rabbeted to receive the sides and are secured to the sides with three square wooden pins at each joint. The one-board bottom is nailed to the four sides. The top is formed of two longitudinal boards to the underside of which a transverse cleat is nailed at either end. Two small snipebill hinges attach the top to the back. The ends of the hinges that protrude through the top are neatly clinched into the hollow at the inner side of the half-round molding worked along the back edge. Where the left hinge comes through to the inside of the back, a depression was gouged out to reduce the thickness of the board. The front is fitted with a lock and the interior with a lidded till on the left. The till side and bottom are slotted into the front and back of the box; the bottom extends under the side, which is slightly canted. The till lid is round-tenoned into the front and back, and its edge is molded with a shallow cyma reversa and a fillet. The front and side edges of the top of the box have a broad ovolo molding, and the corresponding edges of the bottom are beveled. Scribed lines and compass points from the laying out of the design remain visible.

CONDITION

The upper end of the front and back boards is pulling away from the sides. The two boards of the top have separated, and on the inside are remnants of paper that was glued on to cover the gap. Small modern nails were added in the top boards and the cleats at either side of the gap. The lock appears to be original, but the plate with the staple is missing from the top. At some point the top was nailed shut, and there are two screw holes at upper center of the exterior of each side, perhaps from a closing or carrying device. The front edge of the bottom is heavily worn. Residues of dark wax are visible in recesses of the carving and in the pores and nicks of the top.

INSCRIPTIONS

Joiner's assembly marks are scratched on the two abutting boards at each inside corner and consist of a long single, double, and triple line and a large X, respectively. Partly legible numbers and undecipherable markings in white chalk are on the inside of the top, and there are numbers and letters on the exterior of the back.

WOODS

WHITE OAK; bottom, EASTERN WHITE PINE.

DIMENSIONS

OH. 7⅛ (18.1); OW. (top) 26¼ (66.7); CW. 23⅜ (59.4); OD. (top) 17⅛ (43.5); CD. 16⅜ (41.6).

EXHIBITION

"The Art of Joinery: Seventeenth-Century Case Furniture in the American Wing," MMA, 18 October 1972–18 March 1973.

REFERENCES

Kent 1910, p. 6; Safford 1972 (exh. cat.), no. 17 and fig. 5; Safford 1980, fig. 4.

PROVENANCE

Ex coll.: H. Eugene Bolles, Boston.

Gift of Mrs. Russell Sage, 1909 (10.125.5)

1. See Follansbee and Alexander 1996. Objects in this group not shown in that article are in Lockwood 1913, fig. 17; Nutting 1928–33, no. 12; and Randall 1965, no. 1. See also in this catalogue nos. 21 and 45.
2. The boxes are in Randall 1965, no. 1, and Follansbee and Alexander 1996, fig. 3. For a detail of the construction of the chest, see Follansbee and Alexander 1996, fig. 14; the cupboard is fig. 2.

72.

Box

Dedham or Medfield, Massachusetts, 1660–85
Attributed to the Thurston shop tradition

Foliated S-scrolls, as single elements, or paired as on this box, were widely used in seventeenth-century carved decoration. Each craftsman or shop tradition, however, gave the motif an individual interpretation. The particular version seen here, which occurs also on one other box and at least six chests, has been attributed by Robert Blair St. George to John Thurston (1607–1685), of Dedham and Medfield, Massachusetts, who emigrated to New England in 1637 from County Suffolk, England, where S-scrolls carved in a generally similar manner can be found.[1] The carving assigned to the Thurston shop comprises almost exclusively foliated S-scrolls, paired, as they are on cat. no. 72, to create an anthemion-like motif. They are all related but show some variation from piece to piece and often within a piece, for while the scrolls were laid out with a compass, the foliage was carved freehand. Most consistent are the groups of three lower leaves. As can be seen here, each group is outlined with cuts made with round gouges and the three leaves separated—for most of their length but characteristically not at the tip—by lines cut with a V-shaped gouge. Only on the center panel of two chests is there any significant variation in those elements: there, the uppermost of the three leaves ends in a scroll.[2] It is principally in the upper portion of the foliate motifs that variety is introduced, the outline of the scrolls and the lower leaves having established the base pattern. On this box, that carving consists of a pyramid of seven small leaves or petals. A virtually identical design is on the other box in this shop tradition, which is initialed "AH" and similarly constructed of thin boards and with the same type of idiosyncratic pintle hinges (see *Construction*); related schemes are on two of the chests.[3]

72

Carved in that location on the remaining chests are various flowerlike composites of petals and leaves on a central stem. A motif of that type occurs above the initials on the AH box, but there is no indication of carving under the lock above the initials on cat. no. 72. On both boxes the foliage typically lies quite close to the scrolls, leaving little ground visible; that ground, as on all Thurston pieces, was left rough and not textured with a punch.

CONSTRUCTION
The four sides are made of thin riven boards that taper somewhat from bottom to top. The front and back are simply butted to the sides (which are ca. ½ in. thick) and nailed in place with three rosehead nails at each joint; the front and back boards (ca. ⅜ in. thick) were apparently deemed too thin for a rabbet to be cut at either end. The bottom is nailed to the four sides, and its projecting front and side edges are beveled. The top—a single tangent-sawn oak board—has a cleat at either end that is nailed on with three nails from below and one from above at the back, and is shaped at the back to receive a pintle. Because the back of the box is too thin to allow for the insertion of a wooden pin, the pintle is an extension of the back board, which was cut so that a small section running with the grain protrudes at the top to serve as a pin. The lower edges of the cleats are finished with a small chamfer.

CONDITION
The top, which has splits at each end, and the cleats are original. The right pintle has been broken and repaired. The back has split in two lengthwise and has large losses along the upper edge of the gap.

Screws replace nails or have been added in the back, left front corner, and right cleat, and there are added nails in the cleats, back, and bottom. Nails from the back have split out wood at the rear of the left side. Part of the mechanism of the lock is missing, as is the hinged portion of the hasp; the portion of the hasp inside the lid has been renailed or is not original. There are extensive remains of black paint on the ground and in the recesses of the carving and traces of red on the surface. The paint appears to be modern, but the color scheme may well be original.[4]

INSCRIPTIONS
The initials of the unidentified first owner, "MH," are carved on the front of the box. MMA Hudson-Fulton exhibition identification numbers are inscribed in orange crayon on the underside of the bottom (H. F 40.14 and, within a circle, 468) and inside the bottom (H. F 40.14).

WOODS
Front, sides, back, top, left cleat, WHITE OAK; right cleat, RED OAK; bottom, SOUTHERN YELLOW PINE.

DIMENSIONS
OH. 9½ (24.1); OW. (top) 26¾ (67.9); CW. 24 (61); OD. (top) 15½ (39.4); CD. 14¾ (37.5).

EXHIBITIONS
"Hudson-Fulton Exhibition," MMA, 20 September–30 November 1909; "The Art of Joinery: Seventeenth-Century Case Furniture in the American Wing," MMA, 18 October 1972–18 March 1973.

REFERENCES
Hudson–Fulton Celebration 1909 (exh. cat.), no. 81; Halsey and Cornelius 1924 (and 1925, 1926, 1928, 1932), fig. 3 (1938, 1942, fig. 13); Cornelius 1926, pl. I; Safford 1972 (exh. cat.), no. 15; St. George 1979a, figs. 21, 30-o (detail of carving); St. George 1979b, no. 63; Safford 1980, fig. 3; M. B. Davidson and Stillinger 1985, fig. 126 (the corresponding caption is wrongly numbered 125).

PROVENANCE
Ex coll.: H. Eugene Bolles, Boston.

Gift of Mrs. Russell Sage, 1909 (10.125.680)

1. St. George 1979a lays out the basis of the Thurston attribution and the craft practices of that shop tradition and illustrates the then known Thurston pieces and details of all of the carving. St. George 1979b shows three of the same objects (nos. 61–63). An additional chest with Thurston-style carving and construction is offered in *Fine Americana*, auction cat., Sotheby's, New York City, 28–31 January 1994, lot 1202. Also known are several chests with related carving that have been attributed to John Houghton (1624–1684), who was presumably trained by Thurston (for example, St. George 1979a, figs. 10, 11).

2. St. George 1979a, figs. 13, 30-d (detail of panel); and a chest auctioned at Sotheby's in 1994 (see n. 1 above).

3. The AH box (St. George 1979a, figs. 22, 30-p [detail of carving]) was formerly at the Art Institute of Chicago, Chicago, Illinois; its present location is unknown. Cleats hinged in the same manner and other structural similarities occur on a box at the Yale University Art Gallery (G. W. R. Ward 1988, no. 2), which is carved with generally related leafage but within geometric scrolls and appears to be by a joiner trained in a similar County Suffolk tradition. For the two chests, see St. George 1979a, figs. 18, 30-m, and figs. 20, 30-l.

4. As communicated to the writer by Robert F. Trent (5 May 2005), the analysis of the surface of a Thurston chest (in a private collection) revealed a similar red and black scheme.

73.

Box

Windsor, Connecticut, 1680–1700
Attributed to the Stoughton shop tradition

This piece shares stylistic and structural features with two boxes in private collections, one of which has a history of ownership by Rev. Timothy Edwards (1669–1758), first pastor of Windsor's Second Congregational Church. On the basis of Edwards's close ties to the Stoughton family of woodworkers and of two chests with related carving whose Windsor histories also interconnect with the Stoughtons, Joshua W. Lane and Donald P. White III have attributed the style of carving represented by these pieces to the shop tradition established in Windsor by Thomas Stoughton III (1624–1684).[1] In terms of their construction, all three boxes are distinguished by having the bottom board rabbeted around the perimeter to accept the four sides (rather than being simply butted to the sides) and by the sharp bevel on the projecting front and side edges of the bottom (compare cat. nos. 74, 75). The MMA box, unlike the two related examples, was never fitted with a till, and it has lost the cleats underneath its top, but there is clear evidence on the lid that the cleats had the same substantial width as those on the Edwards box and were nailed on in the same manner. Also, a hole bored on the upper left side of the present box suggests there was a corresponding hole in the cleat to accommodate a locking device, as there is on the Edwards box. The front corners of the three boxes are all similarly notched with small concave gouge cuts, and the broad margin on either side of the carved reserve is decorated with the same pattern of scratched intersecting lunettes and a punched star motif at the base of each arc.

Although the ornamental tulip-and-leaf vocabulary of the carving on these boxes has some affinity with that on the boxes—also from Windsor—in the Moore shop tradition (cat. nos. 74, 75), the carving has a quite different character. On this and the related boxes, the design is organized along definite vertical and horizontal axes, and the curves of the larger motifs are more flowing and form perfect arcs, whether or not they were scribed with a compass. The carved foliage on the front of each of the boxes has its own distinct pattern, but in each case it comprises three groupings similar in width, one or two of which consist of a tulip atop a vertical stem that emerges from a small, low mound and bears opposed tulips or leaves. On the Edwards box the design is composed of three separate stalks, the center one ending in a rosette rather than a tulip. On the MMA box the two outer stalks are linked by a horizontal vine from which issues a large central tulip. On the third box there is a central vertical stem terminating in a large tulip and, below, a stalk that springs laterally from each of a pair of opposed stylized leaves or flowers. On all three boxes the ground of the carving has been stippled with a punch. The squat, bulbous tulips on this piece have parallels on the Edwards box, and the large asymmetrical tulips with an elongated petal that ends in a scroll have counterparts on the panels of the two chests with drawers also attributed to the Stoughton shop tradition. Those chests are closely related to the so-called sunflower chests (see cat. nos. 92, 93) both in their construction and in the panel carving, and the initials with scalloped edges and the vine above them on this box are akin to the initials and vine on the center panel of cat. no. 93.

CONSTRUCTION

The front and back are rabbeted to receive the sides and are secured with five T-headed nails at each corner. The top is attached to the back with two snipebill hinges. There is evidence that the cleats were a good 7/8 inch wide and were secured with three T-headed nails down through the top and a nail (presumably a rosehead) up through each end of the cleat. The bottom board is rabbeted on the upper surface to accept the four sides and is nailed in place from below. The bottom protrudes on the front and sides, and those edges are beveled. No layout lines for the carved design are visible, but the main tulip is well centered and the tulips on a vertical stem are equidistant from the center. The ground was stippled with a punch that made a series of impressions at a time. The outer side of the back shows extensive torn grain from riving.

CONDITION

The top is original but has lost its cleats and was once nailed shut. All the nails in the back and several in the bottom have been replaced. The original back nails caused a few splits (now glued) at the back of the left side. Just below the rim at the front of the left side is a large bored hole; in all likelihood it originally lined up with a hole in the cleat, which allowed the top to be locked with a peg inserted through both holes. There is a nail hole in the right side in about the same location. One or more nail holes in each corner of the bottom suggest that the box was at one time attached to another object. The bottom has splits at either end, and the front edge has suffered losses. The box has been stripped and probably waxed but retains a dark coating on the beveled edges of the bottom and on parts of the exterior of the top. Numerous drips from the stripping stain the inside of the top and of the bottom, and there are gray green residues around the inside edge of the top and under the edges of the bottom.

INSCRIPTIONS

The initials "HS" of an unidentified first owner are carved at the center of the front and form part of the design. On the inner side of the right side is a paper sticker with identification numbers from the Wadsworth Atheneum "Connecticut Furniture" exhibition.

WOODS

Front, sides, back, WHITE OAK; top, bottom, SOUTHERN YELLOW PINE.

DIMENSIONS

OH. 7¾ (19.7); OW. (top) 27⅛ (68.9); CW. 23⅞ (60.6); OD. (top) 17¾ (45.1); CD. 16½ (41.9).

EXHIBITION

"Connecticut Furniture: Seventeenth and Eighteenth Centuries," Wadsworth Atheneum, 3 November–17 December 1967.

REFERENCES

Lockwood 1923, fig. 13 (attributed to Nicholas Disbrowe, Hartford, Connecticut); Halsey and Tower 1925, fig. 191; Kirk 1967 (exh. cat.), no. 2; Hornung 1972, no. 933.

PROVENANCE

Ex coll.: H. Eugene Bolles, Boston.

Gift of Mrs. Russell Sage, 1909 (10.125.9)

1. Lane and White 2003, pp. 57–64; the boxes are nos. 24 and 26, and the chests are nos. 23 and 25. A card tacked to the inside of the lid of the Edwards box is inscribed in ink (script): "A Travelling Trunk / Which belonged to the family / of Rev. Timothy Edwards of East / Windsor, Conn. / It was not improbably used / by President Jonathan Edwards / while in Yale College 1716–1820 [*sic*]. / A. C. Thompson." (Windsor's Second Congregational Church, of which Timothy Edwards was the first pastor, was located in an area that later became East Windsor.)

74.

Box

Windsor, Connecticut, 1680–1710
Attributed to the Moore shop tradition

Shallow carving similar to that seen here, consisting of vines that bear stylized tulips and leaves in sometimes fanciful shapes, ornaments a group of about thirty boxes, including this example and cat. no. 75, and two chests with drawers.[1] The designs on the front of the boxes and of the chests' drawers are symmetrical: vines in mirror image extend to either side of a central schematic flower on a vertical stem that is distinguished by having opposed scallops and diamond-shaped interstices up the middle. Here the vines each form a shallow arc; they may also undulate sharply, or ramify as on cat. no. 75. The central motif is laid out with a line down the middle of the front and a line on either side of it that angles out from bottom to top, here all scored very

deeply. There is no evidence on this box of any other layout lines for the design (but a scribe line down each end of the front to guide the placement of the nails remains visible). The carving was done freehand with gouges, and the outlines of the motifs were determined by the curves of the various gouges used. The tulips are asymmetrical and quite squat, and they vary in shape and in the number of their petals. The vines sprout numerous small leaves similar to some of the tulip petals and larger leaves in odd amorphous shapes, such as those that flank the central flower. Typically, some of the petal and leaf tips are ornamented with a gouged crescent and a small round punch. An unusual detail on this box is the scalloped outline of the vertical edges of the reserve. There, as

73

74

on the stem of the central motif, each scallop is punctuated with a punched dot. The design on each box in the group differs to a greater or lesser degree in terms of the density of the ornament, the configuration of the vine, the shapes of the individual elements, and the detailing of the carving (compare cat. no. 75). Clearly the group is the work of more than one craftsman. The carving on this box does not fill the space as convincingly as on many of the other examples; it is somewhat tentative, with the vines terminating in a weak, nondescript tripartite form.

The particular style of vine-and-tulip carving represented by this group of boxes and chests was attributed in 1985 by William N. Hosley Jr. to Windsor, Connecticut, and has recently been ascribed more specifically by Joshua W. Lane and Donald P. White III to a shop tradition established there by Deacon John Moore (1614–1677) and carried on by several generations of apprentices. Moore came from County Suffolk in England and was an original settler of Windsor. The attribution to the Moore shop tradition is based on two boxes in the group that have histories going back to the seventeenth century. One came down in the Moore family and the other in the Loomis family, which included woodworkers connected to the Moores through marriage and perhaps apprenticeship.[2]

CONSTRUCTION

The front and back are rabbeted to accept the sides and secured with four T-headed nails at each corner. The bottom is nailed to the four sides, and the cleats are nailed to the underside of the top. The cleats have a concave profile at the front and back and taper in width and height toward the front. The top is attached to the back with two snipebill hinges. The ovolo molding on the front and side edges of the top is demarcated with just a scribed line. The corners of the front are notched with small V-shaped cuts. A punch probably containing a series of small squares was used to texture the ground of the carving. On the interior, there is at the right rear corner a small, squared recess (ca. ½ in.) cut out on the inner top edge of the back board contiguous to the rabbet.

CONDITION

Both the top and the bottom have warped; the top has pulled away from the right cleat and the bottom from the front and the back. The hinges are loose and, except for the portion of the left hinge attached to the back board, may not be original. A nail has been added to the right cleat; several of the nails in the back joints are replaced, as is one in the bottom. The top is battered along the front edge and is further marred by deep gouges at the right front corner. The carving has suffered some small losses. The box has been stripped and is now waxed. It retains traces of red paint and dark residues of another coating.

INSCRIPTION

The initials "SS" of an unidentified owner are carved in the large leaves that flank the center tulip; the letter on the right is more deeply incised.

WOODS

Front, sides, back, cleats, WHITE OAK; top, bottom, SOUTHERN YELLOW PINE.

DIMENSIONS

OH. 6¾ (17.1); OW. (top) 21¼ (54); CW. 19⅜ (49.2); OD. (top) 13⅛ (33.3); CD. 12⅞ (32.7).

PROVENANCE

Ex coll.: Mrs. J. Insley Blair, Tuxedo Park, New York; her daughter Mrs. J. Woodhull Overton, Balmville, New York.

Mrs. Blair purchased the box in 1925 from C. W. Fancher, Goshen (probably New York). The box was on loan from Mrs. Overton to the MMA from 1952 until it became a gift.

Gift of Mrs. J. Woodhull Overton, 1966 (66.190.2)

1. For the approximate number of boxes, see Lane and White 2003, p. 18. Among the related boxes are those in the Connecticut Historical Society, Hartford (acc. nos. 1960-13-3, 1985-82-0), Mattatuck Museum Arts and History Center, Waterbury, Connecticut (cited in G. W. R. Ward 1988, pp. 63–64, n. 1), Old Sturbridge Village, Sturbridge, Massachusetts (Filbee 1977, p. 36), Saint Louis Art Museum, Saint Louis, Missouri (Roberts 1980, p. 6), Winterthur Museum (acc. no. 54.102.2), and Yale University Art Gallery (G. W. R. Ward 1988, no. 4); two in private collections (Nutting 1928–33, no. 133; and *Three Centuries of Connecticut Furniture* 1935, no. 22 [also in Lane and White 2003, no. 4]); and the two boxes mentioned in n. 2 below. One of the chests, with a history in the Gaylord family of Windsor, is at Old Sturbridge Village (Lane and White 2003, no. 1), and the other is in a private collection (*Great River* 1985, no. 80 [also in Nutting 1928–33, no. 11]). Also attributed to this shop tradition is a joined table (Lane and White 2003, no. 2).

2. For the Hosley attribution, see *Great River* 1985, no. 80. For the Moore shop tradition, see Lane and White 2003, pp. 10–19. The Moore box is on long-term loan to the Windsor Historical Society from Grace Episcopal Church in Windsor (Lane and White 2003, p. 19). The Loomis box is the property of the Village of Unadilla, New York. It descended in the family to attorney David Phelps Loomis (1827–1898) of Unadilla. The writer is indebted to Patricia Sheret, Unadilla Village historian, for making the box available for examination in 1995 and providing information on its history, and to the library staff of the New York State Historical Association, Cooperstown, for further Loomis family genealogy. The box is currently on extended loan to the Farmers' Museum in Cooperstown. See Lane and White 2003, pp. 18–19. The box's existence was noted in Way 1992, p. 89.

75.

Box

Windsor, Connecticut, 1680–1710
Attributed to the Moore shop tradition

While this box and cat. no. 74 are both the product of the Windsor school of craftsmanship that has recently been identified as the shop tradition established by John Moore, the two were clearly carved by different joiners. The design on this box is livelier and more intricate, and it is worked with greater assurance. The composition is quite dense, creating somewhat the effect of an overall pattern. Relatively little of the ground shows, and, exceptionally, that ground has not been worked with a punch, as it has on cat. no. 74 and on many other related boxes. The carving also differs in that the tips of the petals and leaves lack the gouged crescents that in most cases decorate those elements, and they are ornamented

with just a small round punch mark that is normally used in conjunction with the crescents. That same round punch characteristically accents the opposed scallops that invariably run up the middle of the central flower's stem. On this box it punctuates as well the similar scallops that, unusually, appear along the bottom in two groups of three.

Other design and structural features of this piece are common in general to the large group of boxes in the Moore shop tradition (see the entry for cat. no. 74). The rectangular area to be carved was divided by vertical scribe lines into four equal segments, with the central flower laid out in addition with two diagonal lines. The front corners of the box are

75

notched with small, closely stacked V-shaped cuts. The ovolo molding on the front and sides of the top is just minimally defined—with a scribe line rather than a fillet—and the front and side edges of the bottom board protrude strongly and are similarly shaped. The cleats underneath the top are typically rather thin and taper in height and width toward the front. By far the most distinctive trait of this group of boxes is the quirky, small cubelike recess cut into the inner top edge of the back at one corner, either the left one (as in this box) or the right (as in cat. no. 74). It has no conceivable practical purpose and appears to be a sort of trademark of this shop tradition.[1]

CONSTRUCTION

The front and back are rabbeted to receive the sides and secured with three T-headed nails at each joint. Similar nails secure the bottom to all four sides and the cleats to the top. The top is attached to the back with two snipebill hinges. As on cat. no. 74, the ovolo molding on the front and sides of the lid is delimited only by a scribe line, and the cleats, on which the beveled ends are here just slightly concave, taper toward the front. On the inner side of the back there is at the left corner a rectangular recess (ca. ¾ in. high) cut out at the top edge contiguous to the rabbet. The notches on the front corners are V-shaped. Portions of the vertical scribe lines that mark either side of the carved reserve and divide it into four equal parts remain visible, as do the two diagonal lines that lay out the width of the central flower.

CONDITION

The top has warped and pulled away from the cleats at the front and back, and the left front corner has sustained losses. There is heavy wear around the hinges, which are loose but appear to be original. A nail is missing at the back of the right cleat. In the back, an added nail in each corner compensates for the loss of three originals. The reason for the two or three cut nails in the upper front corner of each side is unclear. Three large holes bored through the bottom are modern and may have served to secure the box to another object. There are heavy stains on the inside of the bottom, its front edge is badly nicked, and small metal gliders have been added under the corners. The carving has numerous small losses. The oak has a dark reddish color; the box has probably been oiled and waxed.

WOODS

Front, sides, back, cleats, WHITE OAK; top, bottom, SOUTHERN YELLOW PINE.

DIMENSIONS

OH. 9⅛ (23.2); OW. (top) 29⅝ (75.2); CW. 27⅜ (69.5); OD. (top) 16 (40.6); CD. 15⅛ (38.4).

EXHIBITIONS

On loan to the MacPheadris-Warner House (now Warner House), Portsmouth, New Hampshire, from 1946 to 1972; "Woodworkers of Windsor: A Connecticut Community of Craftsmen and Their World, 1635–1715," Flynt Center of Early New England Life, Historic Deerfield, and Windsor Historical Society, Windsor, Connecticut, 25 April 2003–15 April 2004.

REFERENCES

Kent 1910, p. 6; Lockwood 1923, fig. 14 (attributed to Nicholas Disbrowe, Hartford, Connecticut); Hornung 1972, no. 932; Lane and White 2003 (exh. cat.), no. 3.

PROVENANCE

Ex coll.: H. Eugene Bolles, Boston.

Gift of Mrs. Russell Sage, 1909 (10.125.10)

1. This type of notch is illustrated in Lane and White 2003, p. 19.

76.

Box

New England, 1650–1700

Both the front and the sides of this box are fully ornamented, the front with a design of opposed lunettes framed by gouge carving and the sides with a series of roundels with gouge-work flowers set between channel moldings. The moldings above and below the roundels are composed of a smaller convex profile on either side of a larger one; and at the bottom of the sides is a convex-concave sequence that is repeated at the top and bottom of the front, where the convex portion is ornamented. The gouge carving was all worked with the same-size tool and comprises units of an oblong groove, one end of which is rounded and followed by a crescent-shaped cut—whether it decorates the front corners, defines the flowers on the sides, forms an imbricated pattern on the upper front or an elaborated bead-and-reel design on the lower front. The arcs of the lunettes were deeply incised with a V-shaped gouge, whereas the lighter outline of the stylized tulip within each lunette was made with strikes of round gouges. The center of the tulip is decorated with a circular stamp that contains small punches regularly disposed in rows, and the same stamp fills the spandrels and forms a border along the bottom of the front.

Two boxes with opposed lunette carving on the front similar to that on the present example are known. They differ in that they have plain sides and that the band of gouging at the bottom of the front is identical to that at the top, but the edges of the top and bottom boards appear to have been finished in the same manner as on cat. no. 76.[1] All three were probably made in the same shop, the location of which is uncertain. The decoration on this box, while it employs traditional methods and designs, has distinctive features, but they offer no clear clue as to where the piece was made. Gouge carving is commonly seen embellishing moldings, but no counterpart to the roundels on the sides of this box are known to the writer. Likewise, opposed lunettes are a conventional pattern, but their delineation with multiple incised lines and the use of a tulip within the lunette rather than the usual trefoil motif sets this interpretation apart.[2]

CONSTRUCTION

The front and back are rabbeted to receive the sides, and the front is secured with three T-headed nails at each joint, the back with three rosehead nails. The bottom is nailed to the four sides with roseheads. The top is attached with two snipebill hinges. The front and side edges of the top are partly beveled, as are the side edges of the bottom. A small concave molding and a wider convex one run along the top of the front edge of the bottom. The notches on the front corners and the gouge carving were all executed with a 5/16-inch-wide gouge.

Scribe lines and compass points from the laying out of the designs remain visible on the front and sides. The boards that form all four sides are somewhat wedge-shaped and have the thicker end at the bottom; they retain evidence of riving, and the outside of the back was left just roughly finished with a hatchet.

CONDITION

The top is old and probably original. It has split lengthwise into four sections, which are held together by the replaced pine cleats and by two broad transverse oak braces and two short pine blocks nailed to the underside. Only those portions of the snipebill hinges attached to the back look original; hinges of another type were at one time nailed to the top and back. The back has one missing and one added nail. The lock set into the outer side of the front was the first; the one to the left, recessed into the inner side of the front, was added later. Both are now inoperative, and the top was at one point nailed shut. The box has been stripped and appears to have been oiled and waxed. There are remains of red paint on the front and sides.

INSCRIPTION

On the inside of the bottom is a small paper sticker with the printed number 191.

WOODS

Front, sides, back, WHITE OAK; top, bottom, SOUTHERN YELLOW PINE.

DIMENSIONS

OH. 8 5/8 (21.9); OW. (top) 26 3/8 (67); CW. 24 5/8 (62.5); OD. (top) 15 3/4 (40); CD. 15 1/8 (38.4).

EXHIBITION

On loan to the MacPheadris-Warner House (now Warner House), Portsmouth, New Hampshire, from 1946 to 1972.

REFERENCES

Lockwood 1913, fig. 232; Kettell 1929, pl. 104; Manca 2003, fig. 13.

PROVENANCE

Ex coll.: H. Eugene Bolles, Boston.

Gift of Mrs. Russell Sage, 1909 (10.125.3)

1. One box is at the Henry Ford Museum (Bishop 1975, p. 13); the other is advertised in *Antiques* 70 (November 1956), p. 401, and *Antiques* 72 (August 1957), p. 97, by John Kenneth Byard.
2. Gouge carving is found on the moldings of furniture from Connecticut (G. W. R. Ward 1988, no. 20; Lane and White 2003, p. 31 and nos. 11, 13) and from two counties in Massachusetts, Essex (see cat. no. 108) and Plymouth (St. George 1979b, nos. 7–10). It fully decorates the rails and stiles on two pieces, one attributed to Plymouth County, the other to Providence, Rhode Island (St. George 1979b, nos. 43, 81). Other known examples of opposed lunettes are unrelated to those on this box; they are carved on pieces from Plymouth County (St. George 1979b, no. 73) and Essex County (Lockwood 1926, fig. LXXVII; Trent, Follansbee, and A. Miller 2001, figs. 66, 75); see also cat. no. 97.

76

77

77.
Box

Hampton, New Hampshire, 1660–1710

This box can be linked to Hampton, New Hampshire, through a related example (present location unknown), on which the front is divided likewise into three fields and similarly carved in the two outer ones with a tulip-and-leaf motif and in the center with a large heart flanked by foliage and accompanied in that case not by one but by several smaller hearts. The front of that box is decorated, in addition, with a band of intersecting lunettes across the top and columns of "X"s forming diamonds, which are very close in character and execution to those same elements on cat. no. 91, a chest.[1] There is evidence that the

main motifs on this box were laid out in part with a compass. The carving appears to have been executed by first outlining the designs with a V-shaped gouge (probably the same used to delimit the three fields) and then shaving down one or both edges of the grooves to add some rudimentary modeling. A similar type of elementary relief can be observed on the small circles and semicircles of cat. no. 91. Other touches of ornament on this box front include a small punched triangle in each corner of the tulip-and-leaf fields and some hatching within the triangular forms between the tulip leaves. There is also a herringbone pattern, now largely effaced, along the bottom (see *Construction*), which provides a further link to cat. no. 91.

CONSTRUCTION

The front and back are rabbeted to receive the sides and are secured to the sides with small wooden pins. Similar pins fasten the cleats to the top and the top to the cleats. The top, a single board, is attached to the back with snipebill hinges. The one-board bottom is secured to each of the four sides with a single rosehead nail. The front edge of the top is molded with a large ovolo and a fillet. The ends of the top and of the front are notched with deep, acute V-shaped cuts. Short diagonal lines made with the strike of a chisel run along the bottom of the front board and the top of the adjoining beveled edge of the bottom board to form a herringbone pattern.

CONDITION

The joints of the front have been reinforced near the top with one or two nails. In the back joints all but one pin are missing, and the nails that took their place have not prevented the upper half of the board from strongly pulling away from the sides. As a result, the top no longer reaches the front. The right cleat is missing, and a nail has been added at each end of the left one. The bottom has three added nails. The surface appears to have been heavily oiled and waxed.

WOOD

EASTERN WHITE PINE.

DIMENSIONS

OH. 9 (22.9); OW. (top) 26 3/8 (67); CW. 24 1/4 (61.5); OD. (top) 16 (40.6); CD. 15 1/4 (38.7).

REFERENCES

Lockwood 1913, fig. 233; Anderson 1974, pp. 116–17 (illus.; also shows a reproduction of the box, for which plans could be purchased).

PROVENANCE

Ex coll.: H. Eugene Bolles, Boston.

Gift of Mrs. Russell Sage, 1909 (10.125.4)

1. The box is illustrated in Jobe 1993, ill. no. 1A, described as in the collection of Hollis E. and Trisha Brodrick. In a telephone conversation with the present writer (31 July 2000), Hollis Brodrick said that he no longer owned that box and also that he had at one time a second box with related carving. His impression was that the carving on the MMA box, though similar, was by a different hand. When asked, he could not recall if either or both of the boxes were joined with wooden pins, like cat. no. 77.

78.
Box

Northern Essex County, Massachusetts, 1680–1700

Only a small minority of the seventeenth-century boxes that have survived are decorated with applied ornament rather than carving, and this and four related examples represent the sole group of such boxes that can be attributed to the same school of craftsmanship. They can be linked to the unidentified shop in northern Essex County, Massachusetts, that produced cat. no. 58, a table, and that is known particularly for its cupboards, which are exceptionally varied and elaborate in form and decoration (see the entry for cat. no. 58).

The center motif on the front of this box highlights the taste among the more prosperous Essex County inhabitants during the last quarter of the seventeenth century for furniture that was initialed, or dated, or both—usually on small panels or insets. It is manifest on many of the objects from the shop that made this box and also on pieces by other craftsmen (see cat. no. 79). Here, applied moldings create a small rectangular "panel" containing a plaque carved with initials, presumably of the first owner. The panel is centered by a boss and flanked by identical applied ornament: an arrangement of buttons

around a horizontal half turning that is analogous in profile to the half column at each end of the front, except that the grooved ball at the bottom of the latter has been eliminated. The half columns, discounting the uppermost knop or finial, are symmetrical on either side of a deeply grooved barrel shape. They are a shortened variant of turnings that flank the drawer below the middle shelf on several of the cupboards. The turnings in this school of craftsmanship are complex and varied, characterized not by set and repeated patterns but rather by innumerable reformulations of ring, reel, ball, and baluster forms. The moldings are typically of oak. The base molding on this box (fig. 143), which reads from the bottom up as a fascia, ovolo, cavetto, astragal, and small cavetto, has the same profile and is virtually the same size as the base molding on a cupboard in a private collection, and the molding around the center panel, which has a convex, concave, convex outline, is similar to the molding worked on the arches on that same piece.[1] One of the other boxes in this group has a base molding that is a close match. On the remaining boxes, as is the case

78. See also fig. 143.

on some other pieces, the main convex-concave profiles are similar but not the elements that flank them. The four other boxes in the group are ornamented entirely in the small-panel style seen on some of the cupboards and chests in this shop tradition, each box with a different design and turnings. The lids all have or originally had cleat-pin hinges.[2]

CONSTRUCTION

The front and back are rabbeted to receive the sides, and the front joints are secured with three T-headed nails, the rear joints with four. The top revolves on pintles that are socketed in the sides of the box and engage the back end of the cleats, where the cleats are elliptical in shape and notched on the rear edge near the top. The upper edge of the back board has been rounded to allow the top to rotate more easily. The bottom consists of two ¼- to 5/16-inch-thick boards that are joined with a tongue and groove and nailed to the four sides. The edges of these thin bottom boards are hidden on the front and sides by an applied molding attached with T-headed nails. Inside there is a till with a lid on the right.

CONDITION

The top appears to be original but reworked. Once probably formed of two boards, it is now in three sections: two are separated less than halfway back by a ½-inch-wide full-length strip of new wood; and in the remaining rear portion, which has a large knot near the back edge, there is a sharply diagonal full-length glue joint. Both the inner and the outer surfaces of the top have been replaned. The cleats are now attached to the top with modern screws; each retains one original nail. The hinge pins are new. The lidded till is a replacement that was installed in a manner that did not require any disassembly of the box. The bottom has several added nails. The base molding appears to have been taken off and reattached; the nails look old, but they all show the imprint of a modern nail set. On the front, the right half column and some of the bosses are replaced. The molding around the panel and all the applied turnings except the central boss have been secured with small modern wire nails. Records indicate that there was black paint on the applied turnings when the box was acquired; it was taken off prior to or in 1937, when modern varnish then on the box was removed and the wood was rubbed down with linseed oil. There is now brown stain or colored varnish on the plaque and remains of similar coloring on the turnings and on the top.

INSCRIPTIONS

The initials "SP" of an unidentified owner are carved in the plaque in the center of the front. Large joiner's assembly marks are scratched on the two abutting boards at each inside corner and consist, respectively, of a long diagonal line, a pair of such lines, an oval, and three lines crossed by a diagonal. MMA Hudson-Fulton exhibition identification numbers (H. F. 40.1[8?]) are inscribed in orange crayon on the inside of the back.

WOODS

OAK, probably WHITE OAK (not microanalyzed); turnings, probably plaque, MAPLE.

DIMENSIONS
OH. 8⅞ (22.5); OW. (top) 29⅝ (75.2); CW. 26¾ (67.9); OD. (top) 17⅝ (44.8); CD. 16⅞ (42.9).

EXHIBITIONS
"Hudson-Fulton Exhibition," MMA, 20 September–30 November 1909; "The Art of Joinery: Seventeenth-Century Case Furniture in the American Wing," MMA, 18 October 1972–18 March 1973.

REFERENCES
Hudson-Fulton Celebration 1909 (exh. cat.), no. 82; Lockwood 1913, fig. 229; I. P. Lyon 1938c, fig. 52; Williams 1963, no. 50 (the drawings of the moldings are not accurate); Safford 1972 (exh. cat.), no. 18.

PROVENANCE
Ex coll.: H. Eugene Bolles, Boston.

Gift of Mrs. Russell Sage, 1909 (10.125.684)

1. For related turnings, see, for example, a cupboard in the Museum of Fine Arts, Boston (Randall 1965, no. 20; Trent, Follansbee, and A. Miller 2001, fig. 91). The cupboard with the same moldings as cat. no. 78 is dated 1683 (Nutting 1928–33, no. 447; Trent, Follansbee, and A. Miller 2001, fig. 27).
2. The boxes are two at the Wadsworth Atheneum (Nutting 1928–33, no. 159, initialed "HS"; Williams 1963, no. 49, initialed "SS," dated 1694, and with a closely related base molding); one at the Winterthur Museum (B. Ward 1986, no. 7); and one (present location unknown), initialed "SE," dated 1684 (DAPC, no. 66.2835).

79.
Small cabinet

Salem, Massachusetts, dated 1679
Attributed to the Symonds shop tradition

This richly decorated cabinet, its front a miniature architectural facade, achieves a visual impact that far transcends its actual small size. Made in 1679, in all probability for Ephraim and Mary Herrick of Beverly, Massachusetts, this is one of four related cabinets, all initialed and dated, that have been linked to original owners living in Salem, Massachusetts, and adjoining towns in Essex County. Two others are inscribed with the same year, one owned by Joseph and Bathsheba Pope of Salem Village (now Danvers) and at the Peabody Essex Museum, the other bearing the initials of Thomas Hart of Lynnfield and at the Winterthur Museum. The fourth cabinet, also at the Winterthur Museum, is dated [16]76 and first belonged to Thomas and Sarah Buffington of Salem.[1] The cabinets form part of a larger group of case furniture that is attributed to the Symonds family shop tradition and includes chests with drawer, chests of drawers (see cat. nos. 108, 109), and cupboards, some of which also have histories of ownership in Salem and its vicinity. The founder of this school of joinery, which appears to have set the style for the region, was John Symonds (before 1595–1671), who came to Salem in 1636 from Great Yarmouth, County Norfolk, England. He trained two sons, James (1633–1714), who inherited his father's tools and worked in Salem, and Samuel (1638–1722), who moved to Rowley Village in central Essex County. All three had apprentices, and James in turn trained two of his sons.[2]

As illustrated by the facade of the present cabinet, with its paired half columns, corbels, or brackets, and dentil molding, the overall designs of this school of joinery are architectural in concept. The decoration comprises, on the one hand, elements that freely reflect classical forms and, on the other, geometric patterns created by applied mitered moldings. Distinctive in the former category is the type of molding used under the top of the cabinet, which features a bold projecting convex profile with diagonal saw cuts to suggest dentils. Particularly characteristic of the applied geometric patterns is the octagonal sunburst motif seen on the door's panel. As is typical of the seventeenth-century applied-ornament style in general, the individual appliqués are made of several kinds of wood that originally differed in color and added to the complexity of the design. On the doorframe, the four walnut brackets, the red-cedar top molding, and the ebonized turnings play against one another and the oak ground; on the panel, red-cedar moldings abut both maple and walnut plaques, and the ground is not oak but pine, as it is also on the Hart cabinet.

All four cabinets have a similar format, the same interior arrangement of ten small drawers all constructed identically and fitted with brass ring pulls, and like hinges (fig. 81). The ornament on the two other 1679 cabinets matches that on the present piece, except that their bottom rails bear applied glyphs and bosses rather than the single turning seen here, which,

79. See also figs. 62, 81, 133, 138.

with its rhythmical alternation of convex and concave forms, complements the dentils under the top. The 1676 Buffington cabinet, however, differs on the exterior from the three others in several respects, most notably in the door panel, on which applied moldings form small cruciform motifs, and in the carving on the sides, which features an elaborate arrangement of rosettes, trefoils, and quatrefoils—two designs that do not occur on any other Symonds pieces or, for that matter, on any other New England furniture. The carving on the three 1679 pieces employs the widespread scheme of paired S-scrolls, in an interpretation that relates to the Buffington carving insofar as it also incorporates loops and trefoil motifs and as the design is not set within a rectangular field but is delimited by the outlines of the carved elements (fig. 62). Among the surviving furniture attributed to the Symonds school only these cabinets are ornamented with carving.

The dates on the cabinets, which mark the beginning of a quarter-century-long fashion for dated furniture in Essex County, indicate that they were made by the second generation of joiners in the Symonds shop tradition. Exactly what style the progenitor, John Symonds, transferred to Salem and imparted to his sons and apprentices is not known. In all probability it included a decorative vocabulary composed of architectural forms and both carved and applied geometric patterns that was influenced by the type of Netherlandish-inspired design seen in the elaborate paneling of a room of about 1595–1600 from the William Crowe House in Great Yarmouth, England, and now at the MMA.[3] The carving on the earliest of the cabinets—the most complex and reminiscent of strapwork—comes the closest to recalling frieze carving in such woodwork and invites the speculation that it represents a distinct learned pattern that John Symonds brought with him to Salem. The simpler S-scroll motif is a generic design common in many parts of Old England, including East Anglia, and in New England.[4]

Cabinets of a similar square format and scale as this example were made also in Boston and in Pennsylvania (see the entry for cat. no. 82) and have English antecedents.[5] They were probably used for the safekeeping of documents and small valuables of all kinds, but the amount of decoration lavished upon this and the related pieces indicates that they were clearly meant to serve also as showpieces that proudly proclaimed their owner's identity in the central medallion. The owners of the Symonds cabinets did not belong to the region's elite but were farmers in comfortable circumstances.

CONSTRUCTION

The top and bottom, each formed of two boards, are butted and nailed to the sides, as are the two horizontal boards that constitute the back. Rosehead nails are used throughout the case, except for the T-headed nails that secure the top. The door consists of a panel with deeply beveled edges on the inner side and a frame, the mortise-and-tenon joints of which are double-pinned. It is attached with two dovetail hinges, and the left stile is rabbeted to fit against the front of the left case side, which is nearly ½ inch deeper than the right side. The lock was meant for a door hinged on the opposite side; consequently it and the keyhole escutcheon are inverted. The visible face of the lock's plate is decorated along all four sides with two rows of three parallel scratched lines similar to those on the lock of cat. no. 97. The two original feet are attached with dowels that go up through the bottom of the case and all the way down through the foot. On the interior (fig. 81) are ten drawers on which the front and back fit between the sides and the bottom extends under all four sides. They are held together with thin, wirelike iron nails, the upper ends of which are clinched. The end-grain edges at the back of the drawers are chamfered. Each drawer front is scribed diagonally from corner to corner to mark the center, where a pull—a brass curtain ring—is attached with wire cotter pins. The upper full-width drawer divider is joined to the two main vertical partitions with a halved joint; otherwise the dividers and partitions are butted and nailed together. The whole unit is secured to the case with two nails driven through the case sides into each end of the two full-width dividers. The edge of the top is rounded on all four sides, and that of the bottom is beveled. On the door, the molding under the top has a prominent semicircular profile with diagonal kerfs followed by a fascia and a cyma reversa (fig. 138), and the moldings of the octagons have an astragal, a fillet, and a cyma reversa—a profile peculiar to this and the related cabinets (fig. 133). The cyma is the same as that at the bottom of the corbels. On the sides, compass points from the laying out of the carved designs remain visible. The width of the motifs was adjusted to the width of each side board, the borders remaining constant. A star or flower punch decorates the ground.

CONDITION

There are two added nails in the top and several in the back, and the nails of the bottom have been reset. The two right feet are replacements, and the joints of all four feet have been reglued. On the door, the inner edge of one section of molding on the inner octagon is new, as is one ray of the sunburst. The panel and the corbels at the base of the stiles have splits. Those corbels have been reattached more than once; they and many of the other applied elements are now secured with modern nails. Some of the nails in the hinges are new, as are those in the escutcheon, which may also be replaced. All but one of the drawer pulls are original. The cabinet has been waxed and perhaps also oiled. The black paint on the applied turnings and the old feet has probably been renewed, that on the front edge of the drawer dividers is a modern addition. The nature of the dark color on the ground of the carving has not been determined.

INSCRIPTION

The initials and date "7 H 9 / E M" (see *Provenance*) are carved on the center plaque of the door.

WOODS

Top, bottom, sides, frame of door, drawers, drawer dividers and partitions, RED OAK; back, door panel, EASTERN WHITE PINE; corbels, triangular plaques, rays of sunburst, BLACK WALNUT; top molding, probably moldings of octagons, EASTERN RED CEDAR; turnings, probably octagonal plaque, MAPLE.

DIMENSIONS

OH. 17¾ (45.1); OW. (top and bottom) 17¼ (43.8); CW. 15¾ (40); OD. (top and bottom) 9⅝ (24.4); CD. 8⅛ (20.6).

EXHIBITION
"The Art of Joinery: Seventeenth-Century Case Furniture in the American Wing," MMA, 18 October 1972–18 March 1973.

REFERENCES
Park 1960b, fig. 12; Safford 1972 (exh. cat.), no. 19 and fig. 2; Schwartz 1976, no. 15; Chinnery 1979, fig. 3:300 (misidentified as made for a member of the Hart family); M. B. Davidson 1980, fig. 70; Safford 1980, fig. 8; M. B. Davidson and Stillinger 1985, fig. 123 (detail of front), fig. 127 (open); *The Joseph and Bathsheba Pope Valuables Cabinet,* auction cat., Christie's, New York City, 21 January 2000, figs. 3, 5, 11, 14; Safford 2000, pl. II; Willoughby 2000, fig. 2; MMA 2001, fig. 12.

PROVENANCE
Ex coll.: H. Eugene Bolles, Boston.

In a search of the vital records of Salem, Beverly, and Ipswich, Massachusetts, Benno M. Forman found only one couple living in 1679 whose names correspond to the initials "H" over "E M": Ephraim and Mary Herrick of Beverly. Ephraim Herrick (baptized 1638–1693), whose father, Henry (1604–1671), came to Salem in 1629 and was an early settler of the area that later became Beverly, married Mary Cross (1640–after 1710) of Ipswich in 1661. Regrettably the probate inventory of neither has survived. They had eight children between 1662 and 1683, none of whom was born in 1679. Called a yeoman in his time, he was a farmer like his father, who was described by a family historian as "in easy circumstances but not distinguished by wealth or by civil rank."[6]

Gift of Mrs. Russell Sage, 1909 (10.125.168)

1. All four are in Willoughby 2000, figs. 1–4. For the Buffington cabinet, see also Forman 1968, pp. 111–13, Fairbanks and Trent 1982, no. 485, B. Ward 1986, no. 6, and Trent 1989, no. 3; for the Hart cabinet, see also Kirk 1982, nos. 575, 576; for the Pope cabinet, see also *The Joseph and Bathsheba Pope Valuables Cabinet,* auction cat., Christie's, New York City, 21 January 2000, lot 111 (includes comparative illustrations of the other 1679 cabinets).
2. On the other case furniture, see the entries for cat. nos. 108, 109. For the Symonds family and school of joinery, see Forman 1968, pp. 42–46 (Benno M. Forman was the first to identify this Salem school and ascribe it to the Symondses); Trent 1981; and Trent 1989.
3. Trent 1989, figs. 1, 2. The accession number of the paneling is 65.182.1.
4. Two East Anglian examples are in Kane 1973a, p. 10, figs. 1, 2.
5. A Boston cabinet, of walnut and with paneled sides, is in the Museum of Fine Arts, Boston (Fairbanks and Trent 1982, no. 293); another is in a private collection (Trent 1989, p. 35). Kirk 1982, nos. 577–79, shows an English example, the drawers of which are secured with the same type of nails as those of the Salem cabinets and have similar pulls.
6. Forman 1968, p. 113; Jedediah Herrick, *Genealogical Register of the Name and Family of Herrick, from the Settlement of Henerie Hericke, in Salem, Massachusetts, 1629 to 1846* (Bangor, Maine, 1846), pp. 8, 11, 68; Walter Goodwin Davis, *The Ancestry of Phoebe Tilton, 1775–1847, Wife of Capt. Abel Lunt of Newburyport, Massachusetts* (Portland, Maine, 1947), pp. 129, 131; *Essex County, Massachusetts, Probate Index, 1638–1840,* transcribed by Melinde Lutz Sanborn from the original by W. P. Upham (Boston, 1987), vol. 1, p. 438.

80.

Box

Connecticut, probably Saybrook, 1705–15

The box's history of ownership in Saybrook, Connecticut, indicated by the inscriptions inside its lid, is supported by the maker's use of yellow poplar and chestnut—woods associated with the Connecticut shore and the painted furniture of the Guilford-Saybrook area (see cat. nos. 101, 107). The decorative painting on the box is similar to that of the Guilford-Saybrook school in some of its aspects but differs in others. The floral ornament consists of seven different spray or vine designs—three on the front and two on each side—rather than a single pattern on each surface. On the front, a bunch of branches with thin pinnate leaves on the left is balanced by one with branches bearing small elliptical leaves on the right; in between is a vine on which the main motifs in the upper portion are clusters of small petals or leaves and a large round flower and in the lower portion large speckled forms that might have once been thistle buds. The vine has its base left of center and, like the two groups of branches, shows roots at the bottom; if those roots were attached to mounds, no evidence of them remains. The floral arrangements on the sides, which emerge from mounds, feature tulips and carnations and clusters of petals or leaves. The motifs, laid out first in white, are detailed with veins, dots, or solid-colored centers set against the white or completely covered with red or green, as in the Guilford-Saybrook tradition, but the white undercoat is a thin rather than a thick layer. The painting also diverges from the practices of that school compositionally in that the individual schemes are all to a lesser or greater degree asymmetrical. In addition, few of the stems flow in even curves; they tend to meander, and some appear stiff. With due allowance made for the condition of the painting, some of the motifs reveal a better sense of design than others.

The box itself, fitted with two lidded tills and an elaborate cast escutcheon of a type found on high-style case furniture, was made to be more than an ordinary object.[1] Some of the

80

painted ornament does not seem to be up to the same level. This prompts the speculation that the decoration may represent, at least in part, the work of an amateur, perhaps Rebecca (Clarke) Lynde, with whom the box is so closely identified in the inscriptions. Her social and economic standing would have allowed her to have painting lessons (see *Provenance*). Her husband's younger brother Nathaniel Lynde (1692–1749) was a joiner and may have been the maker of the box.[2]

PAINTED DECORATION
The designs, with the possible exception of the frond motif on the left of the front, are laid out in lead white, and the colors—red (vermilion) and green (which appears to be a copper chloride pigment)—are applied over the white. The layers of the white and the red and green paint are all relatively thin. Whether or not there was a colored ground coat is unclear; cross sections show some dispersed unidentified yellow (perhaps an organic pigment or yellowed varnish) in the wood pores under the decoration, but no actual layer. There are numerous losses to the overlying colors and to the white, particularly at center front and on the lower rear portion of the right side. The surface is coated with one or more layers of yellowed varnish, which is quite thick on the front and thinnest on the left side, where the red and green are the brightest. Most of the other areas of green are very dark. Some of the small dark dabs in the floral forms of the center front appear to be black paint that was added, perhaps to fill out worn motifs at a time when the black on the base molding was touched up or renewed. The inside of the top and much of the interior of the box is covered with red paint (red lead and some lead white) that goes into the wood pores with no intervening layer visible in cross section. It appears to be of the eighteenth century and lies under all the inscriptions. There

are traces of a red pigment (not analyzed) on the exterior of the top, but the order of the pigment and several degraded finish layers is not clear.

CONSTRUCTION
The front and back are rabbeted to accept the sides, and the upper edge of the bottom is rabbeted to accept all four sides. T-headed nails secure all joints as well as the front and side base moldings and the cleats underneath the ends of the top. The top is attached with two snipebill hinges and fitted with a staple to engage the lock in the box front. There is a narrow till at either end, both originally with a lid. On each till, the side and bottom are let into the front and back of the box; the side is nailed to the bottom; and the hole in the back for the rear pintle of the lid was drilled through. A shallow cyma reversa molding is run on the edge of the remaining (left) lid. The base molding consists of a small fascia followed by a cavetto and an ovolo. A broad chamfer finishes the outer straight edge of each cleat and a narrow one the corresponding inner edge. The cast-brass escutcheon is secured with small rosehead nails.

CONDITION
The top, cleats, and hinges are original and so are in all probability the escutcheon, lock, and staple. The lock is no longer operative, and a hole has been drilled through each cleat into the corresponding side for the insertion of a locking device. The lid of the right till is missing. The base molding on the left side and at the left front corner is replaced; the other sections have added nails. There are splits in the back and at the rear of the left side and losses where nails come through in the right cleat and in the bottom of the right till. A wide shrinkage crack extends the length of the box bottom, which has stains, as does the inside of the tills. The exterior of the box is nicked and scratched. (See also *Painted decoration*.)

INSCRIPTIONS

Inscribed in pencil on the interior of the lid in eighteenth-century script are: (in the center, large) "RC"; (in the upper left corner) "Reb . . . ah Ly . . . de [partly effaced] / WL / AL / RL" (the script *L* in the last two initials is almost entirely effaced and followed by a later, hand-printed roman L); (across the center) "Ob^tt Jan 20 1716"; (across the bottom in a somewhat uncertain hand) "Rebekah Lynde Died Jan: 20 1716 / Uxorum optima   Etatis 29." On the interior of the lid in white chalk and over the pencil inscriptions are illegible writing and markings. On the exterior of the back is a daisylike flower on a stem in chalk. On the inside of the till lid are a series of score marks in chalk and numbers in pencil.

WOODS

YELLOW POPLAR; bottom, CHESTNUT; tills, WHITE OAK.

DIMENSIONS

OH. 6 5/8 (16.8); OW. (top) 22 3/4 (57.8); CW. 20 (50.8); OD. (top) 16 1/8 (41); CD. 15 1/4 (38.7).

REFERENCE

Downs 1945, p. 72.

PROVENANCE

Ex coll.: Mrs. J. Insley Blair, Tuxedo Park, New York.

According to the inscriptions inside the lid, the box originally belonged to Rebecca Clark(e) (1687–1716), daughter of Major Samuel Clark (1655–1736) of Saybrook, Connecticut, and granddaughter of John Clark (ca. 1625–1677), who in 1646 moved from Hartford to Saybrook, where he was an extensive landowner. She married Samuel Lynde (1689–1754) of the same town in 1710. He had graduated from the Collegiate School in Saybrook (later Yale College) in 1707 and

became a judge like his father, Nathaniel (1659–1729), who had left Boston after his marriage in 1683 to settle in Saybrook on land deeded to him by his father. Samuel was well off and well connected: he was the namesake of a wealthy merchant uncle (1653–1721) of Boston, who also had investments in Saybrook, and his mother was the only daughter of Deputy Governor Francis Willoughby of Charlestown, Massachusetts. Rebecca had three children: a son, Willoughby (1711–1753), and two daughters, Abigail (1713–1736) and Rebecca (1715–1739). Samuel remarried twice.[3] The box was on loan to the MMA from Mrs. Blair between 1939 and 1945, when it became a gift.

Gift of Mrs. J. Insley Blair, 1945 (45.78.8)

1. For the same escutcheon on English furniture, see R. Edwards 1964, p. 201, fig. 11; and Bowett 2002, pls. 7:19, 7:73. It has been noted by the present writer on only one other American piece, a high chest of drawers signed by Edmund Titcomb of Newbury, Massachusetts (Forman 1985, fig. 24; Benes 1986, no. 64).
2. *Vital Records of Saybrook, 1647–1834* (Hartford, Conn., 1952), p. 49; Trent 1977, p. 97.
3. Prentiss Glazier, *Clark—Clarke Families of Early Connecticut* (Sarasota, Fla., 1973), pp. 23–24; "Cemetery Inscriptions from the Towns of Saybrook, Essex, and Westbrook, in Middlesex County, Connecticut" (typescript, 1907–9, New York Genealogical and Biographical Society, New York City), pp. 24–25; *Vital Records of Saybrook*, pp. 32–33, 143; *Commemorative Biographical Record of Middle-sex County, Connecticut: Containing Biographical Sketches of Prominent and Representative Citizens, and of Many of the Early Settled Families* (Chicago, 1903), vol. 2, pp. 526–27; Edward Elbridge Salisbury and Evelyn McCurdy Salisbury, *Family Histories and Genealogies* (New Haven, Conn., 1892), vol. 1, pt. 2 (containing a series of genealogical and biographical monographs on the Lynde, Digby, Newdigate, Hoo, and Willoughby families), pp. 377, 396–98, 402. The date of Rebecca's death in the cemetery inscription is "1715–16" (giving the year according to both the Old Style [Julian] calendar and the New Style [Gregorian] calendar, the one now in use); in the vital records, it is entered as 1716 (New Style) as in the box-lid inscriptions.

81.

Small chest of drawers

Windsor, Connecticut, or vicinity, 1735–50

The motifs on the front of this small chest of drawers, like those on cat. no. 112, have parallels in the pastoral scenes that became popular in Boston embroidery in the second quarter of the eighteenth century, in which similar human figures, animals, birds, and trees are to be found. Here the ornament is disposed to suggest such scenes rather than to produce an effect of randomness, as on cat. no. 112. In each of the three tiers—two on the upper drawer and one on the lower—all of the elements are supported by a common stretch of ground that extends across the whole drawer, and in the middle tier is a narrative of a hunter following a dog chasing a stag rather than an arrangement of several distinct motifs. How closely the style and technique of the painting originally matched

that on cat. no. 112 and if it was done by the same hand are difficult to say because of the poor condition of the ornament. The same holds true for the floral painting on the top of the chest—a well-balanced, asymmetrical composition of varied flowers and leaves emerging from a mound, which appears to be derived from the same type of printed designs as the flowers in vases on cat. no. 112. Judging from what remains of the original paint, the bouquet was rendered in a relatively naturalistic manner and with a reasonably delicate touch. The designs and the painting on the sides—at least in their present state—have a somewhat different character, which raises some questions. On the left side, a tree trunk toward the front appears to bear grapes, leaves, and tendrils that provide a

81

perch for a bird, but on closer inspection the grapes and leaves spring from more faintly painted vines that rise from the ground at center between the trunk and a strawberry plant at the back. Since there is considerable repainting and the composition is out of the ordinary, one wonders to what extent the present scheme represents the original design. The motif on the right side—a bush over which two butterflies hover—appears uncommonly dense, with compact foliage of uniform oval leaves that look largely repainted; its good-sized, round flowers, left with numerous losses, are unidentifiable.

The most unusual feature of this piece is the applied gilt-paper ornament. Straight, narrow strips border the drawer fronts and subdivide the upper one, accent the drawer divider, and form a double band around the floral motif on the top. Strips that are scalloped on one edge run along either side of

the arris of the top molding and down the vertical edges of the front and sides. Six escutcheons, the two larger ones of which have a keyhole cutout, punctuate the drawer fronts. This paper ornament—gilt not with gold but with a copper alloy known as Dutch gold or German gold—was most likely added in the nineteenth century to spruce up the piece. In all probability there was originally a half-round molding applied to the front edge of the sides and drawer divider, as there invariably is on other small board chests of the period, and such a molding—placed horizontally and not askew like the paper border—divided the upper drawer front. Gilt-paper ornament has not been encountered on any other eighteenth-century American furniture and is known on only one other American piece—a center table (of about 1830–50) at the Winterthur Museum.[1] While Dutch gold was to be found in

Boston by the 1680s and was used there on japanned furniture in the early eighteenth century (see cat. no. 125), and although such leaf was being applied to sheets of paper by the end of the seventeenth century in Europe, the availability of ready-made gilt paper borders and decorative appliqués probably first dates to the late 1700s or early 1800s, when fancy work in paper became very popular.[2] In the March 1810 issue of his *Repository of Arts* Rudolph Ackermann advertised paper borders in colors and gold available in various widths and many patterns, and the June issue of that London publication included an insert of several pages with line drawings of embossed paper ornaments that ranged from plain stars to classical figures obtainable also in colors and gold.[3]

PAINTED DECORATION

The ground coat contains black particles (probably a carbon black) and a small percentage of red particles (perhaps red ocher). The designs appear to have been laid out in white (lead white) with red (vermilion) and green (a copper green) applied over the white. Particulars of the technique or of the coloration of the motifs are difficult to determine because of extensive losses, inpainting and repainting, and surface coatings. The designs are covered by more or less thick, darkened finish layers, which were reduced somewhat in the cleaning of the surfaces undertaken at the MMA in 1980. Among those layers (the stratification of which is confused) is what appears to be a brown glaze, found over much of the surface, and in some areas a green glaze. The repainting on the sides and top includes some obviously new detailing, such as veining on leaves; and on the foliage of the trees on the front there are small added branches, mostly obscured by dark finish layers. The new paint on the other motifs on the front primarily reinforces the outlines of individual elements and fills in some of the areas of loss in red or green with no delineation. The gilding on the glued-on paper borders and escutcheons, which are most likely not original, has been identified as Dutch gold, an alloy of copper and zinc (in a ratio of about ten to one). Most of the gilding has been lost; where it remains, in isolated spots, it shows traces of green glaze. The paper itself, now covered largely by just one or more layers of finish, has breaks and losses.

CONSTRUCTION

The top and bottom are joined to the sides with through dovetails. The back (now missing) was nailed to a rabbet in the top and sides. The drawer divider (2 in. deep) is let into the sides with a sliding half-dovetail joint. Drawer runners are nailed to the sides behind the divider. Both drawers ride on the bottom of the sides. The sides are dovetailed to the front and back—with three keys in the upper drawer and two in the lower. At all but one of the joints, the upper key is smaller than the lower one(s); they all protrude at the back. The longitudinal drawer bottoms are slightly beveled to fit into a groove in the front and sides and are nailed at the front and back. Both drawer fronts angle inward on all four sides and each is fitted with a lock.

A small block is glued to the underside of the top to catch the bolt of the upper lock. The top molding consists of an ovolo, fillet, cavetto, and ovolo.

CONDITION

The back is missing and the bottom molding is replaced. The top right molding has a split at the front, a loss at the back, and added nails. On the drawers there are a few added nails in the dovetail joints, and the nails at the front of the bottoms are probably added as well. The upper lock is a replacement. The escutcheons are of the period and may or may not be original. There is no evidence the drawers ever had pulls. The drawer runners have added nails. Light brown stain has been applied to parts of the interior and drawers. (See also *Painted decoration*.)

INSCRIPTION

Inscribed in black crayon on the exterior of the right side of each drawer is "H 244."

WOODS

Top and sides of case, top molding, drawer fronts, drawer divider, runners, SOFT MAPLE; bottom of case, sides, back, and bottom of drawers, SOUTHERN YELLOW PINE.

DIMENSIONS

OH. 16¼ (41.3); OW. (top molding) 18⅜ (46.7); CW. 16¼ (41.3); OD. (top molding) 10¾ (27.3); CD. 9¾ (24.8).

EXHIBITION

"Connecticut Furniture: Seventeenth and Eighteenth Centuries," Wadsworth Atheneum, 3 November–17 December 1967.

REFERENCE

Kirk 1967 (exh. cat.), no. 54.

PROVENANCE

Ex coll.: Louise R. (Mrs. Charles O.) Cornelius, New York City and Washington, Connecticut.

The chest was on loan to the MMA from Mrs. Cornelius from 1933 until it was purchased from her in 1938.

Rogers Fund, 1938 (38.97)

1. Fennimore 1991, fig. 3.
2. For a 1684 Boston painter's inventory that includes Dutch gold, see Fairbanks 1982, p. 449. For gold leaf (usually not true gold) applied to sheets of paper in the late 1600s, see Haemmerle 1961, p. 131. Rolled strips of paper with gilt edges were used in quillwork contemporary with this chest (Krill 2002, p. 150), but the present writer has not seen any paper strips in quillwork that have a full surface rather than just an edge gilt.
3. *Repository of Arts, Literature, Commerce, Manufactures, Fashions, and Politics*, vol. 3, no. 15 (March 1810), pp. 192–94 (actual samples of gold borders are affixed to a sheet inserted between pages 192 and 193), and vol. 3, no. 18 (June 1810), insert between pages 396 and 397. See also Krill 2002, fig. 147 and pp. 187–93.

82.

Small cabinet or spice box

Philadelphia, 1710–30

In Pennsylvania, a small cabinet containing drawers of various sizes behind a door or doors that locked was usually called a spice box, and inventory listings of a "spice box on a frame" most likely referred to an item like cat. no. 82. The term "spice box," which harks back to a time when spices were a precious commodity and required safekeeping, continued in use in Pennsylvania well into the nineteenth century, even though there is evidence that in the eighteenth century such cabinets stored valuables and small items of all kinds, from gold cuff links and silver spoons to needlework pocketbooks, spectacles, and sundry keepsakes. Spice boxes served a practical purpose, but the careful workmanship and elaboration expended on many of them and the fact that they were usually placed in the parlor (or the best room) indicate that they were also meant for display; their ownership reflected a certain degree of prosperity.[1]

Pennsylvania spice boxes, like their New England cognates, were derived from seventeenth-century English examples. In New England, small cabinets like cat. no. 79 went out of fashion in the early 1700s and few examples are known; in Pennsylvania, however, spice boxes continued to be produced and were so designated throughout the eighteenth century, and their design evolved over time. The majority retained the basic format of a square or rectangular case with door supported on feet, while the form of the foot and the scheme of the ornamentation changed with changing styles. This is one of a relatively small number of examples where the cabinet is set on a stand or frame rather than just on feet and which take the form of miniature versions of full-size case furniture. It is one of five published spice boxes on which the frame replicates the lower case of a William and Mary–style six-legged high chest. The cabinet on the four others has a single door, rather than two, as seen here.[2] Paneled double doors occur more often on the somewhat more numerous spice boxes supported by later-style frames with cabriole legs, and they recall the two-door design of the upper unit of a desk and bookcase, a form that was very rare in American furniture before the Queen Anne style came into fashion, in the 1730s.[3] This evidence suggests the present piece was made late in the William and Mary period.

Cat. no. 82 as it now appears is not as unified in its design as it once was. Originally, around the lower case drawer openings was applied a molding that most likely had a half-round profile and echoed the ovolo around the door panels and the astragal at the top of the mid-molding. Moreover, the eye was not distracted by the present obtrusive hardware; the upper case was fitted with modest, plain butt hinges mounted on the inner side of the case and doors and with probably narrower if not smaller escutcheons. The frame duplicates in miniature some of the features that distinguish such Philadelphia high chests as the one made about 1726 by John Head (d. 1754) for Caspar Wistar (Philadelphia Museum of Art).[4] Design parallels include the overall form of the trumpet legs with their bold, elegant flare and the pointed peak of the central arch of the front skirt (see cat. no. 131 and fig. 43). Structurally, the primary and secondary woods are the same, and so are, in the lower case, the manner of dovetailing the sides to the front, the drawer openings cut out of the solid front and widely separated, the absence of transverse partitions, the way in which the drawer runners are attached, and the fact that the mid-molding, with a characteristic cavetto at the bottom, is all part of the lower case. Precedent for the light-dark-light inlaid stringing on the drawer fronts can be found on another Philadelphia high chest, which, like cat. no. 82, has stretchers that are straight on the inner side.[5] The arrangement of the interior drawers—around a central square drawer—follows English seventeenth-century practice and is generally similar to that on cat. no. 79 (see fig. 81).

CONSTRUCTION

The piece is built in two parts, which are now fastened together, probably by glue. On the upper case, the top is joined to the sides with through dovetails and the bottom is presumably joined in the same manner. The back, formed of two vertical boards, is nailed to the rabbeted edge of the top and sides and to the bottom. The doors are framed with through tenons, which are not pinned; the ovolo molding that surrounds the fielded panels is worked on the edge of the stiles and rails, and the joints are mitered (see fig. 164). On the interior, the horizontal dividers and vertical partitions that form the compartments holding ten small drawers are slotted into one another and into the case sides; the whole unit was slid in from the back. A slat under the top at the front provides support for the cornice molding and stops the doors; drawer guides extend behind it at each end. Along the front on the inside of the bottom is a similar slat and behind it a drawer runner at each side. On the lower case, the back is joined to the sides, and the sides to the front, with half-blind dovetails. The front is a single board in which the drawer openings have been sawn out. The top consists of a thin longitudinal board that fits into a rabbet on the upper edge of the four sides. A vertical block that extends to the top of the case is glued in each corner and inside the front between the drawers. The drawers are supported by L-shaped runners that are rabbeted to fit against the blocks. They are nailed in place at the front and similarly attached to the rear blocks or let into the back board. A guide is glued to the top above each

82

drawer. The round upper tenons of the legs are housed partly in the blocks and partly in the case sides; the lower tenons extend through the stretchers and feet. The stretchers are half-lapped at the corners. The skirt is finished with a nailed-on edging strip. On the drawers of both the upper and the lower cases, the sides are joined to the front with half-blind dovetails and to the back with through dovetails, and the top of the sides is rounded. The lower inner edge of all four sides is rabbeted to receive the bottom, which is glued in place. On the inside of the fronts, kerfs from the sawing of the dovetails extend in for about ½ inch. Except for the front, the drawers are all made of thin (3/16 to ¼ in.) stock, as are the dividers and partitions in the upper case.

CONDITION

The hinges, escutcheons, lock in the right door, and bolt in the left door are all replacements, and so are all the turned wooden knobs on the interior drawers and the metal knobs on the drawers of the lower case. The upper portion of the mid-molding has an atypical profile, but the molding clearly predates the replacement of the hardware

and, like the cornice, is probably original. Scribe lines indicate there was originally a narrow (¼ in.) molding applied around the drawer openings of the lower case. The back of the upper case has been off and renailed. On the lower case, the lower rear corner of the left side is pieced, and one drawer guide is missing. The right half of the front stretcher is new and perhaps also the right stretcher. The right center leg and foot look replaced, as do one or more caps above the legs. The other legs, feet, and caps show losses, splits, and repairs. It is not clear if the wedges in some of the tenons that pass through the feet are original or added. Two interior drawers are new; three others and the lower left exterior one have replacements. The piece has been stripped and has a glossy modern finish, but dark residues of an earlier coating remain in recesses and on the legs and feet.

INSCRIPTIONS

Modern numbers in pencil are inscribed on the underside of the drawers, and corresponding numbers are written on the cases. Four of the dividers also have unrelated scratched numbers.

WOODS

Upper case top, sides, doors, slats at front of top and bottom, front one-quarter of dividers and partitions, lower case front and sides, legs, stretchers, feet, caps at top of legs, all drawer fronts, all applied moldings, BLACK WALNUT; upper case bottom, lower case back and interior vertical blocks, all drawer runners and guides, SOUTHERN YELLOW PINE; upper case back and rear three-quarters of dividers and partitions, lower case top, all drawer sides, backs, and bottoms, ATLANTIC WHITE CEDAR.

DIMENSIONS

OH. 28⅞ (73.3); upper case: OW. (cornice) 16⅛ (41), CW. 14 (35.6), OD. (cornice) 8½ (21.6), CD. 7⅜ (18.7); lower case: OW. (mid-molding) 16⅛ (41), CW. 15 (38.1), OD. (mid-molding) 8½ (21.6), CD. 8 (20.3).

REFERENCES

Lockwood 1913, fig. 77 (with doors open); Stockwell 1939, fig. 2; Williams 1963, no. 53; Schwartz 1976, no. 34.

PROVENANCE

The donor (Mrs. Manfred P. Welcher) was residing in Hartford, Connecticut, at the time the gift was made. It is not known how she acquired the cabinet. She was a daughter of art dealer and collector Samuel Putnam Avery, who was a founder and trustee of the MMA.

Gift of Mrs. Fanny Avery Welcher, 1911 (11.183)

1. The prime reference for Pennsylvania spice boxes is Griffith 1986. See also Hornor 1935, pp. 69–70; Stockwell 1939; Schiffer 1966, pp. 265–66; and Schiffer 1974, pp. 121–22, 141. A "Spice Box on a Frame" is listed in an inventory of 1720 (Hornor 1935, p. 70) and another in one of 1749 (Schiffer 1974, p. 121). For contents, see Griffith 1986, pp. 14–15 and fig. 1; and Lindsey 1999, no. 12.
2. For the four others, see Hornor 1935, pl. 3; Griffith 1986, nos. 47, 48; and one in *Antiques* 103 (April 1973), p. 618, advertised by Joseph Sprain. One New England piece generally similar in form is known (Fales 1976, no. 422). Two further Pennsylvania examples in the William and Mary style have no door in the upper case and a base with baluster legs and one long drawer (Griffith 1986, no. 49; Lindsey 1999, no. 41 and fig. 165).
3. Similar rectangular double doors with fielded panels are on a spice box with a cabriole-leg base at the Philadelphia Museum of Art (acc. no. 1994-157-1); other two-door examples are in Rodriguez Roque 1984, no. 33, and Griffith 1986, nos. 51–55.
4. The high chest was ordered from Head by Wistar (who later became a glass manufacturer) in 1726, the year he was married (Lindsey 1999, no. 38 and fig. 167).
5. Ibid., no. 37.

Chests and Chests with Drawers

Nearly every seventeenth-century household owned at least one chest, a basic form of storage furniture known in antiquity and in use throughout the Middle Ages. Chests most often contained linen and clothing but served to store all manner of personal belongings and household goods as well. They ranged from paneled examples elaborately ornamented to simple nailed pieces, and different types were found within the same home. In the single downstairs room of a blacksmith's house in Hingham, Massachusetts, for example, there were in 1675 "2 Joyned Chests and one Box and a deale [pine] Board Chest."[1]

The better-quality and more highly valued seventeenth-century case furniture was joined, using the frame-and-panel method of construction. Rails and stiles were secured with mortise-and-tenon joints to form rectangular frames, which were grooved on the inner side to hold a panel; the panel was left loose within the grooves so that it could expand and contract according to atmospheric conditions without splitting (see fig. 84). Chests built in this manner, traditionally of riven oak, were sturdy and durable. They involved considerably more labor and were thus more expensive than board pieces, as a 1681 Dedham, Massachusetts, inventory listing of "a joyned Chest. 8/ˢ a plain Chest. 4/ˢ" makes clear.[2]

Chests, however built, had, like boxes, a lift top attached with snipebill hinges or cleat-pin hinges. The interior was often fitted at one or both ends with a till—a rectangular receptacle, sometimes lidded, attached near the top—in which to keep smaller, select objects that it might be difficult to find and retrieve from under other items in the large chest cavity. As a further convenience, one or two discrete compartments—drawers—were sometimes added below the chest. The chest with drawer form was introduced to England by Continental artisans in the 1500s and entered the vocabulary of English craftsmen in the 1600s. Judging by the number of surviving examples, joined chests with drawers were particularly in favor in New England during the last three decades of the seventeenth century. It may be that the popularity of the form at that time represented, at least in part, a conservative response to the chest of drawers (a case containing only drawers), which was the most advanced and fashionable form of case furniture in the colonies in the second half of the seventeenth century.

Some joined chests and chests with drawers were just minimally embellished with chamfered edges and channel moldings, but most that have survived, and all those in the collection, are more extensively ornamented. The Museum's examples all come from New England, and the various decorative styles and structural particularities they exhibit reflect directly or at a little remove the diversity of local or regional craft practices brought to America by immigrant woodworkers from different parts of England. Among the chests decorated solely with carving, the most richly ornamented in terms of the variety of motifs and the degree of relief is the prime example at the head of this chapter, attributed to William Searle or Thomas Dennis, joiners who brought to Ipswich, Massachusetts, the florid style in which they had been trained in County Devon, England (cat. no. 83). The shop tradition they established, of which two lesser examples are also in the collection (cat. nos. 84, 85), represents probably the clearest instance of the direct transfer of a particular English regional style to America. Two chests—one made with four rather than the more usual three front panels—attributed to the New Haven, Connecticut, area but not to any specific shop, exhibit somewhat less elaborate carved schemes (cat. nos. 86, 87). Their designs appear to have their source in other counties in the west of England, as do the simpler patterns on two chests associated with nearby areas of the Connecticut shore (cat. nos. 88, 89). The carving on yet another example from south-central Connecticut, however, relates to patterns favored in County Suffolk, in the east of England (cat. no. 90). Two chests with drawers in the collection that come from Hampshire County, Massachusetts, in the Connecticut River valley are part of a large group of so-called Hadley chests, which, in that quite isolated, rural area, carried on the seventeenth-century tradition of joined construction and carved floral decoration into the early decades of the eighteenth century (cat. nos. 95, 96). A combination of carving and applied ornament distinguishes the numerous so-called sunflower chests made in Hartford County, Connecticut, immediately to the south, during the last quarter of the seventeenth century. Three examples of this school of craftsmanship are here included (cat. nos. 92–94). Neither the sunflower nor the Hadley design has any known direct antecedent, and each appears to have resulted from a convergence of two or more joinery traditions. Decorative schemes consisting solely of applied mitered moldings and turnings were brought to the colonies by craftsmen trained in urban areas of England. Design elements introduced by London joiners to Boston are illustrated by two chests with drawers from that area (cat. nos. 98, 99), which feature a two-panel front—a formula common on Boston chests of drawers. No chest made in the standard three-panel format with applied geometric decoration is in the collection. The use of inlay in seventeenth-century colonial work is rare. When it occurs, as on a chest with drawer that is the only piece in this chapter not attributed to a particular school or locality, it consists of geometric patterns used in combination with other modes of decoration—in this instance, carving (cat. no. 97).

Chests constructed of boards that were simply nailed together were the most common and most affordable, but relatively few examples in the seventeenth-century style are known and only one is in the collection (cat. no. 91). Made by joiners or carpenters, they were most often of pine, like the Museum's example; but unlike this one, they generally had side boards that were oriented vertically and extended down to form feet. While many board chests were probably plain and strictly utilitarian, most that have survived were embellished with molding planes, incised or stamped ornament, or in rare cases applied ornament. The incised decoration on the front of the Museum's chest with its four rectangular divisions alludes to the facade of a joined chest.

On seventeenth-century case furniture, paint generally served to pick out parts of the design or to provide a single-color coat on plain board pieces. Floral painted motifs began to appear about 1700, first on some joined chests and then as a popular mode of decoration on board examples. The collection

is rich in furniture with painted decoration from the early eighteenth century. Of the five chests with drawer so ornamented in this chapter, three are the product of a major school of floral painting centered in the Guilford-Saybrook area of coastal Connecticut, the earliest being joined and dated 1705 (cat. nos. 100–102); the fourth represents a different coastal Connecticut shop tradition (cat. no. 103); and the fifth, dated 1735, exhibits the distinctive style of painting associated with Taunton, Massachusetts (cat. no. 104).

By about 1725, frame-and-panel chests and chests with drawers were no longer being made in New England, even in rural areas. Board examples, however, nailed and then also dovetailed, continued to be produced throughout the eighteenth and much of the nineteenth century, persisting, like some of the early colonial chair and table forms, at the economical or vernacular level.

1. A. L. Cummings 1964, p. 5.
2. Ibid., p. 32.

83.

Chest

Ipswich, Massachusetts, 1663–80
Attributed to William Searle (d. 1667) or Thomas Dennis
(1638–1706)

The richness and vigor of the carving make this the premier example in the Museum's American furniture collection of the carved seventeenth-century style. The chest is a prime representative of the Ipswich, Massachusetts, school of craftsmanship, long identified with William Searle and Thomas Dennis. Their elaborately carved furniture illustrates unequivocally the direct transmission of an English regional style to the New World.

The body of work ascribed to the Searle-Dennis school encompasses two wainscot chairs, about fifteen chests, including cat. nos. 83–85, several boxes, and two tape looms. The attribution is based on five pieces—the two chairs, a chest, a box with drawer, and one of the tape looms—that were inherited by various Dennis descendants and that, as Irving P. Lyon demonstrated in 1937, can be traced back to the progenitor of the family in America, Thomas Dennis, a joiner.[1] The work of this school has since been the focus of much scholarly attention.[2] Information on its protagonists, however, remains limited. Nothing is known of Dennis before the fall of 1663, when he was living in Portsmouth,

New Hampshire, and entered into a transaction with William Searle, who was likewise a joiner and had come to Ipswich from Boston earlier that year.[3] Dennis moved to Ipswich about 1668, when he married Searle's widow, Grace (1636–1686). Among the possessions she inherited from her first husband was a chair that, given its very high valuation, was undoubtedly richly carved. Thus, at least one of the pieces that descended in the Dennis family was very likely made by Searle.[4] Searle came from Ottery St. Mary, County Devon, where he was married to Grace Cole in 1659. Dennis, who worked in the same style, must have also learned his trade in Devon.[5]

The carving on Searle-Dennis furniture clearly has its source in a tradition of florid carving that flourished in Devonshire at the beginning of the seventeenth century and was centered in Exeter. One of the defining motifs of that tradition, which found expression in both stone and wood and in funerary monuments and church and domestic interiors as well as in furniture, is a strapwork pattern closely similar to one that adorns the Dennis family chairs and box, a box at

83. See also figs. 55, 136.

Historic New England, and a chest at the Winterthur Museum. The Exeter school, from whatever sources it actually evolved, reflects the type of complex Mannerist decoration brought to London by Continental immigrant craftsmen in the 1560s and promulgated by northern European pattern books. The strapwork pattern in question may have been derived from a design published in Amsterdam by Jan Vredeman de Vries (1527–1604) and Cornelis Bos (1506?–?1564) in the early 1560s. The pattern, as formulated in Exeter, was most likely transferred to New England by Searle and Dennis in the form of a learned motif with a memorized layout scheme that was part of their decorative repertoire.[6]

The strapwork design of circles alternating with rectangles utilized on the lower rail of the present chest (fig. 55) does not occur on any other surviving Searle-Dennis piece but was a common motif in Devonshire on furniture and interior woodwork. The guilloche pattern, which adorns the upper rail, was likewise part of that English regional decorative vocabulary, and it is found in a more elaborate version—enclosing four different kinds of rosettes—on the drawer front of the Dennis family box.[7] The panels on the chairs and on the large majority of the chests feature what is generically a tree-of-life motif—an arrangement of flowers and leaves issuing from a vase (of which here only the opening is schematically indicated), which was a popular seventeenth-century device in many mediums. Five such floral designs occur on the Searle-Dennis pieces.[8] The scheme on the center panel of the present chest, notable for the stems of leaves that pass under one another at the center and through a loop at the bottom, is also found, in a somewhat different interpretation, on the back of the Dennis family chair at the Peabody Essex Museum. The design on the outer panels of this chest is the most common one and occurs in several versions (see cat. no. 85). Here, large paired leaves dominate the center of the panel, and the frond within the arch recalls, in the way in which the leaflets overlap, the carnation depicted in one of the alternate patterns that is carved on the Dennis family chair at the Bowdoin College Museum of Art, Brunswick, Maine, and a chest at the Winterthur Museum. A lozenge design is utilized on the panels of some of the chests (see cat. nos. 84, 85) and various motifs beyond those seen or mentioned here can be found on rails, stiles, and muntins.

The Searle-Dennis school is remarkable for the number of motifs within its repertoire and for their range, which far exceeds that of any other shop tradition in seventeenth-century America, and the best of its carving exhibits a degree of relief, such as that seen on the large paired leaves on this chest's panels, that is rare in colonial work of this period. To the large number and diversity of the individual decorative elements on the front of this chest have been added variations in the delineation of similar forms: the leaves on the stiles above the roundel are detailed differently from those below, as

are the large paired leaves on the center panel from those on the outer panels; on the lower rail the half roundels at each end contain foliage rather than a pinwheel, and those two patterns alternate on the semicircles along the top and bottom of the rail.

All the various elements on the facade have been masterfully arranged into a carefully balanced composition that vividly expresses the taste for complexity and virtuosity inherent in the aesthetics of the seventeenth-century style. The sinuous curves of the corner brackets lead the eye in and upward to the center panel and up through its lower S-scrolls to the well-articulated dominant motif of paired leaves that is echoed on the outer panels. The horizontal scrolls at the top of the center panel allude to the guilloche on the upper rail, which is recalled on the stiles and to which the strapwork on the lower rail provides a counterpoint. The whole front resonates with an intricate interplay of variations on primarily rounded figures and leaf forms.

Attempts to separate the work of Searle and Dennis have so far not been conclusive.[9] What can be said of this chest is that the nature of the motifs, the vigor of the composition, and the assured handling of the carving indicate that it was executed by an immigrant joiner while the English tradition from which it stemmed was still quite fresh in his mind, be it that of Searle or Dennis.

CONSTRUCTION

The back, like the front, has three panels, and the sides have two; the mortise-and-tenon joints of the frame are secured with two pins, except for the joint of the bottom front rail to the left stile, which has three. The joints are about 5/16 inch wide, the most common width in furniture of this period. The framing members on the front are all similar in width and the panels equal in size. The top is formed of three longitudinal riven boards, the butted edges of which are held together with whittled oak dowels. Originally the cleats under either end of the top were each secured with five wooden pins, and the top was attached to the case with three snipebill hinges. The bottom consists of six transverse boards joined with a tongue and groove, one of the center boards having a tongue on either side. The boards are beveled to fit into a groove in the front and side rails and in both the narrow and the broad inner face of all four stiles. They are secured to the underside of the rear rail with rosehead nails, each sunk in a large gouged hole that considerably reduces the thickness of the board and the length of nail required. The grooves for the bottom are cut 1¼ inches up from the lower edge of the front and side rails, and the bottom of the rear rail is level with the upper edge of the grooves. The side of each bracket is tenoned to the stile and the tip nailed to the rail. There was a till on the right that had a slanted lid; its side was let into grooves in the rails and the bottom into grooves in the stiles. On the chest sides, the center of the rails and of the muntins is worked with a channel molding that has an ovolo on each side. The rails are ornamented, in addition, near the edge facing the panels, with a molding that consists of a cyma reversa and two small beads, and the same molding runs down the stiles. A molding with a cyma reversa followed by a single larger bead and a chamfer (fig. 136) edges the muntins and the bottom of the lower rails. On the front, the muntins are just edged with a similar bead and a narrower chamfer. The last three molding profiles appear to be particular to the Searle-Dennis school (see the entry for cat. no. 84). The edges of the stiles and rails that surround the panels are not ornamented in any manner. On the interior, virtually all edges are finished with a narrow chamfer. The stiles are rectangular, and all surfaces of the framing members and panels are planed.

CONDITION

The chest is missing 2 to 3 inches from the bottom of the feet, which are somewhat shorter on the left than on the right side of the case. The top is original but is now nailed to replaced cleats and attached with large modern butt hinges; the portion of the original snipebill hinges affixed to the rear rail remains in place. A section along the lower edge of the left end of the upper front rail that was missing was replaced in chestnut in 1972. The lock and its staple are missing, as is the till, which was lost before sections of an 1852 newspaper were glued to the interior to cover shrinkage gaps in the bottom and between the right back panel and back stile. Parts of the frame and a few panels have splits and small losses at the edges; a large split at the top of the right rear stile is repaired with nails. Screw holes on the back of the upper rear rail probably stem from when, several decades past at the MMA, small objects displayed on the top were strapped to the case. Several areas of wood weakened by worm damage have been solidified. The front of the top is worn and heavily gouged, and the lower edge of the bottom front rail is battered. The surface has been amply waxed and perhaps also oiled. No traces of paint are evident.

INSCRIPTIONS

MMA Hudson-Fulton exhibition identification numbers are inscribed in orange crayon on the inner side of the left upper rail (H. F. 40.19). Inscribed in white chalk on the outside of a back panel are numbers, and on the inside of the top there are various markings.

WOODS

WHITE OAK and RED OAK.

DIMENSIONS

OH. 29¾ (75.6); OW. (top) 49⅛ (124.8); CW. 47 (119.4); OD. (top) 21¼ (54); CD. 20¾ (52.7).

EXHIBITIONS

"Hudson-Fulton Exhibition," MMA, 20 September–30 November 1909; "The Art of Joinery: Seventeenth-Century Case Furniture in the American Wing," MMA, 18 October 1972–18 March 1973; "A Bicentennial Treasury: American Masterpieces from the Metropolitan," MMA, 29 January 1976–2 January 1977; "American Furniture and the Art of Connoisseurship," MMA, 7 April–4 October 1998.

REFERENCES

Hudson-Fulton Celebration 1909 (exh. cat.), no. 68; Lockwood 1913, fig. 8; Halsey and Cornelius 1924 (and 1925, 1926, 1928, 1932, 1938, 1942), fig. 1; Cescinsky and Hunter 1929, p. 41; MMA 1930, fig. 1; Dyer 1931a, p. 36; I. P. Lyon 1937b, fig. 5; E. G. Miller 1937, no. 595; "Antiques

in the American Wing" 1946, p. 246, no. 4; Bjerkoe 1957, pl. III, no. 2; Comstock 1962, no. 47; Hornung 1972, no. 897; Safford 1972 (exh. cat.), no. 5 and fig. 4 (detail); *Bicentennial Treasury* 1976 (exh. cat.), fig. 1; Schwartz 1976, no. 6; Chinnery 1979, fig. 4:194; M. B. Davidson 1980, fig. 69; Safford 1980, fig. 2; Fairbanks and Trent 1982, p. 516, fig. 65; St. George 1983, figs. 10, 15–17 (details of bracket, bottom, and top); M. B. Davidson and Stillinger 1985, fig. 129 and p. 22 (detail); Tarule 1992, pp. 200–201; Heckscher 1998, pls. I, Ia (detail); Safford 2000, pl. III; MMA 2001, fig. 11; Manca 2003, fig. 23.

PROVENANCE

Ex coll.: H. Eugene Bolles, Boston.

Gift of Mrs. Russell Sage, 1909 (10.125.685)

1. For the Dennis family pieces, see I. P. Lyon 1937a, fig. 1 (chair, Peabody Essex Museum), fig. 2 (chair, Bowdoin College Museum of Art, Brunswick, Maine), fig. 3 (chest, Chipstone Foundation), fig. 4 (box, Bowdoin College Museum); and Park 1960a, fig. 1 (tape loom, Bowdoin College Museum). For other chests, see I. P. Lyon 1937b, fig. 6 (Wadsworth Atheneum), fig. 10 (Peabody Essex Museum), fig. 16 (location unknown); I. P. Lyon 1938a, fig. 23 (Bowdoin College Museum); Fairbanks and Trent 1982, p. 515, fig. 64 (Ipswich Historical Society, Ipswich, Massachusetts); B. Ward 1986, no. 1 (Winterthur Museum); and, in this catalogue, nos. 84, 85, and chests cited in the latter entry. For the other tape loom, see Fairbanks and Trent 1982, no. 478. For boxes, see Jobe and Kaye 1984, no. 1 (Historic New England), and Jobe et al. 1991, no. 4 (Milwaukee Art Museum, Milwaukee, Wisconsin); there is a similar one at the Art Institute of Chicago, Chicago, Illinois (acc. no. 1946.564). Lyon, after assigning the family pieces and furniture with related carving to Dennis (I. P. Lyon 1937a, 1937b, and 1938a), also attributed to him many other objects that, in fact, represent the range of styles made in Essex County, Massachusetts, during the last third of the seventeenth century (I. P. Lyon 1938b, 1938c, and 1938d).
2. Keyes 1938; Park 1960a and 1960b; Forman 1968, pp. 58–62; Fairbanks and Trent 1982, nos. 474–78; St. George 1983; B. Ward 1986, no. 1; Forman 1988, pp. 135–36; Tarule 1992.
3. Park 1960a, p. 42. The document of 1663, long assumed to represent the sale of Searle's house and land in Ipswich to Dennis (I. P. Lyon 1937a, p. 231)—which then leaves unexplained where in Ipswich Searle lived until he died—probably indicates rather that Searle put up his property in Ipswich as collateral for a loan of eight pounds from Dennis (Tarule 1992, p. 122).
4. Fairbanks and Trent 1982, no. 474.
5. According to a genealogy of the Searle family, William Searle was born in Ottery St. Mary in 1634 and married Grace Cole in 1659, as recorded in the parish register (Park 1960a, p. 42). However, W. F. Bennett, clerk to the Ottery St. Mary Urban District Council, in a letter of 14 October 1970 to Benno M. Forman states that what he found in the records was a listing for a William Searle who was born in 1611 and married a Grace Cole in 1659 (letter in the registrar's object file, acc. no. 82.276, Winterthur Museum); in that case Searle would have been about fifty when he emigrated with his young wife. While Bennett found no record of a Dennis in Ottery before 1660, the surname means "man from Devon" (Wells-Cole 1981, p. 3).
6. Wells-Cole 1981. The printed design in question is illustrated in Fairbanks and Trent 1982, p. 376, fig. 46.
7. Wells-Cole 1981, pp. 3, 5, 7, pl. 14. An elaborately carved English cupboard (advertised in *Antiques* 122 [November 1982], p. 929, by Fallen Oaks Limited) exhibits two strapwork patterns—the one related to that on the Dennis family pieces and the other related to the one on cat. no. 83—showing that both were part of the same decorative vocabulary.
8. An English chest in the Devonshire style dated 1671 provides close parallels with two of those patterns (Kirk 1982, fig. 8; Forman 1988, fig. 62).
9. Fairbanks and Trent 1982, nos. 474–78; St. George 1983, p. 18B; B. Ward 1986, no. 1; Tarule 1992, pp. 160–209, 370.

84.

Chest

Ipswich, Massachusetts, 1670–90
Attributed to the Searle-Dennis shop tradition

In its joinery and the profile of its moldings this chest is closely related to cat. no. 83 and several other chests that are among the finest examples of the Searle-Dennis school of craftsmanship, but its carving, which is very poor in quality, bears no comparison and is something of a puzzle. The manner in which the top is made—with oak boards doweled together and secured to the cleat under each end with wooden pins—is the same as on cat. no. 83 and on a chest at the Winterthur Museum. The design of the cleats—which have a small notch followed by a shallow ogee curve at the front and are just rounded at the back—is similar to that on the latter.[1] The construction of the chest bottom—with tongue-and-groove joints between its transverse boards and the boards let into grooves in the front and side rails and all four stiles and secured at the back with countersunk nails—matches that on cat. no. 83, the Winterthur Museum chest, and one at the Ipswich Historical Society, Ipswich, Massachusetts.[2] The channel molding with a cyma reversa and two small beads that ornaments the sides of this piece is a distinctive one that occurs on the three chests just mentioned, as well as one at the Wadsworth Atheneum and cat. no. 85, and has otherwise not been noted on American joined furniture.[3] Possibly another peculiarity of this school is that the cyma reversa utilized as an edge molding on many of the chests—a common profile for this type of molding—ends in a slanted, or chamfered, edge. The smaller edge molding of a bead and a chamfer on the front of this chest is the same as that on the front muntins of cat. no. 83 and the Winterthur chest, and it appears to be a profile particular to this shop tradition as well. The extensive use to which an edge molding has been put on the facade of this piece, where it not only surrounds the panels but also runs the full length of the rails and stiles, is highly unusual—in seventeenth-century joinery in general and particularly in the Searle-Dennis shop tradition, in which an edge molding may finish the muntins but the edges around the panels are otherwise just chamfered or most often left totally plain.[4]

Of the carved motifs utilized on this chest the most common within the Searle-Dennis repertoire are the foliate S-scrolls, arranged in a single band or paired. The design of intersecting lunettes on the top rail, however, occurs on only three other chests in this shop tradition.[5] In each case the foliage on the present chest is lacking in definition; that within the lunettes suffers in particular in comparison to the nicely detailed and modeled leaves on the chest at the Ipswich Historical Society.

One other chest, dated 1692 and at the Peabody Essex Museum, is carved with a lozenge motif on all three panels rather than just one or two, as on cat. no. 85 and its related examples.[6] The design on all those pieces is similar, except that on the center panel of the Peabody Essex Museum chest a lunette containing foliage has been substituted for the three leaves that normally emerge from each side. The pattern on the present chest diverges noticeably from the usual model: the lozenge has been reduced in size and the larger of the three leaves that extend out from each side has been elongated and carved without a rounded central vein (compare cat. no. 85); in addition, a trefoil within an arch—a motif that occurs in the west of England but is not otherwise known on Searle-Dennis furniture—has been appended at the upper and lower apex of the lozenge.[7] The cruciform motif within the center lozenge also differs from the usual scheme. It resembles that on an elaborate English cupboard that has no provenance but is carved with the two strapwork patterns associated with Devonshire that occur on Searle-Dennis pieces (see the entry for cat. no. 83).[8]

The design of the panels on this chest is not a successful one. Neither is its execution, which shows a lack of competence. The difficulty the carver had in controlling the lines made with his V-shaped gouge, especially the curved ones, is painfully apparent in the arches. Since there is evidence that the panels were nailed down for carving and no indication that the chest has been apart, the poor quality or divergent design cannot be explained by assuming that the carving on the panels was added later. The proliferation of edge molding on the facade—and consequent absence of brackets—as well as the variant lozenge motifs are departures from the Searle-Dennis shop's usual practices. This would suggest that the carving is probably not that of an apprentice, who presumably would have been executing standard shop designs. It is thus more likely the work of a journeyman.[9] It is also possible that the chest was made in another shop by an unidentified craftsman from Devonshire trained in a related joinery tradition.

CONSTRUCTION
The chest has three panels in the front and back and two on each side. On the frame, the mortise-and-tenon joints of the side muntins are secured with one pin rather than two. The top, attached with two snipebill hinges, is formed of two longitudinal riven boards, butted and held together with two whittled oak dowels, and it is fastened to each cleat with four wooden pins. The bottom, except for the fact that

84

it consists of four rather than six transverse boards, is constructed in exactly the same manner as that on cat. no. 83. There is a till on the right, which once had a horizontal lid; its bottom extends under the side. On the chest sides, a channel molding with an ovolo at either side is run along the center of the rails and muntins, and a molding with a cyma reversa and two small beads is worked on the four stiles and on the rails near the edge facing the panels, with both profiles similar to those on cat. no. 83. The edge molding on the side muntins and the bottom of the side and front rails consists of a cyma reversa and a chamfer. A bead and a chamfer, a profile also found on cat. no. 83, are worked on the edges of the front muntins, both front edges of the

front stiles, and along the bottom of the upper front rail and the top of the lower front rail. On the interior, all the framing members except the front rails are finished with a narrow chamfer. Holes in the corners of the front panels indicate they were nailed down for carving. All surfaces of the frame and panels are planed; the right rear post is not entirely rectangular.

CONDITION

The top and its cleats appear to be original. One of the dowels joining the boards of the top has broken, and the top is now fastened to the cleats with nails in addition to the wooden pins, which look reset or replaced. The slightly arched profile of the upper edge of the cleats probably dates from the time of the repairs. There are abrasions on the inner side of the cleats caused by an MMA mechanism to lock the top, which proved ineffective. The hinges are replaced, the lock is not the first, and the escutcheon is not old. The lid of the till is missing. The stiles have splits at the joints. A split in the lower front rail has been repaired from the inside with nails. All edges are considerably nicked, and the bottom of the lower front rail and the side of the right front stile appear to have been bashed. There are losses at the bottom of the feet where the wood has deteriorated, as it has along the top of the upper rear rail. The chest has probably been stripped. It retains some dark residues, perhaps of a degraded finish, but no apparent traces of paint. The surface has been waxed and perhaps also oiled. The inner side of the bottom and of the lower rails is heavily stained.

INSCRIPTION

A circle enclosing a partial compass-scribed rosette is scored on the back of the right rear stile.

WOODS

RED OAK and WHITE OAK.

DIMENSIONS

OH. 28 1/2 (72.4); OW. (top) 41 7/8 (106.4); CW. 40 (101.6); OD. (top) 19 3/4 (50.2); CD. 18 7/8 (47.9).

REFERENCES

Kent 1910, p. 6; Dyer 1931a, p. 37; I. P. Lyon 1937b, fig. 9; St. George 1983, fig. 18 (detail of cleat, misidentified in the caption as a detail of cat. no. 83); M. B. Davidson and Stillinger 1985, fig. 17; Tarule 1992, pp. 201–2.

PROVENANCE

Ex coll.: H. Eugene Bolles, Boston.

Gift of Mrs. Russell Sage, 1909 (10.125.24)

1. For the Winterthur chest, see St. George 1983 and B. Ward 1986, no. 1. For details of the top of cat. no. 83, see St. George 1983, figs. 16, 17; for a detail of the cleat on the present chest (not cat. no. 83, as captioned), see fig. 18.
2. St. George 1983, figs. 11, 14 (details of the bottom of the Winterthur chest), fig. 15 (detail of the bottom of cat. no. 83); Fairbanks and Trent 1982, p. 515, fig. 64 (Ipswich Historical Society chest), and p. 548, fig. 80 (detail of the bottom of that chest). Several other chests have the bottom let into grooves in the stiles, but those boards are plain-butted or replaced.
3. For that molding on the Wadsworth Atheneum chest, see I. P. Lyon 1937b, fig. 6. A similar molding occurs on an English chest at the Wadsworth Atheneum (Kirk 1982, fig. 10) with Devonshire-style carving that differs in some elements from that of the Searle-Dennis school, which suggests that in Devon this profile was not limited to one shop but was a local or regional one. A molding analogous in profile to one used on cat. no. 83 (fig. 136) but not on cat. no. 84 also occurs on that English chest.
4. The only related usage is on the sides of the chest that descended in the Dennis family and is now at the Chipstone Foundation (I. P. Lyon 1937a, fig. 3), on which a similar molding was run clear across the lower edge of the upper rail and the upper edge of the lower rail.
5. They are those at the Ipswich Historical Society (see n. 2 above) and the Chipstone Foundation (see n. 4 above); for the third, see I. P. Lyon 1937b, fig. 16 (location unknown).
6. I. P. Lyon 1937b, fig. 10.
7. The information on this motif was provided to the writer by Anthony Wells-Cole, 4 October 1977.
8. The cupboard is advertised by Fallen Oaks Limited in *Antiques* 122 (November 1982), p. 929.
9. At least one of Dennis's two sons, John (1672–1757), was a joiner, presumably trained by his father (Park 1960b, p. 350; Fairbanks and Trent 1982, p. 514). One journeyman appears in the Ipswich records, Josiah Lyndon, who left that town in 1672 (Forman 1968, p. 60). There may well have been other apprentices and journeymen in the shop.

85.

Chest with drawer

Ipswich, Massachusetts, 1685–1700
Attributed to the Searle-Dennis shop tradition

This is one of six chests in the Searle-Dennis shop tradition (see the entry for cat. no. 83) on which the facade features a lozenge motif and a pattern of a stalk of leaves and flowers within an arch—one scheme in the center panel and the other in the two outer ones. Four of these chests were designed with a drawer (here missing). One of the six, a chest at the Museum of Fine Arts, Boston, and the only one to retain its drawer, is carved with four different motifs on the frame.[1] On this and the remaining examples, the carving on the framing members is reduced to two patterns: in each case there are foliate scrolls on the lower rail and "scissor" scrolls

on the stiles, muntins, and upper rail. The latter design, in which one scroll overlaps the other, is quite distinct from the type of paired foliate S-scrolls seen on the muntins of cat. no. 84, for instance. Both schemes occur throughout the body of Searle-Dennis pieces. On the scissor motif, the number of leaves that emerge from the opposed scrolls varies from one to five, depending primarily on the width of the element being decorated. That the use of only a single leaf seen on this chest, which is made of narrow stock, is just one option and does not of itself indicate a deterioration of the pattern is shown by a similar version of the design on the muntins of a

85

much more elaborately and competently carved chest at the Winterthur Museum.[2]

There are, however, several design and structural features on these chests that taken all together do point to a weakening of the Searle-Dennis tradition and suggest that these pieces, particularly the five with similar carving on the frame, belong to the later years of the shop's production. The decorative scheme on the frame of those five appears to represent a standardized formula, and the carving on their arched panels, especially in the area just below the frond at the top, is weak in concept and seems to indicate a poorly recollected or understood source. On the present chest and one designed without a drawer in the Museum of Fine Arts, Boston, the notion of leaves and flowers all emerging from the same base has been lost: the frond within the arch is totally detached from the central stem and hovering above a cup-shaped element that may allude to a calyx, as it appears to do on the center panel of a chest at the Chipstone Foundation. On the two chests within this group that were sold at Sotheby's

in 1978 and 1981 and are now in private collections the central stem extends up through the cup shape to connect to the frond.[3] The carving on those two chests, on that without a drawer at the Museum of Fine Arts, Boston, and on the present one is distinguished by being ornamented throughout with punched dots, which are used less extensively on several other pieces. A punch that impresses a small circle occurs on many of the other objects in the Searle-Dennis tradition. Structurally, this group of six chests exhibits traits that depart from the careful oak joinery seen in cat. no. 83, for example. They all use some pine, and this chest and the one sold at Sotheby's in 1981 incorporate, in addition, a considerable amount of maple, which strongly suggests production at the end of the seventeenth century. The back on both of the auctioned pieces has been reduced to a single horizontal panel. Bottom boards are just butted, and on this and the chest auctioned in 1981 the construction of the bottom has been further simplified by having the boards nailed to a rabbet on the front and side rails rather than set in a groove. The chest with drawer form appears not to have been part of the Searle-Dennis shop's original joinery tradition but rather to represent an evolution in the shop's designs in response to outside influences. No changes were made to the basic chest structure to accommodate the drawer: the sides of the chest were not extended down to hide it, and on the front no rail was added below it. The drawer is treated as a mere appendage, and the one surviving example is simply nailed together.

The present chest has many replacements but is not of dubious origin. Evidence of a change in the design of the facade—the use of narrower muntins and panels of different width than originally planned (see *Construction*)—occurs also on a chest at the Peabody Essex Museum.[4] It points up the fact that in the Searle-Dennis school of joinery there does not seem to have been a shop standard for stock size per se or for one framing member relative to the others, or for the size of panels in themselves or in respect to one another, or for the overall dimensions of the chests, which vary considerably.

CONSTRUCTION

The chest has three panels in the front and back and two on each side. On the frame, the mortise-and-tenon joints of the side muntins and of the lower side rails to the rear stiles are secured with one rather than two pins. The chest's joints are about 3/8 inch wide. On the front rails, the mortises were cut, and the pin holes drilled, for muntins approximately the same width as those in the back and considerably wider than those actually used, which would have made the three front panels about equal in width, as they are in the back. Whatever prompted the change in design, it resulted in the muntins' having joint pins off to one side. The top is attached with two snipebill hinges. The bottom consists of three transverse boards that come together with butt joints. They are nailed to a rabbet at the bottom of the front and side rails and to the underside of the rear rail and are slightly beveled to fit into grooves in the stiles. The bottom of those grooves is about level with the bottom of the front and side rails. Originally the chest had a side-hung drawer supported on runners that were let into the stiles 2 inches below the bottom of the lower rails. Inside, there is a lidded till on the right. A molding with a cyma reversa followed by two small beads, similar to that on cat. nos. 83 and 84, is worked on the side rails. The side muntins are edged with a cyma reversa and a narrow chamfer. The edges of the front muntins are finished with a broad chamfer on the exterior and interior and those of the rear muntins, on the exterior. Most other edges on the interior have a slight chamfer. The framing members are planed on all sides; the inside corner of the right front stile is not square.

CONDITION

H. Eugene Bolles said that the chest was in bad condition when he acquired it (Bolles notes, MMA Archives). The structural repairs he recorded include taking the piece apart (almost all of the joint pins look new) and several obvious replacements: the top, which was missing and now consists of a single pine board without cleats, the till, the panel toward the front on the left side, and sections of the front stiles are all new. On both front stiles there is a splice that angles from just behind the front face at the top down to the back for about 10 inches. In addition, the inside corner of the left stile is pieced for 4 inches above the chest bottom, and a nearly 5-inch-high section of the whole

right stile at the level of the lower rails has been replaced and has new carving. The bottom is attached with modern screws; the center board is clearly new, the two other boards, once nailed, may be reused. The upper rear rail has a repaired split and a patch at one hinge, and the lock is missing from the upper front rail. A groove at the left end of that front rail, probably cut for the side of a till, has been filled, as have the grooves in the stiles that housed the drawer runners. Two of the front panels have splits. The carving has minor losses. Bolles had the chest refinished, and he recorded that under several coats of paint "the original black and red decoration was perfectly apparent." In a 1910 photograph (see *References*), some areas of the ground of the carving are dark, others lighter—presumably black and red. Whatever the age of the paint he found and whether or not he had it renewed, it appears to have been removed or overpainted by 1913, when the chest was rephotographed. The ground is now all covered by pinkish red modern paint, the same, no doubt, as that described in 1933 as Indian red mixed with some white. The moldings on the sides retain residues of black. The exterior of the sides and the interior of the chest are varnished.

INSCRIPTIONS

Carved on the left front foot is the initial "S" and on the right front foot "C."

WOODS

RED OAK and WHITE OAK; front stiles, upper rear rail, HARD MAPLE; bottom, EASTERN WHITE PINE.

DIMENSIONS

OH. 28¼ (71.8); OW. (top) 42¼ (107.3); CW. 40⅜ (102.6); OD. (top) 20¾ (52.7); CD. 19 (48.3).

EXHIBITIONS

On loan to the Pierce-Hichborn House, Boston, from 1950 to 1979; "American Furniture and the Art of Connoisseurship," MMA, 7 April–4 October 1998.

REFERENCES

Kent 1910, p. 6; Lockwood 1913, fig. 9; Cescinsky and Hunter 1929, p. 42; Lee 1930, p. 74; Dyer 1931a, p. 37; I. P. Lyon 1937b, fig. 11 (this and the previous references reproduce the 1910 photograph); Tarule 1992, p. 202; Heckscher 1998, pls. II, IIa (detail).

PROVENANCE

Ex coll.: H. Eugene Bolles, Boston.

Gift of Mrs. Russell Sage, 1909 (10.125.23)

1. Two of the chests are at the Museum of Fine Arts, Boston (Fairbanks and Trent 1982, no. 476 [with drawer]; Randall 1965, no. 7 [with brackets]). The others are in I. P. Lyon 1937b, fig. 8 (known only from that photograph; according to the caption, had brackets); and offered in *Fine Americana*, auction cat., Sotheby Parke Bernet, New York City, 27–29 April 1978, lot 1043 (had drawer), and *Fine American Furniture and Related Decorative Arts*, auction cat., Sotheby Parke Bernet, New York City, 29 April–1 May 1981, lot 877 (had drawer).
2. For the Winterthur chest, see B. Ward 1986, no. 1.
3. For the chest without drawer at the Museum of Fine Arts, Boston, and the two sold at Sotheby's, see n. 1 above; for the Chipstone Foundation chest, see I. P. Lyon 1937a, fig. 3. On the Museum of Fine Arts, Boston, chest with drawer (see n. 1 above) the stem extends to the frond through a leaf form.
4. The Peabody Essex Museum chest (I. P. Lyon 1937b, fig. 10) retains two sets of layout lines for the muntins (Tarule 1992, p. 192). No such lines remain visible on cat. no. 85.

86.

Chest

New Haven, Connecticut, or vicinity, 1650–80

The facade of this chest, richly decorated with five distinct carved motifs, vividly exemplifies the arrangement of ornament characteristic of seventeenth-century design, in that each pattern is contained within the limits of a structural element and defines that member, with, in this case, a different motif adorning the upper rail, lower rail, stiles, muntins, and panels. Out of this multiplicity, which reflects the predilection in this period for complex ornamental schemes, a vibrant whole is achieved through the recall and opposition of forms: the rounded arches of the panels are echoed in the lunettes of the upper rail and the arcs created by the paired leaves on the lower rail, and also in the full circles of the rosettes, which appear in three different contexts and contrast with the elliptical shape of the paired leaves; stylized, deeply veined leaves occur in various forms, with looser designs on the rails opposed to tighter renderings on stiles and panels, and with triangular leaf clusters that allude to the geometry of the lozenges on the muntins.

The chest front presents nearly the full complement of motifs that constitute the decorative vocabulary of a school of carving that has been attributed to New Haven, Connecticut, or environs and that includes elements with some three-dimensional relief.[1] The patterns seen here plus foliate S-scrolls occur in various combinations (but not all on the same piece) on at least three other chests, including cat. no. 87, and on two wainscot chairs.[2]

The chests share not only ornamental features but structural ones as well, such as the manner in which the bottom is constructed and the use of just one pin in the side muntin, and sometimes additional, joints. Included in this group by Patricia E. Kane in 1973 was a chest at the Yale University Art Gallery that has similar construction and motifs, but also differences in details of the carving and distinctive rail and stile moldings not seen on the other objects. Found in Windsor, Connecticut, about 1880, it has recently been attributed by Joshua W. Lane and Donald P. White III to a shop tradition established in Windsor by John Rockwell (1588–1662), a woodworker probably unrelated to the unidentified joiner(s) responsible for the New Haven school but trained in the same English regional style.[3] The New Haven group, even discounting that piece, exhibits variations in the execution of some of the motifs and appears to be the work of more than one craftsman (see the entry for cat. no. 87).

The lunette motif appears on all of the pieces. On the chests—this example, one in the New Haven Museum, one at

the Amity and Woodbridge Historical Society, Woodbridge, Connecticut, and cat. no. 87—it occurs on the upper rail and is executed in a similar manner, with the arches decorated at the vertex, midway down the side, and at the base with a punched dot flanked by semicircles impressed with strikes of a gouge. The leaves within the lunettes and the other foliage on this chest are enriched with a similarly impressed small design that consists of a dot within an arc and, usually, a second arc perpendicular to the convex side of the first (fig. 56). Such motifs occur on all the objects in this group, and a variant pattern with a straight line in place of the second arc decorates the petals of all of the rosettes. Paired leaves like those that extend across the bottom rail as on a chain occur on all the pieces; the panels feature either a rounded arch decorated with stylized leaves and a rosette or paired S-scrolls; and the stiles and muntins, except on one chair, are ornamented with either of the two patterns used on the present chest.

The most distinctive of the motifs is that of lozenges alternating with rosettes seen on this chest's muntins, the stiles and muntins of the New Haven Museum example, and the stiles of one of the chairs. The interpretation of the design on the present chest differs from that on those two pieces in several respects: here the rosette is not surrounded by a flat band; the design within the lozenge is simpler; and the interstices are filled with a schematic leaf rather than a semicircle with punchwork. The general scheme of a roundel alternating with another motif on stiles and muntins can be found, together with other design elements used on this group, on English furniture from the West Country, particularly Gloucestershire and Somerset. Significantly John Rockwell, with whom the similar carving tradition in Windsor has been associated, came from County Somerset. An antecedent for the delineation of the imposts of the arches on this chest with parallel diagonal lines can also be found on a West Country chest.[4] On the present piece, the bases of the arches are rendered with analogous angled lines so that the arches appear to be quasi levitating and are decidedly further removed from architectural reality than those on cat. no. 87. As on all of the objects in this group, the rosettes and the long leaves on the stiles and arches of this chest have some three-dimensional shaping, but the foliage in the spandrels is more schematic than on cat. no. 87, and the leaves on the lower rail are more lightly carved than usual, having just a single gouged vein on either side of the central one and being otherwise decorated with impressed dots and arcs. Overall, this chest's strength lies not in the details of the carving but in the rich and complex patterning of its varied motifs.

CONSTRUCTION

The chest is framed with four equal panels in the front and four in the back that vary somewhat in width. On the front and back, the muntins have the same width as the upper rail, which measures less than the stiles and more than the lower rail, but the stock of the back is somewhat lighter. The mortise-and-tenon joints of the side muntins and of all but one of the back muntins are secured with one rather than two pins. The cleated top is formed of two boards and attached to the back rail with three snipebill hinges. The bottom consists of eleven front-to-back boards joined with a V-shaped tongue and groove, including a wedge board near the center with a tongue on either side. The boards are attached with rosehead nails to a rabbet on the front rail and to the bottom of the other sides; accordingly, the lower front rail extends down a good ½ inch farther than the other rails. There is a till without a lid on the right; its side is canted and nailed to the bottom. The edges surrounding the front panels are finished with a molding that now reads as an ovolo and small fascia (originally a cyma reversa?) on the stiles, a similar but smaller profile on the muntins, and a chamfer on the bottom rail. On the sides, all the edges around the panels are finished with a chamfer, and on the outside of the back, the edges of the rails and muntins are chamfered. Numerous layout marks for the carving remain on the panels and on the top rail, where vertical scribe lines at 5-inch intervals mark the center of each lunette and of each intervening leaf motif, and the width of the latter motif equals the lunette's radius. Holes in the corners of the panels indicate they were nailed down for carving. The oak is riven, and the framing members are not entirely squared; the stiles vary in cross section. Torn grain and hatchet marks are much in evidence on the inside of the chest and outside of the back. Some of the wood contained large wormholes when worked.

CONDITION

The top (pine), which has two transverse braces on the interior, a badly worn rear edge, and a few screws replacing nails in the cleats, is old but not original. A large split has occurred at the top of the right front stile (repaired with nails) and at the top of the left rear stile. There are gaps at the sides of the front and two of the back panels as a result of shrinkage and a scanty allowance of wood. A small section at the upper left corner of the far left front panel has been lost. Two nails are missing from the bottom and two may have been added. The till is loose in its grooves and is held in place with modern wedges. The reason for a gouged hole that extends from the inner lower edge of the upper back rail into the top of the far left back panel is unclear. The chest stands with the left feet about ½ inch higher than the right. The surface appears to have been oiled and waxed.

INSCRIPTIONS

Written in pencil on the inside of the rear board of the top is "3½ bush corn." Glued to the inside of the upper right rail is a Connecticut tercentenary paper exhibition label inscribed in ink: "C.T. 97 / Mrs. Geo. C. Bryant." On the underside of the bottom is written in red paint "72 / MRS. G. C. BRYANT." A piece of paper glued to the inside of the top is inscribed in ink (script): "This chest is exactly like one now / in Memorial Hall at Deerfield / which was taken from the house / where the Indians made the famous / attack in 1704. However this chest / is

perfect while the one in Deerfield / has the top missing, and the feet / which were continuations of the stiles / are worn away or sawed off. The / design and execution of the carving / are unusually fine, combining several / patterns, all of an early date. Chests / were carved in the arch design with / three or four panels, but seldom as / elaborate as these, which were probably / made before 1650. / (From Furniture of the Olden Times by Frances Morse)."[5]

WOODS

RED OAK and WHITE OAK.

DIMENSIONS

OH. 28⅞ (73.3); OW. (top) 60⅞ (154.6); CW. 58¼ (148); OD. (top) 21⅝ (54.9); CD. 21 (53.3).

EXHIBITIONS

"Three Centuries of Connecticut Furniture, 1635–1935," Morgan Memorial, Hartford, Connecticut, 15 June–15 October 1935; "The Art of Joinery: Seventeenth-Century Case Furniture in the American Wing," MMA, 18 October 1972–18 March 1973; "Furniture of the New Haven Colony: The Seventeenth-Century Style," New Haven Colony Historical Society (now New Haven Museum), New Haven, Connecticut, 16 April–31 August 1973.

REFERENCES

Three Centuries of Connecticut Furniture 1935 (exh. cat.), no. 2; Downs 1948, p. 80; "Connecticut Chest" 1949; Safford 1972 (exh. cat.), no. 3; Kane 1973a (exh. cat.), no. II; Kane 1973b, fig. 1; Safford 1980, fig. 1; M. B. Davidson and Stillinger 1985, fig. 124 (detail of carving).

PROVENANCE

Ex coll.: Mrs. George Clarke Bryant (Florence Adele Farrel Bryant), Ansonia, Connecticut.

According to a 1937 letter from Helen D. Baldwin to Mrs. Bryant (ADA files), the chest had belonged to Baldwin's father, who had purchased it about 1888 from Bellostee Hall Clark (1816–1894), a neighbor in Cheshire, Connecticut. The chest had come to him from his parents, Billina (1786–1866) and Hannah Atwater (b. 1790) Clark. Billina was the son of Amasa Clark (1758–1833) and grandson of Stephen Clark (1724–1800). Stephen's grandfather Ebenezer Clark settled in New Haven in 1638 and moved to Cheshire before 1700. While the chest may have come down in the Clark family, it could just as well have entered the family collaterally.[6]

Gift of Mrs. George Clarke Bryant, in memory of her husband, 1947 (47.133.3)

1. Kane 1973a, p. 8 and nos. II–IV, VI, VII; Kane 1993, addendum, fig. 1. Irving P. Lyon, who was investigating chests of this type and their histories in the 1930s, believed then that they came from New Haven or vicinity but never published his findings (letter of 26 February 1937 to Joseph Downs; ADA files).
2. The other chests are at the New Haven Museum (Kane 1973a, no. III), and the Amity and Woodbridge Historical Society, Woodbridge, Connecticut (Kane 1993, addendum, fig. 1); the chairs are both on loan to the New Haven Museum from private collections (Kane 1973a, nos. VI, VII). Not located is a chest that is mentioned in I. W. Lyon 1891, p. 7, and that, according to a 1937 letter from Helen D. Baldwin to the donor of this chest (see *Provenance*), is recorded in Lyon's notes as belonging to William Doolittle of Cheshire about 1883. A chest formerly in the Goss collection, Guilford, Connecticut (present location unknown), has structural similarities and carving only on the upper rail (lunette design) and muntins (large palmette without rosette).

86. See also fig. 56.

3. Kane 1973a, no. V; also G. W. R. Ward 1988, no. 20. Lane and White 2003, pp. 42–43 and no. 17. This chest also differs somewhat structurally, in that the side rails as well as the front rail are rabbeted to receive the bottom.

4. The similarities of this New Haven group to West Country furniture was noted by Anthony Wells-Cole (conversation with the writer, 4 October 1977). For furniture from that area in general, see Wells-Cole 1976a and Chinnery 1979, pp. 454–59. For a generically related muntin design, see Wells-Cole 1976a, no. 2; see also the bottom rail of cat. no. 83, a chest in a County Devon tradition. For the imposts, see Wells-Cole 1976a, no. 26.

5. The inscription is largely a verbatim quote of the text in Morse 1902, p. 11, that refers to a chest owned by the Pocumtuck Valley Memorial Association, which belongs to a different shop tradition (Lane and White 2003, no. 14).

6. The unusual spelling of the names Bellostee and Billina (which differs from the Bellosta and Bellina in Mrs. Baldwin's letter) is that used in a family Bible. This and further family information were kindly provided by Abbott Lowell Cummings (letter of 26 November 2005 to the writer). The life dates of Stephen and Amasa Clark and the information on Ebenezer Clark are from Kane 1973a, no. II.

87.

Chest

Probably New Haven, Connecticut, or vicinity, 1670–90

This chest is a product of the same New Haven, Connecticut, school of joinery as cat. no. 86 but is by a different hand. The two pieces match closely in construction and in the handling of most of the corresponding patterns on rails and uprights, but the carving on some elements of this piece is a little more accomplished: the lines of the midrib on the long leaves, for instance, are on the whole surer, and, above all, the arches on the panels are rendered with greater verisimilitude. On the panels of both chests are incised lines that issue from the bases and imposts and echo the curve of the arch—meant, perhaps, to give an illusion of perspective—but the delineation of the bases and imposts on the two pieces differs sharply. Here those elements are each represented by horizontal grooves beveled on one side and series of incised vertical lines that together suggest three courses of masonry. The concept is similar to that seen on the arches of a chest at the Yale University Art Gallery, which reflects the same West Country English regional style as the New Haven pieces and has recently been attributed to a Windsor, Connecticut, shop tradition, but the carving is here a little cruder; the horizontal grooves on the Yale piece are more regular, and both bases and imposts have a rounded profile on the inner side of the archway.[1] In both cases the grooves are a simplified substitute for the molded bases and imposts in more accurately rendered architectural arches, an American example of which occurs on an early New Haven chest in a different English regional carving tradition.[2] The date range assigned to this chest reflects the fact that the wood used for at least one of the back panels was mill-sawn, as the parallel marks on its outer side attest; sawmills are not known to have been operating in the New Haven area before the 1670s.[3] Notwithstanding its history of ownership in East Hampton, Long Island, this chest was probably made in or near New Haven by a joiner different from the maker of cat. no. 86 but one with similar training. There were close ties between the Connecticut shore and eastern Long Island, and the present chest may have been ordered from New Haven or come to the Stratton family collaterally from a Connecticut family.[4]

The history of the chest illustrates common themes in the survival and then preservation of seventeenth-century furniture. The chest remained in the homestead of descendants of the original owners until the 1870s, by which time it was no longer part of the house furnishings but was being used as a grain box—not discarded so long as it could serve some purpose. The homestead was then in the hands of an older unmarried descendant, who, when a buyer appeared, sold the chest (see the entry for cat. no. 19 for a similar situation). The purchaser in this case was not an early collector or dealer but a member of another branch of the family. How he happened to find it is not known, for his written account of the event has been lost, but his hobby was family history and the year was 1876. One can therefore speculate that with his antiquarian interests heightened by the American Centennial he was seeking out old family dwellings in search of family relics. For the new owner the chest became a family icon, its status validated by its inclusion in a local Centennial exhibit, in time for which he had had the initials and dates of its purported earlier owners inscribed inside the lid, ending with his own and "1876." Typically he pushed the chest's original ownership back to the earliest family members in America and assumed it had crossed the Atlantic with them, which at the time added to its prestige, writing that it had come "with the first English settlers of East Hampton" (see *Provenance*).

CONSTRUCTION

The chest has three equal panels in the front and three in the back that differ somewhat in width; the framing members also vary in width. The mortise-and-tenon joints of the side muntins, the lower left rail, at the back of the lower right rail, and at the right end of the lower rear rail are all secured with just one pin rather than two. The bottom is formed of seven transverse boards joined with a V-shaped

87

tongue and groove (one of the middle boards having a tongue on each side) and attached with rosehead nails to a rabbet on the front rail and the bottom of the other rails. Accordingly, the front rail extends down a good ½ inch farther than the other rails. Inside, there is a till without a lid on the right; its side is canted and nailed to the bottom. (A groove to accept the side of a till—cut in error—is on the inner left end of the lower rear rail.) A molding that now reads as an ovolo and a small fascia (originally a cyma reversa?) is worked at the bottom of the lower front rail and on the edges of the frame along the top and sides of the front panels and the top of the side panels. The other edges around the front and side panels are chamfered, as are most of the edges on the outside of the back and the interior of the chest. Many of the framing members are not entirely squared; the stiles range in cross section from nearly rectangular to pentagonal with a strongly angled inner face. The side panels are thin and barely beveled on the inner side. While most of the stock appears to have been riven, there is evidence of mill sawing on the outer side of one back panel, and possibly a second.

CONDITION

The top (chestnut) is a replacement now attached with two new snipebill hinges at the locations in the back rail of the original ones. When acquired, the chest was fitted with modern hardware that

consisted of strap hinges and a large ornamental hasp that extended from the middle of the top down the center front to the bottom rail. Holes in the back rail, top, and chest front left by the removal of that hardware have been patched. Other repairs include the filling in on the upper front rail of the recess left by a missing lock, the plugging of two holes in a right side panel, and a small strip nailed along the inside bottom of the lower right rail. The bottom has several holes and a few added nails. The purpose of a chiseled recess on the inner side of the top of the left rear stile is unclear. The stiles have splits, and the wood of the bottom and of the feet, which have lost some height, has deteriorated and been solidified. Thick, dark varnish recorded as being on the chest when it was received has been removed but traces remain. The surface is quite uneven in color and appears to have been oiled and waxed. The interior looks varnished.

INSCRIPTIONS

A partially completed, compass-scribed flower within a circle is on the exterior of the upper right rail, and two scribed concentric circles are on the outside of the left back panel. Initials and dates carved on the inside of the top read as follows: "J.S.1648 J.S^Jr^1660 16SS89 JS[conjoined]1700 / M1731S PS[conjoined]1775 PSH[conjoined] 1800 / 18SVS76 / 19RCS10" (see *Provenance* and *References*).

WOODS

WHITE OAK and RED OAK.

DIMENSIONS

OH. 24½ (62.2); OW. (top) 47⅜ (120.3); CW. 46 (116.8); OD. (top) 20¼ (51.4); CD. 19½ (49.5).

EXHIBITIONS

On loan to the MacPheadris-Warner House (now Warner House), Portsmouth, New Hampshire, from 1946 to 1972; "Furniture of the New Haven Colony: The Seventeenth-Century Style," New Haven Colony Historical Society (now New Haven Museum), New Haven, Connecticut, 16 April–31 August 1973; "5000 Years of Art from the Collection of The Metropolitan Museum of Art," organized by the MMA and the American Federation of Arts and shown at five museums in the United States, 10 October 1981–14 November 1982; "Colonial East Hampton, 1640–1800," Guild Hall Museum, East Hampton, New York, 10 October 1998–10 January 1999.

REFERENCES

Harriet Russell Stratton, comp., *A Book of Strattons . . . and a Genealogical History of the Early Colonial Strattons in America,* vol. 1 (New York, 1908), p. 116 (line drawing of chest showing hasp; captioned, "An Oak Chest Belonging to One of the Descendants of Richard Stratton. Tradition says, 'Brought from England by Richard Stratton in 1643.'"); Ralston 1931a; Halsey and Cornelius 1932, fig. 1A (1938, 1942, fig. 2); Kane 1973a (exh. cat.), no. IV; Schwartz 1976, no. 7 (top open showing initials and dates); *Art from the Collection of The Metropolitan Museum of Art* 1981 (exh. cat.), no. 65; Stein 1998 (exh. cat.), pp. 14–15 (top).

PROVENANCE

Ex coll.: George Coe Graves, Osterville, Massachusetts.

The donor acquired the chest in 1931 from Charles Woolsey Lyon, a New York City dealer. Lyon had just bought it from Mrs. A. Vidal Davis, of Natchez, Mississippi, who provided information on the chest's history. Née Eliza Macrery Britton Stratton (1884–after 1931), Mrs. Davis had received the chest at the death of her brother Sidney Vanuxem Stratton (1886–ca. 1928); he had received it in 1918 from his uncle Sidney Vanuxem Stratton (1845–ca. 1918), a bachelor and family historian. According to the elder Sidney Stratton (notes in ADA files), he purchased the chest in 1876 from Phoebe Stratton (1804–d. unmarried 1879), of East Hampton, Long Island, New York, granddaughter of Matthew Stratton, to whom it had "descended through the families there." Phoebe's Stratton forebears had settled and remained in East Hampton: John Stratton (1621 London–ca. 1684), in East Hampton by 1649; Stephen Stratton (d. 1697); John Stratton (d. 1775); Matthew Stratton (1730–1799), whose first wife was Phoebe

(d. 1775); John Stratton (1764–1848), her father. The Sidney V. Strattons belonged to a branch of the family descended from Richard Stratton (1619 London–ca. 1674 East Hampton), the first John's brother, that moved to New Jersey and eventually also to Mississippi.

According to the elder Sidney's notes, the chest was lent in 1876 to Eliphalet Platt Stratton (b. 1844) of College Point, New York, "at the time when the families of Queens County, L. I. determined to send relics to their Centennial Fair." This was the "Long Island Centennial Exhibition" held in conjunction with the "Grand Spring Exhibition of the Queens County Agricultural Society" in Mineola, on 21–22 June 1876. As reported in the *Flushing Daily Times* (22 June), included among the relics shown was "an old oak chest" having carved "inside the lid the successive dates at which the chest has been transferred from one Stratton to the next succeeding Stratton." After the exhibit the chest resided until 1885 in the library of the Camden, New Jersey, home of Charles Preston Stratton (1828–1884), Sidney's uncle, and then, since Sidney did not have a home of his own, it was lent until 1918 to Charles's son, Richard Cooper Stratton (m. 1912), whose initials were added to the lid in 1910. All but Richard's initials were doubtless inscribed at the time of the Centennial: they are all carved in similar modern characters and arranged in a pattern ending with "18SVS76" alone at center bottom. The inscriptions appear to represent a history pieced together from traditional information rather than actual genealogical data. They seem to indicate that the chest passed from the first John Stratton to his son John (1645–1735), when the latter was fifteen, to John Jr.'s brother Stephen, and on down to Matthew and to his wife, who predeceased him by many years. Some of the dates are mystifying, and if "PSH" stands for the vendor Phoebe, there is no record that she was married. However, her sister Mary (1814–1875) married a Huntting.[5]

The Sylmaris Collection, Gift of George Coe Graves, 1931 (31.30)

1. Kane 1973a, no. V; G. W. R. Ward 1988, no. 20; Lane and White 2003, no. 17.
2. Kane 1973a, no. I. For examples on West Country chests, see Chinnery 1979, figs. 4:80, 4:81, 4:86.
3. Fairbanks and Trent 1982, no. 482; Kane 1993, p. 101.
4. For instance, Thomas Osborne, a tanner, moved from New Haven to East Hampton in 1650 and is thought to have taken with him a chest elaborately carved in another style (Kane 1973a, no. I).
5. Letter of 17 May 1931 from Mrs. A. Vidal Davis to Charles W. Lyon, and copy of notes about the chest by Sidney V. Stratton (both in ADA files). Sidney Vanuxem Stratton, *Stratton Genealogy of Long Island, N.Y.* (n.p., 1901), copy at the New York Genealogical and Biographical Society, New York City, annotated and paginated by Herbert Parvin Gerald, pp. 2–3, 48–49, 53–56, 78, 84, 90–91; Harriet Russell Stratton, comp., *A Book of Strattons . . . and a Genealogical History of the Early Colonial Strattons in America* (New York, 1908–18), vol. 1, pp. 102–3, 117–18, 122–26, 132–33, and chart C, vol. 2, pp. 246–47, 277. The writer is indebted to Robert C. Friedrich of the Queens Borough Public Library, Jamaica, New York, for the identification of the Centennial Fair and for the newspaper account.

88. See also fig. 135.

88.
Chest

Guilford, Connecticut, or vicinity, 1670–1700

The school of joinery active in and around Guilford, Connecticut (see also the entry for cat. no. 113), produced chests in a variety of forms and designs. They range from relatively plain examples, with each front panel carved in a large, paired S-scroll motif or in a double-heart pattern, such as that on cat. no. 89, to an elaborate chest with two drawers ornamented with both applied elements and carving at the Old Dartmouth Historical Society, New Bedford, Massachusetts (see the entry for cat. no. 140). The latter is, in effect, a shorter version of the three-drawer form of cupboard that together with the type illustrated by cat. no. 113 represents the highest achievement of this tradition.[1]

The present chest originally sported an applied ornament at the center of each panel—probably a turning like that on the upper side panels of cat. no. 113, which would fit well within the given space. Such accents, their rounded forms

contrasting with the peaked profile of the muntins' channel moldings, would have both heightened the relief of the facade and enlivened its play of horizontals and verticals. The foliate S-scrolls carved on the upper rail line up with the horizontal ones on the panels, and the scrolls at the top of the right and center panels mirror the corresponding scrolls on the rail above so as to form the paired motif that is typical of Guilford carving. The vertical S-scrolls, slightly shorter in length, are opposed on the right panel but not on the others. A chest known only through a photograph has a similar panel design and a history in the Robinson family of Guilford. It also has a peg hole in the vertical space at the center of each panel, indicating the loss of applied ornament. In that case, the vertical scrolls form an opposed pair on all three panels, and the scrolls on the upper rail are shorter and grouped in two series of three on either side of a central space inscribed "1682."[2]

A combination of decorative elements that did not require the tools or skills of a turner is exhibited on several chests with one drawer on which S-scroll motifs are complemented by peaked rectangles or squares that are carved from the solid wood and simulate the applied glyphs and square bosses seen on the cupboards. The rectangles are used to divide the S-scrolls on a rail or drawer front, and on one piece a single long rectangle forms the sole ornament on each of two horizontal front panels. A series of squares may ornament the front stiles and muntins, and in two instances they fill a lozenge that decorates the front panels.[3] The shape of those carved geometric forms recalls the profile of the peaked channel molding that is a characteristic of the Guilford school and that adorns muntins, as on the present chest and cat. no. 89, and also the rail below the panels on the chests with one drawer. The same type of peaked molding distinguishes three chests that have been attributed to a Windsor, Connecticut, shop tradition established by an English immigrant joiner from County Somerset, but there appears to be no direct relationship between the two groups of objects; the correspondence probably reflects the emigration of two joiners from the same region of England to different areas of Connecticut.[4] The similarity between the foliate S-scroll motif on two chests and a chair with New Haven–style carving related to cat. nos. 86 and 87 and those in the Guilford tradition is more likely to be an indication of interaction between the two schools of craftsmanship, given their close proximity one to another. While there are some differences in the outline and articulation of the foliage, in both cases the scrolls are complemented by quarter circles and half circles in the corners and along the edges of the carved reserve.[5]

CONSTRUCTION
The chest has a single panel in the back and one on either side, each composed of two horizontal boards. The mortise-and-tenon joints (which are only about ¼ in. wide) are all secured with two small—about ¼-inch—pins. The panels and the muntins are thin. The top is a single board. The bottom consists of four transverse boards joined with a V-shaped tongue and groove, including a narrow wedge board with a tongue at either side. It is beveled to fit into a groove in the front and side rails and in all four stiles and is nailed to the underside of the back rail. The grooves in the stiles are V-shaped rather than rectangular and appear to have been chiseled, not planed. The grooves that housed the slightly canted side of a lidded till on the right are also V-shaped. A wide channel molding peaked at the center runs down the middle of the front muntins. The edges of those muntins, the lower edge of the bottom front rail and of the top and bottom side rails, and the lower inside edge of the upper rear rail are finished with a broad ovolo and a small cavetto, forming a cyma reversa, a common profile on edge moldings. A narrower molding with a cyma reversa and a fillet (fig. 135) is worked on the stiles and upper front rail where they edge a panel. At the bottom of the front and side panels the rail is chamfered. A small chamfer finishes the inside edges of the muntins and side rails. Holes at the sides of the front panels suggest

they were nailed down for carving. Scribe lines from the laying out of the designs remain visible on the panels and upper front rail. Some of the framing members were only partially squared. The outer surface of the back was left very rough and unfinished. The bottom boards are probably mill-sawn.

CONDITION
A small plugged hole at the center of each panel no doubt originally held a wooden pin that attached a now lost applied ornament; no evidence of its shape remains. The chest has been completely apart, the joint pins reset or replaced, and the joints of the frame and of the boards in the panels glued. Two of the mortises have broken through. The chestnut top—split and held together with battens, now attached with strap hinges, patched at the right front corner, and missing its cleats and part of the left edge—is old but not original; the rear rail retains evidence of one more set of hinges than the top. The wider of the bottom boards have split into sections and all have been reattached with modern nails and screws. The till is missing. A patch has been applied over a large hole gnawed in the back panel just above the bottom rail. The outer corners of the front stiles are heavily nicked. The feet have lost some height. Four screw holes at the center of the outside of each lower side rail are probably from the attachment of a handle for carrying. The reason for a nail hole one-third and two-thirds of the way up the inside of each stile is unclear, as is that for a large drilled hole (now filled) in the left front muntin. The chest has been stripped and has been waxed and probably oiled. There remain traces of red paint.

INSCRIPTIONS
MMA Hudson-Fulton exhibition identification numbers are inscribed in orange crayon on the inside of the top (H. F. 40.2) and on the underside of the bottom (460 / H. F. 40.2). Incised restorer's marks (one to four notches) match up the rear stiles with the side rails, and the lower front rail with the front panels and muntins.

WOODS
Stiles, rails, muntins, panels, WHITE OAK and RED OAK; bottom, CHESTNUT.

DIMENSIONS
OH. 25¾ (65.4); OW. (top) 51 (129.5); CW. 47½ (120.7); OD. (top) 23¼ (59.1); CD. 21½ (54.6).

EXHIBITIONS
"Hudson-Fulton Exhibition," MMA, 20 September–30 November 1909; on loan to the Society for the Preservation of New England Antiquities (now Historic New England), Boston, for exhibition in the Jackson House, Portsmouth, New Hampshire, from 1948 to 1972; "The Art of Joinery: Seventeenth-Century Case Furniture in the American Wing," MMA, 18 October 1972–18 March 1973.

REFERENCES
Hudson-Fulton Celebration 1909 (exh. cat.), no. 69; Lockwood 1913, fig. 13; Cornelius 1926, pl. I; Dyer 1931a, p. 38; Hornung 1972, no. 896; Safford 1972 (exh. cat.), no. 6.

PROVENANCE
Ex coll.: H. Eugene Bolles, Boston.

Gift of Mrs. Russell Sage, 1909 (10.125.668)

1. Kane 1973a, no. XVI, and G. W. R. Ward 1988, no. 23 (paired S-scroll motif); Kane 1993, addendum, fig. 2 (Old Dartmouth Historical Society).
2. The photograph is in the Lyon Family Papers, box 11, Downs Manuscript Collection, Winterthur Museum. As noted by Irving P. Lyon, the chest is illustrated in Mary Gay Robinson, "Thomas Robinson, of Hartford, Conn., 1640, and Guilford, 1664, and Some of His Descendants," in *The Robinson Family Genealogical and Historical Association*, vol. 1 (New York, 1902), p. 35. The chest probably once had a drawer. Its front stiles are carved with alternating glyphs and rosettes, which look questionable.
3. I. W. Lyon 1891, fig. 6; Kane 1973a, nos. XIV, XV; Kane 1993, addendum, fig. 5; Lyon Family Papers, box 11, photograph of chest belonging to Mrs. William B. Church, Meriden, Connecticut.
4. Lane and White 2003, pp. 42–48.
5. Kane 1973a, nos. III, VII; Kane 1993, addendum, fig. 1.

89.
Chest

Guilford, Connecticut, or vicinity, 1670–1700

The double-heart motif on the panels of this piece occurs as the sole carved ornament on four other chests, one of them said to have descended in the Walker family of New Haven, Connecticut, and another having a traditional history of ownership in the Eliot family of Guilford.[1] Indeed, these chests have many affinities with the large group of furniture attributed to the Guilford area that features a distinctive interpretation of the very common S-scroll motif (see the entries for cat. nos. 88, 113). The broad front muntins with a peaked channel molding are similar to those on cat. no. 88, for example; the moldings around the panels are identical; and the bottom was constructed in the same manner, including the use of a V-groove in the stiles. The deep rails and relatively small panels on the sides of this piece recall the heavy framing on the doors of cat. no. 113. There is also a close correspondence in the carving between some of the pieces in the two groups. The foliage within the hearts on this and two of the related chests is virtually identical to that at the base of the paired S-scrolls on cat. no. 113 (see fig. 63), for instance, and on many other objects from the so-called Guilford school; the foliate pattern has the same number of lobes, and they are similarly shaped and veined. A chest with drawer ornamented with the double-heart motif on the panels and the paired S-scrolls on the drawer front further points to the interconnectedness of the two groups of furniture.[2]

Although the hearts can be read as abbreviated paired S-scrolls, the double-heart pattern was a separate design in its own right, characterized by not being set within a rectangular reserve but having the field of the carving conform to the outlines of the scrolls. The source of the pattern can be found in the west of England, particularly Gloucestershire and Somerset. The carving on two of the related chests, distinguished by a somewhat different version of the motif in which the heart shapes are squatter and the foliage has fewer lobes, closely resembles that on a pulpit at Upleadon, Gloucestershire, dated 1661.[3] Interestingly those two chests

are also set apart by having a paneled top—common practice in English but not American joinery. They probably represent a direct transference of an English tradition, whereas the carving on this and the other related chests may represent the motif as it evolved in Connecticut.

CONSTRUCTION

The front and the back each have three vertical panels, and each side has a single horizontal panel, with all the muntins and side rails a good 6 inches wide. The mortise-and-tenon joints (nearly 3/8 in. wide) are all double-pinned. The top is attached with snipebill hinges. The original bottom, which no doubt consisted of several transverse boards, was let into a groove in the front and side rails and in both inner faces of the stiles and nailed to the underside of the rear rail; the grooves in the stiles are somewhat V-shaped rather than rectangular. There was a lidded till on the right with a slightly canted side. A channel molding that is peaked at the center runs down the middle of the front muntins. The edges of those muntins and the lower edge of the bottom front and of the top and bottom side rails are finished with a broad ovolo and a small cavetto. A narrower molding with a cyma reversa and a fillet is worked on the stiles and the upper front rail where they edge a panel. At the bottom of the front and side panels the rail is chamfered. On the interior, there are edge moldings around the back panels similar to those on the facade, and most of the framing members of the front and sides are finished with a chamfer. The stiles are basically rectangular in cross section. Some effort was made to dress the framing members on the exterior of the back, but not the panels.

CONDITION

The top (yellow poplar) is a replacement, and the top of the upper rails has been partly planed down to accommodate it. There is evidence on the upper rear rail of two previous sets of hinges, on the front rail of a missing lock and keyhole escutcheon, and on the interior of a lost till. The bottom is replaced. It consists of two longitudinal reused pine boards nailed to the underside of the rear rail and to the inner side of the side rails; it fits against a rabbet formed at the bottom of the front rail by removing the wood below the original groove. Slats have been nailed to the inside of the lower front and side rails abutting the bottom to close gaps. There are splits in several panels and in the frame at the joints, and a few mortises

89

have broken through. A section of the left rear stile has broken off at the joint with the lower back rail, where the wood has deteriorated; the joint pins have been lost and the tenon is exposed. A thin, narrow board nailed to the back of the adjoining rear panel along its left edge helps keep the panel in place and covers a gnawed hole. The surface shows numerous scratches, including a doodle of a boat on the upper left rail, and presents an uneven appearance. Before the chest came to the MMA, it was partially stripped of red paint (not original), which remains on the sides, at the edges of the front panels, and in thick residues on the ground and in the recesses of the carving.

WOOD
Stiles, rails, muntins, panels, RED OAK.

DIMENSIONS
OH. 25¾ (65.4); OW. (top) 48⅜ (122.9); CW. 47⅝ (121); OD. (case) 21¾ (55.2).

EXHIBITIONS
On loan to the MacPheadris-Warner House (now Warner House), Portsmouth, New Hampshire, from 1946 to 1956 and to the Columbia County Historical Society (for exhibition in the Van Alen House),

Kinderhook, New York, from 1968 to 1972; "The Art of Joinery: Seventeenth-Century Case Furniture in the American Wing," MMA, 18 October 1972–18 March 1973.

REFERENCES
Lockwood 1913, fig. 12; Safford 1972 (exh. cat.), no. 4; Kane 1973a, p. 49, fig. 5.

PROVENANCE
Ex coll.: H. Eugene Bolles, Boston.

Gift of Mrs. Russell Sage, 1909 (10.125.25)

1. For the four chests, which all have the same moldings and bottom construction as cat. no. 89, see Kane 1973a, no. XX, and G. W. R. Ward 1988, no. 22 (formerly Eliot family; Yale University Art Gallery); Kane 1993, addendum, fig. 4 (formerly Walker family; Newark Museum, Newark, New Jersey); Kane 1973a, no. XIX, and G. W. R. Ward 1988, no. 21 (Yale University Art Gallery); and Kane 1973a, p. 49, fig. 4 (formerly Art Institute of Chicago, Chicago, Illinois).
2. See Kane 1993, addendum, fig. 3 (Museum of Fine Arts, Boston).
3. The two chests in question are in Kane 1973a, no. XIX, and Kane 1993, addendum, fig. 4; for the pulpit, see Wells-Cole 1976a, fig. 15. Other interpretations of this motif on furniture from the west of England are in Wells-Cole 1976a, nos. 3, 8, 25, and Chinnery 1979, fig. 4:57.

90. See also figs. 57, 58, 84, 125.

90.

Chest

South-central Connecticut, possibly Milford, 1660–1700

The attribution of this piece to an area of Connecticut within the confines of the New Haven Colony is based primarily on the similarity of the lozenge design on the front panels to that on a chest with a history of ownership in the Merwin family of Milford, Connecticut. The border is the same, characterized by deep V-shaped grooves that, where they are interrupted, terminate in a convex contour cut with a small round gouge, and by a small triangle that projects into the field of the carving at the center of each side (fig. 57). The cruciform arrangement of schematic flowers is analogous to, though not identical with, the design on the Merwin chest, which has a more complex center and is denser overall.[1]

Like virtually all the carving on seventeenth-century American furniture, this lozenge motif was a learned pattern laid out with a rule and a compass. A partially carved design on the inner side of one of this chest's back panels provides a record of how the maker of this piece proceeded (compare figs. 57, 58). The middle of each side of the panel was marked, and a vertical and a horizontal line were scribed between those points to locate the center and to provide the axes for the floral pattern. Next the diagonal lines that form the lozenge were scored between dots impressed on the axes at a fixed distance out from the center of the panel. Then four circles and arcs meant to serve as guides for the curved stems at the center were scribed with a compass, as were arcs for the elliptical tip of the flower at each corner. At that point the craftsman began cutting with strikes of a chisel and gouges—a corner at a time—the outlines of the carved reserve and of the terminal tripartite motif, executing the floral elements freehand except for the end petal. The carving was abandoned (and the board then reused) perhaps because the joiner came to realize that he had not allowed for a border around the floral scheme; the carved reserve on the back panel is the size of the full motif on the front panels. Eventually all the contours of such a design would be cut in deeply and the ground between the various elements removed, as it was on the front panels. In this case, the ground was left quite rough and not finished with a punch.

While the lozenge motif on this and the Merwin piece come out of the same design tradition, the two chests are dissimilar in other aspects of their decoration, including the molding profiles, and in some of their structural features. They were made in different shops and probably some years apart. The Merwin chest, with a tight pattern of S-scrolls carved on the upper front rail and more refined construction, appears to be the work of an immigrant joiner, who may have learned his craft in County Suffolk, England.[2] The present chest is more likely the work of a second- or third-generation joiner. The shapes of some of the floral elements look awkward compared to those on the Merwin piece, and the design is looser and less intricate. The lack of vigor of the cruciform pattern, the abstract character of the lunettes on the upper front rail, and the simple method of attaching the bottom all militate against the chest's representing a joinery tradition transferred directly from England. The lunettes, which are delineated only with incised lines (those depicting the veins of the leaves are stopped in the same manner as the broken lines in the border) appear to be a simplified version of a more elaborate pattern. The columns of diamond shapes on the front muntins were applied with a punch—a quick and easy way to obtain a decorative effect. The maker of this piece appears to have absorbed the influence of more than one school of joinery. Of the features that this chest does not share with the Merwin example, several are characteristic of chests in other New Haven Colony shop traditions; namely, the lunette design; joints secured with only one pin (see cat. nos. 86, 87); and broad front muntins (see cat. nos. 88, 89).

CONSTRUCTION

Like the front, the back has three panels, broad, 5-inch muntins, stiles nearly as wide, and rails up to 1 3/8 inches thick. The mortise-and-tenon joints of the front and rear rails are each secured with one larger than usual pin, those of the side muntins with one small pin, and the remaining joints with two small pins. The left rear stile—one of two on this piece that are not rectangular but partly wedge-shaped—was installed with the angled surface at the back and the thinner end facing out, with the result that the tenon of the upper side rail protrudes at the back. The top is attached with two snipebill hinges. The present bottom, a single board, is nailed to the underside of the four rails; the rails have neither grooves nor rabbets to indicate that the original bottom was attached in another fashion. A lidded till is on the left;

the bottom is let into grooves in the stiles, and the side is nailed to the bottom and to the inner side face of the stiles. A channel molding consisting of an ovolo, tiny fillet, and cavetto is run on the lower front and side rails, twice on the front and once on the side of the front stiles, and twice on the front of the rear stiles. A cyma reversa ending with a fillet is used as the edge molding on the till lid, the front and side muntins, the upper front rail above the panels, and along the inner edge of the front stiles, where it is contiguous with the channel molding. The lower front rail is chamfered below the panels. The molding down the center of the front muntins consists of three reeds. The lozenges on either side of it are each made up of a regular grid of dots impressed with a single punch. On the inner side of the right back panel are the beginnings of a carved design similar to that on the front panels (fig. 58); the carving was scrapped, perhaps because of a miscalculation of size, and the board was trimmed at the bottom and reused.

CONDITION
The top (yellow poplar), though split, warped, battered, and patched at the hinges, does not look original, and neither do the lock and escutcheon. The chest bottom (yellow poplar) and the till side are replacements. The mortise in the left rear stile for the lower side rail has broken through, and a lower corner of the right rear panel is missing. The grooves for the panels are all run the full length of the stiles and quite near the outer surface, resulting in splits at the top and bottom of the stiles and in losses at the corners of the feet; the feet have been shortened and some of the corners have been patched. The outer edges of the front stiles are heavily nicked. In 1972 the chest front was removed and disassembled in order to reveal its construction and display it in the MMA exhibition "The Art of Joinery" (fig. 84). The smaller joint pins were replaced in the reassembly. Some but probably not all of the joints had been previously apart. Most of the panels include a lighter color stripe down one side, which is probably sapwood. The chest has been stripped. It retains a few traces of red paint. The back and parts of the interior have been stained.

INSCRIPTIONS
There are joiner's or early restorer's assembly marks at the joints of the right front stile and side rails (chiseled single and double lines) and of the lower front rail and muntins (single and double scratched lines that begin with a deep, pricked hole).

WOODS
Stiles, rails, muntins, panels, till, WHITE OAK and RED OAK.

DIMENSIONS
OH. 27 (68.6); OW. (top) 54 3/8 (138.1); CW. 50 7/8 (129.2); OD. (top) 19 1/4 (48.9); CD. 18 3/4 (47.6).

EXHIBITIONS
On loan to the MacPheadris-Warner House (now Warner House), Portsmouth, New Hampshire, from 1946 to 1972; "The Art of Joinery: Seventeenth-Century Case Furniture in the American Wing," MMA, 18 October 1972–18 March 1973; on loan to the Dorothy Whitfield Historic Society (for display in the Hyland House), Guilford, Connecticut, from 1975 to 1991.

REFERENCES
S. Chamberlain and N. G. Chamberlain 1972, p. 71 (as exhibited in the Warner House, Portsmouth, New Hampshire); Safford 1972 (exh. cat.), no. 14 (a detail of the disassembled chest front is on the cover); St. George 1979a, figs. 7, 31-f (detail of the left front panel); Kane 1993, addendum, fig. 8.

PROVENANCE
Ex coll.: H. Eugene Bolles, Boston.

Gift of Mrs. Russell Sage, 1909 (10.125.27)

1. For the Merwin chest (New Haven Museum), see St. George 1979a, fig. 6, and Kane 1993, addendum, fig. 7. To compare the panel carving, see St. George 1979a, figs. 31-e, 31-f.

2. The Merwin chest bottom, composed of five front-to-back boards joined with a V-shaped tongue and groove, is set into a groove in the front, side, and rear lower rails (see Kane 1993, p. 109, for a detailed description of the construction). The upper edge of the lower front rail is chamfered all the way across, and the joints of that rail with the muntins are mitered. All the frame joints are secured with two pins. See St. George 1979a, figs. 1, 5 and pp. 3–4, for generically related lozenge carving from Medfield, Massachusetts, attributed to a Suffolk tradition.

91.

Chest

Hampton, New Hampshire, 1660–1710

Chests made of sawn boards (usually pine) that are simply nailed together were the most basic form of case furniture in the seventeenth century. This highly ornamented board chest, however, is far from a commonplace, purely utilitarian piece. The decorative scheme on the front is designed to give it the look of a more expensive joined and carved chest. The front is divided into the equivalent of four panels, each carved with a lozenge containing compass work, and the borders around the front follow an arrangement of decorative elements observed on the rails and stiles of some elaborately carved joined chests, in that one pattern is used at the top, a different one at the bottom, and a third on either side (compare cat. nos. 83, 86).

This is the most ornate of a group of four related chests that has been attributed to Hampton, New Hampshire. One of the chests descended in the Marston family (private collection) and another in the Hobbs family (New Hampshire Historical Society, Concord), both of that locality. The third (Concord Museum, Concord, Massachusetts) was found in Hampton in the early twentieth century, and the present chest can be traced back to a dealer in a nearby town.[1] All of the chests feature four panels with a six-rayed compass-work flower within a circle that is surrounded by four small circles, and on all but one, that motif is within a diamond with circles or semicircles at the apexes, as seen here. The four chests also all have the same border of intersecting lunettes across the top, but none other has a decorative border along the bottom and the sides. The band along the bottom of this example is composed of series of parallel lines that form segments of herringbone pattern and diamond and "X" motifs; the lines are just incised, like most of the decoration. The diamonds formed by the "X" motifs that go up the sides, however, have been given some relief in the way of rough faceting. The small circles and semicircles on all of the chests have been rudimentarily rounded, possibly to suggest bosses. On this chest at any rate, those motifs have in addition been textured with random stamping, perhaps with a nail, and similar pricking occurs along some of the lines of the bottom border and of the lunettes at extreme left.

Three boxes can be associated with this same shop tradition, though they may not all be by the same hand (see the entry for cat. no. 77). Hearts are one of the principal motifs on those boxes, and it should be noted that midway up each band of diamonds on this chest is a small inverted heart. A painted box decorated with a heart and a design of concentric circles containing wavy lines and ellipses that belongs to a group of painted furniture attributed to Hampton points to the existence of a local vocabulary of ornament shared by more than one craftsman or shop over a period of time.[2]

CONSTRUCTION
The chest is made of single, wide mill-sawn boards. The front and back are rabbeted to accept the sides and secured with three large rosehead nails at each corner. The bottom, $1\frac{1}{4}$ inches thick, is nailed on from below. The top is attached to the back with two snipebill hinges. There is a lock in the front and a till on the left. The till bottom and side are let into the front and back of the chest. Short slats to support a shelf are nailed to the front and back below the till. A series of twelve square notches is cut along the ends of the front. The front and side edges of the bottom were originally broadly beveled.

CONDITION
Added nails reinforce the right front corner and the two in back. The top has a full-length split and replaced cleats; it has lost the staple that catches the bolt of the lock, and was once nailed shut. The hinges in the back board are loose, and there is a repair at the left one. The lid of the till is missing, as is the shelf below the till. The reason for nails (cut) and nail holes in the upper central portion of the inside of the

91

back board is unclear. Two pairs of nail holes (including one remaining wrought nail) in the bottom, each about 7½ inches in from one end of the board, suggest the chest was at one time nailed to another object or to long transverse blocks that served as feet. The front edge of the bottom is heavily worn and battered. The top is worn and stained and retains evidence of white paint rings that were on the chest when it was acquired and were removed in 1980. The exterior of the chest appears to have been oiled and waxed; the interior is marred by stains of various kinds.

INSCRIPTION
"F C Higgins / Exeter" is inscribed in pencil in large script on the outside of the back.

WOOD
EASTERN WHITE PINE.

DIMENSIONS
OH. 18 (45.7); OW. (top) 45¾ (116.2); CW. 43 (109.2); OD. (top) 18¾ (47.6); CD. 18 (45.7).

EXHIBITIONS
On loan to the Society for the Preservation of New England Antiquities (now Historic New England), Boston, for exhibition in

the Jackson House, Portsmouth, New Hampshire, from 1948 to 1972; "Portsmouth Furniture: Masterworks from the New Hampshire Seacoast," Currier Gallery of Art, Manchester, New Hampshire, Wadsworth Atheneum, and Portland Museum of Art, Portland, Maine, 15 September 1992–11 July 1993.

REFERENCES
Cescinsky and Hunter 1929, p. 44; Kettell 1929, pl. 27; Lee 1930, p. 74; Jobe 1993 (exh. cat.), no. 1.

PROVENANCE
Ex coll.: H. Eugene Bolles, Boston.
    According to the inscription on the back, the chest was at one time owned by Frank C. Higgins, who was an antiques dealer in Exeter, New Hampshire, in the early twentieth century.[3]

Gift of Mrs. Russell Sage, 1909 (10.125.22)

1. On the three other Hampton chests, in the order mentioned, see Jobe 1993, fig. 27 and pp. 86–87; "Accessions" 1948, p. 19; and Kettell 1929, pl. 28.
2. The box, now in the collection of Historic New England, is in "Early New Hampshire Painted Decoration" 1964, p. 85. For Hampton painted furniture, see also Brazer 1930.
3. Jobe 1993, p. 88, n. 5. Bolles recorded that he bought a Newport bureau-table from Higgins (Bolles notes, MMA Archives; Heckscher 1985, no. 135).

92.

Chest with drawers

Wethersfield, Connecticut, or vicinity, 1675–1700

This chest is part of a large group of furniture ornamented with a similar distinctive and striking combination of carved and applied decoration. The group, most recently estimated at about eighty-five pieces, includes six cupboards, a small number of chests without a drawer or with one drawer, and primarily chests with two drawers, like the present example.[1] The design of these chests, which vary primarily in elements of the carving (see cat. no. 93), presents a regulated, complex ornamental scheme. The two outer front panels invariably feature a large tulip on a central stem, and the middle panel is typically carved with three round flower heads with concentric rows of small petals (fig. 64). The carving is very stylized. The ancillary flowers often have fantastical shapes in the spirit of the hybrid forms seen in grotesques, and the applied turnings represent highly manipulated classical columnar forms. The whole is a well-organized composition with the strong horizontals of the moldings on the rails balanced by the half columns on the stiles and muntins. The triangular arrangement of the three flowers in the center panel is echoed in the disposition of the octagonal panels, with an upper center panel placed above the pair of simulated panels on the front of each long drawer—the one pyramidal scheme enunciated in carving, the other by means of applied moldings. Color, supplied by paint, originally added another layer of patterning to the design. (The traces that remain on this chest are virtually all modern.) The rare pieces that retain original paint confirm the use of color that is generally reproduced on these chests, as, for example, on cat. no. 93: all turned elements, the triangular plaques in the corners of panels, and the channel and applied moldings on the frame are ebonized and the panel moldings painted red and with series of black wavy lines that were probably meant to simulate another exotic wood, such as snakewood.[2]

Commonly called "sunflower" furniture—so dubbed in the early 1900s, even though the carved rosettes bear no actual resemblance to that flower—this group has attracted the attention of collectors and scholars for more than a century because of its visual appeal, the large number of surviving examples, and the continuing quest to determine the origin of the design and the artisan(s) who introduced and produced it.[3] As early as 1891 Irving W. Lyon knew of some forty chests of this type and noted that they had been found only in Connecticut and mainly in Hartford County. The histories of ownership that have since become known usually point more specifically to Wethersfield as the locus of this shop tradition,

an attribution now generally accepted. A key piece and the earliest datable example is a cupboard that has a tradition of ownership by Rev. Joseph Rowlandson and is thought to have been made between his arrival in Wethersfield in April 1677 and his death in November 1678.[4] Houghton Bulkeley in 1958 proposed Peter Blin (ca. 1640–1725) as the joiner responsible for this school of craftsmanship, equating a chest that had descended in the family of Rev. Gershom Bulkeley of Wethersfield with a chest credited to Blin in a 1681 entry in an account book kept by Peter and Gershom Bulkeley, but the evidence is far from conclusive. Peter Blin, who had arrived in Wethersfield by 1675, was one of several woodworkers active in that town during the last three decades of the seventeenth century. He appears to have been French-speaking, but nothing is known of his training nor anything definitive about his background.[5]

The source of the sunflower chest design remains elusive; no prototype for this combination of carved motifs and applied ornament has been identified to date. Most likely the scheme does not have a direct antecedent in toto but represents a convergence of two or more joinery traditions that occurred in Hartford County in the Connecticut River valley. With regard to the carving, John T. Kirk noted several decades ago that tulips combined with rosettes are to be found on furniture from the north and west of England.[6] Recently, Joshua W. Lane and Donald P. White III have attributed two chests with similar tulip and rosette motifs on the panels, but ornamented solely with carving, to a Windsor, Connecticut, shop and proposed that chests in that tradition, which are closely related to the sunflower type in their construction, served as the primary basis for the design.[7] The scalloped initials and the vine with tulips on a box that can be attributed to that same shop tradition (cat. no. 73) are similar to the initials and vine on the center panel of cat. no. 93. Whatever the genesis of this style of furniture and whoever first produced it, the large number of pieces involved makes it highly unlikely that the sunflower chests were all made by one craftsman or shop. How many artisans were involved in the production, who they were, in which Hartford County towns they worked, and how they were interconnected are all still open questions.

CONSTRUCTION

This chest corresponds to cat. no. 93 in all details of construction—excepting replacements—from the type of nails used in specific locations, to the trimming of the back of the chest bottom boards in situ and scratched "V"s on drawer sides. It is similar in dimensions and proportions and in the profiles of the moldings and turnings. On this piece, however, the four turnings that flank the center panel are original and each is secured with a T-headed nail (fig. 64)—a manner of attachment characteristic of original large applied half columns on this type of chest.

CONDITION

The top is old but may not be the first. It has been cut and reworked at the front and pieced for 4 inches at the back. The cleats, which each have a strip of new oak along the top and are now attached with a modern screw at each end, are probably contemporary with the top. That part of the hinges attached to the rear rail is original. The keyhole in the top front rail (for a missing lock) has been filled. Many of the frame joints appear to have been apart and repinned. Splits in several panels have been glued. There is a patch on the inner corner of the left rear stile at the level of the medial rails. A narrow strip at the left end of the chest compartment bottom is new, and the bottom has been renailed to the rear rail. The lid of the till and the top ½ inch of the side are also new. The lower back—now a single board nailed to the stiles and medial rail—is a replacement. The original board fit into grooves in the stiles. Those grooves, which extended to the bottom of the stiles so the board could be slipped into place from below (see the entry for cat. no. 93), have been filled at the level of the feet. The drawer runners are replaced, and the grooves in the drawer sides have been repaired with a strip glued to the upper edge. The face of the upper drawer front is patched for 4¾ inches from the right end. The bottom of the lower drawer has been pieced for about ⅝ inch at the front and has splits. On both drawers, new nails have been added to the bottom and some of the corner joints. The drawer pulls are replaced, and there is a large plugged hole to the right of three of them. There is evidence that at some point the case had a bottom. The four half columns that flank the center panel (two of which have a patch on the lowest ring) are original, as is probably the large boss on each side of the chest. The other turnings, the applied case and panel moldings, and the triangular plaques are all replaced (yellow poplar) and attached with modern nails. A 1909 photograph (see *References*) shows the chest as received, with heavy paint (modern, since it covered replacements) on all of the applied elements, and the panel moldings decorated with dark squiggly lines. By 1927 those lines had been removed, and now the chest retains only vestiges of black on the turnings, triangular plaques, and applied and channel moldings on the frame, and a reddish tone on the drawer and panel moldings. The present surface probably dates from the 1930s when, according to records, modern varnish then on the chest was removed and the piece rubbed down with linseed oil. The inside of the chest compartment looks varnished, and there is brown stain inside the drawers and the lower case and on the outside of the back.

INSCRIPTIONS

A large V (an original joiner's mark) is scratched at the top of the exterior of each side of the upper drawer. An X is chiseled into the underside of the bottom of the lower drawer. Small roman numerals (restorer's reassembly marks) are incised at many of the frame's joints. MMA Hudson-Fulton exhibition identification numbers (H. F. 40.23) are inscribed in orange crayon on the outside of the upper back panel.

WOODS

Stiles, rails, muntins, drawer divider, front and side panels, drawer fronts and sides, center plaques on drawer fronts, cleats, till, WHITE OAK; top,

back panel, chest compartment bottom, drawer backs and bottoms, SOUTHERN YELLOW PINE; half columns flanking center panel, MAPLE.

DIMENSIONS

OH. 39⅛ (99.4); OW. (top) 47⅝ (121); CW. 44⅝ (113.3); OD. (top) 22⅛ (56.2); CD. 20 (50.8).

EXHIBITION

"Hudson-Fulton Exhibition," MMA, 20 September–30 November 1909.

REFERENCES

Hudson-Fulton Celebration 1909 (exh. cat.), no. 72; Kent 1910, p. 7; Lockwood 1923, fig. 1 (attributed to Nicholas Disbrowe, Hartford, Connecticut); Halsey and Tower 1925, fig. 193; Cornelius 1926, pl. VII (this and the previous references reproduce the 1909 photograph); MMA 1930, fig. 2; Salomonsky 1931, pl. 70 (1909 photograph and measured drawings); Dyer 1935, fig. 1; M. B. Davidson 1970, fig. 5.

PROVENANCE

Ex coll.: H. Eugene Bolles, Boston.

Gift of Mrs. Russell Sage, 1909 (10.125.689)

1. This estimate is from Schoelwer 1989, p. 21.
2. The prime example with original paint is a cupboard at the Yale University Art Gallery (G. W. R. Ward 1988, no. 195). For the use of snakewood on English seventeenth-century furniture, see Bowett 1998. Snakewood has also been identified on a Boston chest of drawers (G. W. R. Ward 1988, no. 51).
3. See Schoelwer 1989 for the most complete discussion of this group of furniture and a critical evaluation of the principal literature and attributions made.
4. I. W. Lyon 1891, pp. 15–16, 24–25. This cupboard is in Nutting 1921, pp. 128–29; Nutting 1924, no. 201, which gives a fuller history; and Nutting 1928–33, no. 450. See also Dyer 1935, which includes, in addition, the histories of the other known cupboards. For other pieces with histories, see Kane 1970, pp. 74–77; and G. W. R. Ward 1988, no. 196.
5. Bulkeley 1958; the chest is shown also in Kirk 1967, no. 15. The evidence is inconclusive on several counts: the entry is in the hand of Peter Bulkeley —not Gershom, in whose family the chest descended (Kane 1970, p. 74); the price (ten shillings) seems low for a new carved chest (Schoelwer 1989, p. 27); finally, if the chest is indeed the one in the account book, the fact that the carving presents a slight variant of the standard design—most obviously in both the arrangement and the delineation of the "sunflowers" in the central panel—suggests that the shop that made it was not at the center of the production of this furniture. For Blin and other Wethersfield craftsmen, see Sweeney 1995, pp. 147–54, 164, n. 17.
6. Kirk 1965, pp. 790–95. The rosettes on sunflower chests have been considered Tudor roses (in a few instances, the panels with tulips include thistles [see cat. no. 107]) and were identified by Benno M. Forman as marigolds (Benno M. Forman Papers, box 13, Downs Manuscript Collection, Winterthur Museum). Marigolds have been identified as a Huguenot emblem, and this interpretation has been applied to the rosettes on these chests based on the assumption that Blin had Huguenot connections (*Great River* 1985, no. 78; for the misuse of the Huguenot appellation, see Schoelwer 1989, pp. 26–28). Most likely the rosettes did not have any particular connotations at that point in time. Tulips and rosettes were widespread, long-lived traditional motifs, and generically similar carving can be found on northern European furniture; see, for example, Drepperd 1940, fig. 1B; Ottenjann 1954, pp. 30, 31 and nos. 51–53.
7. Lane and White 2003, pp. 57–59 and nos. 23, 25. Thomas Stoughton III (1624–1684) is credited with founding that shop tradition. The Stoughton family came from County Suffolk, England, about 1630. It is not known to whom Thomas was apprenticed. In terms of construction, one of the two chests (Connecticut Historical Society, Hartford; Lane and White 2003, no. 23) varies from the standard sunflower formula in that the drawer bottom is nailed to a rabbet in the front, but one of the drawer sides retains a scratched joiner's "V" marking similar to that on cat. no. 92.

92. See also fig. 64.

93.

Chest with drawers

Wethersfield, Connecticut, or vicinity, 1675–1700

A small group of chests with two drawers conform to the so-called sunflower design represented by cat. no. 92, except for the carving in the center panel, which features instead of the usual three rosettes the initials of the first owner(s) surrounded by tulips. The chests inscribed with two initials were probably made for young women, as were many of the "Hadley" chests (see the entry for cat. no. 95), but the one example carved with three initials belonged to a couple, who may have been Samuel and Rebecca Wright, married in Wethersfield, Connecticut, in 1686.[1] The tulips around the initials are typically arranged to form a wreath, as seen here, but in each case the details of the carving vary, as they do on the panels with the rosette motif. Throughout the large body of work in the sunflower tradition (see the entry for cat. no. 92), while the tulip design in the two outer panels of the same chest was made to match, it is never entirely the same from one piece to another. The carving was laid out individually each time and executed largely freehand. This chest sheds light on how at least one carver proceeded: the forward of the two lower panels on the left side of the case retains on the inner side a partially carved tulip design (fig. 60). This makes cat. no. 93 of special interest.

Why the carving on that panel was abandoned is not known, but a good board was not to be wasted, and so it was reversed, cut down, and reused. The evidence remaining on that panel shows that the laying out of the pattern consisted of scribing the perimeter of the carved reserve and then dividing the space in two vertically with two converging lines that define the central stem. The two pricked points at the bottom that marked the lower end of those lines have here been obliterated, but they can still be seen on finished panels on this and most of the chests. Less than a quarter of the way down, there is a horizontal line; on this line the compass point from which the arc for the left half of the bottom of the tulip was scribed remains visible. The upper outline of the tulip was no doubt also drawn with a compass that was positioned on the same line, but the beveling of the edges of the board has removed the evidence. It appears that the line around the perimeter of the carving was then cut with strikes of a chisel and the scribed outline of the tulip incised with strikes of one or more gouges. With the basic shape of the main flower in place, the carver next started working freehand from the bottom up using the contours of different-size gouges to outline the motifs and working both sides of the panel.[2] Eventually the full design would have been outlined with deep cuts and the ground between the various elements removed; the ground would then

have been stippled with a punch that typically made several impressions at a time (fig. 59).

The elements sketched out at the base of the abandoned carving represent motifs that are standard in that location on virtually all the chests: a small mound from which the central stem emerges and above that, a short arched stem on either side that holds a tulip. In fully carved designs, those tulips have outer petals of a conventional form, as is indicated by the lower one outlined on this panel, but issuing from the middle are shapes that with few exceptions bear little relationship to anything in the plant world.[3] The carvers seem to have exercised most freedom in filling the space between the givens of the tulips at the base and the large upper one, devising any number of whimsical, part-tulip forms. The main tulips vary considerably in how they were elaborated and in size: the layout of the one on the partially carved panel does not correspond to that on the chest's outer front panels. On the latter, the tulip extends down much farther, which allows it to incorporate within its outline a smaller tulip that is related in scale to those on the center panel.

While the details of the carving impart an individual touch to each piece, the many chests in the sunflower tradition are remarkably consistent in other elements of the design and in their construction. The profiles of the channel and applied moldings and of the applied turnings are the same throughout, but occasionally channel moldings are used on the medial and lower side rails instead of applied projecting moldings or are omitted from the upper rails. The chests adhere closely to a standard structural formula. The main framing members are characteristically of a uniform width, the panels measure twelve inches in height, and the center panel is typically somewhat wider than the outer ones, most often in the eleven to ten ratio seen on this chest and on cat. no. 92. The bottom of the chest compartment, the back, and the drawers are all constructed in the same distinctive manner (see *Construction*) with only rare minor variations.[4]

CONSTRUCTION
The frame is constructed with standard mortise-and-tenon joints; those of the bottom rails, drawer divider, and side muntins are secured with just one pin. The stiles are pentagonal; they and the upper and medial rails, the muntins, and the rectangular plaques on the drawer fronts all have the same width (3⅜ to 3½ in.). The cleated lid is attached to the back with two snipebill hinges. The back at chest level consists of a horizontal panel, deeply beveled on all four sides of the exterior. The bottom of the chest compartment is formed by three

93. See also figs. 59, 60, 95, 109.

front-to-back boards joined with a V-shaped tongue and groove. They are beveled on the underside to fit into a groove in the front rail and stiles, the side rails, and the rear stiles. The end boards were inserted first, followed by the narrower center wedge board fashioned with a tongue on either side. The boards were then attached to the bottom of the rear rail with rosehead nails. Finally, as evidenced by saw marks, their back edges were trimmed in situ flush with the rail (fig. 95). At drawer level, the back is formed by a single board feathered on the ends and set into a groove in each stile. The grooves originally extended down through the feet so that the board could be slid in place from below. There is no rear bottom rail. The chest interior is fitted with a lidded till on the right; the till side is nailed to the bottom. The two drawers are side-hung (fig. 109) and slide on runners that are

let into the stiles. The drawer sides each fit against a rabbet in the front and are secured with two T-headed nails. The back is rabbeted to accept the sides and is attached with two rosehead nails. The bottom—one longitudinal board beveled on four sides—is set into a groove in the front and nailed with roseheads to the sides and back. The channel molding run on the front and side top rails and the side muntins has an ovolo at each side and two thin ridges in the middle. The profile of the applied rail moldings (which conforms to that of original examples) consists, from the bottom up, of an ovolo, cavetto, astragal, and fillet—a sequence of contours common on a smaller scale on panel moldings (see fig. 131). The panel and drawer moldings have an ovolo-and-cavetto outline, and the molding worked on the cleats has a similar contour. The left cleat has a bored hole near the front that lines up with one in the rail, which allows the top to be locked with the insertion of a peg. Similar holes in related pieces suggest this is the original locking system. Many of the framing members—of riven oak—were not entirely squared and are somewhat wedge-shaped. The pine boards were mill-sawn.

CONDITION

The top is old but may not be original. A narrow strip across the back is replaced, and patches and wear in the top and upper rear rail give evidence of two previous sets of hinges. The cleats appear to be contemporary with the top. The recess on the inner side of the front rail for a missing lock has been filled. The lid of the till is new. There is a small patch in the chest compartment bottom at center front. Nails have been added to prevent the lower back board from sliding down. The drawer runners are replaced. On both drawers, the grooves in the sides have been repaired with a filler strip glued to the upper edge, the bottoms have added modern nails, and the knobs are new. On the upper drawer, the top of the right side is patched for about 4 inches at the front and a glued-on block has been added under the bottom at center front. On the lower drawer, the underside of the bottom has been partially replaned. All four feet are pieced at the bottom and partly spliced up to the bottom rails. The six half columns flanking the panels are replaced, as are probably all of the smaller turnings and bosses. The moldings applied to the rails (cherry) are definitely new, but many of the small applied moldings and triangular plaques show some signs of age. The replacements and no doubt also the structural repairs predate the publication of the chest by Irving W. Lyon in 1891 (see *References*). Whether the restoration occurred before or after he acquired the piece is not known. The chest now has a modern varnish finish. None of the black paint on the turnings, triangular plaques, and channel and rail moldings, some of which is flaking, is original, nor is the red on the small applied moldings. The ground of the carving has a mahogany color. The interior of the chest cavity has been varnished.

INSCRIPTIONS

The initials "DC" of an unidentified first owner are carved on the center panel as part of the design. A large V (or X?), an original joiner's mark, is scratched at the top of the exterior of each side of the upper drawer. Scored on the inside of the lower back board is a large sawyer's tally mark: XIII. Inscribed in pencil in very large script on the replaned underside of the bottom of the lower drawer is "1 B B" (nineteenth century).

WOODS

Stiles, rails, muntins, drawer divider, front and side panels, drawer fronts and sides, center plaques on drawer fronts, cleats, till, WHITE OAK; top, back panel, lower back board, chest compartment bottom, drawer backs and bottoms, SOUTHERN YELLOW PINE; panel moldings, triangular plaques, ATLANTIC WHITE CEDAR.

DIMENSIONS

OH. 39⅝ (100.6); OW. (top) 48 (121.9); CW. 45¼ (114.9); OD. (top) 21¼ (54); CD. 20⅛ (51.1).

EXHIBITION

"The Art of Joinery: Seventeenth-Century Case Furniture in the American Wing," MMA, 18 October 1972–18 March 1973.

REFERENCES

I. W. Lyon 1891, fig. 9 and pp. 15–16; Lockwood 1923, fig. 12 (attributed to Nicholas Disbrowe, Hartford, Connecticut); Lockwood 1926, fig. VI; Safford 1972 (exh. cat.), no. 9 and fig. 1; MMA 1975, p. 21; Schwartz 1976, no. 8; Safford 1980, fig. 5; M. B. Davidson and Stillinger 1985, fig. 128 and p. 23 (detail).

PROVENANCE

Ex coll.: Dr. Irving W. Lyon, Hartford, Connecticut; his son Dr. Irving P. Lyon, Buffalo, New York; Mrs. J. Insley Blair, Tuxedo Park, New York; her daughter Mrs. J. Woodhull Overton, Balmville, New York.

Irving W. Lyon purchased the chest in 1880 in Farmington, Connecticut (see *References*). Mrs. Blair purchased it from his son in 1923. The chest was on loan to the MMA from Mrs. Overton from 1952 until it became a gift.

Gift of Mrs. J. Woodhull Overton, 1966 (66.190.1)

1. The two-drawer chests are initialed: "DH" (private collection); "HW" (Historic Deerfield; Fales 1976, no. 354); "LW" (advertised by Ricco-Johnson Gallery in *Antiques* 123 [January 1983], p. 147); "MG" (advertised by H and R Sandor in *Antiques* 124 [July 1983], p. 7); "SB" (private collection; the present writer thanks William N. Hosley Jr. for bringing this chest to her attention); "W/SR" (American Museum in Britain, Bath, England; Kane 1970, pp. 75, 77, and Chinnery 1979, fig. 4:211). Chests with no drawer and somewhat variant decoration are initialed, respectively: "HS" (Monkhouse and Michie 1986, no. 1); "IB" (Bishop 1975, p. 12); "WB" (Nutting 1928–33, no. 60).
2. For a drawing showing the different-size gouges probably used in the carving of the tulip design on a chest at the Yale University Art Gallery, see Schoelwer 1989, fig. 8.
3. In a few instances, notably on a cupboard at the Yale University Art Gallery (G. W. R. Ward 1988, no. 195), those flowers are replaced by thistles.
4. The width of the boards of the chest compartment bottom may vary, for example, or the drawer bottom may be nailed to a rabbet on the front as on a chest in a private collection (*Important American Furniture, Silver and Decorative Arts*, auction cat., Christie's, New York City, 2 June 1983, lot 367).

94

94.
Chest

Hartford County, Connecticut, 1680–1710

The large body of so-called sunflower furniture made in the Connecticut River valley encompasses only a small number of chests without drawer(s) and they, for the most part, deviate to a greater or lesser degree in their ornamental scheme from the prototypical design represented by cat. no. 92. This example is one of two such chests on which applied elements rather than carving decorate one or, as on the other chest, two front panels.[1] Here, applied plaques in a cruciform pattern divide the center panel into smaller panels, each centered by a boss, in a pattern similar to that on the upper center panel of sunflower cupboards. The carving on the two outer panels lacks the clarity of line of the standard tulip design and provides a somewhat weak accompaniment to the strong visual statement made by the geometric central panel. The main tulips have fussy and rather frenzied outlines rather than assured contours that describe clear arcs, and the lower flowers are mainly composed of short, tight curves as well.

The carving is ornamented throughout with a star punch, and the center of the main tulip is decorated with a pinwheel design in which each of the six spokes is formed of a curve and countercurve incised with strikes of a gouge. The scribing that marked the position of the central stem consisted of a single vertical line, rather than the two converging lines that were the norm (see the entry for cat. no. 93 and fig. 60), which is another indication that the maker of this chest was working in a shop related to but not at the core of the sunflower tradition. The profiles of the moldings on this piece are those characteristic of that tradition, but the turnings on the muntins deviate from the standard pattern, in that the columnar segment lacks the pronounced taper of those in the sunflower design and the astragal is near the top of the column. Closer in concept to a classical model, they appear to reflect outside influences and may be an indication that the chest was made toward the end of the sunflower tradition.

Related turnings are on a chest without drawer(s) at the Connecticut Historical Society, Hartford, that has tulip carving similar in character to that on this piece.[2]

CONSTRUCTION

The chest is framed with standard mortise-and-tenon joints and is similar to cat. nos. 92 and 93 in the pentagonal shape of the stiles, the width of all of its framing members, and the single horizontal panel in the back. The height of the panels is also the same, but on the front the center panel is slightly narrower, rather than clearly wider, than the outer ones. The bottom consists of one mill-sawn board, roughly beveled on all four sides and nailed to the underside of the rails. There is a lidded till on the right. The half columns that flank the center panel are attached with T-headed nails. Parts of the scribed lines that defined the rectangular reserve of the carving are still visible, as is the incised point at the middle of the bottom edge that marks the lower end of the vertical line on which the stem of the main tulip was centered. Despite the layout lines, the bottom edge of the reserve on the left panel was cut too far to the right. The upper rear rail is unusually thick at the top and strongly wedge-shaped. Several of the oak components contain large wormholes that were in the wood before it was worked.

CONDITION

The top and its cleats and hardware are replaced, as is the till. The frame has probably been apart and many of the pins renewed. A few nails in the bottom are missing, and some have been added and replaced. There is a large gnawed depression at the top of the upper rear rail. The pairs of half columns on the muntins look old; at some point after the chest came to the MMA they were taken off and their position within each pair switched and then reattached, possibly with the same nails; the renailing caused a long split in the far right turning. The turnings on the front stiles (hard maple) are newer, as are most of the bosses. On the center panel, the upper vertical plaque is replaced and two large nails that at one time secured the plaque in the middle have been removed. Many but not all of the applied moldings on the panels show wear; some of the small nails added to those moldings have been taken out. The base molding looks old but has been renailed. The chest has a modern finish. It retains evidence of stripping and some sanding. Some red paint remains on the panel moldings and thinner or thicker black on the turnings and channel and base moldings. The interior of the chest has been coated, perhaps with oil.

INSCRIPTIONS

A printed paper label glued to the inside of the upper back rail reads: "Included in the collection of Antique Furni- / ture transferred to Mr. H. E. Bolles, and Mr. / Geo. S. Palmer." It is inscribed in ink (script) at the top "Oak Chest, 2 Carved panels" and signed in ink at the bottom

"Walter Hosmer." MMA Hudson-Fulton exhibition identification numbers are inscribed in orange crayon on the outside of the back panel (H. F. 40.34 / 498) and under the bottom (H. F. 40.34). A Connecticut tercentenary paper exhibition label attached with thumbtacks to the inside of the upper left rail is inscribed in ink: "C. T. 43 / Metropolitan / Museum."

WOODS

Stiles, rails, muntins, front and side panels, WHITE OAK and RED OAK; back panel, bottom, EASTERN WHITE PINE; base molding, panel moldings, plaques on center panel, ATLANTIC WHITE CEDAR; left turning on left muntin, BIRCH.

DIMENSIONS

OH. 25¾ (65.4); OW. (top) 48⅜ (122.9); CW. 44⅜ (112.7); OD. (top) 20¾ (52.7); CD. 19 (48.3).

EXHIBITIONS

"Hudson-Fulton Exhibition," MMA, 20 September–30 November 1909; "Three Centuries of Connecticut Furniture, 1635–1935," Morgan Memorial, Hartford, Connecticut, 15 June–15 October 1935.

REFERENCES

Hudson-Fulton Celebration 1909 (exh. cat.), no. 70; Kent 1910, p. 7; Lockwood 1913, fig. 20; Lockwood 1923, fig. 16 (attributed to Nicholas Disbrowe, Hartford, Connecticut); Halsey and Tower 1925, fig. 190; Cornelius 1926, pl. VII; *Three Centuries of Connecticut Furniture* 1935 (exh. cat.), no. 14 (incorrectly described as a chest with drawer).

PROVENANCE

Ex coll.: Walter Hosmer, Hartford, Connecticut; H. Eugene Bolles, Boston.

Bolles and his cousin George S. Palmer, of New London, Connecticut, purchased Hosmer's collection in 1894.

Gift of Mrs. Russell Sage, 1909 (10.125.700)

1. For chests without drawer(s) and variant carving, see Nutting 1928–33, no. 60 (two outer panels with applied ornament); Nutting 1928–33, no. 41 (also in Connecticut Historical Society 1958, pp. 20–21); and Bishop 1975, p. 12, and Monkhouse and Michie 1986, no. 1 (both with channel moldings rather than applied turnings on the frame). On the chests in Nutting 1928–33, no. 62, and Kirk 1967, no. 15, the carving deviates only slightly from the norm.
2. Nutting 1928–33, no. 41; Connecticut Historical Society 1958, pp. 20–21. The turnings flanking the center panel on Nutting 1928–33, no. 60 (see n. 1 above) also have less taper. That such turnings may be indicative of a late date is suggested, for example, by chests of about 1700 that are offshoots of the sunflower tradition and include painted decoration (Kirk 1967, nos. 18, 46).

95. See also fig. III.

95.
Chest with drawers

Hampshire County, Massachusetts, 1700–1725

In 1883 the Hartford, Connecticut, collector Henry Wood Erving acquired from an old house in Hadley, Massachusetts, a chest with carving similar to that seen here and on cat. no. 96. He referred to it thereafter as his "Hadley" chest, and his geographic designation soon became a generic name for furniture decorated with such tulip-and-leaf motifs.[1] So-called Hadley pieces, made between about 1680 and 1730 in the Connecticut River valley—from Suffield and Enfield in the south to Deerfield and Northfield in the north, then all part of Hampshire County, Massachusetts—represent the largest surviving body of American joined furniture. Related through ornament and features of construction, this group has been estimated at as many as two hundred and fifty objects and consists principally of chests with drawer(s) but includes also boxes, tables, chests of drawers, cupboards, and a settle.[2]

Produced in many different shops and over several decades, this large body of work shows stylistic and structural variations. Accordingly it has been divided into different groups—by Patricia E. Kane, who in 1974 sorted the chests visually into six major types with a few subtypes, and by Philip Zea in 1984, who, taking into account also construction, separated the then known objects into sixteen carved variants plus four types of uncarved pieces.[3] In either classification, this chest falls into the largest stylistic group, one that comprises some sixty examples and is characterized by a repeat tulip-and-leaf motif in flat carving over the entire facade. Typically the leaf has three incised scrolls on either side of the central vein and a pair at the tip, and the tulip has a pair of scrolls in the center petal and a line around each outer petal that ends in a scroll at the base (see fig. 61 for similarly detailed leaves and tulips on cat. no. 96). The center panel exhibits a pair of leaves without tulips, above initials of the first owner or owners: usually just two initials—in many cases, when identified, those of a young unmarried woman—or, very rarely, three, indicating a married couple. Structurally, these chests are distinguished by the through chamfering of the framing members of the facade and the particular manner of constructing the chest compartment bottom and the back illustrated by this example (see *Construction*); by a drawer on which the side is joined to the front with a single dovetail; and by channel moldings that normally consist of three V-shaped grooves. This group has been variously subdivided according to details of the carving, such as the type of incised lines in the uncarved voids below and between the motifs, the design elements formed by the negative spaces at the center of rails and drawer fronts, and the use of single or double stalks in the outer panels, and also according to where on the drawer side the dovetail is positioned. The present chest is one of many with a mushroomlike negative space at the center of the horizontal members, but it differs from most others with that feature (including cat. no. 96) by having the dovetail in the side of the drawer below rather than above the groove.[4] An unusual aspect of the flat carving on this general group of Hadley chests is that the sunk ground does not simply serve to define the design; some areas, such as the above-mentioned mushroom shapes and the heart at the top of the center panel on this chest, become part of the decorative scheme.

Hadley chests testify to the persistence of seventeenth-century joinery well into the eighteenth century in a region of New England that remained relatively isolated and was dominated by the economic and political influence of one family, the Pynchons.[5] In their ornament, however, chests of the type represented here, which were probably made between about 1700 and 1725, have drifted from strictly seventeenth-century aesthetics and traditional craftsmanship. The decoration relies for its effect no longer on a diversity of elements in an arrangement that defines the individual structural components but on an allover repeat pattern that was, moreover, laid out

with a template rather than a rule and compass. On this piece, the design on the top rail runs over onto the stiles, and typically there are negative spaces that straddle joints, including, here, those of the drawer fronts and stiles, and the heads of the joint pins were trimmed to conform to the carved pattern—all of which tends to visually negate rather than reinforce the structural divisions of the chest front. Compared, for example, to "sunflower" chests (cat. nos. 92, 93), the panels are small relative to the framing members, so that more of the facade is on the same plane. This greater emphasis on uniformity and a flat surface, which suggests the influence of the William and Mary style, was originally countered in part by painting the carving of particular structural elements in different colors, primarily red and black—an effect that is totally missing from this piece and imperfectly represented on cat. no. 96.

CONSTRUCTION

The frame is made of heavy stock (the pentagonal stiles measure about 4 by 2½ in.) and is assembled with mortise-and-tenon joints 5/16 inch wide; those of all four bottom rails, the drawer divider, and side muntins are just single-pinned. On the front, the stiles, the top and medial rails, and the muntins are chamfered their entire length on the edges that face the panels; accordingly, the outer shoulders of all of the tenons are cut at a 45 degree angle and extend to overlap the chamfer and form a mitered joint (see fig. 86), and on the drawers the ends of the front extend beyond the sides and are beveled on the inner face to form a lip that covers the chamfered edge of the stiles. The cleated top is attached to the back with two snipebill hinges. There is a lock in the top front rail. The back at chest level consists of a horizontal panel deeply beveled all around on the inner side. The bottom of the chest compartment is formed of three front-to-back boards that are joined with a half lap, set into a groove in the front rail, and nailed to the bottom of the medial rear rail. The back at drawer level consists of two horizontal boards butted together, beveled on the outer edges, and nailed to the stiles and medial and bottom rails. The drawers are side-hung. The sides are each joined to the front with a single dovetail below the groove, which is about two-thirds of the way up (fig. 111). The back is butted to the sides and nailed on from the back. The bottom, formed of a wide longitudinal board at the front and a narrow one at the back joined together with a half lap, is nailed to a rabbet in the front and the bottom of the other sides. The drawer runners are let into the stiles and nailed; they extend to the chest sides, where they conform to the contours of the panels and muntins. The channel molding worked on the side rails and the side face of the front and rear stiles consists of three V-shaped grooves, the edge molding on the side muntins of a cyma reversa. The remaining edges around the side panels are finished with a wide chamfer that is stopped at the rails and muntins. The inside edge of the top of the stiles has a narrower chamfer.

CONDITION

The top is old and may be the first. It is pieced at the left front corner, and there is a new strip along the back to which the hinges are now attached (only the section of the right hinge in the rear rail looks original); the left cleat is contemporary with the top, the right is newer, and the staple that engages the lock has been replaced. At the top of the left rear stile there is a third hole (empty) drilled at the joint with the back rail. The chest bottom and the lower back have missing and added nails. The front of the upper drawer has suffered losses at the left corners. On both drawers, the front is pulling away from the sides, the heavily worn grooves in the sides have been repaired with a tapered strip nailed to the upper edge, and there are missing and added nails in the back and bottom. Three of the pulls are definitely new. The feet have lost at least 2 inches in height, and the wood at the bottom is partly rotted; the color on the inner sides of the feet and bottom rails suggests time spent in a damp environment. The exterior of the chest appears to have more than one layer of finish and is uneven in color; a dark brown coating remains on the ground and in recesses of the carving but has been partly removed in other areas. Most interior surfaces including the drawers have some sort of coating, and many show fine light-and-dark speckling; the underside of one drawer has large white splotches.

INSCRIPTION

The initials "MW" of the first owner are carved on the center panel as part of the design.

WOODS

Stiles, rails, muntins, drawer divider, front and side panels, drawer fronts and sides, drawer runners, cleats, WHITE OAK and RED OAK; top, back panel, chest compartment bottom, drawer bottoms, SOUTHERN YELLOW PINE; lower back boards, drawer backs, EASTERN WHITE PINE.

DIMENSIONS

OH. 41 3/8 (105.1); OW. (top) 45 (114.3); CW. 42 (106.7); OD. (top) 18 3/8 (46.7); CD. 18 (45.7).

EXHIBITION

"The Art of Joinery: Seventeenth-Century Case Furniture in the American Wing," MMA, 18 October 1972–18 March 1973.

REFERENCES

Luther 1935, p. 117, no. 92; Safford 1972 (exh. cat.), no. 10; Schwartz 1976, no. 9.

PROVENANCE

Ex coll.: William Smith, Hartford, Connecticut; Mrs. J. Insley Blair, Tuxedo Park, New York.

The chest has no known family history, and the statement by Clair Franklin Luther (see *References*) that it was possibly made for Mehitable Warner (b. 1683), daughter of Daniel and Martha Boltwood Warner, who in 1703 married Preserved Clapp of Northampton, Massachusetts, is conjecture based on a coincidence of initials. Mrs. Blair's notes (ADA files) state that the chest had formerly been in the collection of William Smith. From 1939 to 1948, when it became a gift, the chest was on loan to the MMA from Mrs. Blair.

Gift of Mrs. J. Insley Blair, 1948 (48.158.9)

1. The primary source is Erving 1935, p. 40. Recounted in Luther 1935, pp. 12–13.
2. The principal literature on this furniture includes: Luther 1935 (109 chests catalogued); Kane 1975 (126 chests listed); Zea 1984 (a total of about 175 objects estimated); Zea 1987 (closely based on the preceding); Zea and Flynt 1992 (a total of about 250 objects estimated). The settle was acquired by Historic Deerfield in 2001 (acc. no. 2001.41).
3. Kane 1975, pp. 86–98, 110–19 (two further groups include variants and untraced chests); Zea 1984, pp. 78–140.
4. Kane assigned this chest to her group 3D (Kane 1975, p. 114). Zea assigned it to a group represented by no. 9 in his 1984 thesis (the ISM chest [private collection]; Luther 1935, p. 95, no. 50), but the drawer construction does not conform to that of the latter piece (Zea 1984, p. 118).
5. Zea 1987, pp. 19–31.

96.
Chest with drawer

Hampshire County, Massachusetts, 1700–1725

This chest and cat. no. 95 both belong to the large category of "Hadley" chests that is characterized by flat overall tulip-and-leaf carving, but the two were most likely not made in the same shop. According to Philip Zea, at least six different shops were producing this type of chest in the Hadley-Hatfield-Deerfield area of the Connecticut River valley during the first quarter of the eighteenth century.[1] While the construction of this general class of chests is consistent in most of its aspects (see the entry for cat. no. 95), there are

variations in the dovetailing of the drawers. Here the drawer sides are joined to the front with a small dovetail above the groove, whereas on cat. no. 95 it is below the groove. The latter method is exceptional; the usual alternative to the type of dovetailing seen on this chest is a larger dovetail bisected by the groove. The profile of the edge molding on the side muntins of the two chests under discussion is also not the same. The templates for the basic tulip-and-leaf design used on both chests are a close match, but there are differences in the elements that were executed freehand, such as the incised lines in the uncarved voids below and between the motifs, details of the center panels, and the pattern within the roundels. The two chests also differ in the manner in which the tulip-and-leaf pattern is disposed over the facade. On the present example the design on the top rail does not run across the stiles, as on cat. no. 95, but is cut off at the end of the rail—across the base of a leaf (fig. 61). The pattern on the medial rail terminates at the same point—because of the large pinwheel motif at the center—and does not correspond to the layout on the drawer and bottom rail. On the stiles the design continues to the top, and the tulips face in rather than out. While the same or similar templates were used on a large number of pieces, this type of manipulation of the repeat motif together with variations in the freehand elements of the carving prevented a tiresome uniformity of design.

The use of a template means that the size of the motif is fixed and cannot be adapted to the particular space to be ornamented, in the way it can when a design is laid out with a rule and compass. Consequently the tulip-and-leaf motif on Hadley chests is either truncated or added to, according to the dimensions of the structural member that it adorns. On this chest, for example, the same height pattern—which presumably corresponds to the template—occurs on the top rail, stiles, and outer panels; it has been trimmed slightly along the bottom edge on the medial rail and more obviously so on the bottom rail; on the muntins the space below the tulips and leaves has been enlarged, as it has on the drawer, where, in addition, the tulips have been extended upward. Characteristically a band across the top of the top rail and stiles and the top of the drawer front has been left uncarved.

The tulip-and-leaf motif exemplified by this chest and cat. no. 95 and the use of a template represent in all probability a style of carving and a shop practice that evolved in the Connecticut River valley from earlier schools of joinery and were not an established tradition that was transferred as such from the Old World to the New. Antecedents have been found for the undulating vines characteristic of a subgroup of Hadley chests associated with Hatfield and for the type of leaves with convex stems on chests attributed to Springfield, but no direct source is known for the particular tulip-and-leaf design that distinguishes the large group of Hadley chests under discussion.[2] In their construction, chests like this example and cat. no. 95 incorporate the practices of more than one school of joinery. The structure of the "Hatfield" chests has similarities with that of sunflower chests (see the entry for cat. no. 93), and the construction of the chest compartment bottom and of the back of chests such as this example is related to that of the Hatfield group.[3] The use of dovetails in the drawers and the through chamfering of framing members on the facade of Hadley chests such as this one represent one or two other strains of craftsmanship.[4]

CONSTRUCTION

This chest is similar to cat. no. 95 in most aspects of its structure. On the facade, the framing members have the characteristic through chamfers and the joints are mitered (fig. 86). The front panels have the same dimensions (10 by 8 in.), but the uprights of the frame are somewhat wider, making for a greater overall width of the case. As on cat. no. 95, the panel of the upper back is installed with the beveled edges on the inside. The chest compartment bottom differs in that the two outer boards are unusually wide and the center one measures only about 3 inches. The most significant difference occurs in the drawer, where the sides are joined to the front with a small dovetail placed above the groove—a much more common arrangement than that on cat. no. 95; and in this instance the drawer bottom is a single board. The profile of the channel moldings is the same (exceptionally, that molding runs the length of both the back and the outer side of the rear stiles), but not that of the edge molding on the side muntins, which here consists of an ovolo, fillet, cavetto, and bead. Still clearly visible on this piece are the layout lines characteristically scribed on the front framing members of this class of Hadley chests as guides for the cutting of the mitered mortise-and-tenon joints: lines on the tenoned members perpendicular to, and a short distance in from, each end that mark where the tenon begins and the extent of the overlapping shoulder (fig. 61). Some of the wood used for this chest contained large wormholes before it was worked.

CONDITION

The top (southern yellow pine) is probably an old replacement. The present lock in the front rail and the staple in the top are inoperative; an earlier lock is missing, and the lid is patched where a previous staple was attached. The rear 1½ inches of the drawer bottom has split off and been reattached with wooden dowels. The drawer appears to have been taken apart for that repair; the bottom and back have missing, reset, and replaced nails, and the sides look partly reworked and their dovetail joints have been reglued. The age of the runners is uncertain. The knobs are new. The board of the lower back has one missing and two replaced nails. When the chest was acquired, it was painted in the manner described in 1891 by Irving W. Lyon (see *References*): on the front the carving, but not the ground, was black on the frame and red on the panels and drawer, and on the sides the frame was red and the panels black. That paint has since been partly removed and the chest now has a modern finish over remains of black and red that do not look old. The color scheme is one found on pieces that retain original paint, but whether or not the new paint on this chest was applied according to such evidence is uncertain, for no older paint remains visible to the eye. The interior of the chest compartment has a finish coating, and stain has been applied to the inside and outside of the drawer and to the back of the case.

INSCRIPTIONS

The initials "EG" of the first owner are carved on the center front panel as part of the design. A printed paper label glued to the inside of the upper back rail and missing the lower right corner, reads: "Included in the collection of Antique Furni[-] / ture transferred to Mr. H. E. Bolles, and M[r.] / Geo. S. Palmer. It is the original piece illus[-] /trated in 'Colonial Furniture of New England[,'] / by Dr. Lyons." It is inscribed in ink (script) at the top "Oak Chest, One Draw / Decorated, red and black" and signed in ink at the bottom "Walter H[osmer]." The printed "illustrated" is crossed out and replaced in ink with "To," and "on page" is written after "Lyons." MMA Hudson-Fulton exhibition identification numbers are inscribed in orange crayon inside the lid (H. F. 40.16) and on the

96. See also figs. 61, 86.

underside of the drawer bottom (468, in a circle). Identification numbers applied at the Preservation Society of Newport County (see *Exhibitions*) are inscribed in paint and in chalk on the outside of the back.

WOODS
Stiles, rails, muntins, front and side panels, drawer front and sides, drawer runners, WHITE OAK; left and right board of chest compartment bottom, lower back board, drawer bottom, SOUTHERN YELLOW PINE; back panel, center board of chest compartment bottom, EASTERN WHITE PINE; drawer back, YELLOW POPLAR.

DIMENSIONS
OH. 33¼ (84.5); OW. (top) 46⅞ (119.1); CW. 43½ (110.5); OD. (top) 20¼ (51.4); CD. 19⅞ (50.5).

EXHIBITIONS
"Hudson-Fulton Exhibition," MMA, 20 September–30 November 1909; on loan to the Preservation Society of Newport County from 1950 to 1972.

REFERENCES
I. W. Lyon 1891, p. 16 (not illus.; paint described); *Hudson-Fulton Celebration* 1909 (exh. cat.), no. 71; Kent 1910, p. 7; Lockwood 1913, fig. 27

(initials read as "EC"); Lockwood 1923, fig. 2; Halsey and Tower 1925, fig. 192; Cornelius 1926, pl. VII; Lee 1930, p. 74; Luther 1935, p. 135, no. 18 (not illus.; initials read as "EC").

PROVENANCE
Ex coll.: Walter Hosmer, Hartford, Connecticut; H. Eugene Bolles, Boston.

Bolles and his cousin George S. Palmer, of New London, Connecticut, purchased Hosmer's collection in 1894.

Gift of Mrs. Russell Sage, 1909 (10.125.682)

1. Zea 1984, pp. 116–19; Zea and Flynt 1992, p. 16.
2. A relationship between carving on furniture from the north of England and that of the Connecticut River valley was noted several decades ago by John T. Kirk (Kirk 1965, pp. 790–95; Kirk 1982, pp. 95–104). Three first-generation joiners in Hampshire County, Massachusetts, can be linked to the northern English counties of Yorkshire and Lancashire (Zea 1987, pp. 10–12). Undulating vines occur also on chests attributed to Windsor, Connecticut, shop traditions associated with County Suffolk in East Anglia (Lane and White 2003, nos. 1, 23, 25). Leaves related to those on Springfield, Massachusetts, chests occur in the north of England (Kirk 1982, figs. 255, 257) and, as pointed out by Patricia E. Kane (Kane 1975, pp. 81–88), those in the County Devon style of carving in which William Searle and Thomas Dennis of Ipswich, Massachusetts, were trained also

have similarities (see cat. nos. 83, 85). A box with related leaf carving has been attributed to the Windsor, Connecticut, shop tradition of joiner John Drake (1592–1659) and his sons, who came from County Devon (Lane and White 2003, no. 21). Other immigrant woodworkers in the Connecticut River valley originated in several other parts of England.

3. The drawers of Hatfield chests (for example, one in the Carnegie Museum of Art, Pittsburgh, Pennsylvania; Luther 1935, pp. xv–xvi, no. 6) are constructed in the same manner as those on cat. nos. 92 and 93; the chest compartment bottom is similar, except that the joint between the boards

is a half lap and the boards fit into a groove in only the front rail; the upper back is the same, but the board in the lower back is nailed to, not let into, the stiles. On chests such as cat. nos. 95 and 96, the chest compartment bottom is the same as on Hatfield chests, but the back usually differs in that the panel in the upper back is beveled on the interior rather than the exterior of the case, which is uncommon in seventeenth-century joinery.

4. For through chamfering on English furniture, see Kirk 1982, pp. 97–98, 107 (widespread in the northwest of England); and St. George 1979a, pp. 14–16 and fig. 15 (East Anglia).

97.
Chest with drawer

Probably eastern Massachusetts, 1650–1700

No other piece with this combination of carving and inlay is known. That the chest was made in America is established by its use of riven stock and the specifically American woods that it incorporates. The collection from which it came makes a New England origin likely, and some structural traits suggest eastern Massachusetts, but exactly where it was made is uncertain. The only other American joined furniture that combines inlay and carving is a group of chests attributed to Springfield, Massachusetts, and dating to about 1700. On those pieces the carving, which on two of the panels consists of a symmetrical pattern within a diamond surrounded by gouge work and is otherwise in the so-called Hadley tulip-and-leaf pattern, is accompanied not only by inlay on the muntins but also by applied half columns on the muntins and stiles. The Springfield chests represent a confluence of diverse traditions.[1] This chest, however, appears to have a single stylistic source and to come from the shop of an immigrant joiner. Most likely he came from the north of England, for panels carved with similar cruciform foliate designs within a diamond occur frequently on Yorkshire furniture, and some chairs and chests with such carving from that region also have framing members ornamented with bands of inlay.[2]

The inlay on this chest differs from that on other American joined pieces, be it the Springfield chests, on which the inlay is also formed of diagonal strips but angled in the opposite direction, or furniture from the New Haven, Connecticut, area (see the entry for cat. no. 116), in that its alternating light and dark wood consists of cedar and walnut rather than of the sapwood and heartwood of walnut. The carved designs are carefully laid out; the repeat lunette motifs are equal in size and terminate at the same point at each end. The two-plane carving is enhanced by a little modeling at the center of

the diamond motif and in the pinwheels, and it is embellished with three different punches: a round stamp imprinting a cross or a flower, a small rectangular stamp making two rows of three depressions, and a larger one impressing a pattern of four parallel lines of five marks, which resemble the pricks in the punched ground. The basic vocabulary of the carving—symmetrical stylized foliage within a diamond, pinwheels, and intersecting and opposed lunettes—was widespread and occurred in many different interpretations in England and America. On this chest the diamond motif includes a pinwheel on each side and contains carving that echoes the trefoils in the lunette patterns, but what most distinguishes the design is the reference to strapwork in the continuous band that outlines the diamond and encircles the pinwheels. The combination of carved motifs on a chest advertised in *Antiques* in 1986 that has a diamond pattern on the panels and opposed lunettes with trefoils on the top rail comes the closest to that on the present example, but the execution of the carving differs considerably. The version of opposed lunettes on that piece, which has narrower bands defining the arcs, smaller trefoils, and a half circle instead of a small trefoil in the interstices, is similar rather to that on two cupboards from northern Essex County, Massachusetts.[3] The much denser lunette carving and the more elaborate panel design on the present chest come out of a different shop. Two structural features point to eastern Massachusetts as the most likely place of origin of this chest. The drawer built with single large dovetails suggests the Boston area, although by about 1700 such construction was also employed elsewhere, and the use of cedar for the drawer bottom—a characteristic of Plymouth County furniture (see the entry for cat. no. 114)—suggests southeastern Massachusetts.[4] Wherever it may have been made, this chest

97

appears to be a lone survivor and to represent a transferred English tradition that did not take root and develop into an American school of joinery.

CONSTRUCTION

The mortise-and-tenon joints of the medial and bottom front rails are secured with one pin, all others with two. The back, which consists of three panels at the storage-compartment level, is joined with the framing members flush on the interior and with joint pins driven from the inside out. The front and back panels are quite thick, the sides ones thin and just slightly beveled. The grain of the panels runs horizontally in the back and vertically on the front and sides. The top is formed of three longitudinal boards and is attached with two snipebill hinges. The upper back edge of the top rear rail and of the rear stiles is broadly chamfered. The storage-compartment bottom consists of transverse boards joined with a V-shaped tongue and groove, beveled and let into a groove in the front rail, and nailed to the bottom of the back rail. There is a lidded till on the left, the side of which is slightly canted. The drawer sides are each joined to the front with one large dovetail that is bisected by the groove for the runner. The back is rabbeted to accept the sides and nailed on from the back. The bottom is formed of five transverse boards that are joined with a V-shaped tongue and groove, beveled to fit into a groove in the front, and nailed to the other three sides. The runners are let into the stiles.

The channel molding run on the upper side rails consists of a narrow, flat band with two beads on one side and an ovolo on the other; that worked on the lower side rails and down the middle of the side muntins has a small cyma reversa at each side. The molding on the edge of those muntins is formed of a cyma reversa, a bead, and a fillet. On the interior, the edges of the rear muntins and lower rear rail are finished with a broad chamfer; some of the other edges are lightly chamfered. The carving on the panels was laid out with a large scribed rectangle divided into four equal rectangles that were bisected diagonally to form the diamond. On the top rail and drawer front, evidence remains of the vertical lines scribed for the even spacing of the motifs and of the horizontal lines on which the point of the compass was placed to draw the arcs. The plate of the lock in the upper front rail is ornamented along the side and bottom edges with two rows of three parallel scratched lines similar to those on the lock of cat. no. 79. The stiles are rectangular in section, but most of the other framing members are somewhat wedge-shaped, and surfaces that do not show are only roughly dressed. The cedar bottom boards of the drawer were riven.

CONDITION

Structural repairs made to the chest, which appears to have been at least partially apart, include reinforcement with massive oak bracing. Two transverse braces ($2\frac{1}{4}$ by 2 in. in section) in addition to heavy new cleats—all attached with large modern screws—now hold together the three boards of the top, on which the glued joints have been reworked and the inner side replaned. The top is old and may be original. A narrow strip has been added at the back to which the current hinges are attached; holes in the top and the back rail from a previous set of hinges align. A frame, lapped at the corners and set on top of the chest compartment bottom, is screwed to the side muntins and front rail, and the bottom boards (chestnut) are now attached to the framework with modern nails. The bottom boards, while they all have older nail holes, are at least in part replaced; two were mill-sawn, two hand-sawn, and the underside of the narrow center board was just finished with a hatchet. The till is replaced. A heavy brace attached with screws extends across the back of the bottom front rail and stiles. Nail holes on the back of the rear stiles suggest that at one time, but probably not originally, a board was nailed on at drawer level. The right back corner of the right front foot is pieced. On the drawer, the dovetail joints have been reinforced with glue and modern nails, and the groove in each side has been widened. A narrow slat has been nailed to the top of the back, and a brace to the inside of the back at the bottom. The bottom has modern added nails. The drawer pulls and runners are replaced. The moldings and the present plaque on the drawer front were installed at the MMA. When the chest was acquired, the drawer had a broader center plaque (not original) and no moldings (see *References*). What indications there may have been for the use of moldings on the drawer is not known; no evidence remains as to whether or not the front panels had moldings. Several sections of inlay on the bottom rail and lower portion of the left stile are made of cherry instead of cedar and must be replacements. At the center of the medial rail, where a few walnut and cedar sections are grouped together instead of alternating, loose inlay was probably reglued incorrectly. The facade is uneven in color since a greater amount of a mahogany-color coating remains on the carved areas than on the elements with inlay. The surface has been heavily waxed and perhaps also oiled.

INSCRIPTIONS
There are modern restorer's pencil markings on the interior.

WOODS
Stiles, rails, muntins, panels, top, drawer front, sides, and back, WHITE OAK and RED OAK; drawer bottom, ATLANTIC WHITE CEDAR; light inlay, CEDAR, probably EASTERN RED CEDAR; dark inlay, BLACK WALNUT.

DIMENSIONS
OH. 28⅞ (73.3); OW. (top) 49¼ (125.1); CW. 46¼ (117.5); OD. (top) 22 (55.9); CD. 20½ (52.1).

REFERENCES
Lockwood 1913, fig. 15; Halsey and Cornelius 1928 (and 1932), fig. 2 (1938, 1942, fig. 16); Cescinsky and Hunter 1929, p. 41; Dyer 1931a, p. 38; E. G. Miller 1937, no. 596 (this and the preceding references show the drawer without moldings); Hjorth 1946, fig. 1 and pp. 96, 98 (measured drawings).

PROVENANCE
Ex coll.: H. Eugene Bolles, Boston.

Gift of Mrs. Russell Sage, 1909 (10.125.31)

1. Zea and Flynt 1992, fig. 3 and pp. 15–16.
2. For such pieces with inlay, see *Oak Furniture from Yorkshire Churches* 1971, nos. 7, 18; Chinnery 1979, figs. 4:126, 4:127; Kirk 1982, fig. 276 and nos. 442, 443. For related diamonds with pinwheels, see Kirk 1982, figs. 258, 261; with roundels at the sides, Kirk 1982, fig. 282.
3. *Antiques* 129 (April 1986), p. 720 (Peter Eaton advertisement). For the Essex County cupboards, see Trent, Follansbee, and A. Miller 2001, figs. 66, 75. The interpretation of the opposed-lunette motif on a chair attributed to Hingham, Massachusetts, comes the closest to that on cat. no. 97 (St. George 1979b, no. 73). For other versions, see cat. no. 76; Lockwood 1926, fig. LXXVII; and Nutting 1928–33, nos. 58, 162.
4. The same type of dovetailing is on the drawers of carved chests attributed to Braintree, Massachusetts (Follansbee and Alexander 1996), and is typical of Boston-area chests with applied ornament, such as cat. nos. 98, 99, and 111. Examples from other areas dating from about 1700 include the Springfield chests (see above at n. 1) and cat. no. 100, for instance. Cedar used structurally and not just ornamentally occurs also on some Boston furniture (Fairbanks and Trent 1982, no. 493; G. W. R. Ward 1988, no. 51; Jobe et al. 1991, no. 3).

98.
Chest with drawers

Boston or vicinity, 1670–1700

This is one of six chests of rather small and squarish proportions that are related in their panel and drawer designs and in the profiles of their turned ornament and channel and applied moldings. The group includes cat. no. 99, a chest at the Yale University Art Gallery that has, exceptionally, high turned front feet and one drawer rather than two, and three examples in private collections, one of which has not two but three front panels.[1] The drawers on at least three of the other examples are constructed in the same manner as those on the present piece, which includes drawer backs quickly thinned down at each end with a hatchet; the case back of at least two others is just nailed on, as it is on the present chest. The Yale chest, like this one, is distinguished by the use of hemlock for the boards of the back, chest bottom, and drawer bottom.[2]

The design of this group and the use of dovetails in the drawer construction point to an origin in or around Boston.[3] The raised chest panels created by applied plaques and beveled and mitered moldings and the beveled drawer moldings featured on these chests are derived from the urban joinery tradition that had been transferred to Boston by London-trained craftsmen by about 1640. That style is epitomized by a chest of drawers with doors at the Yale University Art Gallery and a chest of five drawers at the Museum of Fine Arts, Boston, both of which make use of walnut and exotic

98. See also figs. 67, 110, 131.

woods, but is manifest primarily in walnut and cedar chests of four drawers that evolved from those more elaborate forms. In its overall configuration, cat. no. 98 is indebted to those four-drawer chests that, like the Yale and Museum of Fine Arts chests, have a prominent, deep second drawer with projecting applied moldings simulating two panels and a shallow top drawer—to which the panels and top rail on the present piece correspond—and that are divided visually and sometimes also structurally into an upper and lower case of approximately the same height—an arrangement here echoed in the division of the front and in the two virtually equal side panels. Also reflecting the influence of those chests

of drawers are the two-panel configuration of the chest front as well as broad side panels that are left plain.[4]

The half spindles on this and the related chests do not conform to the profile of the standard Boston applied turning, which features a column surmounted by an urn. Characterized by an inverted cup at the top of a columnar segment that tapers toward the bottom (fig. 67), they are in a different London-style design—one quite common on English, but not on American, furniture. The only close American parallels appear on firebacks dated between 1655 and 1662 and attributed to Hammersmith, the ironworks at Saugus, Massachusetts. Robert F. Trent has proposed that the patterns for those cast backs were made by London-trained joiners and turners in Boston.[5] The turnings on the firebacks are surmounted by solid or openwork motifs that correspond to the appliqués used above this form of applied turning on some English furniture; interestingly, they relate in their general outlines to the tongue-shaped elements on cat. no. 99 and at the base of the corbels on this piece. The replaced corbels on this chest conform to the shadow lines of the previous, presumably original, applied elements, of which the profile is unknown; most likely they protruded very little, as on English furniture.[6] More generally related turnings are on a cupboard attributed to Boston, on cupboards from the Guilford, Connecticut, area—for example, cat. no. 113—and on the style of case furniture from coastal Plymouth County, Massachusetts, here represented by cat. nos. 114 and 115.[7]

CONSTRUCTION

The mortise-and-tenon joints of the top rails are secured with two pins, all others with one. The pins, except for those in the muntin joints (diam. a scant ¼ in.), are big (diam. ⅜ in.), and several at drawer level were not trimmed on the interior and protrude as much as 2 inches. The grain of the two front panels runs vertically, that of the two side panels, horizontally. The top is formed of three longitudinal boards and is attached with snipebill hinges. The back consists of two horizontal boards, each beveled on four sides, butted at the medial rail, and nailed to the frame. Two transverse boards joined with a half lap make up the chest compartment bottom; they are nailed to a rabbet on the upper edge of the front and side rails and to the top of the back rail. The drawers are side-hung, and each side is joined to the front with a large dovetail, through the center of which the groove for the runner passes (fig. 110). The back is beveled at each end and nailed to the sides. The bottom is formed of two transverse half-lapped boards that are beveled to fit into a groove in the front and nailed to the other sides. The runners are let into the stiles. The front panels are built up with a central rectangular plaque surrounded by a beveled molding and a separate inner molding that, like all the other small applied moldings on the chest, consists of an ovolo, cavetto, bead, and fillet—a common profile (fig. 131). On the bottom drawer that same profile is worked on the inner edge of the beveled molding. The moldings applied to the front rails are each attached with three large T-headed nails. The one above the drawers has a cyma reversa, a fillet, and a fascia on either side of the central band and that between the drawers just an ovolo. The channel molding worked on the front and side rails has an ovolo at each side; that in the front muntin consists of just a concave profile. The stiles are rectangular. Hidden surfaces of the case and drawers were left entirely unfinished or just roughly dressed with a hatchet.

CONDITION

The top is old and may be original, but the cleats are new. The joints between the boards have been reworked and one has a filler strip, and there is a patch at the right front corner and the left hinge. At some point the top was nailed shut all around. The chest compartment bottom has a gnawed hole at the separated joint of the two boards. Nails have been added to the back. The upper drawer has been partially apart, a section of the upper edge at the left end of the front pieced, and one bottom board (split in two) renailed. The lower drawer bottom has splits and an added nail. Two of the drawer runners are new and two have been reversed. The feet have been shortened, and two have losses at one corner. A 1911 MMA photograph shows the chest as acquired—with numerous applied elements missing—and one taken in 1915 (both in ADA files) as it appears today, except probably for the surface. Replacements made during that interval include: the corbels, the outlines of which were faintly visible; nine of the twelve small half spindles, of which two took the place of damaged ones that were discarded; all the round bosses and all the moldings inside the beveled ones on the chest panels; three triangular plaques and all the moldings on the upper drawer, on which those moldings that remained (about a third) were removed (a few short sections appear to have been reused in the corners of the chest panels); three drawer knobs; the vertical moldings of the lower right side panel; and the base molding, of which only a thin upper strip had survived. The exterior is quite heavily scratched and gouged. It has been stripped and has a modern finish. There are varying amounts of black paint on the turnings, corbels, triangular and narrow rectangular plaques, and the moldings on the front rails; some remains of red brown paint on small moldings; and a few traces of bright red elsewhere. The center of the front panels looks stained, and stain has been applied to the outside of the back and some interior surfaces.

INSCRIPTIONS

A joiner's mark is scribed on the upper edge of each drawer side toward the front: V with the point facing out on the lower drawer; V facing the same way with a line down the middle on the upper drawer. Modern restorer's markings in pencil (one and two dashes) are on the underside of the bottom of the upper drawer. The letter "M" (modern) is scratched once on the top and twice on the top left rail. Identification numbers applied at the Preservation Society of Newport County (see *Exhibitions*) are inscribed in paint and in chalk on the outside of the back.

WOODS

Stiles, rails, muntin, drawer divider, top, drawer fronts, sides, and backs, beveled moldings on front panels, moldings on lower drawer, center plaques on drawer fronts, RED OAK; front and side panels, SOUTHERN YELLOW PINE; back, chest compartment bottom, drawer bottoms, HEMLOCK; molding above and between drawers, old small moldings on front and side panels, plaques at center of front panels and old plaques on upper drawer panels, drawer runners, EASTERN WHITE PINE; large turning on left stile, POPLAR (*Populus* sp.).

DIMENSIONS

OH. 36¼ (92.1); OW. (top) 36½ (92.7); CW. 34¾ (88.3); OD. (top) 21¼ (54); CD. 20¼ (51.4).

EXHIBITIONS

On loan to the Preservation Society of Newport County from 1950 to 1972; "The Art of Joinery: Seventeenth-Century Case Furniture in the American Wing," MMA, 18 October 1972–18 March 1973.

REFERENCE

Safford 1972 (exh. cat.), no. 8.

PROVENANCE

Ex coll.: H. Eugene Bolles, Boston.

Gift of Mrs. Russell Sage, 1909 (10.125.33)

1. See G. W. R. Ward 1988, no. 24 (chest at Yale University Art Gallery). For the three in private collections, see Lockwood 1901, fig. 8 (chest then owned by Lockwood; "found in the vicinity of Boston"); Lockwood 1913, fig. 25 (owned by Mr. Henry Wood Erving; "found in the vicinity of Boston"); *Catalogue of Antiques and Fine Art* 1, no. 4 (July–August 2000), p. 9 (chest with three panels; Anthony S. Werneke advertisement).

2. The writer has not examined the two chests published by Lockwood (see n. 1 above). The construction of the four other chests is similar, except that the back of the example advertised by Werneke has two panels instead of nailed boards.

3. For dovetailed drawers in seventeenth-century New England, see Forman 1970, pp. 12–16, and Forman 1985, pp. 13–14.

4. The London craftsmen generally credited with the transfer of this style are joiners Ralph Mason and Henry Messinger, who were in Boston in 1635 and by 1641, respectively, and turner Thomas Edsall, in Boston in 1635

(Forman 1985, pp. 13–14). For this London style and the Yale chest, see Fairbanks and Trent 1982, no. 481, and G. W. R. Ward 1988, no. 51; for the Museum of Fine Arts chest, see Randall 1965, no. 38, and Fairbanks and Trent 1982, no. 493. Examples of this type of four-drawer chest are Fairbanks and Trent 1982, no. 256, and Jobe and Kaye 1984, no. 11.

5. The firebacks are in Fairbanks and Trent 1982, no. 381 and figs. 32–35. On the Saugus ironworks, see Geib 1982. At least one London turner other than Thomas Edsall (see n. 4 above) was in Boston early on: Robert Windsor, who immigrated some time before 1644 (Forman 1985, p. 14).

6. For related English turnings and appliqués, see R. Edwards 1964, p. 199, figs. 3, 4, and Kirk 1982, figs. 159, 317; the appliqués on cat. no. 98 may have been similar to those on fig. 317.

7. For the Boston cupboard, see Arkell and Trent 1988, figs. 1, 9; *Fine American Furniture, Folk Art and Folk Paintings*, auction cat., Sotheby's, New York City, 26 June 1987, lot 183; and also Trent and Podmaniczky 2002, fig. 9.

99.

Chest with drawers

Boston or vicinity, 1670–1700

On this chest, on cat. no. 98, and on related examples, the traditional chest with drawer(s) form—typically having a three-panel front and a horizontal emphasis—has been modified to reflect the squarish proportions and, in all but one case, the bilateral vertical division of the facade that characterize chests of four drawers made in Boston (see the entry for cat. no. 98).[1] Emulating the look of the more fashionable chest of drawers form, this type of piece provided a degree of stylishness to clients with a conservative taste and pocketbook. Made without walnut or other imported woods, with a nailed rather than a paneled back, and with little or just hasty finishing of most hidden surfaces, these chests aimed at economy. The extent of the use of pine or another softwood in these chests suggests that they probably do not date from before the 1670s. Pine is employed not just in hidden parts of these pieces but also for the front and side panels, all the small mitered moldings and applied plaques, and, on this example, for the beveled drawer moldings as well. Thus the decorative effects usually achieved in the applied-ornament style in large part through the use of woods that differed in color and texture were accomplished on this group of objects to a greater extent with paint. The reliance on pine and on paint became common on mid-level joined furniture produced in Boston and vicinity toward the end of the seventeenth century, as is evident in chests of drawers of the type represented by cat. no. 111.

While this piece is similar to cat. no. 98 and related chests in its construction and the profile of its turnings and moldings, it differs from the others in that its crossetted upper panels are centered with a diamond plaque and lack the somewhat greater mass and higher relief provided by a rectangular field framed by beveled moldings. Half spindles flanking the chest panels that are more attenuated than usual and beveled moldings on the lower drawer that are relatively narrow also

make for a somewhat lighter-looking facade. The heavy moldings applied to the front rails, however, are the same as on related chests. They have distinctive profiles that do not correspond to those on any moldings on Boston chests of drawers. However, moldings of a similar character are to be found on a cupboard of a type attributed to Cambridge, Massachusetts, and on the group of chests-on-frame represented by cat. no. 106.[2]

CONSTRUCTION

The chest is similar to cat. no. 98 in most aspects of its construction. The pins in the mortise-and-tenon joints are the same two sizes, and several pins at drawer level were likewise not trimmed on the inside; here, however, some of the joints of the bottom rails, in addition to those of the top rails, are double-pinned. The grain of the wood in the front panels runs horizontally rather than vertically. The construction of the back and of the bottom of the chest compartment corresponds to that of cat. no. 98 and so does that of the drawers, including the strong beveling of the ends of the back. On this chest there is a case bottom consisting of three butted transverse boards slightly beveled at the edges and nailed to the underside of the rails. The molding applied to the front rail above the drawers differs somewhat, in that the center band is wider and has just a cyma reversa and fillet on either side. The base molding consists of a cyma recta.

CONDITION

The top (pine) and its cleats are replacements; that part of the snipebill hinges that is attached to the rear rail is original. The character and color of the wood on the underside of the chest compartment bottom and of the drawer bottoms and on the inner side of the lower back board raise questions; but the frame is intact, the construction of the chest corresponds closely to that of cat. no. 98, and in the drawers and left rear stile X-radiographs show no previous nails or empty nail holes, so that those boards must be presumed legitimate. The upper left drawer runner is new. The right end of the molding above the drawers is patched, and one corner on each of two feet is pieced. The case bottom (pine) appears to consist of reused wood and was probably

99

added. A photograph of the chest as acquired (first published in 1921; see *References*) shows the piece lacking all the circular bosses, one rectangular plaque, and nine sections of molding on the front chest panels, and seven segments of molding and one applied turning on the upper drawer. The replaced turning is plainly new but was given some wear. The moldings missing in that photograph and now in place on the panels and upper drawer are not crisply new and may have been distressed; possibly some had simply come unglued, since a few have traces of green paint like those that were in situ. All the vertical sections of molding around the panels on the case sides are obviously modern. The drawer pulls are probably all replaced. The chest, when H. Eugene Bolles had it, was entirely painted green.[3] It has been stripped and has a modern finish. There are varying amounts of black paint (some under residues of green) on the half spindles, bosses, triangular and long rectangular plaques, and front case moldings, and a few traces of red on the panels.

INSCRIPTIONS
A joiner's mark is scribed on the upper edge of each drawer side toward the front: on the upper drawer, V with the point facing out; on the lower drawer, V facing the same way, plus a vertical line on one side. Scored on the underside of one board of the lower drawer bottom are large sawyer's tally marks: || and || crossed by a diagonal line. Identification numbers painted on at the Preservation Society of Newport County (see *Exhibition*) are on the outside of the upper back board.

WOODS
Stiles, rails, muntin, drawer divider, drawer fronts, sides, and backs, center plaques on drawer fronts, RED OAK; front and side panels, back, chest compartment bottom, drawer bottoms, drawer runners, all moldings, plaques on front chest panels and upper drawer panels, appliqués at top of front stiles, EASTERN WHITE PINE; large turning on left stile, POPLAR (*Populus* sp.).

DIMENSIONS
OH. 36⅝ (93); OW. (top) 37⅞ (96.2); CW. 36 (91.4); OD. (back to rail moldings) 21⅜ (54.3); CD. 19⅞ (50.5).

EXHIBITION
On loan to the Preservation Society of Newport County from 1949 to 1972.

REFERENCES
Nutting 1921, p. 35; Nutting 1924, no. 49; Nutting 1928–33, no. 52; Dyer 1931a, p. 37 (this and the previous references show the chest as acquired); S. Chamberlain and N. G. Chamberlain 1972, p. 81 (as exhibited in the parlor of Whitehall Museum House,

Middletown, Rhode Island); Hornung 1972, no. 887; Shea 1975, p. 108.

PROVENANCE
Ex coll.: H. Eugene Bolles, Boston.

Gift of Mrs. Russell Sage, 1909 (10.125.32)

1. For London-style Boston chests with drawer(s) of a traditional format, see Jobe and Kaye 1984, no. 6, and Forman 1985, figs. 10, 11, 13.
2. Trent 1975, fig. 3 (also in Nutting 1928–33, no. 460).
3. Letter of 9 January 1910 from Bolles to Henry W. Kent (Bolles correspondence, MMA Archives).

100.

Chest with drawer

South-central Connecticut, dated 1705

Embellished with painted designs and inscribed "1705," this is one of six joined chests bearing a date between 1704 and 1706 that are an early manifestation of the principal school of ornamental painting in south-central Connecticut in the first three or four decades of the eighteenth century (see also cat. nos. 101, 102, 107). Three of the other examples—at the Art Institute of Chicago, Chicago, Illinois, East Hampton Historical Society, East Hampton, New York, and Museum of Fine Arts, Boston—are inscribed "1704," one at the Connecticut Historical Society, Hartford, "1705/6," and one sold in 1996 at Sotheby's, "1706."[1] In form and construction these pieces are an offshoot of the school of joinery that produced the numerous so-called sunflower chests in Hartford County (see the entries for cat. nos. 92, 93), with which they conform structurally, except for minor changes that represent an updating of the seventeenth-century model.[2] The primary difference is that drawer sides are joined to the front with a dovetail rather than being nailed, and that on this example and some others the front and side panels are of pine rather than oak.

In terms of its overall composition, the painted decoration on the front panels of the present piece is indebted to that same tradition. The design on the outer panels of a thistle on a straight stalk that issues from a small mound and has two pairs of symmetrical stems with leaves and flowers (fig. 70) echoes the arrangement of the carved tulip motif on sunflower chests, which sometimes includes thistles. Closely related painting is on the Connecticut Historical Society

chest and the one sold at Sotheby's. The circular pattern on the center panel recalls the carved ring of tulips enclosing initials on cat. no. 93, for instance. A ring motif, each in a different design, ornaments the center panel of all but the Art Institute of Chicago chest. Other than on the present piece, the circular band is surrounded by flowers, and on the chest in the Museum of Fine Arts, Boston, on which all three panels have the same ring design, those flowers are clearly tulips. The decoration on the drawer—a vine extending symmetrically to either side of a central motif, in this case a carnation—was, like a stalk of flowers emerging from a mound or vase, a widespread and long-lived decorative device popular in various mediums throughout the seventeenth century. Large leaves and tulips of the type seen on the side panels of this piece, just outlined in white or filled in, as here, occur only on some of these dated chests.[3]

The six chests in this group, when viewed chronologically, show in their decorative elements a gradual diminution of the influence of the seventeenth-century style and a movement toward William and Mary–style design concepts. The Art Institute of Chicago chest retains some carving and applied half columns. It and the East Hampton Historical Society example still have drawer fronts divided into two simulated panels by a central plaque. All three 1704 objects, each with two drawers, have horizontal moldings applied to the rails similar to those on sunflower chests. The three later chests, all with just one drawer, lack such moldings. On this example, a channel molding in the standard sunflower school profile is worked on the front frame and the side rails and, in the seventeenth-century manner, stresses the exact extent of each individual framing member; on the front, the molding is painted with wavy white lines so as to stand out from the remainder of the frame covered with red and green dots. On the 1705/6 and 1706 chests, the frame is entirely devoid of moldings and on the front it is uniformly stippled with white and green or red dots so that it no longer reads as separate rails and stiles but as a single unit.

The dated chests form part of a broader ornamental tradition that encompasses two other groups of painted case furniture: the largest is represented by cat. nos. 101 and 107, and the third by cat. no. 102. These objects are all linked by a common painting technique, a shared decorative vocabulary, and certain structural traits.[4] The painted ornament on this chest well illustrates the characteristics of that technique. On a thin ground coat—in this case a reddish brown—the floral designs on the facade, except for some of the small elements, are first delineated in a thick coat of white. The colors—here red and two shades of green—are then applied in relatively thin layers over the white. The colors may completely cover the white undercoat, as they do on the solid red or green leaves on the drawer front, but more often they are used in numerous particolor combinations set off by the white. Examples of such detailing on this chest are: on the drawer, the longitudinal division of small leaves into a white and a colored field; on the outer front panels (fig. 70), a diaper pattern in green with dabs of red in the interstices on the thistles; thick green veins over red hatching on the leaves flanking each thistle; red and green dots on the tulips at the bottom of the stalks; and on the carnations above the tulips, cross-hatching in lighter green on the lower petals followed by a tier of petals in solid, deeper green and white center petals with red stripes. Thus, through a fanciful, arbitrary use of color, a limited palette achieves lively, varied effects.

PAINTED DECORATION
The ground coat is a thin red-brown layer that contains iron earth pigment. The other pigments are lead white, vermilion, and copper green. There are two shades of green: a darker bluish green that contains only copper green pigment and a lighter green, in which that pigment is mixed with lead white. The two greens and the vermilion are used both over the white and, for small elements only, directly on the ground. Examples of the latter are the pairs of small light green leaves that alternate with white ones on the outer panels and the dark green and red dots on the front uprights and rails and within the circular band on the center panel. (The intersecting diagonal scribed lines that located the center of that panel and the compass point from the scribing of the circles remain visible.) Some of the dots on the frame have worn off, as has a considerable amount of the white in the channel moldings. Much of the green now looks nearly black, and all the paint on the panels is partly obscured by a brownish glazelike finish layer, the age of which is uncertain. When in 1990–91 the chest was cleaned by Peter Fodera (Fodera Fine Art Conservation, New York City), that coating was left in place since it seems to be bound to the paint

underneath. It varies in thickness, and the colors of the designs vary accordingly. It is responsible, in part if not entirely, for the strong orange-brown cast of the designs on the side panels, which are broadly brushed in thin white in a repeated application. On the front panels it has developed vertical craquelure along the grain of the wood. Only traces of this coating were found on the drawer, where many of the leaves that are now white have probably lost an upper layer of color. Some inpainting was done at that time to integrate the tonality of the drawer front with the rest of the piece, and the surface of the chest was given a protective coating.

CONSTRUCTION
The chest has three equal panels in the front (12 by 11 in., twice the height of the drawer) and two horizontal panels on each side. The mortise-and-tenon joints are secured with two pins, except for one in back that has three. The top is attached with two snipebill hinges. The construction of this piece is related to that of cat. nos. 92 and 93: the back is built the same way, as is the chest compartment bottom, except that here the three bottom boards are roughly all the same width and do not fit into a groove in the stiles. The side-hung drawer differs in that the sides are attached to the front with a single dovetail key reinforced by a T-headed nail and that the front of the bottom has a shallow rabbet on the upper edge in addition to a bevel on the underside. The profile of the channel molding on all the front framing members and the side rails corresponds to that on cat. nos. 92 and 93. The edges of the stiles and rails surrounding the side panels, except that of the bottom rail, are chamfered.

CONDITION
The top (southern yellow pine), stained and deeply scratched and with a narrow new section at the back, is a replacement; the portion of the hinges in the rear rail is original. A lock is missing from the front rail; the keyhole escutcheon is a later addition. The applied moldings on the front panels are replaced; those that surrounded the drawer front are missing. A thin slat is nailed in place across the front of the upper side of the chest compartment bottom to cover several large holes along the bottom's front edge. The board of the lower back has pulled away from the groove in the left stile and is now secured with nails. It is riddled with wormholes, and its upper and lower edges are crumbling; some wormholes are evident in most of the lower half of the piece. On the drawer, both back corners have splits and losses, the bottom has cracks, there a few added nails, and the knobs are replaced. The left drawer runner is new, and two added drawer stops are nailed to the case back. There are losses on the left rear foot. The interior surfaces of the piece have been gone over with a red brown stain. On the chest compartment bottom are residues of paint and other substances that dripped on the lower back board. (See also *Painted decoration*.)

INSCRIPTION
The initials "EL" of the unidentified first owner above the date 1705 are painted in white on the center front panel.

WOODS
Stiles, rails, muntins, drawer front and sides, right drawer runner, WHITE OAK; all panels, lower back board, chest compartment bottom, drawer bottom and back, SOUTHERN YELLOW PINE.

DIMENSIONS
OH. 32½ (82.6); OW. (top) 48⅜ (122.9); CW. 45 (114.3); OD. (top). 20⅛ (51.1); CD. 19¼ (48.9).

100. See also fig. 70.

EXHIBITION
"The Art of Joinery: Seventeenth-Century Case Furniture in the American Wing," MMA, 18 October 1972–18 March 1973.

REFERENCES
Lockwood 1913, fig. 38; Raymond 1922, p. 122; Halsey and Tower 1925, fig. 30; Cescinsky and Hunter 1929, p. 42; "Antiques in the American Wing" 1946, p. 249, no. 15; Margon 1954, no. 31; Williams 1963, no. 71; Margon 1965, pp. 85, 90; Kirk 1967, no. 44; Safford 1972 (exh. cat.), no. 7 and fig. 7; Schwartz 1976, no. 10; Willoughby 1994, p. 54 and fig. 22a; Safford 1998, fig. 3 and pp. 198–99.

PROVENANCE
Ex coll.: H. Eugene Bolles, Boston.

Gift of Mrs. Russell Sage, 1909 (10.125.29)

1. The five are, in the order mentioned, in Kirk 1967, no. 18; Graybeal and Kenny 1987, pl. XIII; Randall 1965, no. 14; Kirk 1967, no. 43, and also Kirk 1982, figs. 174–76 (in color); and *Important Americana*, auction cat., Sotheby's, New York City, 19–21 January 1996, lot 1620.

2. This joinery tradition may have been transmitted to the Connecticut shore by Peter Blin Jr. (1670?–alive 1741), who was presumably trained by his father in Wethersfield, moved to Guilford in about 1695, and worked there until about 1730 (Trent 1994, p. 82).

3. On the sides of the Connecticut Historical Society chest, similar large-scale flowers and leaves are just outlined in white; on the sides of the piece sold at Sotheby's, the motifs on the upper panels are outlined and on the lower panels are partly filled in. The age of the painting on the sides of cat. no. 100 and of the large filled-in leaves on the drawers of the Art Institute of Chicago chest has been questioned (Willoughby 1994, p. 52), but the present writer, particularly since the example that sold at Sotheby's became known, believes the large leaves and flowers on the sides of cat. no. 100 to be of the period. On the sides of the Museum of Fine Arts chest there remain traces of wavy zigzag lines in white; that chest also retains traces of floral painting on the lid.

4. The closest structural parallels are between the dated chests and the joined chests with drawer mentioned in the entry for cat. no. 101, which have the same back, chest bottom, and drawer construction. This chest lacks the scratched joiner's marks on the drawer sides found on other dated chests and on objects in the two other groups (see cat. nos. 101, 107, 102); they have probably been effaced. For a detailed discussion of the structural relationship between sunflower chests, the painted and dated chests, and the Guilford-Saybrook group represented by cat. nos. 101 and 107, see Willoughby 1994, pp. 19–38, 63–67, 123–28. See also cat. no. 102.

101.

Chest with drawer

Connecticut, Guilford-Saybrook area, 1705–25

This small chest decorated with graceful, brightly colored sprays belongs to a sizable group of painted furniture long associated with the towns along the Connecticut shore from approximately Guilford to Saybrook. Of the schools of decorative painting that flourished in Connecticut in the first half of the eighteenth century this one has the largest number of surviving examples and encompasses the broadest range of furniture forms: in addition to three other board chests with drawer of similar small scale and a chest-on-frame (cat. no. 107), the Guilford-Saybrook group to which this piece belongs includes a board chest, a miniature chest, two chests of drawers, a high chest, and at least seven joined chests, nearly all with a drawer.[1] Above all, the decoration on this furniture is noteworthy for the diversity of the designs—featuring mainly flowers and birds—which are more varied than those on any other body of American painted furniture of the period. The flowers and leaves on this chest represent but part of this rich ornamental vocabulary, which is recombined somewhat differently on each piece and elaborated with an imaginative, schematic use of colors. In terms of scale and character, the motifs fall roughly into two categories: good-sized, solid forms, such as the tulips and large curled leaves on this facade and the elements that constitute the pattern on the upper front of cat. no. 107; and lighter motifs composed of a number of small petals or leaves, of which the most common are carnations and various schemes of paired leaves or petals with a bud or open flower in the center (fig. 71). Particularly airy examples of the latter are the flowers with feathery tufts on the sides of this piece. The decoration on this chest is unusual in that a single composition extends over the whole facade, the arrangement nicely balanced between the larger, more solid motifs in the lower half and the lighter elements above. In all other cases, each unit of the facade—be it drawers or chest compartment front—is ornamented with a separate pattern. The designs—whether in the form of a spray or a vine—are typically symmetrical in line and color, except for minor variations in the execution. The sides of this piece are decorated with a small spray; more common on this group of furniture is a bird or an oversized tulip.

The painting technique is the same as that on cat. no. 100, but the support differs, for this Guilford-Saybrook furniture is distinguished by the use of yellow poplar as the principal primary wood; it has a finer texture than oak or pine. On this piece the decoration is executed in two types of red, probably two shades of green, and yellow. The white undercoat is quite thick and slightly raised above the background. Whether or not this aspect of the technique was designed to be an allusion to the raised ornament on japanned furniture it is not possible to say. It seems clear, however, that the popularity of painted furniture in the early eighteenth century was directly related to the fashionableness of japanning and marquetry in that period. The exact source of this style of painting has not been determined, but it may be that it was introduced to the Connecticut shore by Charles Guillam (1671–1727), who has been associated with the Guilford-Saybrook type of decoration since the late 1950s. Guillam, who was in Saybrook by 1703, came from the Isle of Jersey in the Channel Islands. The fact that several mid-eighteenth-century chests with floral painting from the Channel Islands are known raises the possibility that they are descended from an earlier tradition of painted furniture, in which Guillam could have been trained.[2] Whether or not he was responsible for the introduction of this style of painting, the manifestations of this school are too broad and varied overall to have been the work of only one man or shop. It is likely that he was one of several joiners in the area who must have been interacting or working in related shops, given not only the similarity in painting technique and motifs between the Guilford-Saybrook pieces, the group of dated chests to which cat. no. 100 belongs, and the objects represented by cat. no. 102, but also the greater or lesser structural ties between the three groups.

PAINTED DECORATION

The designs are laid out in thick lead white on a black ground—probably a carbon black—that, like the ground of cat. no. 100, is thin and seems to have little binder. The colors are applied over the white, except for parts of the finer detailing, such as some of the red strands in the wispy tufts on the chest sides, which are painted directly on the ground. The color scheme includes probably two shades of green (copper green), as on cat. no. 100; two reds, vermilion and a red that appears to contain lead white and red lead and/or iron earth pigment; and yellow (orpiment). Orpiment was used for the clearly demarcated areas of yellow against a white field on leaves and petals and for the distinct yellow lines within the white field surrounding the green and red on the tulips. The yellow tone in other areas of the design—those where there are no clear boundaries to the color—is probably imparted not by paint but by remains of yellowed finish. In 1992 the chest was cleaned by Peter Fodera (Fodera Fine Art Conservation, New York City), and most but not all of the degraded and uneven finish layers that obscured the designs and the brightness of the colors were removed. In addition, two vertical drip marks through the motif on the right side were inpainted, the ground of the drawer was toned to integrate it with the rest of the piece, and the surface was given a

101. See also fig. 71.

protective coating. During the cleaning of the right side, the outline of a stem and foliage that extended nearly horizontally from either side of the mound and had been sketched in but never executed became faintly visible. No evidence of any prior restoration of the floral elements was found, though some of the background had been toned in. The paint has suffered some losses. Some areas of color detailing are worn thin or missing, and there are small losses throughout where the white undercoat has flaked. It is not certain if parts of the design, such as the stems or small leaves that are now white, were originally meant to be pure white or have lost an overlay of color. However, the definition of the major elements by the use of color reads clearly.

CONSTRUCTION

The front and back are rabbeted to accept the sides and secured to the sides with three T-headed nails at each front joint and four at each back joint. The case bottom, which is beveled on its projecting front and side edges, is nailed to the sides and back. The top, a single board like all components of the case, is attached with two snipebill hinges. The chest compartment bottom is let into a groove in each side and is nailed to a rabbet on the lower edge of the front. The drawer rides on the bottom of its sides along the case bottom. The front is rabbeted at each end and extends over the case sides. Each side is joined to the front and back with one large dovetail reinforced by one or two nails;

at the back, the dovetails protrude. The bottom is formed of two longitudinal boards joined by a half lap, beveled underneath to fit into a groove in the front and sides, and nailed to the back. The three old feet are drilled completely through and doweled to transverse battens attached to the underside of the bottom.

CONDITION

The top appears to be original, but the cleats (oak) and hinges are replaced. The battens (oak) under the bottom are new, as is the left front foot. The other three feet look old and are possibly original. There is a split across the right rear corner of the case bottom. The back edge of the chest compartment bottom has been damaged by rodents. The drawer appears to have been apart; some of the interior surfaces look replaned and there are replaced nails. One back corner has splits and the other a loss, and a thin strip at the bottom of each side has been replaced, as have the pulls. (See also *Painted decoration.*)

INSCRIPTIONS

On the exterior of each drawer side is a scratched joiner's mark that consists of a full-height vertical line near the front and from the top of that line a diagonal one that extends down to the bottom rear corner— shorthand to indicate what is the outer side, front end, and top of the board when the drawer is assembled. Inscribed in chalk on the exterior of the chest back are the large script initials "GS." A printed paper label glued to the inside of the back reads: "Included in the collection of Antique Furni- / ture transferred to Mr. H. E. Bolles, and Mr. / Geo. S. Palmer." The top of the label is inscribed in ink (script) "A Box, painted decoration," and the bottom is signed "Walter Hosmer." Incised on the top edge of the front board is "T ELEZI" (modern).

WOODS

Case front, sides, and back, chest compartment bottom, drawer, YELLOW POPLAR; top, case bottom, SOUTHERN YELLOW PINE; old feet, BIRCH.

DIMENSIONS

OH. 19⅛ (48.6); OW. (top) 29 (73.7); CW. 25¾ (65.4); OD. (top) 16⅝ (42.2); CD. 15⅞ (40.3).

EXHIBITION

On loan to the Monmouth County Historical Association, Freehold, New Jersey, from 1947 to 1978.

REFERENCES

Nutting 1921, p. 45; Nutting 1924, no. 38; Nutting 1928–33, no. 65; Kettell 1929, pl. 36; Safford 1998, fig. 4 and pp. 199–201; Safford 2000, pl. IV.

PROVENANCE

Ex coll.: Walter Hosmer, Hartford, Connecticut; H. Eugene Bolles, Boston.

Bolles and his cousin George S. Palmer, of New London, Connecticut, purchased Hosmer's collection in 1894.

Gift of Mrs. Russell Sage, 1909 (10.125.16)

1. The three small board chests with drawer are in the Winterthur Museum (B. Ward 1986, no. 9) and a private collection, and in Nutting 1928–33, no. 103; the board chest is in a private collection (Kirk 1967, no. 37); the miniature chest is in the Henry Ford Museum (Kirk 1967, no. 38); the two chests of drawers are at Historic Deerfield (Fales 1976, no. 368) and the Wadsworth Atheneum (Fales 1972, no. 22); the high chest is in the Winterthur Museum (Fales 1972, no. 29). The joined chests are at the Acton Public Library, Old Saybrook, Connecticut (W. L. Warren 1958a, fig. 4), Henry Ford Museum (Fales 1972, no. 28), Henry Whitfield State Historical Museum, Guilford, Connecticut (W. L. Warren 1958a, fig. 3), and Yale University Art Gallery (G. W. R. Ward 1988, no. 32); in W. L. Warren 1958a, figs. 1, 2, and also Kirk 1967, nos. 39, 40; and offered in *Important American Folk Art and Furniture*, auction cat., Sotheby Parke Bernet, New York City, 27 January 1979, lot 324.
2. For a review of the literature on this group of furniture, information on Guillam and other joiners in that area, and one of the Channel Islands chests, see Trent 1994. Another chest is in *The 48th Annual Winter Antiques Show* (New York, 2002), pp. 100–101 (Robert Young Antiques advertisement). Robert Young knows of several other such chests (conversation with the present writer in January 2002).

102.

Chest with drawer

South-central Connecticut, 1720–35

The painting technique employed on this chest is that of the Guilford-Saybrook school, and the motifs are related, but various factors seem to indicate that this piece was not made in the same shop or shops as cat. nos. 101 and 107 and that it represents a later expression of that school of painting. The ornamental vocabulary on this chest is more limited and the compositions are more formulaic, suggesting a waning of the tradition. The floral elements on the front are virtually all variations and elaborations on a three-leaf or three-petal form, such as that seen next to the tulips on cat. no. 101 or on the lower drawer of cat. no. 107. Nevertheless, the designs on the facade do not lack in visual interest. The various interpretations of the tripartite motif, which are painted in different stylized color schemes and attached to vines that describe crisp compass curves (fig. 72), appear to be flitting across the surface in a sprightly manner. On each side of the chest is a tree with a more relaxed spread of branches and bearing solid-colored leaves (white, red, or green) that are uniform in size and shape—a pattern not encountered on the main Guilford-Saybrook group. In its construction as in its decoration, this chest reveals the hand of a maker who received training in the Guilford-Saybrook school of crafts-manship but also absorbed other influences. The joiner's marks on the sides of the drawer are similar to those on the

102. See also fig. 72.

drawers of cat. nos. 101 and 107, for instance (see *Inscriptions*), but this piece differs from those examples and others in the main Guilford-Saybrook group in that the primary wood is pine rather than yellow poplar and that the dovetailing of the drawer is a little more refined.[1]

Originally the painted designs on this chest stood against a ground that was yellow rather than the usual red brown or black. Only one other piece within this tradition—a joined chest with drawer at the Yale University Art Gallery—is known to have such a ground color. Interestingly the motifs on the front panel of that chest, except for the central roses and leaves, are similar to those seen here, but it is difficult to say exactly what the relationship is between the two.[2] About nine other case pieces with painting related to that on the present chest but on a ground that looks darker are known. They include a small board chest with drawer, a board chest,

a box, and a high chest of drawers of the same format as the painted example at the Winterthur Museum (see the entry for cat. no. 101), all of which have the same type of motif on the sides as this example; and, in addition, five board chests with two drawers that do not appear to have been ornamented on the sides. The small chest with drawer, which is similar to cat. no. 101 in form and size but not in certain aspects of its construction, is initialed and dated 1730.[3] That date confirms what the nature of the painted decoration and dovetailing on this piece suggest; namely, that this chest is a relatively late product of the Guilford-Saybrook school.

PAINTED DECORATION
The design elements are laid out in a thick layer of lead white, and the colors—vermilion and a copper green—are applied over the white in thinner layers. The ground was originally yellow: yellow pigment, which appears to be yellow ocher, was detected under magnification

245

in the wood pores of all show surfaces, including the top and cleats; in cross sections it shows under the white of the decoration as a thin coat penetrating the wood. The uppermost part of the left side—under the cleat—still has an overall yellow tone. Otherwise the surface now looks more or less reddish from the color assumed by the wood after the yellow wore off and from later toning in of abraded sections in red. The decoration has suffered considerable losses, not just to the overlying colors but also to the white undercoat. The red areas have fared somewhat better than the green ones, and the green paint that remains looks nearly black. One or more layers of slightly amber finish cover the show surfaces going over paint losses, abrasions, and numerous scratches.

CONSTRUCTION

The case is built of wide single boards, including the back, which extends to within 2 inches of the drawer bottom. The front of the chest compartment, the rail below the drawer, and the back are rabbeted to accept the sides and nailed to the sides with T-headed nails. The chest compartment bottom fits into a groove in each side and a rabbet at the bottom of the front. One nail secures the bottom to the front, and two are driven into the bottom through the back. The cleated top is attached with two snipebill hinges. On the interior there is a lock in the front and a till on the right that originally had a lid; inside the till, a thin strip is nailed to the front and back of the case, its upper edge level with the top of the till side. A hole at the center front of the chest bottom permits a rod to be inserted down through an iron loop on the inside of the drawer front to secure the drawer. The ends of the drawer front are rabbeted and extend over the case sides. The drawer sides are dovetailed to the front and back with three keys at each joint; at the back the dovetails protrude. The bottom consists of a longitudinal board that is beveled to fit into a groove in the front and sides and is nailed to the back. The drawer rides on the bottom of its sides on runners nailed to the case sides. The cutout at the bottom of the case sides that forms the feet is shaped at the apex like the letter "M." The half-round molding above the drawer and the base molding, which consists of an ovolo, a cyma reversa, and a fascia, are attached with nails similar to those that secure the case.

CONDITION

The top has a repaired split at the back edge. The lid of the till is missing. The base molding on the left side is replaced and so is the half-round molding on the front edge of the feet, which are chipped at the bottom. The hinges are original, the pulls on the drawer appear to be the first set, and the lock looks old. A hole has been made through each cleat and corresponding chest side near the front, probably to permit the securing of the top with a rod or pin. A wooden spring lock, added at some point to the underside of the drawer, is partly missing. There is a large knothole at the rear edge of the top, another toward the bottom of the back, and one in the chest compartment bottom that has been plugged. There are modern screw holes on the exterior of the back, probably from the time at the MMA (several decades past) when small objects displayed on the top of the chest were strapped to the case. All the show surfaces are nicked and heavily scratched. (See also *Painted decoration*.)

INSCRIPTIONS

The initials "MD" (the "D" is partly effaced) of an unidentified first owner are painted in red on a white, diamond-shaped reserve below the keyhole. On the exterior of each drawer side is a scratched joiner's mark: from the top of a full-height vertical line near the front a diagonal one extends down to the lower rear corner. The lines on the right side of the drawer are straight, and on the left side they are wavy.

WOODS

Top, case front, sides and back, chest compartment bottom, rail below drawer, drawer front and back, drawer runners, till side, EASTERN WHITE PINE; drawer sides and bottom, molding above drawer, SOUTHERN YELLOW PINE; base molding, till bottom, YELLOW POPLAR; cleats, OAK.

DIMENSIONS

OH. 33 1/8 (84.1); OW. (top) 46 (116.8); CW. 43 3/8 (110.2); OD. (top) 19 (48.3); CD. 17 3/4 (45.1).

EXHIBITION

"Connecticut Furniture: Seventeenth and Eighteenth Centuries," Wadsworth Atheneum, 3 November–17 December 1967.

REFERENCES

Downs 1945, p. 72; M. B. Davidson 1967, no. 67; Kirk 1967 (exh. cat.), no. 42; Anderson 1974, pp. 116–17 (illus.; also shows a reproduction of the chest, for which plans could be purchased); Schwartz 1976, no. 29; Safford 1998, fig. 7 and p. 202; MMA 2001, fig. 21.

PROVENANCE

Ex coll.: Mrs. J. Insley Blair, Tuxedo Park, New York.

According to a letter of 18 December 1964, from William L. Warren, chief curator at Old Sturbridge Village, Sturbridge, Massachusetts, to James Biddle (ADA files), Mrs. Blair purchased the chest from Frederick W. Fuessenich, a collector and dealer of Litchfield, Connecticut. Fuessenich did not remember at that point where he had acquired it. The chest was on loan to the MMA from Mrs. Blair from 1939 until it became a gift.

Gift of Mrs. J. Insley Blair, 1945 (45.78.4)

1. For the use of scratched marks on drawer sides, see also Willoughby 1994, pp. 33–38, 128. Even the deepest drawers of the high chest and chests of drawers in the main Guilford-Saybrook group (see the entry for cat. no. 101) have only two dovetails at each joint.
2. G. W. R. Ward 1988, no. 32. Only the chest portion of that piece has survived; it conforms in the construction of its back and bottom and in the use of yellow poplar to the other joined chests with drawer in the group mentioned in the entry for cat. no. 101.
3. The small dated chest with drawer, unlike cat. no. 101 and the small chests related to it, is made primarily of pine, and its drawer has two dovetails at each corner; it was on loan to the MMA from 1952 to 1985 and is in a private collection (*Property from the Collection of Mrs. J. Insley Blair*, auction cat., Christie's, New York City, 21 January 2006, lot 521). The other objects, in the order mentioned, are in the Winterthur Museum (Bjerkoe 1957, pl. VIII, no. 2), Historic New England (Fales 1972, no. 33), DAPC, no. 65.1832 (a misproportioned rendering of the same high chest is in Hornung 1972, no. 912), the Antiquarian and Landmarks Society, Hartford, Connecticut (W. L. Warren 1958b, fig. 8), and formerly in the Goss collection, Guilford, Connecticut (present location unknown); advertised in *Antiques and the Arts Weekly* (Newtown, Connecticut), 14 October 1977, by Lillian Blankley Cogan; and offered in *Important Americana: The Collection of the Late Dr. and Mrs. James W. Marvin*, auction cat., Sotheby Parke Bernet, New York City, 30 September–1 October 1978, lot 331, and *Fine Americana, American Paintings and Chinese Export Porcelain*, auction cat., Christie, Manson and Woods International, New York City, 24–25 June 1980, lot 724. The paint on some of the chests with drawers appears to have been renewed.

103

103.
Chest with drawer

Connecticut, probably Milford area, 1720–40

The floral ornament on this chest is based on the motif of a three-petaled flower terminating in a fleur-de-lis, elements of which—namely, the fleur-de-lis and its components—are used also as separate decorative entities. The painting is distinguished by having been laid out with templates, as is indicated by the exact replication of forms. There was probably a pattern for each element or pair of identical elements, since individual shapes correspond closely but the spacing between them may vary. The chest, because of extensive paint losses,

now offers only tantalizing hints of what was originally a bright array of floral forms delineated in solid white, red, and green and in white with red and green accents, in rather dense compositions that give somewhat the impression of overall patterns. On the upper front of the chest, the flowers are arranged on irregularly curving and undulating stems attached to a horizontal stem that extends to either side from a central stalk. On the drawer the flower stems are joined to form three separate clusters, and on the case sides they spring from a straight, central vertical stalk. The decorative scheme on the facade includes, in addition, short wavy lines on the moldings and a border of undulating transverse lines down the sides of the facade and around three sides of the keyhole location at center top. In the background of the floral designs on the case sides is a network of interconnected diagonal dotted lines, and on the left side there are also series of short wavy lines. Similar lines decorate the feet.

This is one of nine known board chests—all but one with a drawer—embellished with the same standardized flowers and leaves and similar borders.[1] On all but two of the chests the motif of a three-petaled flower terminating in a fleur-de-lis is identical or virtually identical to that seen here.[2] The two exceptions feature a smaller version of that motif. In addition, four of the chests include a tulip and one a circular pattern formed of hearts. The designs are all symmetrical, but there are variations in the configuration of the layout as well as in the choice and specific arrangement of the motifs. Some of the compositions are less compact than on this piece, and the framework of the design sometimes reads more easily. The scheme on a chest at the Connecticut Historical Society, Hartford, is by far the most straightforward of the nine, and it is atypical in its strict linearity; its floral elements (primarily the smaller version of the motif characteristic of this group) are arranged on straight vertical and intersecting diagonal stems, for which the scribe lines remain clearly visible. Although in terms of its composition the ornament on the Connecticut Historical Society chest is at variance with that on cat. no. 103, and thus seems to be by a different hand, structurally these two pieces and four others are part of the same shop tradition. The front corners of the drawers are all nailed in the same manner from the front and side, for example, and the cutouts that form the feet are similar in shape. The cutouts on the three other chests (one without and two with a drawer) are each in a different pattern, and the drawers in question are dovetailed at the front, indicating that those chests were built by one or more craftsmen with other training.[3]

The Connecticut Historical Society chest is the only one to have an early history. It is said to have come down in the Neddleton family that settled in Milford, Connecticut, in the seventeenth century. Consequently this whole group has become associated with the Milford area. Two other examples have relatively recent histories of recovery that support an attribution of this type of painted decoration to the area of southern Connecticut west of New Haven: one, at the Darien Historical Society, was found in a Scofield family farmhouse in Darien (about 1950) and the other (present location unknown) in a dump in Woodbury (about 1965).[4] The formulaized motifs of this school and its use of templates suggest that it was active some time after the introduction of floral painted ornament along the Connecticut shore. It appears to be, at least in part, derivative. Certain aspects of the painting probably represent

the influence of the Guilford-Saybrook tradition: for instance, the type of color accents on white, such as dots or an inner field of color, leaving a white surround, and the use of borders and dotted zigzag lines.[5] The main motif could have been abstracted from floral forms on cat. no. 102, for example, but the resemblance may also be just coincidental since such flowers were part of a widespread traditional vocabulary.

PAINTED DECORATION

The dark ground coat is thin and contains a mixture of black and red particles (probably a carbon black with an iron earth pigment and red lead). The decoration was executed in white (lead white), red (red lead with lead white), and green (unidentified; no copper was detected in the one sample analyzed). Because of extensive losses—in a few areas ornament and ground have been completely abraded, and in many cases only shadow lines of the motifs remain—it is not possible to know the color scheme of all of the design elements. On the front, there is evidence that the two outer petals of the large tripartite flower were solid red, painted directly on the ground, and the center petal was white with green dots. The other elements only show remains of white, with any color detailing once applied over the white now lost. On the sides, the center petal of the main flower was white with red dots and the petals flanking it white with probably a red inner field. In some cases a small dab of red remains at the point where the fleur-de-lis emerges from the main flower and at the juncture of some of the stems. Some of the wavy dashes in the background of the left side are red, as are some of those on the sides of all the feet. The other background patterning on the sides, the borders on the front, and the wavy lines on the moldings seem to be executed only in white. The dots in the background of the sides and in the center petal of all the main flowers appear to have been small raised blobs, and those in the petals not only raised but also well sunk into the white paint. The surface is entirely covered with a yellowed varnish that goes over considerable residues of an earlier thick, degraded finish. There remain visible on the facade vertical scribe lines that divide the chest and drawer front in two and that delimit the border down their side edges, and lines at center top that demarcate the band that runs down the sides and across the bottom of a presumed keyhole location. There is no clear evidence that the outlines of the motifs were scribed.

CONSTRUCTION

The case and drawer are entirely of nailed board construction. The chest front is rabbeted to receive the sides, but the rail below the drawer and the back (two horizontal boards) are simply butted to the sides. The one-board top is attached with two snipebill hinges. The chest compartment bottom fits into a groove in each side and a rabbet at the bottom of the front and is nailed in place through all four sides. The ends of the drawer front are rabbeted and extend over the case sides. The drawer front is nailed to the drawer sides at top and bottom and each side to the front with a nail in the middle. At the back, the sides are rabbeted and nailed to the back. The lower edge of the front and sides is rabbeted to receive the bottom; the bottom is nailed to the front and back and the sides to the bottom. Drawer and chest bottom are formed of a wide and a narrow longitudinal board. The drawer runners are nailed to the case sides and extend only three-quarters of the way back. The cutout at the bottom of the sides that forms the feet has the shape of the letter "M." The base molding consists of a fillet, cyma reversa, and a fascia. The wood of the lower back board and of the drawer back contains large, exposed insect tunnels, and the workmanship as a whole is elementary.

CONDITION

The top has several splits, a replaced left cleat, loose hinges, and a heavily worn front edge. A hole has been drilled through the right cleat and case side to accept a locking device. A small batten for propping the top open that rotates on a nail on the interior of the left case side has been added. The lower back board has loose and missing nails. The drawer has missing and added nails, and the bottom has probably been at least partly off and reset. There are holes in the drawer front but none from the original attachment of a pull. The half-round molding above the drawer is broken near the center and has many added nails. The entire left base molding is missing and so are sections at the left end of the front molding, the rear end of the right molding, the lower right corner of the drawer front, and the back of the rear feet. There are smaller losses elsewhere on the piece as well as a few splits. The exterior surfaces are marked throughout with deep holes, gouges, and scratches. The outside of the back, the chest and drawer bottoms, and the interior surfaces in the lower portion of the case have all been stained. (See also *Painted decoration*.)

DIMENSIONS

OH. 36½ (92.7); OW. (top) 39⅞ (101.3); CW. 36⅝ (93); OD. (top) 17⅝ (44.8); CD. 16½ (41.9).

WOODS

EASTERN WHITE PINE; rail below drawer, RED OAK; base molding, ATLANTIC WHITE CEDAR.

EXHIBITION

On loan to the Pierce-Hichborn House, Boston, from 1950 to 1979.

REFERENCE

Safford 1998, fig. 8 (drawing of main motif) and pp. 202–3.

PROVENANCE

Purchased from King Hooper Antiques, Boston.

Rogers Fund, 1934 (34.128)

1. The chests are in the Colonel Ashley House, Ashley Falls, Massachusetts, Connecticut Historical Society, Hartford (Kirk 1967, no. 50), Darien Historical Society, Pocumtuck Valley Memorial Association (Fales 1976, no. 382), and a private collection; in Kirk 1967, no. 49 (without a drawer); advertised in *Maine Antique Digest*, May 1984, p. 39D, by John Walton; and offered in *Important Americana: The Bertram K. Little and Nina Fletcher Little Collection, Part I*, auction cat., Sotheby's, New York City, 29 January 1994, lot 291 (see also N. F. Little 1984, p. 196 and fig. 260 [detail of side]).
2. A comparison of patterns made of the flowers and leaves on cat. no. 103 with the motifs on three of the chests mentioned in n. 1 above indicates that the designs on the Pocumtuck Valley Memorial Association chest could have been laid out with the same templates; the larger pair of leaves on the Connecticut Historical Society piece correspond to the pair of petals at the base of the fleur-de-lis on cat. no. 103; and the center petals on the Darien Historical Society chest match those on the present piece, and the paired petals and leaves that flank them are wider but the curves that define them correspond.
3. The chest formerly in the Little collection and the unpublished one in a private collection (see n. 1 above) have dovetailed drawers.
4. For the histories of the three chests, in the order mentioned, see Connecticut Historical Society object file 62-2-2; Darien Historical Society, notes on the collection by Mrs. James Farrell; and references in n. 1 above for a chest formerly in the Little collection.
5. For borders, see the entry for cat. no. 107; for zigzag lines, see Fales 1972, no. 28, for example.

104.

Chest with drawer

Taunton, Massachusetts, dated 1735
Attributed to Robert Crosman (1707–1799)

This board chest with one drawer was fitted with moldings so as to achieve the look of a more fashionable chest of drawers, but the painted ornament negates rather than reinforces that effect; a single pattern covers the whole facade—the lines of its vines originally went across the moldings. The distinctive type of design seen here has long been attributed to Robert Crosman of Taunton, Massachusetts, who was a drummaker and carpenter, like his great-grandfather.[1] Six other chests with closely related painting have been published—five of the same format as cat. no. 104 and a smaller example with two drawers at the Winterthur Museum. The pieces are all inscribed with dates—which range from 1731 to 1742—and some also with initials.[2] The design on this group of seven chests is characterized by having two vines emerge from a stylized triangular mound at the base and rise symmetrically in three tiers of compass-drawn curves. The vines bear tendrils, eight-petaled flowers, and, predominantly, tulips with such a flower at the tip (fig. 73). The decorative vocabulary also includes two types of birds—one with spread wings and one that resembles a chick. The shape of the mound, which is represented by parallel wavy lines, is echoed at center top in the similarly rendered inverted triangle of the reserve for the date (and sometimes initials). Those geometric forms and the pyramidal arrangement of three birds at lower center counterbalance the emphatic curves of the vines.

The painting has a strong linear quality and is distinguished by the use of templates for the tulips and birds and of a standard formula for the layout of the main vines, but no two pieces are exactly alike. The arrangement of the secondary vines differs from chest to chest, as does the particular disposition of flowers and birds. There is also some variation in the depiction of the individual elements. On two of the chests, the outer petals of the tulips are accented with dots rather than a band of color. On the present chest, some of the tulip motifs are delineated in a manner not noted elsewhere: they terminate in only half a flower—larger and with narrower petals than the norm—and on the upper false drawer the center petal of those tulips is replaced by a set of parallel lines. The pair of leaves at the base of those tulips is also unusual and encountered otherwise only on the small Winterthur chest. Paint losses make it difficult to determine how consistent the color detailing was on the objects in this group or its exact nature on some of the individual pieces. In general, only red is in evidence in addition to the white. On the Winterthur chest, however, green is definitely also part of the scheme, as it probably was on cat. no. 104.

This group of seven chests is part of a larger body of painted board furniture attributed to Crosman that includes miniature chests with a drawer, low chests with a drawer, and one small chest of drawers with ball feet, as well as other examples of the format seen here.[3] Structurally, this shop tradition is characterized by the particular manner of joining and pinning the bottom rail to the case, the use of wooden pins in the drawer construction, and the rounded arch at the bottom of the side boards—features illustrated by cat. no. 104. The decorative schemes on the larger group of objects differ from the type on the present chest and appear to be precursors of that design. The simplest and most overtly linear pattern—executed in white with red accents and which occurs primarily on miniature chests with a drawer—consists of a tree or bush that stands on one or more wavy lines and has branches that describe arcs and bear small leaves and/or terminate in a dot (or berry), as do the tendrils on this piece, or in a cluster of three. On some of those chests, including one dated 1728, birds similar to those seen here form part of the ornament.[4] More densely and more elaborately foliated trees are represented on four chests of the same format as cat. no. 104, two of which are dated 1729.[5] Similar foliage—not on tree motifs confined to individual drawers but on vines that continue up the whole facade—is depicted in white, red, and green on the small chest of drawers. It is inscribed on the back "Taun Ton, / R C: /1729." and is the key to the attribution of the whole group.[6]

PAINTED DECORATION

The ground coat is a red layer that contains iron earth pigment and perhaps some red lead. The ornament was executed in lead white and an orange red that is a mixture of red lead and lead white (used both over white and directly on the ground), and perhaps also in green, of which there appear to be a few faint traces. The designs were laid out in white, with all the motifs outlined. It looks as if the tulip petals and leaves were then gone over with a broad brush, leaving just a strip of the ground showing down the middle, and the head and body of the birds painted completely white. The wings and tails of the birds were delineated with parallel lines, and similar lines take the place of the center petal on the larger tulips on the upper false drawer. Compass points from the scribing of the arcs of the vines remain visible, and scribe lines can be detected along the outlines of the birds and tulips, indicating the use of templates. What the full original color scheme was is uncertain because of extensive losses, overpainting (in a darker red), and residues of degraded finish. Evidence remains of orange red down the middle of the tulip petals and leaves, at the flower center and near the tip of the petals on the "daisies," at the tip of the tendrils, and accenting the white, wavy lines that form the mound at the base. Sparse blue green pigment particles were found in the upper portion of the white layer in a sample from the perimeter of the outer petal of a tulip. There is no clear indication of how the body of the birds was detailed or whether there was color on or between the white lines of the wings and tail. It appears that the center portion of the daisy petals was left in the ground color. The ground on the front and sides of the chest is very uneven, ranging from nearly bare wood with possible remains of the original ground coat to areas of thick, dark, degraded finish and later red paint. The surface was lightly cleaned at the MMA in 1980 to make the design more legible.

CONSTRUCTION

The chest compartment front and the back have a shallow rabbet at each end and are nailed to the sides. The front is a single board, divided by an applied molding to simulate two drawers, and is set in a recess on the front of the sides so as to be on the same plane as the inset drawer below. The false drawers are of equal height and ½ inch taller than the real one. The back consists of a wide upper board butted to a narrower one at drawer level. The one-board top is attached with two snipebill hinges. The chest compartment bottom is one longitudinal board that fits into a groove in each side and has a rabbeted front edge that extends under the case front; it is nailed in place through the sides and back, and through the bottom to the front. On the rail below the drawer (3 in. deep), the rear two-thirds are let into a groove in the sides and secured through each side with a square wooden pin; the front third extends the full width of the case, fitting into a recess on the front of each side, and its projecting front edge serves as the base molding. The drawer sides are joined to the front with three dovetails and to the back with two. The bottom is formed of two wide transverse boards butted to a narrow center one, with two of the boards joined by a square wooden pin. It is beveled and let into a groove in the front (and was originally held in the groove by two small pins), is nailed to the back, and fits between the sides and is secured through each side with a small square pin. The drawer rides on the bottom of the sides. The runners are nailed to the case sides behind the rail. The front edge of the rail is shaped to an ovolo. All the half-round moldings on the facade are applied.

104. See also fig. 73.

CONDITION

The top—heavily stained, scratched, and gouged, and with loose hinges—is old but may not be original; and the left cleat is not as old as the top. The segment of molding at the left of the upper false drawer is new. There are small splits in the case and drawer and losses at the bottom of the feet. The drawer pulls are replacements, and the two escutcheons are probably not original and may have been added; between the initials at center top there are the remains of what appears to be a painted escutcheon, but no nail holes from an applied one are visible. All surfaces are scratched and nicked. (See also *Painted decoration*.)

INSCRIPTIONS

The initials "CS" of the unidentified first owner, above the date 1735, are painted at center top of the front. Large scored sawyer's tally marks are on the outer side of the upper back board: a V with a diagonal slash and IIII; and on the inside of the lower back board: II X I. Smaller scratched roman numerals—original assembly marks—match the case and drawer sides and on the drawer are also on the top edge of all four sides and the inner side of the front and back.

WOODS

EASTERN WHITE PINE; case back, drawer bottom, ATLANTIC WHITE CEDAR.

DIMENSIONS

OH. 32½ (82.6); OW. (top) 37¾ (95.9); CW. 36 (91.4); OD. (top) 18⅛ (46); CD. 17⅜ (44.1).

EXHIBITION

On loan to the American Museum in Britain, Bath, England, from 1963 to 1979.

REFERENCES

Antiques 13 (April 1928), p. 341 (advertised by Miss Julia F. S. Snow); Brazer 1933 (then Fraser), fig. 9; Downs 1945, p. 72; Williams 1963, no. 65; Chinnery 1979, fig. 4:230 (as exhibited in the American Museum in Britain).

PROVENANCE

Ex coll.: Mrs. J. Insley Blair, Tuxedo Park, New York.

The chest was advertised in 1928 by the dealer Miss Julia F. S. Snow, of Greenfield, Massachusetts, who was probably the source of the information that it was found near Greenfield, published by Esther Stevens Fraser (later Brazer) in 1933 (see *References*). The chest was on loan to the MMA from Mrs. Blair from 1939 until it became a gift.

Gift of Mrs. J. Insley Blair, 1945 (45.78.5)

1. Brazer 1933.
2. See ibid., fig. 8 ("PC/1731"); Drepperd 1940, fig. 1E ("1731"; formerly MMA); Bishop 1975, p. 30 ("JI/1732"; Henry Ford Museum); *Sack Collection* 1981–92, vol. 10, p. 2659 ("1732"); Brazer 1933, fig. 10 ("AC/1736"; Detroit Institute of Arts, Detroit, Michigan), fig. 11 ("1742"; Winterthur Museum).
3. The files at the Old Colony Historical Society, Taunton, Massachusetts, to which Lisa A. Compton kindly gave the writer access in 1993, then recorded about thirty chests, including unpublished examples not cited in this entry.
4. See Lockwood 1913, fig. 39; Brazer 1933, figs. 1–3, 5 (initialed "IP"); Comstock 1962, no. 180 ("HB"); Fales 1972, no. 44; Greenlaw 1974, no. 72; Cullity 1987, no. 5 ("AD/1728"); D. B. Warren et al. 1998, no. F30; also *American Furniture and Decorative Arts*, auction cat., Skinner, Bolton, Massachusetts, 8 June 1997, lot 26. The branches that end in one or three dots recall those on Pennsylvania furniture with "line-and-berry" inlay (Schiffer 1966, ill. nos. 121, 122, 125–28, 168); possibly the Crosman and Pennsylvania designs were derived from similar British sources, which may have been influenced by bone, ivory, or mother-of-pearl inlay on mid-seventeenth-century English furniture (R. Edwards 1964, p. 199, fig. 3, p. 205, fig. 25).
5. Brazer 1933, figs. 4, 6 (initialed and dated "AW/ 1729"); Fales 1972, no. 45; *Currier Gallery of Art* 1995, no. 34 ("SA/1729"). Similar trees or bushes with small oval leaves—disposed within the confines of individual drawer fronts—occur on several painted chests that include buildings in their decoration and, in one instance, birds (Fales 1972, nos. 41–43; Fales 1976, no. 381; Fairbanks and Bates 1981, p. 50). The place of origin of those chests has not been established, and it is not clear what their relationship to these Crosman pieces might be.
6. Brazer 1933, fig. 7; and *Property from the Collection of Mrs. J. Insley Blair*, auction cat., Christie's, New York City, 21 January 2006, lot 519. The drawers on the signed chest are constructed in the same manner as the one on cat. no. 104, and both pieces have the same type of assembly marks scratched on the case and drawer(s). A chest with drawer with a design that continues over the whole facade and includes tulips and eight-petaled flowers but differs from the type on cat. no. 104 is in Schwartz 1968, fig. 28.

Chests-on-Frame

The three case pieces in this chapter each present a quite different interpretation of a furniture form that consists of a small lift-top chest with drawer raised on integral legs or on a separate framework—a type of structure generally termed a "chest-on-frame" or "chest-on-stand." Two of the chests are in the seventeenth-century style and of joined construction, and they are built as one unit, the legs being extensions of the stiles of the case. They represent a form that, according to the at least two dozen surviving examples, was made only in eastern Massachusetts and from about 1670 to 1710. The Museum's chest-on-frame from the coastal area south of Boston (cat. no. 106), one of about eight with similar turnings and carved and applied ornament, illustrates the usual type of understructure. Its turned legs are braced by perimetric stretchers (commonly called box stretchers), which on this and the related chests are rectangular and sometimes, as probably once here, supported a shelf.

The largest group of joined chests-on-frame, most likely produced in or around Boston, has an undercarriage in the same format, but the stretchers are turned to match the legs instead of being plain. No example of this Boston type, decorated with applied moldings and graining and painted floral motifs, is in the collection. The Museum's other joined chest-on-frame, which is ornamented solely with applied moldings and turnings, cannot be linked to any specific shop tradition or locality (cat. no. 105). It has a base like that on no other example of this furniture form: its legs—the front ones with large separate turned balusters and the back ones with plain stiles—recall those of the lower part of a cupboard with open shelf; the configuration of its turned stretchers has no exact counterpart.

The chest-on-frame never became widespread. It was a specialized form, but what particular function it was meant to serve is not certain. The form may well correspond to the term "chamber table" found in probate records, a designation that suggests a piece proper to the bedroom and a use related to dressing and grooming. Its height and lack of legroom, however, indicate it was not designed to be a dressing table, and the relatively large open cavity of the lift-top storage area (typically without a till) is no substitute for the small compartments and drawers of a dressing box. Regrettably no clear physical or documentary evidence remains as to how it was used. Whatever its purpose, the chest-on-frame offered the advantage of providing storage space at a convenient height.

The structural concept of the one-piece form is related to that of seventeenth-century joined box stools (stools with a hinged seat and a bottom under the rails that creates a box) or tables that incorporate a storage compartment, examples of which are to be found in England, though no American ones are known. Exactly how or to what extent the joined chest-on-frame relates to cabinets-on-stand and chests of drawers on stand—advanced forms that were in style in England in the last three decades of the seventeenth century—is not clear, but those forms made the idea of a storage unit raised on a framework fashionable. The design of the third chest-on-frame in the collection, a painted example in the William and Mary style from the Connecticut shore (cat. no. 107), is unquestionably indebted to that of high chests of drawers. Such an influence is evident in the broad mid-molding and the flat shaped stretchers, and in the fact that it is built in two sections. This piece also has no known close parallel.

105.

Chest-on-frame

Eastern Massachusetts, 1670–1700

What purpose this small chest with drawer on high legs was intended to serve and how it was originally designated is not entirely clear. As proposed by Benno M. Forman, this furniture form—described structurally as a "chest-on-frame," "chest-on-frame with drawer," or "chest-on-stand"—may correspond to the term "chamber table" found in inventories of the late seventeenth and early eighteenth centuries. This nomenclature suggests a piece specifically associated with a bedroom, and

Forman speculated that it served perhaps as a washstand and held ewers and basins, or possibly stored chamber pots. It is too high and does not provide enough legroom to be sat at for dressing or any other activity.[1]

Surviving examples point to its popularity and manufacture in Boston and in Massachusetts port towns to the north and south of that urban center between about 1670 and 1710. Two, including one dated 1690, are in a distinct style identified with northern Essex County.[2] One group of about eight was very likely made in the Hingham-Scituate area of Plymouth County (see the entry for cat. no. 106). The largest number is of a type probably produced in and around Boston. Characterized by two front panels with applied moldings that typically form an archlike hexagon above a drawer with two simulated panels and by one-panel sides, they stand on bases turned in either a ball pattern or in one comprising vase shapes and rings. Some examples retain painted floral ornament in the front panels and graining elsewhere.[3]

No other chest with the same understructure or applied ornament as this example is known, and it is difficult to assign it to a particular locality in eastern Massachusetts.[4] The legs and stretchers of the other such joined pieces resemble those of a table. The construction seen here, however—broad rear legs that are a continuation of the upper stiles and separately turned pillars in the front legs—is similar to that of the lower portion of most cupboards with an open bottom shelf. The arrangement of the stretchers, which includes both a longitudinal and a transverse medial member, also has no counterpart among the other examples of this furniture form.[5] Probably so designed to provide extra stability to a frame on which the front legs are not of one piece, it also allowed for the attachment of a turning at the center—a conceit found on some William and Mary–style dressing tables (see cat. no. 128). The stretcher turnings are in the ball pattern promulgated by Boston back stools (see cat. nos. 23, 24). The other turnings do not match those attributed to any particular locality or shop tradition. The closest comparison is with turnings on Essex County furniture. Pillars of an overall related vase form with a deep, rounded groove occur on cupboards made in Salem and in the northern portion of that county, but none terminate at the bottom with the double torus molding seen here or have two tightly spaced rings at the top or multiple fillets on the vase's shoulder (fig. 45). Applied turnings that end at the top with a tall conical shape leading to a knob like those flanking the panels (fig. 68) and some that have an elongated vase form (though usually the inverse of that on this piece) occur on some northern Essex County work, but none provide a close parallel in their entirety.[6] Most distinctive is the design on the center panel. While an octagonal panel with a sunburst motif is characteristic of many pieces in the Symonds tradition of Salem (see cat. no. 79), its interpretation here, with the rays emerging from a molded circle and formed of triangular plaques edged by moldings, is quite different. A precedent for a circular turned molding centering an octagonal panel can be found on a Boston chest with drawers, on which the circle is divided into quadrants by inset keystones as it is on the English (probably London) chests from which that motif was derived.[7] If cat. no. 105 was made in Boston, one would expect the drawer to be dovetailed at the front. Instead, it is nailed, and the nails are driven in through the

front, which is typical of a group of case furniture from Plymouth County (see cat. nos. 114, 115), although such construction did occasionally occur elsewhere in eastern Massachusetts.[8] Wherever it originated and whatever its purpose, when all of its ornament was in place and a play of wood colors and painted surfaces enhanced the design, this was a very stylish piece.

CONSTRUCTION

The chest's mortise-and-tenon joints are secured with one pin, except for those of the deep lower side rails, which extend to the bottom of the mid-molding and have full-height tenons, each held in place by three pins. The back consists of a single panel that is level with the three front ones, but the panel on each side is 2 inches taller. A slat applied across the bottom of each side panel makes the side and front panels look the same height. The lid rotates on wooden pintles that are fixed in the rear stiles and go through the cleats. The chest compartment bottom is formed of three transverse boards butted together, beveled to fit into a groove in the front rail, and nailed to the bottom of the back rail. The drawer is side-hung. The front and back are rabbeted at the ends to accept the sides and nailed in place through the front and the back. The drawer bottom is one longitudinal board beveled to fit into a groove in the front and nailed to the bottom of the other sides. The runners are let into the stiles and nailed at the front, and drawer stops are nailed to the front of the rear stiles. The turned pillars of the front legs are separate pieces joined to the stiles above and below with a round tenon; the front feet are one with the lower stiles. The longitudinal medial stretcher is one piece, the transverse stretcher consists of two sections. The rear stretcher, joined flush with the front of the stiles like the rear rails, protrudes at the back, particularly at the thinner left stile. The applied moldings on the drawer, side panels, and outer front panels consist of a cyma reversa and a bead and those that form the points of the sunburst, of an ovolo, fillet, and cavetto. The arch and the spandrels on the left front panel are made from a single, applied piece of oak. The molding worked on the arch and that on the roundel of the center panel are formed of two and three convex contours, respectively.

CONDITION

The top, which is split and has been reversed from front to back, is old and may be original. The cleats are new and different from the replacements shown in a photograph published by Wallace Nutting (see *References*), and the pintles are not at the original location in the stiles. On the rear stiles, the top back edge has been cut down, there are patches at the hinges, and most of the mortises have broken through at the back. A lock is missing from the top front rail. The middle board of the chest compartment bottom is questionable. On the drawer, the back is replaced, the right side has a large loss at the lower back, the bottom has splits and many added nails, and the knobs are not original. The feet have lost some height. Losses to the applied ornament are numerous. Most of the remaining elements have now been secured with nails. The age of the wooden pins that attach the center plaque on the drawer front and the slats at the bottom of the side panels is unclear. Shadow lines indicate that moldings formed an octagon around the sunburst design in the center front panel and cut the corners of the side panels, which are centered by a lozenge. In both cases, the corners were filled with triangular plaques, one of which has survived on the right side, where the slat at the bottom of the panel is missing, as is the mid-molding that was attached to it.

105. See also figs. 45, 68.

Originally there was also a molding at the bottom of the front and sides of the case. The turnings applied to the rear stiles are modern. The other half spindles are older, and those on the drawer front and muntins show considerable wear. A turning is missing from the center of the stretchers. The exterior of the piece, including the back, is covered with brown paint or stain that postdates virtually all losses and signs of wear and over which there is a coat of varnish. Under the brown are remains of red and black paint.

INSCRIPTIONS
Scratched joiner's marks (single slashes and Xs) match the drawer sides to the front.

WOODS
Rear stiles, upper front stiles, rails, muntins, panels, drawer sides, drawer runners, applied arch, WHITE OAK; top, chest compartment bottom, drawer bottom, slat at bottom of left side panel, mid-molding,

plaque at center of drawer front, SOUTHERN YELLOW PINE; drawer front, drawer moldings, outer front panel moldings, EASTERN WHITE PINE; lower front stiles and feet, stretchers, POPLAR (*Populus* sp.); pillars of front legs, turning to immediate left of center panel and left one on drawer front, MAPLE.

DIMENSIONS

OH. 35⅝ (90.5); OW. (top) 26½ (67.3); CW. 23⅞ (60.6); OD. (top) 18 (45.7); CD. 17½ (44.5).

EXHIBITION

"The Art of Joinery: Seventeenth-Century Case Furniture in the American Wing," MMA, 18 October 1972–18 March 1973.

REFERENCES

Nutting 1921, pp. 86–87 (this and the following two references show the earlier replaced cleats); Nutting 1924, no. 116; Nutting 1928–33, no. 207; I. P. Lyon 1938c, fig. 50; Safford 1972 (exh. cat.), no. 13; MMA 1975, p. 21; Schwartz 1976, no. 21.

PROVENANCE

Ex coll.: Chauncey C. Nash, Milton, Massachusetts; Mrs. J. Insley Blair, Tuxedo Park, New York; her daughter Mrs. J. Woodhull Overton, Balmville, New York.

Mrs. Blair purchased the piece in 1923 from Collings and Collings, New York City dealers. According to Wallace Nutting, it was found in York, Maine.[9] It was on loan to the MMA from Mrs. Blair from 1939 to 1949 and from Mrs. Overton from 1952 until it became a gift.

Gift of Mrs. J. Woodhull Overton, 1969 (69.209)

1. Forman 1987, pp. 152–54.
2. Nutting 1928–33, nos. 210, 211; I. P. Lyon 1938b, figs. 32, 31.
3. For representative examples of the Boston group, which numbers more than a dozen, see Schwartz 1956, p. 344; *Sack Collection* 1981–92, vol. 6, p. 26; Monkhouse and Michie 1986, nos. 21, 22; Forman 1987, fig. 7; D. B. Warren et al. 1998, no. F27. A type of chest with drawer with painted decoration and fielded side panels relates to this group (Jobe and Kaye 1984, no. 7).
4. A similar piece (Fairbanks and Trent 1982, no. 252; *Highly Important American Furniture, Silver, Folk Art and Decorative Arts*, auction cat., Christie's, New York City, 19–20 January 1990, lot 670) was determined to be modern (Solis-Cohen 1990).
5. Nearly all chests-on-frame have just perimetric stretchers. Other exceptions are the two examples cited in n. 2 above, one of which (dated 1690), has a transverse medial stretcher. The other has H-stretchers.
6. For Salem pillars, see I. P. Lyon 1938d, fig. 54; for northern Essex County examples, see Trent, Follansbee, and A. Miller 2001, figs. 33, 43, 86. For applied turnings, see, for example, Trent, Follansbee, and A. Miller 2001, figs. 34, 40, 28.
7. See Jobe and Kaye 1984, no. 6, and Forman 1985, figs. 1, 10, 11.
8. The drawer front is nailed to the sides, for example, on a northern Essex County chest of drawers at the Peabody Essex Museum (Trent, Follansbee, and A. Miller 2001, fig. 16) and on a chest with drawers from Middlesex County, Massachusetts, at the Concord Museum, Concord, Massachusetts, and a related cupboard base at the Museum of Fine Arts, Boston (Wood 1996, no. 2 [chest] and fig. 2.1 [cupboard base]; for the cupboard base, see also cat. no. 141, ill. 141d).
9. Nutting 1921, p. 86, and Nutting 1924, no. 116.

106.

Chest-on-frame

Massachusetts, probably Hingham-Scituate area, 1670–1700

This small chest-on-frame with high turned legs is one of at least eight such pieces similar in design and construction.[1] They are characterized by a facade that features two horizontal panels above a drawer carved in a lunette motif and by applied ornament that consists of bosses and turnings in a repeat ball pattern. They all have the same type of heavy moldings attached to the front rails, and identical channel moldings run on the side rails. The lid is pintle-hinged. The chest bottom is let into a groove in the front rail and generally also in the side rails. In some cases, the rectangular stretchers support a shelf, as they probably once did here. The drawer may or may not be side-hung, but it is consistently assembled in the same manner, with the two nails that secure each side to the front set into lightly gouged holes. Unusual structural traits that distinguish this group are the use of riven maple and the fact that the back panel is installed with the beveled edges on the inner side; it was common practice to have the bevels on the outside of the back so that the neater flat surface of the panel(s) is visible when the chest is opened.[2]

The turnings on the legs represent a distinct version of the seventeenth-century formula of an inverted vase over a short cylinder or barrel form, a pattern that occurs with some frequency and in various interpretations on furniture that has been associated with the towns on the southern shore of Massachusetts Bay. What primarily sets the turnings on this and the related chests apart is the nature of the columnar element at the base: it is not cylindrical but tapers, echoing the lines of the vase (see also cat. no. 47).[3] This same feature characterizes the arm supports on a joined chair that descended in the Lincoln family of Hingham.[4] A box at Historic New England with lunette carving similar to that on these chests and a history in the Briggs family of Scituate further points to the probable origin of these pieces in the coastal area immediately south of Boston.[5] The carving on the box is somewhat more competent than that on the drawers of the chests, in that the lobes of the leaf decoration are more evenly disposed and precisely defined. The execution on the drawers appears cruder, as the tips of the foliage have irregular,

106

often blunted shapes. While on the majority of the drawers the three lunettes are quite evenly spaced, here they were not carefully laid out, and in the execution, which started at the right, the one at the left had to be compressed to fit the remaining space. On the box, as on nearly all the chests, the field of the carving follows the contours of the foliage at the top and is indicated at the sides and bottom by only a line—just the scribed line defining the perimeter or that line gone over with a V-shaped gouge, which in this case the craftsman had obvious difficulty in controlling.

Lunettes enclosing leaf decoration appear to have been particularly favored in County Dorset, but they were a common motif throughout England, and such designs occur on furniture from various parts of New England (see cat. nos. 71, 86, for instance).[6] The use of heavy applied moldings on the front rails may indicate the influence of the style of case furniture that dominated the coastal towns of Plymouth County, Massachusetts, and is represented in this catalogue by two cupboards (nos. 114, 115). As for the profile of the moldings, there is just a very general similarity between the overall contours of the top one, which serves as an architrave, and of the bottom one, which functions as a base molding, and any in that shop tradition. The molding above the drawer with a cyma reversa on either side of a fascia clearly relates to a different school of joinery; it is akin to the symmetrical moldings on cat. nos. 98 and 99, attributed to Boston or vicinity. Although the exact purpose of the type of chest seen here is not clear and what it was called is not entirely certain, it seems to have been a specialized form, the production of which was generally limited to Boston and coastal towns north and south of that metropolitan center (see the entry for cat. no. 105).

CONSTRUCTION

The mortise-and-tenon joints of the four top rails, of the front muntin, and of the lower rear rail to the right stile are secured with two pins, all others with one. The stiles are square and one with the turned legs and feet. The top rotates on wooden pintles that are fixed in the rear stiles and go through the cleats; the upper back edge of the rear stiles and top rail has been rounded. The upper back consists of a single panel that is beveled on the inner side. A board is nailed to the back of the stiles at drawer level. The chest compartment bottom is formed of butted transverse boards beveled to fit into a groove in the front rail and nailed to a rabbet at the bottom of the rear rail. There is a groove in the corresponding side rails, but it is not level with that in the front rail and thus not functional. On the drawer, the sides each fit against a rabbet on the front and are secured with nails set in shallow gouged holes, and the back is butted to the sides and nailed from the back. The bottom is formed of one longitudinal board nailed to a rabbet on the front and to the bottom of the other sides. The drawer rides on the bottom. The drawer runners are beveled at each end and nailed to the stiles and the guides above them are let into the stiles and nailed. The moldings applied to the front rails are attached with rosehead nails. They and those around the front panels all consist of a fascia and the same cyma reversa, with the top rail molding having an overhanging ovolo above the fascia and the mid-molding a cyma on either side of the fascia. A channel molding with a narrow central band and a small cyma reversa at either side is worked on all the side rails and all four stretchers. The edges around the side panels are all chamfered. There is evidence of riving on the back of the maple drawer front and bottom front rail as well as on the oak panels. The left front leg has large flat areas on the turning and was probably not well centered on the lathe.

CONDITION

Most of the joints have separated somewhat. The top, split and with losses at the front, may be a reused board, and the cleats and pintles are new. The chest compartment bottom consists of an original wide board that is split and heavily renailed at the back and two newer narrower boards. The lower back board (spruce) is a replacement. On the drawer, the upper edges have been gnawed, the nails securing the sides to the front have been replaced, and the bottom is split and has missing and added nails; remnants of tacked-on fabric and numerous tacks remain on the interior. The left drawer runner is probably replaced. Nail holes on the upper surface of the stretchers suggest the piece once had a bottom shelf. Modern metal gliders have been added under the feet. The left molding on the left front panel is definitely replaced. The applied bosses vary in character and age. Some are now attached with large modern nails, as are the panel moldings and the upper applied turning on the right stile. In each cleat there is a bored hole that goes through the top side rail for the insertion of a rod to lock the top; a similar hole in each lower side panel goes through the drawer guide and drawer side. Most of the surface is covered with a dark and blistered degraded finish that goes over red paint that was applied to the turnings and moldings as well as to the case and does not look old.

INSCRIPTIONS

Inscribed in pencil on the back of the top rear rail and in black crayon on the back of the rear panel and on the underside of the drawer bottom is "H 89" (all modern).

WOODS

Panels, moldings on front rails, RED OAK and WHITE OAK; front stiles, top front rail, all side and rear rails, front and side stretchers, right drawer runner, ASH; rear stiles, medial and bottom front rails, muntin, rear stretcher, front and sides of drawer, SOFT MAPLE; top, wide board of chest compartment bottom, drawer back and bottom, drawer guides, EASTERN WHITE PINE; lower applied turning on left stile, POPLAR (*Populus* sp.); panel moldings, ATLANTIC WHITE CEDAR.

DIMENSIONS

OH. 34⅛ (86.7); OW. (top) 28¼ (71.8); CW. 24⅞ (63.2); OD. (at top molding) 16¾ (42.5); CD. 15⅞ (40.3).

REFERENCES

Nutting 1921, p. 89 (erroneously identified as owned by Miss C. M. Traver, New York City); Nutting 1924, no. 117 (owned by Mrs. J. Insley Blair); Nutting 1928–33, no. 208 (formerly owned by B. A. Behrend); Andrus 1951, p. 246; Andrus 1952, p. 166; M. B. Davidson 1967, no. 20; Fales 1972, no. 5; Chinnery 1979, fig. 3:416.

PROVENANCE

Ex coll.: B. A. Behrend, Brookline, Massachusetts; Mrs. J. Insley Blair, Tuxedo Park, New York.

According to Mrs. Blair's notes (ADA files), she purchased the piece from Behrend in 1923 and "Behrend bought it from Miss Fraser.... If alive, Miss Fraser would know its history." Miss Fraser was probably Boston decorator Esther Stevens Fraser (later Brazer), an author and also a dealer.[7] The table was on loan from Mrs. Blair to the MMA from 1939 to 1949, when it became a gift.

Gift of Mrs. J. Insley Blair, 1949 (49.155.2)

1. The other examples are: one each at Historic Deerfield (Fales 1976, no. 350) and the Philadelphia Museum of Art (Nutting 1921, p. 88); two at the Winterthur Museum (B. Ward 1986, no. 4; Cullity 1994, no. 150); and one formerly at the MMA (MMA 1930, fig. 4). For the others, see Lockwood 1913, fig. 234; and Keyes 1936, figs. 2a, 2b. A variant example with ball-turned stretchers and a drawer (dovetailed) with applied ornament is at the Shelburne Museum, Shelburne, Vermont (Winchester 1957, p. 442). Wallace Nutting reproduced this type of chest (Nutting 1930 [1977 ed.], p. 56, no. 920; he also advertised his reproduction in *Antiques* 9 [January 1926], p. 64).
2. Riven maple occurs on this and at least two other chests in the group: one at Historic Deerfield (Fales 1976, no. 350) and one at the Winterthur Museum (Cullity 1994, no. 150).
3. A frame with drawer (supporting a box) at the Museum of Fine Arts, Boston (Randall 1965, no. 5), and one in a private collection also have similar turnings, as does a small table with drawer advertised by Lillian Blankley Cogan in *Antiques* 100 (November 1971), p. 696.
4. St. George 1979b, no. 74.
5. Jobe and Kaye 1984, no. 2. A chest in *Important Americana: The Collection of the Late Dr. and Mrs. James W. Marvin*, auction cat., Sotheby Parke Bernet, New York City, 30 September–1 October 1978, lot 304, has similarly carved lunettes on the top rail but no history; its other carved motifs are, however, generally related to those on a chest probably made in Plymouth, Massachusetts (St. George 1979b, no. 41).
6. Wells-Cole 1976b.
7. According to Benno M. Forman (letter of 8 November 1976 to the present writer), the Henry F. du Pont correspondence at the Winterthur Museum confirms that E. S. Fraser (later Brazer) was a dealer.

107.

Chest-on-frame

Connecticut, Guilford-Saybrook area, 1705–25

The painted ornament on the upper front of this chest, with its crowned rose, thistle, and fleur-de-lis, is the most distinctive of the designs on the Guilford-Saybrook group of furniture (see the entry for cat. no. 101). The pattern has a bold graphic quality that retains its appeal even when losses and changes have occurred to the paint, as they have on the present example. Its source is surely a printer's ornament; exactly the same motif appears as a headpiece in seventeenth-century books published in England.[1] Designs derived from this device appear on a majority of the Guilford-Saybrook pieces mentioned in the entry for cat. no. 101 and are exclusive to this group. They vary in their interpretation of the pattern, which seems to indicate that it was considered just a decorative scheme and that its original allusion to the union of England (Tudor rose) and Scotland (thistle) under James I in 1603 and to earlier claims of the crown in France (fleur-de-lis) had been lost. Only on this piece and a joined chest with drawer at the Henry Ford Museum does the painted decoration closely follow the printed design, with a thistle on the right, rose on the left, and large leaves flanking the central crown (and they are, incidentally, the only ones that have initials). Other versions of this pattern are totally symmetrical, in accord with all the other floral compositions of this school of painting. In four instances roses take the place of the large leaves and the vines each terminate in a thistle. On three other chests the design lacks the fleur-de-lis and the lateral crowns, and the vines bearing a pair of roses and thistles each spring from a central crown placed on what looks like a baluster support. On several objects, just roses or thistles are combined with other floral elements.[2] Such variations suggest more than one hand at work and/or evolution over time.

Overall, the painting on this chest is not as well executed as that on cat. no. 101, making due allowance for its condition. The thick vines of the main motif have uneven edges, for example, and the veining of the leaves at center top is quite heavy-handed. The vines on the lower drawer, which issue from a central mound from which rises a carnation, as on the drawer of cat. no. 100, show little variety in their floral elements. The same two flower forms are repeated and have a consistent color scheme: a tripartite motif always with a solid red center petal flanked by solid green ones; and tufts of somewhat stiff red, green, and white filaments. All together, however, the three superimposed floral patterns, playing out their different rhythms as they flow out from the central axis, make for a lively facade. The sides of this piece, like those of

five other chests, are decorated with birds. Each is a somewhat different version of a generic fowl with fanciful stylized plumage, which on both birds on this chest features a speckled body and green tail feathers veined in red that resemble elongated leaves. The flowers and birds on the Guilford-Saybrook pieces and the concept of a spray or vine emerging from a vase or a mound come out of a traditional vocabulary that was popular in numerous mediums throughout the 1600s and indebted to printed ornament designs that were in wide circulation from the Renaissance on and in which flowers and birds abounded. Most likely many of the design elements on these chests were just part of the painter's learned vocabulary, which he might enlarge by selecting a compositional scheme or particular flowers or other motifs from printed or other sources to adapt and incorporate into his repertoire. The copying of a total pattern as on the upper front of this chest was probably exceptional.[3]

The painted decoration on the top of this chest—a border, now only partly visible, that runs around the perimeter and in addition describes a quarter circle inside each corner—has a quite different, up-to-date derivation. The border, which consists of white transverse dashes between red lines, recalls the cross-banding found on inlaid English furniture of the late 1600s.[4] That the Guilford-Saybrook furniture was influenced by contemporary high-style case pieces and aspired to fashionability is made patently clear by the fact that a high chest of drawers (at the Winterthur Museum) is part of this group.[5] Such influence is evident not only in the painted border but also in the form of the present piece, which, like a high chest, is made in two sections, has a broad molding at the juncture of the two cases, and shaped flat stretchers joining the legs. No other American chest of precisely this form is known. It could have been devised locally as an updating of the one-piece joined chest-on-frame (cat. nos. 105, 106); or, maybe more likely, the scheme of a chest with drawer on a separate early Baroque base with drawer was introduced from abroad, from Britain or perhaps with Charles Guillam from the Channel Islands (see the entry for cat. no. 101).[6] The use of a shaped stretcher at the back is unusual and so is the form of the turnings on the legs. The legs follow the general William and Mary–style formula of opposed balusters centered on a ring, but here the balusters are straight-sided and the thinner rather than the thicker end faces the center. Possibly the pattern came from outside the Anglo-American tradition.[7] However, the upper portion down through the center ring resembles the lower half of the legs on the Winterthur Museum high chest, and it may be that the legs on cat. no. 107 represent such a profile transposed to the standard bilateral table-leg scheme of the period—as another allusion, one might speculate, to fashionable urban furniture.

PAINTED DECORATION

The ground is a thin layer of black—probably a carbon black—as on cat. no. 101, and the designs are similarly laid out in a thick coat of lead white, over which most of the color detailing—in vermilion and a copper green—is applied. Painted directly on the ground in red and green are the dots around the crowns on the upper front and the fine lines of the wispy elements on the lower drawer, and in red, the lines that demarcate the border on the top. In 1980 the painted surfaces were cleaned at the MMA, and some of the discolored coatings that obscured the designs were removed (as was overpainting that concealed the large leaves flanking the central crown and the mound on the left side), but one or more layers of yellowed varnish of varying thickness still coat most of the surface. That varnish seems to be responsible for the yellow and brown-yellow seen over most of the white areas (no pigment could be identified in samples taken from two of those areas). The green on the upper front, except for that of the pair of large leaves, now looks nearly black. Losses, both to the red and green detailing and to the white underpaint, also have altered the appearance of the decoration and diminished its impact—most noticeably on the upper drawer, where the carnation in the center is almost totally devoid of color and the two large inner leaves, once well-defined green shapes with red veins that counterbalanced the outer red leaves with green veins, are now mostly indistinct. On the lid, most of the border has worn off.

CONSTRUCTION

The piece was built in two sections: a chest with a drawer and a frame with a drawer, kept aligned by two dowels that joined the backs of the two units. On the upper case, the front of the chest compartment, the rail below the drawer, and the back are rabbeted to accept the sides and nailed to the sides with large T-headed nails. The one-board, cleated top is attached with two snipebill hinges. The storage compartment bottom and the case bottom are let into grooves in the sides; at the front they fit against a rabbet at the bottom of the front board and at the top of the rail below the drawer, respectively, and each is secured with one nail driven from the front. The drawer slides on the bottom of its sides on the case bottom. The ends of the drawer front are rabbeted and overlap the case sides. The drawer sides are joined to the front and back with a single dovetail reinforced with a T-headed nail. The bottom is beveled to fit into a groove in the front and sides and nailed to the back. It is formed of two longitudinal boards joined by a half lap, whereas all other components of the upper case are single boards. The molding below the drawer is attached to the base of the upper case and consists of a large cyma recta preceded by a small ovolo and followed by an outer ovolo that is a separate piece. On the frame, the rails are joined to the stiles, which are one with the turned legs, with large (7/16 in. wide) mortise-and-tenon joints secured with two pins on the sides and back and one pin on the front. The drawer is side-hung. It is dovetailed like the upper drawer (but the nails are roseheads) and the bottom is similar, except that its two boards are joined with a spline. The runners are let into the stiles and nailed in place. The stretchers, each one a solid piece, come together at the corners in a half lap. A round tenon at the bottom of each leg passes through the stretcher joint and into the foot, which is drilled through

to the bottom. The top turning of the feet has been trimmed where it protruded beyond the stretchers. The inner surface of the rails has been left entirely rough.

CONDITION

On the upper case, the top and its cleats and hinges are original. The right cleat has some added nails and the back, replaced nails. A small slat nailed across the inside of the back just below the chest compartment bottom, which has a large gap at the back, is probably a later addition. Repairs to the drawer include adding a new strip at the bottom of each side and a patch on the upper edge of the right side, gluing the joint of the bottom boards, and renailing the bottom to the back. At one point the drawer was nailed shut with a nail driven through the right side of the case into the drawer side. The molding at the base of the upper case has been reattached; the outer section is new (pine). On the frame, the dowels in the back rail that kept the upper case in place have been broken off. The applied half-round molding on the right side is new. The front stretcher is replaced, but the other three, all similar, are old and may be original; the feet show reasonable wear. The rear dovetails of the drawer each have an added nail; the spline in the drawer bottom is replaced and the bottom has been renailed. The left drawer runner has been repaired. The pulls on both drawers are replacements. (See also *Painted decoration*.)

INSCRIPTIONS

The initials "HW" (the "W" partly effaced) of an unidentified first owner are painted on the upper front. On the exterior of each side of the lower drawer is a wavy, diagonal, scratched line that is a remnant of an original joiner's mark similar to that on the drawer of cat. no. 102. On the upper drawer there are a large and a smaller X scratched on the inner side of the left side and on the outer side of the right side (probably restorer's marks). A printed paper label glued to the inside of the back reads: "Included in the collection of Antique Furni- / ture transferred to Mr. H. E. Bolles, and Mr. / Geo. S. Palmer." The top of the label is inscribed in ink (script) "A Box and Stand, / with painted decoration," and the bottom is signed "Walter Hosmer." Large, modern, undecipherable markings in chalk are inside the lid and on the underside of the upper case bottom.

WOODS

Top, front, sides, back, and rail below drawer of upper case, rails, stretchers, and applied molding on lower case, both drawers, YELLOW POPLAR; bottom of chest compartment, bottom of upper case, CHESTNUT; legs, feet, BIRCH; cleats, ASH; drawer runners, OAK; applied molding at base of upper case, ATLANTIC WHITE CEDAR.

DIMENSIONS

OH. 36¾ (93.4); OW. (moldings) 30¼ (76.8); upper CW. 26⅞ (68.3); lower CW. 29 (73.7); OD. (lower molding) 19½ (49.5); upper CD. 17⅜ (44.1); lower CD. 19 (48.3).

EXHIBITION

"Connecticut Furniture: Seventeenth and Eighteenth Centuries," Wadsworth Atheneum, 3 November–17 December 1967.

REFERENCES

Lockwood 1913, fig. 237; Nutting 1928–33, no. 217; Kettell 1929, pl. 44; MMA 1930, fig. 5; Margon 1954, no. 149; Schwartz 1956, p. 342; Kirk 1967 (exh. cat.), no. 36; Margon 1971, pp. 128–29 (includes measured drawings); Fales 1972, no. 26; Hornung 1972, no. 916; Safford 1998, figs. 5, 6 (drawing of border on top), and pp. 199–202.

PROVENANCE

Ex coll.: Walter Hosmer, Hartford, Connecticut; H. Eugene Bolles, Boston.

Bolles and his cousin George S. Palmer, of New London, Connecticut, purchased Hosmer's collection in 1894.

Gift of Mrs. Russell Sage, 1909 (10.125.15)

1. Fales 1972, no. 23 and p. 24; Kirk 1982, fig. 166 and p. 74.
2. For the Henry Ford Museum chest, see Fales 1972, no. 28. For representative variations on this pattern, see Fales 1972, nos. 29, 27, 31.
3. Any pattern—printed, such as headpieces (see the citations in n. 1 above and Beck 1992, pp. 91, 123, for example), or on an actual object—could provide design ideas. But similarities between painted motifs on furniture and those in needlework suggest that English and European pattern books for embroiderers (such as Shorleyker 1632; see Beck 1992, p. 33, and King and Levey 1993, pls. 61, 62), or individual sheets of motifs, or perhaps textiles themselves, were likely sources.

4. A diagram of the border is in Safford 1998, fig. 6. A similar border occurs on the sides of a board chest in the Guilford-Saybrook group (Fales 1972, no. 27). On drawers of a related high chest in the Winterthur Museum, chests of drawers, and joined chests with drawer, a border with a scroll motif alludes to the banding on the drawers of American as well as English veneered furniture (Fales 1972, nos. 29, 22, 28).
5. Fales 1972, no. 29.
6. A Welsh chest-on-frame has the same general form (R. Edwards 1964, p. 205, fig. 25), indicating that similar objects were being made on the more vernacular level in Britain. Two painted Channel Islands pieces that have been published also consist of a chest with drawer on a frame with drawer but are of a later date; the frames have cabriole legs (Trent 1994, figs. 4–7 [dated 1754]; *The 48th Annual Winter Antiques Show* [New York, 2002], pp. 100–101 [Robert Young Antiques advertisement]). They may be late expressions of an earlier Channel Islands tradition, for chests with the same general arrangement but earlier-style bases can be found in Normandy, France (Le Clerc 1924, pl. 27; Lavallée 1990, fig. 21).
7. Similar, but single, straight-sided balusters are on a Norman chest-on-frame (Le Clerc 1924, pl. 27).

Chests of Drawers

The most advanced form of seventeenth-century-style case furniture made in America was the chest of drawers—also called a case of drawers, the two terms apparently interchangeable at the time. This fashionable form was, up to the late 1600s, generally found only in more affluent homes, where it was the most up-to-date case piece in the household. Records document the presence of a few chests of drawers in eastern Massachusetts already in the 1640s. The early examples recorded were in all likelihood English and part of the household furnishings brought by wealthy immigrants, although by the 1640s there were craftsmen in Boston capable of producing this furniture form.

The colonial joined chest of drawers was derived from the earliest English type, which was formulated in London in the early decades of the seventeenth century and introduced to Boston by London-trained joiners, who were present there by 1640. The English prototypes of that time were made in two sections, the upper containing a shallow drawer above a very deep one, and the lower one, three drawers hidden behind doors. They had architectural facades that were richly ornamented with mitered moldings and applied turnings and included exotic woods and often also bone or ivory inlay. One Boston chest of drawers that closely follows this format is known.[1] Carefully crafted and incorporating exotic woods (but no inlay), that sophisticated piece represents a high point in seventeenth-century American joinery. A lower, one-case version of the chest of drawers with doors, which includes geometric inlay, has also survived.[2] It represents a different school of English urban craftsmanship and was made in the New Haven, Connecticut, area.

The other known American seventeenth-century-style chests of drawers were built without doors, and all but one, from Philadelphia,[3] originated in eastern Massachusetts, principally in the Boston area, the style and furniture-making center of New England. One Boston chest without doors adheres to the five-drawer format and incorporates some exotic woods.[4] The type favored in Boston by about 1660-70 was a shorter, four-drawer model of squarish proportions. Like the five-drawer version, it was designed in two sections (if not structurally, then visually) and featured a deep second drawer, its front divided into two simulated panels by beveled moldings; the woods of choice were walnut and cedar. More than a dozen Boston chests of this format, which also has English antecedents and of which one Philadelphia example

is known (see above), have survived, but none is in the collection. The Museum's two chests of drawers in the London-derived Boston style are part of a larger group in a variant design that evolved in the late 1600s. This type has a symmetrical drawer arrangement—two shallow drawers between two deep ones—and was made of oak and pine and meant to be painted. Most often, as on one chest in the collection, the original decorative scheme has been lost (cat. no. 111). The other chest is a prime exception in that it retains its elaborate painted ornament, which includes graining and floral motifs that appear to take their cue from imported veneered and inlaid furniture (cat. no. 110).

The fashion for chests of drawers spread from Boston to other port towns in eastern Massachusetts. A considerable number of joined oak examples were made during the last quarter of the seventeenth century in Essex County, where the form was interpreted according to the local decorative idioms. Two are in the collection, and they exhibit the style that prevailed in Salem (cat. nos. 108, 109). Each of the chests has four drawers graduated in a somewhat different sequence, but on both, the geometric patterns of applied mitered moldings typically alternate between a two-panel and a three-panel scheme and the ornament includes applied columnar turnings. The facades, basically architectural in concept, are definitely busier than those of the more sober and monumental Boston chests; and their design is stylistically earlier than that of the Museum's late Boston-style examples.

Although joined chests of drawers began to be supplanted in fashionable circles during the 1690s by the high chest of drawers of dovetailed board construction and in the William and Mary style, they continued to be made as a conservative alternative during the early decades of the eighteenth century. Also, as the use of chests of drawers—low or high—became more widespread after 1700, board versions constructed of pine or other inexpensive woods and designed to be painted came to be made. The last chest of drawers in this chapter, from the Windsor, Connecticut, area, is such a piece (cat. no. 112); it alludes to the high chest in the vertical emphasis of its five-tier format and to japanned work in its painted decoration.

1. G. W. R. Ward 1988, no. 51 (Yale University Art Gallery).
2. Fairbanks and Trent 1982, no. 482 (Museum of Fine Arts, Boston).
3. Lindsey 1999, no. 24 (Philadelphia Museum of Art).
4. Fairbanks and Trent 1982, no. 493 (Museum of Fine Arts, Boston).

108.

Chest of drawers

Salem, Massachusetts, 1675–1700
Attributed to the Symonds shop tradition

Related to a small cabinet in the collection (cat. no. 79) in its octagonal panel, in the character of its applied turnings and top molding, and in the use of corbels, this is one of some eleven chests of drawers with applied decoration in a style that is attributed to the Symonds shop tradition (see the entry for cat. no. 79) and found favor in Salem, Massachusetts, and its surrounding towns during the last quarter of the seventeenth century. The chests, each with four tiers of drawers and usually two short drawers in the top tier, all differ to a greater or lesser degree in the individual elements of their decorative scheme and in the height of the drawers, suggesting that they represent a regional style rather than the product of a single shop. This is one of six examples on which the four tiers are graduated sequentially with the deepest at the bottom (see cat. no. 109 for the alternate arrangement).[1] In this case, there is but little difference in height between the second and third drawer, but the two are not interchangeable. All but one of the chests share the same overall design concept, in that the tiers alternate, starting from the top, between two and three decorative panels and in that the designs on the two-panel tiers are more open and provide a counterpoint to the others. Here, as on more than half of the chests, the top and the third drawer are in the same pattern.

The front of this chest presents a vivid example of the type of complexity and artifice that informs the applied-ornament style of the Symonds shop tradition. Within an architectural framework there is an intricate play of geometric shapes created by applied mitered moldings that oppose and echo one another and achieve an equilibrium. Whereas on the bottom drawer the outer panels are wider than the center one and show a small rectangle in each corner that is void, on the second drawer the relative size of the panels is reversed and the outer panels have corners filled with plaques. The panels with void corners on the bottom drawer form the base of a triangular scheme that has at its peak the middle panel of the second drawer, which contains four rectangles, each centered by a small boss, and which is a counterpoise to the octagonal panel in the bottom drawer. The latter originally displayed a sunburst of eight applied triangular rays and is at the apex of an inverted triangle formed by the panels with filled corners.

The applied half columns on the chests of drawers, like those on the small MMA Symonds cabinet and the three related examples in other collections (see the entry for cat. no. 79), were influenced by Boston models. However, on cat. no. 108 and some of the other Symonds furniture, they depart from those prototypes in that they have additional rings and reels above and below the shaft of the column (fig. 69), the number here varying according to the requisite height of the turning. A few of the Symonds pieces, namely, three chests with drawer and two cupboards, bear turnings in a different pattern—one that features a tight sequence of urns, rings, and reels.[2] This type of turning, which was probably in the joinery tradition imparted by the immigrant progenitor of this school, is the likely source of the multiple rings that sometimes appear, as they do here, on the Symonds Boston-style columnar turnings.

The molding under the top—replaced, but in a design the writer believes to be original to the piece (see *Condition*)—is similar in its profile and sawn dentils to that on the MMA's cabinet and the other small Symonds cabinets mentioned above, but it shows additional elaboration. The cyma reversa molding at the bottom is adorned with gouge work and the fascia, somewhat wider than on cat. no. 79, is ornamented with a chevron pattern made with a small, round punch and with a small star or flower motif impressed with a stamp. Similar star or flower decoration is evident on the ground of the carving of all four cabinets, and on the cabinet dated 1676 at the Winterthur Museum it was applied to the carved elements as well. The molding under the top of a chest at the Ipswich Museum, Ipswich, Suffolk, England, that contains one drawer above three drawers behind doors and has applied geometric ornament appears to be generically similar. It has convex sawn dentils above a flat band with what looks like a chevron design. If the chest originated in the Ipswich area, it suggests that this kind of molding was a regional type in East Anglia and not restricted to the design tradition of a particular shop.[3]

CONSTRUCTION

The case has four panels on each side and two large horizontal panels in the back. It contains two short above three long drawers, which from the top down measure $5\frac{1}{4}$, $7\frac{1}{8}$, $7\frac{3}{8}$, and $8\frac{5}{8}$ inches in height. The mortise-and-tenon joints of the front rails and drawer dividers are single-pinned; all others, including those of the muntin between the short drawers, are double-pinned. The bottom of the case is formed of several transverse boards butted together and nailed to a rabbet on the bottom of the front and rear rails. The drawer fronts are rabbeted to receive the sides, and the sides to accept the backs, and each joint is secured with two to four countersunk rosehead nails. On the two short drawers the bottom (longitudinal) is beveled to fit into a groove in the front and is nailed to the other sides (fig. 108). On the long drawers the bottom fits against a rabbet in the front and is nailed to all four sides. The bottom of the top long drawer consists of three

108. See also figs. 69, 108.

transverse boards joined with a half lap, that of the two lower drawers of a single longitudinal board that retains some bark on either side. The drawers are side-hung. The runners at the sides of the case are slotted into the stiles. A wide center runner serves both short drawers; it is let into a groove in the muntin at the front and protrudes at the back through a loose-fitting opening in the upper panel. The top front molding has a prominent semicircular profile followed by a fascia and a cyma reversa, and the beak molding between the middle drawers, a fillet, ovolo, cavetto, and fillet. Between the other drawers is a half-round molding and at the base a large cavetto. The moldings applied to the drawer fronts consist of an ovolo, fillet, and cavetto.

On the case sides, all the framing members are decorated with a channel molding that has an ovolo at either side, and the edges around the panels are finished with a cyma reversa. The edges of the rear rails are chamfered on both the inner and the outer side. The end-grain edges of the drawer linings have a small chamfer. The drawer fronts are thick, and they and some of the sides are not fully squared on the interior.

CONDITION
A 1909 photograph of the chest shows it as it was acquired, with a top molding and corbels (inverted) similar to those now on the piece

(see *References*). Probably not long thereafter, that molding was replaced with one with serrated ornament similar to a molding on a cupboard in the collection (cat. no. 115), and the corbels were replaced with pairs of half columns. In 1993 these alterations were reversed by replicating the earlier top molding (in cedar) and the corbels (in walnut).[4] Most likely at the time of the first alterations, the cavetto base molding that according to the 1909 photograph had survived on the front was discarded and a new molding (oak) was applied to the front and sides, bail handles were removed and drop pulls reinstalled, and the left end of the mid-molding was patched. The top (pine), the rear feet (walnut), and probably the front feet (maple) are replacements. The runners for the long drawers are new (walnut) and the grooves in the sides of those drawers have been widened. The drawer bottoms have some missing, replaced, and added nails. The bottom of the right top drawer has a narrow strip added at the back. Although the bottoms vary in their construction, they all appear to be original. A thin strip nailed across the top of the lower back panel and a patch at the right edge cover losses. There are missing and added nails in the case bottom. A good half of the applied turnings and at least one of the decorative plaques are replacements. The moldings between the drawers (walnut) do not look original and neither do many of those on the drawer fronts. The turnings, plaques, and drawer moldings are all attached with modern wire nails. The chest has been aggressively stripped. The surface has been heavily waxed and perhaps also oiled. There are some remains of black paint on the applied turnings, moldings on the case sides, and front feet, and a few traces of red on the plaques and drawer moldings. A dark stain has been applied to the outside of the back and inside of the bottom.

INSCRIPTIONS

A compass-drawn design of two circles within an ellipse is scribed on the outside of the upper back panel. MMA Hudson-Fulton exhibition identification numbers are inscribed in orange crayon on the inside of the bottom of the top left drawer (H. F. 40.20) and in white on the underside of the case bottom (471). Inscribed in pencil on the underside of the top right drawer is "Dec. 20th 1620" (modern).

WOODS

All framing members, side panels, drawer fronts and sides, plaques behind turnings on drawers, original drawer runners, RED OAK; back panels, case bottom, drawer bottoms and backs, EASTERN WHITE PINE; geometric plaques on drawers, BLACK WALNUT; old moldings on drawers, ATLANTIC WHITE CEDAR; turnings on middle full drawer, MAPLE.

DIMENSIONS

OH. 42⅞ (108.9); OW. (top) 46¼ (117.5); CW. 43¾ (111.1); OD. (at corbels) 21⅛ (53.7); CD. 19¾ (50.2).

EXHIBITIONS

"Hudson-Fulton Exhibition," MMA, 20 September–30 November 1909; "The Art of Joinery: Seventeenth-Century Case Furniture in the American Wing," MMA, 18 October 1972–18 March 1973.

REFERENCES

Hudson-Fulton Celebration 1909 (exh. cat.), no. 114; Kent 1910, p. 9; Lockwood 1913, fig. 49; Halsey and Cornelius 1924 (and 1925, 1926, 1928, 1932), fig. 2 (1938, 1942, fig. 17); MMA 1930, fig. 3; E. G. Miller 1937, no. 607; I. P. Lyon 1938d, fig. 58; Hornung 1972, no. 901 (the preceding references show the chest as acquired; this and the following show early MMA alterations); Safford 1972 (exh. cat.), no. 11 and fig. 3; Chinnery 1979, fig. 3:414.

PROVENANCE

Ex coll.: H. Eugene Bolles, Boston.

Gift of Mrs. Russell Sage, 1909 (10.125.686)

1. Related to cat. no. 108 in their drawer arrangement are chests at Historic New England (Trent 1989, no. 5); the Massachusetts Historical Society, Boston (I. P. Lyon 1938d, fig. 59); the Museum of Fine Arts, Boston (Randall 1965, no. 25); the Wadsworth Atheneum (Nutting 1928–33, no. 221; I. P. Lyon 1938d, fig. 57); and the Yale University Art Gallery (G. W. R. Ward 1988, no. 53). For the other chests of drawers, see cat. no. 109.
2. The chests with drawer are: one at the Museum of Fine Arts, Boston (Fairbanks and Trent 1982, no. 484); and two at the Winterthur Museum (I. P. Lyon 1938c, fig. 49; Trent 1989, no. 1). The cupboards are: one at the Nelson-Atkins Museum of Art, Kansas City, Missouri (I. P. Lyon 1938d, fig. 55); and one at the Peabody Essex Museum (I. P. Lyon 1938d, fig. 54; Trent 1989, no. 4).
3. Filbee 1977, p. 99. The present writer did not succeed in obtaining any information on this chest.
4. The contours and ornamentation of the molding were based on the 1909 photograph and the profile of the corbels on that photograph and on the corbels on a chest at Historic New England (see n. 1 above). When the modern elements were removed there was no evidence on the surface of the rails and stiles to suggest that the molding in the 1909 photo was not the first. Another Symonds-school chest of drawers (private collection; I. P. Lyon 1938d, fig. 56) has an original molding that is similar except that the fascia is not ornamented (conversation with Alan Miller, 9 March 2000).

109

109.

Chest of drawers

Salem, Massachusetts, 1675–1700
Attributed to the Symonds shop tradition

Like cat. no. 108, this piece belongs to a group of some eleven chests of drawers attributed to the Symonds shop tradition (see the entry for cat. no. 79), but it differs in several respects from the subject of the previous entry. The drawers on this and four other chests are not graduated progressively. Instead, the top tier, which here exceptionally contains one long rather than two short drawers, and the third tier are shallower than the second and bottom tier, and within each pair the lower tier is typically deeper than the upper.[1] Whatever the drawer-height formula, the alternation between two and three simulated

panels on the drawer fronts remains the same, and the decoration on the bipartite drawers either takes the form of the pattern on cat. no. 108 or consists of a molding only around the perimeter of each panel, as on the present chest. The type of molding invariably used in the latter scheme—one beveled on the outer portion and with a complex profile on the inner edge—recalls those that form the strongly protruding designs on Boston chests of drawers, which appear to have influenced the makers of the Salem-style chests. On this example, the moldings project but little, for the bevel is

267

narrow and not, as is normally the case, wider than the inner profile. The bold, rather weighty effect these moldings usually achieve is also diminished by the modern paint that now divides them visually into two bands, although they are one piece entirely of the same wood.

The modern paint and finish on the facade distort the more balanced and subtle play of colors and textures originally provided by the natural character of the different woods employed. On this and at least three of the other Symonds chests of drawers, the variously shaped panels formed by the applied moldings have thin facings of walnut or cedar.[2] Thus, probably in emulation of fashionable walnut Boston chests of drawers, little oak is visible on this facade—only that of the front stiles and of the vertical plaques on the drawers, against which the ebonized half columns are set. Here the outer panels of the second drawer and all those of the bottom drawer are faced with walnut and surrounded by cedar moldings and walnut plaques. The panels of the shallower drawers, which have walnut moldings, are faced with cedar. So is the octagonal panel, on which the alternation of woods begins at the center with a walnut medallion and ends with cedar corner plaques. Although the second and bottom drawers of this chest and cat. no. 108 have a similar arrangement of wider and narrower panels that contrast void corners with those filled with plaques and fall into opposing triangular schemes, here the design elements are not entirely in equipoise. The facade has a focal point—the octagonal panel, more densely ornamented than the others—which draws the eye upward and leads it to the pair of half columns, or perhaps originally a corbel, at center top.

In this last aspect of the design and in several of its other traits, this piece relates more closely to a Symonds cupboard at the Peabody Essex Museum that has three drawers in the lower case than to the other chests of drawers.[3] The chest's top molding has the same profile and simulated dentils along the bottom as that under the cupboard's middle shelf. There is also the possibility that the chest's turnings, which are all replaced, were originally in a pattern comprised of multiple reels and urns such as that seen on the cupboard. Structurally, the back of this chest contains three vertical oak panels separated by wide muntins like that of the lower case of the cupboard and in contrast to the other Symonds chests of drawers, which have two horizontal pine panels in the back. Other similarities are the use of just a single pin in the joints of the top side rails and the joiner's marks to guide the assembly of the frame. Finally, this piece differs from the other chests of drawers in that its drawers do not contain any pine but are made entirely of riven oak, like those of the cupboard and the Symonds chests with a drawer. This exclusive use of oak seems to indicate a shop preference and not in and of itself an earlier date of manufacture, for one of the chests with drawer is dated 1700–1701.[4]

CONSTRUCTION

The case contains four long drawers that from the top down measure 5, 7¾, 5½, and 8¼ inches in height, respectively. It has four panels on each side and three vertical panels in the back that have approximately the same width (7 in.) as the rear rails and muntins. The mortise-and-tenon joints of the front rails, drawer dividers, and top side rails are single-pinned, all others double-pinned. The case bottom consists of one longitudinal mill-sawn board nailed to a rabbet in the front rail and to the bottom of the other rails. On each drawer, the ends of the front and back are rabbeted to accept the sides; the sides are secured to the front, and the back to the sides with two to four slightly countersunk rosehead nails. The drawer bottoms are formed of five or six riven transverse boards that are joined with a tongue and groove and nailed to a rabbet in the front and the bottom of the other sides. The drawers are side-hung. The bottom drawer is supported by two runners on each side. The runners are let into the stiles. The top front molding consists of an ovolo, fascia, cyma reversa, fascia, and fillet, and the lower, broader fascia bears vertical and diagonal lines incised with strikes of a chisel. Between the middle drawers is a beak molding comprised of a fillet, cyma reversa, cavetto, and fillet. Between the other drawers is a half-round molding and at the base is a large cavetto. On the two shallow drawers, the bevel and inner molding are one piece. The profile of the latter—ovolo, cavetto, bead, fillet—is the same as that of the applied moldings on the deeper drawers, except for the cyma reversa of the small octagon. The drawer fronts have walnut or cedar facings the shape of the panels formed by the moldings; the facings do not extend to the edge of the drawer front. The channel and edge moldings on the case sides match those on cat. no. 108. The edges of the rails below the side panels and all edges around the exterior of the back panels are chamfered. Some of the timber used was not entirely squared, notably that of the thick drawer fronts. There is some defective wood, particularly in the drawer bottoms.

CONDITION

The case has been apart and the joint pins reset or replaced. The top is new (pine) and attached from below with screws set in holes drilled and gouged out in the side and rear rails. The front feet (birch) and the rear stiles below the bottom rails are also modern. The case bottom is probably a reused board (pine). On the drawers, the bottoms all have missing and added nails, the bottom of the second drawer has been off, and the back of the bottom drawer has been partly replaned; all have been varnished on the interior. All but one runner, which is replaced, have an added strip glued to the upper surface, and the grooves in the drawer sides have been widened accordingly. The drawer pulls, some of which have been reattached, appear to be original; there is no evidence of pulls of a larger size or other type. When the chest was acquired, the top drawer was flanked and centered by corbels anomalous in profile (see *References*). Probably quite early in the chest's MMA history, they were removed, pairs of half columns were put in their place, and a keyhole from a later lock was filled. All the other applied turnings (maple) are also modern. The top front molding is old and probably original. The moldings between the drawers show wear (the left end of the mid-molding is pieced) but their age is uncertain. The base molding (walnut) is a replacement. On the shallower drawers, three vertical segments of the moldings are not as worn as the others. On the deeper drawers, many of the moldings do not have strong wear, but most of those that form the octagons look old. The chest appears to have been stripped at some point. At present there is black paint on all the turned elements, the half-round front moldings and the base molding, the outer portion of the moldings on the shallower drawers, the applied geometric plaques, the channel moldings on the sides, and the molded edge of the top. Regardless of the wood, the inner portion of the moldings on the shallower drawers and all the moldings on the deeper drawers have a reddish tint probably imparted by a colored varnish that also appears to cover the cedar facings. A photograph of the chest as received (see *References*) shows no contrast between the outer and the inner portions of the moldings on the shallower drawers, for example, suggesting that the present look, in part or whole, was acquired, probably early on, at the MMA.

INSCRIPTIONS
On the interior of the chest are joiner's assembly marks, consisting of from one to three incised notches in three different sizes, that match up the tenoned and the mortised members of many of the frame's joints. Penciled arabic numbers and Xs and Os on the frame, side panels, and drawer runners date from modern restorations, as does the penciled number 3 on the underside of each bottom board of the second drawer and the line drawn across all the boards.

WOODS
All framing members, side and back panels, drawers, drawer runners, plaques behind turnings on drawers, RED OAK; some of the facings, moldings, and geometric plaques on drawer fronts, BLACK WALNUT; top front molding, probably molding on middle drawer divider, some of the facings, moldings, and geometric plaques on drawer fronts, EASTERN RED CEDAR.

DIMENSIONS
OH. 40 3/8 (102.6); OW. (top) 44 (111.8); CW. 42 (106.7); OD. (top) 21 7/8 (55.6); CD. 20 1/2 (52.1).

EXHIBITION
On loan to the MacPheadris-Warner House (now Warner House), Portsmouth, New Hampshire, from 1946 to 1972.

REFERENCES
Cornelius 1926, pl. XIII; Cescinsky and Hunter 1929, p. 43; Hjorth 1946, fig. 3 (this and the previous references show the chest as acquired); Wendell 1965, p. 715 (as exhibited in the Warner House).

PROVENANCE
Ex coll.: H. Eugene Bolles, Boston.

Gift of Mrs. Russell Sage, 1909 (10.125.38)

1. Of the four other chests, one is in the Museum of the City of New York (acc. no. 49.411) and another in a private collection (I. P. Lyon 1938d, fig. 56). One was formerly at Old Sturbridge Village, Sturbridge, Massachusetts. The fourth, offered in *American Furniture and Decorative Arts,* auction cat., Skinner, Bolton, Massachusetts, 10 June 2001, lot 248, differs in that the second drawer is somewhat deeper than the bottom one.
2. Walnut facings are on the drawer fronts of the chests at Historic New England (Trent 1989, no. 5), the Museum of Fine Arts, Boston (Randall 1965, no. 25), and the Yale University Art Gallery (uppermost drawers only; G. W. R. Ward 1988, no. 53). The chest in a private collection (I. P. Lyon 1938d, fig. 56) has both walnut and cedar facings (the present writer thanks Alan Miller for information on this piece).
3. The cupboard descended in the Putnam family and probably first belonged to Benjamin Putnam (1664–1715) of Salem Village, now Danvers (I. P. Lyon 1938d, fig. 54; Trent 1989, no. 4). The design on the drawers of a related but restored cupboard at the Nelson-Atkins Museum of Art, Kansas City, Missouri (I. P. Lyon 1938d, fig. 55), is questionable and offers no comparison, nor does that of an MMA cupboard (Lockwood 1913, fig. 170), the upper portion of which Benno M. Forman associated with the Putnam example (Forman 1968, pp. 139–41) but that has completely replaced drawers.
4. The 1700–1701 chest with drawer is at the Concord Museum, Concord, Massachusetts (Wood 1996, no. 3). Others are at the Peabody Essex Museum (Willoughby 2000, fig. 9); in *Sack Collection* 1981–92, vol. 10, p. 2544, and Willoughby 2000, fig. 5; and cited in the entry for cat. no. 108, n. 2.

110.

Chest of drawers

Eastern Massachusetts, probably Middlesex or Essex County, 1700–1720

Only a few of the many known chests of drawers of this format (see also cat. no. 111) retain original painted ornament, and on none other has decoration survived that is as elaborate as that on the present piece.[1] It features two types of graining and floral motifs and includes an unusual number of different pigments. Even after losses and changes due to deterioration and overpainting, the surface remains surprisingly colorful, and when the paint was all strong and fresh the effect must have been quite dazzling. On the deep drawers, the small moldings interposed between the broad beveled moldings with red graining on a yellow ground and the simulated panels with multicolor floral sprigs on a red ground were a bright orange (fig. 74). That same orange originally served as the ground of the vine motifs on the shallow drawers, where it contrasted with moldings that were a vivid green, as were the leaves in the floral sprigs. The center plaques on the shallow drawers were once the same yellow as the beveled moldings, and they visually connected the top and bottom drawer. The red of the side panels matches that of the graining and the ground of the deep drawers, but a brighter red and a different orange were used in the sprig and vine designs (see *Painted decoration*).[2]

The influence of William and Mary–style furniture and its English antecedents is evident on this joined chest, both in elements of its overall design (see the entry for cat. no. III) and in its painted decoration, which alludes not only to figured veneers, such as those on Boston high chests, but also to more elaborate inlaid ornament. The dark semicircles and light colored dashes painted on the side panels recall the round or oval figure of so-called oystershell veneer, with its differently colored heartwood and sapwood. This type of veneer is not known on American pieces but is found on English furniture of the last three decades of the seventeenth century, where it frequently occurs in conjunction with brightly colored floral marquetry set against a dark ground. The decoration on this chest of drawers, with sprigs on the deep drawers that emerge from a corner, as does some of the floral marquetry, was apparently meant to evoke such fashionable furniture both in its designs and in the tones of the background on the drawers.[3] Probate inventories indicate that inlaid furniture—no doubt imported—was to be found by the mid-1690s in eastern Massachusetts in stylishly furnished, affluent homes.[4]

The floral sprays on the deep drawers are delineated in a manner not encountered on other New England painted furniture; they are outlined in black, and the colors are applied within those lines. The painting of the undulating vines on the shallow drawers—a traditional motif—reflects more standard practice. The sprigs appear to have been taken from a line design—but interpreted freely, with the number of petals in the flowers varying and the three leaves at the base representing perhaps a misunderstood fleur-de-lis. The simplified flowers that terminate those sprays are generically related to those with a large center and a dark inner portion of the petals surrounded by a lighter band seen in drawings for japanning or on lining papers of the period, for instance.[5] However, the way they are rendered here, with the outer band filled with dots, is quite distinctive. The only flowers known that are worked in a generally similar manner are on cat. no. 122, a high chest painted with designs that emulate japanning. The painting on the two pieces does not otherwise bear comparison; that on the high chest is much more proficient. The decoration on this chest is executed at the basic level of a painter-stainer and may or may not be the work of the joiner who made the piece.[6]

A chest of drawers at the Winterthur Museum, of the same form, proportions, and construction as the present example, now shows no painted motifs on the drawer panels but retains graining. On the top, black graining on a tan ground surrounds a design that consists of a full circle in the middle, and half and quarter circles around the perimeter, each painted red and outlined by a black band. This type of geometric scheme, found in inlay on English furniture, resembles the painted pattern originally on the lower sides of cat. no. 141, a cupboard (see also the entry for cat. no. 107). The Winterthur chest and the present one are closely related

structurally and were perhaps made in the same shop. They both, exceptionally, have channel moldings on the side rails; their panel moldings and top and base moldings have like distinctive profiles; they include more oak than usual; and the drawers are similarly built and numbered.[7] The construction of the drawers on these two pieces—not dovetailed at the front, but nailed—would seem to preclude their having been made in Boston or Charlestown. But where in the broader environs of that metropolitan center they originated is uncertain. On the one hand, the extensive marking of joints for assembly, the numbering of the drawers, and the use of mill-sawn oak seen on the two chests have parallels in furniture of northern Essex County (see cat. no. 58); on the other hand, the painted design on the top of the Winterthur chest is similar in concept to that found on pieces from southern Middlesex County (see cat. no. 141).

PAINTED DECORATION
The pigments have been identified as follows: a carbon black (frame, moldings on frame and side panels, crescent design on side panels, outlines of sprigs, vine on second drawer, dots on third drawer); iron earth red (graining, ground of panels and of center plaques on deep drawers, ground of side panels, trial brushstrokes); yellow ocher (ground of graining, center plaques on shallow drawers, trial brushstrokes); red lead mixed with lead white (orange of moldings on deep drawers, ground of panels on shallow drawers); copper green (moldings on shallow drawers, leaves and buds of sprigs); lead white (vine on third drawer, white details on dark vine and on sprigs, light dashes on sides); vermilion (red on sprigs and on white vine); realgar (orange on sprigs and on the flowers of both vines). When the chest entered the collection, it was covered with heavily degraded varnish that obscured the designs. That varnish was almost entirely removed between 1994 and 1997 after investigation and sampling of the surface.[8] The paint has suffered losses and undergone changes, some of which markedly alter the original color scheme. The green has darkened to the point where it almost all looks black; on the moldings of the shallow drawers it was slightly retouched to indicate the original color. Red overpaint covers the center plaques (originally yellow) and the ground of the vines (originally orange) on both shallow drawers. Much of the orange on the moldings of the deep drawers has been lost. Smudged graining on the top drawer (which appears to predate Mrs. J. Insley Blair's acquisition of the chest) suggests an early attempt at cleaning or damage from stripping of the top. There are traces of red in the wood pores of the top, which is now devoid of paint.

CONSTRUCTION
The chest has one panel on each side and one in the back and contains four full drawers—two shallow ones in the middle, each a little more than half the height of the two others. The joints of the side and back rails, which are deep, are secured with two pins, the others with one. Each panel is a single board; the fielded side panels are beveled on both the outer and the inner side; the back one is plain and beveled mainly on the inside. The back extends to just below the top of the bottom drawer (fig. 97). The one-board top is attached to the rails with T-headed nails. The drawers are side-hung. The sides fit against a rabbet in the front, are butted to the back, and extend somewhat beyond the back. Each joint is secured through the side with two rosehead nails that are set in deep, gouged holes (fig. 106).

110. See also figs. 74, 97, 106, 134, 142.

The drawer bottoms, formed of three or four transverse boards joined by a tongue and groove, are nailed to a rabbet in the front and to the bottom of the other sides. The runners are let into the stiles and nailed. At the center of each drawer front is an applied plaque. The applied beveled moldings on the deep drawers are separate from the inner moldings, which are identical in profile to the moldings on the shallow drawers and those around the edge of the side panels and consist of a wider and a narrower convex profile and a small cavetto, with a fillet between each element (fig. 134). A related sequence of an ovolo, then two convex contours, and a cavetto on a larger scale constitutes the molding under the top and, inverted, the base molding (fig. 142). The half-round molding around the raised field of the side panels is the same as that around the drawers. The channel molding on the side rails has a small cavetto at either side. The drawer fronts are wedge-shaped with the thick end at the bottom. The framing members and the four sides of the drawers are generally well planed, and some of the edges are lightly chamfered. There is evidence of mill sawing on the pine side panels and also on some of the oak bottom boards of the drawers.

CONDITION
The top is stained and warped, and has a shim under the right end. It is old, but holes filled with wooden pegs just inside the front and side rails raise doubts about its being original to the piece. If there was a previous top, however, it was not attached to the rear stiles, the tops of which are now visible, and the nails in the top board that secure it to the rails are T-headed ones similar to those in the base molding, which look original. The front feet (maple) are replacements; they were perhaps once just extensions of the stiles. All the drawer runners have been reversed; in their former position a nail had been added through each into the case side. Several drawer stops have been nailed to the case back. A small section of the beveled molding at the lower left corner of the top drawer is pieced. There is a joint in the middle of the bottom section of the half-round molding on the left side, suggesting a replacement. At what point all the applied elements on the drawer fronts and side panels were secured with small nails is uncertain. The escutcheons look old. There are no traces of previous escutcheons placed so that the keyhole could be functional, and no locks. Some of the pulls may be original. (See also *Painted decoration*.)

INSCRIPTIONS
There is wavy trial brushwork in red paint on the exterior of the right side of the bottom drawer and in yellow paint on the outside of the back panel. Incised joiner's layout marks, consisting of one to three notches and one and two Xs, are at the joints of: the left front stile and the side rails; the right front stile and the side rails, front rails, and drawer dividers; and the right rear stile and the upper side rail and the lower back rail. In addition, there are joiner's marks consisting of one to four notches incised down the middle of the inside of the back: one notch on the upper rail; two notches above three notches on the panel; four notches on the lower rail. The top drawer is similarly numbered inside the front with one notch; the shallow drawer with darker decoration has two notches inside the front (light) and three inside the back; the shallow drawer with lighter decoration has three notches inside the front and sides; the bottom drawer has four notches inside the front and sides.

WOODS
All framing members, drawers, drawer runners, top, RED OAK and WHITE OAK; side and back panels, some case and panel moldings and center plaques on drawers, EASTERN WHITE PINE; some case and panel moldings and center plaques on drawers, SOUTHERN YELLOW PINE.

DIMENSIONS
OH. 40 (101.6); OW. (top) 40½ (102.9); CW. 38 (96.5); OD. (top) 22 (55.9); CD. 20⅞ (53).

EXHIBITION
"The Art of Joinery: Seventeenth-Century Case Furniture in the American Wing," MMA, 18 October 1972–18 March 1973.

REFERENCES
Downs 1949, p. 15 and illus. on p. 17; Andrus 1951, p. 242; Andrus 1952, p. 165; Comstock 1962, no. 64; Safford 1972 (exh. cat.), no. 12; Butler 1973, p. 13; Schwartz 1976, no. 11; Safford 1980, pl. 1; Safford 1998, fig. 1 and pp. 194–97, and also illus. on p. 155.

PROVENANCE
Ex coll.: Mrs. J. Insley Blair, Tuxedo Park, New York.
    Mrs. Blair's notes on this chest (ADA files) only state: "No data. Came from Boston." It was on loan to the MMA from Mrs. Blair from 1939 until it became a gift.

Gift of Mrs. J. Insley Blair, 1948 (48.158.11)

1. A chest at the Brooklyn Museum, Brooklyn, New York (Schwartz 1956, p. 344), has fleur-de-lis and bird motifs on the drawer panels and graining on the front and sides; one at the Leffingwell House Museum, Norwich, Connecticut, has similar decoration under a modern finish that makes it difficult to judge the age of the painting; graining remains on a chest at the Winterthur Museum (acc. no. 56.10.3) and traces of graining on one at Colonial Williamsburg (acc. no. 1976-437).
2. See also Safford 1998, fig. 1 and pp. 194–97, and also illus. on p. 155.
3. For example, Macquoid 1905, figs. 44, 45; Bowett 2002, pls. 2:38, 4:20, 4:21, 4:24. For an English joined oak chest of drawers that has drawer fronts with beveled moldings painted to imitate tortoiseshell, see Knell 1992, pl. V.
4. Forman 1970, pp. 23–25.
5. Stalker and Parker 1688 (1971 ed.), pl. 13; Kirk 1982, fig. 229.
6. For painter-stainers, see A. L. Cummings 1971a.
7. For the inlay, see n. 3 above. On the Winterthur chest (acc. no. 56.10.3) the back panel is a single mill-sawn oak board, but only the sides of the drawers are of oak. The transverse boards of the drawer bottoms are joined by a tongue and groove, as on cat. no. 110, and the drawer numbers are similarly incised down the center of the case back.
8. Safford 1998, fig. 1 and illus. on p. 155, show the chest partly cleaned.

III

III.

Chest of drawers

Boston or vicinity, 1695–1720

Characterized by a deep top and bottom drawer and two shallow ones in between and a single fielded panel on each side, chests of four drawers of the type represented here enjoyed considerable popularity in and around Boston at the end of the seventeenth century and in the early eighteenth century, as is evidenced by the large number, more than two dozen, that are known. While they may vary in their details, they all have the same configuration of drawers, each with two simulated panels, which on the deep drawers have broad, beveled perimetric moldings. The design plays on the

opposition of the drawer heights, here as in many cases in a two-to-one ratio, and of the width of the shaped panels—with the greater being on the shallower drawers—and it counterbalances the angled planes of the beveled moldings on the drawers with those of the fielded panels on the sides.

The bipartite drawer fronts, beveled moldings, and small applied moldings in geometric designs of this chest form are ultimately indebted to the school of joinery established in Boston by London-trained craftsmen by the mid-seventeenth century (see the entry for cat. no. 98). Out of that school came the handsome four-drawer chests on which the second drawer is the deepest and most ornamented and that feature walnut and cedar and are sometimes made in two cases.[1] Chests like the present example and cat. no. 110 represent a further and last major stage in the evolution of the Boston joined chest of drawers derived from that tradition. While they use the same type of moldings on the drawer fronts and have similar overall proportions and dimensions as the walnut group, they exhibit certain later stylistic and structural traits. The aesthetic is no longer entirely that of the seventeenth-century style. Symmetry rather than a balancing of disparate elements underlies the configuration of the drawers. Furthermore the drawers are not divided into distinct tiers by horizontal moldings that extend across the stiles but are tied together by a half-round molding on stiles and drawer dividers, as they are on William and Mary case furniture, the influence of which is also reflected in the use of narrow stiles.[2] Fielded panels, which occur on the sides of a few of the walnut chests of drawers and which on this group are given emphasis by the addition of applied moldings around the raised center, are likewise not part of the traditional Boston seventeenth-century joinery vocabulary and also represent newer stylistic influences.[3]

Structurally, these chests are characterized by the extensive use of pine—typically only the frame is of oak—and by a back that extends down to just beyond the top of the bottom drawer and that, like the side panels, consists of a single panel formed of one wide mill-sawn board. The drawers, which are all side-hung, vary in their construction and offer clear evidence that this form of chest represents a regional style made in a number of different shops. This is one of at least ten examples with the drawer sides joined to the front with one large dovetail, suggesting manufacture in Boston or its immediate vicinity.[4] On others, the front joint is nailed—either through the side, as on cat. no. 110, or in a few instances through the front.[5]

With the panels, drawer fronts, and all the applied elements of pine, such chests lacked the coloristic effects traditionally provided in joined furniture in the applied-ornament style by the use of several different kinds of woods. They were painted instead. In the rare cases where the paint has survived, as on cat. no. 110 or a chest at the Brooklyn Museum, Brooklyn, New York, the sides and beveled moldings are grained to simulate a richer wood and the drawer panels have painted motifs. The Brooklyn Museum chest, which is very close in construction, dimensions, and molding profiles to the present example, has fleurs-de-lis on the panels of the deep drawers and birds on the shallow drawers; this piece appears to have been once also ornamented with birds.[6] Solidly built of local woods and with a decorative surface, chests of this type provided an attractive, less expensive alternative to both the joined walnut chests of drawers and to the newer William and Mary–style high chests. The design of these chests and the chest of drawers

form in and of itself had urban connotations that placed these pieces at a level above other late joined case furniture from eastern Massachusetts with applied moldings and painted ornament.[7]

CONSTRUCTION

The chest contains four long drawers—two shallow ones in the middle, each half the height of the two others. The mortise-and-tenon joints of the back and side rails, which are quite deep, are secured with two pins, those of the front rails and drawer dividers, with one. One board broadly beveled around the perimeter of the outer side forms the single vertical panel on each side of the case and the single horizontal panel of the back. The back extends down just far enough for the lower rail to cover the top of the bottom drawer. The top of the case consists of a front board nearly 20 inches wide with a narrow glued-on section at the rear. The drawers are side-hung, and each side is joined to the front with one large dovetail reinforced with a sprig; the groove for the runner passes through the center of the dovetail. On the shallow drawers, the dovetails are half-blind; on the deep drawers they go through and are concealed by the applied beveled moldings. At the rear, the sides are rabbeted, secured to the back with T-headed nails, and extend somewhat beyond the back. The drawer bottoms run transversely and are attached to a rabbet in the front and to the bottom of the other sides with rosehead nails. On the third drawer, the boards are joined with a half lap; on the others, they are just butted. The drawer runners fit into grooves in the stiles. The molding below the top features a cyma recta, a fillet, and a fascia, that at the base a cyma reversa followed by an ovolo and a fillet. The small moldings on the drawer fronts have the common ovolo, cavetto, bead, and fillet configuration. On the deep drawers they are separate from the beveled moldings, which are attached with wooden pins, and at the center of all the drawers is an applied plaque. The half-round molding on the raised field of the side panels and on the front stiles and drawer dividers is the same. The stiles are square and well planed, the inner side of the rails and the underside of the drawer bottoms are just roughly finished with a hatchet, and evidence of mill sawing remains on the top and panels.

CONDITION

According to a 1911 MMA photograph (ADA files), the chest, when acquired, was missing a front corner of the top, a portion of the moldings, and most of its hardware. The top (pine), which appears to be old but is probably not original, was removed for repairs and now has a transverse brace on the underside to stabilize a large split on the right and is pieced at the right front and left rear corners. A slat nailed to the bottom of the lower back rail is probably added. The drawers have suffered from usage and rodents. The heavily worn grooves in the drawer sides have been repaired with a tapered strip at the top of the groove. The lower edge of the front of the second drawer is partly pieced. The drawer bottoms all have splits and missing and added nails. The upper three sets of runners are new. The front feet (maple) do not look original. Several segments of the upper portion of the top molding have been replaced. Seven of the small triangular plaques, about one-third of the moldings on the shallow drawers plus a short section on the top drawer, and the side base moldings, all missing in 1911, are new. The front base molding (oak) shows some wear and has a profile found on some related chests, but it is probably not original. Although no evidence of it remains, there was probably once an applied molding around the perimeter of the side panels. All the present drawer pulls and one of the escutcheons were installed at the MMA. Old holes from nails or screws that once fastened the drawers shut go through the right side panel into each right drawer side. When the MMA secured the drawers and small objects displayed on the top several decades ago, screw holes were drilled in the back. The chest is heavily scratched and dented. In the 1911 photograph it appears to be covered with paint or a dark, degraded finish. It was stripped at the MMA and is now stained brown; no clear traces of paint are visible. The exterior of the back, interior of the case, and parts of the drawers have also been stained.

INSCRIPTIONS

Incised on the outside of the back of the top drawer is a large sawyer's tally mark: || crossed by a diagonal line. Inscribed on the outside of the upper back rail are the numbers 612 once in white chalk and 6 within a circle followed by "IP." twice in black; and on the outside of the back panel, in black, the number 1 within a circle (all modern). In pencil on the bottom of the top drawer is the mark B and on the outside of the back of the bottom drawer an X (both modern).

WOODS

All framing members, old drawer runners, RED OAK; side and back panels, drawers, top molding, half-round moldings, old applied elements on drawer fronts, EASTERN WHITE PINE.

DIMENSIONS

OH. 36 (91.4); OW. (top) 40 (101.6); CW. 36⅞ (93.7); OD. (top) 21½ (54.6); CD. 19¾ (50.2).

EXHIBITIONS

On loan to the Art Institute of Chicago, Chicago, Illinois, from 1926 to 1958 and to the Litchfield Historical Society (for display in the Tapping Reeve House) from 1968 to 1972.

PROVENANCE

Ex coll.: H. Eugene Bolles, Boston.

Gift of Mrs. Russell Sage, 1909 (10.125.37)

1. Jobe et al. 1991, no. 3, for example.
2. There are a few exceptions—chests of drawers with older-fashion broad

stiles and horizontal moldings that extend across them (for example, a chest in a private collection; and others in Nutting 1928–33, no. 224; Monkhouse and Michie 1986, no. 8; and G. W. R. Ward 1988, no. 56).

3. Fielded panels frequently occur in Dutch joined work of the seventeenth century and are characteristic of Dutch-influenced colonial furniture (see cat. no. 118). In England such panels began to be popular in the 1660s (Chinnery 1979, p. 118, diagram 2:16d), and in New England they began to appear in furniture and interior woodwork at the end of the century. An early example of the latter is the room paneling from the ca. 1695–1700 John Wentworth house, Portsmouth, New Hampshire, installed at the MMA. A painted version of raised panels is on a door of perhaps ca. 1680 at the Paul Revere House (A. L. Cummings 1979, fig. 270).

4. They are at the Brooklyn Museum, Brooklyn, New York (Schwartz 1956, p. 344), Colonial Williamsburg (Gustafson 1977, p. 910), Leffingwell House Museum, Norwich, Connecticut, Los Angeles County Museum of Art, Los Angeles, California (R. Davidson 1968, p. 54), New-York Historical Society, New York City (acc. no. 1944.199), North Andover Historical Society, North Andover, Massachusetts (Kettell 1929, pl. 34), Rhode Island School of Design (Monkhouse and Michie 1986, no. 8), and Yale University Art Gallery (G. W. R. Ward 1988, no. 56); and offered in *Important American Furniture, Silver, Prints, Folk Art and Decorative Arts*, auction cat., Christie's, New York City, 27 January 1996, lot 290.

5. Other chests with drawer sides nailed to the front are at the Chipstone Foundation (Rodriguez Roque 1984, no. 3), Historic Deerfield (Fales 1976, no. 374), the John Whipple House, Ipswich, Massachusetts, and the Winterthur Museum (acc. no. 56.10.3); and formerly at the Art Institute of Chicago, Chicago, Illinois (*New Hampshire Weekend Americana Auction*, auction cat., Northeast Auctions, Manchester, New Hampshire, 4–5 August 2001, lot 358), and Wadsworth Atheneum (Nutting 1928–33, no. 228). Those with drawers nailed through the front are in a private collection; in DAPC (no. 76.1329); and offered in *The Collection of the Late Lillian Blankley Cogan*, auction cat., Christie's, New York City, 7 September 1992 (sale held on premises, Farmington, Connecticut), lot 320. Chests of which the drawer construction is not known to the present writer are in DAPC (no. 66.166); Nutting 1928–33, nos. 224, 229; Frazier 1983, pl. IX; and N. F. Little 1984, fig. 248; advertised in *Antiques* 67 (February 1955), p. 113, by Florene Maine; and offered in *The Myron and Maureen Taplin Collection*, auction cat., Skinner, Bolton and Boston, Massachusetts (sale held on premises, Cranston, Rhode Island), 8 July 1989, lot 186.

6. For the Brooklyn Museum chest, see n. 4 above. In the inventory of the H. Eugene Bolles collection made at the time of the acquisition (MMA Archives) the description of cat. no. 111 includes "bird decorations." Although no such decoration is evident in the photograph of the chest taken in 1911, before the MMA restoration, it was presumably discernible on the actual piece.

7. See Jobe and Kaye 1984, no. 7.

112.

Chest of drawers

Windsor, Connecticut, or vicinity, 1735–50

The painted ornament on this chest of drawers imitates japanning in the disposition of the motifs and in the disregard for scale (see the entry for cat. no. 125). The decorative elements on the front are not organized into coherent designs, as they are on most furniture with floral painting of the first half of the eighteenth century, but disposed in a seemingly haphazard arrangement of multifarious individual motifs that include sprays and vases of flowers, trees, buildings, human figures,

dogs, birds, and butterflies—no two exactly alike. The scheme is not entirely without a plan: the motifs at the ends of the drawers in the top tier are similarly arranged with a spray at the outer and a tree at the inner edge; and on the long drawers there is a vase with flowers at one end and a tree at the other, which alternate sides at each tier. But the overall effect is one of randomness and whimsicality. The decorative vocabulary, however, with the exception of the buildings, which do strike an exotic note, is not derived from japanning;[1] nor is the use of colors, which here appears to reflect the tradition of floral painting that flourished along the Connecticut shore in the early decades of the eighteenth century (see cat. nos. 100–102, 107). Whether or not there was any close relationship—in the delineation of flowers, for example—it is impossible to say because of the extensive losses and repainting.

The motifs correspond overall to those found in embroidery, and similar printed designs or drawings probably served as sources for both. The forms of the trees and the figure of a lady under a tree and of a man holding a pole with a fishing or a butterfly net relate directly to those in the so-called fishing-lady needlework pictures produced in girls' boarding schools in Boston in the mid-eighteenth century. This piece and cat. no. 81 are the only known examples of furniture painted in colors with designs of the type used in such embroidery. The Boston pictures are modeled on pastoral scenes that came into fashion in English embroidery during the first quarter of that century. The vocabulary of both the English and the Boston pictures includes animals, birds, butterflies, such as those seen here, and also buildings, which in the English prototypes are often turreted; such motifs had antecedents in needlework of the 1600s, which sometimes combined elements without regard to scale, as is typical of japanned work.[2] As for the floral schemes, the vases containing bouquets of mixed flowers have their ultimate source in printed designs of the sixteenth and seventeenth centuries. The free-floating naturalistic sprays with undulating stems, such as the small ones toward the center of the drawers and the large ones on the case sides, represent a type of pattern that was favored in England in the first quarter of the eighteenth century and popular in American embroidery in the second and third quarters.[3]

This chest of drawers has a history in the Windsor, Connecticut, area, as do three pieces that are part of a small group of case furniture also decorated with imitation japanning, but of a different character. The group consists of two high chests of drawers with cabriole legs, one at the MMA and one at the Winterthur Museum dated 1736, and four chests of drawers that probably began life as the upper case of a high chest, three of which are dated between 1735 and 1738.[4] The decoration on those pieces, executed in white on black, is the work of another painter, but it documents the taste for japanning in the Windsor area in the second quarter of the eighteenth century. The fact that the high chests are in the Queen Anne style introduced in Boston about 1730 is further evidence that Windsor clients and craftsmen in this period were set on keeping abreast of urban fashions. This piece aims to achieve stylishness primarily through its decoration, not its form. The chest with five tiers of drawers is a conservative design that evolved in the early eighteenth century to simulate the vertical emphasis of high chests. A somewhat earlier example from the Connecticut River valley at Historic Deerfield—a joined chest of drawers with similar proportions and disposition of drawers made in Hampshire County, Massachusetts—has a grained surface that suggests the figured veneers on fashionable William and Mary–style high chests.[5]

PAINTED DECORATION
The ground coat is a relatively thick, brown layer that contains iron earth pigments. The design elements, except for the leaves, are laid down first in lead white, over which detailing is applied in red (vermilion mixed with some lead white and possibly red lead) and, according to the remaining evidence, on the front only, also in green (a copper green). The green of the leaves consists of a mixture of copper green and lead white and is painted directly on the ground. The paint in the decoration is heavily crackled and has extensive losses both to color detailing and to the white ground, and it has considerable restorations. Some of the white areas—mainly on the sides—have been touched up. Most of the red has been overpainted or repainted (in a vermilion that differs from the earlier paint used) in a manner that may, or in some cases probably does not, conform to the original scheme. The green of the leaves has darkened, and what paint remains and the lacunae have been gone over with what appears to be a brown glaze. While the motifs as such still read quite clearly in spite of losses—and they do not seem to have been altered in their overall design by the restorations—the details of the original execution and its quality are unclear. The background is very uneven in color and sheen and is badly streaked; the finish layers vary in thickness and appear to have been touched up. The surfaces were lightly cleaned at the MMA in 1980, and the decorative elements only received a protective coat of modern varnish.

CONSTRUCTION
The sides are joined to the top with half-blind dovetails and the bottom to the sides with through dovetails. Each of those elements is a single board, with the bottom extending only to within 2 inches of the back. The back, formed of horizontal boards (three wide and one narrow), is nailed to a rabbet in the top and sides. The five tiers of drawers are graduated in increments of 5/8 inch. The drawer dividers (ca. 6 in. deep) fit into grooves in the sides; drawer runners are nailed to the sides behind the dividers. The vertical partition in the top tier extends to the back and is nailed in place through the top, divider, and back. A center runner that serves both short drawers is nailed to the bottom of the partition. The bottom drawer runs on transverse battens at each end of the upper side of the case bottom; the battens are nailed on from below and their top is flush with that of the base molding. The round tenons of the feet come up through the case bottom to the top of the battens. On the drawers in the upper two tiers, the sides are joined to the front with one dovetail, on the others with two. On all the drawers, the back corners each have a single large dovetail that is worked on the back board and not on the side. The bottom is nailed to a rabbet in the front and to the bottom of the other sides with sprigs and has a runner strip under each side. All but one drawer bottom (a single board) consist of a wide longitudinal front board and a narrow one at the back. The top and sides of the drawer fronts angle inward, and the top edges of the sides and backs are chamfered. A half-round molding is applied to the front of the case sides and partition; it is worked directly on the front edge of the drawer dividers. The top molding consists of a fillet and cyma reversa, the base molding of a fillet, bead, cyma reversa, and fascia.

112

CONDITION

The joints of the case were reglued at the MMA in the 1970s, as were the top side moldings and the feet. The back was reattached with mostly new nails; it had become loose because the sides of the case have shrunk, and the drawers, when pushed in so that they do not protrude at all at the front, put pressure on the back. In addition, the missing right rear corner of the bottom board was replaced. At what point sprigs, which appear to be handwrought, were added to the dovetails of the case bottom, through the case sides into some of the drawer dividers, and to some of the joints of the drawers is unclear. The sprigs, probably also added, that secure the runner strips to the underside of the drawers show considerable wear. A dovetail in one drawer is partly pieced; others have small losses. The front of the top long drawer has a surface patch at the left end; the side edges of many of the drawer fronts are badly chipped, and the larger losses have wax fill. The drawer bottoms all have shrinkage cracks, and there are several splits in the case as well. The molding on the vertical partition is new. The feet (maple) are probably not original. All the hardware is replaced. The pulls are at least the third set; the first was also of the drop variety. The outer surfaces are nicked and scratched, and the top is very uneven in color. (See also *Painted decoration*.)

INSCRIPTIONS

There are several large, scored sawyer's tally marks on the case: X I X on the underside of the bottom; III . . . X inside the top back board (partly planed off); and X inside the second back board. The drawers are numbered on the underside with scratched lines (not original): one to four lines on the full drawers and one and two on the short drawers. There are modern restorer's chalk numerals on feet and battens.

WOODS

SOUTHERN YELLOW PINE; battens on case bottom, OAK.

DIMENSIONS

OH. 49½ (125.7); OW. (base molding) 43⅜ (110.2); CW. 41¾ (106); OD. (base molding) 17½ (44.5); CD. 16⅜ (41.6).

EXHIBITION

"American Japanned Furniture," MMA, 20 March–30 April 1933 (lent by Mrs. J. Insley Blair).

REFERENCES

Downs 1933, p. 48; Downs 1945, p. 72; "Antiques in the American Wing" 1946, p. 249, no. 13; Downs 1946, fig. 2; M. B. Davidson 1967, nos. 65, 65A (detail); Kirk 1967, no. 56; Fales 1972, no. 87; M. B. Davidson 1980, fig. 82; M. B. Davidson and Stillinger 1985, fig. 139; T. P. Kugelman and A. K. Kugelman 2005, no. 4.

PROVENANCE

Ex coll.: Mrs. J. Insley Blair, Tuxedo Park, New York.

According to a letter of 18 December 1964 from William L. Warren, chief curator at Old Sturbridge Village, Sturbridge, Massachusetts, to James Biddle (ADA files), the chest was sold to Mrs. Blair by Frederick W. Fuessenich, a collector and dealer of Litchfield, Connecticut, who had purchased it from the Stoughton family in East Windsor Hill, Connecticut. According to information from Mrs. Blair (ADA files), the chest came from the Skilton family of East Windsor. Stoughtons were among the original settlers of Windsor (see the entry for cat. no. 73). The chest was on loan from Mrs. Blair to the MMA from 1939 to 1945, when it became a gift.

Gift of Mrs. J. Insley Blair, 1945 (45.78.3)

1. The building motifs are reminiscent of those illustrated in Stalker and Parker 1688 (1971 ed.), for example.
2. For Boston fishing-lady pictures, see Ring 1993, vol. 1, p. 45 and figs. 40–51; for English prototypes, p. 12 and fig. 11. For an English picture of the 1600s, see King and Levey 1993, pl. 69.
3. On printed designs as a source, see Beck 1992, pp. 90–94. For the English and American embroidered floral sprays, see King and Levey 1993, p. 19 and pls. 91–95; Peck 1990, nos. 66, 68, 69.
4. On the high chests with cabriole legs, see Heckscher 1985, no. 152; Fales 1972, no. 88. On the four other chests, see J. L. Cummings 1938; and Kirk 1967, no. 55 (not dated).
5. Zea 1987, fig. 16.

Cupboards and Kasten

Until about 1600 the term "cupboard" referred to open shelves used to display items of silver and to hold cups and glasses and other vessels connected with dining (literally, a board for cups). The standard format in the late sixteenth and early seventeenth centuries in England was a joined three-tiered structure built as one unit, with turned pillars between the shelves at the front corners and a long drawer below the middle shelf. By the early 1600s it became increasingly common to enclose the upper portion or both the upper and lower portions of the piece with a doored compartment, and "cupboard" began to take on its modern meaning.

No American joined cupboard with just open shelves is known. Colonial examples, normally built in two parts, have one or both units enclosed. The four seventeenth-century-style cupboards in the collection, all from New England, each present a different variation on the common two-part scheme in which the upper stage is fitted with a recessed storage compartment and has turned pillars that support the front corners of the top (called the cupboard's head at the time); the lower is either open or enclosed. A cupboard from the Guilford, Connecticut, area (cat. no. 113) illustrates one of the two usual configurations of the upper storage unit: it is trapezoidal in shape. The lower portion of this piece is enclosed in the traditional manner: it has two doors that open on a single compartment with a shelf. The cupboard features a bold carved torus molding that conceals a drawer under the middle shelf. The concept is similar to that of the hidden drawer, usually with a carved ovolo-shaped front, found in the same location on English cupboards with open shelves. Two of the cupboards in the collection have an upper recessed compartment that is straight across the front—the design option favored by the Plymouth Colony, Massachusetts, school of joinery that produced these pieces. On one of them the lower case contains three tiers of drawers (cat. no. 114). The cupboard with drawers, a type known primarily in New England and not Old England, no doubt represents a response to the more fashionable chest of drawers form. It is not coincidental that it is found in Boston, where the production of the chest of drawers was centered in this period, and in surrounding counties influenced by Boston-style joinery, and also in the vicinity of New Haven, Connecticut, where at least one stylish joined chest of drawers was made. The second cupboard in that same tradition, whose designs are characterized by distinctive serrated moldings, is open below and follows the standard scheme of rear legs formed by the stiles and front legs that consist of separate turned pillars (cat. no. 115). The open lower case on the Museum's fourth joined cupboard (cat. no. 116), which has a trapezoidal upper section and originated in the New Haven area, is anomalous. All four of its legs are turned and of one piece with the stiles and feet, and instead of featuring a large baluster, they are in a repeat pattern. Among the cupboard configurations not represented in the collection the highly complex and varied structures produced by an unidentified shop in northern Essex County, Massachusetts, are particularly noteworthy (see the entry for cat. no. 58). Mention should also be made of the unusual arrangement of an open upper section and an enclosed lower one that occurs on a rare cupboard attributed to Virginia.[1]

Cupboards were most often listed in probate inventories without further description, but a variety of designations are also to be found—such as "court," "livery," "press," "standing," or "side" cupboard. How specific or consistent a meaning those terms had, it is difficult to judge. Large joined cupboards were expensive and found in wealthier seventeenth-century homes. As a form, cupboards were not as stylish as the elaborate, more up-to-date chests of drawers, but they were imposing, prestigious pieces. The cupboard stood most often in the parlor or hall where the household dined, and served to store the textiles and vessels and utensils used at mealtime. The top, which was usually covered with a cupboard cloth and sometimes also provided with a cushion, offered a surface for the display of silver, glass, or ceramics or for the deposit of other items—a law book, for instance, as recorded by Boston diarist Samuel Sewall.[2] One wonders what it was that enticed a child in Sewall's household to clamber "to the Cupboard's head upon a chair [and] break . . . her forhead grievously."[3] Probate inventory listings of cupboards given a low valuation—in kitchens, for instance—suggest that simple examples in pine were being made and used alongside the expensive joined oak ones. However, the pine cupboards of board construction that have survived, like the one in the collection (cat. no. 117), are late, rural expressions of the form, made in the eighteenth century after joined oak cupboards had generally become outmoded.

The press—a large two-doored case piece for the hanging of clothing or the storage of linens—is only occasionally mentioned in seventeenth-century colonial inventories. This type of cupboard does not seem to have been very popular in England, and hardly any joined oak colonial examples in the Anglo-American tradition are known. On the Continent, however, linen and clothes presses, often monumental in scale, were a major furniture form, and the traditions of France (the armoire), the Netherlands (the kast), and Germany (the *Schrank*) brought to America by immigrant craftsmen all influenced colonial furniture to a lesser or greater degree. Among the seventeenth-century-style presses, a southern example represents a blending of French and English features,[4] and one New York piece is in a design for which European prototypes have yet to be discovered.[5] Four other seventeenth-century joined oak presses from New York, including one in the collection, are Dutch-style kasten. The Museum's example (cat. no. 118) is representative of the form in general in its strongly architectural design, its large overhanging cornice, and its interior originally fitted with shelves for linens. Like the three other oak kasten, it includes structural features not characteristic of Anglo-American work, but it stands alone in having a striking painted surface that simulates stone.

Painted furniture was produced in the Netherlands, but it was made of softwoods and provided an economical alternative to joined hardwood pieces. The two kasten painted in grisaille and of nailed board construction that conclude this chapter represent that tradition. They are ornamented on the doors and sides with large pendants of fruit in architectural niches that simulate in paint opulent Baroque carving. One, which

has squarish proportions dominated by a large ovolo frieze (cat. no. 119), is painted in the same style as four other American examples, three of them in the taller format characteristic of eighteenth-century kasten. The painting on the other, which has lost its frieze, is by a different, less professional hand (cat. no. 120). Kasten, virtually all of hardwoods and not painted, continued to be made in the areas of New York and New Jersey settled by the Dutch into the early nineteenth century and have survived in large numbers. The Germanic counterpart, the *Schrank*, which was usually a clothespress (fitted with pegs) rather than a linen press, was made mainly in Pennsylvania and during the last two-thirds of the eighteenth century.

1. Fairbanks and Bates 1981, p. 18 (Museum of Early Southern Decorative Arts, Winston-Salem, North Carolina).
2. Sewall 1973, vol. 1, p. 345.
3. Ibid., p. 122.
4. Fairbanks and Bates 1981, p. 20, and J. R. Melchor and M. S. Melchor 1986 (Museum of Early Southern Decorative Arts, Winston-Salem, North Carolina).
5. Failey 1976, no. 37 (Winterthur Museum).

113.

Cupboard

Guilford, Connecticut, or vicinity, 1670–1700

The large torus molding below the middle shelf, which incorporates a drawer, is the salient and most distinctive feature of this cupboard. The use of such a molding, which occurs on richly ornamented English cupboards of the late sixteenth and early seventeenth centuries, is rare in American furniture and found primarily on this and five or more related cupboards.[1] These pieces also differ from virtually all other American cupboards in that the turned pillars are one with the front corner blocks to which the top rails that form the frieze are tenoned and in that the middle shelf is part of the upper case.[2] The rather stark cylindrical form that characterizes the pillars on this group of objects (fig. 48) and especially the strong horizontal emphasis of the torus and the flat expanses of the unusually broad framing members of the doors give these pieces a massive appearance. The applied arch motif that ornaments the upper panels has substantial proportions as well, and on the upper door—the focal point of the design—the small archway, solidly surrounded by a heavy frame, looks like a well-fortified entrance. The arches typically have a boss in each spandrel and a keystone that reaches down as far as the imposts and is followed by a half spindle that extends to

the base. The narrow, plain band around the upper door panel seen here, however, which was worked from the solid wood of those rails and stiles, does not occur on any of the other cupboards in the group. The carved ornament consists solely of foliate S-scrolls utilized in different ways—opposed laterally on the frieze, in opposed mirrored pairs on the torus molding, and singly on the upper stiles. Although the motif is a common one, its interpretation on this and the related cupboards is distinctive, characterized by a frond that ends in a curved band that becomes half of an open loop when the scrolls are paired and by the use of full, half, and quarter circles between elements (fig. 63). On the torus molding the astragal (worked from the solid wood) is situated slightly above the middle[3]—probably as an optical device so that it appears to be in the center when seen from above—and the height of the scrolls in the space above and below, which here differs by a quarter inch, has been adjusted accordingly. The S-scrolls on this piece have been dimensioned to fit into seven different-sized areas and well illustrate how a motif that is laid out with a rule and compass can be readily adapted to the size of a specific space.

113. See also figs. 48, 63, 93.

This and the related cupboards form part of a larger group of furniture that is carved with similar S-scrolls, which in many cases have an oval drop beyond the open loop, as on cat. no. 140. The carving is often but not always combined with applied ornament. Included in the group are various types of chests, several boxes, and also two monumental cupboards with three drawers in the lower case.[4] The overall form of those cupboards—a facade all on the same plane and drawers in the lower case—and the heavy base and mid-moldings suggest the influence of London-style chests of drawers of the mid-1600s. The applied half spindles in the arches of this cupboard and similar ones on other pieces in the group, including the two cupboards with three drawers, also reflect a London-style design (see the entry for cat. no. 98). Other elements of the decoration that distinguish this school of joinery—carving and peaked moldings—appear to have their source in provincial traditions of Gloucestershire and Somerset in the west of England (see the entries for cat. nos. 88, 89). Thus this school of joinery may represent the confluence of an urban applied-ornament style and a West Country tradition of craftsmanship.[5]

Those cupboards and chests that have family histories point to the Guilford area of Connecticut as the locus of this school of joinery, which probably encompassed several shops.[6] The group as a whole not only is related stylistically but also shares several structural features that distinguish this tradition of craftsmanship. Applied half spindles and bosses, like those on the upper panels of the present cupboard, are attached with wooden pins, as are case moldings, like the cornice and architrave on the top rails. A chiseled V-shaped channel may be used instead of a planed rectangular groove to house boards, as, in this instance, those of the bottom of the lower case. Large panels, such as those on the upper and lower sides and on the back of this cupboard, are made up of two or more boards. Chestnut, which appears to have been mill-sawn, is included in this and many of the other pieces. In terms of workmanship, this school of joinery favors small joint pins and habitually shows a total lack of effort to finish wood surfaces that are not visible, such as the back of this cupboard (fig. 93). In this last respect, this group of furniture represents the opposite end of the spectrum from cat. nos. 114 (see fig. 94) and 115, with their careful finishing of all parts.

CONSTRUCTION

The cupboard is built in two sections, with the middle shelf part of the upper case. The two were originally held in place by wooden dowels fixed in the upper case and inserted into holes in the four lower stiles. On the upper case, the two-panel back, the front and side rails that form the frieze, and the front corner blocks, which are one with the turned pillars, are joined as one unit, and the front and splayed sides of the storage compartment, which has pentagonal front stiles, are framed as another. The back edge of the rear stiles of the splayed sides is angled to fit against the rear panels, and the two are held together with nails driven in from the back. The middle shelf is nailed on from

below into the rails, pillars, and rear stiles of the case. Both the top and middle shelves are made of a wider front and a narrower back board. The soffit of the overhanging top consists of thin longitudinal boards nailed to the top of the upper rail of the splayed sides and let into a groove in the front and side frieze rails. On the interior are two narrow shelves at the back, the upper supported by the upper rails of the sides, the lower by slats nailed to the rear stiles of the sides. The moldings on the top rails and the applied arches, half spindles, and bosses on the panels are all attached with wooden pins.

On the lower case, the back has two panels and the sides one. The bottom consists of three transverse boards that come together at one joint with a tongue and groove and at the other with a half lap. It is beveled to fit into a V-shaped channel in the rear and side rails and is nailed to a rabbet in the upper edge of the front rail. The runners for the side-hung drawer are let into the stiles and at the front are nailed in place. The torus drawer front extends over the stiles. The drawer sides are each secured to the front with a tenon that fits into a shallow mortise and is wedged in place from the outer side. The back is butted to the sides and nailed from the back. The bottom, made of several longitudinal boards, is beveled to fit into a groove in the front and sides and is nailed to the back. Originally below the drawer there was a dust board made of transverse boards nailed to a rabbet in the front rail and at the back to a longitudinal brace that was nailed to a recess in the stiles, as on a related cupboard at the Stowe-Day Foundation, Hartford, Connecticut.[7] The large torus molding on each side of the case is attached at the back with two rosehead nails from the inside and at the front with two T-headed nails from the outside.

On both cases, the mortise-and tenon joints are not quite 5/16 inch wide and the pins that secure them are small (no more than 1/4 in.); one, in the left joint of the bottom front rail, was left untrimmed. The joints of the rail above and below the upper door and the rail below the drawer are secured with only one pin; those of the muntins of the back lack pins. The doors revolve on pintle hinges. The door panels are made of a single board, the upper and lower side panels each of two boards, and the back panels, of two or three. The cornice consists of a cyma reversa (formed by a broad ovolo and a narrow cavetto) followed by a small fascia flanked by tiny ridges. The architrave has a fascia above the identical cyma profile, and the same cyma is run on the lower edge of the front and side bottom rails. A narrower cyma reversa edges the stiles where they abut the lower side panels and the hinged side of the doors. There is evidence of mill sawing on some of the chestnut boards. The riven oak is often not entirely squared, and surfaces that do not show have been left totally unfinished.

CONDITION

The cupboard has many repairs and replacements, but the mortise-and-tenon joints have not been apart. On the upper case, the top and the middle shelf each have splits and one front corner pieced; they are old, but perhaps not original. The top has been secured to the rails and to three added transverse braces with large modern screws. The middle shelf has similar screws going up into the rails of the splayed sides and at each end down into an added transverse brace that both stabilizes the boards and keeps the upper case in place. The boards of the soffit, except for the narrow one in the front, look replaced, and one is missing. There is a long surface patch on the front of the left stile of the back. On the door, the outer half of the right stile and a narrow outer strip on the left stile are new, as are the pintles and the knob. On the interior, the left support of the lower shelf is a replacement. Some of the glyphs on the frieze are replaced and one is missing. On the panels, three of the bosses, probably a few of the bases and capitals of the columns, and perhaps two of the keystones are replaced. Some of the original applied elements have been reattached, with nails added to the moldings.

On the lower case, the drawer front, which at one time had a knob, is patched at the joints with the sides, which are secured with new wedges. The back and a narrow strip at the rear of the bottom are clearly new; at least one of the other three bottom boards, which are doweled together, is suspect. The grooves in the drawer sides that engage the runners have been so widened by wear that they hardly serve, and the lower edge of the right drawer side has been worn off in part up to the groove holding the bottom. A dust board below the drawer and the brace to which it was nailed at the back have been lost. The outer two-thirds of the right stile of the right door are replaced, as are the pintles on both doors; the applied panel moldings, bosses, and the knob are new. A large hole in the right rear panel (deteriorated wood) and a gnawed hole in the left side panel have been patched on the inside. A slat simulating a muntin added to each side panel (and removed in 1995) previously hid the latter hole. The joint of the bottom boards to the rear rail has been reinforced with nails; the boards are old but possibly not original. The bottom 3 to 4 inches of the feet have been pieced.

Records indicate that in 1937 modern varnish then on the cupboard was removed and the piece was rubbed down with linseed oil and turpentine. Either then or earlier, red and black paint noted as being on the cupboard when it was acquired, which was no doubt new or renewed, was removed. There now remain only traces of red on the glyphs of the frieze, the keystones and columns of the upper panels, and the lower door moldings, and there is some black on the applied half spindles and bosses, but virtually none on the pillars.

INSCRIPTIONS
MMA Hudson-Fulton exhibition identification numbers are inscribed in orange crayon on the back of the upper rear rail (H F 40.36A) and of the left rear panel (502, in an oval) of the lower case and on the back of the right rear panel of the upper case (H F. 40.36B). Large modern initials "SL" are scratched on the underside of the middle shelf.

WOODS
All framing members, front and side panels, one board in a back panel, top and middle shelf, front board of soffit, interior shelves and right shelf support, torus on case sides, drawer front and two boards of drawer bottom, drawer runners, cornice and architrave, arches on panels, old bosses, WHITE OAK and RED OAK; all boards but one in back panels, drawer sides and one board of drawer bottom, lower case bottom, CHESTNUT; pillars and integral upper front blocks, half spindles, HICKORY; right column on door panel, EASTERN RED CEDAR; other old columns, old keystones, and old glyphs, CEDAR.

DIMENSIONS
OH. 56¾ (144.1); OW. (middle shelf and torus) 49⅞ (126.7); CW. 47½ (120.7); OD. (middle shelf and torus) 21 (53.3); CD. 19½ (49.5).

EXHIBITION
"Hudson-Fulton Exhibition," MMA, 20 September–30 November 1909.

REFERENCES
Lockwood 1901, fig. 56; *Hudson-Fulton Celebration* 1909 (exh. cat.), no. 75; Lockwood 1913, fig. 162; Halsey and Tower 1925, fig. 6; Cescinsky and Hunter 1929, p. 49; "Antiques in the American Wing" 1946, p. 246, no. 1; Hornung 1972, no. 884; Kane 1973a, no. X; Schwartz 1976, no. 13; Chinnery 1979, fig. 4:200.

PROVENANCE
Ex coll.: H. Eugene Bolles, Boston.

According to Bolles, the cupboard "was formerly in the Hurlburt collection (Cromwell, Conn.), and bought of him by me nine or ten years ago. It was doubtless made in Connecticut" (Bolles notes, MMA Archives). He considered it his best example of an American cupboard (letter of 15 May 1909 to Henry W. Kent, Hudson-Fulton exhibition correspondence, MMA Archives).

Gift of Mrs. Russell Sage, 1909 (10.125.703)

1. For English cupboards, see R. Edwards 1964, pp. 289–91, figs. 1, 3–6 (the last has generically similar pillars); and Chinnery 1979, figs. 2:169, 3:254, 3:258, 3:259, 4:33.
2. Related cupboards are at the Brooklyn Museum, Brooklyn, New York (Kane 1973a, no. XI), Stanton House, Clinton, Connecticut (Kane 1973a, no. IX; found in Clinton), and Stowe-Day Foundation, Hartford, Connecticut (Kane 1973a, no. VIII; with a history in the Hall family of Guilford); and two are known only through photographs (Lyon Family Papers, box 13, Downs Manuscript Collection, Winterthur Museum), one with a history in the Eliot family of Guilford (see also Kane 1973a, p. 25, n. 18), and one noted as belonging to Dr. W. Harry Glenny, Buffalo, New York. A much altered cupboard is in the Henry Whitfield State Historical Museum, Guilford, Connecticut (Lockwood 1913, fig. 163); the actual condition and the whereabouts of one formerly in the Walter Hosmer collection (I. W. Lyon 1891, fig. 17) is unknown. See the entry for cat. no. 141 for two cupboards with a torus drawer of another type.
3. The same holds true of the Stowe-Day Foundation and Brooklyn Museum cupboards, and probably also of the others, which the writer has not examined (see n. 2 above).
4. For the chests in this group, see cat. nos. 88, 89, and 140. For the boxes, see *Three Centuries of Connecticut Furniture* 1935, no. 6; Kane 1973a, nos. XVII, XVIII; and Failey 1979, fig. 5. For the cupboards with three drawers, see Kane 1973a, nos. XII, XIII; and G. W. R. Ward 1988, nos. 197, 198.
5. Carving on a group of furniture from the nearby New Haven area also shows West Country influence (see cat. nos. 86, 87). Two of New Haven's early immigrant joiners—William Russell (1612–1664/65) and William Gibbons (in New Haven 1640–d. 1689)—came from London (Kane 1973a, pp. 81, 84), and Robert F. Trent has proposed that they established a London-style shop tradition in New Haven that is responsible for this group of furniture in addition to the group represented by cat. no. 116 (Trent 1985, pp. 35–40). The drawer construction on this group of furniture, however—which is nailed and not dovetailed (see the entry for cat. no. 140)—suggests, as does the carving, that the joinery tradition that produced it included a nonurban component.
6. One of the cupboards with three drawers has a history in the Stone family of Guilford, which raises the possibility that its maker was Lieutenant Nathaniel Stone (1649–1709), a joiner in Guilford (G. W. R. Ward 1988, p. 385). (Robert F. Trent has postulated that Stone was apprenticed to one of New Haven's London-trained joiners mentioned in n. 5 above [Trent 1985, p. 39, n. 10]). For the histories of other cupboards, see n. 2 above; for those of chests, see the entries for cat. nos. 88, 89.
7. See n. 2 above.

114.

Cupboard

Plymouth or Barnstable County, Massachusetts, 1670–1700

Moldings that feature carved serrations and series of paired notches are the most distinctive element in the decorative vocabulary of a school of joinery that has long been associated with Plymouth Colony and that encompasses this and at least four other cupboards, including cat. no. 115, and joined chests with drawers as well as other furniture forms.[1] Best known among the objects with family histories that form the basis of the attribution of this group to the coastal towns of that colony is the cupboard at the Wadsworth Atheneum that descended in the Howes family of Yarmouth and Dennis, from whom Wallace Nutting acquired it in 1921. As Nutting proposed, it may be "the Court Cubberd that stands in the new Parlour with the Cloth and Cushen that is on it" bequeathed in 1673 by Thomas Prince, governor of Plymouth Colony, to his fourth wife, Mary Howes. The related cupboard at the Winterthur Museum came down in the Tracy family and the one at the Museum of Fine Arts, Boston, has been linked to the Alden family, both of Duxbury.[2]

The cupboards share similar applied turnings, corbels, and geometric patterns, but except for the serrated moldings it is certain uncommon structural traits more than decorative motifs that set this school of joinery apart. Distinctive peculiarities are rails with integral moldings and double tenons, drawer fronts nailed to the sides (the nails concealed by applied moldings), and the use of white cedar, especially for drawer bottoms (see *Construction* and *Woods*). Another notable characteristic is the high degree of finishing of all parts, visible or not (fig. 94). The schemes that ornament the panels are cruciform patterns, lozenges, arches, and small paired squares or rectangles set below any of the preceding. On the present cupboard, lozenges prevail, and the design of the center panel with its lozenge above two squares reiterates the overall movement of the facade from the bipartite scheme of the lower case to the dominant upper center motif; so does the pyramidal arrangement of the three lozenges on the upper front. The beveled mitered moldings on the drawer fronts, the use of corbels, and the overall patterns of the applied turnings are design elements derived from London-style furniture and characteristic of Boston case pieces. Comparison can be made with the only known cupboard attributed to Boston (at the Chipstone Foundation), which has a trapezoidal upper section and a lower case equipped with four long drawers rather than doors that enclose a storage space. The drawers, like those on the present and related cupboards, are all of equal height

and similarly ornamented with beveled mitered moldings.[3] The cupboard with drawers, a form that seems to have no British prototypes, appears to be an updating of the traditional design in response perhaps to both the prestige and the practicality of chests of drawers. The flat rather than trapezoidal upper front of this and similar cupboards invites the speculation that there was a desire to achieve a look akin to that of a double chest of drawers.[4]

Whether the London-style features of this school of joinery are traits that came directly from London, or via Boston, or possibly by way of a smaller English urban center is uncertain, but they are clearly not the only influence manifest in the structure and design of this group of cupboards. While the securing of front rails to the stiles with double tenons occurs on the Boston cupboard and is a technique that has been noted in London joinery, the drawer construction of this school of craftsmanship does not follow standard London or Boston practice; the drawers are nailed rather than dovetailed.[5] A different, what can be considered rather provincial, sense of design is in evidence. On the lower case of the Boston cupboard, for example, the four-drawer facade and the sides with two-over-two panels are the same height and the middle drawer divider and medial side rails line up. On the cupboards represented by this piece, the front extends down further than the sides and there is no such architectural integrity. The half columns on the lower case are generically similar to their counterparts on the Boston cupboard, but the larger ones on the upper case elaborate on the chaste Boston-London model of an urn above a Tuscan Doric column by including a reel at the top of the column and extra astragals on the shaft (see fig. 65), and they are not as crisply turned.[6] This greater elaboration is in accord with the repeat sawtooth and double-notch motifs of this school of joinery, which impart a fussiness to the design at variance with the sober, measured schemes of contemporary Boston case furniture. A clear source for this type of molding has not been found. Presumably the alternating dark (painted) and light (wood color) serrations seen at present on this group of cupboards and chests represent the original concept and as such would allude to dark and light geometric inlay like that seen on several pieces from the New Haven, Connecticut, area.[7] That patterning, together with ebonized turnings, the probable picking out of other elements with paint, and the more subtle play of the natural color of the different woods used must have created a striking effect, one which the modern paint on this piece has partly obscured.

114. See also figs. 47, 88, 94, 107, 130, 139, 140, 141.

CONSTRUCTION

The cupboard is built in two sections with the middle shelf part of the lower case. The upper case is held in place by the pillars (fig. 47), the round tenons of which fit in the corner blocks above and the middle shelf and stiles below, and originally also by two dowels that joined the back rails of the two cases. The upper case is joined as one unit and has four vertical panels in the back, one panel on each side, and a center panel flanked by two doors in the front. The top is made of two boards. The soffit is formed of a thin longitudinal board that is let into the front frieze rail and is nailed to the top of the upper front rail of the storage compartment. The storage compartment bottom consists of several front-to-back boards that are butted together, fit into a rabbet at the base of the rear muntins, and are nailed to the top of all four rails. The front edge of the bottom serves as a stop for the two doors, which swing on pintle hinges. The interior is divided in two by a center partition made up of several transverse boards that are let into the center back muntin and sandwiched between vertical slats nailed to the upper front rail and let into the bottom. A shallow shelf extends across the back through the partition and fits into a groove in the rear stiles and muntins.

The lower case has four vertical panels in the back and two on each side and two long drawers below two short drawers that are separated by a muntin. The middle shelf is formed of a narrow board at the front and a wider one at the back. On the two drawer dividers and the bottom front rail the molding is one with the framing member, which is joined to the stiles with double tenons (fig. 88): at each end the front portion of the rail extends across the stile like an applied molding and a short distance behind it is a standard tenon that fits into the mortise in the stile; the joint pin passes through the extension and the tenon proper. The drawers are side-hung. The ends of the fronts and backs are rabbeted to receive the sides and are secured to the sides with rosehead nails (fig. 107). Transverse boards butted together and nailed to a rabbet in the front and the bottom of the other sides constitute the bottoms. The runners at the sides of the case are let into the stiles and nailed. The medial runner for the short drawers is let into the muntins at center front and back and nailed in place; neither end has a tenon.

On both cases, the stiles are pentagonal, the tenons only ¼ inch wide, and the pins equally small, except for those in the double-tenoned joints, which are ⅜ inch wide. Those joints and those of the top front rail of the lower case, of the four bottom rails of the upper case, and of the upper front rail and front muntins of the storage compartment are secured with just one pin. The same serrated pattern carved on a plane that angles inward is found on four different moldings. On the most complex—the cornice and the moldings above the front panels and above and below the middle shelf (fig. 139)—the serrations are preceded by a fascia, ovolo, and cavetto, which have been sawn to simulate dentils. On the base molding, the serrations adjoin a cavetto (fig. 141), and on the drawer dividers they are flanked by shallow ovolos (fig. 140); both of those moldings are edged by a fascia embellished with pairs of notches, as are the bottom side rails of the lower case. On the architrave there is a canted fascia at the top, its angle opposed to that of the serrations below. The same common profile—an ovolo, cavetto, and fillet (fig. 130)—occurs on the panel moldings, on the drawers where it is one with the beveled moldings, on the edges of the lower side muntins, and on the front of the interior shelf. The channel molding run on the framing members of the lower sides and upper front and on the inner side of the upper back muntins consists of a relatively narrow center band flanked by cavettos, one somewhat larger than the other. The stiles and rails around the panels of the lower sides, the exterior of the back, and the interior of the storage compartment and its doors have a broad chamfer; a small chamfer finishes many of the other edges, including the upper edges of the drawers. All surfaces, visible or not, have been planed.

CONDITION

Except for its surface, the cupboard has survived in remarkably good condition. In terms of their design, the pillars look inverted, but wear on the shelf shows they have been oriented as now for a long time and they do not fit in another way. In 1972 new rear feet were installed in place of earlier, crude replacements. At the same time, the rear third of the left edge of the top was pieced, three missing segments of molding on the upper side panels and the edges of three sections of molding on the drawers were replaced, as was the missing tip of a turning on one drawer. The rear corbel on the right side is clearly new. There may well be other replacements—the turnings on the front feet perhaps—but it is difficult to judge the age of some of the other applied elements under their paint; the cupboard as a whole does not show heavy wear. The boards of the top have separated and the rear board of the middle shelf has splits; both the top and shelf are attached with T-headed nails (probably original) and wooden pins (probably added). The soffit has a few holes. There is a lock on the right door; it is not the first one, and an earlier keyhole has been filled. Mid-nineteenth-century wallpaper is glued to the bottom of the left half of the storage compartment. One drawer runner has been reattached and there are remains of drawer stops nailed to the bottom rear rail. The cupboard is covered with modern paint that has been varnished. It is painted brown except for all the turnings, the frieze, drawer panels, plaques that form the lozenge on the upper side panels, channel moldings, and serrated moldings (with light, unpainted triangles), which are black.

WOODS

All framing members, panels of back, upper front, and lower sides, front board of middle shelf, drawer sides and runners, center plaques on long drawers, serrated moldings, RED OAK; top, upper side panels, rear board of middle shelf, drawer fronts and backs, EASTERN WHITE PINE; storage compartment bottom, partition, and shelf, soffit, drawer bottoms, ATLANTIC WHITE CEDAR; corbels, applied moldings on panels and drawers, EASTERN RED CEDAR; plaques on upper front panels, BLACK WALNUT; pillars, applied turnings, SOFT MAPLE.

DIMENSIONS

OH. 55⅝ (141.3); OW. (at corbels) 49¾ (126.4); CW. 46¾ (118.7); OD. (at corbels) 23⅛ (58.7); CD. 21¼ (54).

EXHIBITION

"The Art of Joinery: Seventeenth-Century Case Furniture in the American Wing," MMA, 18 October 1972–18 March 1973.

REFERENCES

Andrus 1951, p. 245; Andrus 1952, p. 167; Comstock 1962, no. 77; Safford 1972 (exh. cat.), no. 1 and fig. 6; Schwartz 1976, no. 14; Chinnery 1979, fig. 4:224; Safford 1980, fig. 7.

PROVENANCE

Ex coll.: Mrs. J. Insley Blair, Tuxedo Park, New York.

Mrs. Blair purchased the cupboard in 1924 from Charles Woolsey Lyon, a dealer in New York City. According to her notes (ADA files), the cupboard "came from near Plymouth. Lyon found it in August, 1923." It was on loan to the MMA from Mrs. Blair from 1939 until it became a gift.

Gift of Mrs. J. Insley Blair, 1950 (50.20.3)

1. For this school of joinery, see St. George 1979b, pp. 25–55, wherein it is attributed to the Massachusetts towns of Marshfield, Scituate, Duxbury, Plymouth, Barnstable, and Yarmouth. Plymouth Colony (in existence from 1620 to 1691, when it lost its charter and became part of the Massachusetts Bay Colony) encompassed the present-day counties of Plymouth, Barnstable, and Bristol, which were formed in 1685 (Peggy M. Baker, Pilgrim Hall Museum, Plymouth, Massachusetts, telephone conversation with Cynthia Schaffner, 3 February 2003).
2. The three cupboards mentioned are in Nutting 1922, figs. 1–3 (Prince) and quotation from will on p. 168; Randall 1965, no. 19 (Alden); and St. George 1979b, no. 35 (Tracy). Considerably restored cupboards in this style are at Historic Deerfield (Fales 1976, no. 488) and the Pilgrim Hall Museum (Geller 1970, p. 6); and offered in *Important American Furniture, Silver, Folk Art and Decorative Arts*, auction cat., Christie's, New York City, 23 June 1993, lot 141.
3. Arkell and Trent 1988; *Fine American Furniture, Folk Art and Folk Paintings*, auction cat., Sotheby's, New York City, 26 June 1987, lot 183; Trent and Podmaniczky 2002, fig. 9.
4. Chinnery 1979, p. 373. Two cupboards with drawers from the Guilford, Connecticut, area have a facade entirely on one plane (G. W. R. Ward 1988, nos. 197, 198).
5. A double-tenon joint was noted by Robert Blair St. George on a London chest (Arkell and Trent 1988, p. 2C). At least one Plymouth Colony joiner, William Ford (1604–1676), who worked in Duxbury and Marshfield, Massachusetts, is known to have been London-trained (St. George 1979b, p. 84), raising the possibility of direct London influence (Trent 1985, p. 41). The use of the same type of joint on cat. no. 141, a cupboard from Middlesex County, Massachusetts, more likely reflects Boston influence.
6. Compare, for example, Fairbanks and Trent 1982, p. 540, fig. 73.
7. Kane 1973a, no. XXIII and figs. 7, 8; Fairbanks and Trent 1982, no. 482.

115.
Cupboard

Plymouth County, Massachusetts, possibly Marshfield, 1670–1700

This is the only cupboard with an open shelf in the lower section from the school of joinery that dominated the coastal towns of Plymouth Colony and is commonly identified by its serrated moldings (see also cat. no. 114). When the cupboard entered the MMA collection in 1909, the rails below the two short drawers rested directly on the bottom shelf—the state in which it had been found in the late nineteenth or very early twentieth century (see *Provenance*). In its present configuration it has a height within the range of that of related cupboards with drawers. There is clear evidence on the piece for the pentagonal shape of the then missing portion of the rear stiles and for the channel molding on their front and outer side. The form of the lower pillars, however, which were made to duplicate exactly the upper ones, remains somewhat conjectural.

The cupboards within this style are quite consistent in the dimensions of the cases, in their construction, and in their ornament, but there are some variations that point to the work of different craftsmen or shops. Details on the interior of the storage compartment on this cupboard, for example, suggest it is by a different, less meticulous hand than the one that made cat. no. 114. The shelf across the back, rather than fitting into neat grooves that were planed in the rear stiles and muntins before assembly, as on cat. no. 114, is supported at each end by a recess that was chiseled out in the side panels, and its back edge was cut to conform to the frame. Similarly the rear muntins were not rabbeted at the base to accept the compartment bottom but were quickly taken down. On the cupboard overall, not all of the surfaces were finished quite as

carefully as those on cat. no. 114. Robert Blair St. George has identified three major shop traditions within this regional school: one, the most active in the colony, encompassed the towns of Marshfield and Scituate near the North River; another included Duxbury and Plymouth; and the third, the towns of Barnstable and Yarmouth. On the chests with one tier of drawers attributed to the North River towns, he noted three different ways of securing the medial drawer runner to the lower rear rail, which suggests the work of that many different craftsmen in that area.[1] The expedient manner in which the medial runner was attached to the rear rail on this cupboard may or may not distinguish yet another hand.

The repertoire of serrated moldings of this school encompasses primarily the four types seen on cat. no. 114—which occur with minor variations, such as the addition of a fascia with notches on the molding above and below the storage space seen here (fig. 65) or the use of notches instead of serrations at the bottom of the base molding on some of the cupboards and joined chests with drawers. The moldings appear to be site-specific. Thus this cupboard with an open space in the lower case—the only one in such a design—has a molding below the drawers in a profile not encountered elsewhere. The contour of the channel molding on this cupboard seems to be the standard one in this tradition, while that on cat. no. 114, on which the center band is only slightly wider than the cavettos that flank it, is the exception. The one design element on the present cupboard that suggests a specific place of origin is the scalloped edge of the front and side bottom rails. The scallops are very similar in outline to those on cat. no. 19, a chair-table that has a history in Marshfield, and the lower edge of the seat rails on two joined armchairs probably from Marshfield are cut out in a related pattern.[2] The arch design does not occur as frequently within this serrated-style tradition as lozenge or cruciform patterns, but it does not appear to be exclusive to any particular shop or locality. Typically the panel with the arch includes incised decoration—bands of serrations, as on this piece (fig. 65), or a star or flower motif. Similar serrated bands ornament board chests.[3] As St. George has shown, the shops within this joinery tradition produced a variety of furniture forms and made case pieces at different levels of production.

CONSTRUCTION

The construction of this cupboard is similar to that of cat. no. 114, except for obvious differences in the lower case and for some minor variations. The upper case is held in place with rectangular rather than round dowels joining the back rails. Inside the storage compartment, the partition is sandwiched between two vertical slats at the back as well as at the front; the shelf across the back is cut out to fit around those slats, the muntins, and the rear stiles, and each end rests on a small ledge chiseled out in the side panel and is nailed in place; the front of the rear muntins has been chiseled down at the base, rather than rabbeted, to allow the compartment bottom to rest on the top of the rear rail all the way across. The joints of the front muntins are secured with not one but two pins. On the lower case there is a panel on each side at drawer level. None of the rails are joined with double tenons, and the serrated moldings are all applied. The back end of the medial drawer runner is simply nailed to the underside of the rear rail. The drawer backs are just butted to the sides and the bottoms run longitudinally. The bottom shelf is a single board and is attached with T-headed nails, like the two-board top and middle shelf.

The serrated moldings on the upper case and below the middle shelf correspond to those on cat. no. 114, except for the addition on this piece of a fascia with paired notches on those at the top and bottom of the storage compartment. The molding below the drawers differs; it consists of a fillet, ovolo, fascia with notches, and angled fascia with serrations. The profile of the applied moldings on the panels and that worked on the inner edge of the beveled moldings on the drawers consists of an ovolo and cavetto (fig. 129)—an outline that, like the similar one ending in a fillet on cat. no. 114 (see fig. 130), was common. On the center panel, the lines that define the arch were made with a V-shaped gouge and the serrated design with strikes of a chisel (fig. 65). The channel molding, which on the lower case ornaments the front and outer side of the front feet and rear stiles and the front and side bottom rails, has a wider center band. There is no such molding on the inner side of the upper rear muntins but there is one on the inside of the lower rail of the right door—perhaps an error. The front of the interior shelf has chamfered edges rather than a molding but the inner edge of the soffit board is molded, suggesting it was originally meant to be a shelf. The hidden side of several of the framing members is not entirely squared or planed as carefully as on cat. no. 114.

CONDITION

When the cupboard was acquired, the rails below the drawers were resting on the bottom shelf, with the front pillars and the intervening section of the rear stiles missing, and the feet were shorter and fitted with casters—as documented by a 1910 MMA photograph (ADA files).

When another photograph was made in 1912 (see *References*), the piece had been restored with lower front pillars the exact duplicates of the upper ones and with new plain rear stiles. By 1921 the present replacement rear stiles, which extend from below the drawer through the feet, had been installed and the casters removed from the front feet, which were extended 2½ inches. At some point before the cupboard came to the MMA the segments of the front frieze rail between the corbels were cut out to form the front of two new, hidden drawers. In the process the top was taken off (and then renailed) and the upper part of the partition in the storage compartment was removed to make way for the medial runner and guides.

The left drawer below the middle shelf has a replaced back and splits in the bottom, and both drawer bottoms have added nails. The far left runner has been reversed. The top and the two shelves are old and probably original. A portion of the applied ornament is definitely new: on the front, the pairs of half columns on the stiles at drawer level, both vertical moldings on the left drawer, and the glyph on the keystone of the center panel; on each upper side, all elements below the cruciform design, one-half to three-quarters of the moldings forming that design, one or two square plaques, and the center boss. Both upper pillars have damage probably caused by charring, and one has a replaced tenon; wear on the middle shelf indicates they have spent quite some time in an inverted position. Locks once on the doors are missing and a recess has been cut in the muntin adjoining the right door. The door and drawer knobs are probably all replaced. The upper side panels have each split in two. There is evidence of heavy wear throughout, including small losses, breaks, and repairs. The cupboard has a modern surface. Painted in black are the pillars and applied turnings, the frieze, simulated drawer panels and small panels below the arch, square plaques on the upper sides, channel moldings, and serrations on the applied case moldings. The wood is otherwise a reddish brown color, except for areas that retain dark residues of an earlier coating. The back of the cupboard and the under surfaces of the lower case have been stained.

INSCRIPTIONS

Scored on the underside of the rear board of the middle shelf is a large sawyer's tally mark: || crossed by a diagonal line. On the back of one of the new drawers are carpenter's notations in pencil of the number and size of pieces of lumber needed for a building. Inside the right door are modern doodles in crayon.

WOODS

All framing members, upper front and lower side panels, front board of middle shelf, drawer sides, drawer runners, serrated moldings, corbels, RED OAK; top, upper side panels, rear board of middle shelf, bottom shelf, drawer fronts and backs, shelf and slats holding partition in storage compartment, EASTERN WHITE PINE; upper back panels, soffit, bottom and partition of storage compartment, drawer bottoms, old square plaques on upper sides, ATLANTIC WHITE CEDAR; old applied moldings on panels and drawers, EASTERN RED CEDAR; archway and plaques on front panels, BLACK WALNUT; upper pillars, old applied turnings, keystone of arch, SOFT MAPLE.

DIMENSIONS

OH. 58 (147.3); OW. (at corbels) 49¾ (126.4); CW. 46¾ (118.7); OD. (at corbels) 23 (58.4); CD. 21½ (54.6).

EXHIBITION

"Craftsmen and Community: The Seventeenth-Century Furniture of Southeastern New England," Brockton Art Center—Fuller Memorial

115. See also figs. 65, 126, 129.

(now Fuller Craft Museum), Brockton, Massachusetts, 15 September–30 November 1979.

REFERENCES
Lockwood 1913, fig. 161 (1912 photograph); Nutting 1921, p. 138; Halsey and Cornelius 1924 (and 1925, 1926, 1928, 1932), fig. 6 (1912 photograph); Nutting 1924, no. 198; Halsey and Tower 1925, fig. 21; Nutting 1928–33, no. 456; E. G. Miller 1937, no. 908; Halsey and Cornelius 1938 (and 1942), fig. 4; Schwartz 1958, pl. 3A; St. George 1979b (exh. cat.), no. 18; M. B. Davidson 1980, fig. 72.

PROVENANCE
Ex coll.: H. Eugene Bolles, Boston.

According to Bolles: "This cupboard was bought by me of a dealer in Rockland, Mass., and he told me where he found it. I think it was Scituate or Scituate Harbor. At any rate it was some nearby South shore town. I offered him $50 to find the two missing posts, and he later reported that the former owners knew nothing about them and could not find them" (Bolles notes, MMA Archives).

Gift of Mrs. Russell Sage, 1909 (10.125.48)

1. St. George 1979b, pp. 25–55; for the securing of the medial drawer runners, see nos. 2c, 17a, 20b.
2. Ibid., nos. 15, 16.
3. A single arch is on the center panel of a heavily restored cupboard with drawers at the Pilgrim Hall Museum, Plymouth, Massachusetts (Geller 1970, p. 6), and there is a double arch on several joined chests with one or two tiers of drawers (see St. George 1979b, nos. 17, 54, 58; and *Important Americana: Furniture, Folk Art and Decorations*, auction cat., Sotheby's, New York City, 15 October 1999, lot 90). For board chests with serrated bands, see St. George 1979b, nos. 24–26.

116.

Cupboard

New Haven, Connecticut, or vicinity, 1670–1700

Governor Robert Treat of Milford (see *Provenance*) is said to have first owned this cupboard, which is one of the main representatives of a school of joinery that produced the most sophisticated case pieces made in seventeenth-century Connecticut and the only furniture from that region decorated solely in the applied-ornament style. Other examples are a cupboard said to have belonged to Treat's son-in-law, Rev. Samuel Andrew, also of Milford (Virginia Museum of Fine Arts, Richmond), a cupboard that descended in the Starr family of Guilford (Yale University Art Gallery), and a one-case chest of drawers with doors (Museum of Fine Arts, Boston) that has no early history and is the only known American example of this furniture form. The last two are notable for their striking geometric inlays of light and dark wood (sapwood and heartwood of walnut) on the drawer fronts and at the center of the doors. A joined chest (originally over one or two drawers) found in Middletown, Connecticut, has similar inlay, as does a small cabinet in the New Haven Museum.[1]

Lacking inlay, the decoration on this cupboard is less flamboyant. Like that on most New England furniture in the applied-ornament style, it relied on the differences in hue of walnut, cedar, and oak and on ebonized appliqués to provide coloristic effects, which have regrettably been almost totally lost. However, the impact of the salient rectangular boss at the center of the door, set within a cruciform scheme that is echoed on the side panels, remains strong (fig. 66). The same patterns occur on the upper case of the related cupboards and a variant on the lower doors of the Yale example and on the piece at the Museum of Fine Arts, Boston. Derived from London case furniture, this type of design is found also on Boston work. The present door and those on the Yale cupboard are distinguished by having the stiles tenoned to the rails rather than the reverse. This allows the channel molding on the rails of the upper side panels to carry on across the full width of the central door. All three cupboards are characterized by ogee corbels under the top that are marked by deeply cut vertical lines and by corbels under the middle shelf that feature an ovolo and a broad plane that cants inward. The form of the applied half spindles with their acorn-shaped tops is also distinctive (fig. 66); close counterparts occur on the chest of drawers with doors and a board chest at the Yale University Art Gallery; a slightly different version is on the Yale cupboard. The character of the replaced upper pillars on the present piece runs counter to seventeenth-century practice. One would expect such pillars to be of a baluster type; the original ones were most likely similar to those on the two related cupboards, where the solid mass of the balusters balances that of the bold projecting boss on the door. With the pillars oriented as they currently are on the Yale University Art Gallery cupboard, the rings and reels at the base of the baluster form would have visually connected the turnings of the upper and lower case.[2] A repeat pattern such as that on the legs of this piece is anomalous on a cupboard and seems more appropriate to a table or a stand. Indeed, the only other known New England turnings in this flattened-ball-and-ring pattern occur on two square tables of the same general format as cat. no. 46.[3] The use of four turned legs in the lower case of

116. See also figs. 66, 113, 132.

a cupboard is unusual as well but has a parallel in the example at the Virginia Museum of Fine Arts, which was originally designed to have an open lower shelf.[4] The lightness of the base and the nature of the turnings on its quite slim legs, together with the overall proportions of the piece, which are more vertical than the norm, give this cupboard a stance suggestive of that of a cabinet on stand.[5]

The type of dovetails used in the drawers of the three related cupboards and the chest of drawers with doors (see fig. 113), like the design of the applied ornament, suggests that these pieces originated in a shop tradition that was derived from London-style joinery. Two London joiners were among the early settlers of New Haven, William Russell (1612–1664/65) and William Gibbons (in New Haven 1640–d. 1689). Robert F. Trent has proposed that they transferred to Connecticut this London-style tradition, which differs from the one established in Boston and which he designated a lower level of London joinery.[6] However, since pieces with closely related designs have yet to be documented to London and to the time that those joiners were working there, and since little is yet known of London-style joinery produced in English urban centers outside that metropolis, the influence of other craftsmen, not necessarily from London and who may have emigrated at a later date, cannot be discounted at this point.[7] The three cupboards that have family histories are associated by them not with New Haven but with adjacent towns. Exactly where and by whom in the New Haven area the furniture in this style was made remain unclear. It is probable that this piece was made by a craftsman with a later working career than Russell or Gibbons; it is here dated no earlier than the 1670s since the design of its lower case appears to represent a stylistic shift from a traditional cupboard form. Trent has assigned the same date range to the chest of drawers with doors because its oak top is made of a mill-sawn board.[8]

CONSTRUCTION

The cupboard is built in two stages, with the middle shelf part of the lower case. The upper case is held in place by a rectangular tenon at the bottom of each rear stile that engages the middle shelf and by the upper pillars, turned as separate pieces, which have round tenons that fit into the corner blocks above and the shelf below. On the upper case, the back, which has three vertical panels, the front and side rails that form the frieze, and the blocks above the pillars are joined as one unit, and the front and splayed sides of the storage compartment, which has pentagonal front stiles, as another. The back edge of the rear stiles of the splayed sides is angled to fit against the stiles of the back, and the two are held together by nails driven in from the front. The top is formed of a wide and a narrow board nailed in place. The soffit consists of thin longitudinal boards nailed to the top of the upper rails of the splayed sides and let into a groove in the front and side frieze rails. On the door, the stiles are tenoned to the rails, and the applied beveled rectangle in the center consists of a solid block of wood. The door is pintle-hinged; a vertical slat has been nailed to the inner side of the left front stile of the case to serve as a stop. The side panels are each formed of two vertical boards.

On the lower case, the turned legs and feet are one with the stiles. The present two drawers were originally part of one long drawer, made to run on its bottom, and with the sides joined to the front with three dovetails, the back rabbeted to accept the sides and nailed to the sides, and the bottom formed of thin transverse boards that come together in a V-shaped tongue-and-groove joint and are nailed to a rabbet in the front and to the bottom of the other sides (fig. 113). The middle shelf is made of a wide front board and a narrow strip at the back and is attached with wooden pins; the bottom shelf is a single board nailed to the rails.

On both cases, the mortise-and-tenon joints are narrow (only about $\frac{1}{4}$ in.), and those of the rear muntins and the rails above and below the door and drawers are secured with just one pin. The corbels under the top are made of two superimposed sections, those at drawer level, of four. The top segment in each consists of a fascia, fillet, and cavetto, and the same profile is used for the molding under the middle shelf (and on the related cupboards for the cornice, here lacking). The architrave and the moldings on the upper side panels, four corners of the door panel, and below the drawers all have a particular profile consisting of a fascia, cyma reversa, and fillet (fig. 132). A smaller cyma reversa preceded by an astragal and followed by a fillet is used on the moldings applied to the center block on the door, and the same cyma and a fillet preceded by two fascias constitute the bottom segment of the lower corbels. The moldings on the drawers and side rails at drawer level are formed of an astragal, cavetto, small bead, and fillet—a common profile. The channel molding run on the front and side rails of the upper case and on the front and side rails below the open shelf has a small ovolo on each side. The oak has been planed, except on the inner surfaces of the lower case rails. Fungus-damaged wood was used in two instances.

CONDITION

If the cupboard once had a cornice, no evidence of it remains. The turned pillars of the upper case (sassafras) are replacements. The shelves in the storage compartment and their supports are replaced, as may be the boards of the soffit (oak). The upper rail of the door has a small patch at the left end. The top (yellow poplar) and the middle shelf (walnut), heavily stained and marked, appear to be reused boards. The middle shelf was in place when the long drawer was divided into two, each the width of a simulated panel. What was the center of the drawer front with its applied plaque and corbel has been nailed in place through the shelf and rail from above and up through the rail below. While what was once one drawer front is made of an unusual wood, there is no indication that it is not original. The new inner drawer sides (yellow poplar) are attached from the front and back with cut nails. On the left drawer the bottom has a patch and a new narrow strip along one edge. The outer drawer runners and guides and the center support system are all new. The lower shelf (chestnut) is somewhat questionable; the applied molding on its front and sides is definitely added. A section of the lower turning is missing on two of the feet; all feet have lost some height and were at one time fitted with casters. The reason for a modern screw hole on the inner side of each front stile below the drawers and for nail holes on the lower leg blocks on the front and sides is unclear; possibly they stem from a makeshift enclosing of the lower case. Three short sections of panel molding on the upper case stand out as new, as do the upper segment of three corbels, the main portion of another, and the doorknob. Some of the bosses look replaced. The remaining applied ornament shows reasonable wear. Some has no doubt been reattached and is secured with nails. The exterior of the cupboard and interior of the door have a glossy modern finish. There are remains, particularly on the soffit, of an earlier mahogany-color coating.

WOODS

All framing members, panels, back, bottom, and outer side of drawers, corbels, moldings applied to frame, WHITE OAK and RED OAK; plaques on door and side panels, possibly beveled block on door, BLACK WALNUT; applied panel and simulated panel moldings, possibly right half spindle on left side, CEDAR; drawer front, Lauraceae (laurel family, genus and species not identified).

DIMENSIONS

OH. 57½ (146.1); OW. (corbels at drawer level) 44 (111.8); upper CW. 40⅛ (101.9); lower CW. 41¼ (104.8); OD. (corbels at drawer level) 21⅝ (54.9); upper CD. 18¾ (47.6); lower CD. 20¼ (51.4).

EXHIBITIONS

"The Art of Joinery: Seventeenth-Century Case Furniture in the American Wing," MMA, 18 October 1972–18 March 1973; "Furniture of the New Haven Colony: The Seventeenth-Century Style," New Haven Colony Historical Society (now New Haven Museum), New Haven, Connecticut, 16 April–31 August 1973; "A Bicentennial Treasury: American Masterpieces from the Metropolitan," MMA, 29 January 1976–2 January 1977.

REFERENCES

Nutting 1921, pp. 130, 136; Nutting 1924, no. 214; Nutting 1928–33, no. 466; Keyes 1931, p. 202; Powel 1954, p. 199; Safford 1972 (exh. cat.), no. 2; Kane 1973a (exh. cat.), no. XXI; Kane 1973b, fig. 6; *Bicentennial Treasury* 1976 (exh. cat.), p. 238; Schwartz 1976, no. 12.

PROVENANCE

Ex coll.: Mrs. J. Insley Blair, Tuxedo Park, New York; her daughter Mrs. J. Woodhull Overton, Balmville, New York.

Mrs. Blair purchased the cupboard from Charles Woolsey Lyon, a dealer in New York City, in 1921. According to a letter dated 12 March 1921 from Lyon to Mrs. Blair (ADA files), the cupboard was acquired from Mrs. Albert W. Mattoon of New Haven, Connecticut, and had been for some twenty years on loan from her to the New Haven Colony Historical Society. She had inherited it from Robert Treat Merwin, to whom it had descended from Robert Treat of Milford, governor of Connecticut from 1683 to 1698. A direct line of descent can be established, as follows: Governor Robert Treat (1622?–1710); his son Joseph Treat (1662–1721); his son Joseph Treat (1693–1772); his son Joseph Treat (1722–1791); his son Richard Treat (1761–1832); his daughter Amy Treat (1786–1848), who married in 1803 Thomas Merwin (1782–1842); their son Ira Merwin (1808–1872); his son Robert Treat Merwin (1838–1902); his daughter Alice Northrop Merwin

(b. 1864), who married in 1891 Albert Ward Mattoon (1865–1937) and who sold the cupboard. The 1710 probate inventory of Governor Treat lists "an old cupboard wᵗʰ 2 Cloths" valued at one pound, ten shillings, very possibly this piece, with one cloth used to cover the top and one the open shelf below. Whether or not the "1 Cubbard" valued at one pound listed in the 1721 inventory of his son Joseph is the same piece it is not possible to know.[9] The cupboard was on loan from Mrs. Overton to the MMA from 1952 to 1953, when it became a gift.

Gift of Mrs. J. Woodhull Overton, in memory of Mrs. J. Insley Blair, 1953 (53.197.1)

1. For the two cupboards, in the order mentioned, see Kane 1973a, nos. XXII, XXIII; for the chest of drawers, see Fairbanks and Trent 1982, no. 482; for the cabinet, see Kane 1973a, p. 55, fig. 8. The joined chest (Kane 1973a, p. 55, fig. 7) has recently come to light again (*American Furniture and Decorative Arts*, auction cat., Skinner, Boston, 9 June 2002, lot 99). There are related board chests at the Connecticut Historical Society, Hartford (Connecticut Historical Society 1958, p. 32), Wadsworth Atheneum (Chinnery 1979, fig. 4:227), and Yale University Art Gallery (Kane 1973a, no. XXIV; G. W. R. Ward 1988, no. 33); and in Nutting 1928–33, no. 95. Additional ones are illustrated in Gronning 2003.
2. For the board chest, see n. 1 above. For the present orientation of the cupboard pillars, see G. W. R. Ward 1988, no. 194.
3. One table is at the East Hampton Historical Society, East Hampton, New York (Graybeal and Kenny 1987, pl. VI); the other is in a private collection.
4. See Kane 1973a, p. 53, fig. 6; see also Keyes 1931.
5. For example, the ones in Bowett 2002, pls. 2:35, 2:38. Fashionable on such English stands and other furniture from the 1670–1700 period were legs with twist ornament. Ring-and-ball turnings were sometimes incorporated with such spiral ornament or used as a less labor-intensive and thus less expensive alternative (Chinnery 1979, fig. 4:271; Kirk 1982, no. 690), so the choice of turning pattern on the cupboard legs may not have been coincidental.
6. For Russell and Gibbons, see Kane 1973a, pp. 81, 84. For the attribution and a full discussion of the characteristics of the New Haven–area London-style joinery, see Fairbanks and Trent 1982, no. 482, and Trent 1985, pp. 35–41.
7. G. W. R. Ward 1988, pp. 102, 378–79; Kane 1993, p. 107. Geometric inlay in contrasting woods, but in combination with carving, occurs on English furniture from Yorkshire (Chinnery 1979, figs. 3:267, 4:118, 4:121; and see the entry for cat. no. 97, n. 2).
8. Fairbanks and Trent 1982, no. 482, and Trent 1985, p. 39; there is no record of a water-powered sawmill in the New Haven area before the 1670s.
9. John Harvey Treat, *The Treat Family* (Salem, Mass., 1893), pp. 130, 184–85, 203–4, 249–50, 310–11, 389–90; Miles Merwin (1623–1697) Association, *The Merwin Family in North America* (Hartford, Conn., 1978), pp. 444, 654, 842; *Dictionary of American Biography*, vol. 18 (New York, 1936), pp. 633–34. The 1710 inventory citation is from Kane 1973a, p. 51; the 1721 inventory of Joseph Treat is in the records of the Department of History and Genealogy, Connecticut State Library, Hartford, New Haven Probate District, no. 10686.

117.

Cupboard

Probably eastern New England, 1720–50

This is one of some ten cupboards that recall in nailed board construction the form of seventeenth-century joined oak cupboards. While they vary considerably in proportions, construction, and ornamentation, they all follow the same general formula, in that they have a trapezoidal upper cabinet, a straight-fronted lower cabinet (each with a central door), and a drawer across the bottom, and are built in one piece.[1] They were not lower-level versions contemporary with the oak examples but late expressions of the form for a conservative clientele because they incorporate early-eighteenth-century design elements—most obviously, pillars that feature William and Mary–style opposed-baluster turnings. A good half of the cupboards retain their painted decoration, which is of the type seen on chests of the early decades of the eighteenth century. At the same time, the majority make reference to the panels of seventeenth-century joined case furniture by the use of applied moldings on the front boards; and the painting on the drawer of an example at the Yale University Art Gallery appears to allude to the division into a central plaque and two panels typical of drawer fronts in the applied-ornament style of the seventeenth century. The fielded panels on this example reflect later stylistic influences. While a cupboard at Historic New England has a board with beveled edges applied to the front of each door to simulate a raised panel, the doors on this cupboard are framed and contain actual fielded panels. With a quarter-round molding on the edges of the stiles and rails that surround the panels, the doors relate directly to the type of paneling that came into general use in interior woodwork in the second quarter of the eighteenth century. The drawer construction, with three dovetails at front and back, also suggests that this cupboard probably does not date from before that period. Made primarily of pine, these board cupboards were meant to be painted. Whether this one was once embellished with ornamental painting, or the colors of the new paint that was on the cupboard when it was acquired followed indications of an earlier, or original, scheme is uncertain. The present stripped, mottled surface distracts from the straightforward geometry of the overall design with its play of horizontals and verticals epitomized in the two raised panels, and the rounded contours of the pillars reflected in the arched cutouts for the feet.

Several of the board cupboards can be associated with southern New Hampshire. The Yale example, the most ornate of those known, is linked by both its painting and its history to the Hampton area, and three others that have similar

117

cutouts for the feet are probably from that region. The one at Historic New England, which is quite different in character, is believed to have descended in a family from Epping—a short distance inland from Hampton.[2] This cupboard offers no stylistic or other clues as to where in New England it was made. Whether the taste for cupboards of this format was merely a regional phenomenon centered in coastal New Hampshire and northeastern Massachusetts or was more widespread is not certain, nor is it clear if these board pieces represent a late simplification of joined oak cupboards that occurred in New England or if they are derived from an English provincial type.[3]

CONSTRUCTION

The case is of nailed board construction. The cupboard sides and the canted front boards of the upper cabinet are let into the top; and the upper cabinet bottom, which extends out to form the exposed shelf, the interior shelf and bottom of the lower cabinet, and the case bottom are let into the sides—each element a single board. The other joints of the canted front boards and all those of the lower front boards are simply butted and nailed. The back is formed of two vertical half-lapped boards that are nailed to a rabbet in the top and sides and to the rear edge of one shelf and of the case bottom. The turned pillars are let into the top and exposed shelf with round tenons. The doors are framed with mortise-and-tenon joints that are mitered, have through tenons, and are each secured with one small pin. The doors each open on two snipebill hinges and have a wooden catch on the inner side attached to the protruding end of the knob. The drawer sides are secured to the front and back with three dovetails at each joint; the bottom is one longitudinal board that is beveled to fit into a groove in the front and sides and nailed to the underside of the back. The drawer slides on the bottom of its sides on the case bottom. The feet were formed by cutting out a rounded arch with a smaller arch at its apex at the bottom of the sides and a broad shallow arch at the bottom of the back. The molded edge on the top consists of a cyma reversa. An ovolo is worked on the edges of the stiles and rails that abut the panels, the edges of the exposed shelf, the outer edges of the front boards, and the front of the projecting lower cabinet and case bottoms. The ovolo on the front edge of the sides at drawer level is applied.

CONDITION

The right rear corner of the top has broken off, two other corners have small patches, and at one end there is a patch over what probably started out as a large knothole. A lock once on the upper cabinet door is missing, and the edge of the boards opposite the lock and the doorknobs is heavily worn. The door hinges are original. The knobs on the doors show some age but those on the drawer are modern. The bottom inch or less of the drawer sides is replaced. A long split in the side of the right rear foot has been repaired. There are missing, replaced, and added nails in various locations. Records from the time the cupboard was acquired describe it as repainted with dark red, black, and orange. The paint has since been largely removed (probably before the 1930s

or 1940s). Most of the surface, which is nicked and scratched, now has an uneven reddish brown color. The pillars, which show evidence of sanding, are painted black, and lesser or greater remains of black are on the bevels of the panels, all the moldings, knobs, and the front edge of the feet. The frames of the doors bear traces of orange. The interior of the cabinets and drawer has been varnished and it has drips and splotches from the stripping.

WOODS
EASTERN WHITE PINE; pillars, SOFT MAPLE.

DIMENSIONS
OH. 48¼ (122.6); OW. (top) 37 (94); CW. 34¼ (87); OD. (top) 18 (45.7); CD. 17¼ (43.8).

REFERENCES
Williams 1963, no. 85 (drawings of moldings, which are partly inaccurate); M. B. Davidson 1980, fig. 83.

PROVENANCE
Ex coll.: H. Eugene Bolles, Boston.

Gift of Mrs. Russell Sage, 1909 (10.125.45)

1. Five of the cupboards are thought to have originated in southern New Hampshire: one is at Historic New England (N. F. Little 1984, figs. 258, 259); the four others, all with similarly shaped feet, are at the Museum of Fine Arts, Boston (Randall 1965, no. 24), and the Yale University Art Gallery (G. W. R. Ward 1988, no. 199), and in Nutting 1928–33, nos. 470, 471, and *Maine Antique Digest*, March 2002, p. 9A (sold by Dawson's Auctioneers and Appraisers, Morris Plains, New Jersey, 26 January 2002). The others are at the Henry Ford Museum (Norman-Wilcox 1968, fig. 3) and Wadsworth Atheneum (Nutting 1928–33, no. 473); and advertised in *Antiques* 55 (May 1949), p. 333 (with fielded panels; by Silvermine Tavern Antique Shops), and *Antiques* 110 (July 1976), p. 97 (by Priscilla Drake Antiques).
2. See n. 1 above. For the attribution of the Yale and related cupboards to the Hampton area, see also Brazer 1930.
3. For an English board cupboard, see Brazer 1930, fig. 3.

118.

Kast

Probably New York City or vicinity, 1650–1700

The sole representative in the MMA collection of a New York seventeenth-century joined case piece, this is one of five cupboards that are the only known examples of frame-and-panel oak furniture attributable to New York. Like three of the others, it is a cupboard in the Dutch tradition, a distinctive type called a kast or a kas. Strongly architectural in design, with a large overhanging cornice and a bold projecting base molding, and of imposing size, kasten were made exclusively in the areas of Dutch settlement in New York and New Jersey

and continued to be produced for more than a century after New Netherland became an English colony in 1664. While the numerous American kasten of the eighteenth century all follow the same general formula, each of the four surviving seventeenth-century oak examples differs in its format, reflecting the diversity of kasten made in the Netherlands at that time. One is a four-door example at the Staten Island Historical Society, Staten Island, New York; another, at the Art Institute of Chicago, Chicago, Illinois, is a two-door kast with a drawer and is made in three sections. The third, at the Winterthur Museum, is a smaller piece with two doors and a drawer.[1]

This kast presents a variation on the usual two-door scheme, in that it does not have the drawer that normally spans the case below the cupboard section and lacks a center upright that is identical to the front corner stiles and is commonly attached to the right door. That upright and the stiles typically serve as prominent pilasters that divide and flank the facade and offset the horizontal mass of the heavy top and base moldings. The front of this piece achieves an equipoise by counterbalancing the impressive top and bottom moldings with numerous smaller vertical elements—the door stiles and muntins, the tall, narrow door panels, and the panels of the case stiles. The facade is animated by a play between different planes: the movement back and forth between the protruding double-fielded panels and the receding moldings that surround them, and between the surface of the framing members and the recessed panels on the case stiles and the shallower sunken bands on the doors. It is also significantly enlivened by the remarkable painted decoration, which emphasizes the projection of the panels and adds both color and contrasts of light and dark to the composition.

The large, free-swirling painted patterns are suggestive in their colors of variegated stone rather than wood, with red over white marbleizing on the panels and cornice and black over blue gray on the frame and base molding (fig. 79). Solid red sets apart the inner field of the front panels and solid black the moldings that surround those panels. No other such decoration on joined furniture is known—and it is unusual for a case piece made entirely of oak to be painted over its whole surface—but the marbleizing is part of a long tradition of imitating wood or stone in paint that in America is first evident in the late seventeenth and early eighteenth centuries.[2] The closest comparison is to be found in interior woodwork, such as the bold marbleizing in similar colors on wall paneling from a Connecticut house of 1723 at the Wadsworth Atheneum. The same colors—red and blue gray—were popular for woodwork in Dutch colonial houses of the Hudson River valley.[3] It may be that the kast formed part of a larger interior decorative scheme either at the time it was made or not too long afterward. Cross sections taken of the painted surface seem to indicate that the paint either is original or was applied reasonably soon after the kast was built; there is no discernible layer between the wood and the paint.

The four oak kasten, although they vary in their design, all come out of the same general tradition of joinery distinguished by traits that are not characteristic of Anglo-American seventeenth-century furniture and that reflect direct Continental influences. The most important of these features are fielded panels (on three of the kasten they are double-fielded), and mortise-and-tenon joints that are mitered

(see fig. 164) because the moldings around the panels are run on the edge of the framing members and not applied. Those moldings have an ovolo-and-bead profile (fig. 137) that was widely used in Dutch seventeenth-century carpentry and joinery and that is encountered on other Dutch-influenced American work, such as the grisaille kasten in the collection (cat. nos. 119, 120). The plain recessed bands on the framing members of this kast and the one at the Winterthur Museum also have their source in Dutch kasten and interior woodwork. The present piece has one additional peculiarity that deserves mention—the manner in which the hinges are attached (let into a mortise in the stiles), which occurs on doors and shutters in the Netherlands and is found on cat. no. 132, a New York desk-on-frame.[4]

PAINTED DECORATION
The pigments have been identified as red lead, lead white, and a carbon black; the blue gray appears to be a mixture of the black and the white. The paint has a generally heavy quality, and the red has a particularly grainy texture. There are smaller and larger areas of abrasion throughout the piece, and the front and right base moldings are devoid of any marbleizing. The painted surface was treated by Peter Fodera (Fodera Fine Art Conservation, New York City) in 1988, after structural restoration of the kast at the MMA. A brown surface film of tobacco smoke residue and grime and below it a discolored finish layer were removed, the replaced feet and small restored patches were inpainted, and the surface was given a thin protective coating.

CONSTRUCTION
The kast is built in one piece. It is framed with two medial rails in the back at the level of the intermediary rails that separate the three tiers of two panels on each side. It is made of heavy stock with mortise-and-tenon joints $\frac{1}{2}$ inch wide. The joints of the muntins on the sides and on the doors are not pinned, the corner joints of the left door are secured with three pins, all others with two. The doors are framed entirely with mitered joints. The back is formed of seven vertical boards (one in two sections) joined by tongue and groove and nailed to all four rails; the end boards fit into a groove in the stiles, and one of the intervening boards has a tongue on either side. The top consists of eleven transverse boards joined by tongue and groove and nailed to the top of the four rails. The bottom has ten transverse boards similarly joined and nailed to the top of the back rail and to a rabbet in the front rail. Originally there were two full shelves in the interior which consisted of transverse boards nailed to the top of the medial back rails and at the front to a rabbet in rails that were nailed to the stiles. A front-to-back center brace is let into a recess in the top of the front and rear top rails with single-shouldered tenons. According to the nail holes on one side of that brace (the other side has a chamfered edge) and a shadow line on the front rail, there was originally a partition formed of several vertical boards that divided the space above the upper shelf.[5]

The front and side top and base moldings are each a solid piece and are attached from the inside with large rosehead nails. Above the cyma reversa molding that dominates the cornice are a small cyma reversa and a large astragal and below it, an astragal and a cavetto. The same cavetto is at the top of the base molding, where it is followed by a fascia flanked by fillets, a large ovolo, and a fillet. The two superimposed fields on the door panels are worked from a solid

118. See also figs. 79, 137.

board, and the edge of the inner field is molded with the same cyma that is at the top of the cornice. The molding around those panels—a shallow ovolo, bead, and fillet (fig. 137)—is worked on the edge of the framing members. Those framing members have, in addition, a plain recessed band down the center. The recess that extends the full height of the front case stiles is edged with the same ovolo-and-bead as the framing members of the doors, and the moldings on the horizontal insets that form the simulated panels have the same profile. The molding worked on either side of the recessed band on the side rails, on the edges of the side muntins, and on the lower inside edge of the upper three back rails is a shallow ovolo with just a fillet. The doors are each attached with two butt hinges on which the outer half of the leaves is bent at a right angle; the inner portion of the leaf is recessed into the outer edge of the door or case stile, and the angled section is inserted into a mortise and secured with nails driven through the stile. The case stiles are rabbeted to accept the doors. The top and bottom edges of the doors are cut on an angle so that the rails are wider on the outside than the inside, and the edges of the case rails are angled to conform. The two doors meet at the center in a slightly canted half lap. The kast is made entirely of riven stock. All surfaces have been planed and the framing members are all well squared.

CONDITION

At one point in the kast's history, no doubt to make the piece easier to move, the four case stiles and the side muntins and panels were sawn through just below the top rails, so that once the uppermost row of nails in the back boards was pulled out, the cornice section could be detached. Restorations undertaken at the MMA after the kast was acquired included removing the nails and screwed-on iron plates that then partly reattached the top section and screwing new metal plates to the four stiles to hold it securely in place. Old and new nails and modern screws secured the back boards to the rails, and those into the top rail were replaced with new screws. There are areas of dry rot on the exterior of those boards and on the back of the rear stiles. At the same time, the feet were restored: the short stubs that had survived made it clear that the feet originally were extensions of the molded stiles. Modern shelves were removed from the interior, where the only vestiges of the original shelves are the nail holes in the back medial rails and those in the stiles from the attachment of the missing front shelf rails. The front base molding, which has two large splits, was reinforced from behind with six large screws that pass through the rail. Various nails had been previously added from the exterior to secure both the base and the cornice moldings. Small sections that were missing at the front corners of the cornice, at the top of the right front stile, and at the lower right hinge were replaced. On the doors, one of the small square insets that fill the end of the recessed band in the stiles was replaced, two are missing, and three are previous replacements. The nails that secure the lower hinges in the stiles are replaced. The lock (now attached with modern screws) in

the right door and an elaborate catch in the left door appear to be original. A thin slat has been nailed to the top of the bottom case rail for the width of the left door. (See also *Painted decoration.*)

WOODS

WHITE OAK; uppermost side muntins, RED OAK.

DIMENSIONS

OH. 70 (177.8); OW. (cornice) 67 (170.2); CW. 61 (154.9); OD. (cornice) 25 (63.5); CD. 22⅛ (56.2).

EXHIBITION

"American Kasten: The Dutch-Style Cupboards of New York and New Jersey, 1650–1800," MMA, 19 January–7 April 1991.

REFERENCES

Keyes 1934, fig. 2 (owned by Mrs. Sara M. Sanders); MMA 1988, pp. 56–57; Kenny, Safford, and Vincent 1991a (exh. cat.), no. 3; Kenny, Safford, and Vincent 1991b, pls. V, Va (detail of front); Leath 1997, fig. 8.

PROVENANCE

Ex coll.: Mrs. Sara M. Sanders, Closter (Bergen County), New Jersey, by 1934; Millia Davenport, New City, New York, from about 1938.

The information that the kast was "found near the palisades of the Hudson," published in 1934 (see *References*), probably came from Mrs. Sanders. By the time the kast was acquired by the MMA, an envelope with the history of the piece, which according to the donor had been tacked to the back of the kast, was lost.

Gift of Millia Davenport, 1988 (1988.21)

1. For a full discussion of the kast form in America, see Kenny, Safford, and Vincent 1991a; for the oak examples, see pp. 10–15 and nos. 1–4. The fifth New York oak cupboard (Winterthur Museum; Failey 1976, no. 37) relates to neither English nor Dutch examples.

2. For examples of graining on furniture of that period, see cat. nos. 46, 47, 110, and 141. Early references to marbleizing in America include the 1705 decision by the House of Burgesses in Williamsburg, Virginia, to have "the wanscote and other Wooden work" in part of the Capitol to "be painted like marble" (cited in N. F. Little 1952, p. 7) and a Boston bill of 1707 for "painting 26 yds. green Marble color" (cited in A. L. Cummings 1979, p. 200).

3. Fales 1972, no. 34 (wall paneling); Blackburn and Piwonka 1988, figs. 101, 176 (Dutch colonial woodwork).

4. For more on the joinery of these kasten, see Kenny, Safford, and Vincent 1991a, pp. 11–14. To the discussion of the ovolo-and-bead molding on p. 12 can be added its use on the end rails of a walnut New York oval table with falling leaves at the Winterthur Museum (Kenny 1994, fig. 12).

5. The kast at the Staten Island Historical Society has a partition constructed in this manner; nails driven through the shelf below into the end of the boards secure the partition at the bottom.

119.

Kast

Probably New York City, 1690–1720

Large pendants of fruit in niches, executed in grisaille and strikingly opulent and sculptural, distinguish this and a small number of other American kasten. Painted in white, black, and blue gray, the decoration also includes festoons, swags, smaller pendants, and foliate scrolls—motifs that are part of a Renaissance vocabulary of architectural ornament that spread from Italy throughout northern Europe during the sixteenth and seventeenth centuries. In the Netherlands during the second half of the seventeenth century carved pendants and festoons were popular on the exterior of buildings and in interior woodwork, and they appeared on Dutch Baroque kasten and other furniture of that period as well. At the same time, grisaille painting was widely used in the decoration of interiors, where it served to represent relief ornament, such as the motifs mentioned above, and to simulate figures in the round within niches. Those traditions are the ultimate source of the type of decoration seen here, which is directly indebted to grisaille painting on Dutch kasten.[1]

The relationship between the ornament on the few known Dutch grisaille kasten (two extant and two documented by photographs) and that on this piece is clear.[2] Most of the motifs correspond quite closely. As here, the primary pendants appear three-dimensional, each suspended in a niche from a ribbon and centered by either a large pomegranate or a pear-shaped fruit that rests on a big leaf and is surrounded by apples and grapes (fig. 80); and the festoons and smaller pendants, which contain just apples arranged to form a lozenge, are rendered as reliefs. The painting shows the same arbitrary use of light and shade in the niches, but the arch of the niches is flat at the top and not rounded as on all the American examples. On the whole, the painting on the Dutch kasten is more elaborate and on three of them is done on a darker ground.

This is one of five kasten that vary structurally but are similar enough in their ornament to have been decorated in the same shop or related shops, which suggests that the painting was done by specialists. One, at Gracie Mansion in New York City, is analogous in form to cat. no. 119, having an overall design derived from Dutch oak kasten of the first half of the seventeenth century, characterized by square proportions and a salient ovolo frieze containing a drawer. The three others—taller, built in two sections, with a drawer in the base, and each made in a different shop—correspond in format and construction to American Baroque kasten of the eighteenth century.[3] While some variations are evident in

the ornament on these five pieces, such as in the number and arrangement of the apples in the lower portion of the large pendants, the overall composition of the motifs and the painting technique is the same throughout. The fruit, for instance, is painted in a consistent manner, with the volume of an apple always similarly defined and highlighted and the apple usually turned the same way. The painting on this kast includes several details that give it a greater degree of architectural verisimilitude than that on the related pieces and bring it closest, all told, to the Dutch examples. Only on this kast is there a clear replication—at the center of the drawer—of the acanthus motif that on the Dutch kasten ornaments the frieze above each stile and serves as a capital. The niches on the doors are drawn deep enough to contain a pendant in the round. Those pendants are suspended from keystones (an element present on all the Dutch kasten and also on the doors of the kast at Gracie Mansion), and the pendants on the sides hang from a ring anchored to the top of the arch. In all other instances the pendants in niches on this group of kasten hang from a ribbon not visibly attached to anything. This is the only kast in the group to center a pendant not with a pomegranate but with a pear-shaped fruit that occurs on one of the Dutch examples and is probably a quince. The quince, like the pomegranate, is a symbol of fertility and accords with other evidence that these kasten may have been dowry pieces.[4] One element of the decoration that has no counterpart on Dutch grisaille examples is the perimetric molding on the doors simulated in paint here and on the kast at Gracie Mansion. Actual moldings are applied to the doors on the other three kasten—a feature of high-style Dutch work that occurs otherwise on only a few unpainted American kasten probably made in New York City. This suggests that the grisaille kasten were made in shops that also produced unpainted examples in other woods. It should be noted in that regard that the base molding on the present piece has essentially the same profile as that on two joined oak kasten, cat. no. 118 and an example at the Art Institute of Chicago, Chicago, Illinois.[5]

PAINTED DECORATION

The pigments have been identified as lead white and a carbon black. The kast was given a ground coat of blue gray, which appears to be a mixture of the white and black, and the decoration was executed in white, black, the ground color, and at least one other value of gray. No gray ground is discernible under the black on the architrave, base molding, and the molded edges of the center front upright. The paint shows abrasions throughout, especially on the doors. The surface, which retains an uneven layer of a yellowed finish over the paint, was cleaned of dirt and grime in 1980 and given a thin protective coating.

CONSTRUCTION

The kast is entirely of board construction secured with rosehead nails. The top consists of a wide front board, which is joined by tongue and groove to a narrower rear section made up of two lengths that are lapped and nailed together. The one-board sides are let into grooves in the top, and the bottom and two deep shelves—each a single board—into grooves in the sides. The back is formed of eleven vertical, riven oak clapboards that are simply overlapped and nailed to the top, the bottom, and the two shelves (fig. 96). The narrow boards that serve as front stiles are nailed to the sides, the bottom, both shelves, and probably also the rail that spans the case above the doors and has rabbeted ends that fit against a rabbet in the front edge of each side. The feet are extensions of the side and front boards. Each door is a single board, reinforced on the interior with two battens that are scribed with a grid of rectangles to guide the placement of the nails. The center upright, positioned somewhat to the right of the center of the case, is nailed to the right door. The doors are each attached with two dovetail hinges, one side of which is nailed to a recess in the edge of the door and adjoining batten and the other to a recess in the edge of the front board and an adjoining block. There is a lock in the right door and an iron hook on the left door that once engaged a staple in the lower full shelf. The front ovolo frieze serves as the front of a hidden drawer, which runs on its bottom on supports nailed to the case sides. The drawer front and back are nailed to the sides and bottom; the bottom is a single longitudinal board that extends under the sides and is nailed to them. The drawer back consists of an oak clapboard similar to those of the case back, and another such clapboard constitutes a shallow top shelf supported by slats nailed to the sides.

The frieze on the sides is formed by a board nailed at the bottom to the case sides and at the top to a narrow board nailed to the underside of the case top (fig. 96). The base molding, which has a profile consisting of a cavetto, fascia, fillet, large ovolo, and fillet, is not a solid block but a thick board that angles out, with only the upper part abutting the case and nailed in place. A slat fills the gap between that molding and the case bottom for the width of the doors; there is a similar slat above the doors between the architrave and the rail. The architrave is formed of an astragal, fascia, and cyma reversa molding. The same small cyma edges the center front upright. An ovolo-and-bead molding (see fig. 137) finishes the edges of the door battens and a chamfer the edge of the drawer runners and of the top shelf supports. Tool marks indicate that the rounded contours of the edge of the top, the convex frieze, the astragal of the architrave, and the ovolo of the base molding were shaped with a flat or round plane. The surfaces of the flat boards, including those on the exterior that are painted, were not completely smoothed but retain ridges left by the planing.

CONDITION

The kast, while it has seen heavy usage and has been repaired more than once, has no major replacements. In 1980 the doors were taken off so that the center upright, which had been shifted, could be returned to its initial position and the doors realigned. The three older hinges were reset and a new matching replacement was installed as the fourth; there are patches at the hinge placements and none of the blocks are original. The drawer, which had been nailed shut through the top and at the corners, was released. There is evidence at the center of the drawer front of a missing pull that probably consisted

of an iron ring attached by means of a strap cotter pin through a shaped plate like the one on the kast at Gracie Mansion. Also in 1980, an old replacement of the right rear foot and the adjoining rear corner of the right side was stabilized, and glued-on blocks were added between all of the feet and the base molding. At some earlier time, long modern blocks were glued on behind the front feet; the left base molding and an adjoining 9-inch strip along the top of the front base molding were replaced, as were the slat that fills the gap between the front base molding and the case bottom and the upper batten of the right door; and the lower right corner of the left door was pieced. At various locations modern nails and screws replace or supplement the original nails. The door lock and hook appear to be original, as is, perhaps, one of the hinges. The front of the two deep shelves has been damaged by gnawing (the lower one has a metal patch at center front), and so has the lower left corner of the center upright and adjacent areas of the case bottom and base molding. The top is badly stained. There are spatters of white paint across the top of the back—probably dating from when the wall of a room was painted around the kast. Red brown stain (not original) covers much of the interior. (See also *Painted decoration*.)

WOODS

YELLOW POPLAR; case back, drawer back, uppermost shelf, RED OAK; left drawer side, left drawer support, EASTERN WHITE PINE.

DIMENSIONS

OH. 61½ (156.2); OW. (top) 60⅜ (153.4); CW. 52¼ (132.7); OD. (top) 23 (58.4); CD. 19 (48.3).

EXHIBITIONS

On loan to the New York State Historical Association, Ticonderoga, from 1933 to 1948; "Country Style," Brooklyn Museum, Brooklyn, New York, 1 March–15 May 1956; on loan to Old Bethpage Village Restoration (for exhibition in the Schenck House), Old Bethpage, New York, from 1974 to 1978 and to the Albany Institute from 1981 to 1988; "Remembrance of Patria: Dutch Arts and Culture in Colonial America, 1609–1776," Albany Institute, 9 May–12 October 1986 (see Blackburn and Piwonka 1988); "American Kasten: The Dutch-Style Cupboards of New York and New Jersey, 1650–1800," MMA, 19 January–7 April 1991.

REFERENCES

Davis 1925, p. 6; "Antiques in the American Wing" 1946, p. 249, no. 17; Schwartz 1956, p. 343; M. B. Davidson 1967, no. 63; O'Donnell 1980, fig. 4; Blackburn 1984, fig. 1; M. B. Davidson and Stillinger 1985, fig. 45 (detail); Blackburn 1986, pl. VIII; Blackburn and Piwonka 1988, fig. 283 and p. 30; Kenny, Safford, and Vincent 1991a (exh. cat.), no. 5 and pp. 28–32 passim; Schipper 1995, fig. 10; MMA 2001, fig. 20.

PROVENANCE

Purchased from the dealer Charles R. Morson, Brooklyn, New York.

Rogers Fund, 1909 (09.175)

1. Kenny, Safford, and Vincent 1991a, pp. 4–5, 30–31.
2. For the extant kasten, see Blackburn and Piwonka 1988, fig. 286; and *The Andy Warhol Collection: Americana and European and American Paintings, Drawings and Prints*, auction cat., Sotheby's, New York City, 29–30 April 1988, lot 3189 (present location unknown). The two others are illustrated in Kenny, Safford, and Vincent 1991a, fig. 29 (also in Blackburn 1986, fig. 11, and in Blackburn and Piwonka 1988, fig. 284) and fig. 30 (also in Blackburn and Piwonka 1988, fig. 285).

119. See also figs. 80, 96.

3. For the kast at Gracie Mansion, which belongs to the Art Commission of the City of New York, see Fabend 1981, figs. 1–3; for the three others, see, for example, O'Donnell 1980, fig. 1 (Van Cortlandt House Museum, Bronx, New York), fig. 2 (Winterthur Museum), and fig. 3 (Monmouth County Historical Association, Freehold, New Jersey). For the differences in construction between the last three, see Kenny, Safford, and Vincent 1991a, pp. 29, 35, n. 96.
4. Kenny, Safford, and Vincent 1991a, p. 30.
5. Ibid., pp. 16–18, 29 (perimetric moldings) and no. 4 (Art Institute of Chicago kast).

120.

Kast

Probably New York City or vicinity, 1690–1730

When this kast was intact and still had an overhanging frieze and board feet, it closely matched cat. no. 119 in format, but its decoration was executed by a different and less skilled painter. While the ornamental vocabulary comes out of the same Dutch tradition, the design on the doors lacks both the perimetric molding and a section of wall with a festoon below the niche, which are characteristic of that kast and of four others with related painting;[1] and while the grisaille technique and arbitrary use of light and shade is similar, the ability to render three-dimensional forms is not. This painter seems most at home depicting conventional foliage, swags, and ribbons, which here have a strong graphic quality. The niches on the doors do achieve some illusion of depth. The pendants, however, with their amorphous composition and solid mass of grapes, look more like pasteboards than clusters of fruit in the round. Not just the flatness of the pendants but also the filling of all space with ornament and a certain lack of understanding of architectural conventions give the decoration a rather provincial look in comparison to that on cat. no. 119. On the doors there are birds below as well as above the pendants, and the edges of the pendants teem with leaves and tendrils. The design on the sides is not subsidiary to, but nearly as elaborate as, that on the doors, with a swag in the spandrels, birds above the pendants, and a niche bottom depicted even though the wall behind the pendant is entirely flat. The niche bottom at the base of the front boards that serve as stiles is totally incongruous, and the small round objects (fallen grapes?) at the bottom of all the niches on the facade are an unusual conceit. None other of the known grisaille kasten has a flourish of leaves surmounting the niches on the doors. The ornament on this piece does not appear to have been directly modeled on that of the school of painting represented by cat. no. 119 but rather based on some other prototype or printed sources in the same general tradition.[2]

In its original configuration, this kast was similar in form and dimensions to both cat. no. 119 and an example at Gracie Mansion, New York City, which has painting related to that on cat. no. 119; the first two also share particular structural traits, as once may have the third. Since these traits seem to be almost all part of a broader Dutch-derived woodworking tradition and because of the changes that have occurred in this and the Gracie Mansion kast, it is not possible to tell whether or not these pieces were made in the same shop.[3] The most distinctive feature that this kast and cat. no. 119 have in common is the quick and easy manner of constructing the back by simply overlapping riven clapboards and nailing them in placed (see fig. 96) rather than more laboriously joining the vertical boards with a tongue and groove, as on cat. no. 118, and as is typical of Dutch and eighteenth-century American kasten. The same timesaving method—documented in New York house carpentry in the seventeenth century—is employed on the back of a joined oak kast at the Art Institute of Chicago, Chicago, Illinois, but it has not been encountered otherwise on case furniture.[4] On both the present kast and cat. no. 119, a narrow top shelf is formed of a single such clapboard. The architrave on these two pieces differs somewhat—here it is squatter and includes a small cyma reversa molding immediately below the astragal not present on the former—but both kasten use the ovolo-and-bead molding that is known in America only on Dutch-influenced work (see the entry for cat. no. 118 and fig. 137). Here it ornaments the front corners of the case and on cat. no. 119 the edges of the door battens. The manner of scribing the door battens for the placement of the nails is similar on this and the two grisaille pieces related in format. That this was a traditional rather than individual working method is indicated by analogous scribing on a pair of house shutters.[5] The interior of this kast originally included a feature that is lacking on cat. no. 119: two shallow drawers hung under the upper deep shelf. This type of drawer—most often one long one—is characteristic of Dutch kasten, occurs on the Art Institute of Chicago oak kast, and is standard on American Baroque examples.

PAINTED DECORATION

The pigments have been identified as lead white and a carbon black. There is a ground coat of blue gray, which appears to be a mixture of the white and black, over which the designs are executed in white,

120

black, and blue gray of at least two different values. The architrave (now the top molding), center front upright, and the molded corners and adjacent side edges of the front boards were painted solid black over the gray ground, as was probably the original base molding. The compass-scribed arcs that laid out the arches of the niches remain visible. There are small paint losses due to nicks and abrasions throughout and large areas where the paint has worn off on the center upright and corner edges of the case, at the top of the right door, and in long scrapes on the right side. In 1980 the painted surfaces were cleaned of dirt, and most of a yellow discolored finish was removed, as were later daubs of white paint above the niches on the doors; the front and sides were then given a clear protective coating.

CONSTRUCTION

The kast is of nailed board construction similar overall to that of cat. no. 119, with two deep shelves and the bottom let into the sides (and the sides originally into the top), but here those elements as well as the doors are all made of two boards joined by tongue and groove. The back is formed of eleven vertical riven oak clapboards nailed on in the same manner, and one such clapboard constitutes the narrow top shelf. As on cat. no. 119, the door battens have been carefully scribed with a rectangular grid for the positioning of the nails, but here the battens are made of thin oak most likely cut from clapboards. The doors are each attached with two truncated dovetail hinges nailed to recesses in the edge of the door and the edge of the front

303

board. The lower edge of the doors is flush with that of the case bottom. Three nails that pass down through the bottom along the front probably once secured a rail or slat that extended out under the doors and to which the base molding was attached. On the interior, a support for a side-hung drawer is nailed to the underside of the upper full shelf toward each end, and nail holes in the center indicate there was originally also a middle support and thus not one long drawer but two short ones. The architrave molding consists of an astragal, cyma reversa, fascia, and cyma reversa. The same small cyma (¼ in.) flanks the half-round molding that runs down each side of the center upright. The outer edge of each of the front boards is finished with an ovolo-and-bead molding. The exterior as well as interior surfaces retain visible ridges left by the planing, and the wood of the right door has several noticeable knots.

CONDITION

There is evidence on the upper edge of the back and side boards that the kast has been cut down; it has lost what was in all likelihood an ovolo frieze, probably with a drawer, similar to that on cat. no. 119. The original top boards have been reworked and reused and now abut the architrave. The sides are not let into the top but just butted to it, the side architrave moldings have been off and reattached, and the top is nailed to the back rather than vice versa. Originally the feet were extensions of the side and front boards, as is indicated by the remaining stubs. When received, the kast had lost its base molding and had replaced feet of the platform type characteristic of Long Island, New York, kasten, with a turned foot in front and a rectangular one in back (missing on the right side) connected by a board to make a unit (see *References*). Those feet were repaired and are still in place, and the missing bottom molding and damaged lower rear half of the right top molding were replaced. In 1992 a new bottom molding based on that of cat. no. 119 was substituted for the earlier replacement, which had an inappropriate profile. Two short drawers originally under the upper deep shelf and the center runner that supported them have been lost. The center front upright has a glued split extending more than halfway up. The hinges are original but not all of the nails that attach them. The present lock with its separate added keyhole is a replacement. An iron hook in the left door that now catches a modern screw in the upper shelf looks old; evidence of some other latching system remains on the lower shelf and on the door at that level. A few large chips have broken out at the bottom of the right door, and there are nicks throughout the piece. (See also *Painted decoration*.)

INSCRIPTIONS

On the interior of the upper left side written in white chalk are the numbers 4 and 2 below a bar and some meaningless markings.

WOODS

EASTERN WHITE PINE; right drawer runner, SOUTHERN YELLOW PINE; back, shallow top shelf, top front rail and filler slat above doors, door battens, RED OAK.

DIMENSIONS

OH. 59⅛ (150.2); OW. (top) 57¾ (146.7); CW. 54¼ (137.8); OD. (top) 21 (53.3); CD. 18¾ (47.6).

EXHIBITIONS

"Dutch Colonial Heirlooms," Holland House, New York City, 30 January–29 March 1941; on loan to the Rijksmuseum, Amsterdam, the Netherlands, from 1954 to 1957 and to the Albany Institute from 1962 to 1979.

REFERENCES

Halsey and Tower 1925, fig. 45 (as received); Holland House Corporation of the Netherlands 1941 (exh. cat.), no. 1; Fales 1972, no. 60; Hornung 1972, no. 882; M. B. Davidson 1980, fig. 79; O'Donnell 1980, fig. 5; Fabend 1981, fig. 4; Schipper 1995, fig. 14.

PROVENANCE

According to the donor, the kast belonged to John and Sarah Hewlett of Woodbury, Long Island, New York, and was used in the Hewlett House, from which woodwork is installed in the American Wing of the MMA.[6] The donor was a direct descendant of John Hewlett (1731–1812), who married Sarah Townsend (1736–1808) in 1751.[7] Exactly when the house in question was built and if by this John III or his father, John II, are not clear, but the kast at any rate predates the house. How and when the kast entered the family are not known. This traditional history interestingly implies that an English family that, at least in this line of descent, intermarried with other English families but lived in an area of Long Island settled by both the Dutch and the English, owned a Dutch-style kast.[8]

Gift of Sarah Elizabeth Jones, 1923 (23.171)

1. For the kasten with painting related to cat. no. 119, see that entry. On the three examples with a drawer in the base, the festoon below the niche is on the drawer front.
2. Two further American kasten painted with pendants of fruit, each distinguished by differences in format and motifs and decorated by a different hand, are known (Kenny, Safford, and Vincent 1991a, pp. 29–31). One is at Van Cortlandt Manor, Croton-on-Hudson, New York (Fales 1972, no. 59), and the other is in a private collection (Fabend 1981, fig. 5).
3. For the Gracie Mansion kast, which belongs to the Art Commission of the City of New York, see Fabend 1981, figs. 1–3. The top, bottom, back, shelves, and architrave and base molding appear to be replacements.
4. Kenny, Safford, and Vincent 1991a, pp. 13–14 (overlapping clapboards) and no. 4 (Art Institute of Chicago kast).
5. Blackburn and Piwonka 1988, fig. 101. The battens on the kast in a private collection mentioned in n. 2 above are also similarly scribed.
6. Letter from Sarah Elizabeth Jones to the MMA, dated 26 May 1923 (MMA Archives). For the woodwork, see Peck et al. 1996, pp. 184–89; and ADA files.
7. *A Memorial of John, Henry, and Richard Townsend, and Their Descendants* (New York, 1865), pp. 152–54; "Jones Family Genealogical Charts," file 1 (J 7185), New York Genealogical and Biographical Society, New York City; obituary of Sarah Elizabeth Jones, *New York Times*, 30 December 1935.
8. For other examples of kasten owned in English families, see Failey 1976, pp. 109–10 and no. 30; and Carr 2003.

High Chests of Drawers

The high chest of drawers, built in two sections with an upper case containing generally four tiers of drawers and raised up on a separate base, was introduced to the colonies in the 1690s and became the prime form of case furniture in the William and Mary style in America. The high chest evolved in England during the last third of the seventeenth century. It is related in concept to cabinets-on-stand, which were made in England beginning in the 1660s and were influenced by the fashion on the Continent and in England for setting Far Eastern lacquer cabinets up on Western, often very elaborate, stands. The first two high chests in this chapter represent a stylistically early format, in which a chest of drawers is set on a relatively low frame with a full-width drawer. The lower units are joined, and some of the methods of construction used in the upper cases of these two pieces also carry on seventeenth-century practices. One chest of this type is from New York, the only object here included that did not originate in New England (cat. no. 121). Its upper case is joined, and its base has legs in a spiral pattern—a design favored on English high chests of a similar form (and on English cabinets), and among colonial high chests found only on a small number made in New York. The other is a Boston piece (cat. no. 122) with legs turned in the so-called inverted-cup pattern found on the majority of William and Mary–style high chests. Made of inexpensive woods, which were decoratively painted, its upper case is of nailed-board construction.

On the other chests in this chapter, the upper case is supported by a high base with three side-by-side drawers, a scalloped skirt, flat curved stretchers, and six turned legs, and the upper and the lower case are of dovetailed board construction. This scheme represents the fully developed William and Mary–style high chest of drawers, which expresses the new aesthetic introduced by early Baroque influences in the vertical emphasis of the design, the use of curves in the form and bold contrasts of thick and thin in the turnings, and in dramatic surface decoration. Veneering, particularly with richly figured burl wood such as that on the front of two Massachusetts high chests in the collection (cat. nos. 123, 124), was the chief means of achieving an active and arresting surface. The most lavish and striking effects were provided by japanning, a Western imitation of Far Eastern lacquerwork, which has survived from this period only on pieces from Boston (such as cat. no. 125). The Museum's japanned high chest and the two with burl veneer exemplify a popular, trim model, on which the upper case is finished at the top with just a modest ogee cornice. The usual alternate design, one that is perhaps stylistically somewhat later, features an upper case with a full entablature consisting of a larger cornice, a pulvinated frieze that conceals a drawer, and an architrave. Such an entablature crowns an imposing Boston chest that has no parallel (cat no. 126). No other known William and Mary–style high chest exhibits pilasters or blocked, projecting moldings, and here both occur not only on the front but also on the sides of the upper case. An unusual interpretation of an entablature with a pulvinated frieze occurs on a high chest ornamented with distinctive banding of contrasting light and dark veneer (cat. no. 127). This piece also has no counterpart, and it is not entirely certain where it was made. Relatively little research has yet been done on high chests of this period, and what the stylistic differences are that separate standard-format examples made in New York from those produced in Boston, for instance, has not been clearly resolved. A distinctive style associated with Philadelphia that features high chests made of solid walnut has long been identified. It is not represented in the collection by a high chest, but it is reflected in a dressing table (cat. no. 131) and a small cabinet (cat. no. 82).

The designation "high chest of drawers," now used to differentiate the form under discussion from the chest of drawers as such, dates from the late colonial period ("highboy" is a strictly modern term). In probate documents of the William and Mary period such a distinction, indicated, for example, by a listing of a "chest of drawers and frame," was rarely made. Most often just the term "chest of drawers" occurs, and that it probably refers to the new-fashioned form must be deduced from the high valuation assigned, the overall character of the household's furnishings, or the fact that it is listed together with a table, which, depending on the context, suggests a high chest paired with a dressing table.

In terms of aesthetics, high chests mark a significant break with seventeenth-century-style case furniture and they bring into practice techniques—dovetailed board construction and veneering—associated with cabinetmaking, not traditional joinery. In areas that were influenced in the seventeenth century by London-style joinery, however, some of the defining features of high chests represent an evolution, in which known methods and designs are adapted to new uses, rather than a radical change. The use of dovetails, for example, common in the drawers of Boston joined furniture, was extended to secure the boards that made up the newer style cases. The application of sections of more valuable wood on to a lesser wood on the drawer fronts of some joined case pieces (see the entry for cat. no. 109) lay the groundwork for the veneering of whole surfaces. Also, like the pillars on cupboards, high chest legs were turned as separate units (with round tenons), and the most popular turning pattern for such legs, that with an inverted-cup form above a tapering shaft, enlarged on an earlier London-style design for applied half columns (see the entry for cat. no. 98). The high chest as a form went out of

fashion in England in the 1730s, but in America it remained popular to nearly the end of the eighteenth century, its design and construction evolving with later styles.

121.

High chest of drawers

New York City or western Long Island, 1695–1720

Legs in a twist pattern are this chest's most distinctive feature (fig. 44). Related to spiral columns in European Baroque architecture, such legs, with their strong circular motion and rhythmic alternations of light and shade and contrasts of thick and thin, vividly express the sense of energy and movement that imbues Baroque design. Twist ornament is rare in American furniture, occurring on only about twenty pieces of the early colonial period, ten of them from New York.[1] While lathes to cut spirals were available in Europe and England, there is no evidence that such devices were in use in the colonies at the time; here, spirals appear to have been worked laboriously by hand. The rings and reels at the top and bottom of the legs on this chest were turned and retain tool marks typical of shaping on a lathe, but the spirals were in all probability worked with gouges and rasps, and evidence of rasping remains clearly visible.[2] Spirals were fashioned so as to have either a single twist, like a corkscrew, as here and on all the other New York pieces (high chests and tables), or a double twist, more like a rope, seen on the other American examples (chairs and one or more tables), which come from Boston, Philadelphia, and the South. Various generalizations have been made as to where abroad the single or the double twist was more popular; the single is usually considered to have been favored in France and sometimes on the Continent as a whole, and the double in England. The fact remains, however, that at least in England and the Netherlands both types occur.[3] In England the choice appears to vary according to the furniture form: for chairs, double-twist ornament was almost always preferred, but the single twist is found on the majority of high chests and cabinets-on-stand that have been published, and seen on some tables as well.[4] Thus the single-spiral legs on New York furniture could reflect either the strong presence in that city and area of craftsmen of northern European background or the influence of English-trained artisans, or a conflation of both.

The overall design of this piece is unquestionably English. The high chest form evolved in England, and this example,

like cat. no. 122, represents what is probably the earliest type, which consists of a chest of drawers set on a low joined base supported by five legs and incorporating one long drawer. This and the three other New York high chests with twist legs all have a single drawer in the base but each differs in particulars of design and/or construction. The MMA chest bears close comparison to one of two examples at the Winterthur Museum, more specifically to its lower case (the present upper case does not belong), which is much narrower and more vertical in its proportions but also of sweet gum and yellow poplar and similarly made, and which may have come out of the same shop. The legs of both pieces have ring-and-reel turnings above as well as below the spirals, and the spirals have relatively sharp ridges. As on the MMA chest, the lower mid-molding on the Winterthur example is entirely intergral to the boards that support the upper case, and the manner of their attachment corresponds, as does the construction of the drawer, except that the drawer of the latter is not side-hung. The other chest at the Winterthur Museum—squatter, with just three tiers of drawers in the upper case—is also of sweet gum but has walnut veneer on the front. The fourth high chest is a six-legged example at the Long Beach Museum of Art, Long Beach, California, distinguished by a burl veneer facade and a front skirt shaped to three identical round arches. On the legs of the last two pieces, the turning above the spirals is a short, tapered column.[5]

While this high chest is strictly English in its overall form, it exhibits traits that are not part of the Anglo-American woodworking tradition but are found on other New York furniture of the late seventeenth and early eighteenth centuries and reflect the cultural blending that was occurring in the colony at that time. The use of face-grain plugs to cover countersunk nails has parallels on cat. nos. 65 and 132, for example. The cornice is anomalous in that it is applied slightly below the upper surface of the top (fig. 144). Its profile, however, is related to the beak molding at the top of the veneered Winterthur chest and to the contours of the

121. See also figs. 44, 112, 144.

upper base molding on early-eighteenth-century kasten.[6] The chest's paneled sides and side-hung drawers, while they would seem to indicate manufacture at the cusp of the William and Mary style period, may equally well represent the conservative strain in New York furniture making that continued to employ these seventeenth-century features in the production of kasten several decades into the eighteenth century.

Furniture with sweet gum as the primary wood was made principally in the New York City area and the Hudson River valley (see cat. nos. 132, 65).[7] As mentioned in the entry for cat. no. 132, sweet gum (often called bilsted at the time and now commonly also red gum or gumwood) found favor as an inexpensive substitute for mahogany, but the intent may not always have been to imitate that imported wood. On three of this chest's long drawers, the wood under the escutcheons, which show no evidence of having been replaced, is light in color. The sweet gum under the brasses on a high chest at the Winterthur Museum made by Samuel Clement of Flushing, New York, was likewise found to be unstained and very light in color.[8] The makers of these two pieces seem to have been aiming at a different aesthetic.

CONSTRUCTION

The frame of both the upper and the lower case is constructed with mortise-and-tenon joints that are about ½ inch wide. On the upper case, the stiles are oriented so that the wider face is toward the side. The joints of the side rails are secured with two pins; those of the front rails and drawer dividers and of the vertical partition between the short drawers (all made of 1 by 2 in. stock) with one. The panel on each side is formed of two vertical boards. The back consists of two horizontal boards lapped together and nailed to a rabbet in the stiles. The top, composed of three longitudinal boards, and the bottom, a single board, are nailed to the rails and the back. The drawer runners at the sides of the case are let into the stiles and nailed. The center runner at top is secured to the partition in the front with a halved joint; at the rear, it is housed in the back and secured with a nail through the back.

On the lower case, which is open at the top, the back and side rails and the rail below the drawer are tenoned to stiles that are nearly 2¾ inches square and are one with the legs. Nailed to the top of the stiles and mitered at the front corners are a board across the front and one on each side (all ca. 3¼ in. wide); the outer third of all three has been planed to form the lower mid-molding, and the inner two-thirds are recessed and support the upper case. A slat nailed to the top of the back rail raises the back to the level of the recess. Two strips are nailed to the underside of the upper case so as to fit just inside that slat and prevent the upper case from sliding back. The drawer runners are let into the stiles and nailed. The center front leg is joined to the front rail with a through tenon secured with two pins. The left rear leg is rotated 90 degrees clockwise in relation to the others. The side stretchers are joined to the front and rear stretchers with thin tenons that are double-pinned as well; each stretcher is a solid piece. The feet are attached to the legs each with a round tenon.

On both cases, the drawers are side-hung. The sides are joined to the front with a single dovetail on the lower case drawer, two dovetails on the upper-case long drawers (fig. 112), and two half dovetails on the short drawers. The back—rabbeted in the upper but not the lower case—is nailed to the sides through the back. The drawer bottom, formed of two longitudinal boards, is beveled to fit into a groove in the front and nailed to the other sides. The three long drawers in the upper case have metal locks, the two short drawers, wooden spring locks. The cornice, which consists of a broad shallow ovolo followed by a fillet and a cyma recta, is applied so that ¼ inch of the edge of the top is visible and functions as part of the profile (fig. 144). On the upper mid-molding there is a cyma recta above a fascia. The cornice, upper mid-molding, and all the half-round moldings are attached with sprigs that have been countersunk and the holes neatly filled with small rectangular face-grain plugs. Small sprigs also secure the drawer bottoms; large rosehead or T-headed nails are used elsewhere.

CONDITION

The feet are replaced, and so are the segments of half-round molding on the lower right front stile. The stretchers are pieced at the right front and right rear corners, and there is a repaired break in the front stretcher. On the drawers, some of the bottoms have a few added or reset nails, the bottom of the left short drawer has a patch, and a thin drawer stop has been nailed to the back of the middle long drawer. The chest, when acquired, had bail handles of a later date. For their installation a large recess had been gouged out on the inner side of the drawer fronts at each point of attachment. They were removed and replaced with drop pulls at locations where evidence indicated such pulls had originally been attached, and the remaining holes were plugged. All but one escutcheon appear to be original. The locks on the long upper case drawers are replacements, and the wooden spring locks on the short drawers may be later additions. The show surfaces are considerably nicked and heavily scratched, and the top is marred, in addition, by dark stains or scorching. The exterior has an uneven reddish mahogany color and appears to have been finished with linseed oil and wax. There are dark remains of a degraded finish, particularly on the legs.

INSCRIPTIONS

The chest bears modern inscriptions in white chalk: in large characters on the underside of the bottom of the upper case "880" over a bar over "78" and a number or letter inside the bottom of each drawer to indicate its location.

WOODS

Stiles, all rails, drawer dividers and partition, top, side panels, all drawer fronts, legs, stretchers, all moldings, SWEET GUM; sides, back, and bottom of drawers, back and bottom of upper case, strips under bottom of upper case, YELLOW POPLAR; drawer runners on sides of upper case, SOUTHERN YELLOW PINE; center runner of upper case, runners of lower case, WHITE OAK.

DIMENSIONS

OH. 58¼ (148); upper case: OW. (cornice) 43¼ (109.9), CW. 40¾ (103.5), OD. (cornice) 23½ (59.7), CD. 22⅛ (56.2); lower case: OW. (mid-molding) 45 (114.3), CW. 43¾ (111.1), OD. (mid-molding) 24⅜ (61.9), CD. 23¾ (60.3).

EXHIBITIONS

On loan to the New-York Historical Society, New York City, from 1973 to 1976; "Long Island Is My Nation: The Decorative Arts and Craftsmen, 1640–1830," Museums at Stony Brook (now Long Island Museum of American Art, History, and Carriages), Stony Brook, New York, 21 October 1976–2 January 1977.

REFERENCES

Downs 1937a; Halsey and Cornelius 1938 (and 1942), fig. 18; "Antiques in the American Wing" 1946, p. 247, no. 10; Buhler 1947, fig. 6; Schwartz 1958, pl. 7C; Comstock 1961, fig. 1; Comstock 1962, no. 69; Hornung 1972, no. 907; Butler 1973, p. 22; Failey 1976 (exh. cat.), no. 38; Fairbanks and Bates 1981, p. 54; Johnston 1988, fig. 67.

PROVENANCE

The high chest was bought from Hannah Elizabeth Mitchell (1878–1968), of Port Washington, Long Island, New York, in whose family it had come down. The vendor was a lineal descendant of Robert Mitchill/Mitchell (1670–1748) through the latter's son John Mitchell Sr. (1716–1792), who married Deborah Prince (1717–1806); his son John Mitchell Jr. (1743–1823), who married in 1764 Rebecca Hewlett (1743–1790) and in 1793 her sister Jane Hewlett (1749–1816); his son Whitehead Mitchell (1783–1862), who married in 1815 Margaret E. Cornwell; his son Charles W. Mitchell (1816–1902), who married Hannah Covert (1816–1902); his son the vendor's father, Samuel M. Mitchell (1847–1916), who married Lizzie Senter Robinson (d. after 1936), from Maine. The first four generations were farmers, and the house built by John Sr. in 1769 (demolished late 1950s) in Port Washington remained in the family until Charles W. sold the homestead, about 1887.

Robert Mitchell was of the generation that would have first acquired the high chest. Born in England, he arrived in New York about 1694 and in about 1700 moved to North Hempstead township, Long Island, where in 1713 he was appointed fence viewer and surveyor of highways for Madnan's Neck (now Great Neck) and in 1740 served as a town trustee at Cow Neck (now Port Washington). He married twice, first in 1708 the widow Phebe Denton Thorne (1679–1728) and then in 1729 the widow Hannah Van Wyck Cornwell. All surnames mentioned, except for that of the vendor's mother, are of families that were among the original or early settlers of the Hempstead or Queens, Long Island, area. Whether Robert purchased the chest or it entered the family collaterally at some point (the probate inventory of Phebe's first husband, Richard, has survived and indicates that she did not bring a high chest into the household), the piece was more likely made in Manhattan or its immediate proximity on western Long Island than locally in North Hempstead.[9]

Rogers Fund, 1936 (36.112)

1. For the twenty or so objects, see Kenny 1994, figs. 11, 12 and nn. 10, 19. Not included in n. 19 was the Winterthur Museum chest acc. no. 58.559 (see n. 5 below).
2. For the use of lathes at that time to cut twists, see R. Edwards 1964, p. 626, and Forman 1988, pp. 220, 222. How spirals were laid out and carved is explained in Schramm 1982.
3. Symonds 1934, p. 177; Symonds 1951, p. 91; Forman 1988, pp. 220, 230; Kenny 1994, pp. 123–24; Bowett 2002, p. 73.
4. The presence in the mid-Atlantic colonies of at least one English high chest of the same format as cat. no. 121 and with single-twist legs is documented by the veneered example shipped from London in 1714 to Elizabeth Estaugh of Haddonfield, New Jersey, by her father (Hopkins and Cox 1936, pp. 6–7).
5. Winterthur Museum acc. no. 58.560 (Downs and Ralston 1934, no. 34; Blackburn and Piwonka 1988, fig. 184). Winterthur Museum acc. no. 58.559 (*Fine American and English Furniture and Decorations*, auction cat., Parke-Bernet Galleries, New York City, 13–15 March 1947, lot 619); the drawers on this piece are dovetailed at the front and back. The high chest at the Long Beach Museum (Promised Gift of Thomas H. Oxford and Victor Gail) is made of walnut, yellow pine, and white pine, with walnut and burl ash veneers (Kirk 1982, no. 540); it has not been examined by the present writer.
6. One other case piece with a cornice molding so applied is known to the writer, a chest of drawers in a private collection that is similar to the upper case of cat. no. 121 in drawer construction and in having paneled sides, and is also made of sweet gum and yellow poplar. For the beak-molding profile on kasten, see Kenny, Safford, and Vincent 1991a, p. 76.
7. Its use in Pennsylvania and the South was generally as a secondary wood, as on cat. no. 131; exceptions are, for example: "gum" bedsteads listed in Philadelphia inventories of 1702, 1708, and 1722 (McElroy 1979, pp. 63–64), and a "Spice Box of Sweet Gum" (cited in Griffith 1986, p. 19); or a North Carolina table and board chest (Bivins 1988, figs. 5.35, 5.48).
8. Letter from Benno M. Forman to the writer, August 1978. For the high chest, see Failey 1976, no. 39.
9. Downs 1937a; Charles J. Werner, comp., *Genealogies of Long Island Families* (New York, 1919), pp. 25–26, 37; George L. Williams, *Historic Mitchell Farms: A Port Washington Walking Guide*, The Landmarks of Cow Neck, vol. 3 (Port Washington, N.Y., 1985), pp. 1, 3, 65, 70–71; George L. Williams, "What's in a Name: The Mitchill or Mitchell Family of Cow Neck," *Long Island Forum* 47 (August 1985), pp. 154, 157; letter of 17 May 1993 from John Wellington Mitchell, a nephew of the vendor, to Leslie Symington (ADA files); *Genealogy of the Descendants of Rev. Richard Denton of Hempstead, Long Island, for the First Five Generations*, prepared by George D. A. Combes from manuscript notes of William A. D. Eardeley (Rockville Centre, N.Y., 1936), p. 33; Richard Thorn(e), 1707 inventory, New York State Archives, Albany, New York (J0301-82, Court of Probates, Inventories of Decedent Estates, box 5).

122.

High chest of drawers

Boston, 1710–25

The painted ornament on this chest emulates the brilliance of japanning, using a palette of red, orange, and what was originally a bright yellow to simulate the dazzling effect of lustrous metal. Though none of the motifs are raised, they are all drawn from the vocabulary of japanning; and while their arrangement on the front does not have the whimsical character typical of such work—on each drawer floral groups flank one or two large birds in motion—the interplay of the sprays and birds, which all differ, makes for a lively facade. The sprays, which emerge from a mound or in two instances from a low orientalizing structure, each contain one of two sorts of flowers common in japanning (fig. 77). One resembles a chrysanthemum, which here is painted consistently with petals of two alternating colors—red and orange for the most part, and in a few cases orange and yellow. It is similar in form to flowers on the sides of the lower case and on the front cornice molding of cat. no. 125, for example—a kind that in japanning is found only in areas of flat decoration.[1] The other is a prunus type of blossom that on this chest is depicted with five or six petals that are painted red, or in a few instances orange, and are detailed with black lines and yellow dashes and sometimes dots. In japanning this sort of flower is delineated entirely with black lines on gold and is usually raised. Both kinds of flowers, but primarily the prunus type, are illustrated in the 1688 *Treatise of Japaning and Varnishing* by John Stalker and George Parker, as are birds in flight and on the ground. Birds generically similar to those on this chest and some with an analogous crest are represented in a design book dated 1718 of Jean Berger, a Huguenot painter-stainer in Boston, and may possibly have some bearing on the painting on this piece.[2] The elongated spray on each side of the upper case resembles that on a Boston japanned six-legged high chest. The ornament on the upper facade of that chest is also related, in that each drawer is decorated with a flower or tree motif at each end and one or more birds of the general type seen here in the middle. In addition, there appears to be a gesso ground on the drawer fronts, as on the present example.[3] The two chests may well have been decorated in the same shop. The similarity of the black ground coat on this piece to that on cat. no. 125 and the use of a gesso ground both point to the hand of a japanner. The painting is the work of a specialist; it is executed with proficiency and some flair.

No other such painting is known; but there are closely related examples of this form of high chest, which stylistically is earlier than that represented by cat. no. 125 and is characterized by a joined base with one long drawer, a thin, straight front bottom rail, and five legs. Two walnut chests, similar to this one in construction as well as in form, bear a close comparison, one at Historic Deerfield and the other at the Henry Ford Museum.[4] As on this chest, the upper case of those pieces is not dovetailed, but nailed (even though they are made of a more costly wood) and the drawers are constructed in the same manner. The turned legs on this (fig. 39) and the Henry Ford Museum chest are virtually identical; those on the Historic Deerfield piece are not cut in under the inverted cup and lack the astragal below the cup and, while the other elements are similar, they have somewhat different proportions. The legs on the japanned high chest with related designs mentioned above and those on a japanned one at the Winterthur Museum differ only in the greater height of the tapered segment below the astragal.[5] The profile of the cornice of cat. no. 122 is typical of Boston William and Mary–style high chests and that of the upper mid-molding is generally related. The lower mid-molding (fig. 145), however, differs significantly; it neither has a flat bottom nor protrudes very far. Like that on the Henry Ford Museum piece, which has the same contours, it is more conservative and recalls the lower mid-molding on a seventeenth-century joined Boston

double chest of drawers at the Museum of Fine Arts, Boston.[6] Although the form of the present piece suggests an early date of manufacture, because of the painted decoration, which is closely allied to japanned work, it is dated to no earlier than the 1710s (see the entry for cat. no. 125).

PAINTED DECORATION

On the drawer fronts of the upper case, the black background (probably a carbon black) is applied over a ground coat of gesso. On the remainder of the piece, the black background is painted directly on the wood and appears to consist of a thin medium-poor layer that goes into the wood pores followed by a thicker layer containing much more medium, as on cat. no. 125. The decoration is executed in red (vermilion), orange (realgar), yellow (orpiment, in a medium that appears to contain lead-tin yellow), and black. The use of yellow is restricted to the upper case. The colors there are now muted by a later pigmented finish layer that varies in thickness and imparts a lighter or darker brown cast to the designs and that goes into paint losses and over structural restorations. It is not clear if the variations in color on the mounds are due entirely to later coatings or if there was originally some glazing. The decoration has generally suffered from scratches, dents, and abrasions, but the original paint is almost entirely untouched by restorations. On the gessoed drawer fronts there are, in addition, losses from flaking (down to the wood) and a few possible small areas of red overpaint. On the upper case sides there are deliberate gouges in the centers of the flowers and traces of some childlike drawings in red paint. All of the decoration on the lower case drawer is of a later date. In 1989 the high chest was cleaned by Peter Fodera (Fodera Fine Art Conservation, New York City), who removed the surface wax, oil, and grime that obscured the designs and reduced the heavy varnish layer on the upper case. Inpainting was confined to areas of the black ground, and the surfaces were given a light, clear protective coating.

CONSTRUCTION

On the upper case, the top and bottom are rabbeted to receive the sides; the sides are nailed to the top, and the bottom to the sides, each element a single mill-sawn board. The back consists of two horizontal boards joined by a half lap and nailed to a rabbet on the rear edge of the sides, top, and bottom. The drawer dividers are let into grooves in the sides, and the partition between the two short top drawers fits into a groove in the top and the divider below. The uppermost divider extends almost three-quarters of the way back; the two lower ones, about 6 inches deep, like the partition, have drawer runners nailed to the sides behind them. The upper case rests on its bottom board, which is as thick as the upper mid-molding is high.

On the lower case, the back and side rails and the one front rail (below the drawer) are tenoned to the stiles, and the joints are pinned. A thick single board, secured with one nail into the top of each stile, forms the top of the case; the lower mid-molding is attached to its edges. The drawer runners are nailed to the stiles, and the guides to the side rails. The turned legs have a round tenon at each end. The upper tenons of the corner legs engage the stiles, and that of the center leg goes through the front rail, which is deeper at the middle than at the ends. The lower tenons go through the stretchers and into the feet. The stretchers are joined by a half lap at the corners and each is a solid piece.

The drawers all ride on the bottom of the sides, and the sides are all dovetailed to the front—with one dovetail, except for the two in the bottom drawer of the upper case. The backs are butted and nailed

122. See also figs. 39, 77, 145.

to the sides. The bottoms are beveled to fit into a groove in the front and sides and nailed to the back. On the long drawers of the upper case the bottom is one longitudinal board; on the others the bottom runs from front to back. The top edge of the upper case drawer fronts angles inward; that of all the drawer sides is chamfered. The cornice molding consists of an ovolo and a cyma recta; the upper mid-molding of a horizontal band, a fillet, a cyma reversa, and a fascia; and the lower mid-molding of a horizontal band, a fillet, an ovolo, and a cyma reversa (fig. 145).

CONDITION

The high chest has been subject to heavy wear and appears to have been thoroughly "put in order," in the parlance of the time, before it came to the MMA (1909 registrar records describe it as "repaired"). On the upper case, the left mid-molding and adjoining front tip are replaced, as are the left tip of the front cornice molding and one long and two short sections of half-round molding. At the upper front of each side, a small square patch covers a bored hole that extends through the adjacent drawer side and allowed for the securing of the drawer. In the back, the shrinkage gap between the boards has been filled with a narrow strip. The drawer runners have been replaced and guides added above the drawers. Grooves in the dividers and case bottom worn by the drawer sides have thin wooden fills at the front. On the lower case, there are similar fills, and guides, and, in addition, drawer stops. The right front portion of the front stretcher and the rear outer section of the left side stretcher are replaced. All the drawers have been apart, were renailed, and have strips added under the sides. There are patches at the corners and along edges on the majority of the drawer fronts and along the upper edge of the sides and backs. On the underside of the long drawers of the upper case, small blocks have been added (glued on) along the joint of the bottom to each side. Both sides of the top long drawer are replaced and on the two short drawers the bottoms may be reused boards. On the lower case drawer, the front and bottom look questionable. None of the drawer pulls or escutcheons is original to the piece. All the upper case drawers except the top right one were at one time fitted with locks, which have been lost. The exterior of the chest is heavily scratched, nicked, and abraded, and there are screw holes in the upper back that date from a time when objects displayed on the case were strapped to it. (See also *Painted decoration*.)

INSCRIPTIONS

There are two sets of large, scored sawyer's tally marks: III crossed by a diagonal slash on the underside of the top of the upper case and II crossed by a diagonal that begins at one end of a third vertical slash on the inside of the back rail of the lower case. Scratched on the outer left side of the left top drawer is "I [or J] Seph / L . . ." (script); inscribed in chalk on the outer right side is ". . . Charl . . ." (script) and in ink "SAR." On the outer right side of the right top drawer and of the bottom long drawer of the upper case are modern doodles in ink

and pencil. On the underside of both top drawers are modern restorer's marks in pencil. MMA Hudson-Fulton exhibition identification numbers are inscribed in orange crayon on the back of the upper case (H. F 40.42A / 525 and H. F. 40.42A) and on the back of the lower case (H. F 40.42B / 526).

WOODS

EASTERN WHITE PINE; legs, POPLAR (*Populus* sp.); feet, BASSWOOD.

DIMENSIONS

OH. 51¾ (131.4); upper case: OW. (mid-molding) 37⅞ (96.2), CW. 35⅞ (91.1), OD. (mid-molding) 20⅞ (53), CD. 19¾ (50.2); lower case: OW. (mid-molding) 39¾ (101), CW. 37⅞ (96.2), OD. (legs) 22⅜ (56.8), CD. 21 (53.3).

EXHIBITIONS

"Hudson-Fulton Exhibition," MMA, 20 September–30 November 1909 (not in catalogue but came in for the exhibition); "American Japanned Furniture," MMA, 20 March–30 April 1933.

REFERENCES

Lockwood 1913, fig. 59; Cornelius 1926, pl. XVI; Halsey and Cornelius 1928 (and 1932), fig. 2; Cescinsky and Hunter 1929, p. 181; Kettell 1929, pl. 46; MMA 1930, fig. 7; Williams 1963, no. 80 (drawings of molding profiles have inaccuracies); Hornung 1972, no. 899; Schwartz 1976, no. 33; Safford 1998, fig. 2 (detail of drawer fronts).

PROVENANCE

Ex coll.: H. Eugene Bolles, Boston.

Bolles recorded that he bought the chest from "a dealer in Boston who goes out collecting" (Bolles notes, MMA Archives).

Gift of Mrs. Russell Sage, 1909 (10.125.709)

1. For details of those flowers on cat. no. 125, see Heckscher and Safford 1986, pls. Ia, Ib. See also pl. IIb.
2. Stalker and Parker 1688 (1971 ed.), pls. 2, 6, 9–11, 14. For Berger's design book, see Leath 1994, pp. 149–51; the book also includes several drawings of chinoiserie vignettes copied, like the birds, from some source in Boston.
3. *Important American Furniture, Silver, Prints, Folk Art and Decorative Arts,* auction cat., Christie's, New York City, 27 January 1996, lot 224.
4. They are, in the order mentioned, in Fales 1976, no. 421; and in Nutting 1928–33, no. 329. Several chests of similar format but with scroll legs are known: Isaac Winslow House, Marshfield, Massachusetts, signed by Edmund Titcomb (Forman 1985, fig. 24); Lyman Allyn Art Museum, New London, Connecticut (acc. no. 1937.4.131); Staten Island Historical Society, Staten Island, New York (Dyer 1930b, p. 63); and Wadsworth Atheneum (Hosley 1984, fig. 16). They all vary from one another and from the group represented by cat. no. 122 in certain elements of their construction; the Titcomb chest has structural features not seen by the present writer on any other piece.
5. For the Winterthur chest, see "Sino-American Highboy" 1945.
6. Randall 1965, no. 38. The same type of molding is on an English veneered high chest of similar format but with spiral legs (Bowett 2002, pl. 2:34).

123.

High chest of drawers

Boston, 1700–1730

Raised on a tall stand with arched skirts, boldly turned legs, and shaped, flat stretchers and featuring richly figured veneered surfaces, this style of high chest expresses the new feeling for form and its movement and for dramatic effects characteristic of early Baroque design. The mass of the upper and lower cases—separated by a molding that juts out prominently—is perched somewhat precariously on a narrow point of the legs. The legs themselves, with a profile that juxtaposes strong bulbous shapes and thin tapers, provide similar visual tensions, and, like the high chest overall, they have a high center of gravity. Though the understructure is slight, the rhythms set up by the emphatic curves of the turnings, skirts, and stretchers are decidedly dynamic. The verticality of this piece and the light, open structure of its base are in marked contrast to the earthbound solidity of joined chests, and a different aesthetic is also evident in the character of the surfaces. The high chest presents broad, smooth planes made possible by dovetailed board construction, and the design of the case front is based on principles of harmony and cohesion rather than on a balancing of multiple distinct elements. The drawer fronts are all similarly bordered with walnut veneer in a herringbone pattern, and a half-round molding around the drawer openings draws them all together.

The high chest of drawers, a furniture form that was an English innovation of the period succeeding the restoration of the monarchy in 1660, was introduced in New England in the 1690s, when early Baroque design began to exert stylistic influence in the urban areas of that region. John Brocas (d. 1740), an English cabinetmaker who was in Boston in 1696, may have initiated the production of this new form in New England.[1] The present piece illustrates the basic format—seen repeated with minor variations on numerous surviving examples—that underlies the design of William and Mary–style high chests made in Boston and copied in smaller towns. The upper case contains four tiers of drawers that are graduated, typically in a progression of one inch from the uppermost down, though sometimes, as here, with a little more between the top tier with two short drawers and the second tier. On trim chests with a narrow cornice molding, like this example, the cornice features a cyma profile that is the mirror image of that on the upper mid-molding, and the width of the upper case at the top and bottom moldings is essentially the same. The lower case is generally aligned vertically—more or less closely, and on this piece exactly—with the edge of the upper mid-molding. In the lower case, the standard format calls for a center drawer that is considerably shallower than the two outer ones, and also wider—here by only half an inch. The width of the drawers determines the spacing of the front legs—in this instance almost equal—and the breadth of the arches in the front skirt. Characteristically the center cutout of that skirt has a round arch at the top, and the outline on either side below it is most often an ogee; the simple convex profile on this chest is a rare variant. The paired ogees seen here at the sides of the front are sometimes replaced by a round arch, as on cat. no. 125, and in a few instances a pair of such arches is used instead of ogees at the bottom of the case sides.[2] The front and side stretchers on this chest (replaced) exhibit those other contours, which look inappropriate on this piece since they do not echo the shapes of the skirts. The legs are turned in one of two basic patterns, both characterized by a dominant inverted-cone form: the more common scheme, with an inverted cup at the top of the cone, is represented here (fig. 40); the other, which has a shape that resembles a trumpet, is seen on cat. no. 125. In both patterns a baluster or a ball form and rings are used above and below the main motif. On the present piece, that motif is set between two opposed balusters that are close in form to those on the front legs of contemporary leather and cane chairs (see cat. nos. 27, 32). The vasiform turnings are well executed and give the legs and the whole chest a nice lift.

In terms of its form, this is a neat and elegant piece; but it is less than top quality in its use of woods. Walnut, the wood of choice for William and Mary–style furniture, had to be imported into Boston, and on this high chest it was used sparingly. It is restricted almost entirely to the front—for all the moldings and the herringbone borders—while the case sides and side moldings (except for the applied strip on the lower mid-molding) are of maple stained to match. The patterns created by the burl veneers on the drawers are less well ordered and balanced than those on many other high chests (compare cat. no. 124), whether because of a limited supply, or a frugal use, of figured wood. Only on the middle long drawer is the veneer book-matched and the seam exactly in the middle, but the triangular sections that fill out the upper corners do not carry on the symmetry. The lower case drawer fronts lack a border along the upper edge, which may represent a deliberate design choice or just the fact that sheets of veneer large enough to reach to the top of the drawers were on hand. That border, which tends to be lost in the shadow of the mid-molding, is absent on other high chests as well.[3]

CONSTRUCTION

On the upper case, the top and bottom are joined to the sides with through dovetails, each element a single board. The back is formed of two horizontal boards beveled to fit into a groove in the top and sides and is nailed to the bottom. Glued under the front of the top above each short drawer is a slat, the bottom of which is level with the bottom of the applied cornice molding. The drawer dividers (4 in. deep) are let into the sides; the grooves for the dividers extend to the back and house the drawer runners, which are, in addition, slotted into a full-height vertical strip that is nailed to the side at each back corner (fig. 98). The partition between the two short top drawers (5½ in. deep) is secured to the top above and divider below with a sliding half-dovetail joint. There is no medial drawer runner. The case rests on the bottom board. Affixed to its upper side are runners for the bottom drawer and a slat across the front, the tops of which are level with the top of the applied upper mid-molding.

On the lower case, the back and the front skirt are joined to the sides with half-blind dovetails. Nailed to the top of the case is a framework that consists of a board on each side and one across the front, mitered at the front corners (fig. 104). It supports the upper unit and extends out to form the lower mid-molding. The lower case has no top board to serve as dust barrier; instead, the back of the upper case extends down to meet the lower case back. The vertical transverse partitions between the drawers are rectangular in shape. They are dovetailed to the skirt at the front (fig. 100) and attached to the back with a through half dovetail for the top inch and a dado joint below that. The drawer runners are let into the front skirt and the back. The legs have a round tenon at each end. The upper tenons pass through the square caps at the top of the legs and are socketed into blocks glued to the interior of the case (and perhaps marginally into the case itself). The corner blocks extend to the top of the case and those at center front to the height of the runners (fig. 99). The lower tenons go through the stretchers to engage the feet, which are drilled through. The stretchers are half-lapped at the corners.

On both cases, the drawers run on the bottom of the sides. The sides are joined to the front and back with two or three dovetails, which at the front are half blind and at the rear extend beyond the back to serve as drawer stops (fig. 115). The bottoms—longitudinal in the upper case and transverse in the lower—are beveled to fit into a groove in the front and sides and nailed at the back. The three long drawers were equipped with locks. The top edge of all drawer fronts angles inward, that of the sides is rounded and a bit lower than the front. The cornice and mid-moldings have standard profiles (fig. 147). The cornice consists of an ovolo and cyma recta, the upper mid-molding of a cyma reversa and fascia. On the lower mid-molding, the raised inner portion, which holds the upper case in place and has an inclined surface, is an applied strip, as usual; the ovolo is here worked from the solid wood on the sides, and on the front the solid edge is beveled and capped with an ovolo strip. The thin strip along the edge of the skirts that simulates a bead is attached with small rosehead nails.

CONDITION

The veneer appears to have only a few tiny patches in addition to nicks along the edges. Both sides of the lower case have a large shrinkage crack, and the right side also has a surface patch at the front

and back where dovetails broke through. The front stretcher (probably maple) is new, and the side stretchers (pine), which have splits and new tips, are older but also look replaced. Each is a solid piece rather than being formed of a single outer section and glued-on inner sections, as was common. The edging strip on the skirts and the bottoms of the feet show small losses. There are splits in some of the drawer sides and bottoms and at the bottom of the upper case back, which has added nails, as do some of the drawers, runners, and joints of the drawer dividers. The bottom of the upper case has a gnawed hole in a rear corner, and the back has two knotholes; there are also modern screw holes in the back from the time at the MMA (several decades past) when small objects displayed on the top of the chest were strapped to the case. Many of the drawer pulls appear never to have been removed, but the escutcheons have been replaced and the lock in the top long drawer is missing. The surface has a modern finish that goes over remains of a degraded varnish; dark residues are particularly heavy on the top, legs, and stretchers, and they streak the sides and are embedded in pitted areas of the veneer.

INSCRIPTIONS

Writing in chalk, mostly illegible, is on the inside of the back of the right top drawer ("New . . . ns"); on the inside of the left side of the left top drawer (". . . 25/ . . ."); and on the outer side of the upper case back (". . . /3 day . . .").

WOODS

Herringbone banding, front cornice, front upper mid-molding, applied sections of lower mid-molding, half-round moldings, square caps at top of legs, BLACK WALNUT; figured veneers, upper and lower case sides, cornice and upper mid-molding on sides, side members of framework at top of lower case, MAPLE; legs, feet, POPLAR (*Populus* sp.); edging strip on skirts, HICKORY; all other original elements, EASTERN WHITE PINE.

DIMENSIONS

OH. 62½ (158.8); upper case: OW. (mid-molding) 36 (91.4), CW. 33¾ (85.7), OD. (mid-molding) 19⅞ (50.5), CD. 18⅝ (47.3); lower case: OW. (mid-molding) 39¼ (99.7), CW. 36 (91.4), OD. (mid-molding) 21¾ (55.2), CD. 20 (50.8).

REFERENCES

"Recent Accessions" 1953, p. 261; Schwartz 1976, no. 31; M. B. Davidson 1980, fig. 74; MMA 2001, fig. 13.

PROVENANCE

Ex coll.: Mrs. J. Insley Blair, Tuxedo Park, New York; her daughter Mrs. Screven Lorillard, Far Hills, New Jersey.

Mrs. Blair purchased the high chest from the firm of Collings and Collings, New York City, in 1925.

Gift of Mrs. Screven Lorillard, 1952 (52.195.2)

1. Forman 1985, pp. 17–21.
2. Clunie, Farnam, and Trent 1980, no. 8; and Margon 1965, pp. 46–47.
3. D. B. Warren et al. 1998, no. F34, for example, which exhibits a luxurious use of woods.

123. See also figs. 40, 98, 99, 100, 104, 115, 127, 147.

124.

High chest of drawers

Boston or vicinity, 1700–1730

Striking burl veneers that create a pattern of arches draw immediate attention to the upper front of this high chest. On the long drawers, the veneers are applied in three sections rather than in the usual two joined in the center to form a bilateral design, and on the short drawers, in two instead of one. The most distinctive feature of this high chest, however, is in the design of the lower front. Deviating from the norm, the front skirt consists of three separate pieces rather than a single board, and the sides of the center segment extend only to the bottom of the outer drawers and not down to the legs. This results in a broad central opening that leaves the front-to-back partitions between the drawers very visible, and consequently they have been shaped on the bottom to match the ogival curves of the case sides.

The same front skirt design and shaped partitions occur on a high chest at the Museum of Fine Arts, Boston, which has book-matched veneers on the long drawers, and on a dressing table acquired by H. Eugene Bolles at the same time as this chest (see *Provenance*). Bolles purchased his two pieces in Salem, Massachusetts, and the inscription on the chest indicates it was there in the late nineteenth century, but neither they nor the Museum of Fine Arts chest have an early history.[1] Whether this type of skirt was a variant made in Boston or in a smaller town like Salem that emulated the Boston style is unclear. Few high chests of this period have early histories, but among them are two with links to Salem, one that descended in the Gardner family and one that came down in the Pickering family. They differ from this chest—their front skirt design is similar to that on cat. no. 125—and also one from the other.[2]

Little work has yet been done to sort out William and Mary high chests in the Boston style. The task is not easy, for few of them present stylistic or structural traits as distinctive as those on the lower case of this piece. Turnings are not a reliable indicator of shop origin, since in Boston, at least, legs and feet (called "pillars" and "balls" at the time) were provided by specialists, so that legs of the same profile might be used by different cabinetmakers and an individual shop might acquire legs from more than one turner.[3] There are definite structural differences, but in large part they represent one of two widespread alternatives, as do most of those between this piece and cat. no. 123, for example: the upper case rests either on slats under the bottom board, as on the present chest (fig. 101), or directly on the bottom, which is then built up on the inside with a front slat and drawer runners (see fig. 98);

the framework on top of the lower case that supports the upper unit is either lapped at the front corners, as here (fig. 103), or, less often, mitered (see fig. 104); the drawers either have a nailed bottom and ride on applied runner strips or have a bottom let into grooves and ride on the lower edge of the sides, and the dovetails at the front may go through and be hidden only by the veneer or be half-blind (compare figs. 114, 115);[4] and the lower case drawers run either on a single center support, as on this piece, or on one at each side. Normally the partitions between the lower case drawers are either dovetailed to the front skirt, as on cat. no. 123 (see fig. 100), or, probably more often, nailed, as on cat. no. 125. Here the anomalous three-section skirt is dovetailed to the partitions. A greater number of structural variations occur, for instance, in the manner in which the two short top drawers are supported and separated and in the joint of the partitions of the lower case to the back. It remains to be seen if any local or individual shop traditions can be identified by the presence of particular structural traits in combination with certain stylistic preferences.

CONSTRUCTION

On the upper case, the sides, made of two boards, are dovetailed to the top and bottom, which are both single boards; the dovetails do not show on the top. The back, formed of three vertical boards, is nailed to a rabbet in the top and sides and to the bottom. Under the front of the top above each short drawer is a glued-on slat, the bottom of which is level with the bottom of the applied cornice molding. The middle drawer divider is joined to the sides with a sliding half dovetail, the other dividers with a dado joint. The partition between the two short top drawers is secured to the top and the divider below with a through tenon at the front, followed by a dado. The short drawers slide on the divider, which extends two-thirds of the way back. Runners, 5 inches shy of the back, are nailed to the sides behind the other, shallower dividers (5½ in. deep, like the partition). The bottom drawer rides on the case bottom. The case rests on slats under the front and sides of the bottom board, which are hidden by the upper mid-molding (fig. 101).

On the lower case, the back is joined to the sides with half-blind dovetails. The framework of three boards that is nailed to the top of the case and supports the upper unit and that protrudes to form the lower mid-molding is joined at the front corners with a half lap (fig. 103). The end grain exposed in this type of joint is here concealed by thin ovolo moldings that cap the beveled outer edge of the framework. Transverse boards that fit into a groove on the inner edge of the framework and are nailed to the back enclose the top of the lower case. The front skirt consists of three separate sections, the middle one dovetailed to the vertical transverse partitions between the drawers and each outer one dovetailed to the respective partition

124. See also figs. 101, 103, 114.

and case side. The partitions are joined to the back with a through tenon for the top inch and for the remainder of their height with a sliding dovetail joint that is wedged at the bottom. The lower edge of the partitions is shaped to match the case sides. Each drawer is supported by a center runner that is housed in the back and nailed to a recess in the front skirt. A drawer guide is glued to each case side. The legs, stretchers, and feet are joined in the same manner as on cat. no. 123, except that the blocks in the rear corners extend less than halfway to the top. On all the drawers, the sides are joined to the front and back with two to four through dovetails, which protrude somewhat at the back (fig. 114). The bottom runs transversely and is nailed to a rabbet in the front and to the bottom of the other sides. On the upper case drawers there is a runner strip under the bottom at each side. The three long drawers have locks. The top edge of all drawer fronts angles inward; the top of the sides and back is rounded. The usual edging strip is nailed to the skirts. The cornice and mid-moldings have standard profiles similar to those on cat. no. 123 (see fig. 147).

CONDITION

Photographs of 1909 and 1912 (see *References*) document the "unrestored" condition of the chest when acquired by the MMA (see *Provenance*). Shown missing in those photographs and restored probably soon thereafter are: the right cornice molding (the rear portion of which looks old and may have just become detached) and a wedge on the right end of the front cornice; the vertical applied half-round molding to the right of the left drawer on the lower case; the lower two-thirds of the veneer above the left front leg; numerous small segments of herringbone banding; a few small sections of the edging strip on the skirts and of the caps at the top of the legs; and all but one of the inner glued-on segments of the stretchers. The old portions of the stretchers may be original but with a renewed surface. Significant shrinkage cracks have occurred in the right side and back of the upper case, the left side of the lower case, and two drawer bottoms. The joints of the legs, leg blocks, feet, and a few other elements have been reglued. In the lower case, the drawer guides are replacements, and rodents have made large holes in the top and gnawed the drawer sides. The legs have losses and two contain defective wood. All of the drawer pulls and escutcheons have been off, and they are at least in part replaced. A dark mahogany-color coating, probably applied at the time of the early MMA restorations, was removed from the show surfaces in 1979, and the clear finish underneath was gone over. Mahogany color remains on the under portions of the lower case. Numerous dark stains mar the top of the chest. The legs and feet are uneven in color.

INSCRIPTIONS

A pencil inscription in script on the underside of the middle long drawer, partly effaced by wear, reads: "From / J[oh]n Gi[d?]n[e?]y / Nov. [1?] 18[89? 99?] / Salem / Mass." MMA Hudson-Fulton exhibition identification numbers are inscribed in orange crayon on the outside of the back of the lower case (H. F. 40.37.A. / 506, in an oval) and of the back of the upper case (H. F. 40.37.B). The drawers bear scratched inscriptions indicating their location, and also numbers and symbols in pencil; and inside the upper and lower cases are various markings in pencil and chalk, some corresponding to those on the drawers (all are modern).

WOODS

Figured veneers, MAPLE; herringbone banding, upper and lower case sides, cornice, upper mid-molding, applied elements of lower mid-molding, half-round moldings, edging strip on skirts, square caps at top of legs, old stretchers, BLACK WALNUT; legs, feet, POPLAR (*Populus* sp.); all other original elements, EASTERN WHITE PINE.

DIMENSIONS

OH. 61½ (156.2); upper case: OW. (cornice) 36⅝ (93), CW. 34½ (87.6), OD. (cornice) 20⅞ (53), CD. 19½ (49.5); lower case: OW. (mid-molding) 39¼ (99.7), CW. 36½ (92.7), OD. (mid-molding) 22⅜ (56.8), CD. 20⅞ (53).

EXHIBITIONS

"Hudson-Fulton Exhibition," MMA, 20 September–30 November 1909; on loan to the Dey Mansion, Wayne, New Jersey, from 1946 to 1978.

REFERENCES

Hudson-Fulton Celebration 1909 (exh. cat.), no. 112; Lockwood 1913, fig. 57; Halsey and Tower 1925, fig. 41; Cescinsky and Hunter 1929, p. 180; MMA 1930, fig. 8 (this and the previous references show the chest as received); M. B. Davidson and Stillinger 1985, figs. 35, 36 (detail of leg).

PROVENANCE

Ex coll.: H. Eugene Bolles, Boston.

As Bolles recorded (Bolles notes, MMA Archives), he purchased the high chest (together with a companion dressing table) from a dealer in Salem, Massachusetts, in the "unrestored condition" in which it came to the MMA (see *References*).

Gift of Mrs. Russell Sage, 1909 (10.125.704)

1. For the Museum of Fine Arts chest, see Randall 1965, no. 50. The dressing table (Lockwood 1913, fig. 58) appears to have been the mate to the present high chest. Both pieces were acquired by the MMA as part of the Bolles collection, but the table, which had lost all the veneer from the top and had replaced stretchers, was among a group of objects sold to the Trent House Association, Trenton, New Jersey, in the late 1950s.
2. The Gardner high chest, at the Peabody Essex Museum (Clunie, Farnam, and Trent 1980, no. 8), is distinguished by having a rail above the drawers in the lower case, and side skirts and stretchers cut in a double-arch shape. The Pickering high chest (present location unknown; *Sack Collection* 1981–92, vol. 3, pp. 628–29) lacks such a rail, as do most Boston-style high chests of the period, and exhibits the usual ogival curves on the sides; its drawer construction may be distinctive (see n. 4 below).
3. Jobe and Kaye 1984, pp. 10, 182. Also, it stands to reason that a fair number of legs have been replaced, given the weak nature of the joints in the understructure of William and Mary–style high chests.
4. On cat. no. 126 the construction of some of the drawer bottoms combines the two methods. Drawer construction that differs significantly from standard practice of the period occurs on several pieces on which the drawer front, sides, and back are secured with a tongue-and-groove type of joint: a chest of drawers (perhaps once the top of a high chest) in the Museum of Fine Arts, Boston (Randall 1965, no. 27) and one at one time in the Harold Lehman collection; two high chests sold at Sotheby's in the 1990s (*Fine Americana, Including Furniture, Folk Art, Quilts, Paintings and Silver*, auction cat., Sotheby's, New York City, 23–24 June 1993, lot 405; *Important Americana: American Furniture, Clocks, Decorations, American Folk Art, Folk Paintings and 20th Century Self-Taught Art*, auction cat., Sotheby's, New York City, 17 and 19 January 1997, lot 779); and, according to Benno M. Forman (conversations with the writer in the 1970s), the Pickering high chest (see n. 2 above).

125.

High chest of drawers

Boston, 1710–30

The japanned decoration on this high chest creates a dazzling, fanciful world, in which animals, flowers, and Far Eastern figures and structures, all depicted in gold, happily coexist without any regard to scale. Japanning, a Western imitation of Eastern lacquerwork, was the height of fashion in America during the first half of the eighteenth century. The earliest examples of japanned furniture recorded in New England—in Massachusetts Bay inventories of 1695 and 1698—were in all probability imported, but by 1712 such splendidly showy pieces were being produced in Boston.[1] This example is one of a group of more than a dozen Boston japanned high chests and one dressing table in the William and Mary style.[2] The japanned ornament in this period is virtually always set against a solid black ground, as it is here. Very generally, it is characterized by the large scale of the raised motifs and their use as separate entities that do not form part of a larger narrative.[3] Within this overall scheme the individual pieces exhibit numerous variations.

The raised elements on this chest are of very good size and hold their place with assurance, be they human figures, a camel, overly large birds, or out-of-scale floral groupings. While the motifs are typically disconnected in terms of what they represent, they are here arranged so that their shapes create pleasing undulating patterns that flow across the drawer fronts in a well-paced fashion. In some areas of the decoration the motifs are not as varied, and their placement is less random than is usually the case: although they differ in their details, the two short top drawers mirror one another in overall layout, with a pair of birds on the outer side that dwarf a figure by a fence on the inner (fig. 78), and the two side drawers of the lower case each have an analogous scheme of a bird and a pair of vases. The designs on both case sides are similar, with the upper floral grouping on the left bending toward the front and that on the right, which lacks a bird, toward the back. Inevitably the decoration has undergone changes over the years, and its original effect has to some extent been altered. The raised motifs very likely once stood out less prominently and appeared less isolated than they do now, when, because of restorations, they are largely brighter than most of the finely painted flat ornament that surrounds them, causing the various design elements to seem somewhat out of balance.

Hardly any close replication of motifs is to be found among the known japanned pieces of this period, and the condition of the decoration—restored, showing losses, or obscured by later coatings—often hinders careful comparison of workmanship. The japanning on one William and Mary–style high chest can be identified as the work of a specific craftsman, the example at the Adams National Historical Park in Quincy, Massachusetts; it was signed by William Randall (active ca. 1715–ca. 1735), one of six artisans documented as japanners in Boston before 1730.[4] The decoration on the drawer fronts of that chest, which does not appear to have suffered the repainting evident elsewhere on the piece, bears no close relationship to that seen here in the nature of the motifs or their arrangement and does not provide any basis for an attribution of cat. no. 125 to the Randall shop. In terms of motifs, the ornament on a high chest at the Chipstone Foundation exhibits the greatest affinity to that on this piece.[5] There are some similarities in the flat painted grasses and fernlike plants, the stance of a bird, the extensive use of ceramic forms (but not their individual shapes), and the design of a crouching dog. Unfortunately the dog on the present chest is virtually all repainted, so that details of the original execution by which to judge the hand of the painter have been lost. A high chest at the Virginia Museum of Fine Arts in Richmond does offer some parallels to the motifs on the Randall example, notably, pairs of swans and groups of rocks with trees. That chest bears the name "Scottow" on the back of its drawers and was probably so inscribed to identify it when in the japanner's shop.[6] The Scottows were a family of furniture makers working in Boston in the seventeenth and early eighteenth centuries. A Queen Anne–style dressing table, originally japanned, is inscribed both "Scottow" and "W. Randle," which suggests a working relationship, at least at the time of its making, between the two craftsmen.[7]

The case work on the MMA high chest and that inscribed "Scottow" share several structural particularities, although the latter piece differs in two design features, namely, a larger cornice and legs that very unusually in American furniture have a faceted rather than a turned trumpet-shaped element. The cases of japanned pieces were produced in the same shops as the veneered ones, but were made of less expensive woods—pine, except for maple drawer fronts. On this and the Scottow chest there were also structural shortcuts taken, probably on the premise that they would be concealed by the japanning, which may have been initially so, but is not now the case: the back of the lower section is not dovetailed to the sides with half-blind dovetails; rather, the dovetails are cut on the side boards and they and the end grain of the pins on the back board are exposed, as are the dovetails of the front skirt on the sides. In addition, the two chests share the uncommon feature of a rail above the drawers of the lower case, and both have similar stops at the front of the upper case drawer dividers. This all raises the possibility that the case work of this chest originated in the Scottow shop. However, the more expedient method of constructing the lower case with exposed dovetails appears to have been the practice in more than one shop, for this feature is found on the Chipstone Foundation chest, some of the drawers of which bear the name "Park," presumably that of a cabinetmaker, and has been noted as well on a chest in a private collection.

JAPANNING

The basic sequence of coatings that makes up the japanning on this chest (according to cross sections taken from the case front and drawers) suggests that the gilded decoration was meant to appear suspended over a deep translucent black and not sunk below thick varnish. The ground consists of a thin medium-poor black layer that penetrates the wood pores, above which is a second black layer containing more medium as well as coarser pigment particles. The latter is followed by a thick, clear coating that appears to be made up of numerous layers. Above that lie the raised gesso motifs and the flat painted ornament, both of which show a red-pigmented layer, which seems to have served as ground and/or size, under the metal leaf or powder. The detailing on the raised elements is in black paint. Last comes a clear coating, considerably thinner than the third layer. The black pigment is probably a carbon black and the red is vermilion. The clear coatings are a plant resin. Two different metals were identified in samples taken from the right top drawer: one from the narrow inner band (under the escutcheon) and one from fine foliage (under the left pull) were found to be gold; that taken from the broad outer band was identified as an alloy of copper (90 percent) and zinc (10 percent), a cheaper substitute known as Dutch or German gold.[8]

The japanned surfaces were cleaned and treated by Peter Fodera (Fodera Fine Art Conservation, New York City) in 1985. They had undergone fairly extensive restoration in the past, including the repainting (which appears to follow the original design) of virtually all motifs on the case sides, of those on the front skirt, lower center drawer, and stiles, and of the broad band around the edge of the drawers. A good portion of the raised decoration and some of the flat painting on the drawers had also been renewed. The 1985 treatment stabilized flaking and restored losses, found predominantly in areas of previously reworked gesso ornament. There remain on the drawer fronts numerous original passages, particularly of flat background painting, which is distinguished by its delicacy, in contrast to the heavier repainting. Compare, for example, the legs and feet (original) of the bird at the far right of the right top drawer with those (repainted) of the bird to its left, and the fence (original) on the left top drawer to that (repainted) on the right drawer (fig. 78). Other elements that have not been retouched are the inner band on the drawers, all the banding on the case front and sides, including that along the edge of the skirts, all decoration on the cornice and upper mid-molding, and what remains of the acanthus and palmettes on the legs and feet (fig. 42) and of the kites on the stretchers. The gold ornament varies somewhat in color and intensity, depending both on its age (the renewed areas are generally brighter) and on the thickness of the varnish that now covers the particular area. Whether or not the original decoration used gold of different colors and, if so, what the scheme was, is difficult to determine.[9]

CONSTRUCTION

On the upper case, the top and bottom are joined to the sides with through dovetails; the top and sides are each a single board. The back is formed of two vertical boards beveled to fit into a groove in the top and sides and nailed to the bottom. Two slats in line under the front of the top support the lower portion of the front cornice molding. The drawer dividers are let into the sides; the middle divider has a through half dovetail at the front. The grooves for the dividers run the full depth of the sides. The divider below the two short top drawers extends a good two-thirds of the way back; the two lower dividers are about half as deep, and the grooves behind them house runners. The partition (5 in. deep) between the two short drawers fits into a groove in the top and the divider below and is through-tenoned at the front. Short longitudinal strips are nailed to the top of the dividers and of the case bottom near the front to serve as drawer stops. Thin vertical strips are glued to the inside of each case side at the front (where the surface was worked with a toothing plane) to increase the width of the front edge of the sides. The upper case rests on slats under the front and sides of the bottom board, as on cat. no. 124.

On the lower case, the sides are dovetailed to the back: broad face-grain tails are on the side boards rather than the back board, and the joints are fully exposed. The front skirt is joined to the sides with through dovetails; on the front, each joint is hidden by a facing that simulates a stile. (For the top of the case, see *Condition*.) There is a narrow front rail above the drawers, which is set into the top of the corner leg blocks with a half dovetail and nailed in place. The transverse partitions between the drawers taper in height toward the back; they are let into the back and secured to it each with a toed-in nail and are nailed to the front skirt. The drawers each run on a central support that is housed in the back and has a beveled front end that is nailed to a conforming recess in the skirt. Drawer guides are glued to the case sides. The legs, feet, and stretchers are joined in the standard manner (see the entry for cat. no. 123). Here only the front corner leg blocks go to the top of the case; those in the rear corners and at center front extend to the bottom of the side drawers. At center front there are, in addition, narrow vertical glued-on blocks that reinforce the joints of the center leg blocks and of the partitions to the skirt. No edging strip was ever nailed to the skirts.

On both cases, the sides of the drawers are joined to the front with two to four half-blind dovetails and to the back with through dovetails, except on the center drawer of the lower case, on which the back is dovetailed (with one key) to each side. The drawer bottoms run from front to back and are nailed to a rabbet in the front and to the bottom of the other sides. On the upper case drawers, runner strips are applied under the bottom at the sides. The top edge of the drawer fronts angles inward, that of the sides and backs is rounded and lower than the front; the rear vertical edges are chamfered. All but the right and center drawers of the lower case are or were fitted with a lock. A double bead molding surrounds the drawers. The cornice and mid-moldings have standard profiles similar to those on cat. no. 123 (see fig. 147).

CONDITION

The top of the lower case, which includes the lower mid-molding, is entirely new (yellow poplar). It dates from 1985 and replaces an earlier, inappropriate restoration. The present top, following the evidence provided by the nail holes from the attachment of the original, was constructed in the same general manner as that on cat. no. 124, which served as model. The framework of a board on each side and one across the front is lapped at the front corners, ovolo caps are applied to its outer edge, and transverse boards are let into the inner edge of

125. See also figs. 42, 78.

the frame. Other structural replacements and repairs are smaller in scope. On the upper case, the right cornice molding is modern. The back, which has large losses along each side edge and an added narrow strip in the center, has been off and renailed. The bottom is pieced at the back and has splits and broad transverse grooves routed out on its upper surface. One drawer runner is new. On the lower case, several of the legs and feet have been reattached and several show sections missing in the trumpet turning. The caps at the top of the rear legs are replacements, as may be the right rear leg block. Two of the three remaining narrow reinforcing blocks at center front look modern. The left stretcher has a repaired break, and in 1985 the missing rear portion of the center section of the front stretcher was replaced. There are large shrinkage cracks in both cases and some of the drawers. On the drawers of the upper case most of the bottoms have been renailed and a few are pieced at a side edge, and almost all the runner strips have been renewed. There are large black blotches on the back of the lower case and of some of the drawers; the interior of all drawers has been varnished. The escutcheons are original, as appear to be the remaining locks (two are missing). The pulls are of the period but installed at the MMA in 1932 in place of turned knobs then on the piece. (For the condition of the surface, see *Japanning*.)

INSCRIPTIONS

Three sets of restorer's markings remain visible. Chalk numbers on the drawers and "m" and "k," respectively, on two of the drawer dividers are the oldest. Large numbers (1 to 5) in pencil on the bottom of the upper case drawers and corresponding numbers on the dividers date from the twentieth century, as do scratched, partly effaced notations on the outer right side of several drawers. They are in the same hand as the "4/30 VARNISHED/M [in a circle]" penciled on a piece of paper tape that came off the top long drawer.

WOODS

Drawer fronts, front skirt, front stretcher, all moldings, square caps at top of legs, SOFT MAPLE; legs, feet, POPLAR (*Populus* sp.); all other original elements, EASTERN WHITE PINE.

DIMENSIONS

OH. 62½ (158.8); upper case: OW. (cornice) 38¼ (97.2), CW. 36 (91.4), OD. (cornice) 20⅞ (53), CD. 19½ (49.5); lower case: OW. (mid-molding) 41 (104.1), CW. 37⅞ (96.2), OD. (mid-molding) 22½ (57.2), CD. 21 (53.3).

EXHIBITIONS

"American Japanned Furniture," MMA, 20 March–30 April 1933; "The China Trade and Its Influences," MMA, 23 April–21 September 1941; "A Bicentennial Treasury: American Masterpieces from the Metropolitan," MMA, 29 January 1976–2 January 1977.

REFERENCES

Downs 1940a, fig. 1; *China Trade* 1941 (exh. cat.), fig. 62; Brazer 1943, fig. 2; "Antiques in the American Wing" 1946, p. 248, no. 4; Gaines 1957, fig. 1 (shown in this and the next reference with steps and ceramics on the top); M. B. Davidson 1967, no. 83 and p. 80 (detail of bottom long drawer); Huth 1971, fig. 90; Fales 1972, nos. 79, 79a (detail of middle long drawer); Hornung 1972, no. 911; Fales 1974, fig. 44; *Bicentennial Treasury* 1976 (exh. cat.), fig. 10; Schwartz 1976, no. 32; M. B. Davidson 1980, pl. 18; M. B. Davidson and Stillinger 1985, figs. 137, 158; Heckscher and Safford 1986, pls. I, Ia–c (details) and "Collectors' Notes" 1986, p. 652 (where a typesetter's error is corrected); Greene 1996, p. 56.

PROVENANCE

The high chest has a traditional history of early ownership in the Pickman family of Salem, Massachusetts. The first owner is thought to have been Benjamin Pickman (1672–1719, m. 1704 Abigail Lindall), who was "master of a vessel" in the West Indies and transatlantic trade and lived in Boston and in Salem, where he built a house in 1714. The chest was acquired by the MMA together with a suite composed of a Boston japanned Queen Anne–style high chest, dressing table, and looking glass and a separate English japanned dressing glass. The suite and dressing glass are said to have first belonged to his son Benjamin Pickman (1708–1773, m. 1731 Love Rawlins), also a Salem merchant, who presumably inherited the present chest from his father. All five pieces appear to have come down together, the likely line of descent going through Benjamin and Love's son Benjamin (1740–1819); his son Thomas (1773–1817); to his daughter Mary, who wed in 1851 George Bailey Loring of Salem. Through Loring's daughter Sally they descended to Lawrence Dwight (d. 1918), who bequeathed them to his fiancée, Harriet Amory, later Mrs. Warwick Potter, the vendor. The chest was on loan to the MMA from Mrs. Potter from 1932 to 1936 and from 1937 to 1940, when it was purchased.[10]

Purchase, Joseph Pulitzer Bequest, 1940 (40.37.3)

1. Inventories cited in I. W. Lyon 1891, pp. 79, 94; and Forman 1985, p. 20. The literature on Boston japanning includes Downs 1933; Downs 1940a; Brazer 1943; Fales 1974; Hitchings 1974; Randall 1974; Rhoades and Jobe 1974; Hill 1976; and Heckscher and Safford 1986.
2. Examples in institutions are at: Adams National Historical Park, Quincy, Massachusetts (Randall 1974, figs. 1, 2); Chipstone Foundation (*Important Americana, Furniture, Folk Art and Decorations*, auction cat., Sotheby's, New York City, 15 October 1999, lot 107); Historic Deerfield (Fales 1974, fig. 45; Fales 1976, no. 420); Historic New England (acc. no. 1971.72); Virginia Museum of Fine Arts, Richmond (Flanigan 1986, no. 17); and Winterthur Museum ("Sino-American Highboy" 1945). In private collections are: the dressing table (Flanigan 1986, no. 18) and two unpublished high chests. Other high chests have come up at auction: *American Furniture and Related Decorative Arts: Property of the Links Golf Club, Roslyn, Long Island*, auction cat., Christie's East, New York City, 8 May 1984, lot 135; *Art and the Antiques Weekly* (Newtown, Connecticut), 18 December 1987, p. 141 (advertisement of a sale at Litchfield Auction Gallery, Litchfield, Connecticut, 1 January 1988, ill. of chest from estate of Mary Allis); *Important American Furniture, Silver, Prints, Folk Art and Decorative Arts*, auction cat., Christie's, New York City, 27 January 1996, lot 224; *Antiques* 152 (July 1997), p. 58 (advertisement of the sale at Northeast Auctions, Manchester, New Hampshire, on 2 August 1997, of the collection of Priscilla S. and Howard K. Richmond); *New Hampshire Weekend Auction*, auction cat., Northeast Auctions, Manchester, New Hampshire, 31 October–2 November 2003, lot 1341.
3. Exceptions are one of the unpublished high chests, which has a tortoiseshell ground, and the scene on the top of the dressing table (see n. 2 above).
4. For Randall, see Randall 1974 and Rhoades and Jobe 1974, passim. The others are: Roger Pendleton (d. 1712); Nehemiah Partridge (active Boston 1712–ca. 1714); Joshua Roberts (d. 1719); Robert Hughes (active 1726); and Thomas Johnston (active late 1720s–1767) (Brazer 1943; Hitchings 1974). The design book of the Huguenot painter-stainer Jean Berger (inscribed "Boston, 1718") includes several chinoiserie drawings (Leath 1994, pp. 149–54).
5. See reference in n. 2 above.
6. Flanigan 1986, no. 17.
7. Bernard and S. Dean Levy gallery catalogue, vol. 5 (New York, 1986), p. 15.
8. A sampling and analysis of metals in 1993 revealed that the visual identification of the narrow bands on the drawers as silver published in 1986 (Heckscher and Safford 1986, p. 1046) was incorrect, putting into question the suggestion then made that the faces and hands of figures, which have not been tested, might be silver (Heckscher and Safford 1986, p. 1046). In addition, cross sections of the black ground on the case sides taken in 2004 did not show any red pigment under the black, which refutes the statement made in 1986 that the color then observed in the cracks of the black ground on the sides was a vermilion undercoat (Heckscher and Safford 1986, p. 1047). Among the items listed in the 1719

probate inventory of Boston japanner Joshua Roberts are "7 papers of Jarman [German] Powder . . . 13 books of Leaf Silver, 2 ditto gold, 4 ditto of Jarman ditto" (Brazer 1943, pp. 209–10).

9. For more on the condition and restoration, see Heckscher and Safford 1986, pp. 1046–48; and "Collectors' Notes" 1986, p. 652 (where a typesetter's error is corrected).

10. Downs 1940a, p. 148; John Adams Vinton, *The Giles Memorial: Genealogical Memoirs of the Families Bearing the Names of Giles, Gould, Holmes, Jennison, Leonard, Lindall* . . . (Boston, 1864), p. 330; Heckscher 1985, p. 240; letter from Harriet Amory Potter to Joseph Downs, 7 April [1940] (ADA files). For the objects in the suite, see Heckscher 1985, nos. 155, 156, 210; the English dressing glass is acc. no. 40.37.5.

126.

High chest of drawers

Boston, 1715–30

Strongly influenced by architectural design, this imposing piece represents a unique interpretation of the William and Mary–style high chest form. With fluted pilasters on both the front and sides (all tapering slightly from bottom to top) and dramatic projections in the entablature and the mid-moldings, the chest relies for its impact not just on figured veneers but in large part on bold effects of relief. The play of alternating planes, particularly in the convex frieze, is akin to that seen on later blockfront furniture—but reversed.[1] While the upper case is more massive than usual, it appears to be borne easily by the base, thanks to the lift provided by the attenuation of the legs (fig. 41) and also to the upward movement of the central arch, which leads the eye up the facade to the middle projection in the entablature.

The influence of classical architecture, as set forth in the books of Andrea Palladio (1508–1580) and introduced in England by the architect Inigo Jones (1573–1652), is reflected in other William and Mary high chests only in the profile of the moldings, and most obviously on those with a pulvinated frieze.[2] Here architectural design informs the whole upper facade, which resembles a doorway, with the projection at the center of the entablature recalling a keystone. The profile of the cornice molding, however, which has a boxy, somewhat monolithic appearance, is not one found as such in classical design, nor does it correspond to that on any other high chest. It is anomalous in that it begins with a heavy fascia and consists of two identical sequences—a fascia and a cyma recta of nearly the same height (fig. 102). The upper mid-molding, which also differs from the typical William and Mary pattern, is more modulated. It steps down to the lower mid-molding, which has a standard profile, with a cavetto, cyma reversa, ovolo, and fascia, presenting at the top a mirror image of the ovolo and cavetto of the architrave (fig. 146). The construction of the upper case is as individualistic as

its design. Heavily overbuilt with double sides, it is a very particular solution to assembling a case that includes pilasters using known William and Mary methods of construction. This was most likely a custom piece, and one that involved considerable expense, for it was labor-intensive; the building out of the projections in the moldings entailed the fitting in of numerous mitered strips.

That the chest was probably made to order is in accord with its credible history of having belonged to Edward Holyoke (see *Provenance*). Holyoke (b. 1689, graduated from Harvard College, Cambridge, Massachusetts, 1705) was ordained in 1716 and served as pastor of the Second Congregational Church in Marblehead, Massachusetts, from that year until 1737, when he became president of Harvard, a post he held until his death, in 1769. His first marriage was to Elizabeth Browne (d. 1719) of Marblehead in 1717.[3] The high chest could date as early as that year, even though pilasters are a feature that in American furniture is closely identified with later eighteenth-century styles, beginning with the Queen Anne, which became fashionable in the 1730s. The design of this chest has no known parallel; it differs from the type of updating of the William and Mary high chest form otherwise seen, which incorporates elements typical of Queen Anne high chests, such as an additional tier of drawers in the upper case to achieve taller proportions, two instead of one tier of drawers in the lower case, or the use of cabriole legs. This chest probably reflects instead the influence of the Palladian classicism transferred by craftsmen who immigrated in the 1710s.[4] Well-documented is William Price, who arrived in Boston from London in 1714. A walnut-veneered and japanned desk and bookcase with double-arched pediment and Corinthian pilasters signed and dated by Price the previous year in London shows the style of furniture he was producing before he emigrated. Conversant with the classical orders, he had a successful career in Boston not only as a cabinetmaker, merchant, and map- and printseller, but also as an architectural designer.[5] The scheme of the upper case of this chest relates more directly to architectural practice than to the design of the furniture forms fashionable in London in the 1710s, such as the desk and bookcase and the chest-on-chest, of which there are very few American examples extant that closely follow the style of English prototypes of that period.[6] On the present piece, a classically inspired doorframe was simply grafted on a standard William and Mary high chest, endowing a well-established form with new stylishness. The chest most likely originated in Boston, but manufacture in Marblehead by a craftsman in touch with design developments in Boston is not entirely out of the question.[7] In any case, its idiosyncrasies suggest that it is not the work of a cabinetmaker trained in England.

CONSTRUCTION

On the upper case, the top and presumably the bottom are joined to the sides with through dovetails, each element made of two boards. Immediately flanking the drawers are secondary sides (formed of a thick front board and thinner rear board), which fit into a groove in the top and bottom and have a through tenon at the front. The space between the outer and inner sides is filled at the front with a thick slat, which provides support for the applied pilaster (fig. 102). The back is formed of four vertical boards joined with a half lap, let into a groove in the top and sides, and nailed to the bottom. The drawer dividers (5½ to 7 in. deep) fit into grooves in the inner sides. The grooves extend to the back and house the runners. Level with the divider under the three short drawers there is a rail across the back that is let into the grooves behind the runners. The partitions between the three short drawers are let into the dividers above and below and have a through tenon at the front. Behind each partition is a broad runner that is beveled on each end to fit into a conforming recess in the divider and rear rail and is nailed in place. At the back, drawer stops are attached to the sides and the rear rail. The upper case rests on thick slats under the front and sides of the bottom board (see the entry for cat. no. 124). The moldings are each a solid piece. The cornice, which is supported on the front by a rail (joint to sides unclear) under the top, and the convex frieze molding, which on the front is applied to the front of a hidden drawer, are equal in height (3 in.); the upper mid-molding measures ½ inch less. On both the upper and the lower case, the projecting portions of the moldings are built out from behind.

On the lower case, the back and presumably the front skirt are joined to the sides (each two boards) with half-blind dovetails. A framework of three boards joined at the front corners with a half lap is nailed to the top of the case (fig. 105). It is grooved on the inner edge to hold two longitudinal boards that enclose the top. The lower mid-molding is applied to that framework in two separate sections: the ovolo is glued to the vertical outer edge and the inner strip to the upper surface (fig. 146). The rectangular, vertical partitions between the drawers are nailed to the front skirt and attached to the back with what are probably a half or a full through dovetail at the top and below that, a dado joint. Each drawer is supported by a center runner that is let into the back and joined at the front in the same manner as the upper case medial runners. Drawer guides are nailed to the case

sides near the top. The attachment of the legs, stretchers, and feet is similar to that on cat. no. 123, with all four corner blocks extending to the top of the case.

On both cases, the drawer sides are joined to the front and back with two to four through dovetails. The bottom runs longitudinally on the long drawers and transversely on the others. On the frieze and lower case drawers, the bottom is nailed to a rabbet in the front and to the bottom of the other sides. On the other drawers, the front edge of the bottom is rabbeted and let into a groove in the front. On the upper case drawers there is a runner strip under the bottom at the sides. The top edge of the drawer front angles inward, that of the sides and back is rounded. The dovetails overall are uneven in size, and their angle varies somewhat, as is common in this period. Those on the top of the upper case are narrower than usual—close in size to those on the drawers.

CONDITION

There are small patches in the herringbone bands on the drawer fronts and one in the veneer above the right front leg. Some of the gaps caused by splitting or the separation of boards in the frieze and case sides have been filled. On the upper case, a central transverse brace has been added under the top, which has a full-length crack. One of the boards in the back is entirely replaced; the others have been patched, shifted, and renailed. A block glued to the inside of the back has been added under the middle of the rear rail. Two drawer runners are missing, and the stops are replaced or reattached. On the lower case, the entire right stretcher and the glued-on back portions of the front and left stretchers are new, as are the edging strip on the skirts, the caps at the top of the legs, and probably the drawer stops. Nails have been added to the boards that form the top of the case, to the leg blocks, and to the stretcher joints. The feet were at one time fitted with casters. The drawers have added nails in some of the dovetail joints, bottoms, and runner strips. Some of the strips are replaced, as is the bottom of the frieze drawer, which has been apart. The brasses are old; except for a mismatched plate behind one of the drop pulls, they may be original but reattached. All but the frieze drawer now have locks (modern); only the three long drawers show evidence of earlier locks. The high chest has a modern finish. Dark stain has been applied to the top and back of the piece and the underside of the lower case.

INSCRIPTIONS

Tacked to the inside of the back of the bottom long drawer is a card inscribed in ink (script): "No 92.1918 / Lent to the Society for the / Pres. of N. E. Antiquities by / Mr. Lawrence Park." A small cloth-tape sticker from the Harvard tercentenary exhibition (see *Exhibitions*), inscribed in ink "H T E / 205," became detached from the bottom left drawer and is preserved in the ADA files. Modern restorer's chalk numbers remain legible on the inside of the back of some of the drawers.

WOODS

All veneers, upper and lower case sides, pilasters, all moldings, legs, feet, old stretchers, BLACK WALNUT; all other original elements, EASTERN WHITE PINE.

DIMENSIONS

OH. 69¾ (177.2); upper case: OW. (cornice) 40⅞ (103.8), CW. 37 (94), OD. (cornice) 20 (50.8), CD. 17¾ (45.1); lower case: OW. (mid-molding) 43⅛ (109.5), CW. 39⅝ (100.6), OD. (mid-molding) 21⅛ (53.7), CD. 19¼ (48.9).

126. See also figs. 41, 102, 105, 146.

"Early American Furniture and the Decorative Crafts," Park Square Building, Boston, 8–29 December 1925; "Harvard Tercentenary Exhibition: Furniture, Silver, Pewter, Glass, Ceramics, Paintings, Prints, Together with Allied Arts and Crafts of the Period, 1636–1836," Robinson Hall, School of Architecture, Harvard University, Cambridge, Massachusetts, 25 July–21 September 1936; "Patterns of Collecting: Selected Acquisitions, 1965–1975," MMA, 6 December 1975–23 March 1976.

REFERENCES
Early American Furniture 1925 (exh. cat.), no. 1; *Harvard Tercentenary Exhibition* 1936 (exh. cat.), no. 205; MMA 1975, p. 21; Cooper 1980, fig. 109; Kaye 1982, fig. 6.

PROVENANCE
Ex coll.: J. Lovell Little, Brookline, Massachusetts; Clarence Dillon, Far Hills, New Jersey.

Dillon purchased the high chest from Little in January 1926, at the close of "Early American Furniture and the Decorative Crafts," a loan exhibition where it was offered for sale. Little had acquired the piece in 1919 from Lawrence Park of Groton, Massachusetts, who then had it on loan to the Society for the Preservation of New England Antiquities (now Historic New England). The history of the piece recorded at that time by Park states that he received the high chest in August 1911 from George E. H. Abbot of Groton shortly before Abbot died and that it was originally in the possession of Edward Holyoke (1689–1769), president of Harvard College from 1737 to 1769. The line of descent given by Park indicates that at Holyoke's death the high chest passed to his widow (his third wife, Mary [Whipple] Epes, of Ipswich, Massachusetts) and at her death in 1790 to her granddaughter Mary Holyoke Pearson (1782–1829), who was actually her stepgranddaughter, as Holyoke's only issue to survive childhood were from his second wife, Margaret Appleton (m. 1725, d. 1740) of Ipswich. Mary Pearson's husband, Rev. Ephraim Abbot (1779–1870), inherited the high chest in 1829, and in 1870 it went to his second wife, Abigail (Whiting) Bancroft Abbot (1798–1886), and then jointly to her three children, Lucy Miranda Bancroft Abbot (1832–1908), George Edward Henry Abbot (1838–1911), and Sarah Bass Abbot (1841–1908). Lawrence Park (1873–1924) was related on his mother's side to the Bancroft family.[8]

Edward Holyoke's probate papers do not include an inventory, but in a codicil to his will he bequeaths to his wife all the furniture on an attached list, which enumerates, among many other items, a "Chest of Drawers, Table, Looking Glass" in the striped chamber—a grouping that suggests a high chest and dressing table. The chest may be the MMA piece, as may the chest of drawers in that portion of her furniture (which also includes a "chamber table") that Mary Holyoke bequeathed to Mary Pearson.[9]

Gift of Clarence Dillon, 1975 (1975.132.1)

1. An unusual cabriole-leg high chest made in Portsmouth, New Hampshire, combines pilasters and projecting moldings with a blockfront design (Jobe 1993, no. 16).
2. See Palladio 1570 (1738 ed.), book 4, pls. 36, 41, 63, for examples of a pulvinated frieze. (Book 1 was first published in English in 1663, the complete books in 1715.) This type of frieze was fashionable on English case furniture about 1680–1710. Whether chests with this feature were produced in America as early as those with a small cornice molding, like cat. no. 123, or represent a later stylistic development is unclear. Such convex friezes continued in use on some Queen Anne high chests and beyond that as a capital for pilasters.
3. George Francis Dow, ed., *The Holyoke Diaries, 1709–1856* (Salem, Mass., 1911), pp. xii, xiii.
4. A more provincial understanding of Renaissance architecture is evident in Boston from the late seventeenth century on, as seen in the Ionic pilasters on the Foster-Hutchinson House, of 1685–92 (A. L. Cummings 1971b, pp. 7–10).
5. On Price's 1713 desk, see Forman 1985, figs. 19, 20 and pp. 21–22; on his career, see Waite 1955. The introduction of the Palladian architectural style to Portsmouth, New Hampshire, has been documented to this period—specifically to the arrival of English joiner John Drew in 1715 (Garvin 1993, pp. 17–19).
6. One chest-on-chest, in the Museum of Fine Arts, Boston, is known (E. S. Cooke 1987; Johnston 1988, fig. 82). There are a few desks and bookcases: for example, a variant of the form at the Warner House in Portsmouth, New Hampshire (E. S. Cooke 1987, figs. 9, 10; see also Buckley 1964, fig. 2 and frontispiece, p. 54); and examples in *Philadelphia* 1976, no. 18, and Naeve and Roberts 1986, no. 38.
7. During the 1730s, Boston cabinetmaker Nathaniel Holmes employed craftsmen living outside of Boston, including two in Marblehead, to make furniture that he sold (Jobe 1974, pp. 13–15).
8. Letter of 11 January 1926 from J. Lovell Little to Clarence Dillon and handwritten statement from Lawrence Park dated 3 October 1919 (ADA files); Dow, *Holyoke Diaries*, pp. xii–xiv; Frank Sylvester Parks, comp., *Genealogy of the Parke Families of Massachusetts* (Washington, D.C., 1909), pp. 206–8; Massachusetts Registrar of Vital Statistics, Boston: Deaths, 1908, vol. 45, pp. 177, 198.
9. Middlesex (Massachusetts) County Probate, dockets 11795, 11798 (microfilm, Boston Public Library). A Boston porringer in the MMA inscribed "MH" (acc. no. 33.120.328) also has a George Abbot provenance and a history of having belonged to Mary Holyoke and come down in the same line of descent.

127.

High chest of drawers

Probably eastern Connecticut or Rhode Island, 1715–35

Bold herringbone bands of contrasting light and dark veneer and an unusual configuration of the entablature distinguish this high chest from all other known examples in the William and Mary style. Normally the pulvinated frieze on a high chest (which contains a hidden drawer) is surmounted by a cornice molding that, following English prototypes, begins with an ovolo and cyma recta profile that matches the cornice on cat. no. 123, for example, and terminates with a fascia and a cavetto. Here the cornice lacks the fascia and surmounts a flat frieze above a convex one. It is difficult to know exactly what inspired this scheme, which, though somewhat ungainly, adds stature to the piece.[1] It may be that this chest is a late example, made at a time when the influence of the Queen Anne style was beginning to be felt; it uses book-matched figured walnut veneers, like those that adorn some high chests in that style, rather than burl veneers. The extension of the entablature can then be seen as an emulation of the greater height of high chests in the newer style, with the flat frieze perhaps representing an expanded fascia, here separate from the cornice cavetto, or alluding to the large cavetto molding in Queen Anne cornices. Equally distinctive are the flamboyant maple and red cedar herringbone bands that border and subdivide the drawer fronts, creating central panels not only down the middle of the facade and of the top side drawers, but also, most unusually, of the two outer drawers of the base. Other examples of contrasting herringbone veneer are rare. A striking use of such bands, in conjunction with burl veneers, occurs on a 1733 high chest in the Queen Anne style made in Portsmouth, New Hampshire (private collection). A much narrower and more discreet version is employed on a desk at the Art Institute of Chicago, Chicago, Illinois, on which the bands form central panels on the drawer fronts, as they do here, and which is ornamented, in addition, with star inlays of the type associated mainly with the Boston area.[2]

The origin of this chest—an ambitious, showy piece, a touch provincial in its overelaboration—remains somewhat uncertain. It exhibits some of the features that Benno M. Forman suggested were characteristic of New York, primarily the use of three rather than two drawers in the top tier and the inclusion of a narrow veneered panel down the center of the drawer fronts. On that basis, from 1980 until reevaluated for this catalogue, the chest was identified by the present writer in the gallery label as probably from New York, and it was once published as such by another author;[3] but the evidence

in actuality is far from conclusive. While these traits occur on some high chests that can be associated with New York through their history or the use of woods, they are not present on all chests attributable to New York nor are they exclusive to that region.[4] Philadelphia high chests are often fitted with three drawers in the top tier, and so is, for instance, a Boston example in this catalogue (no. 126). Central veneered panels are to be found on Massachusetts pieces as well, such as the Art Institute of Chicago desk mentioned above, which, very unusually, has three drawers in the top tier, or a high chest with three top drawers at the Chipstone Foundation, which gives no indication of having been made elsewhere than the Boston area.[5]

This chest's secondary woods do not point to an origin in New York. The haphazard use of chestnut and white pine seen on this piece is not characteristic of early colonial furniture from that area. Rather, it strongly suggests manufacture in eastern Connecticut or Rhode Island. While chestnut is occasionally found in Boston joined chests, it occurs in seventeenth- and early-eighteenth-century case pieces mainly in examples from coastal Connecticut (see cat. nos. 113, 88, 140, 107, 80). In mid-eighteenth-century furniture, a random use of chestnut is encountered in New London County, Connecticut, and it is typical of Newport, Rhode Island, work.[6] While the secondary woods cannot be considered proof positive, they do open up the real possibility that this high chest was made in that area, from which no William and Mary–style veneered furniture has as yet been identified. That there was a taste in that region for furniture with dramatic veneers is suggested by a cabriole-leg high chest at the Yale University Art Gallery that is attributed to eastern Connecticut or Rhode Island on stylistic and structural grounds and includes chestnut and a variety of other woods. An individualistic piece like the present one, it exhibits a vivid facade, with dark burl veneers and light herringbone bands that create a panel down the center of the drawers, and includes veneered panels on the case sides for good measure.[7] One other William and Mary veneered high chest (also at Yale) is known that, like cat. no. 127, is distinguished by the haphazard use of chestnut. More sophisticated and conventional in design than the present piece, it appears to be the product of a major urban center.[8] Too little is yet known about Rhode Island case furniture in this period to say whether or not work of that quality was being produced there.

CONSTRUCTION

On the upper case, the top and bottom are joined to the sides with through dovetails, each element consisting of a wide (front) and a narrow (back) board. The back, originally three horizontal boards, is nailed to a rabbet in the top and sides. Under the top, spanning the front of the case, is a narrow board (joint to sides unclear) that provides the substrate for the veneer on the flat front frieze. It abuts a drawer divider above the pulvinated frieze, which is formed by a convex molding that on the facade is applied to the front of a hidden long drawer. The drawer dividers (3 in. deep) are let into the sides, with the one above and below the top long drawer having what is probably a sliding half- or full-dovetail joint at the front, which is hidden on the front by veneer but exposed on the side. The vertical partitions between the three short drawers in line (1 in. deep) are tenoned through the dividers. Behind each partition is a runner that is rabbeted at each end to fit into a recess in the divider and in a rear rail (the same size as the dividers) that is housed in the sides. All other runners are nailed to the case sides. The case rests on slats under the bottom (see the entry for cat. no. 124). The upper mid-molding has a distinct ovolo and cavetto above the fascia instead of the usual cyma reversa.

On the lower case, the back and the front skirt are joined to the sides with half-blind dovetails. A framework of three boards half-lapped at the front corners is nailed to the top of the case. Three transverse boards nailed to a rabbet on the framework's inner edge and through a filler strip to the top of the back enclose the case. A broad ovolo molding is applied to the framework's outer edge, which is a little shy (¼ in.) of the outer edge of the case; the molding is nailed on. The rectangular, vertical transverse partitions between the drawers are nailed to the front skirt and let into the back and secured with a nail through the back. The runners (two for each drawer) are housed in the back and have a beveled front end that fits into a conforming recess in the skirt. The attachment of the edging strip on the skirt, and of the legs, stretchers, and feet is similar to that on cat. no. 123, except that only the front corner blocks extend to the top of the case. On all the drawers, the sides are joined to the front and back with two to four through dovetails. The bottom runs transversely and is nailed to a rabbet in the front and to the bottom of the other sides. The drawer glides on runner strips applied under the bottom at each side. The three long drawers are fitted with locks.

CONDITION

The moldings and veneers have numerous smaller and larger restorations, many of them dating to 1974 and replacing segments shown missing in earlier photographs (see all but the last citation under *References*). The cornice is pieced on the front corners and along the bottom edge of both sides, and the frieze molding and the upper mid-molding at the left front corner. Three of the half-round moldings and part of the fourth on the upper sides are replacements, as are various sections on the facade. The veneer on both front corners of the lower case has large patches, and numerous small areas of herring-bone banding on the drawers, particularly at the corners, are new. Many of the joints have been reglued and moldings reattached. The upper case back, on which part or the entire top board (now in two sections) is replaced, has been reset. The top boards of the lower case have some losses and added nails. The lower mid-molding shows wear, and X-radiographs reveal that it, like the framework, is attached with wrought sprigs and that there is no evidence of previous nailing; however, it is suspect because it is not designed to hold the upper case in place. Perhaps it is an early replacement for an original that was just glued on. Both rear legs have a repaired break above the inverted-cup

turning, and the left one is missing part of the top ring. The rear leg blocks are replacements, as are the square caps at the top of three of the legs. The side stretchers and much of the front one, shown missing in a photograph published in 1913 (see *References*), are new. There is considerable splitting in both cases and in the drawer bottoms. On the drawers, the right side of the frieze drawer is probably replaced, a few of the runner strips look new, and there are added modern nails. The upper edge of the sides of the three short top drawers has been damaged by rodents, and on the lower case left drawer there is a series of holes and nails below the top of the sides, the purpose of which is unclear. The locks appear to be the first set. The brasses have been off and at least some of them are replaced. The chest has a modern finish, under which are dark remains of an earlier coating.

INSCRIPTIONS

Impressed with a chisel on the underside of the right top short drawer is a workman's mark: III. Scratched on the exterior of the right side of the left lower case drawer are compass-drawn concentric partial circles and other markings. Inscribed in pencil on the exterior of the top board of the upper case back is "J. Mills" (script; modern).

WOODS

Herringbone banding, MAPLE and EASTERN RED CEDAR; veneer on flat front frieze, on front edge of upper sides, on all drawer fronts, and on front of lower case, all moldings including convex frieze molding, old square caps at top of legs, BLACK WALNUT; top and sides of upper case, lower case sides, edging strip on skirts, legs, feet, rear stretcher, MAPLE; back of both cases, core of drawer fronts and of flat front frieze, all vertical partitions, drawer runners, some drawer sides, backs, bottoms, and runner strips, slats under bottom of upper case, left and front members of framework and outer boards at top of lower case, EASTERN WHITE PINE; upper case bottom, upper case drawer dividers and rear rail, some drawer sides, backs, bottoms, and runner strips, right member of framework and center board at top of lower case, filler strip at top of lower case back, core of front skirt, CHESTNUT; front leg blocks, POPLAR (*Populus* sp.).

DIMENSIONS

OH. 65 (165.1); upper case: OW. (cornice) 37¾ (95.9), CW. 34⅞ (88.6), OD. (cornice) 21¼ (54), CD. 19½ (49.5); lower case: OW. (mid-molding) 38¾ (98.4), CW. 37¼ (94.6), OD. (mid-molding) 21¾ (55.2), CD. 20⅞ (53).

REFERENCES

Lockwood 1913, fig. 67 (owned by William W. Smith, of Hartford); Andrus 1951, p. 243; Andrus 1952, p. 165; Comstock 1961, fig. 3; Schwartz 1976, no. 30; Johnston 1988, fig. 70.

PROVENANCE

Ex coll.: William W. Smith, Hartford, Connecticut; Mrs. J. Insley Blair, Tuxedo Park, New York.

Mrs. Blair purchased the high chest from Charles Woolsey Lyon, the New York City dealer, in 1923. It was on loan from her to the MMA from 1939 until it became a gift.

Gift of Mrs. J. Insley Blair, 1950 (50.228.2)

1. The same concept taken a step further is seen on a high chest with three drawers in line between the cornice and the pulvinated frieze (Garrett 1978, pl. I).
2. Jobe 1993, no. 15 (high chest); Naeve and Roberts 1986, no. 39 (desk). Herringbone bands in contrasting woods that are let into a solid wood

ground occur on some Chester County, Pennsylvania, furniture dating to the mid-eighteenth century or later (Schiffer 1966, ill. no. 136; Griffith 1986, nos. 44, 45). For inlay in contrasting woods on seventeenth-century furniture, see cat. no. 97.

3. For the features Forman suggested were characteristic of New York, see Kirk 1982, no. 546 and p. 381, n. 11, and G. W. R. Ward 1988, pp. 238–39. For cat. no. 127 published as probably New York, see Johnston 1988, fig. 70. The plates of the drawer pulls are in a design that Forman also associated with New York, but one cannot prove they are original to this piece.

4. While the best-documented New York William and Mary high chest—one at the Winterthur Museum signed and dated (1726) by Samuel Clement of Flushing, New York—has three drawers in the top tier, the drawer fronts do not have veneered herringbone bands or central panels; instead they have inlaid stringing that meets in the center (Failey 1976, no. 39); conversely, a New York chest that has veneered panels down the center of the front has only two short drawers at the top (V. I. Miller 1956, no. 20).

5. Lindsey 1999, no. 38 and fig. 167 (Philadelphia high chest); a veneered high chest with three top drawers at the Art Institute of Chicago, Chicago, Illinois, published as from New York (Naeve 1978, no. 5) has a mid-molding, lower case drawer arrangement, and secondary woods characteristic of Philadelphia. For the chest at the Chipstone Foundation, see Rodriguez Roque 1984, no. 11. A few Boston Queen Anne high chests also have a central veneered panel on the long drawers (Heckscher 1985, no. 157).

6. For chestnut in Boston joined chests, see G. W. R. Ward 1988, no. 51; Jobe et al. 1991, no. 3. For that wood in mid-eighteenth-century eastern Connecticut and Rhode Island pieces, see Myers and Mayhew 1974, nos. 10, 11, 18, 19, 21, and others; and Heckscher 1985, nos. 135, 140, 145, 161.

7. G. W. R. Ward 1988, no. 132. A quite different, very striking use of veneers occurs on a cabriole-leg high chest of walnut, maple, and white pine attributed to Newport, Rhode Island (Beckerdite 2000, fig. 40).

8. G. W. R. Ward 1988, no. 122. Chestnut also occurs in a veneered desk at the Winterthur Museum (*Girl Scouts* 1929, no. 505).

Dressing Tables

Although called a table, the furniture form represented in this chapter is included in the section on case furniture because of its relationship to the high chest of drawers, with which it was often made en suite. That it was meant to be sat at and hence serve as a table is made clear by its design, which differs from that of the lower case of a high chest in having four legs (rather than six) and cross stretchers, which together with the arched skirt assure ample legroom for a sitter. Several terms found in period inventories seem to have referred to this general type of piece: "chamber table" (indicating its use in a chamber, or bedroom); "dressing table" (describing its function, and still current today); and "toilet table." ("Lowboy" is a modern term.) Since valuations for such items ranged considerably, some of the objects so designated were quite possibly of a simpler kind. Very often, however, this furniture form was described merely as a "table," identifiable as the type under discussion because it was listed in conjunction with a chest of drawers (as high chests were commonly called at the time), and, more tellingly, sometimes together also with a looking glass or a dressing box. In rare instances, the relationship was made explicit, as in the "1 chest of Drawers . . . black walnut, 1 table to ditto" listed with a looking glass and two sconces in a 1711 Boston inventory.[1]

Hardly any matching high chests of drawers and dressing tables in the William and Mary style have survived, and none is in the collection. In fact, the Museum lacks any dressing table that can suitably serve as a pendant to any of the collection's high chests, such as a typical Boston-style table with a veneered front and top. The dressing tables in this chapter, three from New England and one from Pennsylvania, all vary to a greater or lesser degree from the more common designs of those regions. One of the New England examples, made probably in Connecticut (cat. no. 128), conforms to the standard overall format of three drawers, a triple-arched front skirt, and bold, separately turned legs, but the proportions of the case and the manner in which the front is constructed are atypical. The base of a table from northeastern New England (cat. no. 130) is anomalous in that while the front skirt is shaped with the usual three arches, calling for three drawers, there is but a single drawer spanning the case. That piece is further distinguished by having an imported Swiss slate top (of the kind found attached to various types of New England frames of the period), suggesting that despite the design of its base, it may have been used as a side or serving table rather than in the bedroom for dressing. The greatest structural divergence from the standard William and Mary formula is exhibited by a small table, most likely from Connecticut, that has the usual three drawers and shaped skirt but is of joined rather than dovetailed board construction (cat. no. 129); its undercarriage consists of turned legs that are one with the stiles and connected by perimetric stretchers, all in an opposed-baluster pattern. As for the Pennsylvania dressing table (cat. no. 131), it conforms closely to documented Philadelphia examples in the distinctive design of its legs, feet, and stretchers, but it stands apart as the only piece in that particular shop tradition that does not follow the usual three-drawer scheme but has a single drawer and a skirt that is mainly straight.

1. Quoted in Forman 1985, pp. 20–21.

128.

Dressing table

Probably Connecticut, 1710–30

Similar to the base of a high chest of drawers, but smaller and with pendants in place of center front legs and with stretchers that are X-shaped, this furniture form was frequently made as a companion piece to the chests, though very few matching pairs from this period have survived, and usually stood in a bedroom. It appears to have been variously described as a "chamber," "toilet," or "dressing" table, but most often called just a "table."[1]

In its overall design this piece illustrates the standard format of William and Mary dressing tables, but in its details it exhibits some particularities. The case is wider and deeper than on most examples, and the arrangement of drawers and arches on the facade shows less variation in height than usual; the center drawer is quite deep in relation to the side drawers and the center arch is relatively broad and shallow. The other arches, shaped to paired ogee curves, have an unusually high and acute peak. The construction of the front deviates from that characteristic of the dressing tables and lower cases of high chests on which the three drawers are close together and separated only by thin transverse partitions with an applied molding on the front edge—the most common design. The front is joined to the sides—as it normally is in such a scheme—with half-blind dovetails, which on a piece made of solid wood like this one are concealed on the front by an applied facing and otherwise by veneer. Atypically, however, here the front does not consist of just a shaped board below the drawers but rather of a board that extends the full height of the case and in which an opening for the three drawers has been sawn out, leaving a "rail" across the top. This type of full front board, but not the manner in which the case is otherwise constructed, is characteristic of Philadelphia tables and high chests, except that they have a separate opening cut out for each drawer (see cat. no. 82). Like many Philadelphia examples (see cat. no. 131), this dressing table has an applied molding under the top in the space provided by the "rail" above the drawers, but here it continues on the sides to the back of the case and may be a later addition. The legs are distinguished by the strongly bulbous base and narrow neck of the vase forms and by the trim contours at the top of the trumpet shape, where the reel below the vase terminates in just a fillet rather than in a ring, as on cat. no. 125 (see fig. 42) and as is almost always the case other than on Philadelphia pieces, on which the leg turnings differ in other details (compare cat. no. 131, fig. 43).

The individual, somewhat hybrid character of the piece, the rather crude dovetailing of the thick-sided drawers, and the various woods employed suggest that it was produced in a small town or rural setting and not in an urban center. The use of cherry and yellow poplar point to a probable origin in Connecticut or in the mid-Atlantic colonies. The birch legs, however, would seem to narrow the choice down to the former region; birch turnings are to be found on some New England pieces in this period (see cat. nos. 107, 130), but to the writer's knowledge none have been identified to date on mid-Atlantic furniture.

CONSTRUCTION

The back and the front are joined to the sides with half-blind dovetails. The front is a single board in which one opening that accommodates all three drawers has been sawn out; what appears to be a rail above the drawers is an integral part of the board. At either end of that board, the front surface has been recessed to allow the applied facing (¼ in. thick) above each leg, which conceals the corner joint, to lie flush. On the interior, the glued-on blocks in the corners extend to the top of the case and those above the pendants to the bottom of the middle drawer. The vertical transverse partitions between the drawers, rectangular in shape, are let into the back and were originally each secured with two nails through the back; they are nailed to the front board. The side drawers are each supported by a single runner, which is on the outer side and rabbeted and nailed to the corner blocks. The two runners for the middle drawer are similarly attached to the center front blocks and are let into the back. The upper tenons of the legs engage the corner blocks, and the lower extend through the stretchers into the feet, which are drilled through. The stretchers consist of two sections, each sawn from a single board and crossed and joined at the center with a half lap. On the drawers, the sides are joined to the front with half-blind dovetails and the back to the sides with through dovetails. The bottom is beveled all around, fits into a groove in the front and sides, and is nailed to the back. The applied molding at the top of the front and sides has a cyma recta profile. The skirts are finished with a nailed-on edging strip.

CONDITION

The top (yellow poplar) is a replacement, screwed on from below through added battens glued to the case sides. The case has been completely apart. The molding under the top (cherry), which has been off and reset, shows some wear but may not be original. Wedges have been added to the dovetails of the back and to the dado joints of the transverse partitions. The blocks (oak), which are questionable, have been reglued. The drawer runners have all been reattached; the outer ones (one oak, one ash) are suspect. Both pendants and the double-bead molding to the right of the left drawer, missing when the table was acquired, are new, and the present brass pulls replace wooden knobs then on the drawers. The turning at the center of the stretchers and the foot below are new; the other feet (birch) are older but probably also replaced. There are small repairs on the edging strip on the skirts, the square caps, and the left rear leg, and a brace (nailed) has been added under the center of the stretchers. The drawers have been apart, nails

128

and wedges added to the joints, the bottoms reset and that on the right drawer (with grain running parallel rather than perpendicular to the front) probably replaced. There are also a few splits, losses, and gnawed edges. The table has been refinished. Residues of an earlier dark coating remain, particularly on the left side, where there is defective wood, and on the legs, stretchers, and feet. The exterior of the back and under surfaces have been stained a dark wood color.

INSCRIPTIONS
On the exterior of both sides of the left drawer is abraded writing in chalk that is illegible except for a large "S." An Old Barracks Museum identification number in ink on cloth tape is under the right drawer (see *Exhibition*). Modern numbers in pencil are on the back of the drawers and corresponding numbers on the partitions.

WOODS
Case front and facing above legs, drawer fronts, case sides, stretchers, CHERRY; case back, drawer sides, backs, and bottoms, partitions, medial drawer runners, YELLOW POPLAR; legs, BIRCH; edging strip on skirts, square caps above legs and pendants, probably double-bead molding, SOFT MAPLE.

DIMENSIONS
OH. 28 (71.1); top: W. 35¾ (90.8), D. 21⅝ (54.9); case: W. 30 (76.2), D. 20⅛ (51.1).

EXHIBITION
On loan to the Old Barracks Museum, Trenton, New Jersey, from 1945 to 1978.

REFERENCES
Lockwood 1913, fig. 74; Cescinsky and Hunter 1929, p. 61 (this and the previous reference show the table as acquired).

PROVENANCE
Ex coll.: H. Eugene Bolles, Boston.

Gift of Mrs. Russell Sage, 1909 (10.125.66)

1. Forman 1987. For rare surviving pairs of William and Mary dressing tables and high chests, see Failey 1976, nos. 39, 40, and Jobe and Kaye 1984, no. 29; see also the entry for cat. no. 124.

129.
Dressing table

Probably Connecticut, 1710–30

This piece offers an unusual interpretation of the dressing-table form. It is a traditional joined table with baluster-and-block turned legs and stretchers that incorporates the drawer arrangement and arched skirt typical of William and Mary dressing tables of dovetailed board construction. The maker appears to have been familiar with the look but not the standard construction of the latter, or perhaps he was just wary of that less-than-solid structural system; the individual, more substantial manner in which he secured the partitions between the drawers to the front suggests he was accustomed to building sound furniture. The table is idiosyncratic not just structurally but also in the design of its turnings, which exhibit a variant of the popular vase-and-ring pattern not otherwise known. While on other table legs in this general scheme the vase forms are invariably centered on a ring and then may be flanked by a reel at top and bottom, here they are centered on a reel that is defined by prominent rings and is flanked by smaller reels; and when a reel is used instead of a ring at the center of contemporary chair stretchers, it is a modest one, as on cat. nos. 27 and 34. The turnings are very competently executed, with well-rounded ogee vase forms set off by the more staccato rhythms of the rings and reels and with variety added by the balusters on the stretchers being either more compressed or more elongated than those on the legs. The tripartite scheme of the turnings relates to the division of the facade, and the round central arch of the skirt is echoed in the reels, noticeably that of the front stretcher. The original top most likely differed in its design from the present one, and it may well be that there was no heavy molding under it and that instead the double-bead moldings extended across the rail above the drawers to the top, as on the base of cat. no. 125, a high chest, or possibly continued across the top of the drawer openings. Only one other joined dressing table of the same general type has been published. With a skirt cut to three round arches on the front and a single round arch on the sides and with legs turned in an urn-and-baluster pattern, it has little bearing on the present example.[1]

The use of cherry and yellow poplar in this table, as on cat. no. 128, suggests manufacture in Connecticut or the mid-Atlantic colonies, while the birch turnings—unquestionably integral to the piece—indicate it was probably made in the former rather than in the latter region, which is in accord with its history of having been found in Guilford, Connecticut. The feet of cat. no. 101 and the legs and feet of cat. no. 107, both chests from that area of coastal Connecticut, are likewise made of birch. The legs on the latter piece do not relate to those on this table, except that they are also an apparently unique interpretation of the standard opposed-vase pattern of the period.

CONSTRUCTION

The sides and the back are joined to the stiles with tenons that extend nearly the full height of the case and are secured with three pins. The mortise-and-tenon joints of the stretchers and shaped front rail are double-pinned; those of the front rail above the drawers have one pin. The present top, which overhangs at the back and has a separate rim on all four sides affixed with nails or screws hidden by face-grain plugs, is attached from below with modern screws. The vertical transverse partitions between the drawers, rectangular in shape, are housed in the back board and were originally each secured with two nails through the back; at the front they are let into the top rail and also into the skirt for the inch or so that they extend down below the side drawer openings, and near the bottom of the openings they are nailed to the skirt in the usual manner. The extreme right and left drawer runners are rabbeted and nailed to the stiles; those on either side of the partitions fit through the back board and at the front end are beveled on the underside and set into conforming notches in the skirt. Drawer guides are glued to the sides of the partitions near the top. The strip edging the front and side skirts is attached with small rosehead nails. On the drawers, the sides are joined to the front with a single dovetail reinforced by sprigs; at the back they are rabbeted and extend somewhat beyond the back, to which they are nailed with sprigs. The bottom is a front-to-back board that is lightly beveled to fit into a groove in the front and sides and is nailed to the back.

CONDITION

H. Eugene Bolles (see *Provenance*) had the table restored. He recorded that it was "taken apart, put together, refinished," and that in addition to "insignificant repairs" new pendants were made and the top (inside the rim) was provided with a new 1½-inch-wide strip across the back (Bolles notes, MMA Archives). The top is otherwise as he found it; it appears to be a reused board (cherry, possibly the original one reworked), to which a rim (maple) was applied; for its attachment with screws from below, three large holes were drilled on the inner side of the case back and two on each side. The cyma recta molding (cherry) under the top, which on the sides angles out beyond the back of the case, is not old. One drawer runner is replaced, as are the blocks (glued to the front skirt) to which the pendants and square caps are attached. There are patches and repairs where the runners come through the back and a small patch at the front of the left partition. The drawers have a few added and replaced nails and show evidence that drop pulls have been reattached several times. There are splits in the case sides and at the joints, many of which have pins that are probably replaced. The surface of the left side is marred by a large bruised area and that of the front

129

skirt and of the top by the exposed tunneling of borers. Worm damage is extensive on the lower left rear leg, where crumbling wood in the foot has been filled. The refinishing appears to have included sanding of the turnings, though they retain residues of a dark coating. The underside of the top and the interior of the drawers have been varnished.

INSCRIPTIONS
Scratched restorer's marks are inside the back of the right and center drawers (X) and the left drawer (X with a bar across center).

WOODS
Front rails, drawer fronts, case sides, CHERRY; case back, drawer sides, backs, and bottoms, partitions, inner drawer runners, YELLOW POPLAR; outermost drawer runners, ASH; stiles and integral legs and feet, stretchers, BIRCH; molding around drawers, SOFT MAPLE.

DIMENSIONS
OH. 27½ (69.9); top: W. 27⅜ (69.5), D. 18¾ (47.6); case: W. 22¾ (57.8), D. 15½ (39.4).

REFERENCES
Lockwood 1913, fig. 76; Cescinsky and Hunter 1929, p. 60.

PROVENANCE
Ex coll.: H. Eugene Bolles, Boston.
   The table is said to have come "from a family in Guilford, Connecticut" (Bolles notes, MMA Archives).

Gift of Mrs. Russell Sage, 1909 (10.125.69)

1. The table (present location unknown) was lent by Luke Vincent Lockwood to the Connecticut tercentenary exhibition in 1935 (*Three Centuries of Connecticut Furniture* 1935, no. 37) and was for a time at the Saint Louis Art Museum, Saint Louis, Missouri ("New England Furniture" 1943, p. 37).

130.

Slate table

Northeastern Massachusetts, coastal New Hampshire, or
adjacent coastal Maine, 1715–35

This is one of a dozen tables distinguished by having a top
with a slate center framed by a border that features marquetry
designs. The tops, either octagonal or rectangular, are affixed
to frames of various forms, nine in the William and Mary style
and three Queen Anne examples with cabriole legs. That
such tabletops were not of colonial manufacture but imported
and set on American frames was first put forward in print by
Luke Vincent Lockwood in the early 1900s, and in 1961
Winslow Ames demonstrated that this type of tabletop was
made in Switzerland, where numerous examples are known,
and that it was a Swiss export item found also on tables in
Germany, Belgium, and Italy. The tops were most likely
shipped down the Rhine to Holland, whence they entered
further trade routes—across the Atlantic, or to Scandinavia,
for instance. There are several examples attached to Norwegian
frames in the Nordenfjeldske Kunstindustrimuseum in
Trondheim.[1]

The tabletops appear to represent a regional style produced
in many different workshops in eastern Switzerland. They
vary considerably in size and proportions but follow a standard
construction formula, and the marquetry designs exhibit
distinctive traditional schemes that are variously interpreted.
The patterns fall into two categories: those drawn from
heraldry, with lions rampant—shown singly, or in confronting
pairs as on this table—being the most common motif, and a
double eagle less frequently used (seen on only one American
table); and Renaissance-inspired designs consisting of
symmetrical arrangements of vines, scrolls, and stylized foliage,
which hark back to so-called moresque marquetry on Swiss
furniture of the 1550s and 1560s and which typically occur in
rectangular panels on the long sides of the tops.[2] The moresque
designs, although generically related, show considerable
individuality. The lion rampant motifs vary mainly in small
details. The version of confronting lions on this table, shaped
like many to straddle a corner, is distinguished by the particular
spiky outline of the lions, with the tail on the right one
consistently differing from that on the left one, and by the
motifs separating the animals—a trefoil between their feet
and a wreath enclosing a trefoil between their raised paws.
Presumably all four panels were made from the same pattern
and small differences between them, most noticeably the
simplification of two of the lower trefoils, probably occurred
in the cutting. Close parallels but not exact duplicates of this
design are found on a table in Munich, Germany, and one in
Trondheim, the variations stemming either from the use of
slightly different patterns or from the individual executions
of a stock pattern.[3]

The colonial port of entry for the Swiss slate tops was most
likely Boston, as suggested by tables with family histories in
that area and by the style of most of the frames. Probate
inventories document the presence of slate tables in Boston
already in the 1690s, but those tables probably had tops of a
different type, for stylistically none of the known frames with
Swiss tops appear to date before 1700.[4] The nature of the slate
tables to be sold at public vendue advertised in the *Boston
News-Letter* of 29 September–6 October 1718 is not known,
but a Swiss slate top at Trondheim dated 1717 suggests
shipments of such tops were occurring at that time.[5]

Of the eight other William and Mary tables, two have
joined frames with one drawer and turned legs and stretchers
with opposed balusters similar in design to those on cat.
nos. 60 and 61; five are dressing tables of the general format
of cat. no. 128, and one is a tea table with dovetailed rails and
trumpet legs and scroll feet.[6] The present table has some
unusual features that suggest its maker was not customarily
producing Boston-style dressing tables and was probably not
working in an urban context, which lends some support to its
history of having been found in Maine. The design is quirky:
first, while the pattern of arches in the front skirt follows the
standard formula for dressing tables with three drawers, this
table has but a single drawer; second, the drawer, quite exceptionally, spans the full width of the case. No space has been
allowed for the facing (a thin plaque when the piece is not
veneered, as on cat. no. 128) regularly applied above the legs
on the front of New England high chests and dressing tables
that simulates a stile and hides the joint of the front skirt to
the sides, which normally has half-blind dovetails. Here the
dovetails, which are irregular in size and rather crude, are fully
exposed.[7] The legs, in essentially the same pattern as those on
cat. no. 126 (see fig. 41) but distinguished by the lack of under-
cutting below the inverted-cup shape, are close in profile to
the legs on a veneered high chest at the Winterthur Museum,
which like the present ones are made of birch.[8] Although not
a wood considered typical of the William and Mary period,
birch does occur in New England furniture of that time,
mostly in turnings, occasionally as a secondary wood, and in
a few instances as a primary wood, as on this table, where it
was in all likelihood stained walnut to match the top.[9]

130

CONSTRUCTION

The back is joined to the sides with three broad half-blind dovetails and the front skirt to the sides with narrower dovetails that are fully exposed. The top is pinned to the sides of the case at front and back. The octagonal frame of the top, which provides the substrate for the veneer and marquetry, appears to be joined with half laps, and the square rim around its perimeter is attached with wooden pins and is joined at each corner with a spline. The slate (¼ in. thick) is supported by one longitudinal and two transverse braces joined together and to the octagonal frame with half laps, and its perimeter rests on a rabbet on the inner edge of the frame. The edge of the slate has a narrow bevel at the top, and the veneer extends over that bevel. There is no rail above the drawer, which spans the full width of the case, and the glued-on block in each corner of the case extends up to just below the drawer runners. The runners are let into the back and at the front are beveled on the underside and fit into a conforming notch in the skirt. The skirt is not edged with a bead strip, but the back edge of the center front arch is chamfered. The upper tenons of the legs are socketed into the corner blocks, and the lower pass through the stretchers and down to within 2 inches of the bottom of the feet, which are drilled through. The cross stretchers are half-lapped at the center. The drawer sides are joined to the front with half-blind dovetails and to the back with through dovetails. The bottom, one longitudinal board, is beveled to fit into a groove in the front and sides and nailed to the underside of the back. The top of the sides is finished with two broad chamfers, the top of the back with one.

CONDITION
The top has been off and reattached with the original pins into the only set of holes in the case sides (as confirmed by X-radiographs). The marquetry shows no losses, but the top is scratched and stained; near one of the pins is a plugged hole; and the underside of the overhang at center back is marred by modern screw holes from the time at the MMA (several decades past) when small objects displayed on the table were strapped to the top. The case has been apart and there is evidence of regluing of joints. Some of the nails that were at one time added to the corner blocks are now missing and some of them have been replaced with screws. The applied double-bead molding to the right of the drawer and an adjoining section at the bottom are new. There are repairs in the square caps at the top of the legs, and the back of the right rear leg is pieced at the very bottom. The feet, the finial at the center of the stretchers (all birch), and the pendants are probably replaced, as are possibly also the legs. The stretchers (cherry) are questionable; they cause the legs to cant in toward the bottom, and they deviate from standard design in that the curves on one edge are not parallel to those on the other. The hardware on the drawer is original. The drawer bottom is split. The table has a modern finish. The base has a reddish hue that is at variance with the color of the walnut of the top. The base has been stripped, and the outer surface of the sides and front appears in addition to have been planed when the case was apart; however, residues of an earlier degraded coating remain on the legs and stretchers. A dark stain has been applied to the exterior of the back and to most hidden surfaces.

INSCRIPTIONS
Scratched on the underside of the slate is the number 8. Scratched restorer's marks are on the back of the case and adjoining underside of the top (X with double lines) and on the back of the drawer (X).

WOODS
Case sides, front skirt, drawer front, legs, BIRCH; case back, drawer sides, back, and bottom, drawer runners, corner blocks, EASTERN WHITE PINE; veneer and solid rim of top, WALNUT; substrate and braces of top, SPRUCE; marquetry woods not identified.

DIMENSIONS
OH. 28¼ (71.8); top: W. 35⅛ (89.2), D. 24⅞ (63.2); case: W. 25 (63.5), D. 16⅞ (42.9).

REFERENCES
Cornelius 1926, pl. XVII; Nutting 1928–33, nos. 1091 (detail of top), 1092 (overall view); Ralston 1931b, fig. 2 (with detail of top); Halsey and Cornelius 1938 (and 1942), fig. 28; "Antiques in the American Wing" 1946, p. 249, no. 11; Ames 1961, fig. 7 (top only); Comstock 1962, nos. 130A, B (with detail of top); M. B. Davidson 1967, no. 74

(top only); Butler 1973, p. 24 (with detail of top); Schwartz 1976, no. 35; M. B. Davidson and Stillinger 1985, fig. 146 (top only).

PROVENANCE
Ex coll.: George Coe Graves, Osterville, Massachusetts.

Graves purchased the table from Charles Woolsey Lyon, the New York City dealer, who had acquired it from Ross H. Maynard in 1923. A letter from Maynard to Lyon, written on Lyon's business stationery and dated 22 December 1923 (ADA files), states that Maynard first found the table in the home of Harry Quinby and his mother in Saco, Maine, in 1916, and that he succeeded in buying it in 1922. He was informed that the table had descended in the Quinby family. Maynard was a collector and dealer in East Middlebury, Vermont, who advertised in the *Antiquarian* in January 1927.[10]

The Sylmaris Collection, Gift of George Coe Graves, 1930 (30.120.56)

1. Lockwood 1901, p. 227, and Lockwood 1913, vol. 1, p. 73; Ames 1961. Letter of 1 June 1967, from Albert Steen, curator of the Nordenfjeldske Kunstindustrimuseum, Trondheim, Norway, to Colin Streeter, in what was then the MMA's Western European Arts Department, and enclosure, a photograph of one tabletop (ADA files).
2. Trachsler 1978, pp. 4–5 and figs. 12, 14–16, 19. The panels on the long sides of the top at Trondheim that is known to the present writer through a photograph (see n. 1 above) contain, exceptionally, pairs of confronting stags rampant surmounting a horned animal courant and flanking a lion (?) rampant.
3. For the tabletop in Munich, see Ames 1961, fig. 6. For the one at Trondheim, see n. 1 above.
4. I. W. Lyon 1891, p. 203. Slate tables are recorded also in Philadelphia in the 1690s (McElroy 1979, p. 67).
5. Dow 1927, p. 107. Full wording of the advertisement is given in "Slate-Top Tables" 1971. The letter from Albert Steen (see n. 1 above) states that one of the tops at Trondheim is dated 1717.
6. Tables with joined frames are in the American Antiquarian Society, Worcester, Massachusetts (I. W. Lyon 1891, p. 204, for its history; and Lockwood 1913, figs. 705, 706), and Museum of Fine Arts, Boston (Randall 1965, no. 74). Examples of the dressing-table type are in the Brooklyn Museum, Brooklyn, New York (Schwartz 1968, figs. 9, 10); Connecticut Historical Society, Hartford (Lockwood 1913, figs. 62, 63); Dietrich American Foundation ("New England Slate-Top Table" 1939, frontispiece); and Winterthur Museum (Cooper 2002, pl. IX); and in a private collection (*Girl Scouts* 1929, no. 513). The tea table is in the Wadsworth Atheneum (Nutting 1928–33, nos. 1093, 1094). For the three Queen Anne examples, see Ginsburg 1962, figs. 1, 2, 4.
7. For dressing tables with similar construction, see E. G. Miller 1937, no. 671; and *Antiques* 129 (May 1986), p. 939 (Kenneth and Paulette Tuttle advertisement). For high chests, see Nutting 1928–33, no. 336; and *Antiques* 126 (October 1984), p. 657 (Bernard and S. Dean Levy advertisement).
8. Acc. no. 66.1306. For the birch legs, see Forman 1988, p. 33.
9. For other birch turnings, see cat. nos. 101, 107, 128, 129; earlier examples are on a late-seventeenth-century table at the Yale University Art Gallery (Barquist 1992, no. 28). Birch is the sole primary wood on a falling-leaf table probably from York, Maine (Jobe and Kaye 1984, no. 59) and forms the case sides of a Massachusetts dressing table (G. W. R. Ward 1988, no. 94).
10. *Antiquarian* 7, no. 6 (January 1927), p. 16. Born in East Middlebury (1868), Maynard owned a house there, apparently known for its antiques, from 1922 to 1945 (letter of 19 October 1995 from Nancy Rucker, Henry Sheldon Museum of Vermont History, Middlebury [ADA files]). He also at one time lived in Boston (see the entry for cat. no. 46).

131. See also fig. 43.

131.
Dressing table

Philadelphia, 1710–30

The legs and feet of this table are in a distinctive pattern found only on Philadelphia furniture. Notably they closely match those on a high chest and dressing table at the Philadelphia Museum of Art that Caspar Wistar ordered in 1726 from Philadelphia cabinetmaker John Head (d. 1754).[1] The legs have an elegant profile, with the outward sweep of the flaring trumpet shape countered by the taper of the grooved baluster above (fig. 43). The design is further charac-

terized by the turnings at the top of the trumpet, which are composed of an ovolo at the flange followed by a fillet and then an ogee that rises to meet the reel below the baluster, and by the elements at the base, which consist simply of an astragal, a shallow reel, and a substantial, rounded ring. That ring, like the one at the top of the leg, does not terminate with a straight cut in but is succeeded by a short segment that tapers down to the diameter of the tenon. Particularly distinctive is the shape of the foot, which is actually a somewhat enlarged version of a portion of the leg—from just above the groove in the baluster down to an inch or so below the rim of the trumpet shape.

This piece is closely related to three other dressing tables in addition to the Wistar example (all with three drawers) in the particular shape of the stretchers as well as in the pattern of the turnings.[2] It also shares with those tables a peculiarity that appears to be associated solely with this distinct form of leg—the addition of a square plinth between the stretcher and the leg, a feature that occurs on two high chests with similar turnings as well.[3] It is not clear if there ever was any ornament at the intersection of the stretchers on this piece. The Wistar dressing table and one of the related ones mentioned above, which is associated with the Galloway family, have an applied diamond-shaped plaque in that location. One-drawer dressing tables with the same type of case construction, legs, and shaped flat stretchers as the three-drawer tables that were made to match the lower case of high chests are rare. Only one other published example attributed to Pennsylvania is known to the writer and several from New England.[4] This table differs from the others in that the design of its skirt does not refer to that of six-legged high chests. Parallels to its skirt profile—straight with a cavetto at either end—are to be found instead on one-drawer Pennsylvania dressing tables that are of joined construction and have baluster-and-block turned legs.[5]

In the construction of its case, the present piece illustrates structural traits that distinguish Philadelphia high chests and related dressing tables in general and that are represented on the base of a small cabinet in the MMA collection as well (cat. no. 82). Typically this table is made of solid walnut, a wood that was plentiful in Pennsylvania, with southern yellow pine and white cedar (the latter for drawer bottoms) as secondary woods; the occurrence of sweet gum is not as common. The use of solid walnut appears to go hand in hand with methods of construction that differ from those characteristic of Boston veneered high chests and dressing tables, and differ also from those on Boston solid walnut examples, which adhere to the same lower-case structural formula as their veneered counterparts. In Philadelphia the sides of dressing tables or of the base of high chests made of solid walnut are dovetailed to the front, as on this piece, with the dovetails characteristically visible on the sides, instead of, as in Boston, the front being joined with half-blind dovetails to the sides and the joint hidden on the front by veneer or an applied plaque. The case front here consists of a single board in which the opening for the drawer has been sawn out and what appears to be a rail above the drawer and a skirt below are all part of that one board. The same holds true when there are the usual three drawers, as on cat. no. 82, in which case a solid band is left between the individual drawer openings,

resulting in drawers that are widely separated—a characteristic of Philadelphia pieces. With this type of construction there are no transverse partitions, just drawer runners and guides. Typically, as on this piece, there is an applied cavetto molding above the drawer(s)—on high chests it forms part of the mid-molding—but on some dressing tables the double-bead molding used on the bottom and sides of the drawer openings continues across the top.

CONSTRUCTION
The back is joined to the sides and the sides to the front with half-blind dovetails. The front is formed of a single board in which the drawer opening has been sawn out. The top is attached to glued-on corner blocks that extend the full height of the case. The drawer runners are nailed to the front corner blocks and are let into the back. A slat nailed to the outer edge of each runner acts as a drawer guide. The upper tenons of the legs are socketed into the corner blocks and probably partially into the case sides. The lower tenons pass through low square plinths and then the stretchers to engage the feet. The cross stretchers intersect with a half-lap joint. The drawer sides are joined to the front with two half-blind dovetails and to the back with two through dovetails; on the inside of the front, kerfs from the sawing of the dovetails extend in for nearly an inch. The drawer bottom consists of seven narrow transverse boards nailed to a rabbet in the front and to the bottom of the other sides. A runner strip is applied under the bottom at each side.

CONDITION
The top has stains and either has been reworked and reset or is a reused board; it is now attached with wooden pins and nails. The vertical sections of the molding around the drawer opening are new. There are cracks in the left side, particularly above the rear leg, on which sections of the top ring turning have split off and been glued. The caps above the legs have repairs and replacements, and small filled holes in the case front and sides above the caps suggest a nail has been driven into the tenon of each leg. On the interior, the upper third of the inside corner of three of the corner blocks has been gouged out. The left drawer runner has been reattached, the right one may be replaced, and a guide has been added under the top on the right. The stretchers have cracked at the center, and the joint has been reinforced underneath with a wooden brace; on the upper surface there is a square patch and evidence of previous repairs. On the drawer, the bottom has been partly reattached and one runner strip is new. The brass hardware is replaced, but the pulls are of the general type originally there; plugged holes remain from the onetime attachment of bail handles. The lock is missing. Metal gliders have been added under the feet. The walnut has a recent coat of shellac applied over very thin remains of finish found under a tacky dark mahogany-color layer that was cleaned off in 1979. Part of the new coating was toned to minimize differences in color due to sun bleaching. Dark stain has been applied to the interior and back of the case.

INSCRIPTIONS
Inscribed in pencil inside the back in modern script is "Chas Demuth." Incised restorer's marks are under the left side and left drawer runner. A William Trent House identification number (see *Exhibition*) in ink on cloth tape is on the back of the case and inside the drawer.

WOODS

Top, sides, front, drawer front, legs, feet, stretchers, square caps at top of legs, plinths, moldings, BLACK WALNUT; case back, drawer sides and back, SOUTHERN YELLOW PINE; runners and guides, PINE; drawer bottom, ATLANTIC WHITE CEDAR; corner blocks, SWEET GUM.

DIMENSIONS

OH. 27½ (69.9); top: W. 33⅞ (86), D. 20¾ (52.7); case: W. 29⅞ (75.9), D. 19⅝ (49.8).

EXHIBITION

On loan to the William Trent House, Trenton, New Jersey, from 1945 to 1977.

PROVENANCE

The table was bequeathed to the MMA by the mother of the artist Charles Demuth. According to her will, it stood in the corner of the dining room in her house in Lancaster, Pennsylvania (now owned by the Demuth Foundation), where Charles had his home and studio. No previous history of the table is known.

Bequest of Augusta W. Demuth, 1943 (43.60)

1. *Philadelphia* 1976, no. 22; Lindsey 1999, no. 38 and fig. 167 (attributed to John Head).
2. One is in the Winterthur Museum (acc. no. 56.38.143); on the others, see *Antiques* 112 (July 1977), p. 1 (David Stockwell advertisement; said to have belonged to the Galloway family of Philadelphia); and *Important Americana, Including Furniture, Folk Art and Folk Paintings, Prints, Silver and Carpets,* auction cat., Sotheby's, New York City, 28, 29, and 31 January 1987, lot 1318.
3. On the Wistar high chest and one in DAPC (no. 75.266) associated with the Richardson family of Philadelphia.
4. The Pennsylvania table is in G. W. R. Ward 1988, no. 98. For New England tables, see, for example, Kirk 1967, no. 171; and D. B. Warren et al. 1998, no. F28. See also no. 130 in this catalogue. For English examples, see Kirk 1982, nos. 1457, 1458, 1460–62.
5. For joined tables with related skirts, see Schaefer 1982, pl. IV; and Lindsey 1999, no. 49.

Desks

In the seventeenth century, the term "desk"—in a domestic context—commonly referred to a box with an inclined lid, a type of piece in use since the Middle Ages that provided a sloping surface on which to write or prop up a book. Usually small and easily portable, such desks were set on a table or other furniture form that brought them to a convenient height. Few American boxes with sloping lids are known. Nearly all surviving boxes have a flat lid, and while some very probably served to store books or writing materials, they were most likely not described in probate documents as desks; for whereas one or more boxes are listed in the majority of seventeenth-century household inventories, desks are mentioned much less frequently.

Toward the end of the seventeenth century, desk boxes began to be placed on their own stand, an early indication of which is a 1672 Boston inventory listing of "a desk wth a fframe."[1] The desk-on-frame included in this chapter (cat. no. 132) dates from several decades later. A very individual piece made in the New York City area, it exhibits in its design and construction the influence of both Continental and English craft traditions. It is unusual also in being constructed in two sections, with an open joined base separate from the desk portion, which is strictly a desk box with an inclined lid that is hinged at the top and has a ledge at the bottom to hold paper or a book. No seventeenth-century-style American desks-on-frame are known, and the majority of William and Mary examples and typically those in succeeding eighteenth-century styles were built in one piece and have the lid hinged at the bottom. While some fashionable desks-on-frame were made in the late colonial period, the form continued in use in large part at lower levels of production, and it persisted through the nineteenth century in utilitarian pieces for business or school.

By the early 1700s, a new form, which combined the desk box with a chest of drawers into one unit, was introduced. This basic scheme, which remained, with stylistic changes, the predominant desk form during most of the eighteenth century, is here illustrated by two examples, one veneered and from the Boston area (cat. no. 133) and the other in solid walnut and probably from eastern Massachusetts (cat. no. 134). On early-eighteenth-century examples, the lower portion of this still familiar form, now commonly called a slant-top or slant-front desk, duplicates the drawer arrangement, and on veneered pieces also the decorative scheme, of the three upper tiers of drawers on William and Mary high chests. The upper section differs fundamentally from the desk box in that the lid is hinged not at the top but at the bottom and falls down to provide a flat writing surface supported by lopers. (The same sort of lid became common also on desks-on-frame.)

The fall-front type of lid, introduced to England from the Continent, was used on English writing cabinets of the last third of the seventeenth century, which had a vertical hinged front and were called scrutoires or scriptores (from the French *escritoire*). Some scrutoires were relatively small in scale and consisted of a cabinet unit set on an open frame. That form has no counterpart in American furniture, but the larger, probably later, type, on which the cabinet rests on a chest of drawers and the top includes a pulvinated frieze with drawer, was made, albeit rarely, in the colonies. Two prime examples, neither in the Museum's collection, are known: one from Philadelphia made of solid walnut and dated 1707, and one from New York with floral inlay.[2]

The large writing cabinet with its facade all on one plane was soon superseded by the desk and bookcase—a slant-top desk with a separate two-door unit set on top containing shelves and slots. The desk and bookcase, of which several American examples in the William and Mary style are known but none is in the collection, became a major form in the late colonial period. It was available in Boston by 1715, when japanner William Randle or Randall (active ca. 1715–ca. 1735) advertised, among other items of furniture, "Escrutoires . . . Writing Desks, Bookcases with Desk," which may have been imported, as were no doubt the looking glasses and glass sconces he was also selling.[3] The advertisement points up the difficulty in interpreting period terminology. What was the form of his "escrutoires," and how did they differ from his "writing desks"?

1. Quoted in I. W. Lyon 1891, p. 114.
2. *Philadelphia* 1976, no. 9 (Colonial Williamsburg); Baarsen et al. 1988, no. 103 (Museum of the City of New York).
3. Dow 1927, pp. 106–7.

132.
Desk-on-frame

New York City or vicinity, 1695–1720

This striking desk has no known close counterpart. It represents a unique coming together of European and English furniture-making traditions that speaks eloquently of the diverse population of craftsmen and clients in the New York colony at the time it was made. The inscription in Dutch inside the lid indicates an owner of Netherlandish descent. In both construction and design, the desk portion of this piece shares some distinctive attributes with a type of early-eighteenth-century kast ascribed to Kings County, New York (now Brooklyn, where the desk was reputedly found in about 1922). The singular manner in which the desk box is joined corresponds exactly to that of the base of those kasten: the front is dovetailed to the sides and the sides to the back, with all joints exposed and showing analogous neatly and consistently cut, sharply angled dovetails. Another telling similarity is the use of simulated panels veneered with a wood richer in color and more highly prized than that of the piece itself, a characteristic of Kings County kasten, on which mahogany panels are applied to the stiles in place of pilasters. On the kasten and on the desk, those panels were probably meant to provide a rich highlight on a case made of local sweet gum, a red-hued wood resembling the more expensive imported mahogany. Here the panels embellish the front of the desk and give the illusion of two drawer fronts, each of which was once fitted with two drop pulls, probably of English manufacture, as the escutcheon appears to be. Finally, the profile of the molding under the sides of the top and the selfsame profile worked on the cleats, with its tight alternations of convex and concave elements, has a crisp, striated appearance akin to that of the moldings on the stiles of the kasten in question.[1]

A sequence of contours identical to that on the desk's cleats is used on the heavy molding under the lid of a flat-topped box, also of sweet gum and yellow poplar, that is joined with similar distinctive dovetailing and was probably made in the same shop.[2] The desk and box also share a further particularity—the effort to conceal as much of the hinges as possible, with the leaves of the butt hinges on the desk set into mortises and the prongs of the snipebill hinges of the box completely embedded. This type of hinge attachment, evident also on cat. no. 118, a kast, is atypical for American furniture, but it occurs in the Netherlands and may have had wider currency on the Continent.[3]

The base of this desk also exhibits features that are not characteristic of Anglo-American furniture and point to direct Continental influence, but in this instance probably to that of craftsmen of French rather than Netherlandish descent—a distinct possibility, given early New York's significant French Huguenot and Walloon population.[4] The design on the upper part of the legs—an urn followed abruptly by a tapered columnar segment—is one encountered primarily in French or French-inspired turnings, which also tend to be alternately quite deeply cut in and strongly projecting, as on the lower half of the legs (fig. 36).[5] Sharp, disklike elements rather than rounded rings characterize the turnings on the stretchers as well (except on the front stretcher, where they have been rounded by wear). Otherwise the ogee vase shapes and the ball, reel, and ring forms and their disposition cannot be differentiated as such from the Anglo-American turning vocabulary of the period. The pattern of repeated arches and pendants on the skirt is unusual and may also be derived from French sources.[6] But the general character of the strongly projecting molding at the top of the base and the manner in which the loose desk box is supported and held in place are indebted to Anglo-American high chests.

The overall form of this piece—basically a seventeenth-century portable writing box or book box with slanted lid, set on its own base—was probably English-inspired. Colonial examples in the William and Mary style are not restricted to any particular region and they vary considerably in their design. One other desk-on-frame unquestionably from New York has been published. It is also made of sweet gum. Its base contains a drawer, and its legs, turned with bold compressed balusters and rings, are connected by plain stretchers. Its lid, like that of cat. no. 132, is hinged to lift upward as on the portable desk boxes, and on both examples there is a molding at the bottom of the lid to hold a book or paper in place.[7]

CONSTRUCTION
The desk and the frame are built as separate units. On the desk, the front is dovetailed to the sides and the sides to the back, with the joints totally exposed. The bottom, formed of three longitudinal boards joined by tongue and groove, is nailed to a rabbet in the front and sides and through a thin strip to the bottom of the back. The top is secured to the sides and back probably with nails; the means of attachment was countersunk and concealed by large, round face-grain plugs—two at either end and two at the back. The cleated lid is composed of three longitudinal boards and is attached to the top with two butt hinges. The leaves of the hinges are let into mortises in the top and lid, respectively, and each leaf is held in place by two nails driven from the top and clinched on the inside. The two simulated panels on the front formed by applied moldings are veneered. The sequence of profiles on those moldings—astragal, cavetto, small bead,

fillet—is repeated on a slightly larger scale on the applied molding at the bottom of the lid, and that same molding is used reversed at the base of the desk; this somewhat larger version, with the addition of a fascia and cavetto at the top, constitutes the profile on the lid's cleats and on the molding under the ends of the top. The ends of the top board and the side and front edges of the lid are finished with a cyma reversa on the horizontal surface and a fillet and an ovolo on the vertical face. The back edge of the top is finished with a single bead. The interior of the desk is fitted with three tiers of small compartments under the top. They are formed by two horizontal dividers, which are slotted into rectangular grooves in the sides, and by vertical partitions (three over two over two), which are cut to fit into V-shaped grooves in the top and dividers. In the lowest tier, the partitions are butted to the bottom board and secured each with a nail from below. A double-bead molding is worked on the front edge of the compartments.

On the frame, the rails (the front and side ones scalloped) and stretchers are joined to the legs with substantial tenons (7/16 in. thick), which are secured with one pin. The rails and stretchers are slightly recessed from the outer edge of the leg blocks, with the result that the stretchers, which are not as thick as the legs, are more or less centered on those blocks. Nailed to the top of the frame and mitered at the front corners are a board across the front and one on each side that support the desk unit. The visible outer portion of those boards shows a plain band followed by the same cyma reversa as that worked on the edge of the lid; the inner portion has been recessed so as to keep the desk in place.

CONDITION

On the desk unit, the molding at the base of each side is a replacement. There is a patch in the lid at the right hinge and at the left end of the lid where two boards have separated, one at the left rear corner of the top, and one at the bottom rear corner of each side. A large modern screw reinforces the attachment of each end of the top and of the molding under the top to the side; similar screws now secure the lid's cleats. Along the joint of the top and the lid are series of small filled holes, possibly from a leather hinge tacked on when the right metal hinge, which has repairs, failed. Toward either end of each panel on the front is a filled hole and on the inside are imprints of cotter pins that once secured drop pulls. The lock and the escutcheon are probably original. On the interior, the bottom boards, which have warped, are heavily stained. Wear shows that at one time the upper two tiers of compartments had drawers; the vendor reported removing modern drawers before the desk came to the MMA. On the frame, the left front foot is replaced and the wood at the bottom of the three other feet, which have lost some height, has deteriorated. Two rings on the turnings have a sizable loss. The pendants vary in age. According to the vendor, the desk was "painted with red house paint" when he first saw it.[8] He had the paint removed; the surface, particularly on the turnings, shows evidence of aggressive stripping. The wood now has a clear modern finish and is quite light in color except where residues of red paint remain, most noticeably on the lid, where the surface is variegated.

INSCRIPTIONS

A chalk inscription in script across the inside of the front of the lid reads: "1[6? or 7?]85 Ocktober 12 geleent aen / Maerte Schenk 5 pont [. . . 12 October lent to Martin Schenk 5 pounds]."[9] Also inside the lid are: (in chalk) "P-Q" and other letters, numbers, and illegible markings; (in ink, small) "£ 322" over a bar over "50"; (in pencil, small) "184[7?]. . ." Written in green paint on the inner right side of the desk

is "1886 / JBH." The four uppermost compartments of the interior are numbered in pencil from 1 to 4 (modern). Large, scored sawyer's tally marks are on the inner left side of the desk (|| crossed by a diagonal slash and || partly cut off) and inside the rear rail of the base (|| crossed by a diagonal slash).

WOODS

SWEET GUM; bottom, dividers, and partitions of desk box, YELLOW POPLAR; veneer of front panels, MAHOGANY (?).[10]

DIMENSIONS

OH. 35¼ (89.5); OW. (lower mid-molding) 34½ (87.6); CW. (desk and frame) 31¾ (80.6); OD. (lower mid-molding) 24⅛ (61.3); CD. (desk and frame) 22¾ (57.8).

REFERENCES

Downs 1944, p. 78; "Additions to the American Wing" 1945; "Antiques in the American Wing" 1946, p. 249, no. 12; Powel 1954, p. 200; Comstock 1962, no. 91; Williams 1963, no. 100 (drawings of molding profiles are incorrect); Margon 1965, p. 71; M. B. Davidson 1967, no. 102; Schwartz 1976, no. 36; M. B. Davidson 1980, fig. 80; M. B. Davidson and Stillinger 1985, fig. 140; Kenny, Safford, and Vincent 1991a, fig. 18 (detail of side); Kamil 1995, fig. 11.

PROVENANCE

Ex coll.: Arthur W. Clement, Brooklyn, New York.

Clement purchased the desk in about 1922 from Harry Mark, a Brooklyn dealer. Mark told Clement that he had found it in a garret in the Courtelyou Road section of Flatbush (Brooklyn) shortly before he sold it. The desk was on loan from Clement to the MMA from 1934 to 1944, when it was purchased from him.

Rogers Fund, 1944 (44.47)

1. For Kings County kasten, see Kenny, Safford, and Vincent 1991a, pp. 19–21 and nos. 8, 9. The escutcheon on the desk is similar to that on no. 9. The same type of exposed dovetailing is also on the front of a dressing table made by Samuel Clement about 1726 in Flushing, New York (Failey 1976, no. 40).
2. The box is shown in Ottoson 1985, fig. 2; it measures, in inches, 8½ high, 16 5/16 wide, and 10 deep and is now in another private collection.
3. Kenny, Safford, and Vincent 1991a, p. 14.
4. For early New York woodworkers, see Forman 1988, pp. 111, 324; and Kamil 1995, pp. 217–22.
5. Comparison can be made with turnings—in the Louis XIII manner—on French Canadian chairs and tables (Palardy 1965, nos. 299–301, 370–72; Webster 1974, p. 30).
6. For a similar skirt on a French table, see Félice 1923, fig. 59. Palardy 1965, no. 456, shows a more distantly related skirt on a small French Canadian chest.
7. Blackburn and Piwonka 1988, fig. 195 (called a Bible desk, referring to a then custom in the Netherlands of leaving the Bible out and open for reading by the head of the family).
8. Letter of 5 October 1944 from Arthur W. Clement to Joseph Downs (ADA files).
9. Janny Venema of the New Netherland Project, New York State Library, Albany, who is experienced in transcribing early Dutch documents, examined the inscription on 15 November 1995. The writer is indebted to her for the present transcription. The date, recorded as 1695 in 1944, is largely effaced on the desk; more is visible in a 1944 photograph (ADA files). The second number is elusive and could be read as 7 rather than 6; in the photograph, the third number looks very much like an 8 rather than a 9.
10. By eye, the wood appears to be walnut or mahogany. Only a tiny sample could be taken for microanalysis by R. Bruce Hoadley; it allowed walnut to be definitely ruled out and mahogany to be a possibility, but the sample was not large enough for a positive microscopic identification of mahogany.

132. See also fig. 36.

133.

Desk

Boston or vicinity, 1700–1730

A trim, simple form enlivened by richly figured veneers, this piece represents the style of desk fashionable in Boston in the early eighteenth century. The typical configuration of two side-by-side short drawers above two long drawers corresponds to that of the three upper tiers on contemporary high chests, such as cat. no. 123, both in the actual height of the individual drawers and in their gradation of generally one inch, which carries on to the height of the front of the well, a space for storage below the lid. In addition, the cyma reversa and fascia profile of the chests' upper mid-molding is used for the desks' base molding. As on high chests, the veneered drawer fronts are edged with banding in a herringbone pattern, and the drawers are encompassed by an applied molding. The double bead used here continues up the slanted edge of the case sides, so that the inset lid has the same recessed look as the drawers, and then extends to the back, concealing the exposed dovetails at either end of the top. The figured veneer on the top is framed by broad walnut cross-banding and that on the lid by a similar, slightly wider border augmented on the inner side by a narrower band that in all probability originally matched the herringbone on the drawers. On the top and the vertical front, the convoluted grain of the burls creates an overall shimmering effect; on the lid, ripples and small eddies coalesce into two large oval whorls that provide the facade with a very distinctive focal point. The four large sections of veneer on the lid are skillfully matched, but the slightly varying width of the sheets caused the middle seam, and concomitantly the escutcheon, to be off center by a quarter of an inch to the right. The identification of burl veneers is at times difficult to establish. In 1975 a sample of the veneer on the right short drawer was identified as European olive—which made cat. no. 133 the only American piece of the period known to include that imported wood—and the desk was subsequently published as having such veneers.[1] However, the 1991 microanalysis of a sample from the upper long drawer did not yield the same result: in that case, it was determined that the wood belonged to the olive family but was not olive, and that it could be ash.[2] Ash would appear to be the more likely wood on an American piece. Olive-wood veneer has been found in the probate inventory of one American craftsman, Charles Plumley of Philadelphia (d. 1708), but it is not possible to know if it was true olive or simply had a grain that resembled it. The context of some of the references to olive-wood furniture in household inventories of the period makes it very likely that the pieces listed were imported and thus probably veneered

with actual olive; but it may well be, as Benno M. Forman suggested, that the term "olive wood" was also used more generically at the time.[3]

While the flat surfaces of the desk exterior derive their effect from the rippling patterning of the veneers, the interior expresses the early Baroque feeling for movement in three-dimensional terms (fig. 82). The outer sections of the interior compartment, here consisting of two stepped pigeonholes over a drawer, characteristically project forward, separated from the recessed center by shaped partitions that in this instance cascade in interrupted reverse curves. The round arch cut on the front of the outer dividers and the paired ogee curves on the valances parallel shapes on the skirts of contemporary high chests and dressing tables. The broad, recessed central section is typically divided into three units, with the middle one—the original configuration of which is in this case uncertain—usually differing in design from the identical arrangement of drawers and pigeonholes on either side of it. The interior of this desk does not rank among the more ornate of the period; they have figured veneers on the drawer fronts and on the prospect door, if there is one.[4] The sides of this case are not of walnut but made of a less valuable wood stained to match. This was common practice, and maple was the wood most often selected. Although poplar (*Populus* sp.) was frequently chosen for the turned legs and feet of case furniture in this period, its use for the sides of this piece is unusual. The use of poplar for case sides has otherwise been noted on a somewhat later veneered high chest and dressing table with cabriole legs at the Yale University Art Gallery.[5]

CONSTRUCTION

The top is joined to the two-board sides with half-blind dovetails, and the one-board bottom and the sides are dovetailed together. The back, made of two horizontal boards, is nailed to a rabbet in the top and sides. The two boards (a wide front one and a very narrow one in back) that form the bottom of the well above the two short drawers are joined to the sides with a sliding half dovetail. The drawer dividers (3½ in. deep) are let into rectangular grooves in the sides, and the grooves extend to the back and house the drawer runners. The vertical partition between the two short drawers (5½ in. deep) is secured to the well bottom above and to the divider below with a through tenon at the front; there are no medial runners behind the partition but drawer guides are nailed to the underside of the well bottom. The upper portion of the case sides is cut at an angle close to 45 degrees; at the top of the vertical front edge, where a small triangular bracket is applied, the sides protrude level with the bottom of the lid. The hinged lid is formed of one or more boards tenoned to a cleat at each

133. See also fig. 82.

end and is fitted with a lock; when open, it is supported by lopers that slide between the case sides and guides glued to the top of the well bottom. The bottom of the desk interior consists of a framework that has side boards tenoned to the front board and a rear board with a cyma reversa molded front edge that extends a short distance over the sides and is affixed to them. The frame is let into the case sides and encloses a sliding panel that gives access to the well below; the panel

runs on rabbets in the sides of the frame and has an applied bead molding at the front.

On the interior (fig. 82), pigeonholes and compartments for small drawers are formed by horizontal dividers and vertical partitions that are slotted into one another and into the case. The whole unit slides in from the back. The valances at the top each serve as the front of a drawer. The central prospect door is pintle-hinged at the bottom and has a lock. Under the lower drawer behind the door is a secret shallow box with a sliding cover. On all drawers, the sides are dovetailed to the front and back, and the grain of the bottom runs from front to back. On the interior drawers, the front dovetails are half-blind, and the bottom of the lower drawers is glued to a rabbet on the edge of all four sides, while on the valance drawers the bottom is let into the front and otherwise glued to rabbets. On the exterior drawers, the bottom is nailed to a rabbet in the front and to the bottom of the other sides, and there is an applied runner strip under each side; a bead molding finishes the back of the upper edge of the front, and the sides and back are about ¼ inch lower than the front. The two short drawers are fitted with locks. The turned tenons of the feet go into the bottom board, passing through a thick transverse batten under each end concealed by the base molding, which consists of an ovolo, a cyma reversa, and a fascia.

CONDITION

The desk has been considerably restored, but its main decorative feature—the burl veneer, applied in thick (ca. ¹/₁₆ in.) sheets—is basically intact (with the possible exception of the triangular piece in the lower left corner of the lid, which could be an original fill or a repair). But the broad cross-banding at either side of the top and lid, the entire inner band on the lid, and some of the herringbone border around the drawer fronts appear to be replacements, and some of the double-bead molding does not look old. The right base molding is new; the front and left ones are older but probably not original. The feet (poplar [*Populus* sp.]) show some wear but are very likely replaced. The pulls and escutcheons are replacements, and the hinges and all the locks are modern.

As for the structure, the upper back board has been off and reattached and the lower board (maple) replaced. All the runners, guides, and stops for the case drawers are new, as are the battens under the sides of the case bottom and a block under the bottom that backs the base molding at center front. The case drawers have been completely apart; the bottoms have been shifted, pieced at one side, and reset with broad new runner strips, and the exterior of the sides has been planed down. The back of the upper long drawer is partly or entirely replaced, and the age of the ash backs of the short drawers and of the oak sides of the lower long drawer is uncertain. The veneered border and baize on the writing surface of the lid are modern. The replacements in the desk interior, which has been probably taken out for repairs, appear to be extensive. Definitely questionable are the prospect door and the drawers and divider behind it and the four small valance drawers. The four lower drawers with straight fronts have replaced (oak, walnut) or reworked (or reused wood; pine) linings. Holes in the case back and in the backs of the interior drawers date from the time at the MMA (several decades past) when the drawers were secured by screwing them shut. The exterior surfaces of the desk have a modern finish. The inside of all interior and case drawers has been varnished as well as the inner surface of the case sides and the top of the well bottom.

INSCRIPTIONS

Modern restorer's markings in pencil (numbers and letters) are on the exterior drawers, the four small interior valance drawers, and the dividers immediately flanking the prospect door.

WOODS

Burl veneer, Oleaceae (olive family), possibly ASH; banding veneer, applied moldings, cap at front of top board, cap on top edge of lid, lopers, front board, front portion of rear board, and facing on top of side boards of interior bottom, well cover, dividers and partitions of desk interior, front of interior drawers, BLACK WALNUT; core of top, core of lid, case bottom, upper board of back, well bottom, case drawer dividers and partition, core of exterior drawer fronts, all bottoms and some sides and backs of exterior drawers, rear portions of bottom and of outer vertical partitions of desk interior, EASTERN WHITE PINE; case sides, POPLAR (*Populus* sp.).

DIMENSIONS

OH. 39¾ (101); OW. (base molding) 33¾ (85.7); CW. 32 (81.3); OD. (base molding) 19⅛ (48.6); CD. 18 (45.7).

EXHIBITION

"A Bicentennial Treasury: American Masterpieces from the Metropolitan," MMA, 29 January 1976–2 January 1977.

REFERENCES

Lockwood 1913, fig. 240; Halsey and Cornelius 1924 (and 1925, 1926), fig. 22 (1928, 1932, fig. 21; 1938, 1942, fig. 26); Halsey and Tower 1925, fig. 42; Cescinsky and Hunter 1929, p. 164; Salomonsky 1931, no. 80 (measured drawing); "Antiques in the American Wing" 1946, p. 249, no. 16; M. B. Davidson 1967, no. 100; *Bicentennial Treasury* 1976 (exh. cat.), fig. 7; Schwartz 1976, no. 37; M. B. Davidson and Stillinger 1985, fig. 136; Johnston 1988, fig. 78.

PROVENANCE

Ex coll.: H. Eugene Bolles, Boston.

Gift of Mrs. Russell Sage, 1909 (10.125.75)

1. The sample was microanalyzed at the Forest Products Laboratory in Madison, Wisconsin. *Bicentennial Treasury* 1976, fig. 7 and last page (Credits); Forman 1985, p. 21, n. 42; M. B. Davidson and Stillinger 1985, fig. 136; Johnston 1988, fig. 78.
2. Microanalyzed by R. Bruce Hoadley.
3. For Plumley, see Hornor 1935, p. 9; for inventory references, see McElroy 1979, p. 68, and Forman 1985, pp. 20–21; for the generic use of the term, see Forman 1985, p. 21, n. 42. For the similarity of some ash to olive wood and its use in English furniture of the period, see Bowett 2002, pp. 119, 306.
4. For veneered interiors, see, for example, *Girl Scouts* 1929, no. 505 (Winterthur Museum); Randall 1965, no. 55 (Museum of Fine Arts, Boston); Naeve and Roberts 1986, no. 39 (Art Institute of Chicago, Chicago, Illinois); and D. B. Warren et al. 1998, no. F35 (Bayou Bend Collection); see also *Antiques* 97 (March 1970), p. 301 (Ginsburg and Levy advertisement), and *Antiques* 159 (January 2001), pp. 80–81 (Anthony S. Werneke advertisement).
5. G. W. R. Ward 1988, nos. 101, 130 (attributed to Connecticut).

134. See also fig. 83.

134.
Desk

Probably eastern Massachusetts, 1720–40

Made of solid walnut and a little wider and deeper than cat. no. 133, and with a lid somewhat less steeply inclined, this desk has a more substantial presence than the showier example with veneered surfaces. The plain, well-proportioned case stands on skillfully turned feet, which appear to be original and which convey the dynamism of early Baroque design in their juxtaposition of the thin, elegant reel of the neck to the bold mass of the flattened ball shape and its compressed, latent energy. The desk form represented by this piece and cat. no. 133—the merging of a slanted-lid writing box with a chest of drawers—was introduced in the colonies in the early 1700s and remained popular throughout the eighteenth century, and the design of the feet, facade, and interior evolved with changing tastes.

One of the features that characterizes William and Mary desks and did not outlive the period was the well, or storage space, below the desk interior accessible through a sliding cover in the bottom of the interior; with the introduction of newer stylistic concepts in the 1730s, the well and the two short drawers below it began to be replaced with long drawers.

That the change in design was still quite new in 1738 is suggested by the description of a desk supplied that year to Boston cabinetmaker Nathaniel Holmes, which includes the specification "no well rume."[1] As the well was abandoned, so, generally, was the sliding cover in the bottom of the desk interior; and taller lopers that matched the height of the drawer they now flanked came into fashion and displaced in most instances the small earlier type seen here. Desks made in Newport, Rhode Island, are notable exceptions; there, cabinetmakers continued to use small lopers and a slide (elements that had little or no effect on the outward design of their pieces) throughout the late colonial period. The slide was probably retained for its practicality; it provides the convenience of having the contents of the top drawer accessible while the lid is down. On some Newport desks, the top drawer can be bolted shut from the inside, so that, as on William and Mary–style desks, the lock on the lid secures not just the interior but also a large storage area below it.[2]

The design element that most distinguishes the interior of the early-eighteenth-century desk (fig. 83)—the projecting stepped unit at either side with its shaped partition—became outmoded, like the well, during the 1730s, when a straight or slightly incurved bank of drawers and pigeonholes gained favor. At the same time, the prospect door began to be hinged on one side rather than at the bottom. The earlier interior scheme lingered on, however, into the 1740s in some urban desks that had otherwise been brought up to date and for considerably longer in some nonurban pieces.[3] Other aspects of the William and Mary desk interior carried on throughout the eighteenth century: the basic division into three sections, namely, a relatively narrow distinct central portion flanked symmetrically by side units of drawers and pigeonholes; valanced pigeonholes; drawer fronts that have a single or a double concave recess, as on this example, or are straight, as on cat. no. 133, and are used at times in combination. Upright document drawers faced with turned half colonettes, common on interiors in later-style desks, although not represented on the early examples in this collection, also have their source in the William and Mary period.[4] How the edge of this desk's lid was originally finished is uncertain because the lid is pieced at the top and sides. Normally, a lid that is inset like this one has a straight edge, not one with an ovolo profile as seen here; and if an ovolo is used, the edge is lipped, as is the case on some William and Mary examples and is standard on eighteenth-century desks in later styles.

CONSTRUCTION

The top is joined to the two-board sides with dovetails that are exposed on the upper surface. The bottom, a single board, is rabbeted at each end and attached to the sides with large rosehead nails. The back, composed of three vertical boards, is beveled to fit into a groove in the top and sides and is nailed to the bottom. The full-depth board

above the short drawers, which forms the bottom of the well, is housed in rectangular grooves in the sides, as are the two drawer dividers (6½ in. deep) and the runners behind them. The vertical partition between the short drawers is secured to the well bottom above and the divider below with a through tenon at the front, followed by a dado joint; there are no medial drawer runners. The incline of the upper front of the case is slightly more than 40 degrees. The hinged lid consists of two longitudinal boards tenoned to a broad cleat at either end. The lopers slide between the case sides and guides glued in place within the well. The bottom of the desk interior is constructed in the same way as that on cat. no. 133, except that the front board of the framework enclosing the sliding well cover is joined to the case sides at the front with a through dovetail and the front edge of the rear board has an ovolo profile. The horizontal dividers and vertical partitions of the interior are slotted into one another and into the case, and the entire unit was slid in from the back. In the center section behind the prospect door, which is pintle-hinged at the bottom, are a valance, which like the others is cut with paired ogee curves, a middle shelf with a similarly shaped front edge, and a shallow drawer at the bottom.

On all the drawers, the sides are joined to the front with half-blind dovetails and to the back with through dovetails. On the interior drawers, the front-to-back bottom is butted to the inner side of the front and nailed to the sides and back. On the exterior drawers, the bottom is a longitudinal board that is beveled to fit into a groove in the front and is nailed to the bottom of the back and sides; runner strips are applied under the sides. The front is fitted with a lock and its top edge inclines inward; the sides and back are lower than the front and their upper corners are chamfered. The nails in both the interior and exterior drawers are sprigs. A thick rectangular block is nailed under each corner of the case bottom, and the turned tenon of the foot extends through the block and the bottom board. The base molding consists of a cyma reversa and a fascia.

CONDITION

The desk, when acquired, was missing the left base molding, the double-bead molding on the drawer dividers (and, if originally there, on the inclined and top edge of the case sides), and the small triangular brackets typically applied to the front edge of the case sides at the top of the vertical face. The left base molding and the double bead on the drawer dividers were replaced, and drop pulls (for which there was evidence when the desk was received) and matching escutcheons were installed in place of the bail handles and escutcheons then on the piece (see References). Also, a shrinkage gap in the lid was eliminated by adding a narrow strip at the top of the upper board. The 1-inch slat that now forms the upper edge of the lid and the thin cap on each side edge are earlier repairs, as are the replaced hinges and lock. The back has a vertical filler strip and two patches and has been renailed. All the runners and stops for the exterior drawers are new; grooves worn in the dividers have been filled and areas damaged by the bolt of the drawer locks, which are old, have been patched. The runner strips on the bottom drawer are almost completely worn off; on the other drawers they are replaced. The drawer bottoms all have a large shrinkage crack, two backs have a patch, and two joints added nails. On the desk interior, the prospect door and the center and near right drawers are replacements. The center valance (behind which are drawer runners) and the far left and right valances are new; the others are older but may not be original. In the well, the guides for the lopers look replaced, and a board has been added across the back. Metal gliders have been added under the feet, which have suffered losses and appear to be original. The top of the case and the bottom of the desk interior are badly stained, and the writing surface of the lid is heavily scratched. The walnut has a modern finish and varies in color because of uneven remains of earlier coatings.

INSCRIPTIONS

A large scored sawyer's tally mark (I crossed by a diagonal slash partly cut off) is on the inner side of the left back board. On the exterior of the back are MMA Hudson-Fulton exhibition identification numbers in orange crayon (H. F. 40.41 / 524, in an oval) and identification numbers assigned by borrowing institutions and variously inscribed in chalk and paint, as well as "MMA" in chalk in large letters. Modern pencil numbers differentiate the two short drawers, and on the inside bottom of the right one and of the near right interior drawer are numbers and letters in blue.

WOODS

Top, sides, lid, lopers, front of well, front of exterior and interior drawers, front board and front of rear board of desk interior bottom, well cover, interior dividers and partitions (except for back portion on some), applied moldings, BLACK WALNUT; case back, bottom, blocks under bottom, well bottom, case drawer dividers and partition, sides, bottom, and back of all drawers, side boards and back of rear board of desk interior bottom, back portion of some interior dividers and partitions, EASTERN WHITE PINE; feet, POPLAR (*Populus* sp.).

DIMENSIONS

OH. 40³⁄₈ (102.6); OW. (base molding) 35³⁄₈ (89.9); CW. 33⁷⁄₈ (86); OD. (base molding) 20³⁄₈ (51.8); CD. 19¹⁄₈ (48.6).

EXHIBITIONS

"Hudson-Fulton Exhibition," MMA, 20 September–30 November 1909; on loan to the Art Institute of Chicago, Chicago, Illinois, from 1926 to before 1950, to the Preservation Society of Newport County from 1950 to 1976, and to the Newport Historical Society from 1976 to 1979.

REFERENCES

Hudson-Fulton Celebration 1909 (exh. cat.), no. 115; Cescinsky and Hunter 1929, p. 163; Williams 1963, no. 99 (this and the previous references show the desk as received).

PROVENANCE

Ex coll.: H. Eugene Bolles, Boston.

Gift of Mrs. Russell Sage, 1909 (10.125.708)

1. Quoted in Jobe 1974, p. 16.
2. See, for example, Rodriguez Roque 1984, no. 27; and Monkhouse and Michie 1986, no. 38.
3. Projecting side units are still used, for example, in two related Massachusetts desks, one of which is inscribed "1739" (Rodriguez Roque 1984, no. 24), and in a Newport desk signed by John Goddard (1724–1785) and dated 1745 (Rodriguez Roque 1984, no. 26). For late, nonurban examples, see Failey 1976, nos. 149, 205.
4. For William and Mary desks with document drawers, see Naeve and Roberts 1986, no. 39; and D. B. Warren et al. 1998, no. F35. A desk and bookcase made in London by William Price in 1713, the year before he emigrated to Boston, provides an English prototype for the colonial desk interior (Bowett 2002, pl. 7:53).

APPENDIX 1
Addenda

In Appendix 1 are seven objects that have been omitted from the main catalogue because of their condition, doubts about their authenticity in part or in whole, or a combination of reasons; they are included in this book because each is in its own way instructive. In addition, all but the first have been previously published, and this appendix allows the writer's assessment of the pieces in question to be recorded. The first is a spindle-back armchair that has suffered losses (and is being left unrestored) but has a credible history of ownership that lends support to the attribution of a particular school of turning to New York (cat. no. 135). A chest with two drawers (cat. no. 140), part of a sizable body of work from the Guilford, Connecticut, area, represents, in the writer's opinion, an instance of nineteenth-century enhancement of a seventeenth-century object that reflects probably both a misunderstanding of its style and a conscious effort to "improve" the piece. A highly restored cupboard attributed to Middlesex County, Massachusetts (cat. no. 141),

enlarges our knowledge of a school of craftsmanship active in that area and provides insights into the collecting and restoration of furniture in the late 1800s and early 1900s. Two additional armchairs, a slat-back (cat. no. 136) and a banister-back (cat. no. 137), contain older and newer elements, but, particularly in the case of the latter, the exact extent of the replacements is difficult to determine, and it is not entirely clear if either of the two pieces falls in the category of "made up from a few old parts" rather than being a badly damaged object extensively restored. A box carved with the "Hadley" motif (cat. no. 139), however, appears to be entirely modern. Finally, the Museum's oft-published large trestle table (cat. no. 138) has been relegated to an appendix because, although both the trestles and the top show signs of wear and age, it is not possible to demonstrate that they started out as a single piece of furniture or conclusively to assign the whole table or a part of it the seventeenth-century date it has usually been given.

135.
Spindle-back armchair

New York, 1670–1710

This chair is not included in the main body of the catalogue because it is being left in the state in which it was received for educational purposes. In this condition its structure is explicit, and its losses are unequivocal.

A grand chair despite the loss of handgrips and what were probably towering multitiered finials, this is one of the rare spindle-back armchairs that can credibly be associated with New York (city or state) through its history. It links to this area a particular school of chairmaking whose style is manifest also in an armchair at the Winterthur Museum and one illustrated by Wallace Nutting.[1] All three chairs follow a similar format of two tiers of three spindles in the back and three spindles between each arm and a rail above the seat—with the difference that on the other chairs the back extends down considerably further than it does here—and all have related turnings. Their spindles are characterized by an elongated baluster set between ball forms; on this chair and the one shown by Nutting there is a thin ring above the lower ball, and here the upper ball is more like a fat ring. While the posts of the Winterthur chair are turned only with ball shapes, the posts of the Nutting example feature, in addition, stout baluster forms like those on cat. no. 135. They are tall and more straight-sided than ogee in profile, and they do not turn out at the top. Of the three chairs, only the Museum's includes a motif of opposed balusters.

This chair also shares some structural traits with the Winterthur example: both have numerous pinned joints and rear posts with a built-in backward slant; while the layout lines on the posts do not correspond, they are similar insofar as nearly every crosspiece is centered on an individual line. The Winterthur chair and that published by Nutting retain their finials, which have a distinctive form consisting of a large sphere set high above two reels and topped with two knobs. Benno M. Forman related this pattern as well as the extensive use of pinned joints on the Winterthur chair to northern European rather than to English influences and then conjectured that the chair was more likely to have a New York than a New England origin.[2] His conjecture is supported by the history of the present chair in the mid-Hudson River valley and perhaps Kings County (now Brooklyn), New York (see *Provenance*), and also by the fact that its feet (original) are turned not just on the front posts but also on the rear posts—a practice associated with Continental rather than Anglo-American craftsmanship (see the entry for cat. no. 9). The balusters on the posts of this chair and its hefty double

arms that are not parallel one to the other may be related to the corresponding elements on cat. no. 1.

An interesting affinity exists between the turnings on this group of three chairs and those on two armchairs attributed to the East Haven–Branford area of the Connecticut shore with a single tier of spindles in the back and single arms.[3] Although the execution of the turnings differs considerably, the opposed balusters on the stiles are similar to those on cat. no. 135; moreover, the finials are generically related to those on the Winterthur and Nutting chairs, and the spindles also consist of an attenuated baluster form with a ring and ball at either end. These similarities raise intriguing, largely unexplored questions about the movement of artisans and goods and the exchange and interaction of craft ideas between New York and Connecticut in this period (on this topic, see also the entries for cat. nos. 1, 9).

CONSTRUCTION
The chair is joined with round tenons that are strongly shaved on the sides; those of the top back rail, all four seat rails, and all four lower stretchers are pinned. The mortises are each centered on an individual scribe line, with the exception of those for the upper front stretcher, for which there are no layout lines. The backward slant of the rear posts is intended. The holes for the spindles of the back are drilled through on the top rail as well as on the two lower rails, probably owing to carelessness rather than for the attachment of decorative knobs on the top rail. The holes render visible the top of the upper spindles and the bottom of the lower spindles, which each have a depression left by the pin on which the spindle revolved in the lathe.[4] The spindles under the arms are all similar in height, even though the distance between the arm and the under-arm rail increases toward the back; the spindles at the back simply show more of the conical turning at the top. Spindles, which did not have to fit tightly into mortises, were often not turned with distinct tenons demarcated by a shoulder, but were just gradually tapered at the extremities. The stretchers are turned and the seat rails shaved.

CONDITION
The finials and handgrips have been summarily sawn off. A spindle under the right arm has been lost, and the top of the front of the arms appears to have been reduced by whittling in addition to wear. The feet have been cut down and shaved all around to fit into modern casters, which were removed at the MMA. Nearly half of the joint pins are missing, and a number of the joints come completely apart. The chair lacks a seat; imprints on the seat rails indicate it was originally of rush. Evidence of light tacking on the top back rail, stiles, and seat rails suggests that at one point padding may have been attached to the back and seat. There are numerous shrinkage cracks in the posts and arms. The surface shows remains of old red paint and of a subsequent coating, and speckles and blotches of other paint.

135

WOODS
MAPLE; lower right arm, HARD MAPLE; seat rails, stretchers, ASH.

DIMENSIONS
OH. 42¼ (107.3); SH. 15⅛ (38.4); SW. front 23¾ (60.3); SW. back 18⅜ (46.7); SD. 17¼ (43.8).

PROVENANCE
The chair came down in the family of Mary C. Hicks (1887 New Hackensack, New York–1989 Wappingers Falls, New York), daughter of J. Edward and Sarah Vermilyea Hicks. According to her written statement (copy ADA files), which records what she remembered hearing from her grandmother Sarah Matilda Van Duyn Hicks,

"This chair belonged to Mary Montfort, the daughter of Dominicus Montfort and Antoinette Van Kleeck. . . . She married Garret Van Dyne. She was my grandmother's grandmother." The ancestry indicated is: Antoinette Van Kleeck (1751 Poughkeepsie, New York–1840 Fishkill Plains, New York), who married in Poughkeepsie in 1771 Dominicus Montfort (1743 Long Island, New York–1815 Fishkill Plains), whose grandfather lived in Kings County, New York; her daughter Mary Montfort (1778 Poughkeepsie–1875 New Hackensack), who married in 1796 in Fishkill, New York, Garret Van Duyn (1773–1831), whose father lived in Kings County; her son James Van Duyn, of Freedom, New York, who married in 1823 Catherine Hansen, of the same town; his daughter Sarah Matilda Van Duyn (b. ca. 1829), of New Hackensack, Mary Hicks's grandmother, who in 1849 married Martin Hicks (b. ca. 1822), of La Grange, New York.[5]

The style of the chair suggests it was made earlier than the generation of Antoinette Van Kleeck. Baltus Barents Van Kleeck (ca. 1645–ca. 1717) was the first of that family to settle in Poughkeepsie, where he purchased land in 1697 and built a stone house in 1702. His family had emigrated from the Netherlands by 1654 and he resided until at least 1675 in Flatbush, Kings County. He married in 1676 Tryntje Jans Buys; their first four children were born in Albany and the rest after 1683, in Bergen (now part of Jersey City), New Jersey, where his wife's family owned land. Baltus's son Barent Van Kleeck (1677–1750), of Poughkeepsie, married in 1701 Antoinette Parmentier (1684 Bushwick, Kings County– after 1737). His son Peter Van Kleeck (1725–1793), who married in 1746 Antoinette Freer (1729 Kingston, New York–1777) and inherited his father's Poughkeepsie house, was the father of Antoinette.[6] The history thus points to an origin for the chair in the mid-Hudson River valley or in Kings County. The Van Kleeck, Parmentier, Monfort, and Van Duyn family members in this line of descent, like many others who settled in the Poughkeepsie area, all had ties to Kings County.

Gift of Vivian R. Roberts, in memory of Mary C. Hicks, 1991 (1991.255)

1. Forman 1988, no. 9 (Winterthur Museum); and Nutting 1921, p. 187, Nutting 1924, no. 302, Nutting 1928–33, no. 1804.
2. Forman 1988, p. 111.
3. Kane 1973a, nos. XXXI (New Haven Museum), XXXII (Bayou Bend Collection).
4. See Forman 1988, p. 95 and fig. 45.
5. Obituary of Mary C. Hicks, *Poughkeepsie Journal*, 7 April 1989; Alvin S. Van Benthuysen and Edwin Robert Van Kleeck, *The Van Kleeck Genealogy* (Brooklyn, N.Y., 1957), pp. 31, 57; Fred Sisser III, *The Monfoort Family of New York and New Jersey: A Genealogy and History of Pieter Montfoort (c. 1689–1780) of Reading Township, Hunterdon County, New Jersey, and of His Ancestors and Descendants* (Somerville, N.J., 1969), pp. 7, 11; Wilson V. Ledley, comp., *New Netherland Families: Van Dien, Van Duyn and Verduyn Families, the First Five and Some Later Generations* (New York, 1960), unpaginated (no. 183 in genealogy); Helen Wilkinson Reynolds, comp. and ed., *Notices of Marriages and Deaths . . . Published in Newspapers Printed at Poughkeepsie, New York, 1778–1825*, Collections of the Dutchess County Historical Society, vol. 4 (Poughkeepsie, N.Y., 1930), p. 109; 1875 New York State Census, Dutchess County, vol. 1, Fishkill, p. 5 (microfilm, reel 1667, serial no. 619); Arthur C. M. Kelly, comp., *Marriage Notices from Dutchess County, New York, Newspapers, 1826–1851* (Rhinebeck, N.Y., 1983), p. 131; 1850 United States Federal Census, Dutchess County, N.Y., National Archives Microfilm Publications, M-432, roll 496.
6. Dorothy E. Smith, *Tangled Roots and Twisted Branches* (Kingston, N.Y., 1987), unpaginated; Prentiss Glazier, *Van Kleeck Family of Dutchess County, New York* (Sarasota, Fla., 1974), pp. 1–2; Van Benthuysen and Van Kleeck, *Van Kleeck Genealogy*, p. 31.

136.

Slat-back armchair

Eastern Massachusetts, 1650–1700 with later alterations

Catalogue no. 136 has twice been published to exemplify the slat-back version of the style of seventeenth-century turned chair that is identified with eastern Massachusetts and more specifically with the Boston area. It was first so illustrated by Irving W. Lyon in 1891 and again nearly a century later by Benno M. Forman, although he was aware that it had been "overrestored" (see *References*). In terms of the design of the posts and slats, this chair can indeed serve as an exemplar. The post turnings are similar to those on cat. no. 2, for instance: the vase shapes have a like squat profile and the urn-and-flame finials differ only in that they are more compressed in height and lack a groove around the terminal knob. The outline of the slats with arc cutouts at the upper corners and their graduation with the largest at the top are characteristic of such slat-back chairs (see cat. no. 10). In most other respects, however, this is a dubious representative of the form.

The right rear post stands out for its lack of wear and is obviously not old. The other three posts, which show age, may have started out life together, although the front posts differ from the left rear one in the grain of the ash and in that the vase turnings are not as well articulated, both at the lip and at the juncture of the base with the cylinder below; piecework by more than one turner in an urban shop could account for such differences.[1] The middle slat (repaired) has a different character than the other two and appears to be of the period. That it has greater claim to legitimacy than the others is supported by X-radiographs of the slat joints, which reveal that the fit of that slat at the top and bottom of the mortise in the left rear post is quite snug, which is not the case with the other slat joints. That the top slat was not the first to be joined to the left rear post is also suggested by the added (second) pin in that joint. The left arm shows greater wear than the right, but both appear to be replacements for what were in all likelihood sawn arms like those on cat. no. 10. An X-radiograph of the rear joint of the left arm shows evidence that a round drilled hole was modified, presumably to accommodate a square tenon, and that the present round tenon does not conform closely to the mortise. It and other X-radiographs also confirm what is in some cases visible to the eye, namely, that the mortises for the arms and stretchers have all to a greater or lesser degree been widened at the opening (probably with a reamer) to better seat those crosspieces. None of the stretchers are original; they vary in diameter and are shaved rather than turned, with the exception of the upper left one. It is a reused, shortened, probably front, stretcher (from this or another chair) with a set of ornamental grooves—a single line flanked by a pair of lines—that was meant to be in the middle but is now off-center toward the back.

When Lyon published this chair he mentioned only that it had a new seat and replaced feet (all with ball turnings)—commonly restored chair parts. (The present replaced feet were installed at the MMA, the front ones still with conjectural turnings.) At the time, the chair belonged to Walter Hosmer, a collector and a craftsman-restorer working in Hartford, Connecticut. According to Lyon, it had been bought in 1889. What condition the chair was in when Hosmer acquired it is not known, and how much of the restoration is his work is unclear. The fact that the stretchers are largely mismatched, that they are irregularly shaved, and that the lower left one is crudely whittled down at either end is at odds with the careful, neat craftsmanship of the restorations on the frame of cat. no. 33, a leather chair that also belonged to Hosmer. One detail, however, recalls the fastidious work seen on that chair: the holes for the pins in the arm joints were drilled through the layout lines that circumscribe the posts, thereby interrupting those lines, but—against all logic—those work lines were then scribed across the end grain of the new, added pins so that the grooves are continuous.

CONSTRUCTION

The posts taper not quite ¼ inch from the top down, mainly above the seat. The rear posts angle out laterally toward the top, but the front ones, because of the length of the replaced front crosspieces, angle slightly inward. No scribe lines marking the height of the mortises for the rectangular tenons of the slats are visible. The other components are all joined with round tenons; the arms and the front and rear stretchers are centered on a work line, and the seat rails and side stretchers are tangential to a line. Of the joints now pinned, originally only those of the uppermost slat were so secured.

CONDITION

The right rear post is new. The top 1½ inches of the middle slat are restored, and the top and bottom slats are not of the period. The arms, seat rails, rush seat, and stretchers are replacements. The right rear and both front posts are pieced 2¾ inches from the bottom up and the left rear post 4 inches from the bottom up. All the joint pins are new; the second pin in the left joint of the top slat and those in the joints of the arms, front seat rail, and lower front stretcher are added. The chair has been stripped and appears to have been finished with oil and wax.

INSCRIPTIONS

A printed paper label (damaged) glued to the back of the bottom slat reads: "[Include]d in the [c]ollection of Antiqu[e] Furni- / [tur]e

136

transferr[ed to] Mr. H. E. Bolle[s], a[n]d Mr. / Geo. S. Palm[er. It is the origin]al piece illus- / trated in 'Colon[ial Furniture of] Ne[w] England,' / by Dr. Lyons." Any notation in ink originally at the top and Hosmer's signature at the bottom have been lost.

WOOD

Old and new elements, ASH.

DIMENSIONS

OH. 45½ (115.6); SH. 17 (43.2); SW. front 22⅞ (58.1); SW. back 17½ (44.5); SD. 15⅝ (39.7).

EXHIBITION

"Hudson-Fulton Exhibition," MMA, 20 September–30 November 1909.

REFERENCES
I. W. Lyon 1891, p. 143 and fig. 57; *Hudson-Fulton Celebration* 1909 (exh. cat.), no. 62; Williams 1963, no. 6; Forman 1988, fig. 39.

PROVENANCE
Ex coll.: Walter Hosmer, Hartford, Connecticut; H. Eugene Bolles, Boston.
    Bolles and his cousin George S. Palmer, of New London, Connecticut, purchased Hosmer's collection in 1894. Irving W. Lyon,

when he published the chair in 1891, stated that it had been bought in Killingly, Connecticut, in 1889 (see *References*).

Gift of Mrs. Russell Sage, 1909 (10.125.677)

1. The work lines on the front posts match those on the left rear post, and the vase turnings are all the same height. On the right rear post, the layout lines correspond from below the vase turning but not from the vase up, and the vase and the finial are both noticeably taller than on the left post.

137.

Banister-back armchair

Northeastern coastal Massachusetts or Portsmouth, New Hampshire, or vicinity, 1720–40 with later alterations

This chair, built on a grand scale, has great immediate visual appeal. It epitomizes the vertical emphasis of early Baroque seating design—with the curves of the feet, the successively more elongated balusters, and then the curves of the arms leading the eye up to the scrolls and plume of the crest rail—and it also vividly conveys the sense of movement introduced by this style in the strong arms and feet that boldly reach outward. Closer inspection, however, reveals that the chair's two dominant stylistic features—the arms and the crest rail—do not hold up under careful scrutiny.

The imposing ram's-horn arms are not original. They are anomalous in being made of oak and are oversized; at the juncture with the stiles they are crudely worked, and, as X-radiographs confirm, changes have occurred in the stiles at those joints. While the age of the crest rail is debatable, the quality of the carving is unquestionably substandard. The delineation of the motifs is inexpert and stiff, with the scrolls incompletely defined along the bottom edge. The detailing executed with a V-shaped gouge was done by a craftsman who appears to have been capable of producing only straight lines with that tool—there are none that curve to reinforce the contours and movement of the motifs (compare figs. 16 and 17). To the modern eye, at least, there is a real disjunction between the crudely carved crest rail and the convincing, very competently worked front posts and stretcher. This opens up the question whether the crest rail may be of late date or may come from another piece.

In terms of its design, cat. no. 137 relates in most of its elements to chairs attributed to the Gaines family or associated more generally with northeastern coastal Massachusetts or Portsmouth, New Hampshire, or vicinity. The type of ram's-horn arm used is similar to that on cat. no. 37, and the crest rail, insofar as it is accented with gouged crescent shapes, recalls that of cat. no. 29. The front stretcher with its distinctive extra half ring before each terminal turning (fig. 28) and the pattern of the arm supports have parallels on Gaines chairs in other collections.[1] The cavettos on the front posts and stretcher have counterparts not just on Gaines chairs but also on some from other shops in the area, and the same holds true for the front feet—the manner in which they are carved, including the deep groove down the central ridge, and the fact that they are worked from a solid block that is one piece with the legs (see cat. no. 30). The rear posts are akin to those on cat. no. 30 in that the legs are entirely vertical and do not end in raked feet, the cylindrical turnings above the seat are not ornamented with grooves, and the ring at the top of the shaft of the columnar turnings is quite prominent. The finials, however, exhibit details not seen elsewhere; namely, an urn that has a double rim and a base that leads in to the reel with two steps that are concave rather than convex.

Not just the crest rail but also other components of the back raise questions; however, reaching definitive conclusions is difficult. The entire piece has been apart, and since the arms, side stretchers (carved to simulate turnings), and in all probability the seat rails are replaced, there are no clearly original elements linking the front and back of the chair. The rear legs have less wear at the bottom than the front feet, but the former are of hard rather than soft maple and it is possible that they were slightly trimmed. The back of the finials shows considerable wear (which appears to be legitimate) and the singed left stile and cracked crest rail indicate the chair has seen usage in its present form before it was acquired by the MMA. The center banister retains tool marks that are not eighteenth century in character, and all of the banisters give pause in

137. See also figs. 17, 28.

terms of their design, because the profile of the lower portion does not reflect the contours of the present stiles as one would expect, but is in the standard pattern of stiles on chairs without arms. Analysis of the surface has been inconclusive; it suggests only that the chair was thoroughly stripped either at the time or after changes were made (see *Condition*).

CONSTRUCTION

The front posts are joined to the arms, and the seat rails and stretchers to the legs with round tenons. On the rear posts the stiles cant backward and the legs and feet are vertical. The joints of the back, including those of the arms to the stiles, have rectangular tenons. The tenons of the crest rail are pinned from the rear, and those at the front and back of the arms, from the outer side. The tenons on the crest rail are at the back edge of the board and have just a front shoulder, as was usual; but those on the stay rail are at the front edge of the board and have no shoulder at the back, having been formed by shaving down the back of the rail at each end. Because the mortises for both crosspieces were cut the same distance in from the front of the stiles, the stay rail is positioned about ½ inch farther back than the crest rail. Consequently, as on cat. no. 30, the banisters are more vertical in their orientation than the stiles. The crest rail is chamfered on the back along the top edge and around the piercings; the stay rail, on the lower edge of the front. The front feet are carved from a solid block that is a good 3¼ inches wide and integral to the legs.

CONDITION
The arms are replacements and so are the side stretchers (not turned but carved, and with pinned joints), and very probably all the seat rails (the front one strongly bowed in), and perhaps the rear stretcher (shaved). The left stile has been singed on the outer side and back from the middle of the block below the finial down through half of the columnar turning. Both finials and uppermost stile blocks show cracks, and in the reel turning of the left finial are small holes that are difficult to explain. The crest rail, secured with new pins, has a crack at each end (repaired with a nail on the left). A screw or nail has been driven through the left stile into the end of the stay rail tenon. The center banister retains what look like marks from a band saw; it and the extreme right one do not match the others in design. A small pin has been added to the right joint of the front stretcher. The front feet are chipped at the bottom, and a small section at the inner front corner of each is pieced. The rush seat is a replacement. The surface shows black paint, quite thin or worn off in some areas. Cross sections of the surface (taken from the right stile, right front leg, crest rail, and center banister) all indicate that directly on top of the wood there is a layer that contains red pigment mixed with black pigment followed by a white layer, clear finish, and then the black paint. Traces of white under the black are visible to the eye on almost all of the chair's components.

INSCRIPTION
A circle has been scribed with a compass on the front of the far right banister.

WOODS
Front posts, front stretcher, stay rail, crest rail (age?), far left banister (age?), replaced side stretchers, SOFT MAPLE; rear posts, HARD MAPLE; replaced arms, RED OAK; probably replaced side and rear seat rails, OAK; probably replaced front seat rail, HICKORY; rear stretcher (age?), ASH; probably replaced center banister, BIRCH.

DIMENSIONS
OH. 48 (121.9); SH. 17¼ (43.8); OW. (arms) 29¾ (75.6); SW. front 25 (63.5); SW. back 17 (43.2); SD. 14 (35.6).

EXHIBITION
"A Bicentennial Treasury: American Masterpieces from the Metropolitan," MMA, 29 January 1976–2 January 1977.

REFERENCES
Cornelius 1926, pl. XVI; Cescinsky and Hunter 1929, p. 39; Dyer 1930a, p. 32; M. B. Davidson 1967, nos. 138, 138a (detail of handgrip); Kirk 1970, fig. 37; Bishop 1972, nos. 47, 47a (detail of handgrip); *Bicentennial Treasury* 1976 (exh. cat.), fig. 5.

PROVENANCE
Ex coll.: H. Eugene Bolles, Boston.

Gift of Mrs. Russell Sage, 1909 (10.125.228)

1. For stretchers, see Rodriguez Roque 1984, no. 75; Jobe 1993, no. 77; and Richards and N. G. Evans 1997, no. 18. For arm supports, see Richards and N. G. Evans 1997, no. 18, fig. 2.

138.
Trestle table

Eastern Massachusetts, possibly seventeenth century to nineteenth century

Seventeenth-century inventory listings of "board and trestles" or "table and trestles" ("table" in this period still being used to denote a board) refer to this type of piece, a knockdown form of table that is documented in England back to the fifteenth century or earlier and that continued to be made into the 1700s, though it was outmoded for fashionable dining in the latter half of the 1500s by long tables with a joined frame and after 1660 by oval tables with falling leaves.[1] Against this background, cat. no. 138, heavily worn and impressive for its length and the architectural quality of its solid trestles, was described by Frances C. Morse in 1902 and Henry W. Kent in 1910 (see *References*) as a rare and venerable example of the earliest form of table known in America. They judiciously did not call it the oldest American table, as it was considered by the

collector H. Eugene Bolles, who discovered it, and as was stated in the catalogue of the 1909 MMA Hudson-Fulton exhibition and repeated in some later publications—a claim that cannot be substantiated.

The table is here published in an appendix because of evidence that the top and trestles have not always been together and because of the difficulty in determining the age of the top and its supports. While it is not possible to rule out entirely that the top and trestles started out as a single piece of furniture—the top of this type of table was meant to be unattached and to stay in place by dint of its sheer weight and mass—there are clear signs that they have, at least for a period of time, had separate existences. The ends of the trestle heads all show holes, nails, and pegs that indicate that the trestles

138

have, for the most part, if not entirely, been attached to something other than the present top; no corresponding nail holes are discernible in either the upper side or the underside of the board, and the only possible correlations of pegs and holes (in terms of distance apart) are not completely convincing (see *Condition*). Given the type of heavy use and abuse the top has suffered, it is probable that it did service at one time in a workshop; Bolles himself, who highly prized the table, described it as looking "worse than a carpenter's bench."[2] The actual age of the board is difficult to establish; one can just note that according to the empty nail holes in one end the cleats appear to have been attached with wrought nails.[3] Only the trestles exhibit any stylistic features, namely, the outline of the foot and head and the form of the pillar, which is rectangular and broadly chamfered except at the top and base and thus appears columnar. They represent basic designs, easily executed by a carpenter, that hark back to medieval tables and continued in use to the seventeenth century and beyond.[4] While the joints of the trestles have been apart, there is no clear indication that the pillars, feet, and heads do not belong together. (The stretcher does not look as old as the trestles.) The trestles show considerable wear, and there is nothing in their design, their wood (oak), or their height that precludes their dating to the seventeenth century. They make for a quite high table, but of a height comparable to that of some large rectangular joined tables made in New England in that period.[5] Tables of the great length of this piece were used there domestically in the

seventeenth century, usually set along a wall, sometimes with a built-in bench behind them.[6]

Two trestle tables in other public collections (Detroit Institute of Arts, Detroit, Michigan, and Museum of Fine Arts, Boston) are related to this example in their long narrow proportions, but they differ in other respects. Both have a base that is relatively lightweight and is a single unit, consisting of a stretcher tenoned and pinned to end-trestles and one or two medial supports that extend between the stretcher and the top. They are made of maple and pine and have been dated to the early eighteenth century.[7] Like cat. no. 138, they were found in an attic, having probably been set aside in later years for occasional use at special gatherings.

CONSTRUCTION
The top is unattached and formed of a single board about 1¾ inches thick, originally with a cleat affixed to either end with four large wrought nails. On the trestles, the post is joined to the foot and head with a thick (1 in.) tenon, which is secured with two large (a good ½ in.) pins. The vertical edges of the posts are finished with a broad (ca. 1½ in.) chamfer, except for the top and bottom 2½ inches, which have a narrow (¼ in.) chamfer. The broad chamfers end with a straight horizontal cut (at a scribe line on the post), and the resulting corners have been slightly trimmed. The stretcher, which retains evidence of mill sawing, is removable; it fits through slots in the posts and is held in place by wedges that pass through the board on either side of the posts. The rectangular slots for the wedges were cut in a somewhat irregular arrangement; there are no scribe lines marking the location of the slots. The upper edge of the stretcher has an ovolo profile.

CONDITION

The top is warped both crosswise and lengthwise. The remaining cleat is now secured with four large replaced nails and has several empty holes from added nails; the other end of the board, missing its cleat, shows square holes from the four large nails that once attached it, plus a hole from a later nail. The upper surface of the top is deeply scarred and defaced by larger and smaller split-out areas, gouges, a few nails, innumerable scratches and knife- or saw cuts, and many holes of various sizes and shapes—some shallow, some going through the board, and some plugged. The side edges show gouges, cuts, and numerous holes—drilled and/or dug out. The feet of the trestles are well worn on the upper surface, and the end of one has been badly battered. At the bottom of the feet and the top of two of the trestle heads, the wood was infested by insects and has partly crumbled and been consolidated. At each end of the trestle heads are two to four nail holes or nails and, in addition, on two of the heads a large hole containing or lacking a peg. The peg holes on one trestle head are the same distance apart as two at the cleated end of the top, but the latter are somewhat staggered. The distance between the two peg holes on the other trestle head corresponds to that between plugged holes at the uncleated end of the top, but they are even more on a diagonal. The two trestles, if attached at those respective locations, would not be entirely perpendicular to the top, making it difficult to join them together with a stretcher. There are few nail holes in either surface of the top, and none of them correlates with the nails or holes in the trestle heads.

All of the joint pins of the trestles have been reset or replaced; on one trestle the lower tenon is new and on another there appears to be a repair to the upper tenon. Unfortunately one cannot determine from photographs of the table as found (see *Provenance*) if the restorations on the trestles predate or postdate its discovery. Where the wedges abut the posts, the posts are worn and in some cases have also been slightly recessed. All of the wedges are modern (1964 at the MMA), replacing earlier replacements. The stretcher does not appear to be contemporary with the trestles, and the numbering on both parts (see *Inscriptions*) is odd; if it is followed, the one trestle that is slightly shorter than the others is positioned at one end, causing the top to be out of balance. The trestles and the stretcher have been colored brown. Particularly on the feet, the stain has been partly worn off and there are areas that are darker in color. The top shows sizable areas of brown stain (similar in color to some on the base) in the center and traces elsewhere and remains of black in the corners and along the side edges; but for the most part, the surface is down to bare wood, except for residues of wax visible on both the top and the base.

INSCRIPTIONS

Incised on the stretcher are three chiseled marks, each at the location of a set of slots for the wedges: I, II, III. Corresponding markings are on the trestles, incised inside the slot for the stretcher. The slots in the stretcher have been marked in pencil with the numbers 1 through 12, and the present replacement wedges are stamped with corresponding numbers. MMA Hudson-Fulton exhibition identification numbers (H F. 40.45) are inscribed in orange crayon on one side of the head of the trestle marked II.

WOODS

Top, stretcher, EASTERN WHITE PINE; trestles, WHITE OAK and RED OAK.

DIMENSIONS

OH. 35½ (90.2); top: L. 143¾ (365.1), OW. (cleat) 25¼ (64.1); trestles: OH. 33½ (85.1); D. 24⅜ (61.9).

EXHIBITION

"Hudson-Fulton Exhibition," MMA, 20 September–30 November 1909.

REFERENCES

Morse 1902, pp. 216–17 (not illus.); *Hudson-Fulton Celebration* 1909 (exh. cat.), no. 86; Kent 1910, pp. 14–15 (not illus.); Lockwood 1913, fig. 672; Halsey and Cornelius 1924 (and 1925, 1926), fig. 13 (1928, 1932, fig. 12; 1938, 1942, fig. 5); Halsey and Tower 1925, fig. 13; Cescinsky and Hunter 1929, p. 29; Kettell 1929, pl. 82 and measured drawing, no. 27; E. G. Miller 1937, no. 1276; "Antiques in the American Wing" 1946, p. 246, no. 2; Hjorth 1946, fig. 5; Comstock 1962, no. 112; M. B. Davidson 1967, no. 45; Hornung 1972, no. 861; Butler 1973, p. 16; Anderson 1974, pp. 114–15 (illus.; also shows a reproduction of the table, for which plans could be purchased); Shea 1975, pp. 21, 151 (includes measured drawings); Schwartz 1976, no. 16; Chinnery 1979, fig. 3:149; Fitzgerald 1982, fig. I–16; G. W. R. Ward 1992, fig. 2.

PROVENANCE

Ex coll.: H. Eugene Bolles, Boston.

The table was found in the attic of an old house in Essex, Massachusetts, where structural changes to the building were said to have trapped it until it was discovered by Bolles at the end of the nineteenth century. A photograph inscribed "Mr. Bolles's table board was found in this house, 18 . . . " (Hudson-Fulton exhibition correspondence, MMA Archives) shows the Cogswell House in Essex (built 1739–derelict and demolished 1924). A set of three photographs donated by Mrs. Luke Vincent Lockwood (ADA files) pictures the table as found in the attic, as far as can be determined in basically the same condition as it is today.[8]

Gift of Mrs. Russell Sage, 1909 (10.125.701)

1. I. W. Lyon 1891, p. 193; R. Edwards 1964, pp. 531–32; Chinnery 1979, pp. 282–87. References to a "table and frame" imply that the base was joined, as is the case with a square table with removable top at the Wadsworth Atheneum (Nutting 1928–33, nos. 824, 825).
2. Letter of 17 May 1909 from Bolles to Henry W. Kent (Hudson-Fulton exhibition correspondence, MMA Archives).
3. While machine-cut nails came into use in the 1790s, handwrought nails continued to be available until at least the 1820s (Nelson 1968). They have, of course, also been reproduced.
4. Trestles with rectangular pillars and the same basic form of foot are represented in a convent scene on an Italian altarpiece of about 1340 (J. Evans 1966, p. 51, fig. 27). Pedestals generally similar to those on cat. no. 138 are on tables and benches at Winchester College (England), probably from the seventeenth century but based on earlier tables (Eames 1977, pls. 70A, 70B, and pp. 226–27).
5. Fairbanks and Trent 1982, nos. 116, 286.
6. A table of this length and such an arrangement are specified in a 1659 Massachusetts building contract (see the introduction to the chapter in this book on tables with a stationary top). The same type of grouping of a long table and bench along a wall can be seen in fifteenth-century manuscripts, for example, in R. Edwards 1964, p. 531, fig. 1.
7. See, in the order mentioned, Nutting 1928–33, no. 800; and Fairbanks and Trent 1982, no. 175.
8. Morse 1902, p. 216; Lockwood 1913, vol. 2, pp. 167–68. That Bolles discovered the table was mentioned by Henry Wood Erving in a paper entitled "Random Notes on Colonial Furniture," which he read in Hartford, Connecticut, on 19 October 1922; the finding of the table is not described in his book of the same title (Erving 1931). The present writer is indebted to Jane C. Nylander for sharing her notes on the Erving paper and for identifying the Cogswell House (Howells 1931, pl. 170).

139

139.

Box

Modern, in the style of Springfield, Massachusetts, ca. 1700

This box exhibits quite a few features that are out of the ordinary. In their totality—if not every one individually—they put the piece into question and point to its having been made at a later date than that suggested by the carved design. The tulip-and-leaf "Hadley" motif on the front (see the entry for cat. no. 95) is in a style attributed to Springfield, Massachusetts: the carving is ornamented with gouged crescents, and the stem and midrib of the leaf are somewhat rounded and have punched decoration. This type of carving occurs on three other known boxes and eight chests made about 1700.[1] The present piece differs from those three examples and other Hadley boxes and from the standard seventeenth-century format in its shallow height, its thin oak bottom that ends flush with all four sides, and its dovetailing. While dovetails are not unknown on seventeenth-century-style boxes (a few from the Guilford, Connecticut, area are dovetailed front and back),[2] they are uncommon. Those on this box are problematic on two counts: first, because dovetails are not used on any other Hadley examples; second, because of their shape. They are narrower at the base and are cut at a more acute angle than is characteristic of the dovetails on the drawers of Hadley chests (see fig. 111) or on New England furniture of the early eighteenth century in general.

The execution of the carving is not very competent, in that the curves that define the motifs are irregular. It differs from the usual Springfield interpretation of the motif in several details, which may signal a misunderstanding by a later carver.

The stem of both tulip and leaf is broader than normal, and the midrib of the leaf is slightly narrower than the stem, whereas the rib commonly swells somewhat as it issues from a narrower stem. The incised line that echoes the shape of each tulip petal is quite far in from the edge, and the ground shows what look like haphazard, individually punched holes rather than several depressions in a row struck with one punch.

The box front lacks a border below the carving, another anomalous feature. The pattern is similar in its horizontal extent to that on the Springfield boxes and also to the center portion of rails and drawer fronts on related chests, but it is not as high, and to make the design fit, the carving of the lower part of the leaves was adapted—not very successfully—to that shallower space. This means that the front was not cut down from a higher, old piece of carving, which is in accord with structural evidence that indicates that the four sides and bottom of the box are contemporaneous. Shrinkage of the bottom has caused the front and back to bow significantly inward, and shrinkage of the front and sides has resulted in a considerable difference in level between the pins and the tails of the dovetail joints. This can only have occurred because the four sides of the box and the bottom were of unseasoned wood when they were assembled.[3] Several aspects of the construction in addition to the atypical dovetailing suggest this box was not made in the late seventeenth or early eighteenth century: the nail at the top left corner of the back, which is loose and easily removed, does not look old; the type of scribing for the hinges is unusual, and the hinges themselves are suspect; and the tooling on some of the surfaces raises questions.

CONSTRUCTION

The front is dovetailed to the sides, and each joint is reinforced near the top with a nail through the side. The back is rabbeted to receive the sides and secured at each end with three nails from the back. The bottom is one board (apparently riven) about ¼ inch thick that tapers at the very front and is nailed to the four sides. The cleated top has a cyma reversa molding on the front edge and is attached to the back with snipebill hinges that are round in cross section throughout. On the outside of the back a straight vertical line scribed the full height of the board marks the location of each hinge. At either end of the back and at the rear of the left side are scored lines similar to those that mark the depth of the dovetails at the front corners.

CONDITION

The front and the back bow inward to the extent that the depth of the box at the center is about ⅜ inch less than it is at the sides. The bowing resulted from the shrinkage of the bottom, which has splits at either end. The back has a nail missing on the left end and one added at the right. The top, on which a long section behind the left hinge has split off and been nailed on, is probably a reused board. On the inner side there is a patch partly under the hasp and evidence of a previous hasp or that this one has been reset. Neither the lock with its fancy keyhole nor the hasp, on which the fixed and hinged portions do not match, look old. The box has been stripped. It has been waxed and perhaps also oiled.

WOODS

Front, back, sides, bottom, cleats, WHITE OAK; top, SOUTHERN YELLOW PINE.

DIMENSIONS

OH. 4¾ (12.1); OW. (top) 25 (63.5); CW. 23⅝ (60); OD. (top) 14 (35.6); CD. 13⅜ (34).

REFERENCES

Nutting 1921, p. 105 (owned by Mr. B. A. Behrend); Nutting 1924, no. 132 (owned by Mrs. J. Insley Blair); Nutting 1928–33, no. 139; Andrus 1951, p. 241 (detail of the front); Andrus 1952, p. 167.

PROVENANCE

Ex coll.: B. A. Behrend, Brookline, Massachusetts, by 1921; Mrs. J. Insley Blair, Tuxedo Park, New York, by 1924.

The box was on loan from Mrs. Blair to the MMA from 1939 to 1948, when it became a gift.

Gift of Mrs. J. Insley Blair, 1948 (48.158.10)

1. Two of the other boxes with Springfield-type carving are at Historic Deerfield (Fales 1976, no. 359) and the Wadsworth Atheneum (Nutting 1928–33, no. 124); the third is in a private collection (*New England, Philadelphia, and New York Cabinetwork,* auction cat., Parke-Bernet Galleries, New York City, 21–22 October 1960, lot 377). The chests are in the Greenwich Historical Society (Luther 1935, p. 97, no. 55), Museum of Fine Arts, Boston (Randall 1965, no. 11), and Wadsworth Atheneum (*Great River* 1985, no. 81); and see Luther 1935, nos. 10, 15, 28, 60, and Zea and Flynt 1992, fig. 3. Other Hadley boxes are at the Connecticut Historical Society, Hartford (Zea and Flynt 1992, fig. 9), Henry Ford Museum (Bishop 1975, p. 12), Historic Deerfield (Zea and Flynt 1992, fig. 10), and the Yale University Art Gallery (G. W. R. Ward 1988, app. 1); see also Lockwood 1913, fig. 230.
2. For example, Kane 1973a, nos. XVII, XVIII.
3. According to R. Bruce Hoadley, the bottom, because it is only half as thick as the front and back, would dry four times as quickly and, as it shrank, cause the front and back boards, which were drying much more slowly and still contained considerable moisture, to bow in (examination of the box with the writer, 5 October 1999).

140.

Chest with drawers

Guilford, Connecticut, or vicinity, 1670–1700 with later alterations

In 1891 Irving W. Lyon published this substantial chest with drawers in the Guilford idiom in his *Colonial Furniture of New England* (see *References*), with no mention made as to whether it had been restored before or after it was bought in 1884. It looks today—at any rate, on the exterior—as it did then and stands as an exemplar of thorough late-nineteenth-century refitting that included disassembly, some replaning, and the staining of surfaces, in addition to the making of repairs and replacements. While it is far from alone among chests from the seventeenth century in having a new lid, till, and feet, various repairs, and a good number of its applied elements replaced, it is relegated to an appendix of this book because it appears also to have added embellishments; some of its ornamentation, in particular that on the front stiles and muntins, does not ring true and is problematic.

The present piece has the same overall format as a chest with two drawers at the Old Dartmouth Historical Society, New Bedford, Massachusetts, and both chests in turn share distinctive design and structural features with two cupboards with three drawers at the Yale University Art Gallery.[1] Most notably similar are the massive angular mid- and base moldings, the horizontal division of the lower side panels, the

140

wedge-shaped cross section and carving scheme of the drawer fronts, and the drawer construction, with its particular manner of lightening the sides at the front joint. Other features that distinguish this piece, such as the attachment of moldings with wooden pins, the large horizontal panels in the back, the till side fitted into a V-shaped groove, a cyma reversa edge molding on the inside of the top back rail, and the use of chestnut, are characteristics of the Guilford school of craftsmanship in general, found on the Old Dartmouth Historical Society chest and on cat. nos. 88 and 113, for example. The front panels of the Old Dartmouth chest, which have somewhat vertical proportions rather than slightly horizontal ones, as here, are ornamented with applied elements in a cruciform pattern, and a single half spindle adorns the muntins and flanks the panels and the drawers—a decorative scheme that recalls that of the Yale cupboards. The panels on

the present chest are carved in a design of foliate S-scrolls similar in concept to that on cat. no. 88. The scrolls throughout the facade are executed in the typical Guilford manner but have added punchwork. A series of large single dots ornaments the first and last lobe of the foliage, as it does on a box or so-called desk in a private collection,[2] and a punch that impresses four smaller dots in a row decorates the serpentine band of each scroll. The carved rosettes on the stiles and muntins, however, strike an incongruous note, and do not make for a convincing design. Neither do the large bosses in line across the upper facade and the heavy applied glyphs flanking the drawers. Square bosses and glyphs are within the Guilford decorative repertoire, but on other pieces applied bosses are used only on panels, not on framing members, and applied glyphs only on the frieze of cupboards, as on cat. no. 113; glyphs, when they occur in other locations, are carved, like those on the top front rail and drawer fronts of this chest. How the stiles and muntins or the center of the panels may have been treated originally is not clear. None of the present appliqués is attached with a wooden pin, as is typical of applied ornament in this shop tradition, nor is there any trace of former pins either on the interior of the chest or under two glyphs that came loose. It may be that this was an economy model and the stiles, muntins, and center of the panels were left plain. If there was any ornament, it had to have been uncharacteristically just glued on.

The rosettes are carved in the same general manner as are the two inner rows of petals on sunflower chests (see the entry for cat. no. 92 and fig. 64) but with fewer petals, which allows us to speculate that the chest was embellished by one of the late-nineteenth-century Hartford, Connecticut, cabinetmakers-restorers who may have reworked the piece and would have been familiar with sunflower-type carving.[3] This is not the only Guilford-style chest adorned with questionable carved rosettes. The front stiles of a chest similar to cat. no. 88 are decorated with rosettes (which have a single row of larger petals) alternating with carved glyphs, both of which look quite out of place. A chest with two drawers of more vertical proportions than the present example and with the same type of mid- and base moldings but paired foliate S-scrolls in the panels is overrun with rosettes in at least two different sizes: they are carved down the front stiles, the front and side muntins, and across the front and side mid-moldings.[4] We may further suppose that a craftsman inspired by the present chest or its illustration in Lyon's book decided to outdo it by far.

CONSTRUCTION

The chest has two panels on each side, the lower of which is divided horizontally by an applied batten and molding, and two horizontal panels in the back; each is a single board. The mortise-and-tenon joints are secured with two small pins, except for the joints of the drawer divider and bottom front rail, which are single-pinned. (In each rear stile at the joint with the medial back rail is a third drilled pin hole; too low for the height of that rail, it is a joiner's error.) The top is attached with two snipebill hinges. The chest compartment bottom consists of several transverse boards joined with a V-shaped tongue and groove; it is nailed to a rabbet on the lower edge of the front rail and to the bottom of the rear rail, and it fits into chiseled V-shaped grooves in the stiles. There is a lidded till on the right, its side slotted into a vertical V-shaped channel in the front and rear rails. The runners for the side-hung drawers are let into the stiles and nailed in place. The front of each drawer is wedge-shaped, with the thicker part at the bottom, and its ends are rabbeted to accept the sides, which are secured to the front with two rosehead nails; the thickness of the sides has been reduced at the front by recessing the outer surface. The drawer back is rabbeted and nailed to the sides. The bottom, made of two longitudinal boards, is beveled to fit into a groove in the front and nailed to the other sides. The molding at the bottom of the front and side top rails, which consists of an ovolo and two fascias, and the mid- and base moldings are attached with wooden pins. On the interior, the lower edge of the top rear rail is finished with a cyma

reversa molding, and most of the other edges are chamfered. The stiles are rectangular, but other framing members taper in thickness and hidden surfaces have been left rough. There is evidence of mill sawing on some of the chestnut.

CONDITION

The chest has been apart, and some of its elements have been replaned—noticeably, the top rear rail, parts of the drawers, and the bottom inner surface of the upper side panels; the medial side rails may be not just reworked but replaced. The top, cleats, till, lock, and feet are replaced. The bottom of the chest compartment has two narrow sections that are new, and the other boards, which could be original, have been renailed probably more than once. The drawers have been completely disassembled and renailed. The knobs are new. The grooves in the sides for the runners have been repaired with a slat along the upper edge. The bottoms have been shifted forward and a strip added at the back. The back of the upper drawer is replaced, and on the lower drawer the upper left corner of the front has been patched. There are gnawed edges on the drawers and nearby rails and large gnawed holes in the runners, which may be original but if so have been flipped and reworked. The mid- and base moldings and the top front molding have been off, and the pins that secure them were reset or renewed. The top side moldings and the newer and perhaps also the older portions of the molding between the drawers are not original, nor are the moldings around the side panels, which have a questionable angular profile. Almost all of the front panel moldings, which appropriately feature a cyma reversa, are clearly new, as are the applied glyphs flanking the drawers. The square bosses show some to little or no wear. The exterior of the chest, including the back, has been mahoganized,[5] and the top, front, and sides have in addition been varnished and waxed. Virtually all interior surfaces have been stained or otherwise coated.

INSCRIPTIONS

On the inner side of the lower drawer are incised nineteenth-century restorer's reassembly marks (one and two notches). On the underside of the chest compartment bottom and the inner side of the lower side panels are restorer's numbers and markings in pencil that are probably more recent.

WOODS

Stiles, most rails, muntins, drawer divider, front and side panels, drawer fronts, top-, mid-, and base moldings, drawer runners, replaced top and cleats, replaced till, replaced feet, WHITE OAK and RED OAK; back panels, older and newer boards of chest compartment bottom, drawer sides, backs, and bottoms, molding between drawers (age?), CHESTNUT; medial side rails (age?), HICKORY.

DIMENSIONS

OH. 39½ (100.3); OW. (top) 50⅜ (128); CW. 47⅛ (119.7); OD. (mid-molding) 23¼ (59.1); CD. 21½ (54.6).

EXHIBITION

On loan to the William Trent House, Trenton, New Jersey, from 1939 to 1977.

REFERENCES

I. W. Lyon 1891, pp. 14–15 and fig. 8; Dyer 1931a, p. 39; Ralston 1931b, fig. 1.

PROVENANCE

Ex coll.: Dr. Irving W. Lyon, Hartford, Connecticut; George Coe Graves, Osterville, Massachusetts.

When Lyon published the chest in 1891 (see *References*) he stated that it "was bought in 1884, in Madison, Conn., where, according to the history obtained, it had been during the last two centuries. It now belongs to the writer." According to notes compiled by his son Irving P. Lyon, it had come from the Munger family descended from Nicholas Munger, who settled in Guilford in 1652.[6] Graves purchased the chest from Charles Woolsey Lyon, New York City dealer and a son of Dr. Lyon, shortly before he gave the piece to the Museum.

The Sylmaris Collection, Gift of George Coe Graves, 1930 (30.120.378)

1. For the chest, see St. George 1979b, fig. 77; and Kane 1993, addendum, fig. 2. For the cupboards, see Kane 1973a, nos. XII, XIII; and G. W. R. Ward 1988, nos. 197, 198.

2. Kane 1973a, no. XVII.

3. The Hartford firm of Robbins and Winship (then Robbins Brothers), which employed cabinetmakers such as Edwin Simons, Walter Hosmer, and Patrick Stevens, was frequently used by collectors and others in Connecticut during the latter part of the nineteenth century and the early twentieth century for the restoration of early furniture (Stillinger 1980, p. 81; G. W. R. Ward 1988, pp. 378–79; Barquist 1992, p. 74). For carving of the "sunflower" type being done there, see Connecticut Historical Society 1958, p. 39.

4. For the chest similar to cat. no. 88, see that entry. The chest with two drawers is illustrated in *New Hampshire Weekend Auctions*, auction cat., Northeast Auctions, Manchester, New Hampshire, 6–7 November 1999, lot 763. It was formerly at Old Sturbridge Village, Sturbridge, Massachusetts, acquired in 1949 from the William F. Hubbard Estate. Hubbard, an early furniture collector, lived in Hartford, Connecticut (letter of 7 October 1971 from Henry J. Harlow to the writer).

5. For other early furniture that was mahoganized in the late 1800s or early 1900s, see Connecticut Historical Society 1958, pp. 52, 72, 98, 129.

6. Lyon Family Papers, box 11, Downs Manuscript Collection, Winterthur Museum.

141.

Cupboard

Middlesex County, Massachusetts, 1680–1710 with later alterations

Although it is quite heavily restored and now only partially reflects its original appearance, this cupboard is a valuable document that expands our knowledge of a school of joinery that was active in Middlesex County, Massachusetts, at the end of the seventeenth century and produced distinctive designs with a quirky combination of painted decoration, carving, and applied ornament. Related objects are a chest with drawers in the Concord Museum, Concord, Massachusetts, that has a traditional history in the Hunt family of Concord; a box in the Winterthur Museum inscribed "A H /1698"; and a cupboard base in the collection of the Museum of Fine Arts, Boston, thought to have been first owned in the Baldwin family of Woburn (illustrated here, 141d).[1] The present cupboard was found in the same area—in Lexington—in "a dilapidated condition" (see *Provenance*). The cupboard as it now stands reflects the restorations that the collector H. Eugene Bolles had carried out after he acquired it (141c) and the subsequent removal at the Museum of Bolles's repainting (see *Condition*).

Thanks to photographs that Bolles had taken of the piece before restoration (141a, 141b) and also to his notes (MMA Archives), one can gain a much fuller idea of the nature of the painted decoration originally on the sides of the cupboard than is revealed by the scribe and shadow lines that now remain. The upper and lower side panels featured designs of a central oval or round figure with quarter circles in the corners, and on the lower panels also half circles on each side, the whole framed by a border. The decoration, according to Bolles, was executed in black, white, and two shades of red. Similar geometric schemes ornament the related objects—the side panels on the chest and cupboard base and the top on the box—which are all also "grained" with dark, wavy parallel lines.[2] The prerestoration photographs indicate that on the sides of this cupboard the framing members were also covered with such graining—executed on a white ground—and, most interestingly, that the side frieze rails bore a design of an undulating vine, two tulips, and probably a lily that simulated in paint the carving on the front.

Most likely the carving on this cupboard was originally enhanced with paint, as it was on the three related pieces, so that color was present on the front as well as the sides. The carved motifs seen here and their particular interpretation all have counterparts on the other objects in the same tradition: single and paired S-scrolls, lilies, tulips, cross-hatching, and, on the torus molding that fronts the top drawer of the cupboard base, large roundels enclosing rosettes. That convex molding differs from the one on the present piece in the arrangement of the roundel and paired scroll motifs and in the fact that it is affixed to the drawer front in two sections divided in the middle by a flat vertical plaque carved with a single S-scroll. A similar plaque is applied to the center of each of the two lower drawers, where it repeats the carving on the stiles and separates two simulated panels formed by applied moldings. On the bottom drawer the panels are rectangular and on the middle

141a. Cat. no. 141 before restoration.

141c. Cat. no. 141 as restored by H. Eugene Bolles.

141d. Cupboard base, probably Woburn, Massachusetts, ca. 1680.
Photograph © 2007 Museum of Fine Arts, Boston.

141b. Side of cat. no. 141 before restoration.

141. See also fig. 49.

drawer they are shaped, with triangular plaques at the sides and rectangular plaques at the center of the top and bottom. The lower drawers of the present cupboard thus had in all probability applied geometric ornament, but its exact configuration and whether or not it was combined with carved central plaques cannot be determined. The bottom front rail on both cupboards has a scalloped edge (but not in the same design), both pieces have similar base moldings, and the moldings that run on the frame around the lower side panels match. The moldings under the middle shelf differ. The one on this piece is integral to the rail, which is secured to the stiles with a double tenon.[3] The bold scale of its incised dentils is in keeping with the large, individually applied dentils under the top that are visible in the prerestoration photographs. The one area for which all evidence of how it was decorated is lacking is the panel of the door. Otherwise one can visualize a plausible reconstruction of the original aspect of this cupboard—an ambitious, colorful, but not very well integrated composite of ornament.

More than one design influence is evident in this cupboard and the related base. One is a tradition of carving that included the use of a drawer with a torus-molded front at the top of the lower case of cupboards—a scheme that is encountered otherwise in New England only on a group of cupboards from the Guilford, Connecticut, area (see the entry for cat. no. 113). (It may or may not be coincidental that on those cupboards, like this one, the pillars are one piece with the corner blocks above them.) Peculiar about the work of this Massachusetts shop is that the torus molding is a separate element applied to the drawer front and that the concept of a convex drawer front was carried over to the drawers of the Hunt family chest.[4] The use of only drawers in the lower case of a cupboard, and of applied geometric ornament and beveled mitered moldings as seen on the Museum of Fine Arts example, point to the influence of Boston case furniture. With that in mind, one sees that the deep second drawer in these two cupboards is not a strange aberration but a reflection of the typical arrangement in four-drawer Boston chests of drawers. The painted ornament on this group of objects is part of a larger trend of decorating joined furniture with graining and painted motifs manifest in the late seventeenth and early eighteenth centuries in eastern Massachusetts (see cat. nos. 46, 110), western Massachusetts, and Connecticut (cat. no. 100). The painting originally on this cupboard when bright and new was probably among the more startling of that period.[5]

CONSTRUCTION

The cupboard is built in two sections with the middle shelf part of the lower case. On the upper case, the frame of the back, the front and side rails that form the frieze, and the front corner blocks are joined as one unit, and the front and splayed sides of the storage compartment, which has pentagonal front stiles, are framed as another. The back edge of the rear stiles of the splayed sides is angled to fit against the stiles of the case back, and the two are held together by nails driven in from the front. The pillars are one with the front corner blocks (fig. 49), and a tenon at the bottom fits into the middle shelf. The side panels are each formed of one horizontal board. The back consists of two horizontal boards with beveled edges nailed to the frame. The soffit is constructed in the usual manner. The mortise-and-tenon joints on both cases are quite wide (3/8 in. or slightly more). The lower case has one panel (a single vertical board) on each side and contains three long drawers—the middle one 3 inches deeper than the top and bottom ones, which are of equal height. The back consists of several vertical boards with beveled edges nailed to the frame. The case bottom, formed of two longitudinal boards, is nailed to the top of the front rail and beveled and nailed to the underside of the side and rear rails.

On the top drawer there is applied to the actual front (to which the sides and bottom are attached) a carved shallow torus molding that overlaps the stiles. The molding under the middle shelf, which consists of three fascias, is one with the top front rail, which is joined to the stiles with a double tenon of the type used on cat. no. 114 (see fig. 88). A broad, convex channel molding runs down the rear stiles of the splayed upper sides and across the middle of the upper rail of all four side panels. Around those panels, an ovolo and a fillet (or possibly a small, shallow cavetto) are worked on the edges of the stiles, and an astragal, cavetto, small bead, and fillet on the edges of the rails. The latter profiles above a large ovolo constitute the base molding. The upper side panels were scribed for a design with an ellipse in the center and a quarter circle in each corner; the lower side panels for a circle in the center, a half circle in the middle of each side, and a quarter circle in each corner; and all side panels for a band around the perimeter.

CONDITION

Illustrations 141a and 141b show the state of the cupboard when Bolles acquired it and before he had it restored. His notes on the restoration (Bolles notes, MMA Archives) state: "The top boards of the top and base were too rotten to use. The two lower drawers were quite old but not original, and I had new ones made. The carved front of the upper drawer had been nailed in place and saved, but the drawer itself was gone. The centre of the door and two of its frames were gone. The carving on the two new door frames was copied from the two old ones. Otherwise it was substantially original. The painted decoration is restored like the original, except on the missing parts which are after the style of the rest." No effort was made to disguise the replacements, which include quite a few not mentioned by Bolles. Also new on the upper case are the upper rear rail, about half of the back, a portion of the right rear case stile and of the rear stile of the right side panel, a splice on the upper right side rail, the soffit, and an interior shelf. Also definitely replaced on the lower case are one board of the back, the drawer runners, and the feet. The middle drawer is actually the one Bolles acquired, but it has been repaired and renailed. The present drawers are all side-hung, and there is no evidence that any of the original ones ran otherwise. The carved torus molding attached to the front of the new top drawer is pieced at the right end and repaired at the left end. There are other small repairs and patches on both cases. The cupboard was almost entirely taken apart, and some of the old components were replaned. Of the applied elements, two of the half columns, the left front square boss, the architrave, and the base molding, in addition to the torus molding, were on the piece when Bolles purchased it. (So was the molding under the middle shelf, which is one with the rail.) All other applied moldings and ornaments are new. The new paint that Bolles had applied to the cupboard (141c) was removed at the MMA by 1916, along with the original decoration that shows in Bolles's prerestoration photographs, assuming that it had been overpainted and not removed beforehand. At present, only the scribed lines of the designs remain, and mainly on the lower panels thin dark residues within the bands that form the geometric patterns. The cupboard has a modern clear finish; the interior has been varnished.

WOODS

Stiles, rails, drawer dividers, upper side panels, torus molding on front of top drawer, old and new elements of door, replaced feet, OAK; upper front corner blocks and pillars, old half columns, SOFT MAPLE; lower side panels, older boards of back, case bottom, replaced upper rear rail of upper case, SOUTHERN YELLOW PINE; architrave, base molding, replaced top, replaced middle shelf, replaced drawers, and most other replacements, PINE.

DIMENSIONS

OH. 57 3/4 (146.7); OW. (middle shelf) 49 3/4 (126.4); CW. 47 (119.4); OD. (top) 22 3/4 (57.8); CD. 21 (53.3).

EXHIBITIONS

On loan to the Society for the Preservation of New England Antiquities (now Historic New England) for exhibition in the Jackson House, Portsmouth, New Hampshire, from 1948 to 1972 and to the Dorothy Whitfield Historic Society (for display in the Hyland House), Guilford, Connecticut, from 1975 to 2000.

REFERENCES

Lockwood 1913, fig. 171 (repainted); Cescinsky and Hunter 1929, p. 51; Williams 1963, no. 86 (drawings of molding profiles are inaccurate).

PROVENANCE

Ex coll.: H. Eugene Bolles, Boston.

Bolles stated: "It was found by a dealer standing outdoors under a tree in Lexington, Mass., in a dilapidated condition" (Bolles notes, MMA Archives).

Gift of Mrs. Russell Sage, 1909 (10.125.44)

1. For the related chest and cupboard base, see Wood 1996, no. 2; for the box, B. Ward 1986, no. 3. The writer is indebted to Robert F. Trent for first bringing the cupboard base to her attention. Trent has suggested Woburn as the most likely location of the shop that made these objects; Woburn, but not the other towns, supported several prominent joiners (Wood 1996, p. 3).

2. The painting on the chest and box is illustrated in Benes 1982, pp. 43, 44, and B. Ward 1986, p. 18. The two shades of red mentioned by Bolles may correspond to the red and orange paint (both containing vermilion) noted on the box (B. Ward 1986, p. 18).

3. The same type of double tenon on a rail with integral molding occurs on a Boston cupboard and is characteristic of joined case furniture from Plymouth Colony, Massachusetts (see the entry for cat. no. 114 and fig. 88).

4. Wood 1996, no. 2. The bottom drawer on the Museum of Fine Arts, Boston, cupboard base is unusual for joined furniture, in that it is not side-hung but rides on its bottom. On all the drawers in that cupboard and on the original one in the chest, the front is nailed to the sides through the front—a mode of construction associated primarily with Plymouth Colony furniture (see cat. nos. 114, 115) but that occurs also elsewhere on furniture from eastern Massachusetts (see cat. no. 105).

5. For a Boston chest of four drawers see, for example, Jobe and Kaye 1984, no. 11; for a less common three-drawer chest, Trent 1985, fig. 18; for painted pieces from western Massachusetts, Fales 1972, nos. 19–21.

APPENDIX 2
Photographic Details

CHAIR FINIALS

CHAIR CREST RAILS

CHAIR STRETCHERS

LEGS

PILLARS

FEET

DECORATIVE DETAILS

INTERIORS

CONSTRUCTION

HARDWARE AND MARKS

Chair Finials

Fig. 1, cat. no. 2.

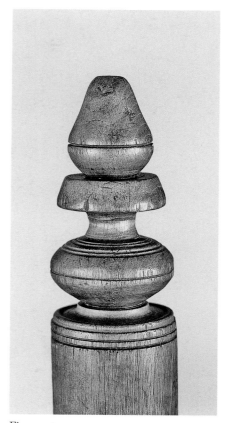

Fig. 2, cat. no. 10.

Fig. 3, cat. no. 4.

Fig. 4, cat. no. 5.

Fig. 5, cat. no. 7.

Fig. 6, cat. no. 12.

Fig. 7, cat. no. 11.

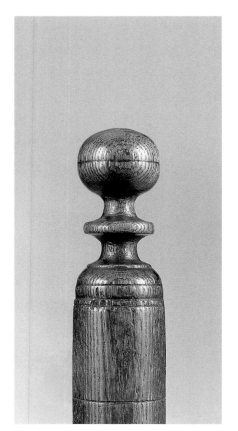

Fig. 8, cat. no. 8.

Fig. 9, cat. no. 15.

Fig. 10, cat. no. 13.

Fig. 11, cat. no. 14.

Fig. 12, cat. no. 17.

Fig. 13, cat. no. 9.

Fig. 14, cat. no. 26-1.

Chair Crest Rails

Fig. 15, cat. no. 27.

Fig. 16, cat. no. 29.

Fig. 17, cat. no. 137.

Fig. 18, cat. no. 28.

Fig. 19, cat. no. 30-1.

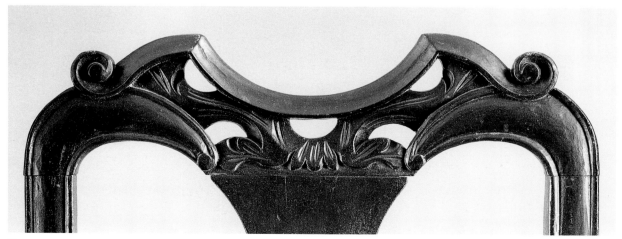

Fig. 20, cat. no. 37.

Chair Stretchers

Fig. 21, cat. no. 26-1.

Fig. 22, cat. no. 20.

Fig. 23, cat. no. 39.

Fig. 24, cat. no. 27.

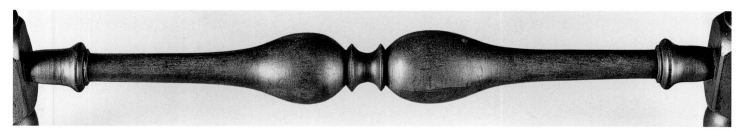

Fig. 25, cat. no. 34.

Fig. 26, cat. no. 32.

Fig. 27, cat. no. 30-1.

Fig. 28, cat. no. 137.

Fig. 29, cat. no. 41.

Fig. 30, cat. no. 37.

Fig. 31, cat. no. 17.

Legs

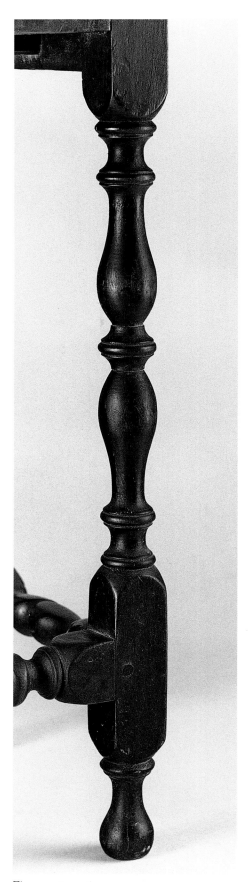

Fig. 32, cat. no. 59.

Fig. 33, cat. no. 60.

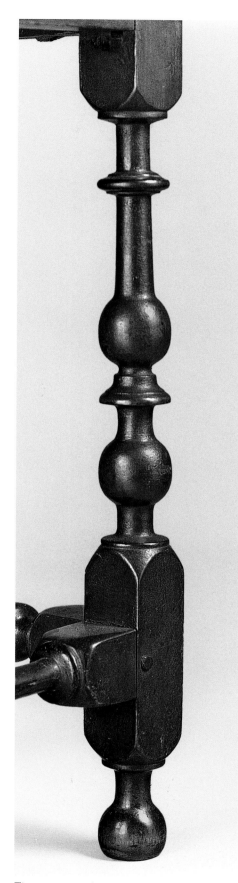

Fig. 34, cat. no. 63.

Fig. 35, cat. no. 65.

Fig. 36, cat. no. 132.

Fig. 37, cat. no. 51.

Fig. 38, cat. no. 64 (foot replaced).

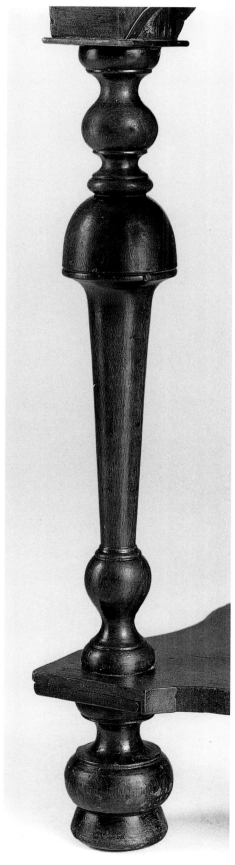

Fig. 39, cat. no. 122.

Fig. 40, cat. no. 123.

Fig. 41, cat. no. 126.

Fig. 42, cat. no. 125.

Fig. 43, cat. no. 131.

Fig. 44, cat. no. 121 (foot replaced).

Pillars

Fig. 45, cat. no. 105.

Fig. 46, cat. no. 58.

Fig. 47, cat. no. 114.

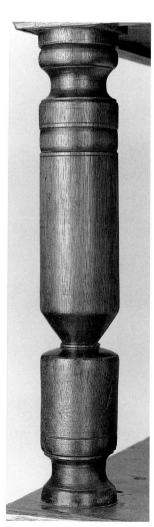

Fig. 48, cat. no. 113.

Fig. 49, cat. no. 141.

Feet

Fig. 50, cat. no. 32.

Fig. 51, cat. no. 36.

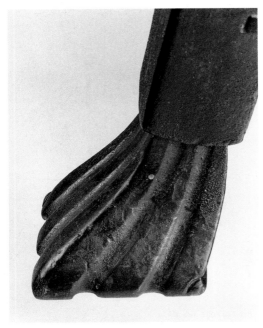

Fig. 52, cat. no. 55.

Decorative Details

Fig. 53, cat. no. 70.

Fig. 54, cat. no. 18.

Fig. 55, cat. no. 83.

Fig. 56, cat. no. 86.

Fig. 57, cat. no. 90.

Fig. 58, cat. no. 90. Right back panel, interior.

Fig. 59, cat. no. 93.

Fig. 60, cat. no. 93. A lower panel on left side, interior.

Fig. 61, cat. no. 96.

Fig. 62, cat. no. 79.

Fig. 63, cat. no. 113.

Fig. 64, cat. no. 92.

Fig. 65, cat. no. 115.

Fig. 66, cat. no. 116.

Fig. 67,
cat. no. 98.

Fig. 68,
cat. no. 105.

Fig. 69,
cat. no. 108.

Fig. 70, cat. no. 100.

Fig. 71, cat. no. 101.

Fig. 72, cat. no. 102.

Fig. 73, cat. no. 104.

Fig. 74, cat. no. 110.

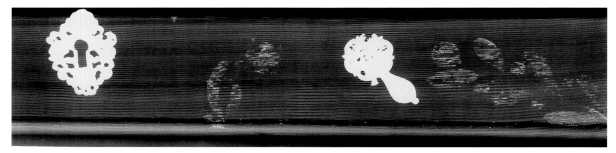

Fig. 75, cat. no. 49. X-radiograph of drawer front.

Fig. 76, cat. no. 46.

Fig. 77, cat. no. 122.

Fig. 78, cat. no. 125.

Fig. 79, cat. no. 118.

Fig. 80, cat. no. 119.

Interiors

Fig. 81, cat. no. 79.

Fig. 82, cat. no. 133.

Fig. 83, cat. no. 134.

Construction

Fig. 84, cat. no. 90. Mortise-and-tenon joint with wooden pin.

Fig. 85, cat. no. 23. Scribe lines for joints.

Fig. 86, cat. no. 96. Joint with chamfered stile and beveled tenon shoulder on rail.

Fig. 87, cat. no. 58. Joiner's assembly marks.

Fig. 88, cat. no. 114. Double-tenon joint.

396

Fig. 89, cat. no. 40. Rectangular tenon at the end of a turned stretcher.

Fig. 90, cat. no. 58. "Gate" support for a hinged table leaf.

Fig. 91, cat. no. 58. Parallel marks produced by sawing in a water-powered mill.

Fig. 92, cat. no. 27. Front of rear leg planed to allow for a right-angle joint with the stretcher.

Fig. 93, cat. no. 113. Back of upper case (left unfinished).

Fig. 94, cat. no. 114. Back of upper case (carefully planed).

Fig. 95, cat. no. 93.

Fig. 96, cat. no. 119. Back formed by overlapping riven clapboards.

Fig. 97, cat. no. 110. Joined chest of drawers, interior.

Fig. 98, cat. no. 123. Upper case of high chest, interior.

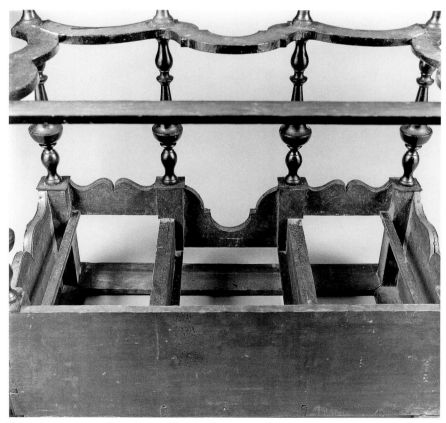

Fig. 99, cat. no. 123. Lower case of high chest, interior (inverted).

Fig. 100, cat. no. 123. Lower case of high chest, joint of partition to front skirt.

399

Fig. 101, cat. no. 124. High chest, juncture of upper and lower case.

Fig. 102, cat. no. 126. High chest, side of upper case constructed of an outer board, inner board, and filler strip in between.

Fig. 103, cat. no. 124. High chest, top of lower case, lapped frame.

Fig. 104, cat. no. 123. High chest, top of lower case, mitered frame.

Fig. 105, cat. no. 126. High chest, top of lower case, lapped frame.

Drawers

Seventeenth-century drawers are generally side-hung — suspended on runners that engage a groove in each side. Later drawers are typically supported from below and run on the bottom or the bottom of the sides.

Fig. 106, cat. no. 110.

Fig. 107, cat. no. 114.

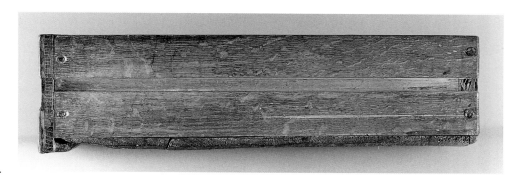

Fig. 108, cat. no. 108.

Fig. 109, cat. no. 93.

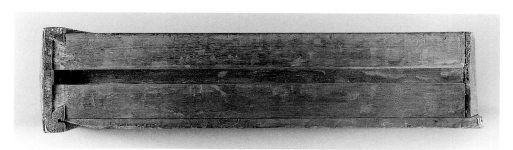

Fig. 110, cat. no. 98.

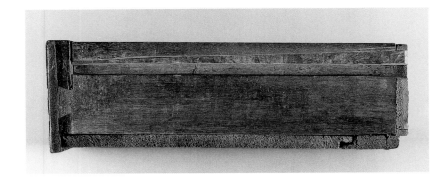

Fig. 111, cat. no. 95.

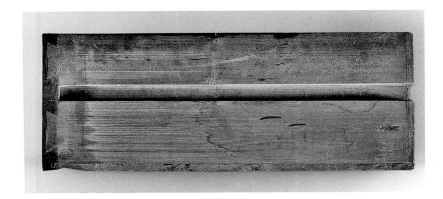

Fig. 112, cat. no. 121.

Fig. 113, cat. no. 116.

Fig. 114, cat. no. 124.

Fig. 115, cat. no. 123.

Hardware and Marks

Fig. 116, cat. no. 49.

Fig. 119, cat. no. 36. Chair number VI in a set.

Fig. 117, cat. no. 63. Rosehead nails and leather washers.

Fig. 120, cat. no. 32. Probably a caner's mark.

Fig. 118, cat. no. 65. Rosehead nails and rivet in center.

Fig. 121, cat. no. 9. Owner's brand.

APPENDIX 3
Explanatory Drawings

GLOSSARY OF FURNITURE TERMS

MOLDINGS

CONVERTING LOGS INTO BOARDS

JOINTS

Glossary of Furniture Terms

The labeled drawings are a guide to the terms for furniture parts used in this catalogue and are not intended to represent an ideal or definitive terminology.

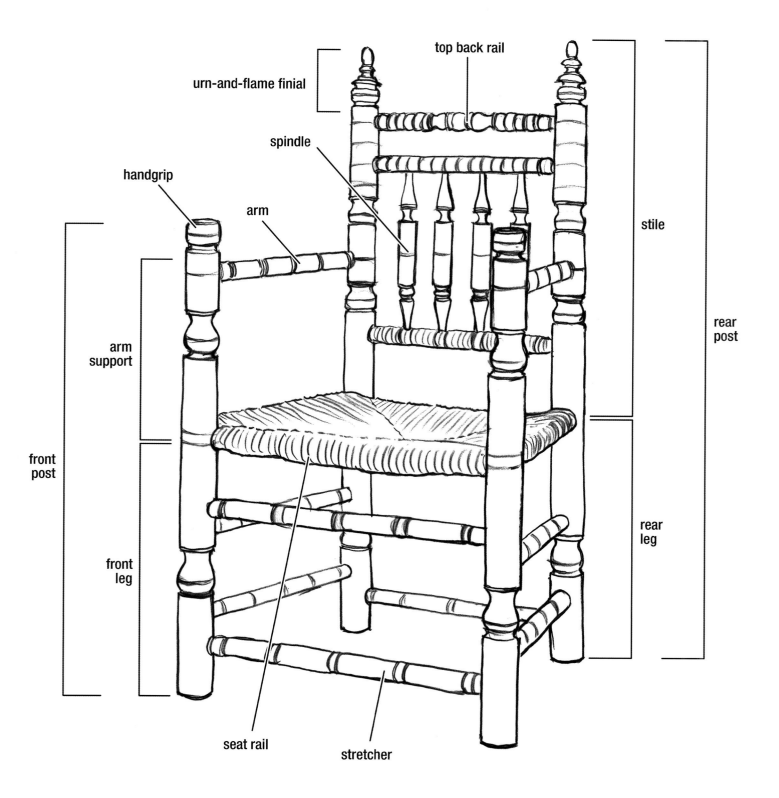

top back rail

urn-and-flame finial

spindle

handgrip

arm

stile

arm support

rear post

front post

rear leg

front leg

seat rail

stretcher

Fig. 122, cat. no. 4. Spindle-back armchair.

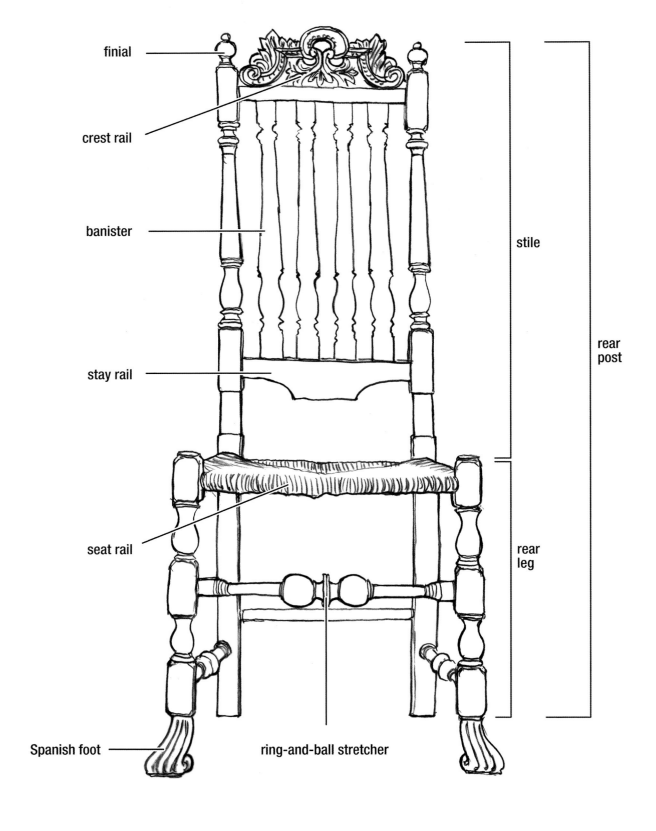

finial

crest rail

banister

stay rail

seat rail

Spanish foot

ring-and-ball stretcher

stile

rear post

rear leg

Fig. 123, cat. no. 30-1. Banister-back chair.

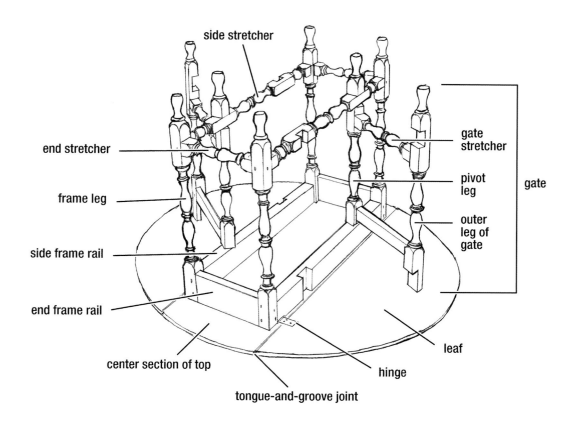

Fig. 124, cat. no. 60. Oval table with falling leaves.

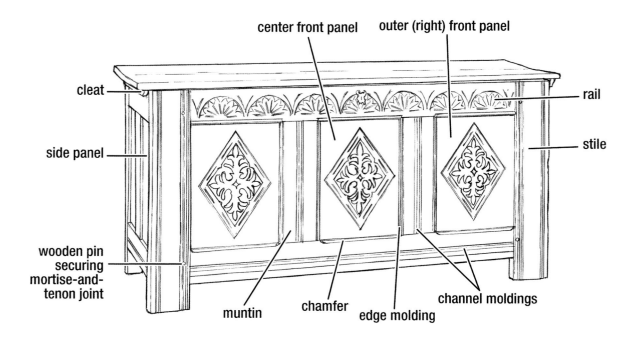

Fig. 125, cat. no. 90. Chest.

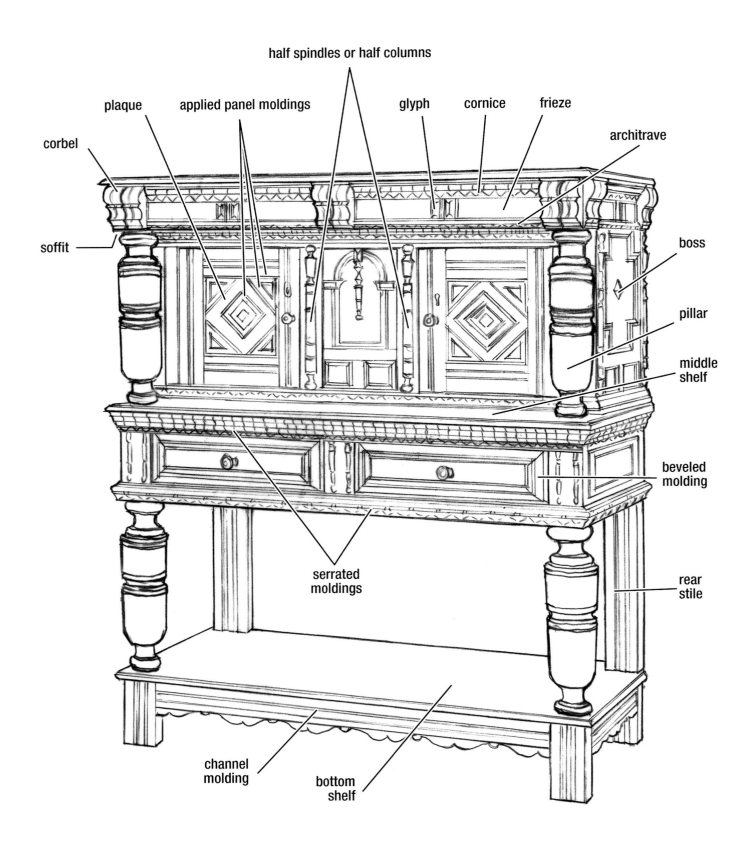

Fig. 126, cat. no. 115. Cupboard.

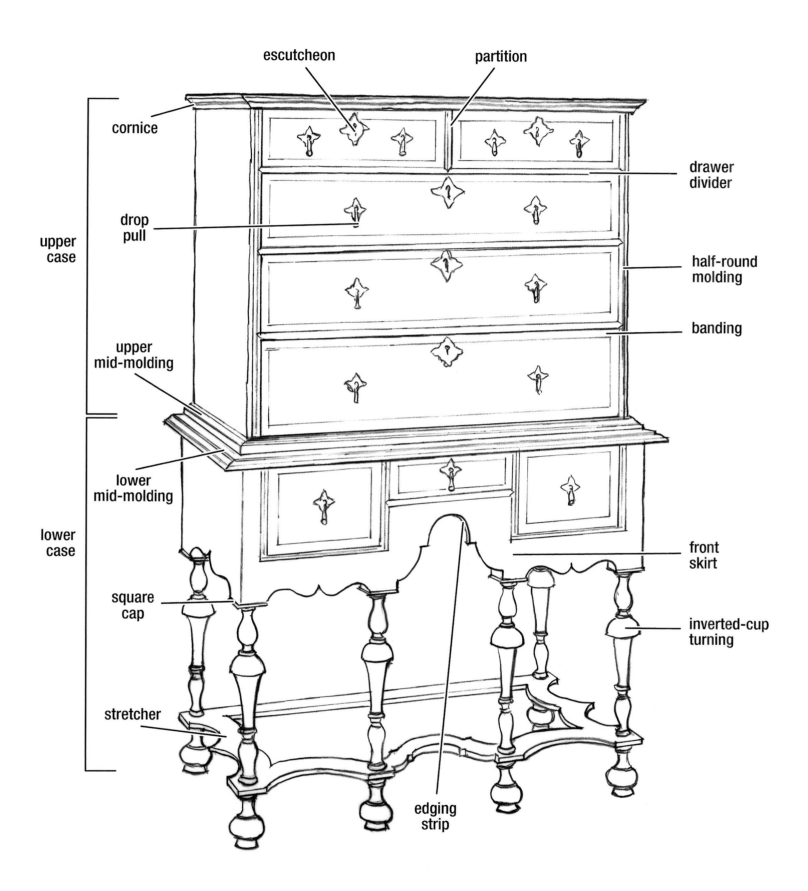

escutcheon

partition

cornice

upper case

drop pull

upper mid-molding

lower mid-molding

lower case

square cap

stretcher

drawer divider

half-round molding

banding

front skirt

inverted-cup turning

edging strip

Fig. 127, cat. no. 123. High chest of drawers.

Moldings

The profiles illustrated (other than those in fig. 128) are taken from objects in the catalogue that retain original moldings. They represent a selection that includes both profiles in widespread use (figs. 129-31, 135, 147) and less common ones peculiar to particular pieces or shop traditions.

Fig. 128. Glossary of common profiles.

Fillet and fascia.   Astragal.   Cavetto.   Ovolo.   Cyma recta.   Cyma reversa.

Seventeenth-century style

Applied panel moldings, shown actual size

Fig. 129, cat. no. 115.   Fig. 130, cat. no. 114.   Fig. 131, cat. no. 98.

Fig. 132, cat. no. 116.   Fig. 133, cat. no. 79.   Fig. 134, cat. no. 110.

Edge moldings, shown actual size

Fig. 135, cat. no. 88.   Fig. 136, cat. no. 83.   Fig. 137, cat. no. 118.

Case moldings, shown actual size

Fig. 138, cat no. 79 (cornice).

Fig. 139, cat no. 114 (cornice).

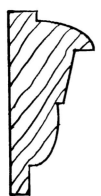

Fig. 140, cat. no. 114 (on drawer divider).

Fig. 141, cat. no. 114 (base).

Fig. 142, cat. no. 110 (base).

Fig. 143, cat. no. 78 (base).

William and Mary style

Case moldings, shown actual size

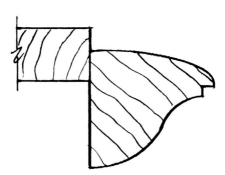

Fig. 144, cat. no. 121 (cornice).

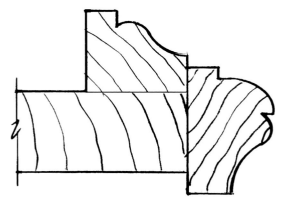

Fig. 145, cat. no. 122 (mid-moldings).

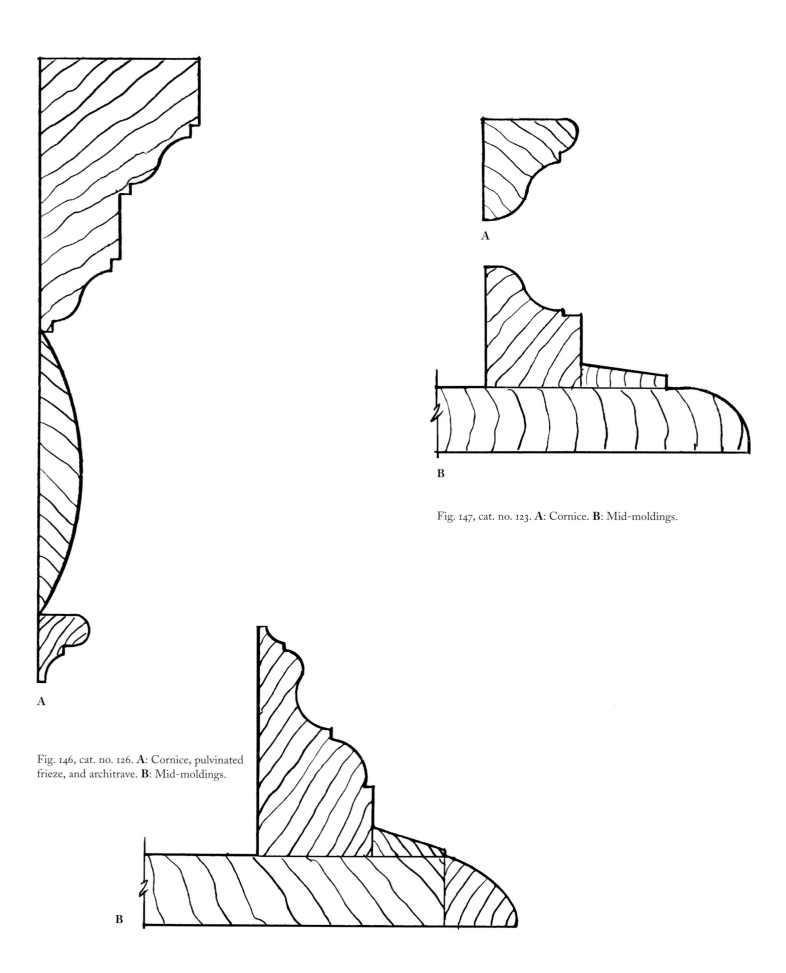

Fig. 147, cat. no. 123. **A**: Cornice. **B**: Mid-moldings.

Fig. 146, cat. no. 126. **A**: Cornice, pulvinated frieze, and architrave. **B**: Mid-moldings.

Converting Logs into Boards

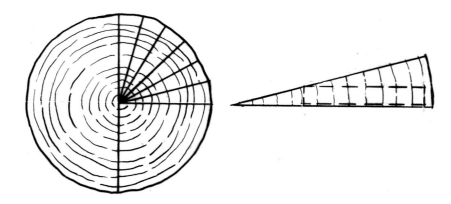

Fig. 148. **Riving.** Some woods, oak in particular, can be easily split, or riven, along the radial plane. When a log is converted into boards by riving, it is first split into longitudinal quarters and then into wedge-shaped sections, which have to be trimmed to produce square or rectangular stock. Nearly all the oak used in American seventeenth-century furniture was riven, and chairs, tables, and case pieces made from such stock may contain boards that taper somewhat in thickness or show torn grain on hidden surfaces. Riving—quicker than sawing but more wasteful of material—was the preferred method for converting oak in the colonies during the 1600s, since wood was plentiful but labor in short supply. Riven oak, which has the growth rings oriented at or close to 90 degrees to the wide face of the board, has little or no tendency to warp. The surface of such a board along the radial plane displays the conspicuous ray flecks that are characteristically visible on oak furniture of the period.

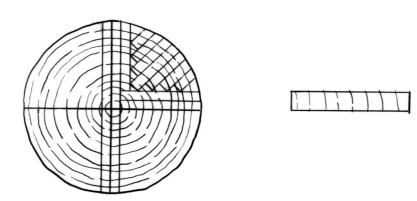

Fig. 149. **Radial cutting, quartersawing, or quartering.** To obtain boards with the wide face along the radial plane by sawing, each sawn quarter of the log is cut in such a way—one of which is illustrated—that the growth rings are oriented at close to 90 degrees, or at any rate at more than 45 degrees, to the wide face. Such radial-cut, quarter-sawn, or quartered wood shows the same ray flecks as riven wood and likewise has little or no tendency to warp. This method makes a more efficient use of material than riving but is more labor-intensive. The size of boards obtainable by riving or radial cutting is less than half the width of the log (once the pith and the bark layer are removed).

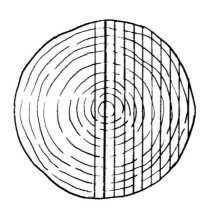

Fig. 150. **Tangent-sawing, plain-sawing, or flat-sawing.** Cutting a log from one side to another into boards parallel to the diameter is the simplest and least wasteful method of sawing. The boards obtained in this manner, with the exception of those down the middle of the log, have the growth rings oriented roughly tangential, or at least at less than 45 degrees, to the wide face of the board and are called tangent-sawn, plain-sawn, or flat-sawn. Much wider boards can be obtained by tangent-sawing than by the other methods, but they shrink more and are more prone to warping than radial-cut or riven wood. Water-powered sawmills, established in the colonies early on, produced tangent-sawn stock. The regular up-and-down movement of their vertical blades left parallel saw marks perpendicular to the length of the board, which often remain visible on unfinished surfaces. Much of the wood other than oak used in early colonial furniture, particularly the pine, was mill-sawn.

Joints

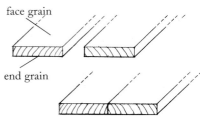

Fig. 151. Butt.

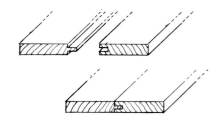

Fig. 152. Tongue and groove.

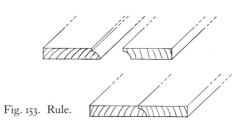

Fig. 153. Rule.

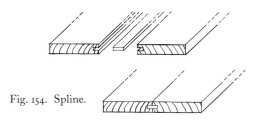

Fig. 154. Spline.

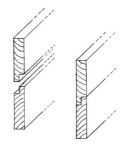

Fig. 155. Half lap.

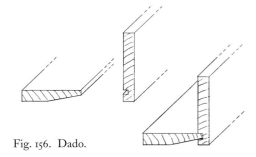

Fig. 156. Dado.

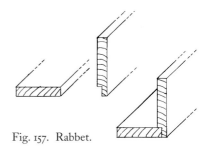

Fig. 157. Rabbet.

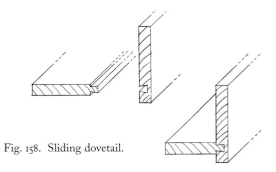

Fig. 158. Sliding dovetail.

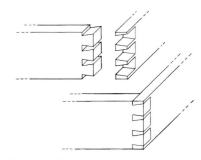

Fig. 159. Through dovetail.

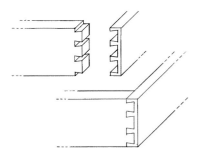

Fig. 160. Half-blind dovetail.

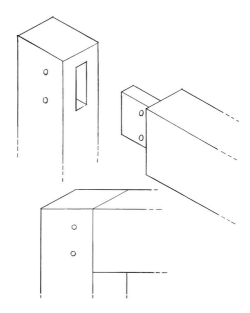

Fig. 161. Rectangular mortise and tenon.

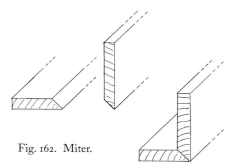

Fig. 162. Miter.

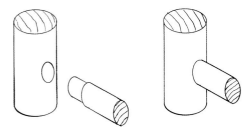

Fig. 163. Round mortise and tenon.

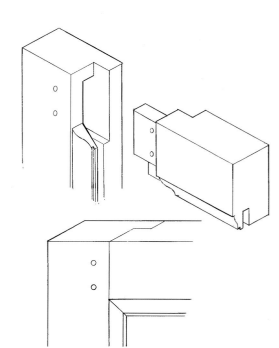

Fig. 164. Mitered mortise and tenon.

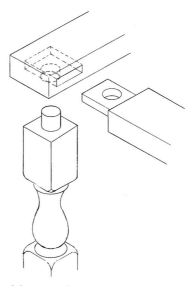

Fig. 165. Mortise-and-tenon joint of horizontal seat rails secured by round tenon of leg.

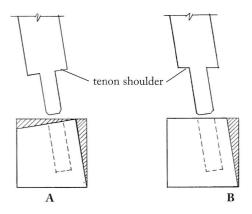

tenon shoulder

A

B

Fig. 166. Methods of joining the side rail and right front leg on a trapezoidal seat. **A**: Rear of leg planed to allow for a right-angle joint. **B**: Oblique tenon shoulders on rail. In both cases, the outer surface of the leg is planed to be in line with the rail.

415

Concordance

Accession number	Catalogue number	Accession number	Catalogue number
09.175	119	* 10.125.218	28
* 10.125.2	70	* 10.125.219	29
* 10.125.3	76	* 10.125.228	137
* 10.125.4	77	* 10.125.235	10
* 10.125.5	71	* 10.125.236	12
* 10.125.9	73	* 10.125.241	15
* 10.125.10	75	* 10.125.327	52
* 10.125.15	107	* 10.125.329	22
* 10.125.16	101	* 10.125.330	21
* 10.125.22	91	* 10.125.668	88
* 10.125.23	85	* 10.125.672	45
* 10.125.24	84	* 10.125.673	62
* 10.125.25	89	* 10.125.676	13
* 10.125.27	90	* 10.125.677	136
* 10.125.29	100	* 10.125.680	72
* 10.125.31	97	* 10.125.681	11
* 10.125.32	99	* 10.125.682	96
* 10.125.33	98	* 10.125.684	78
* 10.125.37	111	* 10.125.685	83
* 10.125.38	109	* 10.125.686	108
* 10.125.44	141	* 10.125.689	92
* 10.125.45	117	* 10.125.691	7
* 10.125.48	115	* 10.125.694	6
* 10.125.66	128	* 10.125.695	35
* 10.125.69	129	* 10.125.697	19
* 10.125.75	133	* 10.125.698	33
* 10.125.101	54	* 10.125.700	94
* 10.125.105	47	* 10.125.701	138
* 10.125.110	51	* 10.125.703	113
* 10.125.114	48	* 10.125.704	124
* 10.125.124	69	* 10.125.708	134
* 10.125.129	59	* 10.125.709	122
* 10.125.130	60	11.183	82
* 10.125.131	61	22.126	42
* 10.125.133	63	23.80.6	34
* 10.125.168	79	23.171	120
* 10.125.182	53	29.133.1, .2	26
* 10.125.195	25	30.120.56	130
* 10.125.207	5	30.120.72	38
* 10.125.208	8	30.120.378	140

*   From the collection of H. Eugene Bolles.

Accession number	Catalogue number	Accession number	Catalogue number
31.30	87	† 52.77.47	3
34.100.16	64	† 52.77.49	4
34.128	103	† 52.77.50	24
35.117	40	† 52.77.51	23
36.112	121	† 52.77.52	50
36.115.2, .3	31	† 52.77.53	49
38.97	81	† 52.77.54	68
40.37.3	125	† 52.77.55	37
41.111	1	† 52.77.57	67
43.60	131	† 52.77.58	27
44.29	36	† 52.77.59	56
44.47	132	† 52.195.2	123
45.46	43	† 52.195.4	55
† 45.78.3	112	† 52.195.5	66
† 45.78.4	102	† 52.195.6	57
† 45.78.5	104	† 52.195.8, .9	30
† 45.78.8	80	† 53.197.1	116
† 47.103.13	44	62.171.23	41
47.133.3	86	† 66.190.1	93
48.61	20	† 66.190.2	74
48.122	32	† 69.209	105
† 48.158.9	95	1975.132.1	126
† 48.158.10	139	1975.310	16
† 48.158.11	110	† 1979.305	17
† 49.155.1	46	1980.499.1	65
† 49.155.2	106	1988.21	118
† 50.20.3	114	1991.255	135
† 50.228.1	39	1995.98	18
† 50.228.2	127	1997.68	9
† 51.12.1	58	1999.219.2	14
† 51.12.2	2		

†   From the collection of Natalie K. (Mrs. J. Insley) Blair.

Abbreviations

Following is a key to the abbreviations used in this book for the names of museums, collections, and one manuscript. Included in the list are those institutions for which the full address is usually not given in the text.

ADA
American Decorative Arts Department
The Metropolitan Museum of Art
New York City

Albany Institute
Albany Institute of History and Art
Albany, New York

Bayou Bend Collection
Bayou Bend Collection and Gardens
Houston, Texas

Bolles notes, MMA Archives
H. Eugene Bolles collection notes (undated manuscript)
The Metropolitan Museum of Art Archives
New York City

Buffalo Historical Society
Buffalo and Erie County Historical Society
Buffalo, New York

Chipstone Foundation
Chipstone Foundation
Milwaukee, Wisconsin

Colonial Williamsburg
Colonial Williamsburg
Williamsburg, Virginia

DAPC
Decorative Arts Photographic Collection
Winterthur Museum and Country Estate
Winterthur, Delaware

Darien Historical Society
Bates-Scofield Homestead
The Darien Historical Society
Darien, Connecticut

Dey Mansion, Wayne, New Jersey
Dey Mansion/Washington's Headquarters Museum
Wayne, New Jersey

Downs Manuscript Collection, Winterthur Museum
Joseph Downs Collection of Manuscripts and Printed Ephemera
Winterthur Library, Winterthur Museum and Country Estate
Winterthur, Delaware

Greenwich Historical Society
Historical Society of the Town of Greenwich / Bush-Holley
Historic Site
Cos Cob, Connecticut

Henry Ford Museum
The Henry Ford
Dearborn, Michigan

Historical Society of Old Newbury
Historical Sociey of Old Newbury
Cushing House Museum
Newburyport, Massachusetts

Historic Cherry Hill
Historic Cherry Hill
Albany, New York

Historic Deerfield
Historic Deerfield
Deerfield, Massachusetts

Historic Hudson Valley
Historic Hudson Valley
Tarrytown, New York

Historic New England
Historic New England
Boston, Massachusetts

Litchfield Historical Society
Litchfield Historical Society and Museum
Litchfield, Connecticut

MMA, the Museum
The Metropolitan Museum of Art
New York City

MMA Archives
The Metropolitan Museum of Art Archives
New York City

Museum of Fine Arts, Boston
Museum of Fine Arts, Boston
Boston, Massachusetts

Museum of Fine Arts, Houston
The Museum of Fine Arts, Houston
Houston, Texas

National Museum of American History
National Museum of American History
Smithsonian Institution
Washington, D.C.

New Haven Museum
New Haven Museum and Historical Society
New Haven, Connecticut

Newport Historical Society
Newport Historical Society and The Museum of Newport History
Newport, Rhode Island

New York State Historical Association, Cooperstown
New York State Historical Association / Fenimore Art Museum
Cooperstown, New York

Paul Revere House
Paul Revere House/Paul Revere Memorial Association
Boston, Massachusetts

Peabody Essex Museum
Peabody Essex Museum
Salem, Massachusetts

Philadelphia Museum of Art
Philadelphia Museum of Art
Philadelphia, Pennsylvania

Pocumtuck Valley Memorial Association
Memorial Hall Museum
Pocumtuck Valley Memorial Association
Deerfield, Massachusetts

Preservation Society of Newport County
Preservation Society of Newport County/The Newport Mansions
Newport, Rhode Island

Rhode Island School of Design
Museum of Art
Rhode Island School of Design
Providence, Rhode Island

Wadsworth Atheneum
Wadsworth Atheneum Museum of Art
Hartford, Connecticut

William Trent House, Trenton, New Jersey
The 1719 William Trent House Museum
Trenton, New Jersey

Winterthur Museum
Winterthur Museum and Country Estate
Winterthur, Delaware

Yale University Art Gallery
Yale University Art Gallery
New Haven, Connecticut

Bibliography

"Accessions" 1948
"Accessions for the Year 1947." *Historical New Hampshire* (New Hampshire Historical Society, Concord), February 1948, pp. 19–31.

Adamson 2002
Glenn Adamson. "The Politics of the Caned Chair." *American Furniture*, 2002, pp. 174–206.

Adamson 2005
Glenn Adamson. "Mannerism in Early American Furniture: Connoisseurship, Intention, and Theatricality." *American Furniture*, 2005, pp. 22–62.

"Additions to the American Wing" 1945
"Additions to the American Wing." *Antiques* 47 (January 1945), p. 50.

Alexander 1989
Forsyth M. Alexander. "Cabinet Warehousing in the Southern Atlantic Ports, 1783–1820." *Journal of Early Southern Decorative Arts* 15 (November 1989), pp. 1–42.

Ames 1961
Winslow Ames. "Swiss Export Table Tops." *Antiques* 80 (July 1961), pp. 46–49.

Anderson 1974
Robert L. Anderson. "Priceless Early American Museum Pieces You Can Copy." *Family Circle* 84 (May 1974), pp. 114–17.

Andrus 1951
Vincent D. Andrus. "Some Recent Gifts of Early New England Furniture." *The Metropolitan Museum of Art Bulletin*, n.s., 9 (May 1951), pp. 241–48.

Andrus 1952
Vincent D. Andrus. "American Furniture from the Blair Collection." *Antiques* 61 (February 1952), pp. 164–67.

"Antiques in the American Wing" 1946
"Antiques in the American Wing." *Antiques* 50 (October 1946), pp. 246–59. Special issue, *The American Wing of The Metropolitan Museum of Art.*

Arkell and Trent 1988
Peter Arkell and Robert F. Trent. "The Lawton Cupboard: A Unique Masterpiece of Early Boston Joinery and Turning." *Maine Antique Digest*, March 1988, pp. 1C–4C.

Art from the Collection of The Metropolitan Museum of Art 1981
Five Thousand Years of Art from the Collection of The Metropolitan Museum of Art. Exh. cat. Organized by The Metropolitan Museum of Art and the American Federation of Arts, New York, and shown at five museums in the United States. New York, 1981.

Baarsen et al. 1988
Reinier Baarsen, Gervase Jackson-Stops, Phillip M. Johnston, and Elaine Evans Dee. *Courts and Colonies: The William and Mary Style in Holland, England, and America.* Exh. cat., Cooper-Hewitt Museum, New York, and Carnegie Museum of Art, Pittsburgh, Pennsylvania. New York and Pittsburgh, 1988.

Bacon 1991
John Mark Bacon. "Delaware Valley Slatback Chairs: A Formal and Analytical Survey." Master's thesis, University of Delaware, 1991.

Bailey 1952
Richard B. Bailey. "Pilgrim Possessions, 1620–1640." *Antiques* 61 (March 1952), pp. 236–39.

Barnes and Meals 1972
Jairus B. Barnes and Moselle Taylor Meals. *American Furniture in the Western Reserve, 1680–1830.* Exh. cat., Western Reserve Historical Society. Western Reserve Historical Society Publication, no. 125. Cleveland, Ohio, 1972.

Barquist 1992
David L. Barquist. *American Tables and Looking Glasses in the Mabel Brady Garvan and Other Collections at Yale University.* With essays by Elisabeth Donaghy Garrett and Gerald W. R. Ward. New Haven, Conn., 1992.

Beck 1992
Thomasina Beck. *The Embroiderer's Flowers.* Newton Abbot, Devon, England, 1992.

Beckerdite 1997
Luke Beckerdite. "Religion, Artisanry, and Cultural Identity: The Huguenot Experience in South Carolina, 1680–1725." *American Furniture*, 1997, pp. 196–227.

Beckerdite 2000
Luke Beckerdite. "The Early Furniture of Christopher and Job Townsend." *American Furniture*, 2000, pp. 1–30.

Beckerdite and A. Miller 2002
Luke Beckerdite and Alan Miller. "Furniture Fakes from the Chipstone Collection." *American Furniture*, 2002, pp. 54–93.

Benes 1982
Peter Benes. *Two Towns, Concord and Wethersfield: A Comparative Exhibition of Regional Culture, 1635–1850.* Exh. cat., Concord Antiquarian Museum, Concord, Massachusetts; Connecticut Historical Society, Hartford; and Wethersfield Historical Society, Wethersfield, Connecticut. Concord, 1982.

Benes 1986
Peter Benes. *Old-Town and the Waterside: Two Hundred Years of Tradition and Change in Newbury, Newburyport, and West Newbury, 1635–1835.* Exh. cat., Cushing House Museum. Newburyport, Mass., 1986.

***Bicentennial Treasury* 1976**
A Bicentennial Treasury: American Masterpieces from the Metropolitan. Exh. cat., The Metropolitan Museum of Art. New York, 1976. Also issued as *The Metropolitan Museum of Art Bulletin*, n.s., 33 (Winter 1975–76).

Bishop 1972
Robert Bishop. *Centuries and Styles of the American Chair, 1640–1970.* New York, 1972.

Bishop 1975
Robert Bishop. *American Furniture, 1620–1720.* Dearborn, Mich., 1975.

Bissell 1956
Charles S. Bissell. *Antique Furniture in Suffield, Connecticut, 1670–1835.* Hartford and Suffield, Conn., 1956.

Bivins 1988
John Bivins Jr. *The Furniture of Coastal North Carolina, 1700–1820.* The Frank L. Horton Series. Winston-Salem, N.C., 1988.

Bjerkoe 1957
Ethel Hall Bjerkoe. *The Cabinetmakers of America.* Garden City, N.Y., 1957.

Blackburn 1981
Roderic H. Blackburn. "Branded and Stamped New York Furniture." *Antiques* 119 (May 1981), pp. 1130–45.

Blackburn 1984
Roderic H. Blackburn. "Dutch Decorative Painted Furniture since the Seventeenth Century." *Decorator* 38 (Spring 1984), pp. 18–27.

Blackburn 1986
Roderic H. Blackburn. "Dutch Arts and Culture in Colonial America." *Antiques* 130 (July 1986), pp. 140–51.

Blackburn and Piwonka 1988
Roderic H. Blackburn and Ruth Piwonka. *Remembrance of Patria: Dutch Arts and Culture in Colonial America, 1609–1776.* With an essay by Mary Black. Albany, N.Y., 1988. Based on an exhibition of the same title at the Albany Institute of History and Art in 1986.

Blades 1987
Margaret Bleecker Blades. *Two Hundred Years of Chairs and Chairmaking: An Exhibition of Chairs from the Chester County Historical Society.* Exh. cat., Chester County Historical Society. West Chester, Pa., 1987.

"Bolles Collection" 1909
"The Bolles Collection of American Furniture and Decorative Arts." *Bulletin of The Metropolitan Museum of Art* 4 (December 1909), pp. 219–20.

Bowett 1998
Adam Bowett. "The Age of Snakewood." *Furniture History* 34 (1998), pp. 212–25.

Bowett 2002
Adam Bowett. *English Furniture, 1660–1714: From Charles II to Queen Anne.* Woodbridge, Suffolk, England, 2002.

Brazer 1930
Esther Stevens Fraser [Brazer]. "Pioneer Furniture from Hampton, New Hampshire." *Antiques* 17 (April 1930), pp. 312–16.

Brazer 1933
Esther Stevens Fraser [Brazer]. "The Tantalizing Chests of Taunton." *Antiques* 23 (April 1933), pp. 135–38.

Brazer 1943
Esther Stevens [Fraser] Brazer. "The Early Boston Japanners." *Antiques* 43 (May 1943), pp. 208–11.

Buckley 1964
Charles E. Buckley. "The Furniture of New Hampshire." *Antiques* 86 (July 1964), frontispiece, p. 54, and pp. 56–61.

Buhler 1947
Kathryn C. Buhler. "Colonial Furniture and Silver: A Study of Parallels and Divergences." *Antiques* 51 (January 1947), pp. 36–39.

Bulkeley 1958
Houghton Bulkeley. "A Discovery on the Connecticut Chest." *Bulletin* (Connecticut Historical Society) 23 (January 1958), pp. 17–19.

Butler 1973
Joseph T. Butler. *American Furniture from the First Colonies to World War I.* London, 1973.

Butler 1983
Joseph T. Butler. *Sleepy Hollow Restorations: A Cross-Section of the Collection.* Tarrytown, N.Y., 1983.

Butt 1929
G. Baseden Butt. "Some North of England Chairs." *Antiques* 16 (November 1929), pp. 388–91.

Carr 2003
Dennis A. Carr. "Going Dutch: The Mott/Willis Family Kast." *Yale University Art Gallery Bulletin*, 2003, pp. 100–103.

Cescinsky and Hunter 1929
Herbert Cescinsky and George Leland Hunter. *English and American Furniture.* Grand Rapids, Mich., 1929.

S. Chamberlain and N. G. Chamberlain 1972
Samuel Chamberlain and Narcissa G. Chamberlain. *The Chamberlain Selection of New England Rooms, 1639–1863.* New York, 1972.

China Trade 1941
The China Trade and Its Influences. Exh. cat., The Metropolitan
Museum of Art. New York, 1941.

Chinnery 1979
Victor Chinnery. *Oak Furniture, the British Tradition: A History
of Early Furniture in the British Isles and New England.*
Woodbridge, Suffolk, England, 1979.

Clunie, Farnam, and Trent 1980
Margaret Burke Clunie, Anne Farnam, and Robert F. Trent. *Furniture
at the Essex Institute.* Essex Institute, Museum Booklet Series, 4.
Salem, Mass., 1980.

"Collectors' Notes" 1986
"Collectors' Notes." *Antiques* 130 (October 1986), pp. 646–47, 652.

Comstock 1942
Helen Comstock. "Transitional Features in American Chairs."
Antiques 41 (May 1942), pp. 312–14.

Comstock 1954
Helen Comstock. "An Ipswich Account Book, 1707–1762." *Antiques* 66
(September 1954), pp. 188–92.

Comstock 1957
Helen Comstock. "Spanish-Foot Furniture." *Antiques* 71 (January 1957),
pp. 58–61.

Comstock 1961
Helen Comstock. "The American Highboy: An Antiques Survey."
Antiques 80 (September 1961), pp. 228–31.

Comstock 1962
Helen Comstock. *American Furniture: Seventeenth, Eighteenth, and
Nineteenth Century Styles.* A Studio Book. New York, 1962.

Comstock 1963
Helen Comstock. "West St. Marys Manor: The Maryland Home
of Lieutenant Colonel and Mrs. Miodrag Blagojevich."
Antiques 83 (February 1963), pp. 186–89.

"Connecticut Chest" 1949
"A Connecticut Chest for the American Wing." *Antiques* 56
(August 1949), p. 127.

Connecticut Historical Society 1958
Connecticut Historical Society. *George Dudley Seymour's Furniture
Collection in the Connecticut Historical Society.* Catalogue
(Connecticut Historical Society), no. 2. Hartford, Conn., 1958.

Connecticut Historical Society 1963
Connecticut Historical Society. *Frederick K. and Margaret R. Barbour's
Furniture Collection.* Catalogue (Connecticut Historical Society),
no. 4. Hartford, Conn., 1963.

C. Cooke and Shorto 1979
Colin Cooke and Sylvia Shorto. "Some Notes on Early Bermudian
Furniture." *Antiques* 116 (August 1979), pp. 328–40.

E. S. Cooke 1987
Edward S. Cooke Jr. "The Warland Chest: Early Georgian Furniture
in Boston." *Maine Antique Digest*, March 1987, pp. 10C–13C.

Cooper 1980
Wendy A. Cooper. *In Praise of America: American Decorative Arts,
1650–1830. Fifty Years of Discovery since the 1929 Girl Scouts Loan
Exhibition.* New York, 1980.

Cooper 2002
Wendy A. Cooper. "H. F. du Pont's Fondness for Furniture: A
Collecting Odyssey." *Antiques* 161 (January 2002), pp. 158–63.

Cornelius 1926
Charles O. Cornelius. *Early American Furniture.* Century Library of
American Antiques. New York, 1926.

Cotton 1990
Bernard D. Cotton. *The English Regional Chair.* Woodbridge, Suffolk,
England, 1990.

Cullity 1987
Brian Cullity. *Plain and Fancy: New England Painted Furniture.*
Exh. cat., Heritage Plantation of Sandwich. Sandwich, Mass.,
1987.

Cullity 1994
Brian Cullity. *A Cubberd, Four Joyne Stools & Other Smalle Thinges:
The Material Culture of Plymouth Colony, and Silver and
Silversmiths of Plymouth, Cape Cod and Nantucket.* Exh. cat.,
Heritage Plantation of Sandwich. Sandwich, Mass., 1994.

A. L. Cummings 1961
Abbott Lowell Cummings, comp. *Bed Hangings: A Treatise on Fabrics
and Styles in the Curtaining of Beds, 1650–1850.* Boston, 1961.

A. L. Cummings 1964
Abbott Lowell Cummings, ed. *Rural Household Inventories,
1675–1775: Establishing the Names, Uses and Furnishings of
Rooms in the Colonial New England Home.* Boston, 1964.

A. L. Cummings 1971a
Abbott Lowell Cummings. "Decorative Painters and House Painting
at Massachusetts Bay, 1630–1725." In *American Painting to
1776: A Reappraisal*, edited by Ian M. G. Quimby, pp. 71–125.
Winterthur Conference Report, 1971. Charlottesville, Va., 1971.

A. L. Cummings 1971b
Abbott Lowell Cummings. "The Domestic Architecture of Boston,
1660–1725." *Archives of American Art Journal* 9, no. 4 (1971),
pp. 1–16.

A. L. Cummings 1979
Abbott Lowell Cummings. *The Framed Houses of Massachusetts Bay,
1625–1725.* Cambridge, Mass., 1979.

J. L. Cummings 1938
J. L. Cummings. "Painted Chests from the Connecticut Valley."
Antiques 34 (October 1938), pp. 192–93.

Currier Gallery of Art 1995
American Art from the Currier Gallery of Art. Exh. cat. by Karen
Blanchfield, John H. Dryfhout, William N. Hosley Jr., and
Carol Troyen. Organized by the Currier Gallery of Art,
Manchester, New Hampshire, and the American Federation
of Arts, New York, and held at the Orlando Museum of Art,
Orlando, Florida, and five other institutions. New York, 1995.

M. B. Davidson 1940
Marshall B. Davidson. "Colonial Cherubim in Silver." *Antiques* 37 (April 1940), pp. 184–86.

M. B. Davidson 1967
Marshall B. Davidson. *The American Heritage History of Colonial Antiques.* New York, 1967.

M. B. Davidson 1970
Marshall B. Davidson. "Those American Things." *Metropolitan Museum Journal* 3 (1970), pp. 219–33.

M. B. Davidson 1980
Marshall B. Davidson. *The American Wing: A Guide.* New York, 1980.

M. B. Davidson and Stillinger 1985
Marshall B. Davidson and Elizabeth Stillinger. *The American Wing at The Metropolitan Museum of Art.* New York, 1985.

R. Davidson 1968
Ruth Davidson. "Museum Accessions." *Antiques* 94 (July 1968), pp. 50, 54, 58, 108, 110, 112, 114.

Davis 1925
Felice Davis. "American Furniture: Assemblage of Colonial Pieces in the New Wing at Metropolitan Museum." *Antiquarian* 5 (August 1925), pp. 5–12, 38.

Decatur 1938
Stephen Decatur. "George and John Gaines of Portsmouth, N.H." *American Collector* 7 (November 1938), pp. 6–7.

***Decorative Arts of New Hampshire* 1973**
The Decorative Arts of New Hampshire: A Sesquicentennial Exhibition. Exh. cat., New Hampshire Historical Society. Concord, N.H., 1973.

Deneke 1979
Bernward Deneke. *Bauernmöbel: Ein Handbuch für Sammler und Liebhaber.* 3rd ed. Munich, Germany, 1979.

Despard and Greatorex 1875
Old New York from the Battery to Bloomingdale. Text by Matilda Despard and etchings by Eliza Greatorex. New York, 1875.

Dilliard 1963
Maud Esther Dilliard. *An Album of New Netherland.* New York, 1963.

Dow 1927
George Francis Dow. *The Arts and Crafts in New England, 1704–1775.* Topsfield, Mass., 1927.

Downs 1933
Joseph Downs. "American Japanned Furniture." *Bulletin of The Metropolitan Museum of Art* 28 (March 1933), pp. 42–48.

Downs 1936
Joseph Downs. "A New England Wing Chair." *Bulletin of The Metropolitan Museum of Art* 31 (April 1936), p. 84.

Downs 1937a
Joseph Downs. "An Early New York Highboy." *Bulletin of The Metropolitan Museum of Art* 32 (February 1937), pp. 40–41.

Downs 1937b
Joseph Downs. "A Gift of Furniture." *Bulletin of The Metropolitan Museum of Art* 32 (August 1937), pp. 199–200.

Downs 1940a
Joseph Downs. "American Japanned Furniture." *Bulletin of The Metropolitan Museum of Art* 35 (July 1940), pp. 145–48.

Downs 1940b
Joseph Downs. "A Loan of American Furniture." *Bulletin of The Metropolitan Museum of Art* 35 (January 1940), pp. 20–21.

Downs 1944
Joseph Downs. "Recent Additions to the American Wing." *The Metropolitan Museum of Art Bulletin*, n.s., 3 (November 1944), pp. 78–83.

Downs 1945
Joseph Downs. "Recent Additions to the American Wing." *The Metropolitan Museum of Art Bulletin*, n.s., 4 (October 1945), pp. 66–72.

Downs 1946
Joseph Downs. "On Collecting American Furniture." *American Collector* 15 (April 1946), pp. 12–14, 22.

Downs 1948
Joseph Downs. "Recent Additions to the American Wing." *The Metropolitan Museum of Art Bulletin*, n.s., 7 (November 1948), pp. 79–85.

Downs 1949
Joseph Downs. "Reports of the Departments: The American Wing." *The Metropolitan Museum of Art Bulletin*, n.s., 8 (Summer 1949), pp. 15, 17.

Downs 1952
Joseph Downs. *American Furniture in the Henry Francis du Pont Winterthur Museum: Queen Anne and Chippendale Periods.* New York, 1952.

Downs and Ralston 1934
Joseph Downs and Ruth Ralston. *A Loan Exhibition of New York State Furniture, with Contemporary Accessories.* Exh. cat., The Metropolitan Museum of Art. New York, 1934.

Drepperd 1940
Carl W. Drepperd. "Origins of Pennsylvania Folk Art." *Antiques* 37 (February 1940), pp. 64–68.

Dyer 1930a
Walter A. Dyer. "The Iconography of the Banister-Back Chair." *Antiquarian* 15 (August 1930), pp. 30–32, 56.

Dyer 1930b
Walter A. Dyer. "Maple: Craze or Appreciation?" *Antiquarian* 14 (April 1930), pp. 62–64, 92.

Dyer 1931a
Walter A. Dyer. "The American Chest: Seventeenth Century." *Antiquarian* 17 (October 1931), pp. 36–40.

Dyer 1931b
Walter A. Dyer. "Butterflies." *Antiquarian* 16 (April 1931), pp. 40–44, 76.

Dyer 1935
Walter A. Dyer. "The Tulip-and-Sunflower Press Cupboard." *Antiques* 27 (April 1935), pp. 140–43.

Eames 1977
Penelope Eames. "Furniture in England, France and the Netherlands from the Twelfth to the Fifteenth Century." *Furniture History* 13 (1977).

***Early American Furniture* 1925**
Loan Exhibition of Early American Furniture and the Decorative Crafts, for the Benefit of Free Hospital for Women, Brookline, Mass. Exh. cat., Park Square Building. Boston, 1925.

"Early American Furniture" 1935
"Masterpieces of Early American Furniture in Private Collections. II." *Antiques* 28 (November 1935), frontispiece, p. 184.

"Early New Hampshire Painted Decoration" 1964
"Early New Hampshire Painted Decoration." *Antiques* 86 (July 1964), pp. 85–86.

R. Edwards 1964
Ralph Edwards. *The Shorter Dictionary of English Furniture, from the Middle Ages to the Late Georgian Period.* London, 1964.

S. C. S. Edwards 1983
Susan Clendon Storer Edwards. "The Mission House, Stockbridge, Massachusetts." *Antiques* 123 (March 1983), pp. 586–93.

Elder and J. E. Stokes 1987
William Voss Elder III and Jayne E. Stokes. *American Furniture, 1680–1880, from the Collection of the Baltimore Museum of Art.* Baltimore, Md., 1987.

Erving 1931
Henry Wood Erving. *Random Notes on Colonial Furniture: A Paper Read before the Connecticut Historical Society in 1922 and Now Revised.* Hartford, Conn., 1931.

Erving 1935
Henry Wood Erving. "Random Recollections of an Early Collector." In *Meeting of the Walpole Society* 1935, pp. 27–43.

J. Evans 1966
Joan Evans, ed. *The Flowering of the Middle Ages.* New York, 1966.

R. T. Evans 1928
Robert Tasker Evans. "When Chairs Were Rare." *Antiquarian* 11 (November 1928), pp. 52–53, 86.

Fabend 1981
Firth Haring Fabend. "Two 'New' Eighteenth-Century Grisaille Kasten." *Clarion*, Spring–Summer 1981, pp. 44–49.

Failey 1976
Dean F. Failey. *Long Island Is My Nation: The Decorative Arts and Craftsmen, 1640–1830.* Exh. cat. Organized by the Society for the Preservation of Long Island Antiquities and held at the Museums at Stony Brook, Stony Brook, New York. Setauket, N.Y., 1976.

Failey 1979
Dean F. Failey. "The Furniture Tradition of Long Island's South Fork, 1640–1800." *American Art Journal* 11 (January 1979), pp. 49–64.

Failey 1998
Dean F. Failey. *Long Island Is My Nation: The Decorative Arts and Craftsmen, 1640–1830.* 2nd ed., with "New Discoveries" (pp. 9-1–9-49). Cold Spring Harbor, N.Y., 1998. [1st ed., 1976.]

Fairbanks 1981
Jonathan L. Fairbanks. "A Decade of Collecting American Decorative Arts and Sculpture at the Museum of Fine Arts, Boston." *Antiques* 120 (September 1981), pp. 590–636.

Fairbanks 1982
Jonathan L. Fairbanks. "Portrait Painting in Seventeenth-Century Boston: Its History, Methods, and Materials." In Fairbanks and Trent 1982, pp. 413–55.

Fairbanks and Bates 1981
Jonathan L. Fairbanks and Elizabeth Bidwell Bates. *American Furniture, 1620 to the Present.* New York, 1981.

Fairbanks and Trent 1982
Jonathan L. Fairbanks and Robert F. Trent, et al. *New England Begins: The Seventeenth Century.* 3 vols. Exh. cat., Museum of Fine Arts, Boston. Boston, 1982.

Fales 1972
Dean A. Fales Jr. *American Painted Furniture, 1660–1880.* New York, 1972.

Fales 1974
Dean A. Fales Jr. "Boston Japanned Furniture." In *Boston Furniture of the Eighteenth Century: A Conference Held by the Colonial Society of Massachusetts, 11 and 12 May 1972*, edited by Walter Muir Whitehill, Brock Jobe, and Jonathan L. Fairbanks, pp. 49–69. Publications of the Colonial Society of Massachusetts, vol. 48. Boston, 1974.

Fales 1976
Dean A. Fales Jr. *The Furniture of Historic Deerfield.* New York, 1976.

Félice 1923
Roger de Félice. *French Furniture in the Middle Ages and under Louis XIII.* Translated by F. M. Atkinson. Little Illustrated Books on Old French Furniture, 1. London, 1923.

Fennimore 1991
Donald L. Fennimore. "Gilding Practices and Processes in Nineteenth-Century American Furniture." In *Gilded Wood: Conservation and History*, edited by Deborah Bigelow et al., pp. 139–51. Proceedings of the Gilding Conservation Symposium at the Philadelphia Museum of Art, October 1988. Madison, Conn., 1991.

Filbee 1977
Marjorie Filbee. *Dictionary of Country Furniture.* London, 1977.

Fitzgerald 1982
Oscar P. Fitzgerald. *Three Centuries of American Furniture.* Englewood Cliffs, N.J., 1982.

Flanigan 1986
J. Michael Flanigan. *American Furniture from the Kaufman Collection.* Exh. cat., National Gallery of Art. Washington, D.C., 1986.

Follansbee and Alexander 1996
Peter Follansbee and John D. Alexander. "Seventeenth-Century Joinery from Braintree, Massachusetts: The Savell Shop Tradition." *American Furniture*, 1996, pp. 81–104.

Forman 1968
Benno M. Forman. "The Seventeenth Century Case Furniture of Essex County, Massachusetts, and Its Makers." Master's thesis, University of Delaware, 1968.

Forman 1970
Benno M. Forman. "Urban Aspects of Massachusetts Furniture in the Late Seventeenth Century." In *Country Cabinetwork and Simple City Furniture*, edited by John D. Morse, pp. 1–33. Winterthur Conference Report, 1969. Charlottesville, Va., 1970.

Forman 1980
Benno M. Forman. "Delaware Valley 'Crookt Foot' and Slat-Back Chairs: The Fussell-Savery Connection." *Winterthur Portfolio* 15 (Spring 1980), pp. 41–64.

Forman 1983
Benno M. Forman. "German Influences in Pennsylvania Furniture." In Scott T. Swank, with Benno M. Forman et al., *Arts of the Pennsylvania Germans*, edited by Catherine E. Hutchins, pp. 102–70. A Winterthur Book. New York, 1983.

Forman 1985
Benno M. Forman. "The Chest of Drawers in America, 1635–1730: The Origins of the Joined Chest of Drawers." *Winterthur Portfolio* 20 (Spring 1985), pp. 1–30.

Forman 1987
Benno M. Forman. "Furniture for Dressing in Early America, 1650–1730: Forms, Nomenclature, and Use." *Winterthur Portfolio* 22 (Summer–Autumn 1987), pp. 149–64.

Forman 1988
Benno M. Forman. *American Seating Furniture, 1630–1730: An Interpretive Catalogue.* A Winterthur Book. New York, 1988.

Frazier 1983
Ronald F. Frazier. "The General Sylvanus Thayer Birthplace." *Antiques* 123 (May 1983), pp. 1027–35.

Gaines 1957
Edith Gaines. "The Step-Top Highboy." *Antiques* 72 (October 1957), pp. 332–34.

Gardner and Feld 1965
Albert Ten Eyck Gardner and Stuart P. Feld. *American Paintings: A Catalogue of the Collection of The Metropolitan Museum of Art.* Vol. 1, *Painters Born by 1815.* New York, 1965.

Garrett 1978
Elisabeth Donaghy Garrett. "Living with Antiques: The Residence of Mr. and Mrs. George J. Dittmar Jr. in Monmouth County, New Jersey." *Antiques* 113 (April 1978), pp. 830–37.

Garvin 1993
James L. Garvin. "'That Little World, Portsmouth.'" In Jobe 1993, pp. 14–35.

Geib 1982
Susan Geib. "Hammersmith: The Saugus Ironworks as an Example of Early Industrialism." In Fairbanks and Trent 1982, pp. 352–53.

Geller 1970
Lawrence D. Geller. *The Pilgrim Hall Museum after 350 Years.* Pilgrim Society Booklet Series. Plymouth, Mass., 1970.

Ginsburg 1962
Benjamin Ginsburg. "Addendum to the Slate-Top Story." *Antiques* 82 (July 1962), pp. 78–79.

Girl Scouts 1929
Loan Exhibition of Eighteenth and Early Nineteenth Century Furniture and Glass . . . for the Benefit of the National Council of Girl Scouts, Inc. Exh. cat., American Art Galleries. New York, 1929.

Gonzales and Brown 1996
Roger Gonzales and Daniel Putnam Brown Jr. "Boston and New York Leather Chairs: A Reappraisal." *American Furniture*, 1996, pp. 175–94.

Graybeal and Kenny 1987
Jay A. Graybeal and Peter M. Kenny. "The William Efner Wheelock Collection at the East Hampton Historical Society." *Antiques* 132 (August 1987), pp. 328–39.

Great River 1985
The Great River: Art and Society of the Connecticut Valley, 1635–1820. Exh. cat. by William N. Hosley Jr. et al. Wadsworth Atheneum. Hartford, Conn., 1985.

Greene 1996
Jeffrey P. Greene. *American Furniture of the Eighteenth Century.* Newtown, Conn., 1996.

Greenlaw 1974
Barry A. Greenlaw. *New England Furniture at Williamsburg.* The Williamsburg Decorative Arts Series. Williamsburg, Va., 1974.

Griffith 1986
Lee Ellen Griffith. *The Pennsylvania Spice Box: Paneled Doors and Secret Drawers.* Exh. cat., Chester County Historical Society, West Chester, Pennsylvania, and Museum of Art, Carnegie Institute, Pittsburgh, Pennsylvania. West Chester, 1986.

Groft and Mackay 1998
Tammis K. Groft and Mary Alice Mackay, eds. *Albany Institute of History and Art: Two Hundred Years of Collecting.* New York, 1998.

Gronning 2001
Erik K. Gronning. "Early New York Turned Chairs: A *Stoelendraaier's* Conceit." *American Furniture*, 2001, pp. 88–119.

Gronning 2003
Erik K. Gronning. "New Haven's Six-Board Chests." *Antiques* 163 (May 2003), pp. 116–21.

Gronning and Carr 2004
Erik K. Gronning and Dennis A. Carr. "Rhode Island Gateleg Tables." *Antiques* 165 (May 2004), pp. 122–27.

Gustafson 1977
Eleanor H. Gustafson. "Museum Accessions." *Antiques* 111 (May 1977), pp. 910–11, 914, 924, 930.

Guyol 1958
Philip N. Guyol. "The Prentis Collection [at the New Hampshire Historical Society]." Reprint, with revisions, from *Historical New Hampshire* (New Hampshire Historical Society, Concord) 14 (December 1958), pp. 9–16.

Haemmerle 1961
Albert Haemmerle. *Buntpapier: Herkommen, Geschichte, Techniken, Beziehungen zur Kunst.* Munich, Germany, 1961.

Halsey and Cornelius 1924
R. T. H. Halsey and Charles O. Cornelius. *A Handbook of the American Wing.* New York, 1924.

Halsey and Cornelius 1925
R. T. H. Halsey and Charles O. Cornelius. *A Handbook of the American Wing.* 2nd ed. New York, 1925.

Halsey and Cornelius 1926
R. T. H. Halsey and Charles O. Cornelius. *A Handbook of the American Wing.* 3rd ed. New York, 1926.

Halsey and Cornelius 1928
R. T. H. Halsey and Charles O. Cornelius. *A Handbook of the American Wing.* 4th ed. New York, 1928.

Halsey and Cornelius 1932
R. T. H. Halsey and Charles O. Cornelius. *A Handbook of the American Wing.* 5th ed. New York, 1932.

Halsey and Cornelius 1938
R. T. H. Halsey and Charles O. Cornelius. *A Handbook of the American Wing.* 6th ed. Revised by Joseph Downs. New York, 1938.

Halsey and Cornelius 1942
R. T. H. Halsey and Charles O. Cornelius. *A Handbook of the American Wing.* 7th ed. Revised by Joseph Downs. New York, 1942.

Halsey and Tower 1925
R. T. H. Halsey and Elizabeth Tower. *The Homes of Our Ancestors as Shown in the American Wing of The Metropolitan Museum of Art.* Garden City, N.Y., 1925.

Harvard Tercentenary Exhibition 1936
Harvard Tercentenary Exhibition: Catalogue of Furniture, Silver, Pewter, Glass, Ceramics, Paintings, Prints, Together with Allied Arts and Crafts of the Period, 1636–1836. Exh. cat., Robinson Hall, School of Architecture, Harvard University. Cambridge, Mass., 1936.

Heckscher 1971a
Morrison H. Heckscher. "Form and Frame: New Thoughts on the American Easy Chair." *Antiques* 100 (December 1971), pp. 886–93.

Heckscher 1971b
Morrison H. Heckscher. *In Quest of Comfort: The Easy Chair in America.* Exh. cat., The Metropolitan Museum of Art. New York, 1971.

Heckscher 1985
Morrison H. Heckscher. *American Furniture in The Metropolitan Museum of Art.* Vol. 2, *Late Colonial Period: The Queen Anne and Chippendale Styles.* New York, 1985.

Heckscher 1998
Morrison H. Heckscher. "American Furniture and the Art of Connoisseurship." *Antiques* 153 (May 1998), pp. 722–29.

Heckscher 2000
Morrison H. Heckscher. "Natalie K. Blair's 'Museum Rooms' and the American Wing." *Antiques* 157 (January 2000), pp. 182–85.

Heckscher and Safford 1986
Morrison H. Heckscher and Frances Gruber Safford. "Boston Japanned Furniture in The Metropolitan Museum of Art." With a conservation note by Peter Lawrence Fodera. *Antiques* 129 (May 1986), pp. 1046–61. See also "Collectors' Notes," *Antiques* 130 (1986), p. 652 (where a typesetter's error is corrected).

Hendrick 1964
Robert E. P. Hendrick. "John Gaines II and Thomas Gaines I: 'Turners' of Ipswich, Massachusetts." Master's thesis, University of Delaware, 1964.

Hill 1976
John H. Hill. "The History and Technique of Japanning and the Restoration of the Pimm Highboy." *American Art Journal* 8 (November 1976), pp. 59–84.

Hitchings 1974
Sinclair H. Hitchings. "Boston's Colonial Japanners: The Documentary Record." In *Boston Furniture of the Eighteenth Century: A Conference Held by the Colonial Society of Massachusetts, 11 and 12 May 1972*, edited by Walter Muir Whitehill, Brock Jobe, and Jonathan L. Fairbanks, pp. 71–75. Publications of the Colonial Society of Massachusetts, vol. 48. Boston, 1974.

Hjorth 1946
Herman Hjorth. "Early American Furniture." *Science and Mechanics*, April 1946, pp. 96, 98, 100, 102–6, 108.

Holland House Corporation of the Netherlands 1941
Holland House Corporation of the Netherlands. *A Loan Exhibition of Dutch Colonial Heirlooms.* Exh. cat., Holland House. New York, 1941.

Holloway 1928
Edward Stratton Holloway. *American Furniture and Decoration: Colonial and Federal.* Philadelphia, 1928.

Hopkins and Cox 1936
Thomas Smith Hopkins and Walter Scott Cox, comps. *Colonial Furniture of West New Jersey.* Haddonfield, N.J., 1936.

Hornor 1935
William MacPherson Hornor Jr. *Blue Book: Philadelphia Furniture, William Penn to George Washington.* Philadelphia, 1935. 2nd printing, Washington, D.C., 1977.

Hornung 1972
Clarence P. Hornung. *Treasury of American Design: A Pictorial Survey of Popular Folk Arts Based upon Watercolor Renderings in the Index of American Design, at the National Gallery of Art.* 2 vols. New York, 1972.

Horton 1967
Frank L. Horton. "The Museum of Early Southern Decorative Arts: The Rooms and Their Furnishings." *Antiques* 91 (January 1967), pp. 72–95.

Hosley 1984
William N. Hosley Jr. "The Wallace Nutting Collection at the Wadsworth Atheneum, Hartford, Connecticut." *Antiques* 126 (October 1984), pp. 860–74.

Howells 1931
John Mead Howells. *Lost Examples of Colonial Architecture.* New York, 1931.

Hudson-Fulton Celebration 1909
The Hudson-Fulton Celebration: Catalogue of an Exhibition Held in The Metropolitan Museum of Art, Commemorative of the Tercentenary of the Discovery of the Hudson River by Henry Hudson in the Year 1609, and the Centenary of the First Use of Steam in the Navigation of Said River by Robert Fulton in the Year 1807. Exh. cat., The Metropolitan Museum of Art. Vol. 2, *Catalogue of an Exhibition of American Paintings, Furniture, Silver and Other Objects of Art, MDCXXV–MDCCCXXV*, by Henry W. Kent and Florence N. Levy. New York, 1909.

Hughes 1962
Judith Coolidge Hughes. "Courting Mirrors: Another European Export Product?" *Antiques* 82 (July 1962), pp. 68–71.

Hurst and Prown 1997
Ronald L. Hurst and Jonathan Prown. *Southern Furniture, 1680–1830: The Colonial Williamsburg Collection.* Williamsburg Decorative Arts Series. Williamsburg, Va., 1997.

Huth 1971
Hans Huth. *Lacquer of the West: The History of a Craft and an Industry, 1550–1950.* Chicago, 1971.

Hyde 1971
Bryden Bordley Hyde. *Bermuda's Antique Furniture and Silver.* Hamilton, Bermuda, 1971.

Iverson 1957
Marion Day Iverson. *The American Chair, 1630–1890.* New York, 1957.

Jeffcott 1944
June Johnson Jeffcott. "We Are Collecting Our Home." *Antiques* 45 (May 1944), pp. 253–55.

Jervis 1974
Simon Jervis. *Printed Furniture Designs before 1650.* Leeds, Yorkshire, England, 1974.

Jobe 1974
Brock Jobe. "The Boston Furniture Industry, 1720–1740." In *Boston Furniture of the Eighteenth Century: A Conference Held by the Colonial Society of Massachusetts, 11 and 12 May 1972*, edited by Walter Muir Whitehill, Brock Jobe, and Jonathan L. Fairbanks, pp. 3–48. Publications of the Colonial Society of Massachusetts, vol. 48. Boston, 1974.

Jobe 1993
Brock Jobe, ed. *Portsmouth Furniture: Masterworks from the New Hampshire Seacoast.* Exh. cat. Organized by the Society for the Preservation of New England Antiquities and held at the Currier Gallery of Art, Manchester, New Hampshire, Wadsworth Atheneum, Hartford, Connecticut, and Portland Museum of Art, Portland, Maine. Boston, 1993.

Jobe and Kaye 1984
Brock Jobe and Myrna Kaye, with Philip Zea. *New England Furniture: The Colonial Era. Selections from the Society for the Preservation of New England Antiquities.* Boston, 1984.

Jobe et al. 1991
Brock Jobe, Thomas S. Michie, Jayne E. Stokes, Robert F. Trent, Anne H. Vogel, and Philip D. Zimmerman. *American Furniture with Related Decorative Arts, 1660–1830: The Milwaukee Art Museum and the Layton Art Collection.* Edited by Gerald W. R. Ward. New York, 1991.

Johnston 1988
Phillip M. Johnston. "The William and Mary Style in America." In Baarsen et al. 1988, pp. 62–79.

Kamil 1995
Neil D. Kamil. "Hidden in Plain Sight: Disappearance and Material Life in Colonial New York." *American Furniture*, 1995, pp. 191–249.

Kane 1970
Patricia E. Kane. "The Joiners of Seventeenth Century Hartford County." *Bulletin* (Connecticut Historical Society) 35 (July 1970), pp. 65–85.

Kane 1973a
Patricia E. Kane. *Furniture of the New Haven Colony: The Seventeenth-Century Style.* Exh. cat., New Haven Colony Historical Society. New Haven, Conn., 1973.

Kane 1973b
Patricia E. Kane. "New Haven Colony Furniture: The Seventeenth-Century Style." *Antiques* 103 (May 1973), pp. 950–62.

Kane 1975
Patricia E. Kane. "The Seventeenth-Century Furniture of the Connecticut Valley: The Hadley Chest Reappraised." In *Arts of the Anglo-American Community in the Seventeenth Century*, edited by Ian M. G. Quimby, pp. 79–122. Winterthur Conference Report, 1974. Charlottesville, Va., 1975.

Kane 1976
Patricia E. Kane. *Three Hundred Years of American Seating Furniture: Chairs and Beds from the Mabel Brady Garvan and Other Collections at Yale University.* Boston, 1976.

Kane 1993
Patricia E. Kane. *Furniture of the New Haven Colony: The Seventeenth-Century Style.* 2nd ed., with addendum. New Haven, Conn., 1993. [1st ed., 1973.]

Kaye 1982
Myrna Kaye. "Concord Case Furniture: Cabinetry Twenty Miles from the Bay." In *The Bay and the River: 1600–1900*, edited by Peter Benes, pp. 29–42. Dublin Seminar for New England Folklife: Annual Proceedings, 1981. Boston, 1982.

Kenny 1994
Peter M. Kenny. "Flat Gates, Draw Bars, Twists, and Urns: New York's Distinctive, Early Baroque Oval Tables with Falling Leaves." *American Furniture*, 1994, pp. 106–35.

Kenny, Safford, and Vincent 1991a
Peter M. Kenny, Frances Gruber Safford, and Gilbert T. Vincent. *American Kasten: The Dutch-Style Cupboards of New York and New Jersey, 1650–1800.* Exh. cat., The Metropolitan Museum of Art. New York, 1991.

Kenny, Safford, and Vincent 1991b
Peter M. Kenny, Frances Gruber Safford, and Gilbert T. Vincent. "The Eighteenth-Century American *Kast.*" *Antiques* 139 (February 1991), pp. 398–411.

Kent 1910
Henry W. Kent. "The Bolles Collection: The Gift of Mrs. Russell Sage." *Bulletin of The Metropolitan Museum of Art* 5 (January 1910), pp. 14–16 and pp. 1, 5–13.

Kettell 1929
Russell Hawes Kettell. *The Pine Furniture of Early New England.* Garden City, N.Y., 1929.

Keyes 1923
Homer Eaton Keyes. "The Editor's Attic." *Antiques* 4 (October 1923), pp. 162–65.

Keyes 1924
Homer Eaton Keyes. "Some Pennsylvania Furniture." *Antiques* 5 (May 1924), pp. 222–25.

Keyes 1927
Homer Eaton Keyes. "New Wings for an Old Butterfly." *Antiques* 11 (February 1927), p. 112.

Keyes 1931
Homer Eaton Keyes. "The Anatomy of a Cupboard." *Antiques* 19 (March 1931), pp. 200–203.

Keyes 1932
Homer Eaton Keyes. "A Study in Differences." *Antiques* 22 (July 1932), pp. 6–7.

Keyes 1934
Homer Eaton Keyes. "Identifying Traits in New York Furniture." *Antiques* 26 (October 1934), pp. 144–46.

Keyes 1935
Homer Eaton Keyes. "The Individuality of Connecticut Furniture." *Antiques* 28 (September 1935), pp. 110–13.

Keyes 1936
Homer Eaton Keyes. "The Editor's Attic." *Antiques* 29 (March 1936), pp. 95–97.

Keyes 1938
Homer Eaton Keyes. "Dennis or a Lesser Light?" *Antiques* 34 (December 1938), pp. 296–300.

Kindig 1978
Joseph K. Kindig III. *The Philadelphia Chair, 1685–1785.* Exh. cat., Historical Society of York County. York, Pa., 1978.

King and Levey 1993
Donald King and Santina Levey. *The Victoria and Albert Museum's Textile Collection: Embroidery in Britain from 1200 to 1750.* London, 1993.

Kirk 1965
John T. Kirk. "Sources of Some American Regional Furniture. Part I." *Antiques* 88 (December 1965), pp. 790–98.

Kirk 1967
John T. Kirk. *Connecticut Furniture: Seventeenth and Eighteenth Centuries.* Exh. cat., Wadsworth Atheneum. Hartford, Conn., 1967.

Kirk 1970
John T. Kirk. *Early American Furniture: How to Recognize, Evaluate, Buy, and Care for the Most Beautiful Pieces—High-Style, Country, Primitive, and Rustic.* New York, 1970.

Kirk 1982
John T. Kirk. *American Furniture and the British Tradition to 1830.* New York, 1982.

Knell 1992
David Knell. *English Country Furniture: The National and Regional Vernacular, 1500–1900.* London, 1992.

Krill 2002
John Krill. *English Artists' Paper: Renaissance to Regency.* 2nd ed. New Castle and Winterthur, Del., 2002.

T. P. Kugelman and A. K. Kugelman 2005
Thomas P. Kugelman and Alice K. Kugelman, with Robert Lionetti. *Connecticut Valley Furniture: Eliphalet Chapin and His Contemporaries, 1750–1800.* With essays by Susan Prendergast Schoelwer, Robert F. Trent, and Philip D. Zimmerman. Hartford, Conn., 2005.

Lane and White 2003
Joshua W. Lane and Donald P. White III. *Woodworkers of Windsor: A Connecticut Community of Craftsmen and Their World, 1635–1715.* Exh. cat., Flynt Center of Early New England Life, Historic Deerfield, Deerfield, Massachusetts, and Windsor Historical Society, Windsor, Connecticut. Deerfield, 2003.

Lavallée 1990
Daniel Lavallée. *Le Meuble haut-normand, des origines à 1700.* Luneray, France, 1990.

Leath 1994
Robert A. Leath. "Jean Berger's Design Book: Huguenot Tradesmen and the Dissemination of French Baroque Style." *American Furniture*, 1994, pp. 136–61.

Leath 1997
Robert A. Leath. "Dutch Trade and Its Influence on Seventeenth-Century Chesapeake Furniture." *American Furniture*, 1997, pp. 21–46.

Le Clerc 1924
Léon Le Clerc. *Le Mobilier normand (ensemble & détails).* Collection de l'art régional en France. Paris, 1924.

Lee 1930
Anne Lee. "Colonial Furniture." *Good Furniture and Decoration* 34 (February 1930), pp. 73–84.

Lindsey 1999
Jack L. Lindsey. *Worldly Goods: The Arts of Early Pennsylvania, 1680–1758.* With essays by Richard S. Dunn, Edward C. Carter II, and Richard Saunders. Exh. cat., Philadelphia Museum of Art. Philadelphia, 1999.

F. Little 1931
Frances Little. *Early American Textiles.* Century Library of American Antiques. New York, 1931.

N. F. Little 1952
Nina Fletcher Little. *American Decorative Wall Painting, 1700–1850.* Sturbridge, Mass., 1952.

N. F. Little 1984
Nina Fletcher Little. *Little by Little: Six Decades of Collecting American Decorative Arts.* New York, 1984.

"Living with Antiques" 1950
"Living with Antiques: The Connecticut Home of Mrs. Katharine Prentis Murphy." *Antiques* 57 (June 1950), pp. 432–36.

Lloyd 1983
Mark Frazier Lloyd. "Germantown, 1683–1983." *Antiques* 124 (August 1983), pp. 254–58.

Lockwood 1901
Luke Vincent Lockwood. *Colonial Furniture in America.* New York, 1901.

Lockwood 1904
Luke Vincent Lockwood. *The Pendleton Collection.* Providence, R.I., 1904.

Lockwood 1908
Luke Vincent Lockwood. "English Furniture of the Eighteenth Century." *Bulletin of The Metropolitan Museum of Art* 3 (June 1908), pp. 111–14.

Lockwood 1913
Luke Vincent Lockwood. *Colonial Furniture in America.* New and enlarged ed. 2 vols. New York, 1913.

Lockwood 1923
Luke Vincent Lockwood. "Nicholas Disbrowe: Hartford Joyner." *Bulletin of The Metropolitan Museum of Art* 18 (May 1923), pp. 118–23.

Lockwood 1926
Luke Vincent Lockwood. *Colonial Furniture in America.* 3rd ed., with supplementary chapters. 2 vols. New York, 1926.

Luther 1935
Clair Franklin Luther. *The Hadley Chest.* Hartford, Conn., 1935.

Lyle and Bloch 1972
Charles T. Lyle and Milton J. Bloch. *New Jersey Arts and Crafts: The Colonial Expression.* Exh. cat. Organized by the Monmouth Museum and the Monmouth County Parks System, Lincroft, New Jersey, and the Monmouth County Historical Association, Freehold, New Jersey, and held at the Monmouth Museum. Lincroft and Freehold, 1972.

Lynes 1933
Wilson Lynes. "Slat-Back Chairs of New England and the Middle-Atlantic States. Part I." *Antiques* 24 (December 1933), pp. 208–10.

Lynes 1934
Wilson Lynes. "Slat-Back Chairs of New England and the Middle-Atlantic States. Part II." *Antiques* 25 (March 1934), pp. 104–7, 116.

I. P. Lyon 1937a
Irving P. Lyon. "The Oak Furniture of Ipswich, Massachusetts. Part I. Florid Type. Dennis-Family Furniture." *Antiques* 32 (November 1937), pp. 230–33.

I. P. Lyon 1937b
Irving P. Lyon. "The Oak Furniture of Ipswich, Massachusetts. Part II. Florid Type. Miscellaneous Examples." *Antiques* 32 (December 1937), pp. 298–301.

I. P. Lyon 1938a
Irving P. Lyon. "The Oak Furniture of Ipswich, Massachusetts. Part III. Florid Type. Scroll Detail." *Antiques* 33 (February 1938), pp. 73–75.

I. P. Lyon 1938b
Irving P. Lyon. "The Oak Furniture of Ipswich, Massachusetts. Part IV. The Small-Panel Type." *Antiques* 33 (April 1938), pp. 198–203.

I. P. Lyon 1938c
Irving P. Lyon. "The Oak Furniture of Ipswich, Massachusetts. Part V. Small-Panel-Type Affiliates." *Antiques* 33 (June 1938), pp. 322–25.

I. P. Lyon 1938d
Irving P. Lyon. "The Oak Furniture of Ipswich, Massachusetts.
    Part VI. Other Affiliates. A Group Characterized by
    Geometrical Panels." *Antiques* 34 (August 1938), pp. 79–81.

I. W. Lyon 1891
Irving Whitall Lyon. *The Colonial Furniture of New England: A Study
    of the Domestic Furniture in Use in the Seventeenth and Eighteenth
    Centuries.* Boston, 1891.

Mackiewicz 1981
Susan Mackiewicz. "Woodworking Traditions in Newbury,
    Massachusetts, 1635–1745." Master's thesis, University of
    Delaware, 1981.

Macquoid 1904–5
Percy Macquoid. *A History of English Furniture.* [Vol. 1], *The Age
    of Oak.* London and New York, 1904–5. [Reprint, Woodbridge,
    Suffolk, England, 1987.]

Macquoid 1905
Percy Macquoid. *A History of English Furniture.* [Vol. 2], *The Age
    of Walnut.* London and New York, 1905. [Reprint, Woodbridge,
    Suffolk, England, 1987.]

"Made in New England" 1944
"Made in New England: Furniture from the Collection of Mr. and
    Mrs. Herbert B. Newton." *Antiques* 46 (July 1944), pp. 26–27.

Manca 2003
Joseph Manca. "A Matter of Style: The Question of Mannerism
    in Seventeenth-Century American Furniture." *Winterthur
    Portfolio* 38 (Spring 2003), pp. 1–36.

Margon 1954
Lester Margon. *World Furniture Treasures: Yesterday, Today and
    Tomorrow.* New York, 1954.

Margon 1965
Lester Margon. *Masterpieces of American Furniture, 1620–1840.*
    New York, 1965.

Margon 1971
Lester Margon. *More American Furniture Treasures, 1620–1840.*
    New York, 1971.

Marsden 2000
Jonathan Marsden. "The Chastleton Inventory of 1633." *Furniture
    History* 36 (2000), pp. 23–42.

Matzkin 1959
Ruth Matzkin. "Inventories of Estates in Philadelphia County,
    1682–1710." Master's thesis, University of Delaware, 1959.

McElroy 1979
Cathryn J. McElroy. "Furniture in Philadelphia: The First Fifty
    Years." *Winterthur Portfolio* 13 (1979), pp. 61–80.

Meeting of the Walpole Society **1935**
The Twenty-fifth Anniversary Meeting of the Walpole Society.
    Boston, 1935.

J. R. Melchor and M. S. Melchor 1986
James R. Melchor and Marilyn S. Melchor. "Analysis of an Enigma."
    Journal of Early Southern Decorative Arts 12 (May 1986), pp. 1–18
    and p. iv.

E. G. Miller 1937
Edgar G. Miller Jr. *American Antique Furniture: A Book for Amateurs.*
    2 vols. Baltimore, Md., 1937.

V. I. Miller 1956
V. Isabelle Miller. *Furniture by New York Cabinetmakers, 1650 to 1860.*
    Exh. cat., Museum of the City of New York. New York, 1956.

MMA 1930
The Metropolitan Museum of Art. *The American High Chest.* Text by
    Ruth Ralston. New York, 1930.

MMA 1975
The Metropolitan Museum of Art. *The Metropolitan Museum of Art:
    Notable Acquisitions, 1965–1975.* New York, 1975.

MMA 1980
The Metropolitan Museum of Art. *The Metropolitan Museum of Art:
    Notable Acquisitions, 1979–1980.* New York, 1980.

MMA 1981
The Metropolitan Museum of Art. *Notable Acquisitions, 1980–1981.*
    New York, 1981.

MMA 1988
The Metropolitan Museum of Art. *Recent Acquisitions: A Selection,
    1987–1988.* New York, 1988.

MMA 2001
The Metropolitan Museum of Art. *A Walk through the American
    Wing.* New York, 2001.

Monkhouse and Michie 1986
Christopher P. Monkhouse and Thomas S. Michie, with John M.
    Carpenter. *American Furniture in Pendleton House.* Providence,
    R.I., 1986.

Mooney 1978
James E. Mooney. "Furniture at the Historical Society of
    Pennsylvania." *Antiques* 113 (May 1978), pp. 1034–43.

Morse 1902
Frances Clary Morse. *Furniture of the Olden Time.* New York, 1902.

Myers and Mayhew 1974
Minor Myers Jr. and Edgar deN. Mayhew. *New London County
    Furniture, 1640–1840.* Exh. cat., Lyman Allyn Museum.
    New London, Conn., 1974.

Naeve 1978
Milo M. Naeve. *The Classical Presence in American Art.* Chicago, 1978.

Naeve 1981
Milo M. Naeve. *Identifying American Furniture: A Pictorial Guide
    to Styles and Terms, Colonial to Contemporary.* Nashville,
    Tenn., 1981.

Naeve and Roberts 1986
Milo M. Naeve and Lynn Springer Roberts. *A Decade of Decorative Arts: The Antiquarian Society of the Art Institute of Chicago.* Exh. cat., Art Institute of Chicago. Chicago, 1986.

Nelson 1968
Lee H. Nelson. *Nail Chronology as an Aid to Dating Old Buildings.* Technical Leaflet, American Association for State and Local History, no. 48. Nashville, Tenn., 1968. Also issued in *History News* 23 (November 1968), pp. 203–14.

"New England Furniture" 1943
"New England Furniture for St. Louis." *Antiques* 43 (January 1943), pp. 37–38.

"New England Slate-Top Table" 1939
"New England Slate-Top Table." *Antiques* 35 (April 1939), frontispiece and pp. 169–70.

New-York Historical Society 1941
The New-York Historical Society. *Catalogue of American Portraits in the New-York Historical Society: Oil Portraits, Miniatures, Sculptures.* New York, 1941.

Norman-Wilcox 1939
Gregor Norman-Wilcox. "American Furniture: Noteworthy and Unrecorded." *Antiques* 36 (December 1939), pp. 282–85.

Norman-Wilcox 1968
Gregor Norman-Wilcox. In "Country Furniture: A Symposium." *Antiques* 93 (March 1968), pp. 360–63.

Nutting 1921
Wallace Nutting. *Furniture of the Pilgrim Century, 1620–1720.* Boston, 1921.

Nutting 1922
Wallace Nutting. "The Prince-Howes Court Cupboard." *Antiques* 2 (October 1922), pp. 168–71.

Nutting 1924
Wallace Nutting. *Furniture of the Pilgrim Century (of American Origin), 1620–1720.* Rev. ed. Framingham, Mass., 1924.

Nutting 1928–33
Wallace Nutting. *Furniture Treasury (Mostly of American Origin).* 3 vols. Framingham, Mass., 1928–33.

Nutting 1930 (1977 ed.)
Wallace Nutting. *General Catalog: Supreme Edition.* Framingham, Mass., 1930. Reprint, rev., Exton, Pa., 1977.

***Oak Furniture from Yorkshire Churches* 1971**
Oak Furniture from Yorkshire Churches. Exh. cat., with an introduction by Christopher Gilbert. Stable Court Exhibition Galleries, Temple Newsam House. Leeds, Yorkshire, England, 1971.

O'Donnell 1980
Patricia Chapin O'Donnell. "Grisaille Decorated *Kasten* of New York." *Antiques* 117 (May 1980), pp. 1108–11.

B. N. Osburn and B. B. Osburn 1926
Burl N. Osburn and Bernice B. Osburn. *Measured Drawings of Early American Furniture.* Milwaukee, Wisc., 1926.

Ottenjann 1954
Heinrich Ottenjann. *Alte deutsche Bauernmöbel.* Hannover, Germany, 1954.

Ottoson 1985
Olga O. Ottoson. "Living with Antiques: The Ryerson House in New Jersey." *Antiques* 128 (October 1985), pp. 755–59.

Page 1969
John F. Page. *Litchfield County Furniture, 1730–1850.* Exh. cat., Litchfield Historical Society. Litchfield, Conn., 1969.

Palardy 1965
Jean Palardy. *The Early Furniture of French Canada.* Translated by Eric McLean. Toronto and New York, 1965.

Palladio 1570 (1738 ed.)
Andrea Palladio. *I quattri libri dell'architettura.* Venice, 1570. 1738 ed., *The Four Books of Andrea Palladio's Architecture.* Translated by Isaac Ware. London, 1738. Reprint of the 1738 ed., *The Four Books of Architecture.* Introduction by Adolf K. Placzek. New York, 1965.

Park 1960a
Helen Park. "Thomas Dennis, Ipswich Joiner: A Re-Examination." *Antiques* 78 (July 1960), pp. 40–44.

Park 1960b
Helen Park. "The Seventeenth-Century Furniture of Essex County and Its Makers." *Antiques* 78 (October 1960), pp. 350–55.

Passeri and Trent 1986
Andrew Passeri and Robert F. Trent. "A New Model Army of Cromwellian Chairs." *Maine Antique Digest*, September 1986, pp. 10C–16C.

Passeri and Trent 1987
Andrew Passeri and Robert F. Trent. "More on Easy Chairs." *Maine Antique Digest*, December 1987, pp. 1B–5B.

Peck 1990
Amelia Peck. *American Quilts and Coverlets in The Metropolitan Museum of Art.* New York, 1990.

Peck et al. 1996
Amelia Peck et al. *Period Rooms in The Metropolitan Museum of Art.* New York, 1996.

Pennington 1988
Samuel Pennington. *April Fool: Folk Art Fakes and Forgeries.* Exh. cat. Organized by the Museum of American Folk Art, New York, and held at Hirschl and Adler Folk, New York. Waldoboro, Maine, 1988.

***Philadelphia* 1976**
Philadelphia: Three Centuries of American Art. Exh. cat., Philadelphia Museum of Art. Philadelphia, 1976.

Pizer, Driver, and Earle 1985
Laurence R. Pizer, Eleanor A. Driver, and Alexandra B. Earle. "Furniture and Other Decorative Arts in Pilgrim Hall Museum in Plymouth, Massachusetts." *Antiques* 127 (May 1985), pp. 1112–20.

Powel 1954
Lydia B. Powel. "The American Wing." *The Metropolitan Museum of Art Bulletin*, n.s., 12 (March 1954), pp. 194–216.

Powers 1926
Mabel Crispin Powers. "The Ware Chairs of South Jersey." *Antiques* 9 (May 1926), pp. 307–11.

Ralston 1931a
Ruth Ralston. "An Early Oak Chest." *Bulletin of The Metropolitan Museum of Art* 26 (June 1931), pp. 144–46.

Ralston 1931b
Ruth Ralston. "The Exhibition in the American Wing of an Anonymous Gift. I. American Furniture and Other Decorative Arts." *Bulletin of The Metropolitan Museum of Art* 26 (February 1931), pp. 31–38.

Randall 1963
Richard H. Randall Jr. "'Boston Chairs.'" *Old-Time New England* 54 (July–September 1963), pp. 12–20.

Randall 1965
Richard H. Randall Jr. *American Furniture in the Museum of Fine Arts, Boston.* Boston, 1965.

Randall 1974
Richard H. Randall Jr. "William Randall: Boston Japanner." *Antiques* 105 (May 1974), pp. 1127–31.

Rauschenberg and Bivins 2003
Bradford L. Rauschenberg and John Bivins Jr. *The Furniture of Charleston, 1680–1820.* 3 vols. The Frank L. Horton Series. Winston-Salem, N.C., 2003.

Raymond 1922
Rachel C. Raymond. "Construction of Early American Furniture. I. Seventeenth Century Types." *Antiques* 2 (September 1922), pp. 120–22.

"Recent Accessions" 1953
"Recent Accessions." *The Metropolitan Museum of Art Bulletin*, n.s., 11 (May 1953), pp. 260–64.

"Recent Acquisitions" 1995
"Recent Acquisitions: A Selection, 1994–1995." *The Metropolitan Museum of Art Bulletin*, n.s., 53 (Fall 1995).

Rhoades and Jobe 1974
Elizabeth Rhoades and Brock Jobe. "Recent Discoveries in Boston Japanned Furniture." *Antiques* 105 (May 1974), pp. 1082–91.

Richards and N. G. Evans 1997
Nancy E. Richards and Nancy Goyne Evans, with Wendy A. Cooper and Michael S. Podmaniczky. *New England Furniture at Winterthur: Queen Anne and Chippendale Periods.* A Winterthur Book. Winterthur, Del., 1997.

Ring 1993
Betty Ring. *Girlhood Embroidery: American Samplers and Pictorial Needlework, 1650–1850.* 2 vols. New York, 1993.

Ripley 1964
S. Dillon Ripley. "An American Triangular Turned Chair?" *Antiques* 85 (January 1964), pp. 104–6.

Roberts 1980
Lynn Springer [Roberts]. "The Cabinetmaker's Art: Selections of American Furniture to the Early Twentieth Century." *Bulletin* (Saint Louis Art Museum), n.s., 15 (Summer 1980), pp. 2–48.

Rodriguez Roque 1984
Oswaldo Rodriguez Roque. *American Furniture at Chipstone.* Madison, Wisc., 1984.

Roth 1964
Rodris Roth. "The Colonial Revival and 'Centennial Furniture.'" *Art Quarterly* 27 (1964), pp. 57–81.

Ryder 1975
Richard D. Ryder. "Three-Legged Turned Chairs." *Connoisseur* 190 (December 1975), pp. 242–47.

Ryder 1976
Richard D. Ryder. "Four-Legged Turned Chairs." *Connoisseur* 191 (January 1976), pp. 44–49.

Sack 1950
Albert Sack. *Fine Points of Furniture: Early American.* New York, 1950.

***Sack Collection* 1981–92**
American Antiques from Israel Sack Collection. 10 vols. Washington, D.C., 1981–92. [Reprint of sales brochures from Israel Sack and other material.]

Safford 1972
Frances Gruber [Safford]. *The Art of Joinery: Seventeenth-Century Case Furniture in the American Wing.* Exh. cat., The Metropolitan Museum of Art. New York, 1972.

Safford 1980
Frances Gruber Safford. "Seventeenth-Century American Furniture at The Metropolitan Museum of Art." *Apollo* 111 (May 1980), pp. 348–53.

Safford 1998
Frances Gruber Safford. "Floral Painting on Early Eighteenth-Century American Furniture at The Metropolitan Museum of Art." In *Painted Wood: History and Conservation*, edited by Valerie Dorge and F. Carey Howlett, pp. 194–205. Proceedings of a symposium at the Colonial Williamsburg Foundation, Williamsburg, Virginia, November 11–14, 1994. Los Angeles, 1998.

Safford 2000
Frances Gruber Safford. "The Hudson-Fulton Exhibition and H. Eugene Bolles." *Antiques* 157 (January 2000), pp. 170–75.

Salomonsky 1931
Verna Cook Salomonsky. *Masterpieces of Furniture Design.* Grand Rapids, Mich., 1931.

Schaefer 1982
Elizabeth Meg Schaefer. "Wright's Ferry Mansion." *Antiques* 122 (December 1982), pp. 1242–51.

Scherer 1984
John L. Scherer. *New York Furniture at the New York State Museum.* Alexandria, Va., 1984.

Schiffer 1966
Margaret Berwind Schiffer. *Furniture and Its Makers of Chester County, Pennsylvania.* Philadelphia, 1966.

Schiffer 1974
Margaret Berwind Schiffer. *Chester County, Pennsylvania: Inventories, 1684–1850.* Exton, Pa., 1974.

Schipper 1995
Jaap Schipper. "Vruchtentrossen in grisaille: Beschilderde kasten uit Nieuw Nederland en Nederland." *Antiek* 30 (October 1995), pp. 98–110.

Schoelwer 1989
Susan Prendergast Schoelwer. "Connecticut Sunflower Furniture: A Familiar Form Reconsidered." *Yale University Art Gallery Bulletin*, Spring 1989, pp. 20–37.

Schramm 1982
Eric Schramm. "Twist Turning: Traditional Method Combines Lathe and Carving." *Fine Woodworking*, no. 33 (March–April 1982), pp. 92–93.

Schwartz 1956
Marvin D. Schwartz. "American Painted Furniture before the Classic Revival." *Antiques* 69 (April 1956), pp. 342–45.

Schwartz 1958
Marvin D. Schwartz. "Furniture, 1640–1840." In *The Concise Encyclopedia of American Antiques*, edited by Helen Comstock, pp. 27–53. New York, 1958.

Schwartz 1968
Marvin D. Schwartz. *American Interiors, 1675–1885: A Guide to the American Period Rooms in the Brooklyn Museum.* Brooklyn, N.Y., 1968.

Schwartz 1976
Marvin D. Schwartz. *American Furniture of the Colonial Period.* The Metropolitan Museum of Art. New York, 1976.

Schwarze 1979–81
Wolfgang Schwarze. *Alte deutsche Bauernmöbel, von 1700 bis 1860.* 2 vols. Wuppertal, Germany, 1979–81.

Scott 1979
G. W. Scott Jr. "Lancaster and Other Pennsylvania Furniture." *Antiques* 115 (May 1979), pp. 984–93.

***Seats of Fashion* 1973**
Seats of Fashion: Three Hundred Years of American Chair Design. Exh. cat., High Museum of Art. Atlanta, Ga., 1973.

Serlio 1537–47 (1611 ed.)
Sebastiano Serlio. *The First Booke of Architecture.* 5 vols. in 1. London, 1611. Reprint, *The Five Books of Architecture: An Unabridged Reprint of the English Edition of 1611.* New York, 1982. Originally published in Italian and French under various titles (Venice and Paris, 1537–47).

Sewall 1973
Samuel Sewall. *The Diary of Samuel Sewall, 1674–1729.* Edited by M. Halsey Thomas. 2 vols. New York, 1973.

Shea 1975
John G. Shea. *Antique Country Furniture of North America.* New York, 1975.

"Shop Talk" 1957
"Shop Talk." *Antiques* 71 (January 1957), pp. 14, 22, 30, 38.

"Shop Talk" 1958
"Shop Talk." *Antiques* 73 (January 1958), pp. 32, 38, 44.

"Shop Talk" 1960
"Shop Talk." *Antiques* 77 (April 1960), pp. 430, 436, 442, 448, 454, 460.

Shorleyker 1632
Richard Shorleyker. *A Schole-House, for the Needle.* London, 1632.

Singleton 1900–1901
Esther Singleton. *The Furniture of Our Forefathers.* 2 vols. New York, 1900–1901.

"Sino-American Highboy" 1945
"A Sino-American Highboy." *American Collector* 14 (September 1945), front cover.

"Slate-Top Tables" 1971
"Slate-Top Tables for Sale in Boston, 1718." *Antiques* 99 (January 1971), p. 94.

Snow 1957
Barbara Snow. "History in Houses: Seventeenth-Century New England and Pennsylvania." *Antiques* 71 (January 1957), pp. 62–65.

Solis-Cohen 1990
Lita Solis-Cohen. "'Made of Whole Cloth,' Says Restorer." *Maine Antique Digest*, May 1990, p. 16A.

Stalker and Parker 1688 (1971 ed.)
John Stalker and George Parker. *A Treatise of Japaning and Varnishing; Being a Compleat Discovery of Those Arts.* London, 1688. 1971 ed., *A Treatise of Japanning and Varnishing, 1688.* Introduction by H. D. Molesworth. London, 1971.

Stayton 1990
Kevin L. Stayton. *Dutch by Design: Tradition and Change in Two Historic Brooklyn Houses. The Schenck Houses at the Brooklyn Museum.* New York, 1990.

Stein 1998
Donna Stein. *Colonial East Hampton, 1640–1800.* Exh. cat., Guild Hall Museum. East Hampton, N.Y., 1998.

St. George 1978
Robert Blair St. George. "A Plymouth Area Chairmaking Tradition of the Late Seventeenth-Century." *Middleborough Antiquarian* 19 (December 1978), pp. 3, 5–7, 10–12.

St. George 1979a
Robert Blair St. George. "Style and Structure in the Joinery of Dedham and Medfield, Massachusetts, 1635–1685." *Winterthur Portfolio* 13 (1979), pp. 1–46.

St. George 1979b
Robert Blair St. George. *The Wrought Covenant: Source Material for the Study of Craftsmen and Community in Southeastern New England, 1620–1700.* Exh. cat., Brockton Art Center—Fuller Memorial. Brockton, Mass., 1979.

St. George 1983
Robert Blair St. George. "The Staniford Family Chest." *Maine Antique Digest*, February 1983, pp. 16B–18B.

Stillinger 1965
Elizabeth Stillinger. "History in Houses: The Dey Mansion in Wayne, New Jersey." *Antiques* 88 (August 1965), pp. 190–94.

Stillinger 1980
Elizabeth Stillinger. *The Antiquers.* New York, 1980.

Stockwell 1939
David Hunt Stockwell. "The Spice Cabinets of Pennsylvania and New Jersey." *Antiques* 36 (October 1939), pp. 174–76.

I. N. P. Stokes 1915–28
I. N. Phelps Stokes, comp. *The Iconography of Manhattan Island, 1498–1909.* 6 vols. New York, 1915–28.

Storey 1926
Walter Rendell Storey. "Table of Many Legs." *Antiquarian* 6 (June 1926), pp. 12–15.

Swain 1987
Margaret Swain. "The Turkey-Work Chairs of Holyroodhouse." In *Upholstery in America and Europe from the Seventeenth Century to World War I*, edited by Edward S. Cooke Jr., pp. 51–63. A Barra Foundation Book. New York, 1987.

Sweeney 1995
Kevin M. Sweeney. "Regions and the Study of Material Culture: Explorations along the Connecticut River." *American Furniture*, 1995, pp. 145–66.

Symonds 1934
R. W. Symonds. "Cane Chairs of the Late Seventeenth and Early Eighteenth Centuries." *Connoisseur* 93 (March 1934), pp. 173–81.

Symonds 1951
R. W. Symonds. "English Cane Chairs." *Connoisseur* 127 (April 1951), pp. 8–15 (part 1); (June 1951), pp. 83–91 (part 2).

Tarule 1992
Robert Tarule. "The Joined Furniture of William Searle and Thomas Dennis: A Shop-Based Inquiry into the Woodworking Technology of the Seventeenth Century Joiner." Ph.D. diss., Union Institute, 1992.

Thornton 1978
Peter Thornton. *Seventeenth-Century Interior Decoration in England, France, and Holland.* Studies in British Art. New Haven, Conn., 1978.

Thornton 1997
Peter Thornton. "The Refined Ladder-Back." *Furniture History* 33 (1997), pp. 75–83.

***Three Centuries of Connecticut Furniture* 1935**
Three Centuries of Connecticut Furniture, 1635–1935. Exh. cat. Organized by the Tercentenary Commission of the State of Connecticut and held at the Morgan Memorial, Hartford. Hartford, Conn., 1935.

Trachsler 1978
Walter Trachsler. *Möbel der Frührenaissance aus der deutschsprachigen Schweiz, 1520 bis 1570.* 2nd ed. Aus dem Schweizerischen Landesmuseum, 13. Bern, Switzerland, 1978.

Trent 1975
Robert F. Trent. "The Joiners and Joinery of Middlesex County, Massachusetts, 1630–1730." In *Arts of the Anglo-American Community in the Seventeenth Century*, edited by Ian M. G. Quimby, pp. 123–48. Winterthur Conference Report, 1974. Charlottesville, Va., 1975.

Trent 1977
Robert F. Trent. *Hearts and Crowns: Folk Chairs of the Connecticut Coast, 1720–1840.* Exh. cat., New Haven Colony Historical Society. New Haven, Conn., 1977.

Trent 1981
Robert F. Trent. "The Symonds Joinery Shops of Salem and Their Works." In *The Peabody Museum of Salem Antiques Show*, pp. 33–36. Salem, Mass., 1981.

Trent 1982a
Robert F. Trent. "The Concept of Mannerism." In Fairbanks and Trent 1982, pp. 368–79.

Trent 1982b
Robert F. Trent. "New England Joinery and Turning before 1700." In Fairbanks and Trent 1982, pp. 501–10.

Trent 1985
Robert F. Trent. "The Chest of Drawers in America, 1635–1730: A Postscript." *Winterthur Portfolio* 20 (Spring 1985), pp. 31–48.

Trent 1987a
Robert F. Trent. "Seventeenth-Century Upholstery in Massachusetts." In *Upholstery in America and Europe from the Seventeenth Century to World War I*, edited by Edward S. Cooke Jr., pp. 39–50. A Barra Foundation Book. New York, 1987.

Trent 1987b
Robert F. Trent. "What Can a Chair and a Box Do for You?" *Maine Antique Digest*, April 1987, pp. 10C–13C.

Trent 1989
Robert F. Trent. "The Symonds Shops of Essex County, Massachusetts." In *The American Craftsman and the European Tradition, 1620–1820*, edited by Francis J. Puig and Michael Conforti, pp. 23–41. Exh. cat., Minneapolis Institute of Arts, Minneapolis, Minnesota, and Carnegie Museum of Art, Pittsburgh, Pennsylvania. Minneapolis, 1989.

Trent 1990
Robert F. Trent. "The Board-Seated Turned Chairs Project." *Regional Furniture* 4 (1990), pp. 42–48.

Trent 1994
Robert F. Trent. "A Channel Islands Parallel for the Early Eighteenth-Century Connecticut Chests Attributed to Charles Guillam." *Studies in the Decorative Arts* 2 (Fall 1994), pp. 75–91.

Trent 1999
Robert F. Trent. "New Insights on Early Rhode Island Furniture." *American Furniture*, 1999, pp. 209–23.

Trent and Goldstein 1998
Robert F. Trent and Karin J. Goldstein. "Notes about New 'Tinkham' Chairs." *American Furniture*, 1998, pp. 215–37.

Trent and Podmaniczky 2002
Robert F. Trent and Michael S. Podmaniczky. "An Early Cupboard Fragment from the Harvard College Joinery Tradition." *American Furniture*, 2002, pp. 228–42.

Trent and Wood 2003
Robert F. Trent and David F. Wood. "The Earliest American Easy Chairs." *Catalogue of Antiques and Fine Art* 4 (Autumn 2003), pp. 161–65.

Trent, Follansbee, and A. Miller 2001
Robert F. Trent, Peter Follansbee, and Alan Miller. "First Flowers of the Wilderness: Mannerist Furniture from a Northern Essex County, Massachusetts, Shop." *American Furniture*, 2001, pp. 1–64.

Trent, Walker, and Passeri 1979
Robert F. Trent, Robert Walker, and Andrew Passeri. "The Franklin Easy Chair and Other Goodies." *Maine Antique Digest*, December 1979, pp. 26B–29B.

Tucker 1925
Henrietta Tucker. "The Cedar Furniture of Bermuda." *Antiques* 7 (February 1925), pp. 80–84.

"Turquerie" 1968
"Turquerie." *The Metropolitan Museum of Art Bulletin*, n.s., 26 (January 1968), pp. 225–39.

Venable 1989
Charles L. Venable. *American Furniture in the Bybee Collection.* Dallas Museum of Art, Dallas, Texas. Austin, Tex., 1989.

Waite 1955
Emma Forbes Waite. "William Price of Boston: Map-Maker, Merchant and Churchman." *Old-Time New England* 46 (October–December 1955), pp. 52–56 and p. iv.

B. Ward 1986
Barbara McLean Ward, ed. *A Place for Everything: Chests and Boxes in Early Colonial America.* Exh. cat., Winterthur Museum. Winterthur, Del., 1986.

G. W. R. Ward 1988
Gerald W. R. Ward. *American Case Furniture in the Mabel Brady Garvan and Other Collections at Yale University.* New Haven, Conn., 1988.

G. W. R. Ward 1992
Gerald W. R. Ward. "The Intersections of Life: Tables and Their Social Role." In Barquist 1992, pp. 14–25.

D. B. Warren 1975
David B. Warren. *Bayou Bend: American Furniture, Paintings and Silver from the Bayou Bend Collection.* Houston, Tex., 1975.

D. B. Warren et al. 1998
David B. Warren, Michael K. Brown, Elizabeth Ann Coleman, and Emily Ballew Neff. *American Decorative Arts and Paintings in the Bayou Bend Collection.* Houston, Tex., 1998.

W. L. Warren 1958a
William L. Warren. "Were the Guilford Painted Chests Made in Saybrook?" *Bulletin* (Connecticut Historical Society) 23 (January 1958), pp. 1–10.

W. L. Warren 1958b
William L. Warren. "More about Painted Chests. Part II." *Bulletin* (Connecticut Historical Society) 23 (April 1958), pp. 50–60.

Waters 1979
Deborah Dependahl Waters. "Wares and Chairs: A Reappraisal of the Documents." *Winterthur Portfolio* 13 (1979), pp. 161–73.

Way 1992
George Way. "The Good Box." *Art and Antiques* 9 (April 1992), pp. 50–53, 89.

Webster 1974
Donald Blake Webster, ed. *The Book of Canadian Antiques.* New York, 1974.

Wells-Cole 1976a
Anthony Wells-Cole, with Karen Walton. *Oak Furniture from Gloucestershire and Somerset.* Exh. cat., St. Nicholas Church Museum, Bristol, Gloucestershire, and Stable Court Exhibition Galleries, Temple Newsam House, Leeds, Yorkshire, England. Bristol and Leeds, 1976.

Wells-Cole 1976b
Anthony Wells-Cole. "Oak Furniture in Dorset: Some Introductory Thoughts." *Furniture History* 12 (1976), pp. 24–28 and pls. 5–10.

Wells-Cole 1981
Anthony Wells-Cole. "An Oak Bed at Montacute: A Study in Mannerist Decoration." *Furniture History* 17 (1981), pp. 1–19 and pls. 1–29.

Wendell 1965
William G. Wendell. "History in Houses: The Macpheadris-Warner House in Portsmouth, New Hampshire." *Antiques* 87 (June 1965), pp. 712–15.

Williams 1963
Henry Lionel Williams. *Country Furniture of Early America.* New York, 1963.

Willoughby 1994
Martha H. Willoughby. "From Carved to Painted: Chests of Central and Coastal Connecticut, c. 1675–1725." Master's thesis, University of Delaware, 1994.

Willoughby 2000
Martha H. Willoughby. "Patronage in Early Salem: The Symonds Shops and Their Customers." *American Furniture*, 2000, pp. 169–84.

Winchester 1957
Alice Winchester. "The Prentis House at the Shelburne Museum." *Antiques* 71 (May 1957), pp. 440–42.

Wood 1996
David F. Wood, ed. *The Concord Museum: Decorative Arts from a New England Collection.* Concord, Mass., 1996.

Zea 1984
Philip Zea. "The Fruits of Oligarchy: Patronage and Joinery in Western Massachusetts, 1630–1730." Master's thesis, University of Delaware, 1984.

Zea 1987
Philip Zea. "The Fruits of Oligarchy: Patronage and the Hadley Chest Tradition in Western Massachusetts." In *New England Furniture: Essays in Memory of Benno M. Forman*, pp. 1–65. Boston, 1987. Special issue of *Old-Time New England* 72.

Zea and Flynt 1992
Philip Zea and Suzanne L. Flynt. *Hadley Chests.* Exh. cat., Israel Sack, New York; Wadsworth Atheneum, Hartford, Connecticut; and Memorial Hall, Deerfield, Massachusetts. Deerfield, 1992.

Zimmerman 2004
Philip D. Zimmerman. "Early American Tables and Other Furniture at Stenton." *Antiques* 165 (May 2004), pp. 102–9.

Index

Page numbers in **boldface** type refer to the main catalogue entry and illustration; page numbers in *italic* type refer to additional illustrations, primarily detail views in Appendix 2. Catalogue items are indexed under the exact name used in the catalogue (e.g., "leather chair"; "small cabinet or spice box"); items are also listed as subentries under the town, county, state, or region in which the item was made (or in which it was probably or possibly made). Persons with the same last name in a descent list are sometimes merged into a family entry (e.g., "Pickman family of Salem"). With only a few exceptions, comparative items are not indexed.

Abbot, George Edward Henry (1838–1911), 326, cat. no. 126
Abbot family of Groton, 326, cat. no. 126
Ackermann, Rudolph, 191
Albertson, Ann (1726–1775), 17, cat. no. 1
Allen, Nathaniel, 87
Alling, Rev. James (1657–1696), 75, 75n9, cat. no. 26
"American Japanned Furniture" exhibition (New York, 1933), 7
Amory, Harriet, 322, cat. no. 125
Andrus, Vincent D., 8
Annable, Esther Knowlton (1824–1894), 147, 147n8, cat. no. 58
Annable family of northern Essex County, 147, cat. no. 58
Antrum, Thomas (d. 1663), 117n1
Appleton, George (1825–1907), 147, 147n8, cat. no. 58
Appleton, Lillie May (Mrs. James Choate Furness) (1858–1930), 146, 147, cat. no. 58
Appleton, Margaret (d. 1740), 326, cat. no. 126
Appleton, Oliver (1677–1760), 147, 147n8, cat. no. 58
Appleton, Samuel (1625–1696), 147, 147n8, cat. no. 58
applied panel moldings [figs. 129–34], *410*
armchairs (armed chairs; elbow chairs; great chairs), 13, 94; terms for parts [fig. 122], *405. See also entries at* banister-back armchair; easy chair; joined armchair; leather armchair; slat-back armchair; spindle-back armchair; splat-back armchair
armoire, 279
astragal molding [fig. 128], *410*
Avery, Samuel Putnam, 194

back stools, 57, 58, 64, 65, 68n4. *See also entries at* Turkey-work chair
Baker, Mrs. George F., 50, cat. no. 17
Baldwin, Helen D., 206, cat. no. 86
Baldwin family of Woburn, cupboard base now in Museum of Fine Arts, Boston [ill. 141d], 367, *368*, 369, 370, 371n4
banister, term, 64. *See also entries at* banister-back; splat-back
banister-back armchair (northeastern coastal Massachusetts or Portsmouth, New Hampshire, or vicinity) (1720–40) [cat. no. 29; fig. 16], 8, 64, **81–82**, 83, 99, 358, *376*
banister-back armchair (northeastern coastal Massachusetts or Portsmouth, New Hampshire, or vicinity) (1720–40, with later alterations) [cat. no. 137; figs. 17, 28], 100, 353, **358–60**, *376*, *379*

banister-back chair (eastern Massachusetts) [cat. no. 28; fig. 18], 64, **79–80**, *377*
banister-back chairs (two) (Bermuda) [cat. no. 31], 64, 80, **86–87**
banister-back chairs (two) (northeastern coastal Massachusetts or Portsmouth, New Hampshire, or vicinity) [cat. no. 30; figs. 19, 27, 123], *12*, 64, 82, **83–85**, 358, *377*, *379*, *406*
banister-back chairs, form, 34, 64, 80; terms for parts [fig. 123], *406*
Barnstable County, Massachusetts, 287n1
    cupboard [cat. no. 114; figs. 47, 88, 94, 107, 130, 139–41], 56, 232, 236, 254, 257, 279, 282, **284–87**, 287, 288, 370, 371n4, *385*, *396*, *398*, *401*, *410*, *411*
Baroque influences, 9, 51, 72, 305, 306, 313, 358
Bassett family of Marshfield, 57, cat. no. 19
Batchelder, Charles H., collection, 54, cat. no. 18
Batchelder (Bachiler), Nathaniel (1630–1710), 54, cat. no. 18
Batchelder family of Hampton, 54, cat. no. 18
beds, 104
bed settle, 117n1
Behrend, B. A., collection, 84, 131, 258, 364; cat. nos. 30, 50, 106, 139
benches ("forms"), 51, 121
Berger, Jean, design book, 310, 312n2, 322n4
Bermuda, banister-back chairs (two) [cat. no. 31], 64, 80, **86–87**
Bible desk, term, 344n7
Biddle, James, 8
bilsted. *See* sweet gum
birch, 332, 334, 336, 338n9
Blair, Mrs. J. Insley (Natalie K.) (1887–1951), collection, 3, 5–6, 8, 20, 22, 24, 50, 66, 70, 78, 84, 100, 106, 117, 124, 130, 131, 140, 141, 142, 146, 162, 163, 164, 178, 189, 224, 229, 246, 252, 256, 258, 272, 278, 286, 293, 314, 328, 364; cat. nos. 2–4, 17, 23, 24, 27, 30, 37, 39, 44, 46, 49, 50, 55–58, 66–68, 74, 80, 93, 95, 102, 104–6, 110, 112, 114, 116, 123, 127, 139
Blaney, Dwight, 6
Blin, Peter (ca. 1640–1725), 219, 220n6
Blin, Peter Jr. (1670–alive 1741), 241n2
board and trestles, term, 360. *See also* trestle table
Bolles, H. Eugene (1853–1910), collection, 3, 4, 5, 6–7, 8, 26, 28, 29, 31, 36, 37, 38, 40, 42, 45, 46, 57, 60, 62, 72, 80, 82, 92, 96, 118, 126, 127, 133, 135, 136, 138, 148, 151, 152, 154, 156, 166, 171, 173, 175, 176, 179, 180, 182, 184, 187, 199, 202, 204, 212, 214, 217, 218, 220, 226, 231, 234, 236, 237, 239, 241, 244, 262, 266, 269, 275, 283, 290, 295, 312, 316, 318, 333, 334, 335, 348, 351, 358, 360, 361, 360, 362, 367, 370, 371; cat. nos. 5–8, 10–13, 15, 19, 21, 22, 25, 28, 29, 33, 35, 45, 47, 48, 51–54, 59–63, 69–73, 75–79, 83–85, 88–92, 94, 96–101, 107–9, 111, 113, 115, 117, 122, 124, 128, 129, 133, 134, 136–38, 141
Boomgaert, Wyntie Cornelise (d. 1700), 17, cat. no. 1
Bos, Cornelius (1506?–?1564), 198
Boston, Massachusetts, 9, 10
    cane chair [cat. no. 32; figs. 26, 50, 120], 64, 76, 80, **88–90**, 90, 95, 100, 105, 108, 156, 313, *379*, *386*, *403*

chest of drawers [cat. no. 111], 234n4, 237, 263, 269, 270, **273–75**

chest with drawers (with diamond plaques) [cat. no. 99], 195, 234, 234n4, 236, **237–39**, 257

chest with drawers (with rectangular fields) [cat. no. 98; figs. 67, 110, 131], 195, 234n4, **234–37**, 237, 257, 273, 282, 306, *390, 401, 410*

desk [cat. no. 133; fig. 82], 342, **346–48**, 349, *395*

easy chair (1715–30) [cat. no. 39; fig. 23], 88, 104, **105–7**, 108, 156n5, *378*

easy chair (1730–40) [cat. no. 40; fig. 89], 78n2, 88, 104, 105, 106n4, **108–10**, *397*

high chest of drawers (1700–1730) [cat. no. 123; figs. 40, 98–100, 104, 115, 127, 147], 305, **313–15**, 316, 318, 320, 326n2, 327, 346, *383, 399, 400, 402, 409, 412*

high chest of drawers (1700–1730; with three-piece front skirt) [cat. no. 124; figs. 101, 103, 114], 305, 313, **316–18**, 320, *400, 402*

high chest of drawers (1710–25) [cat. no. 122; figs. 39, 77, 145], 270, 305, 306, **309–12**, *383, 393, 411*

high chest of drawers (1710–30) [cat. no. 125; figs. 42, 78], *2, 8, 191,* 275, 305, 310, 313, 316, **319–23**, 332, *384, 393*

high chest of drawers (1715–30) [cat. no. 126; figs. 41, 102, 105, 146], 8, 305, 318n4, **323–26**, 327, 336, *383, 400, 412*

joined table with drawer (1680–1710) [cat. no. 48], 121, **126–27**, 128, 130

joined table with drawer (1690–1710) [cat. no. 49; figs. 75, 116], 121, 126, **128–30**, 132, *392, 403*

joint stool [cat. no. 22], 51, **62–63**

leather armchair [cat. no. 34; fig. 25], 64, 78n2, **93–95**, 108, 334, *378*

leather chair (1690–1705) [cat. no. 25], 64, 65, **71–72**, 72, 161

leather chair (1700–1720) [cat. no. 27; figs. 15, 24, 92], 5, 57, 62, 64, 72, 74, **76–78**, 79, 83, 88, 91, 94, 105, 108, 147, 161, 313, 334, *376, 378, 397*

leather chair (1723–45) [cat. no. 33], 42, 64, 76, 88, **90–92**, 94, 95, 95n1, 105, 156, 357

leather chairs (two) (1695–1715) [cat. no. 26; figs. 14, 21], 26, 64, 72, **72–75**, 76, 86, 105, 134, 161, *375, 378*

oval table with falling leaves (1690–1720) [cat. no. 59; fig. 32], *4,* 122, 143, 146, **147–49**, *380*

oval table with falling leaves (1715–40) [cat. no. 60; figs. 33, 124], 143, 146, **150–51**, 151, 162, 336, *380, 407*

slat-back armchair [cat. no. 10; fig. 2], 34, **34–36**, 356, *373*

spindle-back armchair (1640–80) [cat. no. 2; fig. 1], 5, 13, **17–20**, 20, 21, 22, 23, 24n1, 27, 34, 36, 42, 356, *373*

spindle-back armchair (1650–80) [cat. no. 3], 13, **20–22**, 27, 36

splat-back chair [cat. no. 35], 64, 94, **95–96**, 97, 102, 112, 138

square joined table [cat. no. 46; fig. 76], 121, **122–24**, 125, 126, 128, 161, 290, 370, *392*

Turkey-work chair (1660–90) [cat. no. 23; fig. 85], 5, 31, 57, 64, **65–68**, 68, 70, 71, 74, 126, 128, 148, 254, *396*

Turkey-work chair (1680–1700) [cat. no. 24], 5, 30, 64, 65, **68–71**, 74, 126, 148, 161, 254

box (Braintree, Massachusetts; attributed to the Savell shop tradition) [cat. no. 71], 60, 118, 169, **172–73**, 257

box (Connecticut, probably Saybrook) [cat. no. 80], 169, **187–89**, 327

box (Dedham or Medfield, Massachusetts; attributed to the Thurston shop tradition) [cat. no. 72], 169, **173–75**

box (Essex County, Massachusetts, northern) [cat. no. 78; fig. 143], 24, 169, **182–84**, *411*

box (Hampton, New Hampshire) [cat. no. 77], 169, **181–82**, 217

box (modern, in the style of Springfield, Massachusetts) [cat. no. 139], 353, **363–64**

box (New England) [cat. no. 76], 169, **180–81**, 234n3

box (Windsor, Connecticut; attributed to the Moore shop tradition) [cat. no. 74], 169, 175, **176–78**, 179

box (Windsor, Connecticut; attributed to the Moore shop tradition; with dense carving) [cat. no. 75], 169, 175, 176, 177, **178–79**

box (Windsor, Connecticut; attributed to the Stoughton shop tradition) [cat. no. 73], 169, **175–76**, 177, 219, 278

box (Windsor or Killingworth, Connecticut; attributed to the Buell shop tradition) [cat. no. 70; fig. 53], 169, **170–71**, *386*

boxes and other small case pieces [cat. nos. 70–82, 139], 169–94, 363–64

box stools, 253

box with drawer below, form, 169

Bradford, William, chair, 13, 18, 20n5, 36

Braintree, Massachusetts
   box (attributed to the Savell shop tradition) [cat. no. 71], 60, 118, 169, **172–73**, 257
   joint stool (probably the Savell shop tradition) [cat. no. 21], 51, **59–61**, 62, 118, 122, 124, 161

Branford-Saybrook area, Connecticut, spindle-back chair [cat. no. 8; fig. 8], 8, 13, 28, **30–31**, 37, 45, *374*

Breck, Joseph, 7

Brewster, William, chair, 13, 18, 20n5, 36

Bristol County, Massachusetts, 287n1

Brocas, John (d. 1740), 313

Brown, Joseph Jr. (active in 1741), 166n1

Browne, Elizabeth (d. 1719), 323

Bryant, Mrs. George Clarke (Florence Adele Farrel Bryant), collection, 206, cat. no. 86

Buell, Samuel (1641–1720), 170

Buell (Buel), William (1614–1681), 170

Buell shop tradition, Windsor and Killingworth, Connecticut, attributed to, box [cat. no. 70; fig. 53], 169, **170–71**, *386*

butterfly table, term, 144, 164, 165n1

butt joint [fig. 151], *414*

Buys, Tryntje Jans (m. 1676), 356, cat. no. 135

Byrd, William I, 143

cabinets. *See entries at* small cabinet; writing cabinets

cabinets-on-stand, 253, 305

cabriole-leg chairs, 108

cane chair (Boston) [cat. no. 32; figs. 26, 50, 120], 64, 76, 80, **88–90**, 90, 95, 100, 105, 108, 156, 313, *379, 386, 403*

cane chairs, influence, 10, 64, 71, 88

card tables, 143, 146

carvers, 65

case furniture [cat. nos. 70–134, 139–41], 169–351, 363–71
   boxes and other small case pieces [cat. nos. 70–82, 139], 169–94, 263–64
   chests and chests with drawers [cat. nos. 83–104, 140], 195–252, 364–67
   chests of drawers [cat. nos. 108–12], 263–78
   chests-on-frame [cat. nos. 105–7], 253–62
   cupboards and kasten [cat. nos. 113–20, 141], 279–304, 367–71
   desks [cat. nos. 132–34], 342–51
   dressing tables [cat. nos. 128–31], 331–41
   high chests of drawers [cat. nos. 121–27], 305–30

case moldings [figs. 138–47], *411–12*

case of drawers, term, 263. *See also entries at* chest of drawers

cavetto molding [fig. 128], *410*

cedar, 232, 234n4
Centennial Exposition (Philadelphia, 1876), 4, 117
chair crest rails, 64, 81; detail views [figs. 15–20], *376–77*
chair finials, detail views [figs. 1–14], *373–75*
chairmaker, term, 65
chairs (little chairs; small chairs), 13, 27, 64; terms for parts [fig. 123], *406. For specific forms, see entries at* banister-back chair; cane chair; leather chair; spindle-back chair; splat-back chair; Turkey-work chair. *For large chairs, see* armchairs; easy chairs
chair stretchers: detail views [figs. 21–31], *378–79*
chair-table (Plymouth County, Massachusetts, probably Marshfield) [cat. no. 19], 51, **54–57**, 208, 288
chair-tables, form, 51, 54
Chambers, Thomas (active in 1642), 17n6
chamber table, term, 253, 331. *See also entries at* dressing table
Channel Islands influence, 242, 262n6
Charlestown, Massachusetts, spindle-back armchair [cat. no. 2; fig. 1], 5, 13, **17–20**, 20, 21, 22, 23, 24n1, 27, 34, 36, 42, 356, *373*
Cheshire, England, influence, 57
chest (Connecticut, south-central, possibly Milford) [cat. no. 90; figs. 57, 58, 84, 125], 195, **215–17**, *388, 396, 407*
chest (Guilford, Connecticut, or vicinity; with double-heart motif) [cat. no. 89], 195, 211, 212, **213–14**, 216, 282
chest (Guilford, Connecticut, or vicinity; with S-scroll motif) [cat. no. 88; fig. 135], 195, **211–13**, 213, 216, 282, 327, 365, 366, *410*
chest (Hampton, New Hampshire) [cat. no. 91], 181, 182, 196, **217–18**
chest (Hartford County, Connecticut; sunflower chest) [cat. no. 94], 195, **225–26**
chest (Ipswich, Massachusetts; attributed to the Searle-Dennis shop tradition) [cat. no. 84], 195, 196, **200–202**, 202
chest (Ipswich, Massachusetts; attributed to William Searle or Thomas Dennis) [cat. no. 83; figs. 55, 136], 4, 195, **196–99**, 200, 201, 202n3, 203, 217, *387, 410*
chest (New Haven, Connecticut, or vicinity, 1650–80) [cat. no. 86; fig. 56], 195, **205–8**, 208, 212, 216, 217, 257, 283n5, *387*
chest (New Haven, Connecticut, or vicinity, probably 1670–90) [cat. no. 87], 147n5, 195, 205, **208–10**, 212, 216, 283n5
chest, form, 195; board construction, 195, 196, 217; joined, 195; terms for parts [fig. 125], *407. See also entries at* chest with drawer
Chester County, Pennsylvania, 57
chestnut, 187, 282, 327
chest of drawers (Boston or vicinity) [cat. no. 111], 234n4, 237, 263, 269, 270, **273–75**
chest of drawers (eastern Massachusetts, probably Middlesex or Essex County) [cat. no. 110; figs. 74, 97, 106, 134, 142], 5, 122, 147n5, 263, **269–72**, 274, 370, *392, 399, 401, 410, 411*
chest of drawers (Salem, Massachusetts; attributed to the Symonds shop tradition) [cat. no. 108; figs. 69, 108], 7, 24, 180n2, 184, 263, **264–66**, 267, 268, *390, 401*
chest of drawers (Salem, Massachusetts; attributed to the Symonds shop tradition; with walnut and cedar facings) [cat. no. 109], 184, 263, 264, **267–69**, 305
chest of drawers (Windsor, Connecticut, or vicinity) [cat. no. 112], 5, 189, 263, **275–78**
chest of drawers (case of drawers), form, 263; and chest with drawers, 195, 237; and cupboard, 279, 284; versus high chest of drawers, 305. *See also entries at* high chest of drawers; small chest of drawers
chest of drawers on stand, form, 253
chest-on-chest, form, 324, 326n6

chest-on-frame (Connecticut, Guilford-Saybrook area) [cat. no. 107], 187, 220, 239, 240, 241n4, 242, 244, 245, 253, **259–62**, 270, 276, 327, 332, 334, 338n9
chest-on-frame (Massachusetts, eastern) [cat. no. 105; figs. 45, 68], 253, **253–56**, 258, 259, 371n4, *385, 390*
chest-on-frame (Massachusetts, probably Hingham-Scituate area) [cat. no. 106], 124, 237, 253, 254, **256–58**, 259
chest-on-frame (chest-on-stand), form, 253
chest with drawer (Connecticut, Guilford-Saybrook area) [cat. no. 101; fig. 71], 4, 10, 187, 196, 239, 240, 241n4, **242–44**, 244, 245, 246n1, 246n2, 246n3, 259, 276, 334, 338n9, *391*
chest with drawer (Connecticut, probably Milford area) [cat. no. 103], 10, 196, **247–49**
chest with drawer (Connecticut, south-central, 1705) [cat. no. 100; fig. 70], 196, 234n3, **239–41**, 242, 276, 370, *391*
chest with drawer (Connecticut, south-central, 1720–35) [cat. no. 102; fig. 72], 5, 196, 239, 240, 241n4, 242, **244–46**, 248, 276, *391*
chest with drawer (Hampshire County, Massachusetts; "Hadley" chest) [cat. no. 96; figs. 61, 86], 195, 228, **229–32**, *389, 396*
chest with drawer (Ipswich, Massachusetts; attributed to the Searle-Dennis shop tradition) [cat. no. 85], 195, 196, 198, 200, **202–4**
chest with drawer (Massachusetts, eastern, probably) [cat. no. 97], 180n2, 195, **232–34**
chest with drawer (Taunton, Massachusetts; attributed to Robert Crosman) [cat. no. 104; fig. 73], 5, 10, 196, **249–52**, *391*
chest with drawer(s), form, 195, 237
chest with drawers (Boston or vicinity; with diamond plaques) [cat. no. 99], 195, 234, 234n4, 236, **237–39**, 257
chest with drawers (Boston or vicinity; with rectangular fields) [cat. no. 98; figs. 67, 110, 131], 195, 234n4, **234–37**, 237, 257, 273, 282, 306, *390, 401, 410*
chest with drawers (Guilford, Connecticut, or vicinity) [cat. no. 140], 211, 282, 283n5, 327, 353, **364–67**
chest with drawers (Hampshire County, Massachusetts; "Hadley" chest) [cat. no. 95; fig. 111], 195, 222, **227–29**, 229, 230, 232n3, 363, *402*
chest with drawers (Wethersfield, Connecticut, or vicinity; sunflower chest) [cat. no. 92; fig. 64], 8, 9, 175, 195, **219–21**, 222, 225, 228, 232n3, 239, 366, *390*
chest with drawers (Wethersfield, Connecticut, or vicinity; sunflower chest with initials) [cat. no. 93; figs. 59, 60, 95, 109], 9, 175, 195, 219, **222–24**, 225, 228, 230, 232n3, 239, *388, 398, 401*
Clapp, Preserved (m. 1703), 229, cat. no. 95
Clark, Bellostee Hall (1816–1894), 206, cat. no. 86
Clark, Ebenezer (in New Haven 1638–before 1700), 206, cat. no. 86
Clark, John (1625–1677), 189, cat. no. 80
Clark(e), Rebecca (1687–1716), 188, 189, cat. no. 80
Clark, Major Samuel (1655–1736), 189, cat. no. 80
Clark family of Cheshire, Connecticut, 206, cat. no. 86
Clarkson, Emilie Vallete (Mrs. William A. Moore) (1863–1946), 94, 95, cat. no. 34
Clarkson family of New York, 94–95, cat. no. 34
Clement, Arthur W., collection, 344, cat. no. 132
Clement, Samuel (active 1726), 308, 330n4, 344n1
clothespresses, 279–80
Cole, Grace (Mrs. William Searle; later Mrs. Thomas Dennis), 196, 199n5
Collings and Collings, 22, 24, 78, 84, 100, 106, 124, 131, 140, 164, 256, 314; cat. nos. 3, 4, 27, 30, 37, 39, 46, 50, 55, 68, 105, 123

Connecticut
    chest [cat. no. 90; figs. 57, 58, 84, 125], 195, **215–17**, *388*, *396*, *407*
    chest with drawer (1705) [cat. no. 100; fig. 70], 196, 234n3, **239–41**, 242, 276, 370, *391*
    chest with drawer (1720–35) [cat. no. 102; fig. 72], 5, 196, 239, 240, 241n4, 242, **244–46**, 248, 276, *391*
    dressing table (with full front board) [cat. no. 128], 254, 331, **332–33**, 334, 336, 338n9
    dressing table (with joined construction) [cat. no. 129], 331, **334–35**, 338n9
    high chest of drawers [cat. no. 127], 305, **327–30**
    oval table with falling leaves [cat. no. 68], 143–44, 162n2, **164–65**
    See also Branford-Saybrook area; Guilford-Saybrook area; Hartford; Milford; New Haven; New London County; Saybrook; Wethersfield
Connecticut River valley, carving tradition, 227, 229, 230, 231–32n2
construction, detail views [figs. 84–105], *396–400*
Continental influences, 8, 9, 31, 32n3, 44, 198, 306, 354
Cornelius, Charles O., 7
Cornelius, Louise R. (Mrs. Charles O.), collection, 191, cat. no. 81
Cornwell, Hannah Van Wyck (m. 1729), 309, cat. no. 121
Cornwell, Margaret E. (m. 1815), 309, cat. no. 121
Corwithy, Samuel (d. 1659), 117n1
Cotton, Elizabeth (1663–1743), 75, cat. no. 26
couch (southeastern Pennsylvania) [cat. no. 42], 46, 104, **112–13**
couch (southeastern Pennsylvania, probably Philadelphia) [cat. no. 41; fig. 29], 46, 104, **110–12**, *379*
couches (daybeds), form, 104, 110, 112, 112n1
Covert, Hannah (1816–1902), 309, cat. no. 121
cradle (Suffolk County, Massachusetts) [cat. no. 45], 60, 104, **117–19**
Crosman, Robert (1707–1799), 249, 250
Crosman, Robert, attributed to, chest with drawer [cat. no. 104; fig. 73], 5, 10, 196, **249–52**, *391*
Cross, Mary, 187, cat. no. 79
cupboard (Guilford, Connecticut, or vicinity) [cat. no. 113; figs. 48, 63, 93], 8, 147n4, 211, 213, 236, 279, **280–83**, 327, 365, 370, *385*, *389*, *398*
cupboard (Middlesex County, Massachusetts) [cat. no. 141; fig. 49], 6, 122, 147n4, 270, 287n5, 353, **367–71**, *385*
cupboard (New England, eastern, probably) [cat. no. 117], 279, **294–95**
cupboard (New Haven, Connecticut, or vicinity) [cat. no. 116; figs. 66, 113, 132], 147n4, 147n5, 232, 279, 283n5, **290–93**, *390*, *402*, *410*
cupboard (Plymouth County, Massachusetts, possibly Marshfield) [cat. no. 115; figs. 65, 126, 129], 7, 56, 236, 254, 257, 266, 279, 282, 284, **287–90**, 371n4, *390*, *408*, *410*
cupboard (Plymouth or Barnstable County, Massachusetts) [cat. no. 114; figs. 47, 88, 94, 107, 130, 139–41], 56, 232, 236, 254, 257, 279, 282, **284–87**, 287, 288, 370, 371n4, *385*, *396*, *398*, *401*, *410*, *411*
cupboard, forms, 279–80; and chest of drawers, 279, 284; terms for parts [fig. 126], *408*
cupboard base in Museum of Fine Arts, Boston (probably Woburn, Massachusetts) [ill. 141d], 367, *368*, 369, 370, 371n4
cupboards and kasten [cat. nos. 113–20, 141], 279–304, 367–71
Curran, Thomas, 158
Cushing, Caleb (1703–1797), 75, cat. no. 26
Cushing, Rev. Caleb (1673–1752), 75, 75n6, 75n9, cat. no. 26
Cushing, Sarah (1738–1822), 75, cat. no. 26
cyma recta molding [fig. 128], *410*
cyma reversa molding [fig. 128], *410*

dado joint [fig. 156], *414*
Davenport, Millia, collection, 298, cat. no. 118
Davis, Mrs. A. Vidal, 210, cat. no. 87
Davis, B. H., 113, cat. no. 42
daybeds. *See* couches
decorative details [figs. 53–80], *386–94*
Dedham, Massachusetts, box (attributed to the Thurston shop tradition) [cat. no. 72], 169, **173–75**
de Forest, Robert W., 4, 5, 6, 7
de Forest, Mrs. Robert W., 5; collection, 3, 158, cat. no. 64
de Groot, Adelaide Milton, 87, cat. no. 31
Delaware River valley school, slat-back chairs, 44, 46–47, 48, 50n1, 112
Demuth, Augusta W., 342, cat. no. 131
Demuth, Charles, 342
Dennis, Grace Cole Searle, 196, 199n5
Dennis, John (1672–1757), 202n9
Dennis, Thomas (1638–1706), 195, 196, 199n1, 199n3, 202n9, 231n2. *See also* Searle, William, or Thomas Dennis; Searle-Dennis shop tradition
desk (Boston or vicinity) [cat. no. 133; fig. 82], 342, **346–48**, 349, *395*
desk (probably eastern Massachusetts) [cat. no. 134; fig. 83], 342, **349–51**, *395*
desk and bookcase, form, 192, 324, 326n6, 342
desk box, form, 342
desk-on-frame (New York City or vicinity) [cat. no. 132; fig. 36], 8, 159, 296, 308, 342, **343–45**, *381*
desk-on-frame, form, 342
Devonshire, England, 195, 196, 198, 200, 202n3, 231–32n2
Dexter, Mrs. Gordon, collection, 90, cat. no. 32
Dillon, Clarence, collection, 326, cat. no. 126
dining tables, 135, 143
Dole, Jane (m. 1765), 75, cat. no. 26
Dorset, England, 257
dovetail joints [figs. 158–60], *414*
Drake, John (1592–1659), 232n2
drawers, detail views [figs. 106–15], *401–2*
draw (drawing) tables, form, 143
dressing box, form, 169, 253
dressing table (Connecticut, probably; with full front board) [cat. no. 128], 254, 331, **332–33**, 334, 336, 338n9
dressing table (Connecticut, probably; with joined construction) [cat. no. 129], 331, **334–35**, 338n9
dressing table (Philadelphia) [cat. no. 131; fig. 43], 10, 147, 192, 305, 309n7, 331, 332, **339–41**, *384*
dressing table (chamber table, toilet table, lowboy), form, 331
dressing table, with slate top. *See* slate table
Drew, John (in Boston 1715), 326n5
Dunn, Duval, 110, cat. no. 40
Dunn, Mr. F., 142, cat. no. 57
du Pont, Henry Francis, 5
Dutch gold, 190–91, 320. *See also* German gold
Dutch influence, 31, 275n3, 296, 299, 302. *See also* Netherlandish influence
Dutch-style cupboards, 10. *See also entries at* kast
Duxbury, Massachusetts, 287, 287n5
Dwight, Lawrence (d. 1918), 322, cat. no. 125

East Anglia, England, 186, 264
easy chair (Boston, 1715–30) [cat. no. 39; fig. 23], 88, 104, **105–7**, 108, 156n5, *378*

easy chair (Boston, 1730–40) [cat. no. 40; fig. 89], 78n2, 88, 104, 105, 106n4, **108–10**, *397*

easy chairs, form, 104, 105

edge moldings [figs. 135–37], 200, *410*

Edsall, Thomas (in Boston 1635), 237n4

elbow chairs, term, 13. *See also* armchairs

Endicott, Robert B., collection, 48, cat. no. 16

English influences, 8–9, 10. *See also* London; *and entries for specific counties and shires*

Erving, Henry Wood, 227

Essex County, Massachusetts, 182, 186
  box [cat. no. 78; fig. 143], 24, 169, **182–84**, *411*
  chest of drawers [cat. no. 110; figs. 74, 97, 106, 134, 142], 5, 122, 147n5, 263, **269–72**, 274, 370, *392, 399, 401, 410, 411*
  folding table [cat. no. 58; figs. 46, 87, 90, 91], 5, 24, 143, **144–47**, 182, 270, 279, *385, 396, 397*
  joined armchair [cat. no. 18; fig. 54], 8, 51, **52–54**, *387*
  See also Ipswich; Salem

Exeter, England, school of florid carving, 196–98

fall-front desk, 342

falling leaves. *See entries at* oval table with falling leaves

Fancher, C. W., 178, cat. no. 74

Faneuil, Benjamin (in New York 1706), 75n5

Far Eastern influences, 305

fascia molding [fig. 128], *410*

feet, detail views [figs. 50–52], *386*

fielded panels, 275n3

fillet molding [fig. 128], *410*

firebacks, 235–36

Fisher, Captain Daniel, chairs, 27

Fitch, Thomas, 74, 75n5, 90, 104

flat-sawing [fig. 150], *413*

Fleeson, Plunket, 93, 95n1

folding table (northern Essex County, Massachusetts) [cat. no. 58; figs. 46, 87, 90, 91], 5, 24, 143, **144–47**, 182, 270, 279, *385, 396, 397*

folding (folded) table, forms, 143, 146

Ford, Edward, 146, cat. no. 58

Ford, William (1604–1676), 287n5

"forms," 51, 121

Fostor, Captain Hopestill, 62

frame-and-panel construction [fig. 84], 9, 195, *396*

framed table, term, 121

Fraser, Esther Stevens, 258, cat. no. 106

Freer, Antoinette (1729–1777), 356, cat. no. 135

French Canadian furniture, 32n6, 344n5

French influences, 306, 343

Friedley, Durr, 7

Fuessenich, Frederick W., 246, 278; cat. nos. 102, 112

Fulton, Robert, 4

Furness, George Choate (1884–1944), 146, cat. no. 58

Furness, James Choate (1854–1925), 146, cat. no. 58

Furness, Lillie May Appleton (1858–1903), 146, 147, cat. no. 58

Fussell, Solomon (active 1726–ca. 1750), 48–49

Fussell, Solomon, shop of, Philadelphia, probably, slat-back armchair [cat. no. 17; figs. 12, 31], 34, 47, **48–50**, *95n2, 375, 379*

Gaines, John II (1677–1748), 82, 97, 99n1, 102n2

Gaines, John III (1704–1743), 83, 97, 99, 99n1, 102n2

Gaines, John III, shop of, Portsmouth, New Hampshire, attributed to

splat-back armchair [cat. no. 37; figs. 20, 30], 64, 82, 83, 97, **99–102**, 103, 138, 358, *377, 379*
  splat-back chair [cat. no. 36; figs. 51, 119], 64, 82, 83, **97–99**, 100, 102n3, 103, 138, *386, 403*

Gaines, Thomas (1712–1761), 99n1, 102n2

Gaines family, 82, 83, 97, 102n2, 358

Gaines school (Gaines-type) chairs, 82, 83, 84n3, 84n4, 97, 99, 100

Garvin, Francis P., 5

"gate" [fig. 90], 143, *397*

"gateleg" tables, 143. *See also entries at* oval table with falling leaves

German gold, 320, 322n8. *See also* Dutch gold

Germanic influences, 47, 121, 130

Gibbons, William (in New Haven 1640–d. 1689), 283n5, 292

Gloucestershire, England, 202, 205, 213

Goddard, John (1724–1785), 351n3

graining, 122, 125, 126n1, 269, 367

Graves, George Coe, collection, 3, 103, 210, 338, 367; cat. nos. 38, 87, 130, 140

Gravesend, New York, 17n6

great chair, term, 13. *See also* armchairs

Griggs, Martha, 17, cat. no. 1

grisaille painting, 280, 299, 302

Guilford, Connecticut, or vicinity
  chest (with double-heart motif) [cat. no. 89], 195, 211, 212, **213–14**, 216, 282
  chest (with S-scroll motif) [cat. no. 88; fig. 135], 195, **211–13**, 213, 216, 282, 327, 365, 366, *410*
  chest with drawers [cat. no. 140], 211, 282, 283n5, 327, 353, **364–67**
  cupboard [cat. no. 113; figs. 48, 63, 93], 8, 147n4, 211, 213, 236, 279, **280–83**, 327, 365, 370, *385, 389, 398*

Guilford-Saybrook area, Connecticut, school, 187, 196, 242, 244, 245, 246n1, 248, 259n1
  chest-on-frame [cat. no. 107], 187, 220, 239, 240, 241n4, 242, 244, 245, 253, **259–62**, 270, 276, 327, 332, 334, 338n9
  chest with drawer [cat. no. 101; fig. 71], 4, 10, 187, 196, 239, 240, 241n4, **242–44**, 244, 245, 246n1, 246n2, 246n3, 259, 276, 334, 338n9, *391*

Guillam, Charles (1671–1727), 242, 259

"Hadley" pieces, 227–28, 363; chests, 195, 222, 227, 228, 229, 232

half-lap joint [fig. 155], *414*

Halsey, R. T. H., 7

Hammersmith ironworks, 235

Hampshire County, Massachusetts, 227, 231n2
  chest with drawer [cat. no. 96; figs. 61, 86], 195, 228, **229–32**, *389, 396*
  chest with drawers [cat. no. 95; fig. 111], 195, 222, **227–29**, 229, 230, 232n3, 363, *402*

Hampton, New Hampshire
  box [cat. no. 77], 169, **181–82**, 217
  chest [cat. no. 91], 181, 182, 196, **217–18**

Hansen, Catherine (m. 1823), 355, cat. no. 135

hardware, detail views [figs. 116–18], *403*

Hart, Thomas, house, Ipswich, 8

Hartford County, Connecticut, 219, 239
  chest [cat. no. 94], 195, **225–26**

Harvard University, President's Chair, 14

Haskell, Mrs. J. Armory, collection, 115, cat. no. 43

Hawley, Charles (1791–1866), 87, cat. no. 31

Hawley, Samuel (ca. 1647–1734), 87, 87n8, cat. no. 31

Head, John (d. 1754), high chest and dressing table for Caspar
     Wistar, 192, 194n4, 339, 340
Heckscher, Morrison H., 8
Herrick, Ephraim (baptized 1638–1693), 184, 187, cat. no. 79
Herrick, Henry (1604–1671), 187, cat. no. 79
Herrick, Mary Cross (1640–after 1710), 184, 187, cat. no. 79
Hewlett, Jane (1749–1816), 309, cat. no. 121
Hewlett, John III (1731–1812), 304, cat. no. 120
Hewlett, Rebecca (1743–1790), 309, cat. no. 121
Hicks, Mary C. (1887–1989), 355, cat. no. 135
Hicks, Sarah Matilda Van Duyn (b. ca. 1829), 355–56, cat. no. 135
Hicks family, 355–56, cat. no. 135
Higgins, Frank C., 218, cat. no. 91
highboy, term, 305. *See also entries at* high chest of drawers
high chair. *See* slat-back high chair
high chest of drawers (Boston, 1700–1730) [cat. no. 123; figs. 40,
     98–100, 104, 115, 127, 147], 305, **313–15**, 316, 318, 320, 326n2, 327,
     346, *383, 399, 400, 402, 409, 412*
high chest of drawers (Boston, 1710–25) [cat. no. 122; figs. 39, 77, 145],
     270, 305, 306, **309–12**, *383, 393, 411*
high chest of drawers (Boston, 1710–30) [cat. no. 125; figs. 42, 78], 2, 8,
     191, 275, 305, 310, 313, 316, **319–23**, 332, *384, 393*
high chest of drawers (Boston, 1715–30) [cat. no. 126; figs. 41, 102, 105,
     146], 8, 305, 318n4, **323–26**, 327, 336, *383, 400, 412*
high chest of drawers (Boston or vicinity) [cat. no. 124; figs. 101, 103,
     114], 305, 313, **316–18**, 320, *400, 402*
high chest of drawers (New York City or western Long Island) [cat.
     no. 121; figs. 44, 112, 144], 8, 10, 159, 305, **306–9**, *384, 402, 411*
high chest of drawers (probably eastern Connecticut or Rhode
     Island) [cat. no. 127], 305, **327–30**
high chest of drawers, form, 305, 313; and dressing table, 331; influ-
     ence on other forms, 253, 263, 346; miniature, *see* small cabinet or
     spice box; terms for parts [fig. 127], *409*
Hingham-Scituate area, Massachusetts, chest-on-frame [cat.
     no. 106], 124, 237, 253, 254, **256–58**, 259
Hoentschel, Georges, collection, 5
Hogg, Ima, 5
Holly, Mary Stiles (m. 1821), 87, cat. no. 31
Holmes, Nathaniel (active in 1730s), 326n7, 350
Holyoke, Edward (1689–1769), 8, 323, 326, cat. no. 126
Holyoke, Mary Whipple Epes (d. 1790), 326, cat. no. 126
Hopper, Maria, 17, cat. no. 1
Hosmer, Walter, 91, 92, 367n3; collection, 92, 135, 226, 231, 244, 262,
     357, 358; cat. nos. 33, 52, 94, 96, 101, 107, 136
Houghton, John (1624–1684), 175n1
Hubbard, William F., 367n4
Hudson, Henry, 4
Hudson-Fulton exhibition (New York, 1909), 4, 7, 360
Hughes, Robert (active 1726), 322n4
Huguenot artisans, 14, 44n3, 220n6, 310, 343
Hunt family of Marshfield, 57, cat. no. 19
Huntingdon, England, 170
Hurd, Louis, 130, cat. no. 49
Hurlburt collection, 283, cat. no. 113

inlaid furniture, 141, 195, 232, 252n4, 263, 270, 290, 293n7
interiors, detail views [figs. 81–83], *395*
Ipswich, Massachusetts
     chest (attributed to William Searle or Thomas Dennis) [cat. no. 83;
          figs. 55, 136], 4, 195, **196–99**, 200, 201, 202n3, 203, 217, *387, 410*

chest (attributed to the Searle-Dennis shop tradition) [cat. no. 84],
     195, 196, **200–202**, 202
chest with drawer (attributed to the Searle-Dennis shop tradition)
     [cat. no. 85], 195, 196, 198, 200, **202–4**

japanners, in Boston, 319, 322n4
japanning, 242, 275, 276, 305, 309–10, 319–20
Jay, Frances (m. 1723/24), 95, cat. no. 34
Jay, Judith (m. 1735), 95, cat. no. 34
Johnston, Thomas (active late 1720s–1767), 322n4
joined armchair (Essex County, Massachusetts) [cat. no. 18; fig. 54],
     8, 51, **52–54**, *387*
joined armchair (southeastern Pennsylvania) [cat. no. 20; fig. 22], 10,
     51, **57–59**, 114, 130, 141, *378*
joined box stools, 253
joined chair-tables. *See* chair-tables
joined cradle. *See* cradle
joined furniture, compared to turned, 51
joined paneled chairs (wainscot chairs, wooden chairs, wooden-
     bottom chairs), 51. *See also entries at* joined armchair
joined seating with a wooden bottom [cat. nos. 18–22], 51–62
joined settles, 114. *See also* leather settle
joined stools. *See* joint stools
joined table (southeastern Pennsylvania) [cat. no. 50], 32, 121, 126,
     130–31
joined table. *See also entries at* small joined table; square joined table
joined table with drawer (Boston) [cat. no. 49; figs. 75, 116], 121, 126,
     128–30, 132, *392, 403*
joined table with drawer (Boston or vicinity, probably) [cat. no. 48],
     121, **126–27**, 128, 130
joined table with drawer (New York) [cat. no. 51; fig. 37], 7, 121,
     132–33, *382*
joined upholstered chairs, 64. *See also entries at* Turkey-work chair;
     leather chair
joiners, 51, 64–65
joints [figs. 151–66], *414–15*
joint stool (probably Boston or vicinity) [cat. no. 22], 51, **62–63**
joint stool (probably Braintree, Massachusetts, probably the Savell
     shop tradition) [cat. no. 21], 51, **59–61**, 62, 118, 122, 124, 161
joint (joined) stools, form, 51, 59
Jones, Inigo (1573–1652), 323

kast (probably New York City, 1690–1720) [cat. no. 119; figs. 80, 96],
     8, 10, 280, 296, **299–302**, 302, 303, *394, 398*
kast (probably New York City or vicinity, 1650–1700) [cat. no. 118;
     figs. 79, 137], 8, 280, **295–98**, 299, 302, 343, *394, 410*
kast (probably New York City or vicinity, 1690–1730) [cat. no. 120], 8,
     10, 280, 296, **302–4**
kast, form, 279, 280, 295, 308, 343
Kaufman, Hyman, 163, cat. no. 67
Keene, Mr. and Mrs. James O., collection, 32, cat. no. 9
Kent, Henry W., 4–5, 6, 7, 360
Killingworth, Connecticut, box (attributed to the Buell shop tradi-
     tion) [cat. no. 70; fig. 53], 169, **170–71**, *386*
King Hooper Antiques, Boston, 249, cat. no. 103
Kings County, New York (now Brooklyn), 17n6, 343
Kinsman family of northern Essex County, 147, no. 58

Lancashire, England, influences, 47, 57, 141, 231n2
Lawton, Herbert, collection, 141, cat. no. 56

leather armchair (Boston or vicinity) [cat. no. 34; fig. 25], 64, 78n2, **93–95**, 108, 334, *378*

leather chair (Boston, 1690–1705) [cat. no. 25], 64, 65, **71–72**, 72, 161

leather chair (Boston, 1700–1720) [cat. no. 27; figs. 15, 24, 92], 5, 57, 62, 64, 72, 74, **76–78**, 79, 83, 88, 91, 94, 105, 108, 147, 161, 313, 334, *376, 378, 397*

leather chair (Boston, 1723–45) [cat. no. 33], 42, 64, 76, 88, **90–92**, 94, 95, 95n1, 105, 156, 357

leather chairs (two) (Boston, northeastern Massachusetts, or possibly southern New Hampshire) [cat. no. 26; figs. 14, 21], 26, 64, 72, **72–75**, 76, 86, 105, 134, 161, *375, 378*

leather settle (southeastern Pennsylvania) [cat. no. 43], 104, **114–15**

legs, detail views [figs. 32–44], *380–84*

Lehman, Harold M. and Cecile (later Cecile L. Mayer), collection, 112, cat. no. 41

Levin, N. D., 113, cat. no. 42

Lindall, Abigail (m. 1704), 322, cat. no. 125

Little, J. Lovell, collection, 326, cat. no. 126

Little, Walter H. (b. 1863), 75, cat. no. 26

little chairs, term, 13. *See also* chairs

Little family of Newbury, 75, cat. no. 26

Lockwood, Luke Vincent, 3, 4–5, 7, 336

Lockwood, Mrs. Luke Vincent, 362

London influences, 9, 234, 235, 237n4, 263, 273, 282, 284, 287n5, 292

Long, H., collection, 100, cat. no. 37

Long Island, high chest of drawers [cat. no. 121; figs. 44, 112, 144], 8, 10, 159, 305, **306–9**, *384, 402, 411*

Loomis family of Windsor, 177

Lorillard, Mrs. Screven, collection, 5, 84, 140, 142, 163, 314; cat. nos. 30, 55, 57, 66, 123

Loring, George Bailey (m. 1851), 322, cat. no. 125

Loring, Sally, 322, cat. no. 125

Louis XIV style, 9

Lovering family of northern Essex County, 147, cat. no. 58

lowboy, term, 331. *See also entries at* dressing table

Low Countries (Netherlandish) influence, 9, 31, 186, 299, 306

Lynde, Nathaniel (1659–1729), 189, cat. no. 80

Lynde, Nathaniel (1692–1749), 188

Lynde, Rebecca (Clarke) (1687–1716), 188, 189, cat. no. 80

Lynde, Samuel (1689–1754), 189, cat. no. 80

Lynde family of Saybrook, 189, cat. no. 80

Lyndon, Josiah (active 1672), 202n9

Lyon, Charles Woolsey, 66, 146, 210, 286, 293, 328, 338, 367; cat. nos. 23, 58, 87, 114, 116, 127, 130, 140

Lyon, Dr. Irving P., 196, 199n1, 206n1, 358, 367; collection, 70, 71n5, 224; cat. nos. 24, 93

Lyon, Dr. Irving W., 3, 66–68, 92, 219, 230, 356, 357, 358, 364, 367; collection, 66, 70, 224, 367; cat. nos. 23, 24, 93, 140

Maine, southern
oval table [cat. no. 55; fig. 52], 102–3, 122, 137, **138–40**, *386*

slate table [cat. no. 130], 331, 332, **336–38**

splat-back armchair [cat. no. 38], 64, 94, **102–3**, 138

Mannerist influences, 9, 52, 198

Marblehead, Massachusetts, 324, 326n7

marbleizing, 296, 298n2

Mark, Harry, 344, cat. no. 132

marks, detail views [figs. 119–21], *403*

marquetry, 242, 270, 336

Marshfield, Massachusetts
chair-table [cat. no. 19], 51, **54–57**, 208, 288

cupboard [cat. no. 115; figs. 65, 126, 129], 7, 56, 236, 254, 257, 266, 279, 282, 284, **287–90**, 371n4, *390, 408, 410*

Marston, Nathaniel, 94, cat. no. 34

Mason, Ralph (in Boston 1635), 237n4

Massachusetts
spindle-back chair [cat. no. 6], 13, **27–28**

eastern region
banister-back chair [cat. no. 28; fig. 18], 64, **79–80**, *377*

chest of drawers [cat. no. 110; figs. 74, 97, 106, 134, 142], 5, 122, 147n5, 263, **269–72**, 274, 370, *392, 399, 401, 410, 411*

chest-on-frame [cat. no. 105; figs. 45, 68], 253, **253–56**, 258, 259, 371n4, *385, 390*

chest with drawer [cat. no. 97], 180n2, 195, **232–34**

desk [cat. no. 134; fig. 83], 342, **349–51**, *395*

oval table with falling leaves (1690–1720; on trestle base) [cat. no. 66], 143, 146, 159, **161–62**, 164

oval table with falling leaves (1715–40; on trestle base) [cat. no. 67], 143, 146, 159, 161, **162–63**, 164

oval table with falling leaves (1720–50) [cat. no. 62], 143, 146, 150, **153–54**

slat-back armchair (1650–1700) [cat. no. 136], 353, **356–58**

slat-back armchair (1720–50) [cat. no. 15; fig. 9], 32n7, 34, **45–46**, *374*

spindle-back armchair [cat. no. 5; fig. 4], 13, **25–26**, *373*

trestle table [cat. no. 138], 143, 353, **360–62**

northeastern and northeastern coastal regions
banister-back armchair (1720–40) [cat. no. 29; fig. 16], 8, 64, **81–82**, 83, 99, 358, *376*

banister-back armchair (1720–40, with later alterations) [cat. no. 137; figs. 17, 28], 100, 353, **358–60**, *376, 379*

banister-back chairs (two) [cat. no. 30; figs. 19, 27, 123], *12*, 64, 82, **83–85**, 358, *377, 379, 406*

leather chairs (two) [cat. no. 26; figs. 14, 21], 26, 64, 72, **72–75**, 76, 86, 105, 134, 161, *375, 378*

slate table [cat. no. 130], 331, 332, **336–38**

spindle-back armchair [cat. no. 4; figs. 3, 122], 13, **22–24**, *373, 405*

splat-back chair [cat. no. 35], 64, 94, **95–96**, 97, 102, 112, 138

southeastern region
square joined table [cat. no. 47], 60, 121, **124–26**, 128, 161, 256

See also Barnstable County; Boston; Dedham; Essex County; Hampshire County; Hingham-Scituate area; Ipswich; Middlesex County; Plymouth County; Salem; Suffolk County

Mattoon, Albert W. (1865–1937), 293, cat. no. 116

Mattoon, Mrs. Albert W. (Alice Northrop Merwin) (b. 1864), 290, cat. no. 116

Mayer, Cecile L., 112, cat. no. 41

Maynard, Ross H., 338n10; collection, 124, 338; cat. nos. 46, 130

Medfield, Massachusetts, box (attributed to the Thurston shop tradition) [cat. no. 72], 169, **173–75**

Merwin, Robert Treat (1838–1902), 293, cat. no. 116

Merwin family of Milford and New Haven, 215, 293, cat. no. 116

Messinger, Henry (in Boston 1641), 237n4

mid-Atlantic region, settle [cat. no. 44], 104, **116–17**

Middlesex County, Massachusetts, 270, 367
chest of drawers [cat. no. 110; figs. 74, 97, 106, 134, 142], 5, 122, 147n5, 263, **269–72**, 274, 370, *392, 399, 401, 410, 411*

cupboard [cat. no. 141; fig. 49], 6, 122, 147n4, 270, 287n5, 353, **367–71**, *385*

Milford, Connecticut, area
chest [cat. no. 90; figs. 57, 58, 84, 125], 195, **215–17**, *388, 396, 407*

chest with drawer [cat. no. 103], 10, 196, **247–49**

Mitchell, Hannah Elizabeth (1878–1968), 309, cat. no. 121

Mitchell (Mitchill), Robert (1670–1748), 309, cat. no. 121

Mitchell family of Port Washington, 309, cat. no. 121

miter joint [fig. 162], *415*

moldings, profiles [figs. 128–47], *410–12*

Montfort, Dominicus (1743–1815), 355, cat. no. 135

Montfort, Mary (1778–1875), 355, cat. no. 135

Montfort family of Poughkeepsie, 356

Moody, Elizabeth (b. 1799), 75, cat. no. 26

Moody, Molly (1774–1854), 75, cat. no. 26

Moody, Nathaniel (1769–1815), 75, cat. no. 26

Moody, Col. Samuel Jr. (1731–1790), 75, cat. no. 26

Moore, Deacon John (1614–1677), 177, 178

Moore, Sarah (1801–1870), 68, cat. no. 23

Moore, Mrs. William A. (Emilie Vallete Clarkson) (1863–1946), 94,
    95, cat. no. 34

Moore shop tradition, Windsor, Connecticut, attributed to
    box [cat. no. 74], 169, 175, **176–78**, 178, 179
    box (with dense carving) [cat. no. 75], 169, 175, 176, 177, **178–79**

Morgan, J. Pierpont, 5

Morson, Charles R., 300, cat. no. 119

mortise-and-tenon joints [figs. 84, 161, 163–65], 13, 51, *396*, *415*

Munger, Nicholas, 367, cat. no. 140

Munger family, 367, cat. no. 140

Myers, Louis Guerineau, collection, 142, cat. no. 57

nails, 362n3; detail views [figs. 117, 118], *403*

Nash, Chauncey C., collection, 256, cat. no. 105

Netherlandish (Low Countries) influence, 9, 31, 186, 299, 306

New England, 8
    box [cat. no. 76], 169, **180–81**, 234n3
    oval table (on splayed legs) [cat. no. 54], 122, **136–38**, 138, 164
    oval table (on trestle base) [cat. no. 56], 122, **140–41**
    oval table with falling leaves (1720–50) [cat. no. 61], 53, 143, 146,
        151–52, 336
    oval table with falling leaves (1770–1800; butterfly table) [cat.
        no. 69], 143–44, 162n2, 164, **166–67**
    settle [cat. no. 44], 104, **116–17**
    small joined table [cat. no. 53], 121, **135–36**
    eastern region
    cupboard [cat. no. 117], 279, **294–95**
    southeastern region
    slat-back high chair [cat. no. 11; fig. 7], 7, 34, **37–38**, *374*
    spindle-back armchair [cat. no. 7; fig. 5], 13, **28–29**, *374*

New Hampshire
    leather chairs (two) [cat. no. 26; figs. 14, 21], 26, 64, 72, **72–75**, 76,
        86, 105, 134, 161, *375*, *378*
    slate table [cat. no. 130], 331, 332, **336–38**
    splat-back chair [cat. no. 35], 64, 94, **95–96**, 97, 102, 112, 138
    See also Hampton; Portsmouth

New Haven, Connecticut, or vicinity
    chest (1650–80) [cat. no. 86; fig. 56], 195, **205–8**, 208, 212, 216, 217,
        257, 283n5, *387*
    chest (1670–90) [cat. no. 87], 147n5, 195, 205, **208–10**, 212, 216, 283n5
    cupboard [cat. no. 116; figs. 66, 113, 132], 147n4, 147n5, 232, 279,
        283n5, **290–93**, *390*, *402*, *410*

New Jersey, slat-back armchair [cat. no. 16], 34, **46–48**, 112

New London County, Connecticut, 327
    slat-back armchair [cat. no. 13; fig. 10], 34, **41–42**, *375*

Newmarch, Mary (m. 1730), 75, cat. no. 26

Newport, Rhode Island, 327, 350

New York, 8
    joined table with drawer [cat. no. 51; fig. 37], 7, 121, **132–33**, *382*
    oval table with falling leaves [cat. no. 65; figs. 35, 118], 44, 132, 143,
        146, 154, **159–61**, 162, 306, 308, *381*, *403*
    slat-back armchair [cat. no. 14; fig. 11], 34, **43–44**, *375*
    spindle-back armchair [cat. no. 135], 13–14, 16, 353, **354–56**

New York City, 9–10, 306–8
    desk-on-frame [cat. no. 132; fig. 36], 8, 159, 296, 308, 342, **343–45**,
        381
    high chest of drawers [cat. no. 121; figs. 44, 112, 144], 8, 10, 159, 305,
        306–9, *384*, *402*, *411*
    kast (1650–1700) [cat. no. 118; figs. 79, 137], 8, 280, **295–98**, 299, 302,
        343, *394*, *410*
    kast (1690–1720) [cat. no. 119; figs. 80, 96], 8, 10, 280, 296, **299–302**,
        302, 303, *394*, *398*
    kast (1690–1730) [cat. no. 120], 8, 10, 280, 296, **302–4**
    spindle-back armchair [cat. no. 1], 8, 13, **14–17**, 20n3, 24n1, 354
    spindle-back chair [cat. no. 9; figs. 13, 121], 8, 13, 16, 24n1, **31–33**, 44,
        130, 354, *375*, *403*

"New York State Furniture" exhibition (1934), 7

Nicholson, Mr. and Mrs. Eddy, collection, 54, cat. no. 18

Norwich, Connecticut, school, 41–42, 42n3

Nutting, Wallace, 258n1, 354; collection, 18, 20, 100, 284; cat. nos. 2, 37

oak: mill-sawn, 144, 147n5; riving [fig. 148], *413*

Oliver, Mary (m. 1656), 147, cat. no. 58

olive wood, 346

oval table (New England; on splayed legs) [cat. no. 54], 122, **136–38**,
    138, 164

oval table (New England; on trestle base) [cat. no. 56], 122, **140–41**

oval table (Portsmouth, New Hampshire, or southern Maine) [cat.
    no. 55; fig. 52], 102–3, 122, 137, **138–40**, *386*

oval table with falling leaves (Boston) [cat. no. 59; fig. 32], 4, 122, 143,
    146, **147–49**, *380*

oval table with falling leaves (Boston or vicinity, probably) [cat.
    no. 60; figs. 33, 124], 143, 146, **150–51**, 151, 162, 336, *380*, *407*

oval table with falling leaves (Connecticut; butterfly table) [cat.
    no. 68], 143–44, 162n2, **164–65**

oval table with falling leaves (Massachusetts, eastern, probably,
    1690–1720; on trestle base) [cat. no. 66], 143, 146, 159, **161–62**, 164

oval table with falling leaves (Massachusetts, eastern, 1715–40; on
    trestle base) [cat. no. 67], 143, 146, 159, 161, **162–63**, 164

oval table with falling leaves (Massachusetts, eastern, 1720–50) [cat.
    no. 62], 143, 146, 150, **153–54**

oval table with falling leaves (New England, 1720–50) [cat. no. 61],
    53, 143, 146, **151–52**, 336

oval table with falling leaves (New England, 1770–1800; butterfly
    table) [cat. no. 69], 143–44, 162n2, 164, **166–67**

oval table with falling leaves (New York; on trestle base) [cat. no. 65;
    figs. 35, 118], 44, 132, 143, 146, 154, **159–61**, 162, 306, 308, *381*, *403*

oval table with falling leaves (Pennsylvania, southeastern, possibly
    Philadelphia) [cat. no. 64; fig. 38], 94, 143, 146, 154, **157–59**, *382*

oval table with falling leaves (Rhode Island) [cat. no. 63; figs. 34, 117],
    134, 143, 146, **154–56**, *381*, *403*

oval table with falling (hinged) leaves, form, 121, 143; terms for parts
    [fig. 124], *407*

Overton, Mrs. J. Woodhull, collection, 5, 50, 178, 224, 256, 293; cat.
    nos. 17, 74, 93, 105, 116

ovolo molding [fig. 128], *410*

oystershell veneer, 270

Paine, Hannah (m. 1651), 147, cat. no. 58
painted decoration, 128, 169, 196, 253, 263, 280, 305
Palladian style, 323, 326n5
Palladio, Andrea (1508–1580), 323
Palmer, George S., 4, 92, 135, 226, 231, 244, 262, 358
Park (cabinetmaker), 320
Park, Lawrence (1873–1924), 326, cat. no. 126
Parmentier, Antoinette (1684–1737), 356, cat. no. 135
Partridge, Nehemiah (active Boston 1712–ca. 1714), 322n4
Patch family of northern Essex County, 147, cat. no. 58
pattern books, 9, 52, 198, 256
Pavey, Jess, collection, 32, cat. no. 9
Pearson, Mary Holyoke (1782–1829), 326, cat. no. 126
Pendleton, Charles, collection, 3
Pendleton, Roger (d. 1712), 322n4
Penn, William, 143
Pennsylvania, 8
    slat-back armchair [cat. no. 16], 34, **46–48**, 112
    southeastern region
    couch (1710–40) [cat. no. 41; fig. 29], 46, 104, **110–12**, *379*
    couch (1750–80) [cat. no. 42], 46, 104, **112–13**
    joined armchair [cat. no. 20; fig. 22], 10, 51, **57–59**, 114, 130, 141, *378*
    joined table [cat. no. 50], 32, 121, 126, **130–31**
    leather settle [cat. no. 43], 104, **114–15**
    oval table with falling leaves [cat. no. 64; fig. 38], 94, 143, 146, 154, **157–59**, *382*
    round table [cat. no. 57], 122, **141–42**
    See also Philadelphia
Perkins, Sarah (m. 1701), 147, cat. no. 58
Philadelphia, 9–10; chair forms, 46, 47, 57, 87, 93–94; high chests, 147–48, 192, 305, 327, 340
    couch [cat. no. 41; fig. 29], 46, 104, **110–12**, *379*
    dressing table [cat. no. 131; fig. 43], 10, 147, 192, 305, 309n7, 331, 332, **339–41**, *384*
    oval table with falling leaves [cat. no. 64; fig. 38], 94, 143, 146, 154, **157–59**, *382*
    slat-back armchair (probably the shop of Solomon Fussell) [cat. no. 17; figs. 12, 31], 34, 47, **48–50**, 95n2, *375, 379*
    small cabinet or spice box [cat. no. 82], 116, 169, 186, **192–94**, 305, 332, 340
Phillips, Abigail (b. 1851), 57, cat. no. 19
Phillips, John (d. 1658), 57, cat. no. 19
Phillips, Nathaniel (1713–1795), 57, cat. no. 19
Phillips, Nathaniel (1798–1884), 57, cat. no. 19
Phyfe, Duncan, 7
Pickman, Benjamin (1672–1719), 322, cat. no. 125
Pickman, Benjamin (1708–1773), 322, cat. no. 125
Pickman family of Salem, 322, cat. no. 125
pillars: detail views [figs. 45–49], *385*; term, 316
plain-sawing [fig. 150], *413*
plain-top leather chairs, 72–74, 75n5
Plumley, Charles (d. 1708), 346
Plymouth Colony, 13, 117; school of joinery, 7, 54–56, 284, 287, 287n1, 287n5
Plymouth County, Massachusetts, 18, 21, 37, 180n2, 236, 254, 257
    chair-table [cat. no. 19], 51, **54–57**, 208, 288
    cupboard [cat. no. 114; figs. 47, 88, 94, 107, 130, 139–41], 56, 232, 236, 254, 257, 279, 282, **284–87**, 287, 288, 370, 371n4, *385, 396, 398, 401, 410, 411*

cupboard (with open shelf in lower section) [cat. no. 115; figs. 65, 126, 129], 7, 56, 236, 254, 257, 266, 279, 282, 284, **287–90**, 371n4, *390, 408, 410*
    slat-back armchair [cat. no. 12; fig. 6], 24n1, 28, 34, 37, **38–40**, 41, *374*
poplar, 20, 346
Portsmouth, New Hampshire, 84n5, 326n5
    banister-back armchair (1720–40) [cat. no. 29; fig. 16], 8, 64, **81–82**, 83, 99, 358, *376*
    banister-back armchair (1720–40, with later alterations) [cat. no. 137; figs. 17, 28], 100, 353, **358–60**, *376, 379*
    banister-back chairs (two) [cat. no. 30; figs. 19, 27, 123], *12*, 64, 82, **83–85**, 358, *377, 379, 406*
    oval table [cat. no. 55; fig. 52], 102–3, 122, 137, **138–40**, *386*
    splat-back armchair [cat. no. 38], 64, 94, **102–3**, 138
    splat-back armchair (attributed to the shop of John Gaines III) [cat. no. 37; figs. 20, 30], 64, 82, 83, 97, **99–102**, 103, 138, 358, *377, 379*
    splat-back chair (attributed to the shop of John Gaines III) [cat. no. 36; figs. 51, 119], 64, 82, 83, **97–99**, 100, 102n3, 103, 138, *386, 403*
Potter, Mrs. Warwick (Harriet Amory), 322, cat. no. 125
presses, 279–80. *See also entries at* kast
Price, William (in Boston 1714), 323–24; desk and bookcase made by, 323, 351n4
Prince, Deborah (1717–1806), 309, cat. no. 121
Providence, Rhode Island, 166n1
Pynchon family, 117, 228

quartering (quartersawing) [fig. 149], *413*
Queen Anne style: chairs, 10, 32, 48, 64, 88, 95, 99, 108; high chests, 323, 327
Quinby, Harry, 338, cat. no. 130

rabbet joint [fig. 157], *414*
radial cutting [fig. 149], *413*
Ralston, Ruth, 7
Randall (Randle), William (active ca. 1715–ca. 1735), 342; high chest japanned by, 319
Randall family of Marshfield, 57, cat. no. 19
Rawlins, Love (m. 1731), 322, cat. no. 125
Reifsnyder, Howard, collection, 158, cat. no. 64
Renaissance influences, 9, 14, 17, 148, 299
restoration issues, 6–8
Rhode Island
    high chest of drawers [cat. no. 127], 305, **327–30**
    oval table with falling leaves [cat. no. 63; figs. 34, 117], 134, 143, 146, **154–56**, *381, 403*
    small joined table [cat. no. 52], 121, **134–35**, 154
riving [fig. 148], *413*
Robbins Brothers shop (formerly Robbins and Winship), Hartford, 91, 367n3
Roberts, Joshua (d. 1719), 322n4, 323n8
Robinson, Lizzie Senter (d. after 1936), 309, cat. no. 121
Rockwell, John (1588–1662), 205
Rogers, Sarah L. (1812–1898), 57, cat. no. 19
Rogers family of Marshfield, 57, cat. no. 19
round table (probably southeastern Pennsylvania) [cat. no. 57], 122, **141–42**
Rubel, Mrs. Andrew M. (née Jane Moody Little), 75, cat. no. 26
rule joint [fig. 153], 166, 166n1, *414*

rush-seated chairs, 13, 21, 64
Russell, William (1612–1664/65), 283n5, 292
Russia leather, 74, 78n1, 91

Sack, Israel, 99, cat. no. 36
Sage, Mrs. Russell, 3, 4, 8
Salem, Massachusetts
    chest of drawers (attributed to the Symonds shop tradition) [cat. no. 108; figs. 69, 108], 7, 24, 180n2, 184, 263, **264–66**, 267, 268, *390, 401*
    chest of drawers (attributed to the Symonds shop tradition; with walnut and cedar facings) [cat. no. 109], 184, 263, 264, **267–69**, 305
    small cabinet (attributed to the Symonds shop tradition) [cat. no. 79; figs. 62, 81, 133, 138], 4, 9, 169, 182, **184–87**, 192, 233, 254, 264, 267, *389, 395, 410, 411*
Sanders, Mrs. Sara M., collection, 298, cat. no. 118
Sargent, Earle W., collection, 160, cat. no. 65
Savell, William Sr., 118n6
Savell shop tradition, Braintree, Massachusetts, 60, 118, 172
    box (attributed to)[cat. no. 71], 60, 118, 169, **172–73**, 257
    joint stool (probably) [cat. no. 21], 51, **59–61**, 62, 118, 122, 124, 161
Savery, William (1722–1787), shop of, Philadelphia, 112
Saybrook, Connecticut, box [cat. no. 80], 169, **187–89**, 327. *See also* Branford-Saybrook area; Guilford-Saybrook area
Schmuck, Henry (ca. 1801–1838), 68, cat. no. 23
Schmuck, Henry Moore (b. 1831), 68, cat. no. 23
Schrank, 279, 280
Schwartz, Morris, 6, 7, 158, 164–65
Scituate, Massachusetts, 287. *See also* Hingham-Scituate area
Scottow shop, Boston, 319–20
scrutoires (scriptores), form, 342
Searle, Grace Cole (later Dennis), 196, 199n5
Searle, William (d. 1667), 195, 196, 199n3, 199n5, 231n2
Searle, William, or Thomas Dennis, attributed to, chest [cat. no. 83; figs. 55, 136], 4, 195, **196–99**, 200, 201, 202n3, 203, 217, *387, 410*
Searle-Dennis shop tradition, Ipswich, Massachusetts, 195, 196–98, 202n9, 204
    attributed to
    chest [cat. no. 84], 195, 196, **200–202**, 202
    chest with drawer [cat. no. 85], 195, 196, 198, 200, **202–204**
seating furniture, 13–118
    joined seating with a wooden bottom [cat. nos. 18–22], 51–62
    miscellaneous furniture for sitting and reclining [cat. nos. 39–45], 104–18
    turned chairs with a slat back [cat. nos. 10–17, 136], 34–50, 356–58
    turned chairs with a spindle back [cat. nos. 1–9, 135], 13–32, 354–56
    upholstered, cane, and related rush-seated chairs [cat. nos. 23–38, 137], 64–103, 358–60
settees, 112
settle (mid-Atlantic region or New England) [cat. no. 44], 104, **116–17**
settle, form, 104, 114, 116, 117n1. *See also* leather settle
settle chest, 117n1
seventeenth-century style, 8–9, 10
Sewall, Samuel, 13, 279
Shippen, Edward, 149n3
Simons, Edward, 367n3
Skilton family of East Windsor, 278, cat. no. 112
slant-top (slant-front) desk, form, 342

slat-back armchair (Boston or vicinity, probably) [cat. no. 10; fig. 2], 34, **34–36**, 356, *373*
slat-back armchair (Massachusetts, eastern, 1650–1700, with later alterations) [cat. no. 136], 353, **356–58**
slat-back armchair (Massachusetts, eastern, probably, 1720–50) [cat. no. 15; fig. 9], 32n7, 34, **45–46**, *374*
slat-back armchair (New London County, Connecticut) [cat. no. 13; fig. 10], 34, **41–42**, *375*
slat-back armchair (New York) [cat. no. 14; fig. 11], 34, **43–44**, *375*
slat-back armchair (Pennsylvania or New Jersey) [cat. no. 16], 34, **46–48**, 112
slat-back armchair (Philadelphia, probably the shop of Solomon Fussell) [cat. no. 17; figs. 12, 31], 34, 47, **48–50**, 95n2, *375, 379*
slat-back armchair (Plymouth County, Massachusetts) [cat. no. 12; fig. 6], 24n1, 28, 34, 37, **38–40**, 41, *374*
slat-back high chair (probably southeastern New England) [cat. no. 11; fig. 7], 7, 34, **37–38**, *374*
slate table (northeastern Massachusetts, coastal New Hampshire, or adjacent coastal Maine) [cat. no. 130], 331, 332, **336–38**
small cabinet (Salem, Massachusetts; attributed to the Symonds shop tradition) [cat. no. 79; figs. 62, 81, 133, 138], 4, 9, 169, 182, **184–87**, 192, 233, 254, 264, 267, *389, 395, 410, 411*
small cabinet or spice box (Philadelphia) [cat. no. 82], 116, 169, 186, **192–94**, 305, 332, 340
small cabinets, 169
small chairs, term, 13, 27. *See also* chairs
small chest of drawers (Windsor, Connecticut, or vicinity) [cat. no. 81], 169, **189–91**, 276
small joined table (New England) [cat. no. 53], 121, **135–36**
small joined table (Rhode Island) [cat. no. 52], 121, **134–35**, 154
Smith, William, collection, 229, 328, cat. nos. 95, 127
Snow, Julia F. S., 252, cat. no. 104
Somerset, England, 205, 212, 213, 282
spice box, term, 192. *See also* small cabinet or spice box
spindle-back armchair (Boston or Charleston, Massachusetts) [cat. no. 2; fig. 1], 5, 13, **17–20**, 20, 21, 22, 23, 24n1, 27, 34, 36, 42, 356, *373*
spindle-back armchair (Boston or vicinity, probably) [cat. no. 3], 13, **20–22**, 27, 36
spindle-back armchair (Massachusetts, eastern) [cat. no. 5; fig. 4], 13, **25–26**, *373*
spindle-back armchair (Massachusetts, northeastern) [cat. no. 4; figs. 3, 122], 13, **22–24**, *373, 405*
spindle-back armchair (New England, southeastern, probably) [cat. no. 7; fig. 5], 13, **28–29**, *374*
spindle-back armchair (New York) [cat. no. 135], 13–14, 16, 353, **354–56**
spindle-back armchair (New York City or vicinity) [cat. no. 1], 8, 13, **14–17**, 20n3, 24n1, 354
spindle-back armchair, terms for parts [fig. 122], *405*
spindle-back chair (Connecticut, Branford-Saybrook area) [cat. no. 8; fig. 8], 8, 13, 28, **30–31**, 37, 45, *374*
spindle-back chair (Massachusetts, probably) [cat. no. 6], 13, **27–28**
spindle-back chair (New York City or vicinity) [cat. no. 9; figs. 13, 121], 8, 13, 16, 24n1, **31–33**, 44, 130, 354, *375, 403*
splat, term, 64
splat-back armchair (Portsmouth, New Hampshire, attributed to the shop of John Gaines III) [cat. no. 37; figs. 20, 30], 64, 82, 83, 97, **99–102**, 103, 138, 358, *377, 379*
splat-back armchair (Portsmouth, New Hampshire, or southern Maine) [cat. no. 38], 64, 94, **102–3**, 138
splat-back chair (Boston, northeastern Massachusetts, or coastal New Hampshire) [cat. no. 35], 64, 94, **95–96**, 97, 102, 112, 138

splat-back chair (Portsmouth, New Hampshire, attributed to the shop of John Gaines III) [cat. no. 36; figs. 51, 119], 64, 82, 83, **97–99**, 100, 102n3, 103, 138, *386, 403*

spline joint [fig. 154], *414*

Springfield, Massachusetts, 231n2, 232

modern box in the style of [cat. no. 139], 353, **363–64**

square joined table (probably Boston or vicinity) [cat. no. 46; fig. 76], 121, **122–24**, 125, 126, 128, 161, 290, 370, *392*

square joined table (southeastern Massachusetts) [cat. no. 47], 60, 121, **124–26**, 128, 161, 256

square table, term, 122. *See also entries at* square joined table

Stalker, John, and George Parker, *Treatise of Japanning and Varnishing*, 310

Standish, Myles, chair, 20n6

Stanton, Edward (d. 1689), 112n1

Stapleford, Thomas, 149n3

Stevens, Patrick, 367n3

Stokes, J. Stogdell, collection, 59, cat. no. 20

stools, 59, 62, 135; and tables, 121, 134, 135, 136. *See also* back stools; *and entries at* joint stool

Stoughton, Thomas III (1624–1684), 175, 220n7

Stoughton family of East Windsor Hill, 278, cat. no. 112

Stoughton shop tradition, Windsor, Connecticut, attributed to, box [cat. no. 73], 169, **175–76, 177**, 219, 278

Stratton, Eliza Macrery Britton (Mrs. A. Vidal Davis), 210, cat. no. 87

Stratton, John (1621–ca. 1684), 210, cat. no. 87

Stratton, Phoebe (1804–1879), 210, cat. no. 87

Stratton, Sidney Vanuxem (1845–ca. 1918), 210, cat. no. 87

Stratton family of East Hampton, 208, 210, cat. no. 87

stretchers. *See* chair stretchers

Strijcker, Jacobus Gerritsen (ca. 1620–1687), 16, 17, cat. no. 1

Striker, Josephine, 16, cat. no. 1

Striker (Strijcker, Strycker, Stryker) family of New York, 14, 16–17, cat. no. 1

Suffolk, England, influence, 173, 175n3, 177, 195, 216, 220n7, 231n2

Suffolk County, Massachusetts, cradle [cat. no. 45], 60, 104, **117–19**

sunflower chests, 175, 195, 219, 222, 225, 239

sweet gum (bilsted), 308, 309n7

Switzerland, slate tabletops from, 336

Sylmaris Collection, 3

Symonds, James (1633–1714), 184

Symonds, John (before 1595–1671), 184, 186

Symonds, Samuel (1638–1722), 184

Symonds shop tradition, Salem, Massachusetts, 24, 184, 186, 254, 264

attributed to

chest of drawers [cat. no. 108; figs. 69, 108], 7, 24, 180n2, 184, 263, **264–66**, 267, 268, *390, 401*

chest of drawers (with walnut and cedar facings) [cat. no. 109], 184, 263, 264, **267–69**, 305

small cabinet [cat. no. 79; figs. 62, 81, 133, 138], 4, 9, 169, 182, **184–87**, 192, 233, 254, 264, 267, *389, 395, 410, 411*

"table and frame," term, 362n1

"table and trestles," term, 360

tables [cat. nos. 46–69], 121–66

with hinged leaves [cat. nos. 58–69], 143–66. *For specific forms, see entries at* folding table; oval table with falling leaves

with stationary top [cat. nos. 46–57], 121–42. *For specific forms, see entries at* joined table: joined table with drawer; oval table; round table; small joined table; square joined table

See also entries at dressing table; slate table; trestle table

tall-back (high-back) chair, form, 76, 79, 81; versus plain-top, 72

tangent-sawing [fig. 150], 122, *413*

Taunton, Massachusetts, 196

chest with drawer (attributed to Robert Crosman) [cat. no. 104; fig. 73], 5, 10, 196, **249–52**, *391*

"tavern table," 137, 138n1

templates, 228, 230, 247, 250

Temple, Jacob Paxson, collection, 50, cat. no. 17

Thomas family of Marshfield, 57, cat. no. 19

Thorne, Phebe Denton (1679–1728), 309, cat. no. 121

Thurston, John (1607–1685), 173, 175n1

Thurston shop tradition, Dedham and Medfield, Massachusetts, attributed to, box [cat. no. 72], 169, **173–75**

till, term, 195

Tinkham, Ephraim II, 38

"Tinkham" school, 38, 39

Titcomb, Edmund, chest signed by, 189n1, 312n4

toilet table, term, 331. *See also entries at* dressing table

tongue-and-groove joint [fig. 152], *414*

Townsend, Sarah (1736–1808), 304, cat. no. 120

Trace, Jonathan, 44, cat. no. 14

Tracy, Berry B., 8

Treat, Joseph (1662–1721), 293, cat. no. 116

Treat, Governor Robert (1622–1710), 290, 293, cat. no. 116

Treat family of Milford and New Haven, 293, cat. no. 116

trestle-base tables: with falling leaves, 143, 159, 161, 162, 162n1; fixed-top, 140

trestle table (eastern Massachusetts) [cat. no. 138], 143, 353, **360–62**

Tucker, William, 87

Tufts, John, 20, cat. no. 2

Tufts, Peter (d. 1700), 20, cat. no. 2

Turkey work, 65

Turkey-work chair (Boston, 1660–90) [cat. no. 23; fig. 85], 5, 31, 57, 64, **65–68**, 68, 70, 71, 74, 126, 128, 148, 254, *396*

Turkey-work chair (Boston, 1680–1700) [cat. no. 24], 5, 30, 64, 65, **68–71**, 74, 126, 148, 161, 254

turned chairs, 13, 34; with a slat back [cat. nos. 10–17, 136], 34–50, 356–58; with a spindle back [cat. nos. 1–9, 135], 13–33, 354–56

turned furniture, compared to joined, 51

turners, 13, 64–65

upholstered chairs, 64. *See also entries at* easy chair; leather chair; Turkey-work chair

Valentiner, Wilhelm R., 5, 7

Van Cortlandt, Anna Maria (b. 1736), 94, cat. no. 34

Van Cortlandt, Frederick (m. 1723/24), 95, cat. no. 34

Van Duyn, Garret (1773–1851), 355, cat. no. 135

Van Duyn, James (m. 1823), 355, cat. no. 135

Van Duyn family of Poughkeepsie, 356, cat. no. 135

Van Horne, Ann Mary (1778–1856), 94, cat. no. 34

Van Horne, Augustus (1736–1796), 94, 95, cat. no. 34

Van Horne, Cornelius (m. 1735), 95, cat. no. 34

Van Kleeck, Antoinette (1751–1840), 355, 356, cat. no. 135

Van Kleeck, Baltus Barents (ca. 1645–ca. 1717), 356, cat. no. 135

Van Kleeck family of Poughkeepsie, 356, cat. no. 135

Vredeman de Vries, Jan (1527–1604), 52, 198

wainscot, term, 51

wainscot chairs, 51, 52, 57. *See also entries at* joined armchair

Walker, G. W., collection, 84, cat. no. 30

walnut, 10, 51, 64, 313, 340

Warner, Mehitable (b. 1683), 229, cat. no. 95

Webb, Electra Havemeyer, 5

Weil, Henry V., 162, cat. no. 66

Welcher, Mrs. Manfred P., 194, cat. no. 82

Wentworth, John, house, Portsmouth, New Hampshire, 8, 275n3

West Country, England, 205, 208, 282, 283n5

Wethersfield, Connecticut

    chest with drawers (sunflower chest) [cat. no. 92; fig. 64], 8, 9, 175, 195, **219–21**, 222, 225, 228, 232n3, 239, 366, *390*

    chest with drawers (sunflower chest with initials) [cat. no. 93; figs. 59, 60, 95, 109], 9, 175, 195, 219, **222–24**, 225, 228, 230, 232n3, 239, *388, 398, 401*

Whipple family of northern Essex County, 147, cat. no. 58

White, Cornelius (1682–1755), 57, cat. no. 19

White, Daniel (1649–1724), 57, cat. no. 19

White, Joanna (1713–1798), 57, cat. no. 19

White, Peregrine (1620–1704), 57, 117, cat. no. 19

White family of Marshfield, 57, 162, cat. no. 19

wicker cradles and chairs, 104

William and Mary style, 9, 10

Williams, Roger (1603?–1683), 68, cat. no. 23

Willoughby, Francis, 189, cat. no. 80

Windsor, Robert, 237n5

Windsor, Connecticut, shop traditions, 9, 205, 208, 212, 219, 220n7, 231–32n2

    box (attributed to the Buell shop tradition) [cat. no. 70; fig. 53], 169, **170–71**, *386*

    box (attributed to the Moore shop tradition) [cat. no. 74], 169, 175, **176–78**, 179

    box (attributed to the Moore shop tradition; with dense carving) [cat. no. 75], 169, 175, 176, 177, **178–79**

    box (attributed to the Stoughton shop tradition) [cat. no. 73], 169, **175–76**, 177, 219, 278

    chest of drawers [cat. no. 112], 5, 189, 263, **275–78**

    small chest of drawers [cat. no. 81], 169, **189–91**, 276

Wistar, Caspar, high chest and dressing table ordered from John Head, 192, 194n4, 339, 340

Woburn, Massachusetts, 371n1; cupboard base in Museum of Fine Arts, Boston [ill. 141d], 367, *368*, 369, 370, 371n4

wooden (wooden-bottom) chairs, 51. *See also entries at* joined armchair

writing cabinets, 342

Wright, Samuel and Rebecca, 222

Wunsch Americana Foundation collection, 44, cat. no. 14

X-shaped base, 142

yellow poplar, 187, 242

Yorkshire, England, influence, 231n2, 232, 293n7

Photograph and Drawings Credits

Photographs are by Gavin Ashworth, with the exception of those listed below.

Museum of Fine Arts, Boston: cat. no. 141, ill. 141d (cupboard base, probably Woburn, Massachusetts, ca. 1680; oak, white pine; 32 ½ x 50 ¼ x 22 ⅞ in. [82.6 x 127.6 x 58.1 cm]; Gift of Virginia Page Anthony, 1990.337).

The Photograph Studio, The Metropolitan Museum of Art: cat. no. 39 (easy chair frame), cat. no. 40 (easy chair frame); cat. no. 141, ills. 141a, 141b, 141c; figs. 60, 75, 84, 95, 96.

Paul Warchol: fig. 76.

Drawings are by Robert S. Burton.